The Cookie Book

The
Cookie Book

Holly Garrison

Macmillan • USA

MACMILLAN

A Simon & Schuster Macmillan Company
1633 Broadway
New York, NY 10019

Library of Congress Cataloging-in-Publication Data

Garrison, Holly.
The cookie book / Holly Garrison
p. cm.
Includes index.
ISBN 0-02-542745-8
1. Cookies. I. Title.
TX772.G37 196
641.8'654—dc20
96-4767
CIP

Design by Rachael McBrearty

10 9 8 7 6 5 4 3 2 1

Printed in the United States of America

For Lillian G. Tamarin,
the smartest cookie of all,
with gratitude and affection.

Contents

The Cookie Maker's Kitchen

1
Tools 3

Very little kitchen hardware is needed to make cookies. Nevertheless, nothing is more disheartening than discovering at the last moment that there is not the right-size pan, a wire rack, a whisk, or whatever. Taking a few minutes to peruse this chapter can save time and aggravation.

2
Ingredients 9

What are the differences between all-purpose flour and cake flour? How about butter, margarine, shortening, and vegetable oil? Referring to these pages before gathering the ingredients needed for a recipe can help circumvent many a major and minor glitch in the cookie-making process.

3
Terms and Techniques 21

To make good cookies, much depends on understanding fundamental recipe lingo, such as how to grease a pan, separate an egg, or beat a batter. Any unfamiliar idioms in the recipe instructions should be learned—and sometimes practiced—before baking actually begins.

4

Decorating Cookies 25

From tasty toppings to the most elaborate and artful decorations, there are an infinite number of supplies available, and nearly as many ideas and techniques, for those bakers who wish to improve upon the perfection of a plain and honest cookie.

5
Storing, Shipping, and Giving Away Cookies 37

With love . . . your favorite crumbs from home. Unfortunately, this happens. Most cookies are good travelers, but packing them right almost guarantees that they will arrive fresh and intact.

More Than 400 Fabulous Cookie Recipes

6
Drop Cookies 43

These are the simplest of all cookies to make. *Drop* literally means that the batter is dropped onto the baking sheet, and just about anyone can do it. All forms of chocolate-chip cookies are drop cookies. So are hermits, macaroons, jumbles, Florentines, oatmeal cookies, and hundreds of other traditional, cookie-jar classics.

Acknowledgments

When I was asked to write a book including more than 400 cookie recipes, I didn't think it would be all that difficult. But when I actually started to do research and development, then testing, and finally putting what amounted to well over 150,000 words into the computer, it turned out to be a daunting job, and one that took about twice as long as I thought it would.

All of this is to say that *The Cookie Book* would never have been completed in time for publication in 1996 if it hadn't been for a few very patient, dedicated, and talented colleagues and helpers.

First of all, my deepest appreciation goes to Betty Bianconi, who tested and also developed many of the recipes. Often I would fax her a recipe late in the evening, which she would test at midnight so that I could have it back by 6 A.M. the next morning when I started my day. Betty, I simply could not have done it without you. Thank you for bouncing ideas around with me, for sharing your enviable knowledge about baking, and for all your moral support. Thank you, too, for styling so beautifully the cookies that appear on the cover.

Thanks also to Anne Bailey, who contributed so much to this book, but especially the gingerbread house and the biscotti.

And to all my "foodie" friends, who were kind enough to share their expertise, as well as their favorite cookie recipes, thank you so much.

Special thanks to these dear friends: Stephanie Curtis, Linda and Barry Greenhouse, Linda Johnson, Marty Jacobs, and Hoover, who have always been there for me.

Thank you, too, Taco and Ginger, for staying up late and getting up early whenever I did (and for your "opinions" about the dog cookies).

Thank you Mi Ok Song Bruining for your beautiful drawings.

And thanks, as always, to Madeleine Morel, my agent.

Thanks, of course, to "the group."

I am also extremely grateful to everyone at Macmillan Publishing Co., Pam Hoenig especially, for their patience and understanding in giving me the extension of time I needed to do this book after my husband's long illness and death.

And finally, words cannot express my gratitude to Jane Sigal, my wonderful, wonderful editor. When this book is finally put to bed, I should probably treat her to a long cruise, but right now I will send flowers and take her to lunch at Periyali, my favorite restaurant.

The following companies and trade associations were very helpful in providing information and sometimes products: Bard Valley Medjool Date Growers Association; Borden; California Date Administration Committee; California Fig Advisory Board;

California Pistachio Commission; California Prune Board; Crisco; Dairy Management; Dole Food Company; Hamilton Beach/Proctor-Silex; Karo Corn Syrup (Best Foods); KitchenAid; Kretschmer Wheat Germ; Land O' Lakes; Lewis and Neale for the American Spice Trade Association; McCormick Company, Inc.; Nestlé USA; Oregon Hazelnuts/Hazelnut Marketing Board; Texas Peanuts; and The Quaker Oats Company.

Preface

I am not a baker, which may actually be the best reason for me to have written this book. I can identify with the would-be or novice cookie makers reading this more than they can imagine.

I learned my own baking skills in the same way as most home cooks: I watched and helped grownups. When I was a little kid, I liked nothing better than to climb up on a stool and watch my grandmother bake bread. I loved to see her "measure" the flour from a big barrel into an enormous bowl. The bubbling of yeast as it proofed fascinated me. Actually getting to put my hands on the soft, fragrant dough and learning how to knead it was a thrill I will never forget. Then there was the pure magic of watching the dough creep up the side of the bowl. I remember the rush of hot air from the oven, and finally the ultimate reward: a thick slice of aromatic bread spread with butter and fresh-from-the-hive honey that I ate at the kitchen table with my grandfather.

At about the same time, I remember baking Christmas cookies with my mother and, every now and then when we got a yen for them, the Toll House cookies from the recipe on the back of the bag of Nestlé chocolate chips.

That was about it for any training in the art of baking. The rest I learned by observation, reading, and a lot of trial and error, so I think I'm in a good position to know what and how much you probably want or need to know to become a good cookie maker.

Professional bakers spend years in front of hot ovens and in and out of walk-in refrigerators learning and perfecting their craft, since baking is, above all other forms of cooking, as much chemistry as it is art.

Before ever picking up a spoon, the student baker doggedly and methodically learns about each and every baking ingredient: what it is, what it does, how it works, why it doesn't work, how it acts and reacts with every other baking ingredient, and why. I wouldn't actually know, but I've been told that studying at a professional baking school in Europe is as grueling as studying at any medical school.

Is all of this actually necessary in order to make a mouth-watering batch of cookies? Of course not. If it were, there would be precious few cookies to eat in this world. If you can read and are willing to follow a few rudimentary rules, you can be a great cookie baker.

I have tried my best to make every recipe in this book as clear, concise, and self-contained as I possibly can. I don't want you to have to constantly flip back and forth in the book to find out how to do certain steps. Any cookbook with intensive cross-referencing drives me mad, so even though it may be a great reference book, I rarely use it.

Although I have my doubts that anyone actually reads the preface to a book, if you've gotten this far I hope you will also take the time to quickly read over the pages that precede the recipes. I think you will find it helpful when you start looking through the recipes and trying to decide which cookies you want to make.

Writing this cookbook has been fun and quite a challenge. And the cookies certainly do pile up in the process. As Betty Bianconi, the main tester and troubleshooter for the recipes in this book, so aptly put it at one point: "Cookies, cookies everywhere. Even my neighbors won't take any more!" Nor will mine. Right now I think I may never bake, or even eat, another cookie. Well, at least until Christmas. Come to think of it, I guess I really should get started.

Holly Garrison
November 25, 1995

Introduction

Homemade cookies are the ultimate comfort food. With the first bite, they invariably pull us back into our childhood, a time that most of us remember—or want to remember—as being happy, secure, and far less complicated than now.

Cookie recipes are sometimes culinary heirlooms, as irreplaceable as quilts, silver, and other precious possessions that have been passed down from generation to generation. Although I have long since committed my grandmother's recipes to the memory of my Macintosh, the yellowed and tattered handwritten sheets of paper that record them (at least those that she bothered to write down, undoubtedly after some prodding by one of her children) are carefully preserved between sheets of clear plastic.

Fortunately, most cookies are obligingly easy to make and are almost always infinitely better tasting than their commercially packaged counterparts. They may also be the best place for the cook with limited time and culinary skills to learn how to bake, since cookies are, after all, merely little cakes of one sort or another, and most are extremely forgiving of the novice baker's small blunders. Cookies are also conveniently portable, easy to store, relatively indestructible, and, when eaten in moderation, not likely to interfere with anyone's idea of a healthy diet.

Although these days cookie making has evolved into primarily a Christmastime activity, a good cookie knows no season. Cookies, especially homemade cookies, are absolutely wonderful just about anytime you choose to eat one.

FOOTPRINTS IN THE FLOUR

My earliest cookie-making memories go back to the gaily decorated sugar cookies my mother and I made—and I still make—for Christmas, using my grandmother's sugar cookie recipe on page 96.

One of the longest days of my young life, besides Christmas Eve, was the day we baked the Christmas cookies. Watching the big clock above the blackboard, it seemed to me, squirming at my desk, that school would *never* let out. As the little hand finally approached the three, I could almost smell and taste those cookies that would be coming from the oven in a mere hour or two.

Butter and sugar were rationed during World War II, but my mother hoarded—or managed to get hold of somehow—enough of these precious commodities to make a dozen or so batches of our favorite cookies. She not only let me help make the cookies, but, bless her, she even encouraged me to invite two or three of my little friends to "help."

The cookie dough had been mixed the night before and refrigerated, so all that remained to be done after we arrived panting at the back door was the fun stuff: rolling, cutting, decorating, and, of course, plenty of sampling. (This was in the days before the food police outlawed eating raw cookie dough.)

Everything stood waiting for us. The leaves on the drop-leaf kitchen table were up and ready, loaded down with a bag of flour, a wooden dough board, my grandmother's heavy rolling pin, baking sheets, colored sugars, nuts, green and red candied cherries, and the all-important assortment of slightly bent and battered cookie cutters, some of which I still use.

It was well after dark when the final sheet of cookies came out of the oven. Like snow, a fine dusting of flour covered the kitchen, and we kids were half sick from eating raw dough.

I can still see those dozens of beautiful cookies laid out on tea towels on the dining room table before they were carefully tucked into two or three big earthenware crocks. I say beautiful. Well, they looked beautiful to me then and, in my mind's eye, they still do. In truth, many were probably misshapen, with varying thicknesses and haphazardly applied decorations.

For more than fifty years, these same cookies have been part of my cookie-making repertoire for the holidays. Not every Christmas has been particularly joyful for me, and a couple far from it, but I have always somehow managed to make "the Christmas cookies," which magically lifted my spirits.

Often, when I'm feeling out of sorts, I head for the kitchen and make a batch of cookies. Usually I eat only a few and give the rest away. The magic, I've discovered, is in the making, baking, and sharing, as much as in the eating.

Happy is the home where the cookie jar is always brimming, an old saying goes. As this book—I hope—demonstrates, with a few simple ingredients and utensils, and an hour or so to spare, wonderful things can happen.

COOKIES THEN AND NOW

"Mom, where do cookies come from?" is a question that you may very well never be called upon to answer. But if you are mildly curious about the history of cookies, as I was when I embarked upon this book, what I was able to learn was barely enough to fill a small baking sheet.

Tracing the origin of something as ambiguous as cookies has got to be informed speculation at best. A historical culinary source might put it this way:

We can only imagine the smile of surprise and satisfaction when some long-forgotten Neolithic baker tasted the results after accidentally dropping a blob of grain paste onto a hot stone and ending up with what would eventually become one of the world's favorite snack foods.

Historical information like this makes *me* smile.

Another more plausible theory suggests that cookies may have evolved from bakers' test batches, dabs of cake batter that were baked mostly to determine the temperature of the oven. It's a lot easier for me to picture the smile on the face of the baker who discovered that he could sell the test cakes for a larger profit than the cakes.

Other food historians theorize that at least one of the ancestors of today's tender, sweet cookie may have been heavy, twice-baked, rock-hard pieces of dough, with a seemingly endless shelf life, which were the mainstay of the sailing ships' larders on long and perilous voyages. On land, whole armies traveled with little else in their knapsacks. Even then, who can say how many inventive and enterprising cooks may have been industriously experimenting with these unappetizing little biscuits, eventually using some kind of fat and sugar to lighten, tenderize, and sweeten them. Cookies really got going in the late nineteenth century when refined sugar became readily available.

However murky its beginnings, there is no disputing that the cookie, in all its fabulous and friendly forms, eventually became one of the world's favorite confections, often associated with religious festivals and celebrations.

Like so many other things we eat and enjoy today, cookies probably got their start somewhere in the ancient civilized world and, over time, wended their way to northern Europe and eventually to the New World.

In Asian cultures, cookies are conspicuous by their absence. Although something akin to the almond cookie was served by the Chinese in the ninth century, anything made with butter is still in the realm of the extremely exotic in the Far East, where baking itself is not a traditional form of cooking. For the most part, the closest things to cookies in that part of the world are cloying little cakes, often brightly colored, that are based on glutinous rice and bean pastes with plenty of sugar, and are cooked by steaming, simmering, or deep frying.

What may be more remarkable than its history is the evolution of the cookie on its meandering path to America. Try to imagine a world without rugelach from Israel, kourambiethes from Greece, pizelle and biscotti from Italy, macaroons and madeleines from France, shortbread from Scotland, springerle and lebkuchen from Germany, krumkake from Norway, even almond cookies from China. And, finally, from the United States, comes our very own chocolate-chip cookie, indisputably one of the best cookies ever developed.

Cookies have always been the most flexible of baked goods, readily lending themselves to frivolous and symbolic forms, with names often as nonsensical as their shapes.

How the cookie got its American name, though, is a little less speculative. Dutch settlers in New York state were most likely responsible for introducing the word *cookie* into the American vernacular, when *koeptje*, their word for *little cake*, eventually came to be pronounced *cookie*.

WHAT KIND OF COOKIE IS THAT?

Cookies fall into five rather broad categories, which simply refer to the ways in which they are formed, and the way in which the cookies in this book have been presented.

Drop Cookies
Shaped Cookies
Rolled Cookies
Icebox Cookies
Bar Cookies

It is the consistency and texture of the dough that determines the way cookies are formed.

To be dropped onto a baking sheet, a thick, batterlike dough is needed. However, it takes a firmer and more malleable dough to be rolled into a cylinder or thin sheets and then sliced, stamped, or twisted into plain or whimsical shapes.

A very soft dough can be pushed through a cookie press or a pastry tube. Still other cookies are made with batters so thin that, while they are still warm from the oven, they can be shaped into cones, rolls, or even baskets, giving them the perfect configuration for holding delectable fillings.

A few cookies, though, are nonconformists, refusing to be associated with any particular group. These I have lumped together in one catch-all chapter with the imaginative name of "Special Cookies."

My own favorite chapter is a collection of diverse cookie recipes from my "foodie" friends, a knowledgeable group of magazine food editors, cookbook authors, and radio and television personalities. It was fascinating to see the recipes that came over the fax line when I asked each of them if they would like to contribute their favorite cookie recipe to be included in this book.

Considering the level of culinary sophistication of this group, I was surprised (or was I?) that most of the recipes they gave me were for cookies baked by their mothers and fondly remembered from childhood.

The Cookie Maker's Kitchen

1
Tools

If you have ever stepped into a no-nonsense cookwares store, like E. Dehillerin in Paris or Bridge Kitchenware in New York City, you were no doubt overwhelmed by the sheer number of cooking objects for sale, all for the seemingly simple purpose of fixing something to eat. Talk about candy stores for cooks!

If you like to cook, it's easy to be seduced by attractive and intriguing pieces of cookware and gadgets, many of which you may never use, or use only once, but will still have to store. Keep this in mind when you go shopping for cookie-making equipment.

The hardware needed to make cookies is blessedly minimal compared to that used for many other baked goods, and could probably fit neatly into a small cabinet or a deep drawer. If you own even one baking sheet, a bowl, a mixing spoon, and measuring cups and spoons, you probably have all the implements you need right there to turn out dozens of delectable varieties.

If, however, you are interested in making more than supersimple, one-bowl cookies, there are additional baking utensils and small appliances that would be useful to have.

It is not necessary to own every item listed here. The absolute need for some things is obvious, but the best rule is always to read through the recipe you are planning to make—well ahead of actual baking time—to be sure that you have all the equipment and ingredients you'll need.

MAKING GOOD INVESTMENTS

When it comes to cooking equipment, the old cliché about getting what you pay for could never be truer, and the range of prices you can expect to spend for baking sheets, say, can vary wildly, from cheap-cheap to ridiculously expensive.

Flimsy, badly made cooking utensils and equipment are simply not worthy of the cook's time and efforts. These things will probably have to be replaced often, and may even fall apart or stop working at some crucial point. *You should not even consider them.*

Even though I know better, not long ago I bought a really terrific looking, nonstick skillet for the bargain price of $8.99. Although I didn't recognize the brand, the sign advertising the sale at a reputable discount store confidently assured me that the skillet would ordinarily retail for three times as much. The skillet wasn't even a few months old before the nonstick coating started to flake off, so I threw it—and my $8.99—into the trash.

On the other hand, professional equipment, meant for hard use in a restaurant kitchen or bakery, is a waste of money at the other extreme.

Look for a kitchenware store that specializes in home-baking equipment and supplies, where there are knowledgeable salespeople on hand to answer questions.

On page 353–354 is a list of companies that do mail-order business, which you may find helpful if you have trouble locating a well-stocked kitchenware store where you live. However, with Williams-Sonoma stores popping up like mushrooms all over the United States, and catalogs that specialize in nothing but kitchen stuff and exotic ingredients flying through the mail slot every other day, locating these things gets easier and easier all the time.

SPECIAL COOKIE-BAKING EQUIPMENT

Specialized equipment, such as cookie cutters, dough presses, cookie molds, pastry bags, etc., are discussed in the chapters in which they are used, and are listed in the index.

BAKING PANS

Almost without exception, bar cookies are baked in a $13 \times 9 \times 2$-inch metal baking pan or glass baking dish. Some metal pans have nonstick finishes, but I don't use these for making bar cookies, since it's much more efficient to cut the bars right in the pan, a practice that would soon render a nonstick finish useless. Either metal or glass works well, except that because the two conduct heat differently, a lower oven temperature is required when using a glass baking dish, usually 325° for a glass dish and 350° for a metal pan.

BAKING (COOKIE) SHEETS

Baking sheets are most often made of shiny or dark aluminum and less frequently of other metals and alloys. Sometimes they are coated with silicon to prevent sticking, which also eliminates the need for greasing. Baking sheets come in varying sizes and have a lip at one or both ends to facilitate handling.

Jelly-roll pans, which have four low sides, are great for jelly rolls, but not for cookies. Although some bakers will disagree with me, I find that even very low sides can interfere with the heat flow over the tops of the cookies, and can trap just enough moisture during baking to make the cookies perceptibly soggy.

When choosing a baking sheet, look for one that is large and rigid, keeping in mind that it should fit into your oven with about 2 inches all around it to allow proper heat circulation. The 17×14-inch size is about right for most home ovens.

Rigid means 1 to $1\frac{1}{2}$ millimeters (about $\frac{1}{16}$ inch) thick, which will ensure even heat distribution. Flimsier sheets tend to develop hot spots, warp over time, and sometimes even buckle when they get hot, which can do weird things to the cookies as they bake, and none of them particularly good.

The only sure way to test the strength of a baking sheet before you buy it is to grasp it firmly at both ends and twist it. If it gives much or produces a sort of bending-popping sound, you don't want it.

Shiny aluminum baking sheets that deflect heat are the home baker's best choice for cookies and are the kind I prefer and use regularly.

Pans with a dark surface absorb more heat and are usually the professionals' choice, but they can be tricky to work with. Because these sheets don't reflect the heat, the cookies tend to over-brown on the bottoms before they are fully baked.

Double-bottom, insulated sheets are relative newcomers to the baking-sheet market, and can be useful for delicate cookies that might

otherwise darken too quickly, although I have never found these *really* necessary for cookie baking. Double panning, putting two same-size baking sheets together, works just as well.

If you are planning to do much cookie making, I recommend owning four baking sheets. Since only one or two can be in the oven at the same time, having four will permit you to fill two baking sheets while the other two are in the oven. And, since baking sheets have to cool and then be wiped (and sometimes washed) before baking subsequent cookie batches, having four baking sheets is certainly more efficient.

Treat baking sheets respectfully, keeping the surface as scratch-free as possible by removing the cookies with a wide nylon turner made for use with nonstick pans. Wash the sheets in hot, sudsy water using a brush or non-abrasive scouring pad, and they will reward you with years and years of service and thousands of meltingly delicious, golden cookies.

ELECTRIC MIXERS

For all of the recipes in this book that require any substantive mixing or beating, an electric mixer is used.

Battery-Operated or Rechargeable Hand Mixer

These are fine for very light mixing jobs, but aren't nearly strong enough for cookie batters, and certainly not for heavy doughs.

Hand Mixer

If you opt for a hand-held mixer, choose a powerful model that feels good in your hand and has most of its weight in the front over the beaters. Some of these mixers are made so that they stand upright next to the bowl, thus giving you two hands when you need to scrape the bowl or add things. An extra set of beaters is convenient to have.

It usually takes about a third more time to beat or whip with a hand mixer than it does in a stand mixer.

Stand Mixer

A stand mixer does take up a certain amount of counter and/or cabinet space, but it is by far the easiest to use, since the ingredients are merely put into the bowl and the mixer does the work, freeing you to do other things.

One appliance you *don't* want to own is a wimpy mixer. I regularly use two stand mixers: a KitchenAid and a Hamilton-Beach. Both models have powerful motors and don't overheat when called upon to beat heavy mixtures for long periods.

If you plan to do a lot of baking and mixing, you might want to invest in an extra mixer bowl or two, perhaps in different sizes. A second set of beaters is a good idea, too. Having these on hand will save a lot of washing time during the baking session.

The only bad thing, if you can call it that, about the big stand mixers is that if you don't keep a careful eye on what's happening, they can quickly overbeat, something that is not desirable for cookie batters, which is explained more fully on page 21.

It usually takes about a third less time to beat or whip with a stand mixer than with a hand mixer.

FOOD PROCESSOR

This is another appliance that everybody once got along perfectly well without. But why should you? It makes quick work of most chopping, mincing, and grinding jobs, things that an electric blender cannot and was never really meant to do.

GRATER

A common, four-sided grater will perform most of the grating and shredding tasks called for in cookie recipes very efficiently. Graters are usually made of metal, either tinned steel or stainless steel. Choose the latter, even though it is more expensive, since tinned steel tends to rust. (I also have in my cabinet an all-in-one flat grater, but each grating surface is so small that it is difficult to use.)

For cookie making, you will probably only need to use the two largest sides of the grater. The side with the smaller holes grates, making little, crumblike pieces. The other side, with much larger holes, makes larger, strandlike pieces.

ICING SPATULAS

The big icing spatulas that look like long knives with rounded, flexible blades are fine for icing large cake surfaces, but for more delicate cookie icing, you will need a small version that is about the same size as a paring knife. An artist's palette knife or a sandwich spreader also works well for this, and you can also use an individual butter spreader.

KNIVES

You'll need a knife that is long and sharp for cutting and slicing dough. I will assume that you have a sharp paring knife, which will be needed occasionally for small jobs.

MEASURING CUPS

If you haven't had much cooking or baking experience, you may wonder what in the world there is to say about measuring cups. Well, actually quite a lot.

The most common error beginning cooks make is to use glass measuring cups for both liquid and dry ingredients. This may be okay when putting together a dinner casserole, but for reasonably precise measurements, glass measuring cups should be used only for liquid ingredients.

To measure dry ingredients (mainly flour and sugar in cookie making), use nested cups with handles. These are sold in sets in graduated sizes: $1/4$ cup, $1/3$ cup, $1/2$ cup, 1 cup, and sometimes 2 cups. Cooking professionals frequently refer to these cups as Mary Anns. I don't know why.

If you plan to do much cookie baking, you'll want to have a few of both kinds of measuring cups, unless, of course, you don't mind stopping every few minutes to wash and dry frequently used sizes.

MEASURING SPOONS

I think you probably know what measuring spoons are. Beyond that, I'll only say that I prefer those that have rather shallow, narrow bowls (the easier for getting into small jars), that are made from stainless steel or some other dishwasher-safe material. Several sets are nice to have so that you don't have to stop and wash. If the spoons are on a ring, take them apart and use and store them separately. The spoons are almost impossible to deal with when they are flopping around like a bunch of keys, and hard to wash that way, too.

Measuring spoons are used for both liquid and dry ingredients.

METAL COOLING RACK

A cooling rack is a grid of wires attached to a frame with short legs. The wires are close enough together so that the cookies won't fall through. The purpose of a rack is to allow air to circulate around the cookies so that they won't become soggy as they cool. The same theory applies to baking sheets and pans set on racks after they come out of the oven.

To cool cookies, you should have enough rack surface to cool two baking sheets of cookies at once. Racks measuring about 12×18 inches are a good size for this purpose. When buying a rack, make sure that it is sturdy and stands level. If counter space is limited, you might want to consider a double- or triple-decker rack that I have seen advertised in cooking-equipment catalogs.

MIXING BOWLS

I prefer dishwasher-safe, stainless-steel, glass, or earthenware-type bowls with wide bottoms and gently sloping sides. This design is more or less tip-proof and makes it easy to blend batters and doughs, which tend to get stuck around the bottom of steeper-sided bowls. I am not all that enamored of plastic bowls, since even the very best of them are slightly porous, which makes them hard to wash, and they scratch easily. Consequently, they can occasionally

transfer minuscule amounts of grease or perceptible flavors to such things as egg whites and delicate batters.

A set or two of nested bowls (small, medium, large, and extra-large), should be enough to get through most cookie-baking sessions.

OVEN THERMOMETER

A mercury oven thermometer costs only a few dollars and is worth every penny. It is not unusual for the thermostats of even the most expensive and well-insulated ovens to be off by 25° or 50°, which can make a big difference in whether you will be pleased or disappointed with the results of your labors. Before every baking session, the first thing to do is to test the oven temperature with the thermometer. It is also not a bad idea to test between batches to check for any temperature "drifts."

By the way, if your oven is off by more than 50°, it should be recalibrated.

PASTRY (DOUGH) BOARD

A smooth—but not slippery—surface is needed to roll dough. In most cases, a clean, nonporous countertop works just fine, especially a laminated countertop. So does a large wooden board, as long as it has not been used for cutting and chopping, which scars the surface and makes the dough stick. Wooden boards also pick up the flavors of whatever has been chopped on them, so your sugar cookies could taste oddly of garlic. In other words, pastry and cutting boards can't be used interchangeably. Some bakers prefer to work on a marble slab, and that's fine, as long as it is not too highly polished. (Dough slides when the rolling surface is too smooth.)

PASTRY BRUSH

The typical pastry brush looks like a small housepainter's brush. Pastry brushes are usually between 1 and 1½ inches wide with sterilized nylon or natural bristles. You can use a paint brush if you like, but invest in a very good one, or the bristles may fall out. It is useful for greasing pans and applying glazes and other thin coatings. The brush should be run beneath cold water just before using to soften it.

Wash the brush in hot sudsy water and rinse very well, paying special attention to that part of the brush where the bristles are attached to the handle. Shake out the excess water and blot dry. Allow to air dry completely before storing.

Another kind of pastry brush is made with goose feathers. This special brush is used for applying egg glazes, and it's not likely that you would really need one for cookie making.

PIZZA CUTTER AND PASTRY WHEEL

These are surprisingly handy implements to have in the drawer. Both the pizza cutter (with a straight blade) and a pastry wheel (with a decorative edge) can make quick work of cutting a rolled dough into squares or other angled shapes.

ROLLING PIN

The secret to crisp, rolled cookies is evenly thin dough that has a minimum of flour added to it to prevent sticking while it is being rolled. Choose a heavy, straight, wooden pin with sturdy, ball-bearing or axle handles and let *it* do most of the work. Some expert cookie bakers recommend the straight, handleless French pin (not the one that tapers at the ends), which they claim gives them a better "feel" for the dough. I have found my grandmother's big, heavy rolling pin to be entirely satisfactory. It has good-size handles and rolls easily. Its fat cylinder measures about 3½ inches in dia-meter and 14 inches long.

If properly cared for, a good wooden rolling pin will last for several generations, as mine has been proving for nearly a century. Don't soak the pin in water, but wash it *briefly* in hot, sudsy water, then rinse and dry it immediately. Store the pin where it is not likely to get nicked or gouged.

SCALES

Rarely will you have to use a scale in cookie making. The exception might be to weigh nuts.

If you decide to invest in a kitchen scale, unless you need weights right down to the last gram, in which case you will need an expensive beam balance scale, a spring scale is fine for most culinary purposes.

SIFTER

Sifting flour is rarely necessary for cookie making (see "Sifting," page 24), but it is a good idea to have a sifter on hand for those occasional times when sifting is needed.

A good flour sifter should be heavy for its size and have at least a 2-cup capacity, although 3- or 4-cup is better. I find that old-fashioned sifters, those with a crank on the side, are the easiest to work with and the least likely to develop problems. Another good choice is a sifter with a trigger handle. There are also battery-operated sifters that work very rapidly, a helpful feature if you do a lot of baking.

You don't need to wash the sifter after every use and risk getting little clumps of hard "dough" in the screens or in the mechanism. Merely knock the side of the sifter a few times with the palm of your hand to release any remaining flour mixture around the edge of the screen, and store the sifter in a plastic bag.

SPOONS

A couple of sturdy wooden or plastic mixing spoons with reasonably long handles are needed for mixing batters and doughs. You will also want to have one or two hard-rubber spatulas (sometimes known as plate scrapers) for scraping down the sides of mixing bowls and food processor work bowls.

TIMER

A kitchen timer with a loud, persistent bell is not a critical piece of kitchen equipment, but it may actually end up saving quite a few cookies when you become distracted or absorbed in shaping, rolling, or cutting subsequent batches. Most cookies have rather short baking times, and you know the old saying about how time flies when you're having fun!

WIDE (PANCAKE) TURNER

This is sometimes referred to as a wide spatula. It is the best device for moving cut cookies off the rolling surface and onto baking sheets, and then off the baking sheet onto wire racks after they are baked.

WIRE WHISKS

These are not all the same. For mixing dry ingredients, choose a fairly large, bulbous balloon whisk, which has ten or so wire strands, rather than the classic French whisk, which has fewer strands, is more pear-shaped, and is meant for blending sauces.

2
Ingredients

You will probably not find listed here every ingredient that has been used in this book. Some things are so intrinsically common that it would be silly to ramble on about each and every one of them.

To make this book easy to use, I have tried to be explicit in every recipe about exactly what is called for and in what form. Sometimes notes have been added. I have listed only those ingredients here that I think warrant further discussion, in the belief that understanding what certain things are and how they work will make you a more confident cookie maker.

BAKING POWDER

Baking powder is a chemical leavening (rising) agent, and it is one of the most important cookie-making ingredients. Double-acting baking powder (about the only kind the consumer can find in this country these days) means that the first action begins in the mixing bowl as soon as liquid is added. The second action takes place when the heat of the oven releases it. It is this double action that permits the baker to completely mix ingredients and then delay baking until later.

Since baking powder loses its strength over time, it should be used by the expiration date that is stamped on the bottom of the can, or replaced every year. To determine whether or not baking powder is still active, mix 1 teaspoon with $1/3$ cup hot water. If the mixture bubbles furiously, the baking powder is still active and will produce good results.

Storing Baking Powder
Store baking powder in a cool, dry cabinet.

BAKING SODA

Baking soda is another kind of chemical leavening agent with just one action that reacts with acid ingredients by releasing carbon dioxide gas and causing expansion of the batter. Baking soda is also used to neutralize acid ingredients. Often baking soda and baking powder are used together when the baking soda is needed for its neutralizing effect.

Baking soda will not lose strength nearly as quickly as baking powder, but it does not last forever, either. Usually, it just gets old, and considering its almost insignificant cost, it is not a bad idea to replace it every year or so. Baking soda that has been around a while has also undoubtedly picked up some undesirable odors and flavors, which is why it is also used as a refrigerator deodorant. It also forms lumps, which should be sieved out in a strainer before blending it with the dry ingredients.

To make certain that baking soda is still active, place $1^{1}/_{2}$ teaspoons in a small bowl and add 1 tablespoon vinegar. If the mixture doesn't fizz, the baking soda is no longer active.

Storing Baking Soda

Baking soda should be stored in a cool, dry cabinet.

BUTTER AND MARGARINE

I use butter in my baking recipes, but I certainly believe that you should feel perfectly comfortable about substituting margarine if that is what you generally use and prefer, so margarine has been given as a butter alternative in almost every recipe. Whichever one you choose to use, make sure it is top quality, which would be USDA Grade AA butter and a good brand of margarine.

Butter and regular margarine have the same baking properties, except that butter is a natural dairy product and margarine is made from hydrogenated vegetable oils, mostly corn and soy oils. Both are available salted or unsalted, and have about the same number of total fat grams, although butter is higher in saturated fat and also contains some cholesterol.

The recipes in this book call for *salted* butter or margarine. My years as a magazine food editor have convinced me that most Americans use salted butter on the table and for cooking, as well as for baking, which is fine. Salt is frequently used in sweet baked goods, since it tends to define the flavor of sugar (see "Salt," page 17).

Unsalted butter can *always* be substituted for salted butter. Each stick ($^{1}/_{2}$ cup) of salted butter contains about $^{1}/_{4}$ teaspoon of salt, which can be added to the dry ingredients, if you like.

The biggest difference between butter and margarine is that margarine simply does not have the incomparable flavor of butter, nor does it literally melt in the mouth like butter.

Whipped butter or margarine has been beaten and aerated in order to "lighten" it. You can substitute whipped butter or margarine for regular, but—and it's a big but—if you do, you will have to measure it by weight and not by volume. (Eight ounces of whipped butter or margarine equals 1 cup; 8 ounces of regular butter or margarine equals $^{1}/_{2}$ cup.)

Butter-and-margarine blends can be substituted for either butter or margarine, as long as the weights are the same.

Reduced-calorie or low-fat butter or margarine contains significantly less fat than regular butter or margarine, by virtue of adding water and air to them. These are meant for use as spreads. *Do not try to use them for baking!*

Storing Butter and Margarine

Butter has a limited refrigerator life. Store salted butter in the coldest part of the refrigerator for no more than four weeks. Unsalted butter spoils more quickly. It should be stored under the same conditions, but for no longer than two weeks. For longer storage, wrap the butter tightly in aluminum foil and freeze it for up to several months. However, butter that has been frozen spoils more quickly after it has been thawed than butter that has not been frozen.

Margarine will keep for several weeks in the refrigerator and almost indefinitely if it is tightly wrapped in aluminum foil and frozen.

CHOCOLATE

Most people would agree that everything about chocolate is absolutely fabulous. So, it's not surprising that it finds its way into so many cookie recipes. All chocolate comes from cocoa beans and is available in several forms.

Bittersweet Chocolate

Dark chocolate that is not quite as sweet as semisweet. It is the chocolate connoisseur's chocolate, and is available loose and in bars. Bittersweet and semisweet chocolate can be used interchangeably.

Cocoa

This is pure powdered chocolate, or what's left after most of the cocoa butter has been removed. It should not be confused with sweetened cocoa mixes that are used to make drinks. For clarity's sake, cocoa is often referred to as "unsweetened cocoa powder" when called for as a cooking ingredient, and always in this book.

German (Baking) Chocolate

This chocolate is slightly sweeter than semisweet chocolate. It is available in bars and can be used in place of semisweet chocolate.

Milk Chocolate

Very sweet chocolate with milk added to give it a creamy taste and texture. Milk chocolate is not often used as a baking ingredient.

Semisweet Chocolate

When sugar is added to unsweetened chocolate, something almost magical happens. It becomes a true, mouthwatering confection, and the one many people prefer to eat, as is, above all other forms of chocolate and candy, me being one of them.

Semisweet chocolate is available in many forms and in many price ranges. One of the most familiar forms of semisweet chocolate is chocolate chips, the all-time-favorite cookie ingredient. The chips come in two sizes: the regular size we all know and love, as well as miniature chips. Semisweet chocolate is also available in molded squares, in bars, and loose.

Unsweetened Chocolate

Pure chocolate with no sugar added, unsweetened chocolate is too bitter to be eaten by itself as a confection. When called for in cookie recipes, it is almost always melted and stirred into the sweetened batter. The usual sequence is butter, sugar, eggs, chocolate.

Unsweetened chocolate is available molded into 1- or 2-ounce blocks and packed four to eight in a box. It can also be purchased in chunks (loose) at specialty food stores, but then it needs to be cut and weighed before it is used.

White Chocolate

This is really not chocolate at all, but a chocolate derivative, a blend of cocoa butter, sugar, milk, and flavorings. It is available in a number of forms, including chips. White chocolate baking bars have the highest amount of cocoa butter and are the best choice when white chocolate is called for in cookie recipes. The correct term for white chocolate is vanilla-flavored white baking chips or bars.

Storing Chocolate

Store all forms of chocolate in a cool location, ideally between 64° and 76° and at low humidity. The less sugar the chocolate contains, the longer it keeps well. I don't let semisweet chocolate hang around for more than a few months. Unsweetened chocolate, if tightly wrapped, can be kept under ideal conditions for a couple of years.

If the storage area becomes too warm, some of the cocoa butter will rise to the surface of the chocolate producing a whitish film that is known as "bloom." And, although it doesn't look great, bloom doesn't affect the eating or cooking qualities and will disappear when the chocolate is melted.

How to Melt Chocolate

Instructions for melting chocolate have been given in all of the recipes in this book that call for melted chocolate, but I do want to mention a few important things here about the procedure.

Melting chocolate is not as difficult as you may have been led to believe, but you can't be

casual about it, either. The fact is that chocolate *does* scorch easily, so melting it requires extreme care and your *constant* attention. If even a small amount of water should accidentally get into the pan during melting, it will cause the chocolate to "seize" and become thick, grainy, and lumpy. It is almost impossible to rescue chocolate that has seized, so make sure that pans and utensils used for chocolate melting are very dry. (This is one reason I don't like to recommend melting chocolate in a double boiler, with its risk of steam or water landing on the chocolate, although it can be done this way, and does eliminate any danger of scorching.) If, despite your best efforts, the chocolate suddenly becomes pasty and little hard patches appear, you will know that it is scorched. There is no way to rescue or use it. Throw it out and start over.

Use a small, heavy pan for melting chocolate; the less chocolate the smaller the pan should be. (So that the chocolate, as it melts, is not exposed to any more of the hot surface of the bottom of the pan than is necessary.) Break or chop the chocolate into smallish pieces and place them in the pan. Set the pan over *very low* heat and *immediately* begin stirring with a wooden spoon. Keep stirring until the chocolate is nearly smooth. Don't hesitate to lift the pan from the heat and continue stirring if you think things are happening too fast or getting out of control. When the chocolate is nearly melted, remove the pan from the heat and keep stirring until the chocolate has cooled down a little and is smooth and shiny.

Microwave melting: Chocolate can also be melted in a microwave oven, but it still requires constant attention. Place the chocolate in a microwave-safe bowl. Large chunks of chocolate should be cut or broken into smaller pieces. Microwave at medium power, stirring once or twice during melting. One ounce of chocolate will take 1 to 2 minutes to melt; 2 ounces, 3 to 5 minutes; 3 ounces, 4 to 6 minutes. Looks can be deceiving, since, even when it is technically melted, microwave-melted chocolate continues to hold its shape.

COCONUT

I have no doubt that you know what a coconut is. What most people don't know is how to open one, even if you have watched an island boy perform the task dozens of times. It all looks so simple until you try it yourself. When I was a kid, I used to take the coconut outside and throw it down onto the concrete sidewalk in front of the house, which did the job very efficiently, and sometimes this direct approach still seems to me like it might be the most expeditious.

When shredded or flaked coconut is called for, you can follow the lengthy directions given below for doing this yourself, or take the easy way out and use packaged coconut. Commercially packaged coconut is sold in the baking section of the supermarket in bags or cans, either shredded or flaked, and is almost always sweetened. There is really no difference between the two except that the shredded coconut is more strandlike than the flaked coconut. One can always be substituted for the other. If the whole can or package is not used, it should be tightly sealed and frozen.

Unsweetened dried coconut, which is more like fresh, is usually available at health food stores.

How to Open and Grate a Fresh Coconut

Coconuts that come to market have mercifully already been husked. When shaken, you should be able to hear the coconut milk inside.

Place the coconut on a solid work surface and pierce one or two of the "eyes" with an ice pick or a screwdriver. Drain the liquid and discard it.

Wrap the coconut in a dish towel and break it into pieces with a hammer. Remove the flesh from the shell, prying it out with the point of a strong knife. Peel off the brown membrane with a vegetable peeler and cut the white coconut flesh into pieces. Place a few of these pieces in

a food processor and process with the grating or shredding disk. Or, you can do the job on a four-sided grater, but look out for your knuckles.

Storing Grated Coconut

Store fresh grated or shredded coconut in the refrigerator for a day or two in a tightly covered container. What is not used should be eaten almost immediately.

DRIED FRUIT

Dried fruit includes raisins, currants, prunes, dates, figs, apricots, and the list goes on. Lately, blueberries, cherries, and cranberries have taken their place among the dried fruits that are widely available.

Dried does not mean rock hard. Fruit should be mildly aromatic and reasonably pliable. If it has reached the stage where it feels like buckshot, it should be discarded. Dried fruit that has become just a little too firm can be softened by soaking it in boiling water for about 10 minutes; drain and pat dry between paper towels before using.

Storing Dried Fruit

Store dried fruit in the unopened package, or in an airtight container, for up to several months. Loose dried fruits can also be sealed in an airtight plastic bag and frozen for up to one year.

EGGS

Eggs should be fresh, no matter how they are to be used, so buy them often and inspect each one carefully before you leave the egg case to make sure that none are cracked or dirty.

Eggs are important in baking for several reasons: They add richness and act as an emulsifier by binding incompatible ingredients (such as oil and water), as well as providing structure and volume.

Separating eggs and using egg whites are discussed in relation to making meringues on page 69.

The recipes in this book were tested using USDA Grade A large eggs. And one more time:

There is no difference between a white or brown egg, except the color of the shell.

Storing Eggs

Store eggs in the refrigerator in their original carton. If you have eggs on hand and are not sure about their age, there is an easy way to test them. Place the egg in question in a bowl of water. If it remains on the bottom it is very fresh. A less-than-fresh egg will start to rise in the water. If it floats to the surface, or close to the surface, discard it.

EXTRACTS

The most common extract is vanilla extract, and it is called for in almost every cookie recipe in this book. Almond and lemon extracts are also frequently used.

Pure extracts are made by distilling the essential oils of certain plants and dissolving them in alcohol or an alcohol-based liquid. When these oils are not present, or not strong enough to produce extract, food scientists have done a remarkably good job of duplicating them in both natural and artificial flavorings.

McCormick & Company, Inc., currently has more than twenty extracts and flavorings in its line, from vanilla extract to root beer and coconut flavorings.

Extracts should be added only to cool or cooling mixtures. For better distribution in the batter, they are usually blended into ingredients at the creaming stage before the flour is added.

Storing Extracts

Keep bottles of extracts and flavorings tightly closed and store in a cool cabinet.

FLOUR

Wheat flour is the main ingredient in most cookie recipes. Simple enough, except when you are faced with an array of flours on the shelf at the supermarket: all-purpose flour, whole wheat flour, cake flour, bread flour, and self-rising flour.

All-Purpose Flour

Either bleached or unbleached, white, all-purpose flour is the one and only flour called for in almost every recipe in this book. It is ground endosperm, the starchy center of the grain kernel. The endosperm's purpose is to nourish the seed after it sprouts.

There are two very broad categories of white flour—hard and soft—that are determined by the physical hardness of the variety of wheat from which the flour was milled. When bakers refer to "hard" flour, what they actually mean is flour with a high gluten content, gluten being a plant protein that, when moistened and mixed or kneaded, provides the strength, structure, and elasticity needed for bread making. Conversely, "soft" flour has a low gluten content and is used mainly for cakes, pastries, and other baked goods when elasticity is not desirable.

Flour can be a huge consideration when making certain kinds of breads, cakes, and pastries, but is not nearly so important in cookie making.

It was the late Peter Kump, founder of Peter Kump's New York Cooking School, and whose knowledge I deeply respect, who convinced me that the cookie recipes in this book should be tested with two national brands of all-purpose flour: Gold Medal and Pillsbury. However, that is not to say that you must, too. Here is Peter's reasoning, which makes good sense:

All-purpose flour, a blend of hard and soft flours, is milled mainly for general home baking. However, there are no standards as to exactly how much hard flour and how much soft flour constitutes all-purpose flour. It is up to the miller. For example, in the South, where a lot of the flour is used for biscuit making, the millers tend to use more soft flour in their blends. In the North, where bread making is popular, millers generally use more hard flour.

Although George Pillsbury and Betty Crocker might scowl at me for saying so, as far as I can tell, Pillsbury and Gold Medal flours are identical. Because they are milled for countrywide distribution, the blend of flours in these brands is formulated and consistent. However, if you have a favorite regional brand of all-purpose flour, go ahead and use it.

Whole Wheat (Graham) Flour

Whole wheat flour is milled from the entire wheat kernel, and so it contains a little more fiber and has a slightly higher nutritional profile than white flour. But whole wheat flour also has less strength than white flour, so it cannot be substituted for white flour on a one-to-one basis. Do not, in an attempt to healthy-up your cookies a little, substitute whole wheat flour for all-purpose flour. Cookie doughs, although extremely good-natured, are not generally quite so forgiving as to accept random flour substitutions without some alterations to the rest of the ingredients.

Having said that, I will now add that whole wheat flour can be substituted for one-quarter of the amount of all-purpose flour called for in virtually all cookie recipes.

Storing Flour

Store flour in a tightly covered container. Contrary to what some cooks believe, flour does not keep forever, before or after the bag has been opened. After a few months exposed to the air, even in a canister, flour develops a stale taste. Even in an unopened bag, little tenants, for whom flour can provide a very happy home, are bound to appear after a while. A couple of months is the longest I ever keep white flour around after it has been transferred to a canister, and not much longer than that in an unopened bag. If I am not going to be doing much baking, I buy flour in very small quantities, usually two-pound bags.

Fresh flour should not be dumped into the canister over old flour. In fact, it is best if the flour canister is well washed and dried before it is refilled.

If all-purpose or whole wheat flour is to be kept for any length of time, store the tightly closed bag in the refrigerator or freezer for up to one year. As it is needed, the flour can be

transferred to a canister, or even measured directly from the bag. In that case, fold over the top of the bag, tape it securely so that it does not pick up any odors, and return it to the refrigerator. Allow the flour to come to room temperature before using it in a baking recipe so that it does not lower the temperature of the other ingredients.

LIQUEURS

Liqueurs (the sweet stuff you drink after dinner) come in an almost endless variety of flavors, and many distilled spirits, such as brandy and rum, are also good flavoring agents.

Liqueurs should be added only to cool or cooling mixtures. For better distribution in the batter, they are usually blended into ingredients at the creaming stage before the flour is added.

Storing Liqueurs

Store liqueurs in a cool cupboard.

MARGARINE

See "Butter and Margarine."

MOLASSES

See "Sugar and Other Sweeteners."

NUTS

Nuts (nutmeats, technically) are an integral part of many homemade cookies, and make an appearance in many of the recipes in this book. Most nut varieties are familiar to everyone, and I have been quite specific about the form in which they are to be used in the recipes that call for them.

Most nutmeats can be purchased the way they are called for in a recipe, such as blanched, slivered, chopped, whole, halves, and so forth.

Natural refers to the way the nutmeat is found in the shell. Natural almonds, for instance, are almonds that are still covered with thin, brown skins.

Nutmeats come packed in vacuum-sealed cans, jars, or bags, salted or unsalted, and they can also be purchased loose. For baking, use unsalted nuts.

Because nutmeats contain a lot of oil, and some more than others, once they are exposed to the air nutmeats become rancid rather quickly. If you buy loose nutmeats, sniff them first to make sure they are fresh. I assure you that there will not be a doubt in your mind if they are not. Even vacuum-packed nutmeats can become rancid over time.

Storing Nutmeats

Nuts won't keep forever in your kitchen cupboard, either. Sealed in vacuum-packed containers, they will probably keep for a few months, or maybe as long as a year. Loose nutmeats will start losing freshness almost immediately and will generally start turning rancid within a few weeks.

I usually buy nuts in vacuum-sealed plastic bags, and if I have no immediate plans for them, I routinely toss them into the freezer, where they keep nicely for at least a year before they begin to taste "old." So, it's a good idea to jot down the freeze date on a piece of tape and stick it on the bag so that you can keep rotating the stock, so to speak.

Preparing and Shelling Nuts

Certain kinds of nuts, hazelnuts and in-shell pistachios, for example, require a little prep work before they can be used.

Hazelnuts (Filberts)

These are one of the most delicious nuts you will ever put into your mouth. It is always good to buy them when you see them (usually in the fall after the harvest) and stick them in the freezer (for up to one year) until needed. The supply of hazelnuts is limited. So many are used commercially (usually in candy making) that you and I tend to get what's not contracted for by the big guys.

Hazelnuts have one big drawback, though: a bitter, papery brown skin that clings tenaciously to the nutmeat, which you will want to get rid of, or most of it, before using the nuts.

How to Skin Hazelnuts

Preheat the oven to 350°. Place the nuts in a jelly-roll pan and toast them, stirring once or twice, until the skins begin to flake, about 7 minutes. Immediately place the nuts in a wire sieve and rub them together and against the mesh to remove as much of the skins as possible. Or wrap the warm nuts in a kitchen towel and rub them together and against the towel.

Pistachios

Sticking your thumbnail between the halves of a pistachio shell and eating the rich, buttery nutmeats inside can be a lovely, mindless pastime while watching a football game on television. But it's another matter when you need them for a recipe. Some specialty food stores sell shelled pistachio nutmeats, but the chances are you'll have to shell them yourself. However, it takes only about 15 minutes to shell 8 ounces of in-shell pistachios to make 1 cup of nutmeats.

In-shell pistachios are sometimes dyed red. I have no idea how or where this custom started. Their natural color is tan. I make it a point to buy natural, California pistachios, rather than those that are imported.

Pistachio nutmeats are a lovely shade of green, covered with brown skin. Since the skin is not bitter, there's no real reason to remove it, except for eye appeal. The skins on pistachios are fairly loose. You can often just rub it off between your fingers, but blanching them is the easiest way.

How to Blanch Pistachios

Pour boiling water over the nutmeats and let stand for 5 to 10 minutes; drain and cool. Remove the skins by slipping them off between your fingers. After blanching, the nutmeats should be dried in a warm oven. Place in a single layer on a baking sheet and dry them for 1 hour in a 250° oven. Cool completely before storing or using.

Storing Pistachios

In a tightly covered container, in-shell pistachios will keep for about a year in the refrigerator. After shelling, place them in a heavy, airtight plastic bag and freeze for up to one year.

How to Grind Nuts

You can use a food processor to grind nuts, but because nuts contain so much oil, they must be carefully monitored during the grinding process or you will end up with nut paste faster than you can say peanut butter. Use on-off pulses, and give the nuts a good stir from the bottom once or twice during processing. A little of the flour or sugar called for in the recipe added to the nuts before processing also helps to keep them from becoming pasty.

How to Toast Nuts

Toasting nuts brings out their full range of flavor, and also makes them look nice. This is a step that is not necessary when nuts are stirred into the batter, or even used as part of the cookie decorations before baking. However, if the nuts are used after the cookies are baked, they should be toasted.

Nuts can be toasted whole or after they are chopped, slivered, or sliced, on the stove top, in the oven, or microwaved, usually depending on the amount being toasted. For much more than a cup, you may want to use the oven method.

Although it takes a few minutes for the nuts to start toasting, once they do it's only a matter of seconds until they burn, so watch carefully, or, I should say, *smell* carefully, since it's actually the aroma that gives you the best clue as to when the nuts are perfectly toasted.

To pan toast: Place the whole or chopped nuts in a dry skillet that is large enough to hold them in a single layer. Cook over medium heat, stirring and tossing them constantly, just until the nuts begin to smell toasty, about 2 to 3 minutes. Immediately remove from the heat and continue stirring for a minute or so, since the heat retained by the skillet can still cause the nuts to burn.

To toast in a conventional oven: Spread whole, halved, or chopped nuts in a single layer in a shallow pan and place in a cold oven. Set the oven temperature to 350°. Toast nuts, stirring occasionally, until the nuts smell toasty, whole and half nuts for 12 to 15 minutes, and chopped nuts for 9 to 11 minutes. Remove from the oven and continue to stir for a minute or two until the nuts cool down a little.

To microwave toast: Spread the whole or chopped nuts on a microwave-safe plate or tray. Microwave on high power for 4 to 5 minutes for whole nuts or about 3 minutes for chopped nuts, stirring halfway through toasting time.

SALT

A minuscule amount of table salt added to sugar defines sweetness. Some bakers swear by the addition of salt to confectionery products. Others do not, usually those who have been trained in the French methods of baking. The salt can be reduced or omitted from any of the recipes in this book.

SHORTENING

Solid vegetable shortening was developed years ago primarily to replace lard (rendered pig fat). It is available either plain (white and nearly tasteless) or yellow and butter-flavored. Either kind of shortening can be used in place of butter or margarine in most cookie recipes, although there will be some difference in flavor and texture.

Always use a top brand of shortening. Lower-priced brands may have had air or water whipped into them to increase volume, so they weigh less, cup for cup.

Shortening used to be a real pain to work with. It had to be dug out of the can and then transferred to measuring cups and spoons, which made them greasy and hard to wash. Now shortening is also being made in sticks and can be measured the same way as butter and margarine.

The recipes in this book were not tested with shortening unless it was called for in the list of ingredients.

Storing Shortening

After it is opened, shortening can be kept in the can or tightly wrapped for up to a year in a cool cupboard.

SUGAR AND OTHER SWEETENERS

Brown Sugar

In the old days, brown sugar was simply less-refined granulated sugar and, as such, retained some of the molasses. These days brown sugar is made by adding molasses to granulated sugar. Both light and dark brown sugar are available. Although dark brown sugar contains about twice as much molasses as light brown sugar, and has a more pronounced molasses flavor, the two can always be used interchangeably.

Storing Brown Sugar

Once opened, both light and dark brown sugars lose moisture quickly and become rock hard. Store in a tightly closed glass or plastic container. I store brown sugar in the freezer (with the plastic bag in the box taped shut if it has been opened), and bring it to room temperature when needed. (It thaws and softens quickly.) If there are any little hard lumps in the sugar that cannot be easily broken apart with your fingers, discard them. They will never dissolve, either in blending or baking.

To soften brown sugar that has become hard through mosture loss, place it in an airtight container with a fat wedge of apple. After a couple of days, the sugar should be made soft again by the moisture in the apple and ready to use.

Confectioners' Sugar

Confectioners' sugar is also known as powdered sugar and 4X. It is granulated sugar that has been ground to a powdery consistency, and has had some cornstarch added to help prevent lumping and to make it easy to measure and

blend with other ingredients. Confectioners' sugar can develop little lumps after it is opened and these should be sieved out before the sugar is used. In cookie making, confectioners' sugar is used mainly for icings and glazes, where an extremely smooth texture is desirable.

Storing Confectioners' Sugar
Store confectioners' sugar, tightly closed, in a cool, dry place.

Granulated Sugar
This is the same white sugar you stir or don't stir into your coffee, and is the sweetener called for in most cookie recipes, sometimes in tandem with other sweetening agents.

Granulated sugar is refined from sugar cane, and sometimes from sugar beets. It is a simple carbohydrate and its chemical name is sucrose. Besides making cookies taste good, sugar has several important functions in cookie making. It helps to insure tenderness and good texture, provides much of the golden-brown color of baked cookies, increases storage time by retaining moisture, and acts as a creaming agent for fats and as a foaming agent for eggs.

Storing Granulated Sugar
Granulated sugar keeps almost indefinitely, but it can get lumpy under humid conditions. Store it in a moisture-proof container or in its unopened bag or box in a cool, dry place.

Sugar Substitutes
The only similarity between these and sugar is that they both taste sweet. Substitutes absolutely cannot be used for baking, except in recipes that have been especially developed for them.

Superfine Sugar
This is granulated sugar that has been ground into very fine crystals. It dissolves very quickly, which makes it the sugar of choice for meringues. Regular granulated sugar and superfine sugar can be substituted for one another.

Sweeteners, Liquid
In baking recipes, light and dark corn syrup, honey, molasses, cane (table) syrup, and maple syrup are the most commonly used liquid sweeteners. But, since they have a different chemical composition than regular sugar, they cannot be used in place of it.

Molasses is a by-product of refining cane sugar. It is available in three grades: light and dark from the first and second boiling of the cane, and blackstrap, the most potent of the three, obtained from the final boiling. The term "unsulphered" means that sulphur was not used in the refining process. For the recipes in this book use either light, dark, or unsulphured molasses. I prefer unsulphured molasses, which is what I usually call for.

Storing Liquid Sweeteners
Read the label, but generally liquid sweeteners can be stored in a cool cabinet after they have been opened. Maple syrup is one exception; it must be refrigerated.

SPICES
Spices are often at the very heart and soul of many cookies. Here are the mostly commonly used spices in cookie baking, as well as an abridged profile of their flavors and the forms in which they are available:

The flavor of spices, especially ground spices, does not last for very long. Before shopping for baking supplies, check the condition of the spices in your cupboard by rubbing a little of the ground spice between your fingers. Then sniff it

Tip
Bakers often use pepper in sweet baked products to give them a little character. Black pepper, for instance, is the spice that gives gingerbread its characteristic bite.

Spice	Type of Flavor	Forms
Allspice	Predominately clove	Whole and ground with cinnamon and nutmeg overtones
Anise	Sweet, licorice-like	Seeds
Cardamom	Cool, exotic, eucalyptus-like	Seeds and ground
Cinnamon	Sweet, aromatic	Sticks and ground
Cloves	Strong, pungent, but basically sweet	Whole and ground
Ginger	Sharp, spicy sweet; pungent flavor and aroma	Fresh, crystallized pieces and ground
Mace	Similar to nutmeg, but more delicate	Ground
Nutmeg	Strong, sweet, warm	Whole and ground
Black, white, and red pepper	Hot	Whole and various grinds (see Tip)

to make sure that it still produces its characteristic pungent aroma. If not, it's time to buy new.

Storing Spices

Store spices in tightly closed containers in a cool, dark, dry cabinet. Mark the date of purchase on the lid, or label the container, so you have some idea about its age.

VANILLA

See "Extracts."

VEGETABLE OILS

These are not often used in cookie recipes. Vegetable oils absolutely cannot be substituted for butter or other solid fats unless the recipe has been especially developed for them.

ZEST, CITRUS

The colored portion of the outermost peel on citrus fruits is called zest. The white pith that is just beneath is very bitter, so when recipes call for zest, make sure that it does not include the pith. The zest is what carries the essential oils of the fruit, which makes it an intense flavoring agent when it is shredded or grated.

Grated zest has a very intense flavor, often too much flavor that borders on being bitter. It is also difficult to grate the peel without picking up too much of the pith. For a more mellow flavor, the alternative is to shred the zest and then mince it with a sharp knife.

To obtain shredded zest, rub the fruit lightly across the shredding blade of a four-sided grater, then mince the shreds with a sharp knife. Or you can invest in a little zesting tool, which has five little holes in the head and is drawn across the peel to remove just the zest in fine threads, which can then be minced.

Zest should be added only to cool or cooling mixtures. For better distribution in the batter, it is usually blended into ingredients at the creaming stage before the flour is added.

3
Terms and Techniques

After the recipe has been decided upon and all the equipment and ingredients have been assembled, the moment of truth arrives. You will actually start to make cookies!

My grandmother consistently turned out impeccable cookies, cakes, and all sorts of fancy baked goods, and she didn't even *own* measuring cups or spoons, much less *use* them. I'm not sure how she did it, except that she probably learned to bake at about the same time she learned to walk and talk, and had an unerring sense of quantities merely by looking at them or taking them in her hand. I suspect she was not unique among the cooks of her day. But that was then and this is now. What can I say, except that most of us are not nearly that infallible.

I have tried to be very clear in the recipes in this book about what to do, how to do it, for how long, and what to look for or expect, so, hopefully, you will not have to refer to this list very often.

General cookie-making terms and techniques used throughout the book are explained here. Special techniques that are used only when making certain kinds of cookies—techniques such as rolling out dough or beating egg whites—can be found in the chapters that call for them, or you can find them in the index.

BATTER
Batter is thin enough to pour or to drop from a spoon. (See also "Dough.")

BEATING
This is what you do when you really want to mix things up. Beating is a rapid, circular motion that can be done with a heavy spoon, a whisk, or an electric mixer, depending on what is being beaten. Beating also incorporates air into the mixture and helps it to rise. Do not overbeat a cookie batter, which might cause the cookies to rise too much. The general rule after adding the flour is to beat just until well blended and no longer.

BEATING UNTIL
Most cookie recipes start out by beating room-temperature butter (or other solid fat) and sugar together. "Until light and fluffy" or "light and creamy" refers to what you

21

have in the bowl after beating with an electric mixer on medium-high speed for two or three minutes. The term means what it sounds like: The mixture has lightened in color, increased in volume, and looks fluffy or creamy, although there will still be some graininess if using granulated sugar. The purpose of this long beating is to give the fat an opportunity to wrap itself around the sugar without melting, making the two as one. Speeding up the mixer to make the process go faster is not advisable, since the increased friction may only cause the solid fat to melt.

BLENDING

Blending means to mix two or more ingredients until they are completely incorporated with each other.

COMBINING

Combine means to stir two or more ingredients together just until mixed.

COOLING

Most cookies are firm enough when they come from the oven to be transferred immediately to the racks on which they will be cooled. Other cookies need to stay on the baking sheet for one or two to several minutes to firm up a bit before lifting them off. Still others may need to be returned to the oven, on the baking sheet, to soften slightly if they become difficult to remove. In this book, cooling procedures are given for every recipe.

The point of cooling cookies is to make them firm and to allow the steam within them, generated by the baking process, to be completely evaporated before the cookies are stored. Otherwise they will be soggy.

CUTTING IN

This is the method by which solid fat is incorporated into dry ingredients. The easiest way to do this is with a pastry blender, an implement with U-shaped wires attached to a wooden or plastic grip. Using two knives in a crisscross motion also works well.

DOTTING

Dotting means to distribute small pieces of butter (usually) over the surface.

DOUGH

Dough is firm enough to hold its shape. (See also "Batter.")

DRIZZLING

Drizzling means to drip a thin icing or glaze over cookies or other baked goods, usually using the tip of a spoon.

DUSTING

Dusting is to lightly sprinkle a powdery dry ingredient, such as confectioners' sugar or cocoa.

FOLDING

This is one technique where watching it done once is worth a thousand words, so if you know an accomplished baker you can call on for a quick demonstration, do so by all means.

Folding is required when a light, aerated mixture (usually stiffly beaten egg whites or whipped cream) is to be incorporated into a heavier mixture to lighten it, with minimal loss of air.

To fold, spoon about half of the light mixture on top of the heavier mixture. (Make sure to use a large enough bowl.) With a large rubber spatula, cut through the center of the mixture down to the bottom of the bowl, across the bottom of the bowl, and up the side and over. This should be done very gently. Turn the bowl slightly with each fold. Continue in this manner until both mixtures are uniformly combined. Fold in the remaining light mixture until no streaks remain.

Some recipes may instruct you to stir in about a quarter of the light mixture before folding in the remainder as directed above.

GLAZING

Glazing is to lightly coat with thin icing, usually with a pastry brush (page 7) or an icing spatula (page 6).

GREASING BAKING SHEETS AND PANS

The mistake most inexperienced bakers make is greasing baking sheets and baking pans too lavishly, which will result in cookies that spread too much and baking sheets that are hard to clean. If the baking sheet is reasonably unmarred and very clean (that means no areas of baked-on grease here and there), only a very little grease is necessary to keep the cookies from sticking to the sheet after they are baked. If the cookies contain a proportionately large amount of butter or other fat, greasing the baking sheet may not be needed at all.

My choice for greasing both baking sheets and baking pans is flavorless vegetable-oil spray. I know that doesn't sound very gourmet, but the spray works well, it's easy to do, and doesn't impart a bit of flavor to the cookies. Here again, don't overdo it. Follow the label instructions and spray on a *very light* coating, covering the baking sheet, or the area to be greased in the baking pan, evenly and completely.

My next choice would be room-temperature shortening, *very lightly* applied with a crumpled paper towel. You can also use very soft butter or margarine (preferably unsalted, since salted butter and margarine tend to burn), that is rubbed on with a paper towel or applied, very lightly and evenly, with a pastry brush.

Not often, but occasionally, it is necessary to grease *and* flour a baking sheet to keep the cookies from sticking. Grease the baking sheet as described above, then sprinkle a tablespoon or so of flour as evenly as possible over the greased sheet. Tilt the baking sheet in all directions until it is evenly coated with flour. Finally, shake the baking sheet pan over the sink to knock off any excess flour.

If the greasing job has been done properly, the baking sheets will usually need only to be wiped well with paper towels and cooled before being reused for subsequent batches of cookies. Often regreasing is not even necessary.

Alternatives to greasing include covering the baking sheet with aluminum foil, shiny side up to better reflect the heat. Also, the cookies are less likely to stick to the shiny side. The foil needs to be greased just like the baking sheet, but the supposed advantage is that while one batch of cookies is baking, the next can be prepared on sheets of foil. Slide the first batch off and slip the (cooled!) baking sheet beneath the foil for the next batch. Obviously, using foil may save some time, and certainly makes cleanup a breeze, but there is something ecologically bothersome to me about this method. I would just as soon use four baking sheets.

MEASURING

Accurate liquid and dry measurements are important to the success of any recipe and are especially important when baking (read about measuring cups and spoons on page 6).

How to Measure Liquid Measurements

Pour the liquid into a glass measuring cup, which should be set on a level surface. View the cup at eye level to make sure the liquid is even with the gauge marks.

To measure dry ingredients, use dry measuring cups and spoon in the flour, sugar, or whatever dry ingredient you want to measure, mounding it slightly. (Don't use the measuring cup to scoop.) Level off with a spatula or the back of a knife.

To measure stick butter, margarine, and shortening, check the wrappers; quarter-pound sticks are printed with handy measuring marks for tablespoons, $1/4$ cup, $1/3$ cup, and $1/2$ cup. See Appendix A for more information on equivalents.

Shortening from the can or butter or margarine in solid, 1-pound blocks should be measured using dry measuring cups. Firmly press into the measuring cup, making sure there are no pockets of air in the cup; level off with a spatula or the back of a knife.

Measuring spoons are used for both liquid and dry ingredients. When measuring dry

ingredients, level them off with a spatula or the back of a knife. To measure liquid ingredients, fill the spoon as full as possible.

PREHEATING THE OVEN

Give the oven a good 15 minutes to preheat. Many experienced bakers preheat at 25° to 50° over the temperature called for, and then turn the heat down the *instant* the cookies are put into the oven. The theory is that at least this many degrees of heat are lost when the door is opened to put the cookies into the oven. But—and it's another big but—you do have to unfailingly remember to readjust the oven temperature, something novice bakers sometimes forget to do.

ROOM TEMPERATURE (SOFTENED)

This is a term that is usually applied to butter and other solid fats. It means just until soft enough to blend in easily. It does not mean melted or anything close to it. Softened butter or margarine still holds its shape. When it begins to lose its shape, it is starting to melt and may be too soft to cream properly with sugar.

SCALDING

Scalding is to bring a liquid (usually milk or cream) to just below the boiling point, when little bubbles appear around the side of the pan.

SIFTING

The flour milled these days is routinely presifted more than 100 times, so sifting, merely for the sake of removing lumps and little bits of debris like they had to do in the good old days, is no longer necessary.

To sift for the purpose of blending flour with other dry ingredients (baking powder, baking soda, salt, cocoa, etc.), I use a balloon whisk (page 8) to thoroughly mix and aerate the ingredients in a bowl. However, if the recipe specifically calls for sifted flour, that direction should be followed.

WHIPPING

The action of beating rapidly, usually with a balloon whisk or an electric mixer, to incorporate air into a mixture in order to lighten it and increase the volume.

YIELDS

It seems that no matter how many times a cookie recipe is made, the number of cookies it yields is always slightly different, and who knows why. Probably because a teaspoon one time is a teaspoon and a quarter another time the same cookies are baked. Not to worry. This is one very good reason why a range of baking times is given for most cookie recipes. Learn to depend more on how the cookies look and smell, rather than exact baking times.

4
Decorating Cookies

There are few things more naturally beautiful than golden brown, freshly baked cookies as they come from the oven. But within us all, I suppose, lurks the deep-rooted urge to improve upon the perfect. And so we decorate cookies.

I have been given cookies that have been so exquisitely composed and decorated that I could barely stand to eat them. The temptation was go out and buy a frame, or at least a can of shellac to preserve them forever.

When it comes to decorating cookies, you probably have more imagination and artistic talent than you ever realized. Usually it is just a matter of getting a varied selection of decorating supplies and seeing what happens. You may be pleasantly surprised.

Then there's decorating and decorating. The difference between fancy and plain decorations may be going all out with a pastry bag and sparkles, or merely adding a compatible frosting, icing, or glaze to the top of the cookie. Or, for a change, you may decide to sandwich two cookies together with a fluffy filling. Recipes for these "plain" decorations can be found beginning on page 28, as well as other nice-to-have-recipes that can be useful to the cookie maker.

PUTTING ON THE GLITZ

Cookies are not wedding cakes. For the most part, they are a very humble and straightforward food and, as such, should be treated with respect and not gussied up like a loose lady. Drop cookies, icebox cookies, or cookies with very simple shapes will look and taste their best with just a hint of decoration, such as a sprinkling of confectioners' sugar or cocoa powder, or perhaps a few lines of chocolate glaze drizzled over them.

Cutout cookies, however, are the great exception. These include gingerbread people and all the other fancy shapes on which we express ourselves with elaborate decorations for Christmas and other holidays.

What You Need to Decorate Cookies

It's a good idea to keep some basic decorating supplies on hand. Then, when you plan to make cookies, you can get out your box of goodies and sort through it to find just the perfect things, as well as to determine what else you may need.

Here are the things I keep on hand:

- Pastry bags in various sizes
- Disposable pastry bags
- Decorating tips in various sizes with plain and fancy tips
- Small spatulas with straight, angled, and tapered tips
- Paste food colors (about ten colors)
- Liquid food colors
- Decorating comb (to drag through an icing, frosting, or glaze before it is set to produce a pretty, wavy pattern)
- Fluted (serrated) pastry wheel (for cutting dough to produce a fluted edge)
- Tweezers (for handling dragées and other tiny decorations)
- Cookie stamps (page 28)
- Paint brushes for applying glazes, icings, and for painting on decorations
- A variety of sprinkle decorations left over from decorating projects dating from 1967
- Small plastic and cardboard craft stencils; small doilies
- Tubes of ready-made icing in various colors (for little jobs; however, these take forever and a day to dry, so keep that in mind)

Shopping for Decorating Supplies

Start with the cake decorating section at the supermarket. It's a good place to stock up on ordinary sprinkle decorations and tubes of decorating icing.

Candy- and cake-decorating stores are where serious decorators go. I suggest you treat this expedition like a gambling junket to Las Vegas. Take a certain amount of money with you and when it's gone it's gone.

The selections of decorating paraphernalia in these stores can be overwhelming, if not downright intimidating. I am thinking of the New York Cake and Baking Distributors here in New York City, where there are tables and tables of various kinds of sprinkle decorations, and a whole wall of food colorings. And you wouldn't believe the assortment of cookie cutters.

Unfortunately, stores like this exist only in fairly large cities. The next best thing is mail order. Wilton Industries, Sweet Celebrations, and New York Cake and Baking Distributors probably have the best selection anywhere of decorating equipment and supplies. Call or write for their catalogs (see Appendix C, "Shopping and Mail-Order Sources").

A Glossary of the Most Common Sprinkle and Applied Decorations

Dragées (pronounced "drah-zhays"): Round balls in various sizes from small to teensy, in many colors including gold and silver. (The larger sizes are usually placed, not scattered. Use tweezers for this job.)

Jimmies: Tiny, cylinder-shaped pellets in different flavors and colors.

Sprinkles: Colorful, infinitesimal sugar-spheres that are meant to be scattered at random over cookies, cakes, and other confections. Icings and glazes hold them in place.

Nonpareils: Wee sugar balls. Smaller than dragées, larger than sprinkles.

Crystal sugar: A large granulation of sugar, usually brightly colored.

Edible glitter: Sparkly sprinkles

Candy and confections: Tiny candies and other confections in many colors and designs that are often seasonal or made in holiday shapes and colors.

There are also more "natural" options, such as dried fruits, nuts, and seeds, as well as candied cherries and other fruits.

All the Colors of the Rainbow

There are two main kinds of food coloring: liquid and paste.

Liquid Food Coloring

This is what most cooks depend on to color food. However, liquid colorings are only meant to *tint* food, not to actually color it. You can't achieve dark, vibrant colors using liquid food coloring, even if you use a whole bottle. If what you're aiming for is a pretty pastel, use liquid coloring. Add the coloring drop by drop to the mixture that is to be colored until it reaches the shade that you want. Primary colors can be mixed to produce other colors. Do this just the way you were taught to mix water colors in kindergarten: Blue and yellow makes green, red and yellow makes orange, etc.

Paste Food Coloring

This is what serious decorators use. With it you can create a whole range of hues from very pale to very intense. Paste colors come in jars in every color imaginable from buttercup yellow to delphinium blue. These colors are extremely potent. You need to use only a very small amount. One jar could conceivably last a lifetime. The best way to add paste color is to pick up the smallest amount possible on the tip of a toothpick and add it that way to the mixture to be colored. If you are the least bit heavy-handed, you are likely to end up with barn-red frosting when what you really wanted was baby pink.

Cookies as Canvases

Cookies can be decorated either before or after baking. When decorating before baking, the possibilities are somewhat limited, since the heat of the oven can do strange things to many applied decorations. Most unbaked cookies go into the oven decorated with merely colored sugars, candied fruits, or nuts.

Unbaked cookies can also be painted with Pastel Cookie Paint (opposite) or Bright Cookie Paint (page 28), and even decorated with "embossed" designs using Piping Dough (page 28).

Cookies on Cookies

This is a neat little technique that is often overlooked. It is also a good decorating method for children. The principle is simple. Two or three different-size baked cookies are set on top of one another, going from the largest to the smallest. For the best effect, the cookies should be different shapes and different colors. The cookies can be "glued" together with icing, or they can be strung together using ribbon or licorice shoestrings through holes made in the center of the cookies before baking.

Double-cookie scenes can also be easily created. For instance, a boat-shaped cookie sailing on a blue, rectangular cookie sea; one or two small animal shapes in a round- or square-cookie barnyard or corral. The ideas, I promise you, will just keep coming once you begin. Use icing or glaze to "glue" the cookie scenes together.

Stenciling

Place a small stencil (or doily) over the baked cookie. Sprinkle very lightly over the stencil with confectioners' sugar or cocoa powder. Lift the stencil carefully, so as not to smudge the cookie.

You can also "paint" over a stencil for interesting designs.

Colored Granulated and Crystal Sugars

It's a lot cheaper to make your own colored sugars than to buy them. Place the sugar in small bowls, one for each color. Add liquid food coloring and mix with your fingers until you have the shade you want. (In order to keep your fingers from getting stained, pull on plastic gloves before mixing, or use a fork or spoon, although these don't work as well.)

Pastel Cookie Paint

This paint produces delicate colors. In small bowls, thin liquid food colors with water. Apply with a paintbrush to the raw dough.

Bright Cookie Paint

For bright, shiny colors, use this formula to "paint" cookies *before* they are baked.

> **2 large egg yolks**
> **Liquid food coloring**

In a small bowl, lightly beat the egg yolks. Divide the yolks evenly among 4 small bowls, about 1½ teaspoons per bowl. Add food coloring to each bowl and mix until evenly colored. Use a small paintbrush to brush colors on the cookie dough before baking.

To make yellow paint: Add ¾ teaspoon yellow food coloring.

To make red paint: Add ¾ teaspoon red food coloring.

To make green paint: Add a scant ½ teaspoon green food coloring.

To make blue paint: Add a scant ½ teaspoon blue food coloring.

Piping with Dough

This is a tricky little technique that you don't see very often, but it works wonders for decorating cookies before they are baked. By using this dough-type icing, you can pipe simple or intricate raised and colored designs on cookies before they are baked.

> **½ cup (1 stick) butter, at room temperature**
> **½ cup all-purpose flour, sifted if it is the slightest bit lumpy**
> **1 tablespoon light corn syrup**
> **Food coloring**

In a small bowl, with an electric mixer at medium speed, beat together the butter, flour, and corn syrup until smooth. Gradually beat in liquid or paste food coloring to achieve the desired color.

Pipe onto the unbaked cookie in whatever designs you would like.

Stamped Cookies

Stamping is another good technique for decorating unbaked cookies. In your travels through kitchenware stores, you are almost sure to come upon cookie stamps. These are generally round, sometimes square, and about 2½ inches in diameter. The little devices, which have a decorative design cut into them in reverse, are pressed onto a ball of raw cookie dough to make a relief pattern on the cookie top. In olden days, cookie stamps were carved out of wood. Nowadays they are made of glass or ceramic and have little knobs on the top.

You don't need to be limited to using real cookie stamps. Look in kitchen drawers, the toy box, the workshop, and even through costume jewelry to find objects that when pressed into raw cookie dough will make interesting patterns.

Dough that is rolled into a ball and then pressed down (with the bottom of a glass, for instance, or the tines of a fork) before it is baked can almost always be turned into a stamped cookie. You merely roll the dough into a ball and press down onto it with the floured stamp. Before the cookie is baked, the raised portion can be colored with Bright Cookie Paint (opposite) or, for more delicate shades, Pastel Cookie Paint (page 27).

Decorating After Baking

The most fabulous examples of decorated cookies are done after baking. Here is where the royal icings and glazes, as well as the most glittery and glitzy of decorating findings come into play.

Icings can be applied to baked cookies in different ways: They can be spread onto the cookie with a small spatula, or piped or painted on.

Slightly different consistencies are needed for different methods of application, which is just a matter of adding a few drops of water or corn syrup to thin the icing, or more confectioners' sugar to thicken it.

After the cookies are baked, decorations can be applied directly to the surface, or the cookies can be glazed with a white or colored icing before fancy decorations are put down.

Simple Cookie Icing

This icing, which can be used as a background before the baked cookies are decorated, can be tinted with either liquid or paste food color and dries to a hard, shiny finish. It can be used for glazing or piping.

> 1 cup sifted confectioners' sugar
> 1 teaspoon milk
> 2 teaspoons light corn syrup

In a small bowl, with a fork, mix the confectioners' sugar and milk until smooth. Stir in the corn syrup until well blended.

For piping: Use as is.

For painting: The icing must be thinned by stirring in very small amounts of corn syrup until the right consistency is obtained.

To color: Use the tips of toothpicks to add infinitesimal amounts of paste coloring until the desired shade is reached.

Royal Icing

This icing is a joy to use. It tastes good, covers well, and pipes easily. It is also the best "glue" to use for applying decorations and building things, like a gingerbread house.

Make royal icing shortly before you plan to use it. This icing dries out quickly. Keep it covered with a damp towel, pushed down into the bowl close to the icing, at all times. Leftover royal icing made with raw egg whites should be discarded after using.

Royal Icing Made with Egg Whites

Until a few years ago, this was the formulation used by home bakers. But after salmonella awareness, meringue powders have become increasingly popular. (Although the danger of contracting food poisoning from raw egg whites is slight at best, you might prefer the formula using meringue powder.) This icing is the right consistency for piping and "gluing." For painting or glazing, thin slightly by beating in a very small amount of water.

> 3 large egg whites, at room temperature
> 1/2 teaspoon cream of tartar
> One 16-ounce box confectioners' sugar, sifted

In a large bowl, with an electric mixer at medium speed, beat together the egg whites and cream of tartar until frothy. Gradually add the confectioners' sugar until blended. Beat at medium-high speed for 5 to 7 minutes until the icing is glossy and forms stiff, slightly curving peaks when the beaters are lifted.

Yield: About 2 1/2 cups

Tip

For small or spur-of-the-moment piping jobs, use a small, zipper-top plastic bag just as you would a pastry bag. Snip off the tip of one corner of the bag. Fill with icing and seal the top, pressing out the air. Then just pipe away!

How to Use a Pastry Bag

There seems to be an inherent fear among American cooks about using pastry bags. Actually, they are kind of friendly little devices, and if you take the time to learn how to use one, you'll kick yourself for not having done so before.

There are many types of pastry bags available, even disposable ones, and they come in every size for every piping task, from putting down large amounts of cookie dough on the baking sheet, to tiny little bags for the most delicate piping.

Tips also come in a huge variety of sizes and different shapes of openings. For cookie making and decorating, you will only need a very few.

Pastry bags and tips, when you buy them, all come with the manufacturer's directions. Better than that, Wilton has decorating videotapes that you can order (see Appendix C, "Shopping and Mail-Order Sources"). But just to give you an idea how easy it is, at least for simple projects:

- First fit the tube into the pastry bag. This is either done with a coupler or, in some cases, the tube is just slipped down into the tip of the bag.

- Hold the bag down near the tip and fold the top down partway over your hand. Using a rubber spatula or a large spoon, fill the pastry bag about two-thirds full with the icing.

- Pull the bag back up and twist it securely at the point where the icing ends inside the bag.

- Hold the bag as shown in the diagram.

- Assuming that you are right-handed, exert pressure on the icing with the right hand, which keeps the icing moving down into the tip. Use your left hand to guide it. Stop frequently to retwist the bag so that the icing keeps moving down into the tip.

- Use a 90° angle to pipe straight down. This is the position you use to pipe rounds of cookie batter onto a baking sheet. Here's how to do it: Hold the bag so that the tip is just slightly above the surface. Squeeze and continue to squeeze, and at the same time lift the tip so that the batter builds up. When the drop is the size that you want it, stop pressure, then pull away. Use the tip to clean away the little point of dough that forms as you pull away or smooth it with your finger.

- The 45° angle is for writing and piping running decorations. Hold the bag at this angle with the back of the bag facing you. The amount of icing you lay down is determined by how slowly or quickly you keep moving the bag.

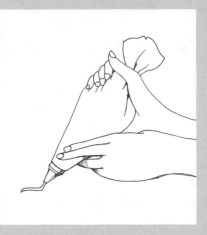

How to hold a pastry bag at a 45° angle

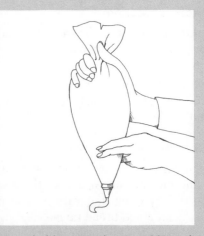

How to hold a pastry bag at a 90° angle

The easiest way to learn how to use a pastry bag is to use it. Make a simple icing and practice on a sheet of waxed paper. Then scrape up the icing, refill the bag, and practice again.

Royal Icing Made with Meringue Powder

Meringue powder has always been used by professional bakers to make royal icing, as it is the right consistency for piping and "gluing." For painting or glazing, thin by adding few drops of water until it is the right consistency. Royal icing made with meringue powder can be kept for a few days in a tightly covered container at room temperature. Rebeat when ready to use, and thin slightly, if necessary.

> 3 level tablespoons meringue powder
> 4 cups sifted confectioners' sugar
> 6 tablespoons warm water

In a large bowl, with an electric mixer at medium speed, beat together the meringue powder, confectioners' sugar, and water until the mixture forms peaks when the beaters are lifted, 7 to 12 minutes, depending on the power of the mixer you are using.

Yield: About 3 cups

MISCELLANEOUS ICINGS, FROSTINGS, GLAZES, AND FILLINGS

One of my pet peeves is cookbooks that require you to flip back and forth to find all the recipes you need to make one thing.

In almost every case in this book where they are called for, I have included icings, glazes, and frostings right there with the recipe where you need it. Occasionally, I have suggested that you look to this chapter for fillings and frostings. In any case, these are recipes that the cookie baker should have for reference and to use as needed.

Flavored Icing and Glaze for Cookies

This is a good formula for making flavored icings and glazes. You can use any liquid you like (usually fruit juices, but sometimes rum or liqueurs) to get the desired flavor. To make a plain glaze, use water. Milk or cream used instead of water makes a richer glaze.

> 1 cup sifted confectioners' sugar
> 2 to 3 tablespoons liquid (see above)
> 1 teaspoon vegetable oil

In a small bowl, with a mixing spoon, beat the confectioners' sugar with the liquid until smooth. Add the oil and continue to beat until the mixture is glossy.

For icing: Use only about 2 tablespoons liquid.

For glaze: Use 2½ to 3 tablespoons liquid.

Yield: About ¼ cup

Basic Cookie Drizzle

This mixture is specially formulated to hold its shape after it is randomly drizzled over the cookie of your choice.

> 3 cups confectioners' sugar, sifted
> ¼ cup milk
> 1 teaspoon vanilla extract
> Liquid or paste food coloring

In a small bowl, stir together the confectioners' sugar, milk, and vanilla until smooth, adding additional milk if necessary, so that the glaze is thin enough to drizzle, but still firm enough to hold its shape slightly. Add food coloring, if desired.

Yield: About 1⅛ cups

Chocolate Glazes

A melted-chocolate glaze is one of the easiest (and most delicious) ways to embellish cookies. It can be spread or drizzled over the cookie tops, or used as a dip or as a filling.

There are two ways to make a chocolate glaze. The first is simply to melt the chocolate and use it as is.

The second method is to melt the chocolate with shortening. (Do not substitute vegetable oil, butter, margarine, or any other fat.) Many bakers prefer this formula, as it makes a shinier glaze that may be a little easier to use.

Dark Chocolate Glaze

1 cup (6 ounces) semisweet chocolate chips, or 6 ounces (6 squares) semisweet chocolate, broken in half
2 teaspoons plain shortening

In a small, heavy saucepan set over very low heat, stir together the chocolate and shortening until melted and smooth.

Milk Chocolate Glaze

1 cup (6 ounces) milk chocolate chips
2 teaspoons plain shortening

In a small, heavy saucepan set over very low heat, stir together the chocolate chips and shortening until melted and smooth.

Basic Buttercream Filling and Frosting

Better watch the kids, or they're likely to finish this off before it even gets out of the bowl.

^{1}/3 cup (^{1}/2 stick plus 1^1/2 tablespoons) salted butter, at room temperature
3 cups sifted confectioners' sugar, divided
2 to 3 tablespoons milk or light cream
1^1/2 teaspoons vanilla extract

In a medium-size bowl, with an electric mixer at medium speed, beat together the butter, 1 cup of the confectioners' sugar, and 1 tablespoon of the milk until light and fluffy, 2 to 3 minutes. Gradually add the remaining 2 cups of confectioners'

sugar and the remaining 2 tablespoons of milk, alternately, until the mixture reaches a soft, spreadable consistency. Beat in the vanilla.

Yield: About 2 cups

Variations

Lemon or Orange Frosting and Filling: Substitute lemon juice or orange juice for the milk. Omit the vanilla. Beat in 1 teaspoon grated lemon or orange zest.

Peppermint: Substitute a few drops of peppermint extract for the vanilla. A tablespoon or two of crushed peppermint candy can also be added.

Mocha: Increase confectioners' sugar to 4 cups; omit the vanilla. In a medium-size bowl, with a whisk, combine the confectioners' sugar with ^{1}/4 cup unsweetened cocoa powder until thoroughly mixed. Substitute ^{1}/3 cup strong coffee for the milk. **Yield:** About 2^1/2 cups

Basic Chocolate Filling and Frosting

This is the best frosting for brownies—and almost anything else. It can also be used as a cookie filling or frosting.

3 tablespoons salted butter or margarine, at room temperature
3 tablespoons unsweetened cocoa powder
1 tablespoon light corn syrup
^{1}/2 teaspoon vanilla extract
1 cup confectioners' sugar, sifted
1 to 2 tablespoons milk

1. In a small bowl, with an electric mixer at medium-high speed, beat the butter, cocoa, corn syrup, and vanilla until smooth. Gradually beat in the confectioners' sugar and enough milk to give the mixture a good spreading consistency.

2. Use at once, or refrigerate, covered, until ready to use. If the mixture stiffens, let stand at room

temperature for about 10 minutes, or until it reaches spreading consistency.

Yield: About 1 cup (enough frosting for two 8- or 9-inch square pans of brownies, or one 13 × 9-inch pan)

Mint Filling or Frosting

This is especially nice to spread between chocolate cookies.

2 cups sifted confectioners' sugar
¹⁄₈ teaspoon salt
3 tablespoons light cream
¹⁄₄ teaspoon peppermint extract
Few drops of liquid green food coloring

1. In a large bowl, with a whisk, combine the confectioners' sugar and salt until thoroughly mixed. Gradually add the cream, stirring with a rubber spatula or a mixing spoon until smooth. Stir in the peppermint extract and green food coloring until completely blended and evenly colored.

2. Use immediately, or refrigerate, covered, until ready to use. If the mixture stiffens, let stand at room temperature for about 10 minutes, or until it reaches spreading consistency.

Yield: About ³⁄₄ cup

Crème de Menthe Filling or Frosting

This is an adult version of Mint Filling or Frosting and has a lot more pizzazz. However, crème de menthe contains alcohol, as I'm sure you know, so this is not a good choice for children's cookies.

3 cups sifted confectioners' sugar
¹⁄₄ cup crème de menthe
¹⁄₄ cup (¹⁄₂ stick) salted butter or margarine, at room temperature

1. In a large bowl, with an electric mixer at medium speed, alternately add the confectioners' sugar and the crème de menthe to the butter until well blended. Beat at medium-high speed until the mixture is smooth and fluffy.

2. Use immediately, or refrigerate, covered, until ready to use. If the mixture stiffens, let stand at room temperature for about 10 minutes, or until it reaches spreading consistency.

Yield: About 1¹⁄₃ cups

Variation

Any liqueur that you like can be substituted for the crème de menthe.

Creamy Mocha Filling

1 cup heavy (whipping) cream
¹⁄₂ cup sugar
6 ounces (6 squares) semisweet chocolate, coarsely chopped, or 1 cup (6 ounces) semisweet chocolate chips
2 tablespoons strong coffee
¹⁄₂ cup (1 stick) salted butter, at room temperature

1. In a heavy, medium-size saucepan over medium heat, stir together the cream and sugar until the mixture begins to boil. Reduce the heat to low and boil gently, without stirring, for 6 minutes. Remove from the heat. Immediately stir in the chocolate and coffee until the chocolate is melted and the mixture is smooth and completely blended. Turn into a large bowl and set aside at room temperature until cool.

2. With a whisk, beat the butter into the cooled chocolate mixture, 1 tablespoon at a time, until the mixture is smooth. Use at once or refrigerate, covered, until ready to use. If the filling hardens, let stand at room temperature for about 10 minutes, or until of spreading consistency.

Yield: About 2¹⁄₄ cups

Marshmallow Creme Filling

This is exactly like the filling you'll find in those popular chocolate sandwich cookies. Wonderful to sandwich anything that you want to take you flying back into your childhood.

> 2 tablespoons salted butter or margarine, at room temperature
> 2 tablespoons plain shortening
> 1/2 cup marshmallow creme
> 3/4 teaspoon vanilla extract
> 2/3 cup confectioners' sugar

In a small bowl, with an electric mixer at medium-high speed, beat the butter and shortening until creamy, about 1 minute. Gradually beat in the marshmallow creme until blended. With the mixer at medium-low speed, beat in the vanilla and the confectioners' sugar. With the mixer at medium-high speed, beat the mixture to a spreading consistency.

Yield: About 1 cup

Ginger-Molasses Buttercream Filling

Very tasty with ginger cookies or fruit-and-nut cookies.

> 3/4 cup sugar
> 1/4 cup water
> 2 tablespoons light corn syrup
> 3/4 cup (1 1/2 sticks) unsalted butter, at room temperature
> 2 teaspoons unsulphured molasses
> 2 teaspoons finely chopped crystallized ginger

1. In a small, heavy saucepan set over low heat, stir together the sugar, water, and corn syrup until the sugar is dissolved. Brush down the side of the pan with a brush dipped in water to remove any sugar crystals. Cook over medium-low heat, without stirring, until the mixture reaches 238° on a candy thermometer, about 10 minutes. Remove from the heat and set aside to cool to room temperature.

2. In a medium-size bowl, with an electric mixer at medium-high speed, beat the butter until creamy, about 1 minute. Gradually beat in the cooled syrup and then the molasses until completely blended. Fold in the ginger.

3. Use immediately, or refrigerate, covered, until ready to use. If the mixture stiffens, let stand at room temperature for about 10 minutes, or until it reaches spreading consistency.

Yield: About 1 1/2 cups

A FEW BASIC RECIPES AND INGREDIENTS

Dried Fruit Puree

This miraculous mixture can be used measure for measure as a replacement for butter or oil in any cookie recipe. Obviously, it will reduce the fat content dramatically.

> 1 1/3 cups (8 ounces) pitted prunes
> 6 tablespoons water

Combine the prunes and water in a food processor. Process with on-off pulses until the mixture becomes pasty. Use measure for measure as a replacement for butter or oil in baking recipes.

A slightly richer variation replaces half of the fat with dried fruit puree. As an example: Instead of 1 cup of butter use 1/2 cup butter and 1/2 cup dried fruit puree. This half-and-half mixture improves texture and flavor, but still cuts the fat dramatically.

Variations

Fig Puree: Substitute figs for the prunes.

Date Puree: Substitute pitted dates for the prunes.

Praline Powder

This wonderful ingredient, as it turns out, is only used in one cookie recipe. But since it has other applications, I thought I'd just leave it here with the following suggestions for how to use it.

1 cup sugar
1 cup natural almonds

1. Lightly butter a baking sheet; set aside.

2. In a medium-size, heavy saucepan, combine the sugar and almonds. Cook the mixture over medium heat, stirring constantly, until the syrup turns a rich amber color. Pour the syrup and nuts onto the prepared baking sheet to cool.

3. When the praline has cooled, break it up into small pieces and pulverize it in a food processor. Store the powder in a tightly covered jar in the refrigerator.

Yield: About 2 cups

- Substitute about one-quarter praline powder for sugar in plain cookie recipes.

- Stir it into icings and fillings.

- Sprinkle it on top of baked or unbaked cookies in place of sugar.

- Pulverize only what you need. Eat the rest like peanut brittle.

Cinnamon Sugar

In a small bowl, thoroughly mix 2 tablespoons granulated sugar with 1 teaspoon ground cinnamon.

Almond Paste

1$^1/_2$ cups whole blanched almonds
1$^1/_2$ cups sifted confectioners' sugar
1 large egg white
1 teaspoon almond extract
$^1/_4$ teaspoon salt

1. In a food processor fitted with a steel blade, process the almonds using on-off pulses until finely ground, stopping once to give the nuts a good stir from the bottom. Add the confectioners' sugar, egg white, almond extract, and salt. Continue to process until the mixture forms a stiff paste.

2. Store in an airtight container or plastic bag.

Yield: About 1$^1/_3$ cups

5
Storing, Shipping, and Giving Away Cookies

Cookies are amenable to just about anything you choose to do with them:
Make the dough tonight and bake the cookies next Tuesday.

Store cookies in a big crock on the counter and most varieties will keep just fine down to the last delicious crumb.

Want to send a few dozen cookies to your cousin in Japan? No problem! Wrap them with reasonable care and call UPS.

And whoever complained about getting cookies as a gift, especially when a little thought has been given to the container in which they are presented?

MIX IT NOW, BAKE IT LATER

Many cookie doughs, with the exception of very thin batters or meringue-based doughs, can be mixed and then refrigerated for several days or frozen for up to three months.

Dough that will be refrigerated for only a few days can be wrapped in plastic wrap. Dough that will be frozen should be tightly wrapped in aluminum foil. If you're not sure when the frozen dough will be baked, label it with the name of the cookie, the freezing date, and even the baking instructions, if you like.

If the recipe calls for the dough to be worked cold, thaw it in the refrigerator for a few hours. If the dough is to be worked at room temperature, thaw it on the kitchen counter. In either case, leave the dough tightly wrapped until you are ready to use it.

PUTTING COOKIES BY

To their credit, most cookies are never around long enough to worry about how to store them for any extended length of time. Most are eaten so quickly that merely putting them into a covered container is enough to keep them fresh for several days. Or, for bar cookies, simply leave them in the baking pan and cover with aluminum foil. See more on storing bar cookies below.

Rule number one: All cookies must be completely cool before they are stored, or they will get soft, stick together, and be generally unappetizing.

Cookies, especially those with a high butter (or other fat) content, will stay fresh for a week, and often longer, in a tightly covered cookie jar, crock, or tin.

Very soft cookies and many decorated cookies should be separated by sheets of waxed paper so that they don't stick together. A shallow container, rather than a deep crock or tin, is preferable for storing very delicate cookies that might crack or break if they were subjected to the weight of many layers of cookies on top of them.

Throughout this book, I have tried to be specific in every case for cookies that require any special storage treatment.

Store soft and crisp cookies separately; otherwise you can guess what happens. Different kinds of cookies also need separate storage facilities so that the flavor of one does not mingle with the flavor of the other.

Soft cookies will stay that way longer if a slice of apple or a piece of bread is put into the container with them and changed every other day.

In a dry climate, store crisp cookies in a loosely covered container. In a humid climate, store them in an airtight container. Crisp cookies that become slightly limp can be recrisped on a baking sheet in a 300° oven for 3 to 5 minutes.

Freezing Cookies

Most cookies can be frozen in airtight containers or zipper-top plastic bags. Place some crumpled waxed paper in the air space at the top of the container, and take the time to push all of the air out of the top of a plastic bag before sealing. Unwrap and thaw at room temperature, then store as you would fresh-baked cookies.

Freezing decorated cookies (especially those with elaborate decorations) is not recommended. If you must, flash-freeze the decorated cookies first on a baking sheet, then transfer them to a shallow storage container (so that there is not too much weight on the bottom layers), separating the layers with sheets of waxed paper. Be warned that no matter how carefully they are handled, frozen decorations have a tendency to fall off. A better method is to freeze undecorated cookies and decorate them after thawing, just as you would fresh-baked cookies.

Cookies that have been dipped in or decorated with chocolate should not be frozen, because freezing will discolor the chocolate.

Storing Bar Cookies

Most bar cookies are cut right in the baking pan, which also makes a good storage container. Let the cookies cool completely and tightly cover the pan with plastic wrap or aluminum foil. Bars will usually stay fresh for up to several days. Bars can also be stored in a tightly covered container, but be sure to separate the bars with sheets of waxed paper so they don't stick together.

Bar cookies with a high fat content (like brownies) can also be frozen. However, those that are low in fat or depend upon fruit or fruit purees for their moistness don't always do so well in the freezer. To freeze, remove the bars from the baking pan and wrap each one securely in plastic wrap or aluminum foil before freezing. Bars should be kept frozen for no longer than three months. Unwrap and thaw at room temperature, although many bars are very tasty when they are served frozen or cold.

COOKIES ON THE GO

Few things are as happily received as a box of homemade cookies. If it's possible to wrap up a little piece of "home" and send it off, cookies are the sure way to do it.

Shipping cookies takes a little care and the right packing materials, but if done correctly cookies can be sent to China and arrive in tip-top condition.

Plain, Sturdy Cookies
Are the Best Travelers

Choose sturdy cookies that store well. Most drop cookies can withstand a bit of jostling, as

can very hard cookies. Cutout cookies can usually handle the rigors of a long haul, but choose small shapes that don't break as easily as large shapes, and those with simple decorations, such as colored sugar, candied fruit, or nuts. Cookies with delicate decorations are obviously not good travelers. Glazes and icings sometimes melt. The plainer, the better is the general rule.

Loose Pack or in a Tin?

Cookies can be packed loose or in a tin or other rigid container. In either case, you will need a *very sturdy* shipping box.

To pack loose cookies, place them back-to-back and wrap each pair in plastic wrap. Line the bottom of the shipping box generously and evenly with a soft packing material, such as bubble wrap, Styrofoam chips, or crumpled newspaper. Arrange the wrapped cookies in snug rows and in single layers, separating each layer with more soft packing material. Leave space at the top of the box for as much packing material as there is at the bottom. Also make sure that the sides of the box are well padded, and be sure to fill any crevices.

Cookies that are shipped in a tin or other rigid container also need to be packed carefully within the tin or box, in layers that are separated with crumpled tissue or waxed paper. The container itself should be placed in the center of the shipping box, surrounded by enough packing material to keep it from moving about.

Bar cookies, if they are good keepers, are also good travelers. It is best to wrap each one individually, and then arrange the bars in fairly tight rows in a shallow box or tin, or even a disposable aluminum pan, as long as the pan is covered with a solid top.

COOKIES: THE BEST GIFT OF ALL

Many a gift-giving dilemma has been neatly solved with a batch of cookies. Of course, it's hard to make freshly baked, homemade cookies any more special than they already are, but if such a thing is possible, then it would have to be by the trappings of presentation.

Clever Containers

Cookies packed in a tin are the obvious, but there are other more interesting containers. Baskets, bowls, crocks, vases, canisters, platters, pitchers, colorful paper or fabric bags, and little shopping bags are all good choices. Flea markets and garage sales are good places to find many of these things at bargain prices. Decorative cloth- or paper-covered closet and drawer organizers make nifty cookie containers. Round hat boxes, for example, come in many sizes that are perfect for cookies. (Just remember to line the insides of the boxes so that they don't get greasy.)

Also consider containers that reflect the recipient's special interest: a watering can, flower pot, or small flower box for someone who enjoys indoor or terrace gardening; a mold, soufflé dish, casserole, colander, pie plate, ice bucket, or other piece of cooking or serving equipment for the person who likes to cook or entertain. Office workaholics would no doubt appreciate desk accessories, a letter box, or desk caddy filled with cookies. (Stationery stores and art supply stores, by the way, are full of interesting possibilities.) For children, a dump truck or a sand pail would be a marvelous way to present cookies.

To make sure that the cookies stay fresh, you may want to put them into plastic bags or wrap them in airtight material before inserting them into the container you have chosen.

Tissues and Bows

Line the container with such things as colored tissue paper, cellophane, fabric, or a pretty dish towel or napkin. If you like, the cookies can be nested in a bed of tinsel, thin strips of tissue, or cellophane "grass."

Wrap or overwrap the cookie container with the same gay ribbons and bows as any other gift.

Cookies as Greeting Cards

I love the idea of using cookies for mounting greeting cards for Christmas, birthdays, Mother's Day, and other special occasions, and they're easy to make.

Roll out plain sugar-cookie dough and use a pizza cutter or pastry wheel to cut the dough in the same shape and slightly larger than the card. After the cookies are baked and cooled, attach the cards with dabs of icing to hold them securely. If you like, a decorative icing design can be piped around the edge to frame the card. Overwrap with clear or colored plastic wrap or cellophane and tie it all up with ribbon.

Little Additions

Sometimes you may want to add a little something extra to your gift of cookies, such as the same-shape cutters, or some other little gadget that was used in the recipe, such as a pastry brush or a pastry wheel. And, of course, *always* tuck in the recipe, written on a card that's ready for the file box.

More Than 400
Fabulous
Cookie Recipes

6
Drop Cookies

If there is such a thing as *the* quintessential cookie, the familiar and friendly drop cookie must be it. When the word *cookie* comes to mind, it's a drop cookie of one kind or another that pops into most peoples' heads. Chocolate chip, oatmeal, peanut butter, jumbles, and many other old-fashioned favorites are drop cookies. These are the cookies that moms have been baking for generations; that fill the family cookie jar; that are baked to give away to special people.

A creamed-butter base is how most drop cookies begin. This base is probably the most often used formulation in cookie making. In fact, most cookies—rolled, refrigerated, shaped, piped, spritzed, or dropped—have their start by first creaming together butter and sugar before the flavorings and finally the flour are added to make a batter. The variations then become almost endless, which is why so many cookie recipes are so remarkably alike.

MIX, DROP, BAKE, COOL, EAT

Drop cookies are by far the easiest and quickest cookies to make. There are exceptions, but for the most part it's usually just a matter of making a batter that is the right consistency for pushing off a spoon and onto a baking sheet. There is generally no chilling or waiting around for something to happen.

QUIET! COOKIE GENIUS AT WORK

Drop-cookie batters also encourage your own inventiveness. Even if you are a novice baker, one day, while mixing your favorite drop cookie, it will occur to you that you have a couple handfuls of chocolate-covered raisins, or pieces of peanut brittle, or gummy bears, or marshmallows, or whatever, that you would like to finish off. You wonder what would happen if you stirred them into the batter. Go ahead and do it. I can assure you that nothing bad will happen and, in fact, something very good may happen.

Bolstered by your success, another time you will be tempted to try something even more daring, like adding the half cup or so of orange juice left over from breakfast to the chocolate-cookie batter. It will probably taste fine, you think, since chocolate and orange flavors go so well together. But the orange juice may make the batter too thin to drop properly. No problem. Taking courage in hand, you simply add a little more flour than the recipe calls for. Bingo! Your own chocolate-orange drops!

WHEN PUSH COMES TO SHOVE

There are any number of little implements you can use to accomplish the simple act of dropping cookie batter onto a baking sheet. In most cases, a plain old teaspoon (the kind you use to stir your coffee) works just dandy.

Sometimes you will be instructed to use another teaspoon to push off the batter. Why, I wonder, when your own finger is so much more efficient? Other methods include a special kitchen gadget that picks up the batter and then pushes it off onto the baking sheet, as well as *very small* ice cream scoops.

I have been making cookies for more than forty years, and the only things I've ever used for this task, besides a trusty teaspoon, is a measuring teaspoon, a measuring tablespoon, and, occasionally, a dry measuring cup, depending on the size cookies, and I suggest you do the same.

Please note: In these recipes, I have been quite specific about what kind of measuring implement to use. If the recipe calls for a teaspoon, use a plain teaspoon. Otherwise follow the instructions to use a measuring teaspoon, or a measuring tablespoon, or whatever is called for.

Also keep in mind that there is plenty of leeway in cookie size. If you want a larger cookie, drop slightly larger mounds of batter onto the baking sheet and leave a little more room between each one. Baking time will probably have to be extended, too. And it's just as easy to make smaller cookies by reversing this procedure.

CHOCOLATE-CHIP COOKIES

These are unquestionably the most famous drop cookies of all time. According to modern legend, which actually happens to be true, we have Mrs. Ruth Wakefield, proprietor of the Toll House Inn between Boston and New Bedford, Massachusetts, to thank for the original chocolate-chip cookie recipe. (Skeptic that I am, I found it hard to believe that there were *no* chocolate-chip cookies before Mrs. Wakefield invented hers, so I wasted a lot of time going through old American and European cookbooks to test my theory. I found *not even one* recipe for drop cookies that included chocolate pieces in the batter.)

Anyway, in keeping with tradition, Mrs. Wakefield baked for her guests at the inn. One day, back in the thirties, while stirring together a batch of Butter Drop Do Cookies (page 45), she was inspired to add pieces of chocolate to them. She cut a bar of Nestlé semisweet chocolate into bits and added them to the batter, expecting them to melt. Instead, the pieces of chocolate held their shape and softened to a creamy texture, and a monumental, new cookie recipe was born that day. Mrs. Wakefield called her creation the Toll House Cookie and it quickly became a widespread favorite.

The rest of the chocolate-chip cookie story is food history: Nestlé, the originators of chocolate chips (which they call morsels), acquired Mrs. Wakefield's recipe. To make the cookie easier to mix, Nestlé first offered a chocolate bar divided into small sections. Then they came up with the idea of making chocolate in tiny pieces (Voila! Chocolate chips!), and forever after the recipe has been printed on the bags containing the ubiquitous little morsels.

The recipes that follow include the original and the more recent version of the Toll House Cookie, as well as some of its hundreds of descendants.

Original Toll House® Cookies

This is the recipe, exactly the way it appeared on Nestlé bags of chocolate chips (which they trade-marked morsels), that was used for many years. Presumably it is identical to the recipe that Mrs. Wakefield developed. It's interesting to note the almost insignificant changes in the current version that follows. (I can't help but wonder what $1/2$ teaspoon of water did for the batter in the original recipe.)

2 ¹/₂ cups sifted flour

1 teaspoon baking soda

1 teaspoon salt

1 cup softened butter or shortening

³/₄ cup granulated sugar

³/₄ cup firmly packed brown sugar

1 teaspoon vanilla

¹/₂ teaspoon water

2 eggs

One 12-oz. pkg. (2 cups) Nestlé Semi-Sweet
  Real Chocolate Morsels

1 cup coarsely chopped nuts

Preheat oven to 375°F. Sift together flour, baking soda, and salt; set aside. Combine butter or shortening, sugar, brown sugar, vanilla, and water; beat till creamy. Beat in eggs. Add flour mixture; mix well. Stir in Nestlé Semi-Sweet Real Chocolate Morsels and nuts. Drop by well-rounded half teaspoonfuls onto greased cookie sheets.

BAKE at: 375°F.

TIME: 10 to 12 minutes.

Makes 100 2-inch cookies.

Today's Nestlé Toll House Chocolate Chip Cookies

· ·

This is the current version of the original, exactly the way it is given on the bags of Nestlé morsels (and the only way they would give me permission to use it). However, we tested this recipe using large eggs.

2 ¹/₄ cups all-purpose flour

1 teaspoon baking soda

1 teaspoon salt

1 cup (2 sticks) butter, softened

³/₄ cup granulated sugar

³/₄ cup packed brown sugar

1 teaspoon vanilla extract

2 eggs

2 cups (12-ounce package) Nestlé Toll House
  Semi-Sweet Real Chocolate Morsels

1 cup chopped nuts

COMBINE flour, baking soda, and salt in small bowl. Beat butter, granulated sugar, brown sugar, and vanilla in large mixer bowl. Add eggs one at a time, beating well after each addition; gradually beat in flour mixture. Stir in morsels and nuts. Drop by rounded tablespoon onto ungreased baking sheets.

BAKE in a preheated 375°F oven for 9 to 11 minutes until golden brown. Let stand for 2 minutes; remove to wire racks to cool completely. Makes about 5 dozen cookies.

Butter Drop Do Cookies

· ·

We can assume that this must be the recipe that Mrs. Wakefield was making when she was divinely inspired to add pieces of chocolate. They have more or less the texture of Toll House Cookies but, without the chocolate chips, they are somewhat flatter in appearance, as well as flavor.

Follow the recipe exactly for the current version of Toll House Chocolate Chip Cookies, but omit the chocolate morsels. The nuts can stay or go. The baking time remains about the same, but you do end up with significantly fewer cookies.

Yield: About 32 to 36 cookies

Tip

For soft chocolate chip cookies, bake at 325°F until light golden brown. For a crisper cookie, bake the same dough at 350°F until golden brown.

Triple Chocolate Chocolate-Chip Cookies

This is an upscale chocolate-chip cookie, very much like those from expensive cookie stores, and a chocoholic's dream come true. They are great tasting, sweet, and, most important, full of chocolate. Just one usually satisfies a nagging sweet tooth and a dual craving for chocolate. The tester's note on this recipe said: "I love chocolate and could only eat a half of one of these at a sitting."

> 6 squares (6 ounces) semisweet chocolate, coarsely chopped
>
> 2 squares (2 ounces) unsweetened chocolate, coarsely chopped
>
> 3 tablespoons salted butter or margarine
>
> $1/3$ cup all-purpose flour
>
> 1 teaspoon baking powder
>
> 2 large eggs
>
> 2 teaspoons vanilla extract
>
> 1 cup sugar
>
> 2 cups coarsely chopped pecans
>
> 6 ounces sweet baking chocolate, chilled until very hard and then chopped into small, even-size pieces

1. Adjust two racks to divide the oven into thirds. Preheat the oven to 325°. Lightly grease two baking sheets.

2. Place the semisweet chocolate, unsweetened chocolate, and butter in a heavy, medium-size saucepan. Set the pan over very low heat and stir constantly until the chocolate is melted. Remove from the heat and set aside to cool slightly.

3. In a small bowl, with a whisk, combine the flour and baking powder until thoroughly mixed.

4. In a large bowl, with an electric mixer at low speed, beat the eggs with the vanilla until frothy. Gradually add the sugar, beating at high speed until the mixture is pale yellow and thick and a ribbon forms when the beaters are lifted, about 5 minutes. Add the slightly cooled, melted chocolate and beat at medium speed until completely blended. With the mixer at medium-low speed, gradually add the flour mixture, beating just until blended. With a mixing spoon, stir in the nuts and pieces of baking chocolate until well distributed throughout the batter.

5. Drop by heaping measuring tablespoonfuls onto the prepared baking sheets, spacing the drops about 2 inches apart. With the back of the spoon, flatten each mound just a little.

6. For a slightly chewy cookie, bake for about 15 minutes until the tops crack. Reverse the baking sheets on the racks and from front to back once during baking. For a crisper cookie, add 5 minutes to the baking time. With a wide turner, transfer the cookies to wire racks to cool completely.

7. Store in a tightly covered container, separating the layers with sheets of waxed paper.

Yield: About 30 cookies

Michael Emerson's "Lotsa Chips" Cookies

Michael is my six-year-old great-nephew, a great little kid, who likes to help his mama Becky bake cookies almost as much as he enjoys hitting golf balls in the backyard.

> 2 cups all-purpose flour
>
> 1 cup regular or quick-cooking (not instant) rolled oats
>
> 1 teaspoon baking soda
>
> 1 cup (2 sticks) salted butter or margarine, at room temperature
>
> 1 $1/3$ cups granulated sugar
>
> 1 cup light brown sugar
>
> 2 large eggs
>
> 1 $1/2$ teaspoons vanilla extract
>
> 6 cups (about 24 ounces) mixed chips (Michael prefers milk chocolate, butter-scotch, and peanut butter)
>
> 2 cups (about 8 ounces) chopped walnuts
>
> 1 cup raisins (optional)

1. Adjust two racks to divide the oven into thirds. Preheat the oven to 325°. Lightly grease two baking sheets.

2. In a medium-size bowl, with a whisk, combine the flour, oats, and baking soda until thoroughly mixed.

3. In a large bowl, with an electric mixer at medium-high speed, beat the butter with the granulated sugar, brown sugar, eggs, and vanilla until very well blended, 2 to 3 minutes. With the mixer at low speed, gradually add the flour mixture to the butter mixture, beating just until blended. With a mixing spoon, stir in the chips, nuts, and raisins until evenly distributed throughout the batter. Drop by heaping measuring tablespoonfuls onto the prepared baking sheets, spacing the drops about 1½ inches apart.

4. Bake for about 12 minutes until lightly browned. Reverse the baking sheets on the racks and from front to back once during baking. With a wide turner, immediately transfer the cookies to wire racks to cool completely.

5. Store in a tightly covered container.

Yield: About 60 cookies

The Famous "Neiman Marcus" Chocolate-Chip Cookies

Neiman Marcus says the often-repeated story about its chocolate chip cookies isn't so, and I believe it, since this is one of the friendliest department stores with which I've ever dealt. Here's an abbreviated version. It seems that "someone" (it has, of course, never been determined exactly "who") ordered the N M chocolate-chip cookies for lunch at the store. After lunch, that person asked for the recipe and was told that the charge for it would be "two-fifty." Assuming that meant $2.50, the person said to put it on his/her credit card. When the monthly statement arrived, it was discovered that "two-fifty" meant $250. To get even, the person decided to spread the recipe far and wide, for free. It is a great recipe, and one that Neiman Marcus has been providing without charge for many years to anyone who asked for it. This recipe divides in half very easily.

> 5 cups regular or quick-cooking (not instant) rolled oats
> 4 cups all-purpose flour
> 2 teaspoons baking powder
> 2 teaspoons baking soda
> 2 cups (4 sticks) salted butter, at room temperature
> 2 cups granulated sugar
> 2 cups light brown sugar
> 4 eggs, lightly beaten
> 2 teaspoons vanilla extract
> 3 cups chopped pecans
> One 8-ounce bar semisweet chocolate, grated
> 4 cups (24 ounces) semisweet chocolate chips

1. Adjust two racks to divide the oven into thirds. Preheat the oven to 375°. Have ready two ungreased baking sheets.

2. In a food processor or blender, process the oats until they are ground to a fine powder.

3. In a large bowl, with a whisk, combine the oats, flour, baking powder, and baking soda.

4. In another large bowl, with an electric mixer at medium-high speed, beat together the butter, granulated sugar, and brown sugar until light and creamy, 2 to 3 minutes. Beat in the eggs and vanilla until well blended. With the mixer at medium-low speed, gradually add the flour mixture, beating until well blended. With a mixing spoon, stir in the pecans, grated chocolate, and chocolate chips until well distributed throughout the batter. Drop by measuring tablespoonfuls onto the ungreased baking sheets, spacing the drops about 2 inches apart.

5. Bake for 12 to 15 minutes until golden brown. Reverse the baking sheets on the racks and from front to back once during baking. With a wide turner, immediately transfer the cookies to wire racks to cool completely.

6. Store in a tightly covered container.

Yield: About 144 cookies

Tips for Baking Drop Cookies

- Read through the recipe completely to make sure that you have all of the equipment and ingredients you will need.

- Baking sheets should be very clean and cool. If the recipe calls for greasing the baking sheets, use only a very light coating of grease or nonstick vegetable spray, otherwise the cookies can spread too much and even run into one another. Greasing *and* flouring is usually only necessary when the batter is very thin.

- Although it is possible to make the drops of batter slightly larger or smaller than the recipe directs, it is important that they all be the same size so that they bake in the same amount of time.

- Don't overcrowd the baking sheets. If there are only a few cookies to be baked, spread them out evenly over the baking sheet so that no big empty spaces are exposed to the oven heat, or use a smaller baking sheet.

- If for some reason you can't finish the cookie making, most shaped-cookie doughs will be just fine if refrigerated until later, or even a few days later, as long as they are tightly wrapped or covered.

- Take the time to reverse the baking sheets on the racks and from front to back as instructed in the recipe. All ovens, even the best of them, have "hot spots," and reversing the baking sheets helps the cookies to bake more evenly.

- Check the cookies for doneness at the first time given when there is a range of times. If only one time is given, set the timer for a couple of minutes before that time. Oven temperatures and other seemingly small factors can affect baking times significantly.

- Most cookies are better when they are a little underbaked rather than a little overbaked. Drop cookies are usually done when they are lightly browned and a slight imprint remains after the cookies are gently pressed with a fingertip. If you are still unsure, remove one cookie from the baking sheet, break it apart, and look inside for any sign of raw dough, keeping in mind that the cookies will continue to bake as long as they are hot and will get significantly firmer as they cool.

- Unless the recipe directs otherwise, drop cookies should be removed from the baking sheet as soon as they come from the oven. If they stick a little, let them cool for a minute or so on the baking sheet and then try again.

- If the same baking sheet will be used for baking successive batches of cookies, make sure that it is clean and completely cool before reusing. Often it is enough to just wipe the baking sheet with a paper towel between batches. Sometimes it is necessary to rinse the sheet briefly in hot water and wipe it dry before regreasing. Occasionally there is enough grease left on the sheet so that regreasing isn't even necessary, but in any case subsequent greasing should always be extra light.

- Most drop cookies can be turned into shaped cookies by merely chilling the batter or adding a little more flour to it. So, in theory, it's possible to take a plain chocolate-chip cookie and roll it between the palms of your hands into a Chocolate-Chip Thumbprint Cookie.

- Most drop cookies can be baked as bar cookies, although you may have to thin the batter just a little so that it can be spread in the pan.

Chocolate Oat-Chip Cookies

The next time you're casting around for a good "cookie-jar" cookie recipe, try this one, or one of the several easy variations that follow.

1 ³/₄ cups all-purpose flour

1 teaspoon baking soda

¹/₂ teaspoon salt

1 cup (2 sticks) salted butter or margarine, at room temperature

1 ¹/₄ cups packed light brown sugar

¹/₂ cup granulated sugar

2 large eggs, lightly beaten

2 tablespoons milk

2 teaspoons vanilla extract

2 ¹/₂ cups regular or quick-cooking (not instant) rolled oats

2 cups (12 ounces) semisweet chocolate chips

1. Adjust two racks to divide the oven into thirds. Preheat the oven to 375°. Have ready two ungreased baking sheets.

2. In a medium-size bowl, with a whisk, combine the flour, baking soda, and salt until thoroughly mixed.

3. In a large bowl, with an electric mixer at medium speed, beat together the butter, brown sugar, and granulated sugar until light and fluffy, 2 to 3 minutes. Add the eggs, milk, and vanilla and beat until smooth. With the mixer on medium-low speed, gradually add the flour mixture, beating just until blended. With a mixing spoon, stir in the oats and chocolate chips until well distributed throughout the batter. Drop by rounded measuring tablespoonfuls onto the baking sheets, spacing the drops about 2 inches apart.

4. Bake for 9 to 10 minutes until lightly browned. Reverse the baking sheets on the racks and from front to back once during baking. Cool the cookies on the baking sheets for 1 minute. With a wide turner, transfer the cookies to wire racks to cool completely.

5. Store in a tightly covered container.

Yield: About 60 cookies

Variations

Bar Cookies: Spread the cookie dough into the bottom of an ungreased 13 × 9-inch baking pan. Bake for 30 to 35 minutes until golden brown. Cool in the pan on a wire rack; cut into bars.

Cherry-Chocolate Chip Cookies: Substitute dried cherries for half of the chocolate chips.

Candy-Chip Cookies: Substitute candy-coated chocolate pieces or small jelly beans for all of the chocolate chips.

Snowflakes: Substitute vanilla-flavored white baking pieces for all of the chocolate chips. Drop by rounded measuring teaspoonfuls onto *ungreased* baking sheets. Bake for 7 to 8 minutes until the edges are a light, golden brown.

White Chocolate Drops

These are very large, very sweet, very rich, and very good.

> 2 cups all-purpose flour
>
> 1 ¹/₂ teaspoons baking powder
>
> ¹/₄ teaspoon baking soda
>
> ¹/₄ teaspoon salt
>
> 1 ¹/₄ cups (2 ¹/₂ sticks) salted butter or margarine, at room temperature
>
> 1 ¹/₂ cups packed light brown sugar
>
> 2 teaspoons vanilla extract
>
> 2 large eggs
>
> 3 cups (18 ounces) vanilla-flavored white baking pieces
>
> 3 cups coarsely chopped pecans

1. Adjust two racks to divide the oven into thirds. Preheat the oven to 350°. Lightly grease two baking sheets.

2. In a medium-size bowl, with a whisk, combine the flour, baking powder, baking soda, and salt until thoroughly mixed.

3. In a large bowl, with an electric mixer at medium speed, beat together the butter, sugar, and vanilla until light and creamy, 2 to 3 minutes. Beat in the eggs, one at a time, until well blended. With the mixer at low speed, gradually add the flour mixture, beating just until blended. With a mixing spoon, stir in the baking pieces and nuts until well distributed throughout the batter. Drop by scant ¹/₄ cupfuls onto the prepared baking sheets, spacing the drops about 3 inches apart.

4. Bake until golden brown, about 15 minutes. Reverse the baking sheets on the racks and from front to back once during baking. Leave the cookies on the baking sheet for 1 minute. With a wide turner, transfer the cookies to wire racks to cool completely.

5. Store in a tightly covered container.

Yield: About 36 cookies

Extra Soft and Chewy Chocolate-Chip Cookies

The tasters told me that this was a cookie to die for. The name says it all. These cookies are supposed to have a very soft, chewy texture, so it is better to underbake them slightly than to overbake them.

  ^{2}/$_3$ **cup all-purpose flour**

  ^{1}/$_4$ **teaspoon salt**

  1 **teaspoon baking powder**

  18 **ounces (3 cups) semisweet chocolate chips, divided**

  4 **ounces (4 squares) unsweetened chocolate**

  ^{1}/$_2$ **cup (1 stick) salted butter or margarine, cut into pieces**

  ^{1}/$_2$ **cup packed dark brown sugar**

  1 **cup granulated sugar**

  3 **large eggs**

  1 **tablespoon vanilla extract**

  1 ^{1}/$_2$ **cups coarsely chopped pecans**

1. Adjust two racks to divide the oven into thirds. Preheat the oven to 350°. Lightly grease two baking sheets.

2. In a medium-size bowl, with a whisk, combine the flour, salt, and baking powder until thoroughly mixed.

3. In a heavy, medium-size saucepan set over very low heat, melt together 1 cup of the semisweet chocolate chips, all of the unsweetened chocolate, and the butter, stirring constantly until smooth. Remove from the heat and set aside to cool to lukewarm.

4. In a large bowl, with an electric mixer at medium speed, beat together the brown sugar, granulated sugar, eggs, and vanilla until blended. With the mixer at medium speed, beat until the mixture forms a thin ribbon when the beaters are lifted, 2 to 3 minutes. With the mixer at low speed, beat in the melted-chocolate mixture until well blended. Gradually add the flour mixture, beating just until blended. With a mixing spoon, fold in the remaining 2 cups of semisweet chocolate chips and the pecans until well distributed throughout the batter. Refrigerate the dough in the bowl for about 15 minutes.

5. Scoop the dough out of the bowl by ^{1}/$_4$ cupfuls and drop onto the prepared baking sheets, spacing the drops about 3 inches apart.

6. Bake for 15 to 20 minutes until barely firm and hairline cracks appear on the tops. Reverse the baking sheets on the racks and from front to back once during baking. Cool on the baking sheets set on wire racks for 5 minutes. With a wide turner, transfer the cookies to wire racks to cool completely.

7. Store in a tightly covered container, separating the layers with sheets of waxed paper.

Yield: About 20 cookies

Cookie Store Chocolate-Chunk Cookies

These are a lot like the chocolate chip cookies I used to buy at David's, a cookie store on Second Avenue that every New Yorker visited as often as possible when chocolate-chip cookies became the rage. They were best eaten warm, right off the assembly line, while the chocolate was still melting, and so are these.

  1 **or 2 pieces (about 12 ounces total) loose semisweet chocolate (page 11)**

  1 ^{1}/$_2$ **cups all-purpose flour**

  ^{3}/$_4$ **teaspoon baking soda**

  ^{3}/$_4$ **teaspoon salt**

  ^{2}/$_3$ **cup (1 stick plus 3 tablespoons) salted butter or margarine, at room temperature**

  ^{1}/$_2$ **cup granulated sugar**

  ^{1}/$_2$ **cup packed light brown sugar**

  1 **tablespoon milk**

  1 **teaspoon vanilla extract**

  2 **large eggs, lightly beaten**

  ^{2}/$_3$ **cup finely chopped pecans**

1. Adjust two racks to divide the oven into thirds. Preheat the oven to 375°. Have ready two ungreased baking sheets. Place the chocolate in the refrigerator to chill while making the batter.

2. In a medium-size bowl, with a whisk, combine the flour, baking soda, and salt until thoroughly mixed.

3. In a large bowl, with an electric mixer at medium speed, beat together the butter, granulated sugar, brown sugar, milk, vanilla, and eggs for about 3 minutes. (The mixture will appear to be curdled.) Gradually add the flour mixture, beating after each addition, just until blended.

4. Remove the chocolate from the refrigerator to a cutting surface. With a long, sharp knife, chop the chocolate into roughly ¼-inch pieces. Immediately stir the chocolate and the nuts into the batter until well distributed throughout. Drop by measuring tablespoonfuls onto the ungreased baking sheets, spacing the drops about 2 inches apart.

5. Bake for 9 to 11 minutes until golden. Reverse the baking sheets on the racks and from front to back once during baking. With a wide turner, immediately transfer the cookies to wire racks to cool completely.

6. Store in a tightly covered container, separating the layers between sheets of waxed paper.

Yield: About 40 cookies

---

2 cups sugar

2 large eggs

2 teaspoons vanilla extract

2 cups (12 ounces) semisweet chocolate chips

1 ½ cups chopped walnuts or pecans

1. Adjust two racks to divide the oven into thirds. Preheat the oven to 350°. Lightly grease two baking sheets.

2. In a medium-size bowl, with a whisk, combine the flour, cocoa, baking soda, and salt until thoroughly mixed.

3. In a large bowl, with an electric mixer at medium speed, beat together the butter, sugar, eggs, and vanilla until light and fluffy, 2 to 3 minutes. With a mixing spoon, stir in the flour mixture just until blended. Stir in the chocolate chips and nuts until well distributed throughout the batter. Drop by heaping teaspoonfuls onto the prepared baking sheets, spacing the drops about 1½ inches apart.

4. Bake for 10 to 12 minutes until lightly browned. Reverse the baking sheets on the racks and from front to back once during baking. With a wide turner, immediately transfer the cookies to wire racks to cool completely.

5. Store in a tightly covered container, separating the layers with sheets of waxed paper.

Yield: About 96 cookies

Two-Chocolate Chews

These chocolate cookies, full of chocolate chips, are about as chocolatey as a chocolate-chip cookie can get.

2 cups all-purpose flour

¾ cup unsweetened cocoa powder

1 teaspoon baking soda

½ teaspoon salt

¾ cup (1 ½ sticks) salted butter or margarine, at room temperature

Tip

If frozen chocolate chips are stirred into the batter just before dropping and baking, they will hold their shape better and have more definition in the baked cookie.

Chocolate-Chip Thins

As you might have guessed, these are the thin, crisp cousin of the plump, chewy, chocolate-chip cookie.

- 1 cup plus 2 tablespoons all-purpose flour
- 1/2 teaspoon baking soda
- 1/2 teaspoon salt
- 1 cup (2 sticks) salted butter or margarine, at room temperature
- 1 cup packed dark brown sugar
- 1 cup granulated sugar
- 1 large egg, lightly beaten
- 2 tablespoons orange liqueur or orange juice
- 1 1/2 teaspoons vanilla extract
- 1 1/2 cups (9 ounces) semisweet chocolate chips
- 1 cup (about 4 ounces) coarsely chopped pecans

1. Adjust two racks to divide the oven into thirds. Preheat the oven to 375°. Lightly grease two baking sheets.

2. In a small bowl, with a whisk, combine the flour, baking soda, and salt until thoroughly mixed.

3. In a large bowl, with an electric mixer at medium speed, beat together the butter, brown sugar, and granulated sugar until light and fluffy, about 5 minutes. Beat in the egg, liqueur, and vanilla until blended. With a mixing spoon, stir in the flour mixture just until blended. Stir in the chocolate chips and pecans until well distributed throughout the batter. Drop the dough by tablespoonfuls onto the prepared baking sheets, spacing the drops about 2 inches apart.

4. Bake for about 8 minutes until nicely browned. Reverse the baking sheets on the racks and from front to back once during baking. Cool on the baking sheet set on a wire rack until the cookies begin to harden, about 2 minutes. With a wide turner, transfer the cookies to wire racks to cool completely.

5. Store in an airtight container.

Yield: About 42 cookies

Dropped Brownie Chews

When my children were growing up, we used to spend part of our summers at a rented house on the Outer Banks of North Carolina. The first year I took along a brownie recipe, and guess what? No baking pan, and everyone dying for brownies. These cookies are a drop version of chewy brownies.

- 1 1/2 cups all-purpose flour
- 1/3 cup unsweetened cocoa powder
- 1/2 teaspoon salt
- 1/4 teaspoon baking soda
- 2/3 cup (1 stick plus 3 tablespoons) solid shortening
- 1 1/2 cups packed light brown sugar
- 1 tablespoon water
- 1 teaspoon vanilla extract
- 2 large eggs, lightly beaten
- 1 cup (6 ounces) semisweet chocolate chips
- 1 cup coarsely chopped walnuts or pecans

1. Adjust two racks to divide the oven into thirds. Preheat the oven to 375°. Have ready two ungreased baking sheets.

2. In a medium-size bowl, with a whisk, combine the flour, cocoa, salt, and baking soda until thoroughly mixed.

3. In a large bowl, with an electric mixer at medium-high speed, beat together the shortening, brown sugar, water, and vanilla until creamy, 1 to 2 minutes. Beat in the eggs until well blended. With the mixer at medium-low speed, gradually add the flour mixture, beating just until blended. Drop by rounded measuring tablespoonfuls onto the ungreased baking sheets, spacing the drops about 2 inches apart. Bake for 7 to 9 minutes or just until set. Reverse the baking sheets on the racks and from front to back once during baking. Cool on the baking sheets for 2 minutes. With a wide turner, transfer the cookies to wire racks to cool completely.

4. Store in a tightly covered container, separating the layers with sheets of waxed paper.

Yield: About 36 cookies

White Chocolate-Chip Cookies

The name pretty much says it all about these cookies. They are very rich, very sweet, and very delicious, especially when they are served on a plate with their dark-chocolate cousins.

    1 ³/₄ cups all-purpose flour
    ³/₄ teaspoon baking soda
    ²/₃ cup (1 stick plus 3 tablespoons) salted
        butter or margarine, at room temperature
    1 cup packed dark brown sugar
    1 teaspoon vanilla extract
    1 large egg, lightly beaten
    ¹/₂ cup sour cream
    1 cup coarsely chopped pecans or walnuts
    1 ¹/₂ cups (10 ounces) vanilla-flavored white
        baking pieces

1. Adjust two racks to divide the oven into thirds. Preheat the oven to 375°. Have ready two ungreased baking sheets.

2. In a medium-size bowl, with a whisk, combine the flour and baking soda until thoroughly mixed.

3. In a large bowl, with an electric mixer at medium-high speed, beat together the butter, brown sugar, and vanilla until creamy, 2 to 3 minutes. Beat in the egg and sour cream until well blended. With the mixer at medium-low speed, gradually add the flour mixture, beating just until blended. With a mixing spoon, stir in the nuts and baking pieces until well distributed throughout the batter. Drop by rounded measuring tablespoonfuls onto the ungreased baking sheets, spacing the drops about 2 inches apart.

4. Bake for 12 to 13 minutes until firm when lightly touched and beginning to brown around the edges. Reverse the baking sheets on the racks and from front to back once during baking. Let cool on the baking sheets for 2 minutes. With a wide turner, transfer the cookies to wire racks to cool completely.

5. Store in a tightly covered container.

Yield: About 24 cookies

Soft Banana Chip Cookies

This recipe is a good example of how versatile a drop cookie can be. In this case, bananas that otherwise might have gone to waste have been mashed and added to the batter. Almost anything goes with drop cookies, as long as the batter "feels" right and is the proper consistency to drop into a mound on a baking sheet.

    2 ³/₄ cups all-purpose flour
    1 ¹/₂ teaspoons baking soda
    ¹/₂ teaspoon salt
    1 cup (2 sticks) plain shortening
    1 ¹/₂ cups sugar
    2 large eggs, lightly beaten
    1 teaspoon vanilla
    ¹/₂ cup buttermilk
    1 cup mashed ripe bananas (about 3 medium
        bananas; make sure they are very ripe)
    1 cup chopped nuts
    2 cups (11 ¹/₂ ounces) milk chocolate chips

1. Adjust two racks to divide the oven in half. Preheat the oven to 375°. Lightly grease two baking sheets.

2. In a medium-size bowl, with a whisk, combine the flour, baking soda, and salt until thoroughly mixed.

3. In a large bowl, with an electric mixer at medium-high speed, beat the shortening and sugar until very well blended, 2 to 3 minutes. Beat in the eggs and vanilla until well blended. With the mixer at medium-low speed, add the flour alternately with the buttermilk and the banana, beating just until blended. With a mixing spoon, stir in the nuts and chocolate chips until well distributed throughout the batter. Drop by heaping teaspoonfuls onto the prepared baking sheets, spacing the drops about 1¹/₂ inches apart.

4. Bake for 8 to 10 minutes until lightly browned. Reverse the baking sheets on the racks and from front to back once during baking. With a wide turner, immediately transfer the cookies to wire racks to cool completely.

Yield: About 84 cookies

Treasure Islands

Most likely this cookie is one of the endless varieties inspired by the chocolate-chip cookie. It happens to be one of my favorites. I like the tart cranberries playing against the almost cloying sweetness of the white chocolate.

1 ^{2}/$_3$ cups all-purpose flour

1 teaspoon baking soda

^{3}/$_4$ cup (1 ^{1}/$_2$ sticks) salted butter or margarine, at room temperature

^{3}/$_4$ cup packed light brown sugar

1 large egg

1 package (10 ounces) vanilla-flavored white baking chips

1 cup raw cranberries, rinsed, picked over, and drained until dry

^{1}/$_2$ cup coarsely chopped pecans

1 teaspoon grated orange zest

1. Adjust two racks to divide the oven into thirds. Preheat the oven to 375°. Have ready two ungreased baking sheets.

2. In a medium-size bowl, with a whisk, combine the flour and baking soda until thoroughly mixed.

3. In a large bowl, with an electric mixer at medium-high speed, beat together the butter and brown sugar until creamy, 2 to 3 minutes. Add the egg and beat until well blended, about 1 minute. With the mixer at medium-low speed, gradually add the flour mixture, beating just until blended. With a mixing spoon, stir in the baking chips, cranberries, pecans, and orange zest until evenly distributed throughout the batter. Drop by heaping measuring tablespoonfuls onto the ungreased baking sheets, spacing the drops about 2 inches apart.

4. Bake for 7 to 10 minutes until lightly browned. Reverse the baking sheets on the racks and from front to back once during baking. With a wide turner, immediately transfer the cookies to wire racks to cool completely.

5. Store in a tightly covered container.

Yield: About 30 cookies

Orange-Cashew Cookies

Rich, buttery cashews are one of the world's most exquisite nutmeats, but rarely are they ever used in cookie recipes—probably because they are *so* expensive. Other nuts can be substituted, of course, but in this case I'd just go for the gold.

1 ^{3}/$_4$ cups all-purpose flour

^{3}/$_4$ teaspoon baking soda

^{1}/$_2$ cup (1 stick) salted butter or margarine, at room temperature

^{2}/$_3$ cup packed light brown sugar

^{1}/$_4$ cup sour cream

1 large egg, lightly beaten

1 teaspoon vanilla extract

1 cup chopped, salted cashews

1 cup (8 ounces) finely chopped candied orange peel

1. Adjust two racks to divide the oven in half. Preheat the oven to 375°. Have ready two ungreased baking sheets.

2. In a medium-size bowl, with a whisk, combine the flour and baking soda until thoroughly mixed.

3. In a large bowl, with an electric mixer at medium-high speed, beat together the butter and brown sugar until creamy, 2 to 3 minutes. Beat in the sour cream, egg, and vanilla until well blended. With the electric mixer at medium-low speed, gradually add the flour mixture, beating just until blended. With a mixing spoon, stir in the cashews and orange peel until well distributed throughout the batter. Drop the batter by rounded, measuring teaspoonfuls onto the ungreased baking sheets, spacing the drops about 2 inches apart.

4. Bake for about 10 minutes until golden. Reverse the baking sheets on the racks and from front to back once during baking. With a wide turner, immediately transfer the cookies to wire racks to cool completely.

5. Store in a tightly covered container.

Yield: About 60 cookies

Candied Fruit Drops

My kids liked the candied cherries that decorated the tops of cookies as much as they liked the cookies, so this cookie pleased them enormously, and still does.

> 2 cups all-purpose flour
> 1/2 teaspoon baking soda
> 1/3 cup (1/2 stick plus 1 1/2 tablespoons) salted butter or margarine, at room temperature
> 1/2 cup packed light brown sugar
> 1 large egg
> 1/3 cup buttermilk
> 1 1/2 cups chopped red and green candied cherries or other candied fruit
> 1/2 cup chopped pecans

1. Adjust two racks to divide the oven in half. Lightly grease two baking sheets.

2. In a medium-size bowl, with a whisk, combine the flour and baking soda until thoroughly mixed.

3. In a large bowl, with an electric mixer at medium-high speed, beat together the butter, brown sugar, and egg until creamy, 2 to 3 minutes. With the mixer at medium-low speed, gradually beat in the buttermilk until well blended. With a mixing spoon, stir in the candied fruit and nuts until evenly distributed throughout the batter. Lightly cover the bowl and refrigerate until the dough is chilled, about 1 hour.

4. Preheat the oven to 375°.

5. Drop the dough by measuring tablespoonfuls onto the prepared baking sheets, spacing the drops about 2 inches apart. With your fingers, flatten each mound of dough slightly.

6. Bake for 8 to 10 minutes until golden brown. Reverse the baking sheets on the racks and from front to back once during baking. With a wide turner, immediately transfer the cookies to wire racks to cool completely.

7. Store in a tightly covered container.

Yield: About 32 cookies

Choco-Coco Drops

Shredded coconut and lots of chocolate chips make these drops chewy and gooey.

> 3/4 cup all-purpose flour
> 1/4 teaspoon baking soda
> 1/8 teaspoon salt
> 1/3 cup (1/2 stick plus 1 1/2 tablespoons) plain shortening
> 2/3 cup sugar
> 1 large egg
> 1 teaspoon vanilla extract
> 1/3 cup sour cream
> 1/2 cup shredded or flaked coconut
> 1 1/2 cups (9 ounces) semisweet chocolate chips

1. Adjust two racks to divide the oven into thirds. Preheat the oven to 350°. Lightly grease two baking sheets.

2. In a medium-size bowl, with a whisk, combine the flour, baking soda, and salt until thoroughly mixed.

3. In a large bowl, with an electric mixer at medium-high speed, beat the shortening until creamy, about 1 minute. Add the sugar, egg, and vanilla and beat until creamy, 2 to 3 minutes. With the mixer at medium-low speed, add the flour mixture alternately with the sour cream, beating just until blended. Stir in the coconut and then the chocolate chips until both are well distributed throughout the batter. Drop by heaping measuring teaspoonfuls onto the prepared baking sheets, spacing the drops about 2 inches apart.

4. Bake for about 10 minutes just until set, but still fairly soft when lightly pressed with a finger. Reverse the baking sheets on the racks and from front to back once during baking. With a wide turner, immediately transfer the cookies to wire racks to cool completely.

5. Store in a tightly covered container.

Yield: About 36 cookies

Hermits

A classic American cookie that probably originated in New England not long after the first settlers arrived, and may have been a forerunner of the chocolate-chip cookie. Although the spices called for in these cookies seem quite commonplace these days, in olden times they were rare and expensive, so these cookies must have been a great luxury.

> 1 ³/₄ cups all-purpose flour
>
> ¹/₂ teaspoon baking soda
>
> ¹/₂ teaspoon ground cinnamon
>
> ¹/₂ teaspoon ground cloves
>
> ¹/₂ teaspoon ground ginger
>
> ¹/₂ teaspoon ground nutmeg
>
> ¹/₂ cup (1 stick) plain shortening
>
> ¹/₄ cup (¹/₂ stick) salted butter or margarine, at room temperature
>
> 1 cup packed dark brown sugar
>
> 1 large egg
>
> 1 teaspoon vanilla extract
>
> 2 tablespoons water
>
> 1 cup raisins
>
> 1 cup coarsely chopped walnuts

1. Adjust two racks to divide the oven into thirds. Preheat the oven to 350°. Lightly grease two baking sheets.

2. In a medium-size bowl, with a whisk, combine the flour, baking soda, cinnamon, cloves, ginger, and nutmeg.

3. In a large bowl, with an electric mixer at medium-high speed, beat together the shortening, butter, and brown sugar until creamy, 2 to 3 minutes. Add the egg, vanilla, and water and beat until very well blended, about 1 minute. With the mixer at medium-low speed, gradually add the flour mixture, beating just until blended. With a mixing spoon, stir in the raisins and nuts until well distributed throughout the batter. Drop by teaspoonfuls onto the prepared baking sheets, spacing the drops about 2 inches apart. Flatten the cookies slightly with the back of the tines of a dinner fork.

4. Bake for about 15 minutes until the cookies feel firm when lightly touched. Reverse the baking sheets on the racks and from front to back once during baking. With a wide turner, immediately transfer the cookies to wire racks to cool completely.

5. Store in a tightly covered container.

Yield: About 48 cookies

Walnut-Apricot Snowcaps

I like to bake these cookies at Christmas. They look quite pretty on a plate of assorted cookies, and everyone loves them. For the holidays, you might also want to decorate them with an assortment of very finely chopped candied fruits or colored sugars, in addition to the walnuts.

> 1 ¹/₄ cups all-purpose flour
>
> 2 teaspoons ground allspice
>
> ¹/₂ teaspoon baking soda
>
> ¹/₂ cup (1 stick) salted butter or margarine, at room temperature
>
> ³/₄ cup granulated sugar
>
> 1 large egg, lightly beaten
>
> 1 teaspoon vanilla extract
>
> 1 ¹/₄ cups chopped walnuts
>
> 1 cup chopped dried apricots or golden raisins

Snowy Glaze

> 1 ¹/₂ cups confectioners' sugar
>
> 1 to 2 tablespoons milk
>
> Very finely chopped walnuts, for decorating cookies

1. Adjust two racks to divide the oven into thirds. Preheat the oven to 350°. Lightly grease two baking sheets.

2. In a medium-size bowl, with a whisk, combine the flour, allspice, and baking soda until thoroughly mixed.

3. In a large bowl, with an electric mixer at medium-high speed, beat together the butter and sugar until light and fluffy, 2 to 3 minutes. Beat in the egg and vanilla until well blended. With the mixer at medium-low speed, gradually add the flour mixture, beating just until blended. With a mixing spoon, stir in the walnuts and dried apricots until well distributed throughout the batter. Drop by rounded measuring teaspoonfuls onto the prepared baking sheets, spacing the drops about 2 inches apart.

4. Bake for about 15 minutes just until set. (The cookies will become firmer as they cool.) Reverse the baking sheets on the racks and from front to back once during baking. With a wide turner, transfer the cookies to wire racks to cool completely.

5. While the cookies are cooling, make the glaze. In a small bowl, beat together the confectioners' sugar and enough of the milk to make a glaze of thick pouring consistency. Drizzle the glaze over the cookies, covering them as much as possible. While the glaze is still moist, decorate the cookies with the finely chopped walnuts. Leave undisturbed until the glaze is completely dry, 1 to 2 hours.

6. Store in a tightly covered container, separating the layers with sheets of waxed paper.

Yield: About 48 cookies

Trail Cookies

These sturdy cookies are great for backpacks and lunch boxes, providing lots of energy on the trail and brain power in the classroom.

> 2 cups all-purpose flour
> 1 cup whole wheat flour
> 1 $^{1}/_{2}$ teaspoons baking powder
> 1 teaspoon baking soda
> 1 teaspoon ground cinnamon
> $^{1}/_{2}$ teaspoon salt
> 2 cups packed light or dark brown sugar
> 1 cup (2 sticks) salted butter or margarine, at room temperature

One 4 $^{1}/_{2}$-ounce jar applesauce-apricot baby food
$^{1}/_{4}$ cup buttermilk
2 large eggs, lightly beaten
2 teaspoons vanilla extract
4 cups 100% natural raisin and date cereal

1. Adjust two racks to divide the oven into thirds. Lightly grease two baking sheets.

2. In a medium-size bowl, with a whisk, combine the all-purpose flour, whole wheat flour, baking powder, baking soda, cinnamon, and salt until thoroughly mixed.

3. In a large bowl, with an electric mixer at medium-high speed, beat together the brown sugar and butter until creamy, 2 to 3 minutes. Beat in the baby food, buttermilk, eggs, and vanilla until well blended. With the mixer at medium-low speed, gradually add the flour mixture, beating just until blended. With a mixing spoon, stir in the cereal until well distributed throughout the batter. Cover the bowl and refrigerate until the batter is cold, 1 to 2 hours.

4. Preheat the oven to 350°.

5. Drop the batter by rounded measuring teaspoonfuls onto the prepared baking sheets, spacing the drops about 2 inches apart.

6. Bake for 10 to 14 minutes until the edges are light golden brown. Reverse the baking sheets on the racks and from front to back once during baking. Cool on the baking sheets for 1 minute. With a wide turner, transfer the cookies to wire racks to cool completely.

7. Store in a tightly covered container.

Yield: About 72 cookies

Tip

Recipes calling for dropping teaspoonfuls or tablespoonfuls of dough onto the baking sheet generally mean tableware and not measuring spoons. This is especially true for old recipes.

Super-Duper Lunch Box Whoppers

Not only are these cookies supernutritious, with all of the ingredients kids love, but they're also sandwiched together with a creamy peanut butter filling.

- ³/₄ cup whole wheat flour
- ¹/₂ cup nonfat dry milk powder
- ¹/₂ teaspoon baking soda
- 2 cups regular or quick-cooking (not instant) rolled oats
- ³/₄ cup (1 ¹/₂ sticks) salted butter or margarine, at room temperature
- ¹/₃ cup packed light brown sugar
- ¹/₄ cup honey
- 2 large eggs, lightly beaten
- 1 teaspoon vanilla extract
- 1 ¹/₂ cups raisins
- 1 cup chopped pecans or walnuts
- 2 cups bran flakes cereal

Peanut Butter Filling

- 1 cup smooth peanut butter
- Confectioners' sugar

1. Adjust two racks to divide the oven into thirds. Preheat the oven to 350°. Lightly grease two baking sheets.

2. In a medium-size bowl, with a whisk, combine the flour, milk powder, and baking soda until thoroughly mixed. Add the oats and whisk until well blended with the flour mixture.

3. In a large bowl, with an electric mixer at medium-high speed, beat together the butter, brown sugar, and honey until creamy, 2 to 3 minutes. Beat in the eggs and vanilla until well blended. With the mixer at medium-low speed, gradually add the flour mixture, beating just until blended. With a mixing spoon, stir in the raisins and nuts, then the bran flakes until well distributed throughout the batter. Drop by rounded measuring tablespoonfuls onto the prepared baking sheets, spacing the drops about 2 inches apart.

4. Bake for 15 to 20 minutes until the edges are lightly browned. Reverse the baking sheets on the racks and from front to back once during baking. Cool on the baking sheets set on wire racks for 10 minutes. With a wide turner, transfer the cookies to wire racks to cool completely.

5. To make the filling, in a small bowl, mix together the peanut butter and confectioners' sugar to taste. With a small spatula or a butter spreader, spread each of the bottom sides of half the cookies with about 2 teaspoons of the filling. Place another cookie, bottom side down, on top of the filling.

6. Store in a tightly covered container, separating the layers with sheets of waxed paper.

Yield: About 24 sandwich cookies

Fresh Apple and Currant Cookies

Because apples are a natural humectant (one substance that helps another to retain moisture), cookies made with apples and other tree fruits stay moist and fresh-tasting for a surprisingly long time, especially if they are stored airtight with a slice of apple. Replace the apple slice every couple of days.

- 2 cups all-purpose flour
- 1 ¹/₄ teaspoons ground cinnamon
- 1 teaspoon baking soda
- ³/₄ cup packed light or dark brown sugar
- ¹/₂ cup (1 stick) salted butter or margarine, at room temperature
- 1 large egg, lightly beaten
- 1 cup chopped walnuts
- 1 cup dried currants
- 1 medium-size apple, peeled, cored, and finely chopped (about 1 cup)

1. Adjust two racks to divide the oven into thirds. Preheat the oven to 375°. Lightly grease two baking sheets.

2. In a medium-size bowl, with a whisk, combine the flour, cinnamon, and baking soda until thoroughly mixed.

3. In a large bowl, with an electric mixer at medium-high speed, beat together the brown sugar and butter until creamy, 2 to 3 minutes. Beat in the egg until well blended. With a mixing spoon, stir in the walnuts, currants, and apple until well blended. Drop by heaping measuring tablespoonfuls onto the prepared baking sheets, spacing them about 3 inches apart. With the back of a spoon, spread each cookie into a 3-inch round.

4. Bake for 15 to 20 minutes until lightly browned. Reverse the baking sheets on the racks and from front to back once during baking. With a wide turner, transfer the cookies to wire racks to cool completely.

5. Store in a tightly covered container.

Yield: About 32 cookies

Tip

Drop cookies can be frozen before baking. Drop the dough onto the baking sheet and freeze until solid. Remove the drops from the baking sheets and seal in airtight containers for up to three months. When ready to bake, arrange the frozen drops on a baking sheet and bring to room temperature, lightly covered, until thawed. Bake as directed.

Applesauce-Raisin Chews

Kids love the soft, chewy texture of these wholesome cookies. Because applesauce is used in place of some of the sugar, they are not quite as sweet as most cookies, either.

>   2 cups all-purpose flour
>   1 teaspoon baking soda
>   1 teaspoon ground cinnamon
>   1 cup (2 sticks) salted butter or margarine, at room temperature
>   1 cup packed light or dark brown sugar
>   1 cup applesauce
>   1 large egg, lightly beaten
>   1 teaspoon vanilla extract
>   2 1/2 cups regular or quick-cooking (not instant) rolled oats
>   1 cup raisins

1. Adjust two racks to divide the oven into thirds. Preheat the oven to 350°. Have ready two ungreased baking sheets.

2. In a medium-size bowl, with a whisk, combine the flour, baking soda, and cinnamon until thoroughly mixed.

3. In a large bowl, with an electric mixer at medium-high speed, beat together the butter and brown sugar until creamy. Beat in the applesauce, egg, and vanilla until blended. With the mixer at medium-low speed, gradually add the flour mixture, beating just until blended. With a mixing spoon, stir in the oats and raisins until well distributed throughout the batter. Drop by rounded measuring tablespoonfuls onto the ungreased baking sheets, spacing the drops about 3 inches apart.

4. Bake for 11 to 13 minutes until light golden brown. Reverse the baking sheets on the racks and from front to back once during baking. Cool for 1 minute on the baking sheet. With a wide turner, transfer the cookies to wire racks to cool completely.

5. Store in a tightly covered container.

Yield: About 48 cookies

Piña Colada Cookies

The beverage of the same name inspired these easy-to-make cookies. The cookie version has the same hint of those tropical flavors that will make you think of an island vacation.

1 ³/₄ cups all-purpose flour

¹/₂ teaspoon baking powder

¹/₂ cup sugar

¹/₃ cup (¹/₂ stick plus 1 ¹/₂ tablespoons) salted butter, at room temperature

2 large eggs, lightly beaten

¹/₃ cup pineapple preserves

¹/₂ teaspoon rum extract

¹/₄ cup flaked coconut

1. Adjust two racks to divide the oven into thirds. Preheat the oven to 350°. Lightly grease two baking sheets.

2. In a medium-size bowl, with a whisk, combine the flour and baking powder until thoroughly mixed.

3. In a large bowl, with an electric mixer at medium-high speed, beat together the sugar and butter until light and fluffy, 2 to 3 minutes. Beat in the eggs, preserves, and rum extract until well blended. With the mixer at medium-low speed, gradually add the flour mixture, beating just until blended. With a mixing spoon, stir in the coconut until well distributed throughout the batter. Drop by rounded teaspoonfuls onto the prepared baking sheets, spacing the drops about 2 inches apart.

4. Bake for 8 to 12 minutes until the edges are lightly browned. Reverse the baking sheets on the racks and from front to back once during baking. With a wide turner, immediately transfer the cookies to wire racks to cool completely.

5. Store in a tightly covered container.

Yield: About 36 cookies

Tip

Ice cream scoops in various sizes are handy for dropping cookies onto a baking sheet. You can also use a pastry bag, fitted with a large, round tip for plain batters that contain no nuts or other lumpy ingredients.

Very Old-Fashioned Dropped Cookies

A cookie very much like this one was probably what the Colonials were munching in the sixteenth century. This is a very old recipe, adapted for today's ingredients and baking methods.

3 cups all-purpose flour

1 teaspoon baking soda

1 teaspoon ground cinnamon

¹/₂ teaspoon ground cloves

¹/₂ cup (1 stick) salted butter or margarine, at room temperature

1 cup sugar

2 large eggs

¹/₂ cup milk

¹/₂ cup unsulphured molasses

³/₄ cup dried currants

1. Adjust two racks to divide the oven into thirds. Preheat the oven to 350°. Lightly grease two baking sheets.

2. In a medium-size bowl, with a whisk, combine the flour, baking soda, cinnamon, and cloves until thoroughly mixed.

3. In a large bowl, with an electric mixer at medium-high speed, beat together the butter, sugar, and eggs until light and fluffy, 2 to 3 minutes. Add the milk and molasses and beat until well blended. (The mixture will look curdled.) With the mixer at medium-low speed, gradually add the flour mixture, beating just until blended.

With a mixing spoon, stir in the currants until well distributed throughout the batter.

4. Drop by level measuring tablespoonfuls onto the prepared baking sheets, spacing the drops about 2 inches apart.

5. Bake for 8 to 10 minutes, until lightly browned and firm to the touch. Reverse the baking sheets on the racks and from front to back once during baking. With a wide turner, immediately transfer the cookies to wire racks to cool completely.

6. Store in a tightly covered container.

Yield: About 70 cookies

Anne Disrude's Sweet Bean Crisps

Anne is one of New York's top food stylists, and I love to watch her work. She is also an imaginative cook. Frankly, this is the first cookie I've ever encountered that included pureed beans in the batter. The crunchy cookies that come out of the oven are as good as they are unusual. Try them.

$^1/_2$ cup golden raisins

1 teaspoon grated orange zest

$^2/_3$ cup sweet Marsala wine

1 $^1/_4$ cups all-purpose flour

2 teaspoons baking powder

$^1/_2$ teaspoon cinnamon

$^1/_2$ teaspoon ground cloves

One 19-ounce can garbanzo beans, drained, rinsed, and patted dry

1 cup milk

1 teaspoon vanilla extract

$^1/_2$ cup (1 stick) salted butter, at room temperature

$^3/_4$ cup packed dark brown sugar

1 large egg, lightly beaten

Confectioners' sugar, for dusting cookies

1. Adjust two racks to divide the oven into thirds. Preheat the oven to 375°. Lightly grease two baking sheets.

2. In a small saucepan, stir together the raisins, orange zest, and Marsala. Bring to a boil; remove from the heat and set aside to cool.

3. In a medium-size bowl, with a whisk, combine the flour, baking powder, cinnamon, and cloves until thoroughly mixed.

4. In a food processor fitted with a steel blade, combine the beans, milk, and vanilla. Process until very smooth, 4 to 5 minutes.

5. In a large bowl, with an electric mixer at medium-high speed, beat together the butter and brown sugar until creamy, 2 to 3 minutes. Beat in the egg until well blended. With a mixing spoon, stir in the cooled raisin mixture, and then the bean puree until very well blended. With the mixer at medium-low speed, gradually add the flour mixture, beating just until blended. Drop by heaping teaspoonfuls onto the prepared baking sheets, spacing the drops about 2 inches apart.

6. Bake for about 25 minutes until the cookies are lightly browned around the edges. Reverse the baking sheets on the racks and from front to back once during baking. With a wide turner, immediately transfer the cookies to wire racks to cool completely.

7. Store in a tightly covered container. Sprinkle with confectioners' sugar before serving.

Yield: About 60 cookies

Tip

Baking two sheets of cookies at the same time simply makes this step go more quickly. Cookies can *always* be baked one sheet at a time in the center of the oven, but the baking sheet should be reversed from front to back midway through baking time for even baking.

Fluffy Sugar Cookies

Bake these cute cookies for the Easter Bunny to tuck into your children's Easter baskets. If you like, you can decorate some of the cookies with jelly beans and sprinkle others with cinnamon sugar, or just leave them plain. (They are also easy enough for the kids to help make them.)

    2 cups all-purpose flour

    $1/4$ teaspoon cream of tartar

    1 cup (2 sticks) salted butter or margarine

    1 $1/3$ cups sugar

    2 large eggs, lightly beaten

    1 teaspoon vanilla extract or $1/2$ teaspoon almond extract

    $2/3$ cup sour cream

    Assorted miniature jelly beans (about 360 jelly beans)

1. Adjust two racks to divide the oven into thirds. Preheat the oven to 375°. Lightly grease two baking sheets.

2. In a small bowl, with a whisk, combine the flour and cream of tartar until thoroughly mixed.

3. In a large bowl, with an electric mixer at medium-high speed, beat together the butter and sugar until light and fluffy, 2 to 3 minutes. Beat in the eggs and vanilla until blended. Beat in the sour cream until blended. With the mixer at medium-low speed, gradually add the flour mixture, beating just until blended. Drop by heaping measuring teaspoonfuls onto the prepared baking sheets, spacing the drops about 2 inches apart. Press three jelly beans into the top of each cookie.

4. Bake for about 10 minutes until the edges begin to brown. Reverse the baking sheets on the racks and from front to back once during baking. With a wide turner, transfer the cookies to wire racks to cool completely.

5. Store in a tightly covered container.

Yield: About 120 cookies

Tip

Room-temperature butter means just that. Butter that is too warm or too cold will not blend properly into the batter.

Orange-Cappuccino Drops

These cookies are unusual in both flavor and texture, which is much softer than most drop cookies. They are a good choice for a simple dessert when served with fruit, sherbet, or ice cream.

    $1/2$ cup (3 ounces) semisweet chocolate chips

    2 cups all-purpose flour

    $1/2$ teaspoon baking soda

    1 cup packed light brown sugar

    $1/2$ cup (1 stick) salted butter or margarine, at room temperature

    $2/3$ cup sour cream

    $1/2$ cup very strong coffee, cooled

    1 large egg

    1 teaspoon vanilla extract

1. Adjust two racks to divide the oven into thirds. Preheat the oven to 375°. Have ready two ungreased baking sheets.

2. In a small saucepan over very low heat, melt the chocolate, stirring constantly until smooth. Remove from the heat and set aside to cool slightly.

3. In a medium-size bowl, with a whisk, combine the flour and baking soda until thoroughly mixed.

4. In a large bowl, with an electric mixer at medium-high speed, beat together the brown sugar and butter until creamy, 2 to 3 minutes. Beat in the sour cream, coffee, melted chocolate, egg, and vanilla until well blended. With the mixer at medium-low speed, gradually add the flour mixture, beating just until blended. (The dough will be soft and sticky.) Drop by teaspoonfuls onto the ungreased baking sheets, spacing the drops about 2 inches apart.

5. Bake for 5 to 7 minutes until the cookies feel set when lightly touched. Reverse the baking sheets on the racks and from front to back once during baking. Do not overbake. With a wide turner, immediately transfer the cookies to wire racks to cool completely.

6. Store in a tightly covered container, separating the layers with sheets of waxed paper.

Yield: About 72 cookies

Vanilla-Butter Wafers

This is one of the world's most perfect cookies, unmatched in its absolute purity and tenderness. This crisp little cookie is as at home on a tea table as it is in a lunch box. Omit the zest, if you want to, or drizzle the baked cookies with melted chocolate (page 32). You can also experiment with different extracts for subtle flavor variations.

> $^1/_2$ **cup (1 stick) salted butter (not margarine), at room temperature**
>
> $^1/_2$ **cup sugar**
>
> **1 large egg white**
>
> **1 teaspoon vanilla extract**
>
> $^3/_4$ **teaspoon grated orange or lemon zest**
>
> $^3/_4$ **cup all-purpose flour**

1. Adjust one rack to divide the oven in half. Preheat the oven to 350°. Lightly grease two baking sheets.

2. In a medium-size bowl, with an electric mixer at medium speed, beat together the butter and sugar until light and fluffy, 2 to 3 minutes. Beat in the egg white, vanilla, and orange zest until well mixed. With the mixer at low speed, gradually add the flour, beating just until blended.

3. Place one of the prepared baking sheets in the oven until it is hot, about 2 minutes. Remove from the oven to a wire rack. Immediately drop the batter by rounded measuring teaspoonfuls onto the hot baking sheet, spacing the drops about 2 inches apart.

4. Bake for 6 to 8 minutes just until the edges are lightly browned. Reverse the baking sheet from front to back once during baking. With a wide turner, immediately transfer the cookies to wire racks to cool. Repeat with the remaining batter using the other baking sheet. (If a baking sheet is to be reused for this recipe, it must first be cooled, cleaned, and regreased.)

5. Store in a tightly covered container.

Yield: About 48 cookies

Maggie's Spur-of-the-Moment Vanilla Drops

To be honest, I'm not sure who Maggie is, or was. However, her recipe for these crisp, mildly spicy Vanilla Drops, which is neatly printed on a tattered card in my file, has gotten a lot of mileage over the years, probably because I always have the simple ingredients to bake them on hand, making this a good choice for spur-of-the moment cookies, and hence the new name. The toppings are nice, but not necessary.

> $2/3$ cup all-purpose flour
>
> 1 teaspoon ground cinnamon
>
> $1/2$ teaspoon ground nutmeg
>
> $1/2$ cup (1 stick) salted butter or margarine, at room temperature
>
> $1/3$ cup sugar
>
> 1 large egg
>
> 1 teaspoon vanilla extract
>
> Walnut or pecan pieces, raisins, diced candied fruit, or candy-coated chocolate pieces, for toppings

1. Adjust two racks to divide the oven into thirds. Preheat the oven to 350°. Lightly grease two baking sheets.

2. In a medium-size bowl, with a whisk, combine the flour, cinnamon, and nutmeg until thoroughly mixed.

3. In a large bowl, with an electric mixer at medium speed, beat together the butter and sugar until light and creamy, 2 to 3 minutes. Beat in the egg and vanilla until light and fluffy, about 2 minutes. With a mixing spoon, gradually stir in the flour mixture just until blended. Drop by rounded teaspoonfuls onto the prepared baking sheets, spacing the drops about 2 inches apart. Lightly press a few chopped nuts or other suggested toppings into the tops of the cookies.

4. Bake for 10 to 12 minutes until the edges are golden brown. Reverse the baking sheets on the racks and from front to back once during baking.

With a wide turner, transfer the cookies to wire racks to cool completely.

5. Store in a tightly covered container.

Yield: About 30 cookies

Rose Petals

These waferlike cookies are best when served as a nibble with tea, or as an accompaniment to a light dessert, such as fruit or sorbet. Rose water gives them their delicate and unusual flavor. This ingredient can be found most easily in specialty food stores that carry an extensive line of flavorings and essences. Middle Eastern grocery stores also stock rose water. Just be certain that the rose water you buy is intended for eating and not for cosmetic purposes. Strengths vary between brands. Start by tasting a drop, then add incrementally and cautiously to the cookie batter.

> $3/4$ cup all-purpose flour
>
> Pinch of ground mace
>
> $1/2$ cup (1 stick) salted butter or margarine, at room temperature
>
> $1/2$ cup sugar
>
> 1 large egg, lightly beaten
>
> $1/2$ teaspoon vanilla extract
>
> $1/2$ to 1 teaspoon rose water (see above)

1. Adjust one oven rack to divide the oven in half. Preheat the oven to 375°. Lightly grease one baking sheet.

2. In a small bowl, with a whisk, combine the flour and mace until thoroughly mixed.

3. In a medium-size bowl, with an electric mixer at medium-high speed, beat together the butter and sugar until light and creamy, 2 to 3 minutes. Add the egg, vanilla, and rose water and beat until fluffy. With the mixer at medium-low speed, add the flour mixture all at once, beating just until blended. From a teaspoon, drop marble-size mounds of batter onto the prepared baking sheet, spacing the drops about 1 inch apart. Place the baking sheet in the refrigerator for about 10 minutes until the batter is firm.

4. Bake for 12 to 15 minutes until the cookies are very lightly browned around the edges. Reverse the baking sheet from front to back once during baking. With a wide turner, immediately transfer the cookies to wire racks to cool completely.

5. Store in a tightly covered container.

Yield: About 24 wafers

Lemony Ginger Drops

Lemon sauce over gingerbread is a time-honored combination, so I think you'll like this version of gingerbread cookies topped with a fresh-tasting lemon icing.

Dough

2 cups all-purpose flour

1 teaspoon baking soda

1 teaspoon grated lemon zest

$^1/_2$ teaspoon salt

$^1/_2$ teaspoon ground ginger

$^1/_2$ teaspoon ground cinnamon

$^1/_4$ teaspoon ground cloves

$^1/_2$ cup sugar

$^1/_4$ cup butter-flavored shortening

$^1/_2$ cup regular or unsulphured molasses

$^1/_2$ cup hot water

1 large egg

Icing

1 cup sifted confectioners' sugar

$^1/_2$ teaspoon shredded and minced lemon zest

1 tablespoon salted butter or margarine, at room temperature

1 tablespoon strained fresh lemon juice

About 1 tablespoon milk

1. Adjust two racks to divide the oven into thirds. Preheat the oven to 375°. Lightly grease two baking sheets.

2. In a medium-size bowl, with a whisk, combine the flour, baking soda, lemon zest, salt, ginger, cinnamon, and cloves until thoroughly mixed.

3. In a large bowl, with an electric mixer at medium-high speed, beat the sugar, shortening, molasses, water, and egg until creamy, 1 to 2 minutes. With the mixer at medium-low speed, gradually add the flour mixture, beating just until blended. Let stand for 5 minutes before dropping by rounded teaspoonfuls onto the prepared baking sheets, spacing the drops about 2 inches apart.

4. Bake for 8 to 12 minutes until the edges are pale golden brown. Reverse the baking sheets on the racks and from front to back once during baking. With a wide turner, immediately transfer the cookies to wire racks to cool completely.

5. While the cookies are cooling, making the icing. In a small bowl, beat together the confectioners' sugar, lemon zest, butter, and lemon juice. Gradually add the milk until the mixture reaches a good spreading consistency. With a small spatula or a butter spreader, spread thinly over the cooled cookies. Let set until the icing hardens, about 1 hour.

6. Store in a tightly covered container, separating the layers with sheets of waxed paper.

Yield: About 36 cookies

Tip

A heavy, plastic bag, with one corner cut off, can be used as a pastry bag for dropping cookies directly onto a baking sheet.

Port and Almond Drops

Almonds and port mark this cookie as coming from Portugal. The port adds just a hint of its flavor.

These are what I think of as adult cookies, not so much because they contain port (the alcohol evaporates during baking), but because they aren't especially sweet and their subtle flavor is better appreciated by an adult palate. This is the perfect cookie to serve with tea or to accompany a healthy-minded dessert, such as fruit or sorbet.

    1/2 cup (1 stick) salted butter or margarine,
      at room temperature
    1/2 cup sugar
    2 large egg yolks
    1 cup very finely chopped blanched almonds
    1/4 cup tawny port
    1 teaspoon shredded and minced lemon zest
    1/2 teaspoon vanilla extract
    1 cup all-purpose flour

1. Adjust two racks to divide the oven into thirds. Preheat the oven to 400°. Lightly grease two baking sheets.

2. In a small bowl, with an electric mixer at medium speed, beat together the butter and the sugar until light and fluffy, 2 to 3 minutes. Add the egg yolks, one at a time, beating well after each addition. With a mixing spoon, stir in the almonds, port, lemon zest, and vanilla. Stir in the flour just until blended. Drop by generous measuring teaspoonfuls onto the prepared baking sheets, spacing the drops about 1 1/2 inches apart.

3. Bake for 8 to 10 minutes until golden. Reverse the baking sheets on the racks and from front to back once during baking. With a wide turner, immediately transfer the cookies to wire racks to cool completely.

4. Store in a tightly covered container.

Yield: About 60 cookies

Raisin and Nut Rocks

Appearance, not texture, is what gives these cookies their name. This is a good all-purpose cookie, crisp on the outside with a soft, chewy center.

    2 cups all-purpose flour
    1 teaspoon ground cinnamon
    1/2 teaspoon ground nutmeg
    1/2 teaspoon baking soda
    1 cup golden raisins
    1 cup chopped pecans
    3/4 cup (1 1/2 sticks) salted butter or marga-
      rine, at room temperature
    1 1/4 cups packed dark brown sugar
    3 large eggs, lightly beaten
    1/3 cup sour cream

1. Adjust two racks to divide the oven into thirds. Preheat the oven to 375°. Lightly grease two baking sheets.

2. In a large bowl, with a whisk, combine the flour with the cinnamon, nutmeg, and baking soda until thoroughly mixed. With a mixing spoon, stir in the raisins and pecans until well distributed throughout the flour mixture.

3. In a large bowl, with an electric mixer at medium speed, beat together the butter and the brown sugar until light and creamy, 2 to 3 minutes.

4. In a small bowl, beat the eggs with the sour cream just until mixed. Add the egg mixture to the butter mixture, beating until smooth. With the mixer at medium-low speed, gradually add the flour mixture, beating just until blended. Drop by teaspoonfuls onto the prepared baking sheets, spacing the drops about 2 inches apart.

5. Bake for 12 to 15 minutes until the cookies are light brown. Reverse the baking sheets on the racks and from front to back once during baking. With a wide turner, immediately transfer the cookies from the baking sheets to wire racks to cool completely.

6. Store in a tightly covered container.

Yield: About 54 cookies

French Chocolate-Nut Cookies

Like many French cookies, these contain only a minuscule amount of flour, which gives them their melt-in-the-mouth texture and *lots* of intense chocolate flavor.

- 1 ¹/₂ cups (9 ounces) semisweet chocolate chips, divided
- 1 ounce (1 square) unsweetened chocolate
- 1 tablespoon salted butter or margarine
- 2 tablespoons all-purpose flour
- ¹/₈ teaspoon baking powder
- 1 large egg, lightly beaten
- ¹/₃ cup packed dark brown sugar
- 1 tablespoon water
- 1 teaspoon vanilla extract
- 1 cup coarsely chopped walnuts

1. In a small, heavy saucepan over very low heat, melt together ¹/₂ cup of the semisweet chocolate chips, the unsweetened chocolate, and butter, stirring constantly until smooth. Transfer to a large bowl and set aside to cool slightly.

2. In a small bowl, with a dinner fork, combine the flour and baking powder until thoroughly mixed.

3. With a mixing spoon, stir the egg, brown sugar, water, and vanilla into the chocolate mixture until well blended. Stir in the flour mixture until completely blended. Stir in the remaining 1 cup chocolate chips and walnuts until well distributed throughout the batter. The dough will be very sticky. Cover and refrigerate until very cold, at least 1¹/₂ hours or overnight.

4. Adjust two racks to divide the oven into thirds. Preheat the oven to 350°. Line two baking sheets with foil, shiny side up.

5. Drop the cold batter by heaping teaspoonfuls onto the prepared baking sheets, spacing the drops about 1 inch apart.

6. Bake for 13 to 15 minutes until the cookies are firm to the touch. Reverse the baking sheets on the racks and from front to back once during baking. Cool on the baking sheets set on wire racks.

7. Store in a tightly covered container, separating the layers with sheets of waxed paper.

Yield: About 36 cookies

Tip
When mixing or holding dry ingredients on a sheet of waxed paper, first fold the waxed paper in half to form a spout for easier pouring.

Chocolate-Hazelnut Chewies

Although there are no chocolate chips in this cookie, you will undoubtedly recognize its well-known ancestor.

> 1 ³/₄ cups all-purpose flour
> ³/₄ cup whole wheat flour
> 1 cup unsweetened cocoa powder
> 1 ¹/₂ teaspoons baking soda
> 1 ¹/₄ cups (2 ¹/₂ sticks) salted butter or margarine, at room temperature
> ¹/₃ cup vegetable oil
> 1 ¹/₄ cups packed light or dark brown sugar
> 1 ¹/₄ cups granulated sugar
> 2 large eggs, lightly beaten
> 2 ¹/₂ teaspoons vanilla extract
> 2 ¹/₂ cups skinned and chopped hazelnuts, toasted (page 16)

1. Adjust two racks to divide the oven into thirds. Preheat the oven to 350°. Have ready two ungreased baking sheets.

2. In a medium-size bowl, with a whisk, combine the all-purpose flour, whole wheat flour, cocoa, and baking soda.

3. In a large bowl, with an electric mixer at medium speed, beat together the butter, oil, brown sugar, and granulated sugar until light and fluffy, 2 to 3 minutes. Beat in the eggs and vanilla until blended. With the mixer at medium-low speed, gradually add the flour mixture, beating just until blended. With a mixing spoon, stir in the hazelnuts until well distributed throughout the batter. Drop by measuring tablespoonfuls onto the ungreased baking sheets, spacing the drops about 2 inches apart.

4. Bake for 8 to 9 minutes until golden brown. The cookies should still be slightly soft when lightly touched. Reverse the baking sheets on the racks and from front to back once during baking. Do not overbake. Cool on the baking sheets set on wire racks for a minute or two. With a wide turner, transfer the cookies to wire racks to cool completely.

5. Store in a tightly covered container.

Yield: About 48 cookies

Chocolate-Dipped Double-Chocolate Oat Drops

All you need to make a batch of these supersimple, crunchy cookies is a spoon, a pan, and a bowl. Talk about easy!

> 4 cups quick-cooking (not regular or instant) rolled oats
> ²/₃ cup packed light or dark brown sugar
> 1 cup coarsely chopped walnuts
> 1 cup flaked coconut
> 2 cups (12 ounces) semisweet chocolate chips, divided
> ¹/₄ cup (¹/₂ stick) salted butter or margarine
> ²/₃ cup light or dark corn syrup
> 2 large eggs, lightly beaten
> ¹/₄ teaspoon salt

Chocolate Dip

> 1 ¹/₂ cups (9 ounces) semisweet chocolate chips

1. Adjust two racks to divide the oven into thirds. Preheat the oven to 350°. Lightly grease two baking sheets.

2. In a large bowl, with a whisk, combine the oats, brown sugar, walnuts, and coconut until thoroughly mixed.

3. In a heavy, medium-size saucepan, melt 1 cup of the chocolate chips with the butter over very low heat, stirring until smooth. With a mixing spoon, stir in the corn syrup, eggs, and salt. Stir the chocolate mixture into the oats mixture until well blended. Stir in the remaining 1 cup of chocolate chips until well distributed throughout the batter. Drop by measuring tablespoonfuls onto the prepared baking sheets, spacing the drops about 2 inches apart.

4. Bake for 15 minutes (the cookies will not change much in appearance during baking) until the cookies are firm to the touch. Reverse the baking sheets on the racks and from front to back once during baking. Cool on the baking sheets

set on wire racks for 5 minutes. With a wide turner, transfer the cookies to wire racks to cool completely.

5. While the cookies are cooling, make the chocolate dip: In a small, heavy saucepan, melt the chocolate over very low heat, stirring constantly until smooth. Dip half of each cooled cookie in the melted chocolate. Place on waxed paper until the chocolate hardens, about 1 hour.

6. Store in a tightly covered container, separating the layers with sheets of waxed paper.

Yield: About 36 cookies

MERINGUE COOKIES

In the strictest sense of the word, meringue cookies may not meet all of the criteria to be called a cookie. But my feeling is that if it *looks* like a cookie and it *tastes* like a cookie, then it must *be* a cookie.

Meringue is what happens when egg whites are beaten with sugar until the sugar dissolves and the whites have had enough air beaten into them to reach their peak volume. You know when this has happened, because the mixture is very stiff, glossy, and moist looking.

Meringue has many lovely applications, the most well known probably being the topping for lemon meringue pie. When used this way, the meringue is baked at a relatively high temperature just until the lemon-custard filling in the pie shell is cooked. The meringue itself browns lightly and remains soft and slightly gooey.

Meringue as cookies is quite another delicious story. In this case, dollops or other shapes of meringue, are baked (or, more accurately, "dried out") slowly at a low oven temperature. The sweet, airy meringue then becomes crisp-crumbly and tender, with a true melt-in-the-mouth texture that is hard to resist and hard to forget.

How to Beat Egg Whites for Meringue

When beating egg whites into a meringue, it is crucial that both the bowl and the beaters are clean and absolutely grease-free. (Most expert bakers routinely wipe the bowl and beaters beforehand with a paper towel dampened with lemon juice or vinegar, just in case.) A metal (copper being the material of choice) or a glass bowl is best for this job, since it is possible for grease to lurk in the pores of plastic bowls, no matter how well they have been washed.

The reason for all of this pickiness is that fat is an egg-white deflator, and even the smallest particle of fat that finds its way into the whites is reason enough for them not to achieve their greatest volume.

If a little speck of the yolk should happen to get into the whites while they are being separated, it can usually be flicked out with a piece of the eggshell.

Eggs separate more easily when they are cold, but beat up to their greatest volume at room temperature, so plan ahead. Transferring the yolk from shell half to shell half is *not* the best way to separate an egg. A better way is to use a little kitchen gadget called an egg separator, or simply break the egg into a small bowl, then transfer it to your hand and let the white slip through your fingers into the bowl in which the whites will be beaten.

Beat, Beat, And Beat Some More

There are several ways to start a meringue, but my method is to beat the room-temperature whites at medium speed until they are frothy. (Sometimes the recipe will direct you to add a little lemon juice or cream of tartar to the unbeaten egg whites for the purpose of added volume and stability, usually when the batters tend to be heavy.)

Either superfine or regular granulated sugar can be used to make meringue. Since superfine sugar dissolves more quickly than regular granulated sugar, it is a better choice for meringue recipes. In either case, the sugar must be added gradually (usually one tablespoon at a time) while beating at medium speed. After all of the sugar has been added, the mixture is beaten at high speed until it forms stiff, unwavering peaks

when the beaters are lifted. This whole process can easily take as long as 15 minutes, so be patient. Some experts recommend that you test the meringue by rubbing a bit of it between your thumb and forefinger until no graininess can be detected, which means that the sugar is completely dissolved and the meringue is perfect.

Another method, known as Swiss meringue, is beating the egg whites and sugar over warm water, which gives the meringue more volume and stability.

To Bake or Not to Bake?

Meringue is not baked in the usual sense. More accurately, it is slowly dried out. Sometimes a meringue is started in a cold oven, other times in a preheated oven, but it is always baked at a low temperature. Then, depending on the recipe, the meringue is removed when baking is complete, or left in the turned-off oven for as long as overnight, and sometimes cooled in the oven with the door left ajar to allow any steam to escape.

Storing Meringues

Meringue cookies keep well in a loosely covered container for several weeks, at least as long as the atmosphere is dry. But, at the first hint of humidity, they will absorb moisture readily and become soft and sticky. In humid weather, even when stored in a tightly covered container, they do not keep well.

A Nutritional Bonus

Because egg whites are virtually fat-free, meringue cookies are also low in fat; how low depending on what's been added to them. Chocolate and nuts, for example, contain significant amounts of fat, which must be factored in. Also, remember that meringue *always* contains sugar calories, and usually quite a few of them.

Meringue Drops

These cookies are sure to be a hit with those people who are obsessive about not eating fat. They are plain as plain can be, but exquisitely delicious, crisp on the outside, soft and a little chewy inside. For the holidays, these are pretty when they are dipped in melted white chocolate with a few white or silver sprinkles on top. If you want to change the color of the meringue, it's easy enough to do. Just add liquid food coloring, very sparingly, at the same time as the vanilla extract.

> 1 large egg white
> 1 cup superfine sugar
> 3 tablespoons boiling water
> 1/2 teaspoon vanilla extract

1. Adjust two racks to divide the oven into thirds. Preheat the oven to 225°. Cover two baking sheets with aluminum foil, shiny side up.

2. In the top of a double boiler, combine the egg white, sugar, boiling water, and vanilla. Set over simmering water, making sure that the bottom of the pan holding the egg white mixture does not touch the water. With an electric mixer at medium speed, beat the egg-white mixture until stiff peaks form when the beaters are lifted, 10 to 15 minutes. Drop the meringue from a teaspoon onto the prepared baking sheets, spacing the drops about 1 inch apart. (The puffs of meringue may be slightly different sizes and shapes, but this will not affect baking time.)

3. Bake for 35 to 40 minutes until the meringues are crisp on the outside, but still white in color. Reverse the baking sheets on the racks and from front to back once during baking. With your fingers, carefully peel the meringues from the baking sheets and place on wire racks to cool completely.

4. Store at low humidity in a loosely covered container.

Yield: About 30 meringues

Linda Hollins's Chocolate Meringues

When I told my niece Linda that I was working on a cookie cookbook, she was anxious to contribute the recipe for these meringues, which she got from her sister-in-law, who got it from her ex-mother-in-law. Well, that's the way it is with homemade cookies. Every recipe comes with its own little story.

> 3 large egg whites, at room temperature
> 1/2 cup superfine sugar
> 1/2 teaspoon vanilla extract
> 2 ounces (2 squares) semisweet chocolate, grated

1. Adjust two racks to divide the oven into thirds. Do *not* preheat the oven. Line two baking sheets with foil, shiny side up; lightly grease the foil.

2. In a small bowl, with an electric mixer at medium speed, beat the egg whites until frothy. Add the sugar, 1 tablespoon at a time, beating for about 1 minute after each addition. Add the vanilla and continue to beat until the whites are glossy and stand in stiff peaks when the beaters are lifted, 5 to 10 minutes. With a mixing spoon, fold in the chocolate just until well distributed throughout the batter. Drop by heaping teaspoonfuls onto the prepared baking sheets, spacing the drops about 2 inches apart.

3. Place the filled baking sheets in the cold oven. Set the oven temperature to 200°. Bake for about 1 1/4 hours (from the time the oven is turned on) until the meringues look very dry and are firm to the touch. With a wide turner, transfer the meringues to wire racks to cool completely.

4. Store at low humidity in a loosely covered container.

Yield: About 42 meringues

Dark Meringue Delights

Because of the brown sugar and walnuts in them, these meringues seem more like "real" cookies than some of the other meringues.

> 1 cup packed light brown sugar
> 1 cup finely chopped walnuts
> 1 large egg white, at room temperature

1. Adjust two racks to divide the oven into thirds. Preheat the oven to 350°. Cover two baking sheets with aluminum foil, shiny side up; lightly grease the foil.

2. In a medium-size bowl, with a whisk, combine the sugar and nuts until well mixed.

3. In a small bowl, with an electric mixer at medium speed, beat the egg white just until soft peaks are almost ready to form. (If the white is beaten too much, the cookies will not hold together.) With a mixing spoon, stir in the sugar mixture just until the batter holds together and forms a ball. Drop by heaping measuring teaspoonfuls onto the prepared baking sheets, spacing the drops about 1 inch apart.

4. Bake for 6 to 8 minutes until puffed and the edges look dry. Remove from the oven and set the pans on wire racks to cool completely. With your fingers, carefully peel the meringues from the baking sheets.

5. Store at low humidity in a loosely covered container.

Yield: About 30 meringues

Tip

Chilled chocolate can be grated and chopped more easily.

Fresh-Orange Meringues

Each of these meringues contains just a little fat (from the almonds) and a fresh, citrusy flavor from the orange peel and extract. They are fabulous.

3 large egg whites, at room temperature
³/₄ cup superfine sugar
¹/₂ teaspoon strained fresh lemon juice
¹/₄ teaspoon orange extract
¹/₄ cup finely chopped candied orange peel
¹/₄ cup finely chopped blanched almonds

1. Adjust two racks to divide the oven into thirds. Preheat the oven to 200°. Cover two baking sheets with aluminum foil, shiny side up.

2. In a large bowl, with an electric mixer at medium speed, beat the egg whites until frothy. Increase the speed to medium-high and beat until the whites hold soft peaks when the beaters are lifted. Add the sugar, 1 tablespoon at a time, beating for about 1 minute after each addition. Add the lemon juice and orange extract. Continue to beat for 5 to 10 minutes, or until the whites are glossy and stand in stiff peaks when the beaters are lifted. With a mixing spoon, fold in the orange peel and almonds until well distributed throughout the batter. Drop the meringue by heaping teaspoonfuls onto the prepared baking sheets, spacing the drops about 1 inch apart.

3. Bake for about 30 minutes until the meringues are firm to the touch, but not colored. Turn off the oven and leave the meringues in the oven for several hours or overnight.

4. Store at low humidity in a tightly covered container.

Yield: About 36 meringues

St. Marcarius's Sugarplum Meringues

I'm not sure who St. Marcarius was, but everyone who has ever eaten one certainly raves about his sugarplums. This is a rather unique cookie, best reserved for very special occasions.

2 teaspoons instant coffee powder (not granules), divided
1 tablespoon warm water
3 tablespoons miniature semisweet chocolate chips
3 tablespoons walnut pieces
1 cup halved pitted prunes
2 large egg whites, at room temperature
¹/₈ teaspoon cream of tartar
¹/₂ cup superfine sugar
Confectioners' sugar, for sprinkling on sugarplums (optional)
Grated semisweet chocolate, for sprinkling on sugarplums (optional)

1. Adjust two racks to divide the oven into thirds. Preheat the oven to 300°. Lightly grease two baking sheets. In a small bowl, dissolve 1 teaspoon of the coffee powder in the warm water; set aside.

2. In a food processor fitted with a steel blade, finely chop the chocolate chips and walnut pieces together using quick on-off pulses. Add the dissolved coffee and continue to process until the mixture forms a paste. Fill the prune halves with the walnut mixture, dividing evenly, and setting each one aside on waxed paper as it is filled.

3. In a large bowl, with an electric mixer at medium speed, beat the egg whites and cream of tartar until frothy. Increase the speed to medium-high and beat until the whites hold soft peaks when the beaters are lifted. Add the sugar, 1 tablespoon at a time, beating for about 1 minute after each addition. Continue to beat for 5 to 10 minutes, or until the whites are glossy and stand in stiff peaks when the beaters are lifted. With a mixing spoon, stir in the remaining teaspoon of instant coffee powder until well blended.

4. Using a dinner fork, dip each filled prune half into the meringue. As the prune halves are dipped, set them on a prepared baking sheet, spacing them about 2 inches apart.

5. Bake for 35 to 40 minutes until dry. Reverse the baking sheets on the racks and from front to back once during baking. With a wide turner, immediately transfer the cookies to wire racks to cool completely.

6. Store in a single layer, loosely covered with waxed paper. The sugarplums will keep for about a week in low humidity. Just before serving, dust with confectioners' sugar and grated chocolate, if desired.

Yield: About 18 cookies

Chocolate-Dipped Meringues

Meringues, chocolate, and nuts are a classic combination. If you want to, you can sandwich these cookies after they are covered with chocolate, bottom to bottom.

> 3 large egg whites, at room temperature
> $1/8$ teaspoon cream of tartar
> 1 cup superfine sugar
> 1 cup finely chopped walnuts
> 3 ounces (3 squares) semisweet chocolate, coarsely chopped
> 1 teaspoon plain shortening

1. Adjust one rack to the lowest oven position. Preheat the oven to 200°. Line a baking sheet with aluminum foil, shiny side up. Lightly grease and flour the foil.

2. In a large bowl, with an electric mixer at medium speed, beat the egg whites with the cream of tartar until frothy. With the mixer at medium-high speed, add the sugar, 1 tablespoon at a time, beating for about 1 minute after each addition. Continue to beat at high speed for 5 to 10 minutes until the whites are glossy and stand in stiff peaks when the beaters are lifted. With a mixing spoon, fold in the nuts just until evenly distributed throughout the batter. With two spoons, using about a heaping measuring tablespoonful of the batter, form the meringue into smooth balls and place them on the prepared baking sheet, spacing the balls about 1 inch apart.

3. Bake for 2 $1/2$ to 3 hours until firm. At the end of the baking time, turn off the oven and leave the meringues in the oven, with the door closed, for about 8 hours or overnight.

4. With your fingers, carefully peel the meringues off the foil and set aside.

5. Melt together the chocolate and shortening in a small heavy saucepan over very low heat, stirring constantly until smooth. Remove from the heat and set aside to cool to lukewarm. With a pastry brush, brush the bottoms of the meringues with melted chocolate. Place the meringues, chocolate side up, on sheets of waxed paper until the chocolate is firm, about 1 hour.

6. Store at low humidity in a loosely covered container, separating the layers with sheets of waxed paper.

Yield: About 27 meringues

Coconut Meringues

Coconut replaces the traditional nut paste in this very sweet and chewy adaptation of a bona fide macaroon, and they are supereasy to make.

> 3 egg whites, at room temperature
> 1/2 cup sugar
> 3 tablespoons all-purpose flour
> 1/8 teaspoon salt
> 1/2 teaspoon vanilla or almond extract
> One 7-ounce bag shredded coconut
>   (about 2 1/2 cups)

1. Adjust two racks to divide the oven into thirds. Preheat the oven to 325°. Lightly grease and flour two baking sheets.

2. In a large bowl, with an electric mixer at medium speed, beat the egg whites until frothy. Add the sugar, flour, salt, and vanilla and beat just until well blended. With a mixing spoon, stir in the coconut until well distributed throughout the batter. Drop by measuring tablespoonfuls onto the prepared baking sheets, spacing the drops about 1 inch apart.

3. Bake for about 15 minutes until set and lightly browned. With a wide turner, immediately transfer the cookies to wire racks to cool completely.

4. Store at low humidity in a loosely covered container, separating the layers with sheets of waxed paper.

Yield: About 18 cookies

MACAROONS

If you can't immediately decide whether you're eating a meringue or a cookie, then it's probably a macaroon, which is vaguely like a meringue, but is made by an entirely different method and has a denser, chewier texture. Nevertheless, because both meringues and macaroons are made using egg whites as the base ingredient, in cooking annals they have been linked together forever and I wouldn't want to be the one to change all that.

Macaroons originated in Italy hundreds of years ago. However, the French, who have always been quick to recognize a culinary masterpiece, adopted macaroons as their own after they were brought to France in the seventeenth century. Although macaroons are made and loved all over France, the most famous ones come from Nancy, where two nuns made and sold them during the French Revolution. In fact, a street in Nancy has been named after the nuns, who were known as the Macaroon Sisters.

Macaroons are made by mixing nut paste (traditionally almond), sugar, and egg white. The egg white acts as a binder and also prevents the nuts from releasing too much oil, but let's not get too technical. A good macaroon is surprisingly simple to make. Sometimes they are shaped, but more often they are dropped from a spoon, and sometimes even piped using a pastry bag.

Real Almond Macaroons

It takes only a few minutes to make your own almond paste, which I think is a little better than the canned version, but you can certainly use the latter. However, my feeling is that if you're going to make *real* macaroons, it pays to take this extra step.

> 1 1/3 cups almond paste (page 35)
> 2 large egg whites, divided
> 1/2 cup granulated sugar
> 1 cup sifted confectioners' sugar

1. Adjust two racks to divide the oven into thirds. Preheat the oven to 350°. Cover two baking sheets with aluminum foil, shiny side up. Lightly grease and flour the foil.

2. In a large bowl, with an electric mixer at medium speed, beat the almond paste with one of the egg whites until smooth, about 1 minute. Add the remaining egg white and about half of the granulated sugar and continue beating until well blended. Gradually add the remaining granulated sugar and the confectioners' sugar, beating just until well blended. Drop by teaspoonfuls onto the prepared baking sheets, spacing the drops about 2 inches apart.

3. Bake for 14 to 16 minutes until shiny and golden. Reverse the baking sheets on the racks and from front to back once during baking. Cool on the baking sheets set on wire racks. Carefully peel the macaroons off the foil with your fingers.

4. Store at low humidity in a loosely covered container, separating the layers with sheets of waxed paper.

Yield: About 40 cookies

Variation

Macaroon Thumbprints: After the macaroons have been dropped onto the baking sheet, coat a finger with confectioners' sugar and make a little indentation in the middle of each cookie. (Coat your finger with confectioners' sugar each time you make an indentation.) After the macaroons have been baked and cooled, fill each indentation with about ¼ teaspoon of seedless raspberry or other jam or jelly, or melted and cooled semisweet chocolate.

Tip

Cold eggs separate more easily, but the whites beat up to their greatest volume when they are at room temperature.

Thin Macaroons

Macaroons are usually plump and chewy. These are thin and crisp.

> 1 ¼ cups whole natural almonds (1 ½ cups ground)
> 1 ½ cups sugar, divided
> 5 large egg whites, at room temperature
> 1 teaspoon vanilla extract
> ½ teaspoon almond extract

1. Adjust two racks to divide the oven into thirds. Preheat the oven to 375°. Lightly grease and flour two baking sheets.

2. In a food processor fitted with a steel blade, process the almonds with about ½ cup of the sugar until finely ground, stopping the processor once and giving the almonds a good stir from the bottom.

3. In a large bowl, with an electric mixer at medium speed, combine the ground almond mixture and the remaining 1 cup of sugar. Add the egg whites, one at a time, beating hard after each addition. (The batter will resemble a thin paste.) Continue beating until the mixture barely holds soft peaks when the beaters are lifted, 3 to 4 minutes. With a mixing spoon, stir in the vanilla and almond extracts until well blended. Drop by measuring teaspoonfuls onto the prepared baking sheets, spacing the drops about 3 inches apart.

4. Bake for 10 to 15 minutes until the cookies are crisp and golden. Reverse the baking sheets on the racks and from front to back once during baking. With a wide turner, immediately transfer the cookies to wire racks to cool completely.

5. Store at low humidity in a loosely covered container, separating the layers with sheets of waxed paper.

Yield: About 40 cookies

Dropped Coconut Macaroons

If you are a purist, you may want to use fresh-grated coconut (page 12) in this recipe, and the macaroons won't be quite as sweet. Otherwise, the packaged coconut works just fine.

> One 7-ounce bag flaked coconut
> (about 2 ¹/₂ cups)
> ¹/₂ cup sifted all-purpose flour
> 4 large egg whites, at room temperature
> 1 teaspoon vanilla extract
> 1 ¹/₂ cups sifted confectioners' sugar

1. Adjust two racks to divide the oven into thirds. Preheat the oven to 325°. Lightly grease and flour two baking sheets.

2. In a medium-size bowl, with a whisk, combine the coconut and flour until thoroughly mixed.

3. In a large bowl, with an electric mixer at medium speed, beat the egg whites until frothy; beat in the vanilla. Gradually add the confectioners' sugar, 2 tablespoons at a time, beating for about 1 minute after each addition. Beat at high speed until the whites are glossy and stand in stiff peaks when the beaters are lifted, about 5 minutes. With a mixing spoon, fold in the coconut mixture until well blended. Drop by measuring tablespoonfuls onto the prepared baking sheets, spacing the drops about 2 inches apart.

4. Bake for about 25 minutes until the macaroons are pale golden. With a wide turner, immediately transfer the macaroons to wire racks to cool completely.

5. Store at low humidity in a loosely covered container.

Yield: About 24 macaroons

Praline Cookies

It's a little bit of a nuisance to make praline powder, but it is not difficult, and there is no substitute. Since only part of the praline powder is called for in the recipe, the remainder (about 1 ¹/₂ cups) can be stored in a tightly covered container in the refrigerator almost indefinitely and used as a topping for ice cream or stirred into whipped cream. Or, only pulverize enough to make the amount needed for the cookies and leave the rest in pieces to eat as candy.

Praline Powder

> 1 cup sugar
> 1 cup blanched almonds

Cookies

> ³/₄ cup all-purpose flour
> ¹/₄ teaspoon baking powder
> ¹/₂ cup (1 stick) salted butter or margarine,
> at room temperature
> ¹/₃ cup sugar
> 1 large egg, lightly beaten
> 1 teaspoon vanilla extract
> ¹/₂ cup praline powder

1. Make the praline powder: Lightly butter a large baking sheet. In a medium-size, heavy saucepan, stir together the sugar and almonds until well blended. Cook over medium heat, stirring constantly, until the sugar melts and the mixture forms a syrup and turns amber-colored. (Once the sugar has melted, things start happening pretty rapidly, so watch carefully so that the syrup does not go beyond this point.) Immediately pour the syrup onto the prepared baking sheet. Set aside to cool and harden, about 1 hour.

2. When the praline has hardened, break it into small pieces and pulverize in a food processor fitted with a steel blade. Measure out ¹/₂ cup of the powder and set aside. Reserve the remaining praline for another use.

3. Adjust two racks to divide the oven into thirds. Preheat the oven to 350°. Lightly grease two baking sheets.

4. In a medium-size bowl, with a whisk, combine the flour and baking powder until thoroughly mixed.

5. In a large bowl, with an electric mixer at medium speed, beat the butter and sugar until light and fluffy, 2 to 3 minutes. Beat in the egg and vanilla until well blended. With a rubber spatula, fold the flour mixture into the butter mixture just until blended. Stir in $1/2$ cup of the praline powder just until blended. Drop the batter by measuring teaspoonfuls onto the prepared baking sheets, spacing the drops $1^1/2$ to 2 inches apart.

6. Bake for about 8 minutes until the cookies are brown around the edges. Reverse the baking sheets on the racks and from front to back once during baking. With a wide turner, immediately transfer the cookies to wire racks to cool.

7. Store in a tightly covered container.

Yield: About 40 cookies

Dutch Caramel-Sugar Drops

After the sugar is caramelized, the rest is easy and the results are worth it.

Caramelized Sugar

$^1/_2$ cup granulated sugar

Dough

1 $^1/_4$ cups all-purpose flour

$^1/_2$ teaspoon baking powder

$^3/_4$ cup (1 $^1/_2$ sticks) salted butter or margarine, at room temperature

$^1/_2$ cup sugar

$^1/_2$ teaspoon vanilla extract

2 tablespoons tepid water

1. Adjust two racks to divide the oven into thirds. Generously grease two baking sheets. Generously grease a 12-inch-square of aluminum foil.

2. To make the caramelized sugar, set a heavy, 10-inch skillet over medium-high heat. Sprinkle the sugar into the skillet. As soon as the sugar starts to melt, tilt the skillet in each direction to mix the sugar crystals with the melted sugar. As soon as all of the sugar is melted and turned an amber color, immediately pour it onto the greased foil. Set aside to cool and harden, about 1 hour. Break up the hardened caramel in small pieces and place in a food processor fitted with a steel blade. Process until coarsely chopped, but not ground.

3. Preheat the oven to 325°.

4. In a small bowl, with a whisk, combine the flour and baking powder until thoroughly mixed.

5. In a medium-size bowl, with an electric mixer at medium-high speed, beat together the butter, sugar, and vanilla until light and fluffy, 2 to 3 minutes. With the mixer at medium-low speed, gradually add the flour mixture, beating just until blended. With a mixing spoon, stir in the caramelized sugar until well distributed throughout the batter. Drop by rounded measuring teaspoonfuls onto the prepared baking sheets.

6. Bake for 12 to 15 minutes until the edges are lightly browned. Reverse the baking sheets on the racks and from front to back once during baking. With a wide turner, immediately transfer the cookies to wire racks to cool completely.

7. Store in a tightly covered container.

Yield: About 36 cookies

Pumpkin-Pecan Drops

Obviously, these cookies would be a natural for Halloween or Thanksgiving. To make them a little less rich, forget the icing. They are almost as good without it, and easier to store.

- 2 cups all-purpose flour
- 1 teaspoon baking powder
- 1 teaspoon baking soda
- $^1/_2$ teaspoon salt
- 1 teaspoon ground cinnamon
- $^1/_8$ teaspoon ground ginger
- $^1/_8$ teaspoon ground nutmeg
- $^1/_8$ teaspoon ground allspice
- Pinch ground cloves
- 1 cup (2 sticks) salted butter or margarine, at room temperature
- 1 cup sugar
- 1 cup solid-pack canned pumpkin
- 1 large egg, lightly beaten
- 1 teaspoon vanilla extract
- $^1/_2$ cup dried currants
- $^1/_2$ cup chopped pecans

Icing

- $^1/_2$ cup light or dark brown sugar
- About $^1/_4$ cup milk
- 3 tablespoons salted butter or margarine
- $^3/_4$ teaspoon vanilla extract
- About 1 cup confectioners' sugar

1. Adjust two racks to divide the oven into thirds. Preheat the oven to 375°. Lightly grease two baking sheets.

2. In a medium-size bowl, with a whisk, combine the flour, baking powder, baking soda, salt, cinnamon, ginger, nutmeg, allspice, and cloves until thoroughly mixed.

3. In a large bowl, with an electric mixer at medium speed, beat together the butter and sugar until light and fluffy, 2 to 3 minutes. Add the pumpkin, egg, and vanilla and beat until smooth. With the mixer at low speed, gradually add the flour mixture, beating just until blended. With a

mixing spoon, stir in the currants and nuts until well distributed throughout the batter. Drop by measuring teaspoonfuls onto the prepared baking sheets, spacing the drops about 1 inch apart.

4. Bake for 10 to 15 minutes until golden. Reverse the baking sheets on the racks and from front to back once during baking. With a wide turner, immediately transfer the cookies to wire racks to cool completely.

5. While the cookies are cooling, make the icing: In a medium-size, heavy saucepan, combine the brown sugar, $^1/_4$ cup milk, and the butter. Cook the mixture over medium heat, stirring constantly, until the sugar has melted. Remove from the heat and set aside to cool. Stir in the vanilla and 1 cup confectioners' sugar. If the icing is too thick to spread, stir in a little additional milk. If it is too thin, add a little more confectioners' sugar. With a small icing spatula or a butter spreader, spread the cookies with icing. Let stand until the icing is set and dry, about 1 hour.

6. Store in a tightly covered container, separating the layers with sheets of waxed paper.

Yield: About 72 cookies

Whoopee Pies

I can't decide if this recipe makes a cookie or a little cake. It certainly doesn't make a pie. But, because it's good, and because you can eat it with one hand, I decided to go ahead and categorize this recipe as a cookie. In any case, you won't be disappointed. I grew up in eastern Pennsylvania, where Whoopee Pies are one of the local treats.

- 2 cups all-purpose flour
- $^1/_2$ cup unsweetened cocoa powder
- 1 $^1/_2$ teaspoons baking soda
- 1 teaspoon salt
- 1 cup sugar
- $^1/_2$ cup plain shortening
- 1 cup milk
- 2 teaspoons vanilla extract

Filling

> $^1/_2$ **cup (1 stick) salted butter or margarine, at room temperature**
> **One 7 $^1/_2$-ounce jar marshmallow creme**
> $^3/_4$ **cup confectioners' sugar**
> $^1/_4$ **cup plain shortening**
> $^1/_2$ **teaspoon vanilla extract**

1. Adjust two racks to divide the oven into thirds. Preheat the oven to 350°. Lightly grease two baking sheets.

2. In a medium-size bowl, with a whisk, combine the flour, cocoa, baking soda, and salt until thoroughly mixed.

3. In a large bowl, with an electric mixer at medium-high speed, beat together the sugar and shortening until very well blended, 2 to 3 minutes. With the mixer at medium-low speed, gradually add the flour mixture and the milk alternately with the sugar mixture, starting and ending with the flour mixture, and beating well after each addition. Beat in the vanilla just until well blended. Drop the batter by heaping measuring tablespoonfuls onto the prepared baking sheets, spacing the drops about 2 inches apart.

4. Bake for about 15 minutes until the cookies spring back when lightly touched. Reverse the baking sheets on the racks and from front to back once during baking. With a wide turner, transfer the cookies to wire racks to cool completely.

5. While the cookies are cooling, make the filling: In a large bowl, with an electric mixer at high speed, combine the butter, marshmallow creme, confectioners' sugar, shortening, and vanilla until light and fluffy, about 2 minutes. Place about 1 tablespoon of the filling on the bottoms of half the cookies. Sandwich together with the remaining cookies, top sides up, pressing them together so that the filling oozes out the sides a little.

6. Store in a tightly covered container, separating the layers with sheets of waxed paper, for a couple of days. Those that are not eaten soon after baking should be tightly wrapped in aluminum foil or plastic wrap and refrigerated or frozen.

Yield: About 20 cookies

Potato Chip Cookies

Back in the fifties, they were putting potato chips in everything, including cookies. These crisp, cookies have a pleasantly sweet-and-salty flavor. "They taste southern," said Annie Bailey, who reinvented this oldie-but-goodie recipe.

> $^1/_3$ **cup granulated sugar**
> $^1/_4$ **teaspoon ground cinnamon**
> $^1/_2$ **cup (1 stick) salted butter or margarine, at room temperature**
> $^1/_2$ **cup packed light brown sugar**
> **2 cups all-purpose flour**
> $^3/_4$ **cup crushed, salted potato chips**
> $^1/_2$ **cup finely chopped pecans**

1. Adjust two racks to divide the oven into thirds. Preheat the oven to 350°. Have ready two ungreased baking sheets.

2. In a small bowl, with a whisk, combine the granulated sugar and cinnamon until thoroughly mixed. Sprinkle onto a sheet of waxed paper.

3. In a large bowl, with an electric mixer at medium speed, beat together the butter and brown sugar until light and creamy, 2 to 3 minutes. Gradually add the flour, beating just until blended. With the mixer at low speed, beat in the potato chips and nuts just until blended. Drop by heaping teaspoonfuls onto the ungreased baking sheets, spacing the drops about 2 inches apart.

4. Rub the bottom of a glass with a little softened butter or margarine. Dip the glass into the sugar mixture. Slightly flatten each cookie with the sugar-coated glass bottom, redipping it into the sugar mixture between each cookie. (If you twist the glass slightly as you do this, it helps to keep it from sticking.)

5. Bake for 10 to 12 minutes until the edges are golden. Reverse the baking sheets on the racks and from front to back once during baking. Cool on the baking sheets for 5 minutes. With a wide turner, transfer the cookies to wire racks to cool completely.

6. Store in a tightly covered container.

Yield: About 68 cookies

Jumbo Blueberry Cookies

Kids love to snack on these giant-size cookies as well as to help make them. In fact, they are a good project for parents and kids, since there is lots of whisking, mixing, and stirring things in. Also, the cookies are big, so the dropping and baking procedure goes fast.

    2 1/4 cups all-purpose flour
    1 teaspoon baking soda
    1 cup (2 sticks) salted butter or margarine,
        at room temperature
    1/4 cup granulated sugar
    3/4 cup packed light brown sugar
    1 package (4-serving size) vanilla-flavor
        instant pudding and pie filling
    1 teaspoon vanilla extract
    2 large eggs, lightly beaten
    1 cup chopped pecans (optional)
    2 cups fresh or frozen (no need to thaw
        frozen berries) blueberries, rinsed and
        picked over

1. Adjust two racks to divide the oven into thirds. Preheat the oven to 375°. Have ready two ungreased baking sheets.

2. In a medium-size bowl, with a whisk, combine the flour with the baking soda until thoroughly mixed.

3. In a large bowl, with an electric mixer at medium speed, beat together the butter, granulated sugar, brown sugar, pudding mix, and vanilla until smooth and creamy, 2 to 3 minutes. Beat in the eggs until blended. With the mixer at low speed, gradually add the flour mixture, beating just until blended. With a mixing spoon, stir in the nuts, if using, and then the blueberries, until well distributed throughout the batter. Scoop the batter out of the bowl by 1/3 cupfuls and drop onto the ungreased baking sheets, spacing the drops about 6 inches apart.

4. Bake for 15 to 20 minutes until golden brown. Reverse the baking sheets on the racks and from front to back once during baking. With a wide turner, immediately transfer the cookies to wire racks to cool completely.

5. Store in a tightly covered container.

Yield: About 16 cookies

Variation

Jumbo As-You-Like-Its: There are any number of things that can be substituted for blueberries: Raisins or currants; dried cherries, cranberries, or blueberries; candy-coated chocolate pieces; even chocolate chips.

Holiday Drops

This cakelike cookie is especially well suited for Christmas, since it contains so many of the ingredients that are associated with this holiday.

    1 cup pitted dates, finely chopped
    1 cup mixed candied fruits, finely chopped
    1/4 cup brandy
    2 ounces (2 squares) unsweetened chocolate
    1 1/2 cups all-purpose flour
    1/4 teaspoon baking soda
    1/4 teaspoon salt
    1 cup packed light brown sugar
    1/2 cup (1 stick) salted butter or margarine,
        at room temperature
    1 large egg, lightly beaten
    1 teaspoon vanilla extract
    1/2 cup whole milk
    1 cup chopped walnuts or pecans
    Candied cherry halves, for decoration
        (optional)
    Walnut or pecan halves, for decoration
        (optional)

1. In a small bowl, combine the dates, candied fruits, and brandy. Cover lightly and set aside for 1 1/2 to 2 hours. (This can be done the day before.)

2. In a small, heavy saucepan set over very low heat, melt the chocolate, stirring constantly, until smooth. Set aside to cool slightly.

3. In a medium-size bowl, with a whisk, combine the flour, baking soda, and salt until thoroughly mixed.

4. In a large bowl, with an electric mixer at medium speed, beat the brown sugar with the butter until light and fluffy, 2 to 3 minutes. Beat in the melted chocolate, egg, and vanilla until blended. With the mixer at medium-low speed, beat in the flour mixture alternately with the milk just until blended. With a mixing spoon, stir in the brandy-soaked fruits and the nuts. Cover the bowl and refrigerate the dough until very cold, about 2 hours.

5. Adjust two racks to divide the oven into thirds. Preheat the oven to 375°. Lightly grease two baking sheets.

6. Drop the batter by generous teaspoonfuls onto the prepared baking sheets, spacing the drops about 2 inches apart. Lightly press a cherry half or a nut half into each mound of dough.

7. Bake for 12 to 15 minutes. Reverse the baking sheets on the racks and from front to back once during baking. With a wide turner, immediately transfer the cookies to wire racks to cool completely.

8. Store in a tightly covered container.

Yield: About 100 cookies

SYRUP COOKIES

The main ingredients in syrup cookies are usually sugar and butter, which are first melted into a thick syrup. Then a small amount of flour is added to make a thin batter. As the heat of the oven spreads the cookie batter over the baking sheet, the batter breaks apart and hardens, and forms a lacy pattern. Syrup cookies are often known as lace cookies or Florentines.

Syrup cookies are extremely fragile. They break and crumble easily, so they need to be handled with extreme care. They don't take well to humidity, either. Any atmospheric dampness will cause them to become sticky and a little limp, at which point they quickly lose their charm. The best way to store these cookies is in a shallow container in one or at most two layers.

Lace cookies can be shaped while they are still warm and pliable, but this does take a certain amount of speed and dexterity. To make shell-shaped cookies, drape the warm cookies over a fat rolling pin and remove them as soon as they are firm enough to do so. They can also be draped over inverted small bowls or custard cups and then used as edible servers for desserts, such as ice creams, mousses, and fruits. The warm cookies can also be shaped into cylinders and filled with whipped cream or other soft mixtures. Shaping cylinders are available from stores or companies that sell a full line of baking equipment, such as Sweet Celebrations, Bridge Kitchenware, or New York Cake and Baking Distributors (see Appendix C, "Shopping and Mail-Order Sources").

Be forewarned that when shaping cookies, you will probably not be able to get all of the cookies off the baking sheets and shaped before they harden too much, which means that the baking sheet will have to be returned to the oven a couple of times to resoften the cookies.

Shaped cookies are largely a labor of love. A good idea is always to make a sample cookie first to see how, and if, things are going to work.

Florentines

Dried fruit and almonds in the batter is what sets Florentines apart from other lace cookies. Although the Italians claim this cookie as their own, neighboring Austrians disagree.

- $^2/_3$ cup minced dried apricots
- $^1/_2$ cup plus 2 tablespoons sugar, divided
- 1 cup sifted all-purpose flour
- 1 cup finely chopped blanched almonds
- $^1/_2$ teaspoon grated orange zest
- 6 tablespoons ($^3/_4$ stick) salted butter or margarine,
- 2 tablespoons honey
- 2 tablespoons heavy (whipping) cream
- 1 tablespoon orange-flavored liqueur

Coating

- One 8-ounce bar semisweet chocolate, broken into small pieces
- 2 tablespoons salted butter or margarine

1. Adjust two racks to divide the oven into thirds. Preheat the oven to 350°. Lightly grease two baking sheets.

2. In a medium-size bowl, toss the apricots with 2 tablespoons of the sugar until well coated. With a mixing spoon, stir in the flour, almonds, and orange zest.

3. In a heavy, medium-size saucepan, place the butter, the remaining $^1/_2$ cup sugar, the honey, and cream. Cook over low heat, stirring occasionally, until the butter and sugar are melted, about 10 minutes. Do not allow the mixture to boil. Remove from the heat and set aside for about 5 minutes to cool slightly. Stir in the apricot mixture and the liqueur until well blended. Drop by $^1/_2$ teaspoonfuls onto the prepared baking sheets, spacing the drops about 2 inches apart. If necessary, flatten each mound of dough slightly with the back of a spoon.

4. Bake for 8 to 10 minutes until lightly browned around the edges. Reverse the baking sheets on the racks and from front to back once during baking. Let cool on the baking sheets for 2 minutes. With a wide turner, transfer the cookies to wire racks to cool completely.

5. Make the coating: In a small, heavy saucepan set over very low heat, melt the chocolate with the butter, stirring constantly until smooth. Remove from the heat and stir briskly until the mixture is very glossy, about 3 minutes. With a small icing spatula or a butter spreader, spread the bottom of each cookie with a thin coating of chocolate. Return the coated cookies to the wire racks, chocolate side up, until the chocolate is firm, about 1 hour.

6. Store in a loosely covered, shallow container, separating the layers with sheets of waxed paper. Florentines do not keep well, so they must be served within a day or two.

Yield: About 65 cookies

Tip

Coffee cans make perfect containers for storing cookies.

Kletskoppen
à la SS *Rotterdam*

Some of the finest food in the world was served to the passengers who traveled on the great luxury liners. These Dutch cookies are a good example. The finished cookies are supposed to be very thin and brittle, so don't attempt to make them on a rainy or humid day, which tends to make them a little limp.

> 1 ²/₃ cups packed light brown sugar
> 1 cup all-purpose flour
> ²/₃ cup finely chopped blanched almonds
> ¹/₄ cup (¹/₂ stick) salted butter or margarine, at room temperature
> 2 teaspoons ground cinnamon
> ¹/₈ teaspoon salt
> About ¹/₄ cup water

1. Adjust two racks to divide the oven into thirds. Preheat the oven to 300°. Lightly grease two baking sheets.

2. In a large bowl, with a mixing spoon, mix together as thoroughly as possible the brown sugar, flour, almonds, butter, cinnamon, and salt. Gradually stir in enough of the water to make a stiff dough. Scoop the dough out of the bowl by teaspoonfuls and drop onto the prepared baking sheets, spacing the drops about 3 inches apart.

3. Bake for 15 to 20 minutes until bubbly and lacy. Reverse the baking sheets on the racks and from front to back once during baking. Cool for about 3 minutes on the baking sheet set on wire racks until they are firm enough to be transferred with a wide turner to wire racks to cool completely. If the cookies become too brittle to remove from the baking sheets, return them to the oven for a minute or so to soften.

4. Store at low humidity in a shallow, loosely covered container, separating the layers with sheets of waxed paper.

Yield: About 42 cookies

Doilies

Even for lace cookies, these are exceptionally lacy. As you might expect, they are especially thin and crisp. Handle them with extreme care.

> ¹/₂ cup all-purpose flour
> ¹/₂ teaspoon ground ginger
> ¹/₂ teaspoon grated lemon zest
> ¹/₄ cup (¹/₂ stick) salted butter or margarine
> ¹/₄ cup sugar
> 2 tablespoons dark corn syrup
> 2 teaspoons brandy

1. Adjust one rack to divide the oven in half. Preheat the oven to 350°. Lightly grease two baking sheets.

2. In a medium-size bowl, with a whisk, combine the flour and ginger until thoroughly mixed. Whisk in the lemon zest.

3. In a heavy, medium-size saucepan, combine the butter, sugar, and syrup. Cook over low heat, stirring constantly, until the sugar is dissolved, 2 to 3 minutes. Remove the pan from the heat and beat in the flour mixture all at once; beat in the brandy. Drop half the batter by teaspoonfuls onto one of the prepared baking sheets, spacing the drops about 3 inches apart.

4. Bake one sheet at a time for about 8 minutes until the cookies are golden. With a wide turner, immediately transfer the cookies to wire racks to cool. Repeat with the remaining batter using the other baking sheet.

5. Store at low humidity in a shallow, loosely covered container, separating the layers with sheets of waxed paper.

Yield: About 16 cookies

Almond Lace Cookies

These are my favorite lace cookies. They have a wonderful buttery, nutty flavor that keeps me and everyone who has ever tried one going back for just one more, and one more after that. I always drizzle these cookies with fine lines of melted chocolate.

> $^3/_4$ **cup whole natural almonds, toasted (page 16)**
> $^1/_2$ **cup sugar**
> **1 tablespoon all-purpose flour**
> $^1/_2$ **cup (1 stick) salted butter or margarine**
> **2 tablespoons heavy (whipping) cream**
> $^1/_2$ **teaspoon vanilla extract**
> $^1/_2$ **cup (3 ounces) semisweet chocolate chips**

1. Adjust two racks to divide the oven into thirds. Preheat the oven to 350°. Lightly grease two baking sheets.

2. Combine the almonds, sugar, and flour in a food processor fitted with a steel blade. Process until the almonds are finely ground, stopping once to give the almond mixture a good stir from the bottom to keep the mixture from becoming pasty.

3. In a heavy, medium-size saucepan, combine the almond mixture with the butter and cream. Cook over medium heat, stirring constantly, until the butter is melted. Remove from the heat and stir in the vanilla. Drop by measuring teaspoonfuls onto the prepared baking sheets, spacing the drops about 4 inches apart.

4. Bake for about 5 minutes until golden and the edges are brown. Reverse the baking sheets on the racks and from front to back once during baking. Cool on the baking sheets for $1^1/_2$ to 2 minutes until slightly firm. With a wide turner, transfer the cookies to wire racks to cool completely.

5. While the cookies are cooling, melt the chocolate in a small, heavy saucepan over very low heat, stirring constantly, until smooth. Drop the melted chocolate from the tip of a spoon in back-and-forth lines across the tops of the cookies. Let stand until the chocolate hardens, about 30 minutes.

6. Store at low humidity in a shallow, tightly covered container, separating the layers with sheets of waxed paper.

Yield: About 36 cookies

Chocolate Lace Cookies

Has there ever been a cookie so perfect that a little chocolate couldn't make it even better? Praise be to the baker who decided to add cocoa to a lace cookie. And, since chocolate and orange flavors are so compatible, there's a little orange zest and orange extract in these, too. Yum!

> **1 cup all-purpose flour**
> $^2/_3$ **cup sugar**
> $^1/_4$ **cup unsweetened cocoa powder**
> $^1/_8$ **teaspoon salt**
> **1 cup honey**
> $^1/_2$ **cup (1 stick) salted butter or margarine**
> **1 teaspoon shredded and minced orange zest**
> **1 teaspoon orange extract**

1. Adjust two racks to divide the oven into thirds. Preheat the oven to 375°. Lightly grease two baking sheets.

2. In a medium-size bowl, with a whisk, combine the flour, sugar, cocoa, and salt until thoroughly mixed.

3. In a medium-size saucepan over medium heat, heat the honey until it bubbles. Remove from the heat and stir in the butter and orange zest, stirring until the butter is melted; stir in the orange extract. Gradually add the flour mixture to the honey mixture until well blended; set aside to cool completely. Drop the cooled batter by teaspoonfuls onto the prepared baking sheets, spacing the drops about 4 inches apart.

4. Bake for 4 to 6 minutes until the cookies are firm. Reverse the baking sheets on the racks and from front to back once during baking. Let the cookies cool on the baking sheets for 1 minute, then remove with a wide turner to wire racks to cool completely. If the cookies become too stiff

to remove from the baking sheets, return them to the oven for a minute or so to soften.

5. Store at low humidity in a loosely covered container, separating the layers with sheets of waxed paper.

Yield: About 60 cookies

Chocolate and Orange Florentines

The batter for these fabulous cookies is superthick with a mixture of candied orange peel and sliced almonds. After the cookies are dropped, the caramel batter spreads out and frames the nuts. Like any lace cookies, these should not be made or stored during humid weather. Moisture robs them of their crispness very quickly.

Candied Orange Peel

    2 small navel oranges
    $^1/_2$ cup water
    $^1/_4$ cup sugar

Batter

    $^1/_2$ cup (1 stick) salted butter or margarine
    $^2/_3$ cup sugar
    2 tablespoons milk
    2 tablespoons light corn syrup
    $^1/_3$ cup all-purpose flour
    1 cup sliced almonds
    1 teaspoon vanilla extract

Filling

    1 cup (6 ounces) semisweet chocolate chips

1. Adjust two racks to divide the oven into thirds. Preheat the oven to 350°. Line two baking sheets with foil, shiny side up, making sure the foil is as wrinkle-free as you can get it.

2. To make the Candied Orange Peel, with a vegetable parer, cut the peel off the oranges in $^1/_2$-inch strips, making sure not to include any of the bitter white pith just beneath. (Scrape away the pith with the tip of a sharp knife, if necessary.) Cut the strips into $^1/_8$-inch bits. In a small saucepan set over very low heat, combine the orange peel, water, and sugar. Cook without stirring until the bottom of the pan is covered only with the glazed peel. *Be careful not to go too far and allow the mixture to caramelize.* Remove from the heat and set aside. When cool, measure out $^1/_4$ cup and set aside. (Any remaining peel will not be used.)

3. To make the batter, in a medium-size saucepan set over medium heat, combine the butter, sugar, milk, and corn syrup. Bring to a boil and cook, without stirring, until the mixture registers 230° on a candy thermometer, or spins a 2-inch thread when dropped from a spoon or a fork. Remove from the heat. With a mixing spoon, immediately stir in the flour, candied orange peel, almonds, and vanilla until well blended.

4. To keep the batter from hardening while you are working with it, set the pan in a deep skillet that has been partly filled with hot water. Drop the batter by level teaspoonfuls on the prepared baking sheets, spacing the drops about 4 inches apart.

5. Bake for 8 to 11 minutes until the cookies are bubbly all over and a light brown, caramel color. Cool completely on the baking sheet. (If you need this baking sheet for subsequent batches, slide the foil off the baking sheet. Cool the baking sheet completely before re-covering with foil.) When the cookies are completely cool and firm, gently peel the foil away from the cookies.

6. In a small saucepan set over very low heat, melt the chocolate chips, stirring constantly until smooth. Remove from the heat and set aside to cool slightly. With a small icing spatula or a butter spreader, spread the chocolate on the flat side of one cookie. Gently press on another cookie, flat sides together. Set aside in a cool place until the chocolate hardens, at least 2 hours.

7. Store in low humidity in a tightly covered container, separating the layers with sheets of waxed paper.

Yield: About 18 sandwich cookies

Cigarettes

Definitely VSO (very special occasion) cookies, the kind you see in the windows of high-end bakeries in Europe, and, if you learn to make them, will seal your reputation as a master baker. Cigarettes can be contrary to make, but once you get the batter formula and the rolling business down pat, they go surprisingly quickly. To get things just right, bake one test cookie first. If it is not crisp enough, add 1 tablespoon of melted butter to the batter. If it is too brittle, add 1 to 2 tablespoons of flour. If you like, one or both tips of the rolled cookies can be dipped in Chocolate Glaze (page 32).

  $1/2$ cup (1 stick) salted butter, at room
     temperature
  $3/4$ cup confectioners' sugar
  4 large egg whites, divided
  $2/3$ cup plus 1 heaping tablespoon all-purpose
     flour, divided
  $3/4$ tablespoon heavy or whipping cream
  $3/4$ teaspoon vanilla extract

1. Adjust two racks to divide the oven into thirds. Preheat the oven to 450°. Lightly grease two baking sheets.

2. In a large bowl, with an electric mixer at medium speed, beat together the butter and confectioners' sugar until creamy, about 2 minutes. Beat in 2 of the egg whites until well blended. Add 1 heaping tablespoon of the flour, beating until well combined. Beat in the remaining 2 egg whites until well blended. With a mixing spoon, stir in the cream and vanilla until blended and smooth.

3. Drop by level measuring tablespoonfuls onto the prepared baking sheets, spacing the drops about 3 inches apart.

4. Bake for 4 to 6 minutes until brown around the edges. With a wide turner, immediately loosen the cookies from the baking sheet, but do not remove them. With your fingers pick up one cookie and place it, bottom side up, on a work surface. Immediately roll the cookie around the handle of a wooden spoon or a $3/4$-inch dowel to form a cigarette shape. Slide the cookie off the handle and set on a wire rack to cool. Quickly repeat the rolling procedure with the remaining cookies. If the cookies become too firm to roll, put them back into the oven for 30 to 60 seconds to soften.

5. Store in a tightly covered container for several days. For longer storage, freeze in tightly sealed plastic bags.

Yield: About 30 cookies

Chewy Oatmeal Cookies

I thought my grandmother's fabulous, chewy oatmeal cookies were lost forever until I came upon this recipe in a turn-of-the-century cookbook. After a few tests and some minor alterations, I think I've duplicated her flourless oatmeal cookies almost exactly.

Before you begin, please note that this batter *must* be refrigerated for at least 8 hours (overnight is better) before baking. Plan ahead and don't try to shorten the chilling time. It takes that long for the moisture in the batter to be absorbed into the oats.

  2 $1/2$ cups regular (not quick-cooking or
     instant) rolled oats
  1 teaspoon baking powder
  4 tablespoons salted butter or margarine,
     at room temperature
  $3/4$ cup packed light brown sugar
  $1/4$ cup granulated sugar
  2 large eggs
  1 teaspoon vanilla extract

1. In a medium-size bowl, with a whisk, combine the oats and the baking powder until thoroughly mixed.

2. In a medium-size bowl, with an electric mixer at medium speed, beat together the butter, brown sugar, and granulated sugar until the mixture comes together and leaves the side of the bowl.

Beat in the eggs, one at a time, beating after each addition until well blended. Add the vanilla and continue to beat until smooth and creamy, about 1 minute. With a mixing spoon, gradually stir in the oats mixture until well combined. Cover the bowl and refrigerate the batter for at least 8 hours or overnight.

3. Adjust two racks to divide the oven into thirds. Preheat the oven to 375°. Lightly grease two baking sheets.

4. Drop the cold batter by scant measuring tablespoonfuls onto the prepared baking sheets, spacing the drops about 2 inches apart.

5. Bake for about 8 minutes until the edges are brown. Reverse the baking sheets on the racks and from front to back once during baking. Cool on the baking sheets set on wire racks for 5 minutes. With a wide turner, transfer the cookies to wire racks to cool completely. Handle the cookies gently, since at this point they will break and crumble easily.

6. Store in a shallow, tightly covered container, separating the layers with sheets of waxed paper.

Yield: About 36 cookies

Quaker's Classic Oatmeal Cookies

Who better to invent what might be the world's best oatmeal cookie? In its own way, this cookie ranks right up there with the famous Nestlé chocolate-chip cookie.

> 3 cups regular or quick-cooking (not instant) rolled oats
> 1 cup all-purpose flour
> 1 teaspoon salt
> 1/2 teaspoon baking soda

> 3/4 cup (1 1/2 sticks) plain shortening
> 1 cup packed light or dark brown sugar
> 1/2 cup granulated sugar
> 1 large egg
> 1/4 cup water
> 1 teaspoon vanilla extract

1. Adjust two racks to divide the oven into thirds. Preheat the oven to 350°. Have ready two ungreased baking sheets.

2. In a medium-size bowl, with a whisk, combine the oats, flour, salt, and baking soda until thoroughly mixed.

3. In a large bowl, with an electric mixer at medium-high speed, beat together the shortening, brown sugar, granulated sugar, egg, water, and vanilla until creamy. With the mixer at medium-low speed, gradually add the oats mixture, beating just until blended. Drop by rounded measuring teaspoonfuls onto the ungreased baking sheets.

4. Bake for 12 to 15 minutes until lightly browned. (For a chewy cookie, bake for about the minimum time. The longer the baking time, the crisper the cookie will be.) Reverse the baking sheets on the racks and from front to back once during baking. With a wide turner, immediately transfer the cookies to wire racks to cool completely.

5. Store in a tightly covered container.

Yield: About 60 cookies

Variation

Oatmeal Cookies Plus: Add 1 cup of any or a combination of the following to the basic dough: raisins, dried cherries or cranberries, chopped nuts, chocolate chips, butterscotch- or peanut butter–flavored chips, or coconut.

Chocolate Oatmeal Cookies

Where there is a plain cookie, there is always the chocolate variation, and oatmeal cookies are no exception.

2 cups all-purpose flour

$^1/_3$ cup unsweetened cocoa powder

1 teaspoon baking soda

1 teaspoon salt

1 teaspoon ground cinnamon

1 cup (2 sticks) plain shortening

1 $^1/_3$ cups sugar

2 large eggs, lightly beaten

$^1/_2$ cup milk

2 cups regular or quick-cooking (not instant) rolled oats

1 cup raisins

1. Adjust two racks to divide the oven into thirds. Preheat the oven to 350°. Lightly grease two baking sheets.

2. In a medium-size bowl, with a whisk, combine the flour, cocoa, baking soda, salt, and cinnamon until thoroughly mixed.

3. In a large bowl, with an electric mixer at medium-high speed, beat together the shortening and sugar until creamy, 2 to 3 minutes. Beat in the eggs until well blended. With the mixer at medium-low speed, add the flour mixture alternately with the milk, beating well after each addition. With a mixing spoon stir in the oats and raisins. Drop by measuring teaspoonfuls onto the prepared baking sheets, spacing the drops about 2 inches apart.

4. Bake for 10 to 12 minutes until firm when lightly touched. Reverse the baking sheets on the racks and from front to back once during baking. Cool on the baking sheets for 1 minute. With a wide turner, transfer the cookies to wire racks to cool completely.

5. Store in a tightly covered container.

Yield: About 72 cookies

Orange-Oatmeal Drops

Someone recently asked me how many versions of oatmeal cookies I thought there were. In my research I easily found dozens and dozens of oatmeal-cookie recipes, and I probably only scratched the surface. However, they are all very much alike, except for stir-in ingredients and special flavors. This, for instance, is just a very basic oatmeal cookie flavored with orange zest and orange juice.

$^1/_2$ cup all-purpose flour

$^1/_4$ teaspoon baking soda

$^1/_4$ teaspoon salt

1 $^1/_2$ cups regular or quick-cooking (not instant) rolled oats

$^1/_2$ cup plain shortening

1 cup packed light or dark brown sugar

$^1/_2$ teaspoon vanilla extract

2 to 3 tablespoons fresh, strained orange juice

1 tablespoon shredded and minced orange zest

1. Adjust two racks to divide the oven into thirds. Preheat the oven to 375°. Lightly grease two baking sheets.

2. In a medium-size bowl, with a whisk, combine the flour with the baking soda and salt until thoroughly mixed. Whisk in the oats until well blended.

3. In a large bowl, with an electric mixer at medium-high speed, beat together the shortening, brown sugar, vanilla, 2 tablespoons of the orange juice, and orange zest until creamy, 2 to 3 minutes. With the mixer at medium-low speed, gradually add the flour mixture, beating just until blended. If the mixture seems dry, beat in a little more orange juice. Drop by heaping measuring teaspoonfuls onto the prepared baking sheets, spacing the drops about 2 inches apart.

4. Bake for about 12 minutes until the edges are lightly browned. Reverse the baking sheets on the racks and from front to back once during baking.

Cool on the baking sheets set on wire racks for about 3 minutes. With a wide turner, transfer the cookies to wire racks to cool completely.

5. Store in a tightly covered container.

Yield: About 36 cookies

Candy Bar Cookies

These cookies are just *so* American. Can you imagine anyone but *us* putting candy bars into cookies? Naturally, you will choose the candy bars you love the best, which melt into the cookies as they bake. I make these with either Fifth Avenues or dark-chocolate Milky Ways.

> **2 or 3 chocolate-covered candy bars**
> **1 1/4 cups all-purpose flour**
> **3/4 teaspoon baking powder**
> **1/2 cup (1 stick) salted butter or margarine, at room temperature**
> **1/2 cup sugar**
> **1 large egg, lightly beaten**
> **1 teaspoon vanilla extract**

1. Adjust two racks to divide the oven into thirds. Preheat the oven to 325°. Lightly grease two baking sheets. With a sharp knife, cut the candy bars into 1/2-inch pieces. (You should have about 1 cup.)

2. In a small bowl, with a whisk, combine the flour with the baking powder until thoroughly mixed.

3. In a medium-size bowl, with an electric mixer at medium-high speed, beat together the butter and sugar until light and fluffy, 2 to 3 minutes. Beat in the egg and vanilla until well blended. With the mixer at medium-low speed, gradually add the flour mixture, beating just until blended. With a mixing spoon, stir in the candy-bar pieces until well distributed throughout the batter. Drop the batter by heaping measuring tablespoonfuls onto the prepared baking sheets, spacing the drops about 2 inches apart.

4. Bake for about 15 minutes until the tops of the cookies are light golden brown. Reverse the baking sheets on the racks and from front to back once during baking. Cool on the baking sheets for 1 minute. With a wide turner, transfer the cookies to wire racks to cool completely.

5. Store in a tightly covered container.

Yield: About 24 cookies

Coconut Jumbles

Even though this recipe calls for ready-to-use, presweetened coconut, which is pretty sweet, these cookies are surprisingly unsweet. If you use fresh-grated coconut, you may want to add another 1/3 cup of sugar.

> **2/3 cup salted butter, at room temperature**
> **2/3 cup sugar**
> **1/2 teaspoon vanilla extract**
> **1 large egg, lightly beaten**
> **2 cups ready-to-use flaked coconut (from a 7-ounce package)**
> **1 cup all-purpose flour**

1. Adjust two racks to divide the oven into thirds. Preheat the oven to 400°. Lightly grease and flour two baking sheets.

2. In a large bowl, with an electric mixer at medium speed, beat together the butter, sugar, and vanilla until light and fluffy, 2 to 3 minutes. Beat in the egg until blended. The mixture will look curdled. With a mixing spoon, stir in the coconut and flour until well blended. Drop the batter by measuring tablespoonfuls onto the prepared baking sheets, spacing the drops about 1 1/2 inches apart.

3. Bake for 10 to 12 minutes until the edges are golden. Reverse the baking sheets on the racks and from front to back once during baking. With a wide turner, transfer the cookies to wire racks to cool completely.

4. Store in a tightly covered container.

Yield: About 40 cookies

Black-and-Whites

These are the hands-down favorite of every American schoolchild. Many people recall buying one black-and-white at the bakery after school, including me. These are traditionally BIG cookies, and they were iced, so I guess we all felt that we got a lot for our money. Black-and-whites are one-bowl cookies and very simple to make.

    2 cups all-purpose flour
    1 teaspoon baking powder
    ¹/₂ teaspoon baking soda
    1 cup granulated sugar
    ¹/₂ cup (1 stick) plain or butter-flavored
        shortening
    ¹/₂ cup buttermilk
    1 ¹/₂ teaspoons vanilla extract
    1 large egg

Icings

    5 to 6 teaspoons water
    1 ³/₄ cups confectioners' sugar, divided
    1 ounce (1 square) unsweetened chocolate,
        broken in half
    1 to 2 tablespoons warm water

1. Adjust two racks to divide the oven into thirds. Preheat the oven to 350°. Lightly grease two baking sheets.

2. In a medium-size bowl, with a whisk, combine the flour, baking powder, and baking soda until thoroughly mixed. With an electric mixer at medium-low speed, beat in the granulated sugar, shortening, buttermilk, vanilla, and egg until well blended, occasionally scraping the side of the bowl with a rubber spatula.

3. Drop the batter by ¹/₄ cupfuls onto the prepared baking sheets, spacing them about 3 inches apart. With the back of a spoon, spread the batter into 2-inch circles.

4. Bake for 15 to 17 minutes until the edges begin to brown and the cookies spring back when lightly touched. Reverse the baking sheets on the racks and from front to back once during baking.

With a wide turner, transfer the cookies to wire racks to cool completely.

5. While the cookies are cooling, make the white icing. In a small bowl, gradually add the water to 1¹/₄ cups of the confectioners' sugar, beating constantly with a spoon until the mixture achieves a good spreading consistency.

6. Turn the cookies over on the racks so that the flat, bottom sides are up. With a small icing spatula, spread half of the bottom sides of the cookies with the white icing. Give the icing time to set, about 20 minutes.

7. To make the chocolate icing, in a very small saucepan set over very low heat, melt the chocolate, stirring constantly until smooth. Remove from the heat. In a small bowl, stir the remaining ¹/₂ cup confectioners' sugar with 1 tablespoon of the warm water until smooth. Stir in the melted chocolate until smooth. Add enough of the remaining warm water to giving the icing a good spreading consistency. With a small icing spatula, spread the other half of the bottom sides of the cookies with the chocolate icing. Set aside until the icings are completely dry, about 1 hour.

8. Store in a tightly covered container, separating the layers with sheets of waxed paper.

Yield: About 14 cookies

Chocolate Cookie Sandwiches

Here is a home-baked version of that very popular chocolate-sandwich cookie with the filling that kids like to eat first.

1 ^{1}/$_2$ cups all-purpose flour
^{1}/$_3$ cup unsweetened cocoa powder
^{1}/$_2$ teaspoon baking soda
^{1}/$_2$ teaspoon salt
^{1}/$_2$ cup (1 stick) plain or butter-flavored
   shortening
1 cup sugar
1 large egg
1 teaspoon vanilla extract
^{1}/$_4$ cup milk
Marshmallow Creme Filling (page 34)

1. Adjust two racks to divide the oven into thirds. Preheat the oven to 375°. Have ready two ungreased baking sheets.

2. In a medium-size bowl, with a whisk, combine the flour, cocoa powder, baking soda, and salt until thoroughly mixed.

3. In a large bowl, with an electric mixer at medium-high speed, beat together the shortening, sugar, egg, and vanilla until light and fluffy, 2 to 3 minutes. With the mixer at medium-low speed, alternately add the flour mixture and the milk, beating until well blended. Drop by teaspoonfuls onto the ungreased baking sheets, spacing the drops about 2 inches apart.

4. Bake for 11 to 12 minutes until just set. (Do not overbake.) Reverse the baking sheets on the racks and from front to back once during baking. Cool on the baking sheet for 1 minute. With a wide turner, transfer the cookies to wire racks to cool completely.

5. Spread the bottom of half the cookies with about 1 tablespoon of the Marshmallow Creme Filling. Cover with a plain cookie, bottom side down.

Yield: About 15 cookie sandwiches

Pennsylvania Dutch Mashed-Potato Cookies

The Germans have long used potatoes to improve the flavor and texture of baked goods, usually bread and often sweet breads. (Knowing the Pennsylvania Dutch as well as I do, I suspect there might also be some waste-not, want-not reasoning behind this as well.) You can use any kind of mashed potatoes you like for this recipe: from-scratch, instant, or even frozen. Just make sure they are at room temperature when you add them to the batter.

2 cups all-purpose flour
3 teaspoons baking powder
^{1}/$_2$ teaspoon salt
1 teaspoon ground cinnamon
1 teaspoon ground nutmeg
^{1}/$_2$ teaspoon ground allspice
^{1}/$_4$ teaspoon ground cloves
^{2}/$_3$ cup (1 stick plus 3 tablespoons)
   salted butter or margarine, at room
   temperature
1 ^{3}/$_4$ cups sugar
1 cup plain, unseasoned mashed potatoes,
   made with just enough milk to make them
   fairly smooth
4 large eggs
1 cup coarsely chopped walnuts

1. Adjust two racks to divide the oven into thirds. Preheat the oven to 375°. Lightly grease two baking sheets.

2. In a medium-size bowl, with a wire whisk, combine the flour, baking powder, salt, and spices until thoroughly mixed.

3. In a large bowl, with an electric mixer at medium-high speed, beat together the butter and the sugar until creamy. Add the mashed potatoes and beat until well blended. Add the eggs, one at a time, beating well after each addition. Gradually beat the flour mixture into the butter mixture just until blended. With a mixing spoon, stir in the walnuts until well distributed throughout the batter. Drop the batter by regular teaspoonfuls onto the prepared baking sheets, spacing the drops about 2 inches apart.

4. Bake for about 12 minutes until the edges are lightly browned. Reverse the baking sheets on the racks and from front to back once during baking. With a wide turner, transfer the cookies to wire racks to cool completely.

Yield: About 72 cookies

My Grandmother's Toasted-Oatmeal Cookies

My grandmother rarely bothered to record her recipes. This one, which is in my Aunt Jo's handwriting, is probably Grandmother's best guesstimate about amounts. The original recipe calls for either lard or meat drippings and sour milk. Maybe that's why mine, despite my best efforts, don't ever seem to taste quite the same as I remember them.

- 1 1/2 cups regular (not quick-cooking or instant) rolled oats
- 2 1/2 cups all-purpose flour
- 1 teaspoon baking soda
- 1 teaspoon baking powder
- 1/2 teaspoon salt
- 1 teaspoon ground cloves
- 1 teaspoon ground cinnamon
- 1 teaspoon ground nutmeg
- 1/3 cup buttermilk
- 3/4 cup plain shortening
- 2 cups packed light or dark brown sugar
- 2 large eggs, lightly beaten
- 1 teaspoon vanilla extract
- 1 cup chopped dates
- 1 cup chopped pecans or walnuts

1. Adjust one rack to divide the oven in half. Preheat the oven to 350°. Lightly grease two baking sheets.

2. Sprinkle the oats in a single layer onto an ungreased baking sheet or jelly-roll pan. Place in the oven and bake, stirring occasionally, until lightly browned, 8 to 10 minutes. Remove from the oven and set aside to cool.

3. Adjust two racks to divide the oven into thirds.

4. In a medium-size bowl, with a whisk, combine the flour, baking soda, baking powder, salt, cloves, cinnamon, and nutmeg until thoroughly mixed.

5. Place the toasted oats in a small bowl. Stir in the buttermilk. Set aside for 5 minutes.

6. In a large bowl, with an electric mixer at medium-high speed, beat together the shortening and brown sugar until creamy, about 2 minutes. Beat in the eggs and vanilla until well blended. Beat in the soaked oats until blended. With the mixer at low speed, gradually add the flour mixture, beating just until blended and smooth. With a mixing spoon, stir in the dates and nuts until well distributed throughout the batter. Drop by heaping tablespoonfuls onto the prepared baking sheets, spacing the drops about 2 inches apart.

7. Bake for about 15 minutes until lightly browned and firm when lightly touched. Reverse the baking sheets on the racks and from front to back once during baking. With a wide turner, immediately transfer the cookies to wire racks to cool completely.

8. Store in an airtight container.

Yield: About 70 cookies

7
Rolled Cookies

Crisp, tender cookies, cut from a rich, thinly rolled dough into myriad shapes and sizes that are very often decorated—sometimes quite elaborately—are the glory of the cookie maker. Since these cookies do take time and a modicum of artistic ability, rolled cookies are understandably the ones that are trotted out only for special occasions.

If any one type of cookie can be considered "difficult" to make, then rolled cookies must be the nemesis of the novice cookie baker. The scary part, of course, is the seemingly simple act of thinly rolling out the dough. Nothing is more frustrating and disheartening than dough that stubbornly sticks to the rolling pin, the rolling surface, and even the cookie cutters. To correct the problem, the inexperienced baker usually keeps adding flour and, after repeated rolling, the cookies, when they finally come from the oven, have the distinct taste and texture of cardboard.

ROLL, ROLL, ROLL THE DOUGH

Two things critical to the success of perfectly rolled dough are the rolling pin and the rolling surface. On page 7, I've discussed the virtues of the big, fat, wooden rolling pin, which I believe is the best tool for rolling out anything. Still, there are alternatives, which you may want to try. The only one that makes any real sense to me is a silicone-coated pin, which won't stick to anything and works very well. Another choice includes a pin with a hollow barrel that is filled with ice cubes. Theoretically, the ice keeps the pin cold, which keeps the dough cold and stickproof. I've also seen marble rolling pins. The idea behind this pin is that marble, besides being heavy, doesn't absorb moisture, and stays cool, especially if it is chilled before using. To be honest, I've not tried either one, so I can't recommend them.

The rolling surface is as important as the rolling pin, since sticking more commonly occurs here than on the pin. A laminated countertop works well as a rolling surface. Some bakers like to use a piece of marble. My only objection to marble is that sometimes it can be too smooth, thus allowing the dough to slide, rather than flatten, as it is rolled, an irritating situation. A large, smooth, wooden surface is ideal for dough rolling, because it has just enough texture to keep the dough in place.

The most foolproof method to keep the dough from sticking to the rolling surface and the pin is to roll it between two sheets of waxed paper, flipping the

93

waxed paper–encased dough over and over, and replacing the waxed paper as it becomes moist and wrinkled, which is often. The waxed-paper method is useful when rolling dark doughs (gingerbread and chocolate, for example), when you want to avoid a film of flour on the baked cookie. (By the way, plastic wrap won't work for this purpose. It wrinkles and the wrinkles transfer themselves to the dough.)

The encouraging truth is that if the dough is made and handled properly, it should roll out very obligingly.

You must use *some* flour when rolling out a cookie dough, but less is more, and as little as possible is what you aim for when it comes to flouring the work surface, the dough, and the rolling pin. Sprinkle a small amount of flour (no more than a teaspoon or two) onto the work surface and spread it around with the palm of your hand. Place the dough on the floured work surface and lightly sprinkle the top of it with flour, spreading it as you did on the work surface. Rub the rolling pin with flour. Give the dough a few whacks with the pin to flatten it slightly and then start to roll. If the dough breaks significantly around the edge or offers much resistance, it is too cold to roll. Allow it a few minutes to warm up a bit.

Roll the dough a couple of times in all directions and then turn it over, adding a wee bit of flour to the work surface and to the top of the dough each time it is turned. Continue in this manner until the dough is as thin as you want it. Don't guess about this. Use a ruler to measure it until your eye and hand become more experienced. At first you may have a little trouble getting the dough rolled out evenly, which takes a little practice and a little patience.

Cut as many cookies as possible from each piece of rolled dough. This not only saves time in the end, but keeps scraps and rerolling to a minimum. Preferably, the dough should be rerolled only once.

The few scraps left over after the second rolling can either be discarded or incorporated into

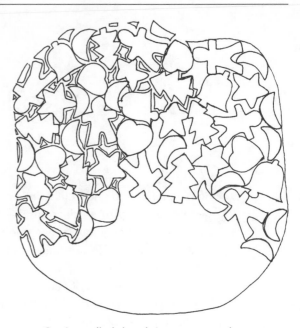

Cutting rolled dough into as many shapes as possible

the next batch of dough. (Or, a better idea, plop the scraps just as they are onto a baking sheet, bake them, and hand them out to the family for immediate sampling and critiquing.)

ABOUT COOKIE CUTTERS

Collecting cookie cutters is great fun. I've been doing it for years and have assembled quite a variety. Once you start looking for them, you will be surprised at just how many shapes and sizes there are available in almost every motif imaginable and for any occasion.

Most cookie cutters are made out of metal, and sometimes plastic. Plastic cutters lack charm, but, if they are decently made, they do the job just about as well as metal cutters, which are usually made from stainless steel, tin-clad stainless steel, and sometimes aluminum. The price of a cookie cutter ranges somewhere between a dollar or two to several dollars, depending on what they are made from and whether

- Making rolled cookies is not a spur-of-the-moment project. Set aside plenty of uninterrupted time. Clear away the work area. This is one baking endeavor for which you need plenty of elbow room and *lots* of counter space. Make sure that you have all the implements, ingredients, and every last little decorating supply on hand before you begin.

- In most cases, making rolled cookies can be broken down into two or three steps. The dough can be made at least one day ahead and refrigerated or frozen. (It takes 3 to 5 hours to thaw frozen dough in the refrigerator, depending on the size of the package.) Then all, or even part of it, can be rolled, cut, and baked when time permits. If the cookies are to be decorated after they are baked, another step can be added, and the decorations done a day or two after baking.

- Most rolled-cookie doughs need to be chilled before they are rolled. Even doughs that don't require chilling won't be hurt by it. Don't be tempted to eliminate or shortcut this important step. There are always exceptions, but, as a rule, *just-made dough is almost impossible to roll!*

  Cut the dough in half or in quarters before wrapping and chilling it. Small amounts of dough are easier to roll out. Leave the dough you are not working with in the refrigerator until you are almost ready to roll it.

- If the cookie cutter sticks to the dough, press the cutting edge into flour as often as necessary.

- Although different-size cookies can be cut together, don't arrange them on the same baking sheet, since smaller cookies take less time to bake than larger cookies. All of the cookies on a single sheet should be approximately the same size and spaced evenly apart.

- Sometimes the cutout shapes are firm enough so that you can simply pick them up with your fingers and arrange them on the baking sheet. Other times you will have to do this with the aid of a wide turner. Except for larger cookies, I find that a small metal sandwich spreader works beautifully for this purpose.

- If there aren't enough cookies to fill up the baking sheet, spread them out evenly so that there are no large, bare spaces, or use a smaller baking sheet.

- When making rolled cookies, it is especially important to reverse the baking sheets on the racks and from front to back during baking. This procedure helps to ensure that the cookies will be evenly baked, and also gives you a chance to check what's going on midway through the baking time.

- Check the cookies after the minimum baking time, or 2 or 3 minutes before the "about" time. When they are baked, rolled cookies are generally firm and lightly browned around the edges, with lightly browned bottoms.

- Although the directions for rolled cookies usually call for transferring them from the baking sheet onto the cooling rack immediately after baking, they may actually be easier to remove if they are allowed to cool for just a minute. Each cookie has its own infinitesimal quirks about what's "immediate," and it's sort of up to you to find out what they are.

- Before using the baking sheets for subsequent batches of cookies, make sure that they are completely cool, clean, and regreased, if necessary. Usually it is just enough to wipe the baking sheets well with paper towels. Regreasing may not even be necessary.

they are made by machine or by hand. Fancy copper cutters cost more. You can also have a good time ferreting out charming old cookie cutters at flea markets and antique shops, and they generally don't cost very much.

These days, cookie cutters are usually open at both ends. I happen to like this feature because it makes it easy to give the dough-shape a little nudge back down onto the rolling surface if it lifts up along with the cutter. Some cutters have

handles, others do not, and it doesn't much matter. Very cheap metal cutters get bent out of shape easily. Buy good quality cutters, especially in those shapes that will be used often, year after year.

It is also a good idea to have some very standard shapes (rounds, mainly) on hand, in three or four sizes, from 1 inch to about 3½ inches, with both plain and scalloped edges, since these shapes and sizes are frequently called for.

Homemade Cutters for Homemade Cookies

You can also fashion your own cookie cutters of sorts by designing and cutting simple shapes from heavy cardboard to use as templates.

A more ambitious project is to make your own "tin" cutters, believe it or not, by using the tops and bottoms of *large* cans (industrial-size cans being the best if you can find a source for them, like a friendly restaurateur). Use tin shears to cut the top and bottom off the can. Don't cut through the rim of the can, but use the shears or other sharp instrument to make a cut in the can about an inch down from the rim on each end. Start cutting evenly around the can at that point. What you will end up with are two large, round cookie cutters, so to speak. Use pliers to bend them into simple shapes.

Rolling Cookie Cutter

Another device for cutting cookies is something called a rolling cookie cutter, which looks something like a rolling pin. The drum roller is basically a conglomeration of raised cookie shapes that is rolled over the dough firmly enough to cut it. Since the shapes on the drum—which range from very simple to very complex—fit together like a jigsaw puzzle, there is not a scrap of dough left over. I haven't been tempted to try this implement, since I like to cut out my cookies the old-fashioned way, but I am told it works like a dream.

Springerle Rolling Pin

Springerle is the name of a cookie that is made by firmly rolling a carved wooden rolling pin over a rectangle of raw cookie dough, which produces square cookies with raised designs on the tops that are very much like stamped cookies.

The custom of making springerle imprinted with the shapes of animals originated with ancient Germanic tribes, who offered them to the gods as a substitute for sacrificing live cattle during the pagan celebration of Julfest.

DECORATED COOKIES

There are limitless ways to beautify cookies, which range from supersimple designs to do with the kids to very elaborate and intricate decorations. The method decided upon usually depends on the amount of time available to do it and, to a greater or lesser degree, artistic ability and an interest in painstakingly producing a work of art that will be briefly admired and then lost to the ages. Most of us fall someplace in the middle.

Decorating cookies is generally easy and fun to do. Many cookies—not just Christmas and other special-occasion cookies—benefit from the addition of something as simple as a sprinkling of colored sugar or a chocolate kiss planted on top.

In Chapter 4, "Decorating Cookies," various methods for decorating cookies, as well as a complete listing of the ingredients and supplies needed to do it, are shown and explained.

My Grandmother's Christmas Sugar Cookies

These are the sugar cookies that I bake every Christmas for my family and, I might add, the first cookies I ever baked. When I first started making them (about a million years ago it seems), I couldn't understand why they puffed up, when my grandmother's were very thin and crisp. As my baking knowledge expanded, the light dawned one day. Grandmother used old-fashioned, single-action baking powder. I was using the modern, double-acting baking powder. I cut the amount of baking powder she called for in half, and the cookies turned out just as I remembered them. This is

something to bear in mind when working with very old recipes.

This is an exceptionally good dough on which to master the skills of rolling and cutting, since it almost always behaves politely. Even if you have to roll it out several times (although once, or twice at the most, is what you should aim for), the cookies will still be very good.

> 4 ¹/₂ to 5 cups all-purpose flour, divided
> 2 teaspoons baking powder
> ¹/₂ teaspoon salt
> 1 cup (2 sticks) salted butter, at room
>   temperature
> 2 cups sugar
> 2 eggs, lightly beaten
> 2 teaspoons vanilla extract
> 2 tablespoons milk

1. In a large bowl, with a whisk, combine 4¹/₂ cups of the flour, the baking powder, and salt until thoroughly mixed.

2. In a large bowl, with an electric mixer at medium-high speed, beat the butter and sugar until creamy, 2 to 3 minutes. Add the eggs, vanilla, and milk and beat until light and fluffy, about 1 minute. With the mixer at medium-low speed, gradually beat in the flour mixture just until blended. If the dough seems soft, add some of the remaining ¹/₂ cup flour, a little at a time, until a small handful can be pressed into a soft dough. Gather the dough into a ball and divide it into quarters. Wrap each quarter in plastic wrap and refrigerate until the dough is very cold, 3 to 4 hours or overnight. (At this point, the dough can be tightly wrapped in aluminum foil and refrigerated for up to one week or frozen for up to three months. If frozen, thaw in the refrigerator before proceeding.)

3. Adjust two racks to divide the oven into thirds. Preheat the oven to 350°. Lightly grease two baking sheets. Have ready an assortment of small, medium, and large cookie cutters in various shapes.

4. On a lightly floured surface, roll one quarter of the dough to a ¹/₈-inch thickness. (Leave the remaining dough in the refrigerator until you are ready to roll it.) Cut the dough into as many shapes as possible. Arrange the shapes on a prepared baking sheet, spacing them about 1 inch apart. Gather the scraps of dough together and reroll once or twice, or incorporate the scraps into the next batch of dough. The cookies can be decorated now or after baking. Repeat with the remaining dough.

5. Bake for 8 to 12 minutes until the cookies are pale golden. Reverse the baking sheets on the racks and from front to back once during baking. With a wide turner, immediately transfer the cookies to wire racks to cool completely.

6. Store in a tightly covered container, separating and cushioning the layers with sheets of waxed paper.

Yield: About 8 dozen cookies of various sizes

Variations

The cherries, nuts, chocolate, and crystallized ginger called for in the following variations should be very finely chopped, almost to the point of being ground, before they are added to the dough. Otherwise, the cookie shapes will be difficult to cut.

How to Make Springerle

Roll out a plain sugar-cookie dough with a regular rolling pin (the dough for My Grandmother's Christmas Sugar Cookies works well for this) into a rectangular shape that is ¹/₄ inch thick and the same width as the springerle pin. Firmly roll the springerle pin over the dough from one short end to the other. (Remember, you only get one shot at this. If you mess up, the dough will have to be rerolled.) With a pizza wheel or the tip of a sharp knife, cut the squares apart and bake the cookies as directed. The raised pattern can be painted or otherwise decorated, or left plain, which is actually more traditional.

Cherry-Chip Sugar Cookies: After the dough has been mixed and before it is gathered into a ball, add 1 cup of minced candied cherries. With the mixer at medium-low speed, blend in the cherries until they are evenly distributed throughout the dough.

Nutty Sugar Cookies: After the dough has been mixed and before it is gathered into a ball, add 1 cup of very finely chopped nuts. With the mixer at medium-low speed, blend in the nuts until they are evenly distributed throughout the dough.

Chocolate Chip Sugar Cookies: After the dough has been mixed and before it is gathered into a ball, add 1 cup of very finely chopped semisweet chocolate. With the mixer at medium-low speed, blend in the chocolate until it is evenly distributed throughout the dough.

Gingered Sugar Cookies: After the dough has been mixed and before it is gathered into a ball, add ½ cup of very finely chopped crystallized ginger.

Stained Glass Cookies

These cookies can be somewhat tedious to make, depending mostly on how involved you want the "stained-glass" designs to be, but the technique itself is rather simple: Tiny shapes are cut out and removed from unbaked cookies and replaced with crushed hard candies in a variety of colors. When the cookies bake, the candies melt, giving the cutouts the appearance of stained glass. Stained-glass cookies are particularly nice to use as tree ornaments, since the light coming through them produces a glorious effect.

Use any plain, rolled-cookie dough, such as the dough for My Grandmother's Christmas Sugar Cookies, and cut into any shapes you want, although round or other simple shapes are easiest to work with and the most traditional.

Cover the baking sheets with aluminum foil, shiny side up. Grease or coat the foil generously with nonstick vegetable spray. In a blender or food processor, crush separately various colors of sour balls or other hard candies. (Or you can put the candies in separate plastic bags and pound the bags with a rolling pin or a hammer until the candies are evenly crushed.) Set the crushed candies aside in separate bowls.

Cut the rolled cookies in the usual manner. Cut out and remove tiny shapes from each cookie to make a stained-glass design. (If you are going to use the cookie for ornaments, don't forget to poke a little hole in the top to attach the hanger.) With a wide spatula, very carefully transfer the cookies to the baking sheets, spacing them about 2 inches apart. With the tip of a pointy knife, pick up a small amount of crushed candy and fill each cutout space with the desired colors, to just slightly beneath the top of the cookie. If the crushed candies mound even slightly, the sugar syrup will run over the surface of the cookie and spoil the appearance.

Bake the cookies as the recipe directs. Remove the baking sheets from the oven and set them on wire racks until the cookies have completely cooled. Pick up the foil from the baking sheet and peel it away from the backs of the cookies. Don't try to lift the cookies off the foil.

Store in a tightly covered container, separating the layers with sheets of waxed paper.

Stacks of Cookies

Having a good sugar-cookie dough to work with allows you to do all sorts of imaginative cookies. This was one of my children's favorites for Christmas, although we sometimes made them for Valentine's Day and Easter, appropriately decorated for the holiday.

The point here is to make three different sizes of sugar cookies. Each one has a hole poked in it and after baking they are stacked and strung together in threes on a licorice shoestring or a piece of ribbon. The shapes of cookie cutters should not be identical, but they should be compatible—a round, a star, a heart shape, a

square—so that they stack up in an interesting manner. The cookies can be decorated before or after baking, depending on which decorating method you choose to use.

Ingredients for My Grandmother's Sugar Cookies (page 96)
Red licorice shoestrings or ribbon

1. Have ready three cookie cutters of more or less the same design in three sizes: small (about 1 to 1½ inches in diameter), medium-size (about 2 inches in diameter), and large (not more than 3 inches in diameter).

2. Make a batch of dough according to the instructions given through step 3, cutting an equal number of cookies in each size. Arrange the cookies on the baking sheets. Poke a hole in the center of each one with a plastic straw.

3. After the cookies have been baked and cooled, string three together on a piece of licorice, starting with the largest cookie first. Tie together tightly with a bow, making sure that the cookies remain stacked. The cookies can also be strung together loosely on the licorice like the keys on a key ring, if you prefer.

Yield: About 32 stacks of three cookies each

Chocolate Sugar Cookies

Although it is possible to get a decent chocolate sugar cookie by merely adding cocoa powder to My Grandmother's Christmas Sugar Cookies, I prefer a slightly richer blend to better support the flavor of the chocolate.

2 ³/₄ cups all-purpose flour
¹/₂ cup unsweetened cocoa powder
1 teaspoon baking powder
1 cup (2 sticks) salted butter or margarine, at room temperature
1 cup granulated sugar
¹/₂ cup packed light brown sugar
1 large egg, lightly beaten
1 teaspoon vanilla extract

1. In a medium-size bowl, with a whisk, combine the flour, cocoa powder, and baking powder.

2. In a large bowl, with an electric mixer at medium-high speed, beat together the butter, granulated sugar, brown sugar, egg, and vanilla until light and fluffy, 2 to 3 minutes. With the mixer at medium-low speed, gradually add the flour mixture, beating after each addition just until blended. Gather the dough into a ball and divide it in half. Wrap each half in plastic wrap and refrigerate until the dough is very cold, several hours or overnight. (At this point, the dough can be tightly wrapped in aluminum foil and refrigerated for up to one week or frozen for up to three months. If frozen, thaw in the refrigerator before proceeding.)

3. Adjust two racks to divide the oven into thirds. Preheat the oven to 375°. Lightly grease two baking sheets; set aside. Have ready an assortment of small, medium-size, and large cookie cutters in various shapes.

4. Between two sheets of waxed paper, roll half of the cold dough to a ¹/₈-inch thickness. (Leave the remaining dough in the refrigerator until you are ready to roll it.) Cut the dough into as many shapes as possible. Arrange the shapes on a prepared baking sheet, spacing them about 1 inch apart. Gather the scraps of dough together and reroll once or twice. The cookies can be decorated now or after baking. Repeat with the remaining dough.

5. Bake for 8 to 9 minutes until firm. Reverse the baking sheets on the racks and from front to back once during baking. With a wide turner, immediately transfer the cookies to wire racks to cool completely.

6. Store in a tightly covered container, separating and cushioning the layers with sheets of waxed paper.

Yield: About 42 cookies

Sugar-and-Spice Cutouts

These cookies are merely a very spicy and more flavorful version of a plain sugar cookie.

- 3 cups all-purpose flour
- 1 1/2 teaspoons ground cinnamon
- 1 teaspoon ground ginger
- 1/4 teaspoon ground nutmeg
- 2 teaspoons baking powder
- 1 cup (2 sticks) salted butter or margarine, at room temperature
- 3/4 cup packed light brown sugar
- 1/2 cup granulated sugar
- 1 large egg
- 1 teaspoon vanilla extract

1. In a medium-size bowl, with a whisk, combine the flour, cinnamon, ginger, nutmeg, and baking powder until thoroughly mixed.

2. In a large bowl, with an electric mixer at medium-high speed, beat together the butter, brown sugar, granulated sugar, egg, and vanilla until light and fluffy, 2 to 3 minutes. With the mixer at medium-low speed, gradually add the flour mixture, beating after each addition just until blended. Gather the dough into a ball and divide it in half. Wrap each half in plastic wrap and refrigerate until the dough is very cold, several hours or overnight. (At this point, the dough can be tightly wrapped in aluminum foil and refrigerated for up to one week or frozen for up to three months. If frozen, thaw in the refrigerator before proceeding.)

3. Adjust two racks to divide the oven into thirds. Preheat the oven to 375°. Lightly grease two baking sheets. Have ready an assortment of small, medium-size, and large cookie cutters.

4. On a lightly floured surface, roll half of the cold dough to a 1/8-inch thickness. (Leave the remaining dough in the refrigerator until you are ready to roll it.) Cut the dough into as many shapes as possible. Arrange the shapes on a prepared baking sheet, spacing them about 1 inch apart. Gather the scraps of dough together and reroll once or twice. The cookies can be decorated now or after baking. Repeat with the remaining dough.

5. Bake for 8 to 9 minutes until firm. Reverse the baking sheets on the racks and from front to back once during baking. With a wide turner, immediately transfer the cookies to wire racks to cool completely.

6. Store in a tightly covered container, separating and cushioning the layers with sheets of waxed paper.

Yield: About 42 cookies

Oatmeal Sugar Cookies

Most people don't expect oats in a rolled cookie.

- 3 cups all-purpose flour
- 2 teaspoons baking powder
- 3/4 cup (1 1/4 sticks) salted butter or margarine, at room temperature
- 1 cup granulated sugar
- 2 large eggs
- 2 tablespoons milk
- 1 1/2 teaspoons vanilla extract
- 3/4 cup regular or quick-cooking (not instant) rolled oats
- Confectioners' sugar, for rolling cookies

1. In a medium-size bowl, with a whisk, combine the flour and baking powder until thoroughly mixed.

2. In a large bowl, with an electric mixer at medium-high speed, beat together the butter and sugar until light and fluffy, 2 to 3 minutes. Add the eggs, one at a time, beating after each addition until blended.

3. In a small bowl, mix the milk with the vanilla. With the mixer at medium-low speed, add the flour mixture alternately with the milk mixture to the butter-and-sugar mixture, beating after each addition just until blended. With a mixing spoon, stir in the oats until well blended. Gather the dough into a ball and divide it in half. Wrap each half in plastic wrap and refrigerate until very cold, about

2 hours. (At this point, the dough can be tightly wrapped in aluminum foil and refrigerated for up to one week or frozen for up to three months. If frozen, thaw in the refrigerator before proceeding.)

4. Adjust two racks to divide the oven into thirds. Preheat the oven to 400°. Have ready two baking sheets. Also have ready an assortment of small, medium-size, and large cookie cutters in various shapes.

5. Generously sprinkle a work surface with some of the confectioners' sugar. Work with one half of the cold dough at a time. (Leave the remaining dough in the refrigerator until you are ready to roll it.) Sprinkle the top of the dough with more confectioners' sugar. Roll the dough to a 1/8-inch thickness. Cut the dough into as many shapes as possible. Arrange the shapes on an ungreased baking sheet, spacing them about 1 inch apart. Gather the scraps of dough together and reroll once or twice. The cookies can be decorated now or after baking. Repeat with the remaining dough.

6. Bake for 6 to 8 minutes until firm. Reverse the baking sheets on the racks and from front to back once during baking. With a wide turner, immediately transfer the cookies to wire racks to cool completely.

7. Store in a tightly covered container, separating and cushioning the layers with sheets of waxed paper.

Yield: About 65 cookies

Peanut Butter Sugar Cookies

The more familiar form of peanut butter cookies are shaped into a ball and then flattened with the tines of a fork.

- 1 1/4 cups all-purpose flour
- 1/2 teaspoon baking powder
- 1/4 teaspoon baking soda
- 1/2 cup smooth peanut butter
- 1/2 cup (1 stick) salted butter or margarine, at room temperature
- 1/2 cup granulated sugar
- 1/2 cup packed light brown sugar
- 1 large egg, lightly beaten

1. In a medium-size bowl, combine the flour, baking powder, and baking soda until thoroughly mixed.

2. In a large bowl, with an electric mixer at medium-high speed, beat together the peanut butter and butter until well blended, about 1 minute. Gradually add the granulated sugar and the brown sugar and beat until light and creamy, 2 to 3 minutes. Beat in the egg until creamy. Add the flour mixture all at once to the peanut butter mixture. With the mixer at medium-low speed, beat just until blended. Gather the dough into a ball and divide it in half. Wrap each half in plastic wrap and refrigerate until cold, about 1 hour. (At this point, the dough can be tightly wrapped in aluminum foil and refrigerated for up to one week or frozen for up to three months. If frozen, thaw in the refrigerator before proceeding.)

3. Adjust two racks to divide the oven into thirds. Preheat the oven to 350°. Lightly grease two baking sheets. Have ready an assortment of small, medium-size, and large cookie cutters in various shapes.

4. On a lightly floured surface, roll half of the cold dough to a 1/4-inch thickness. (Leave the remaining dough in the refrigerator until you are ready to roll it.) Cut the dough into as many shapes as possible. Arrange the shapes on a prepared baking sheet, spacing them about 1 inch apart. Gather the scraps of dough together and reroll once or twice. The cookies can be decorated now or after baking. Repeat with the remaining dough.

5. Bake for 12 to 15 minutes until lightly browned. Reverse the baking sheets on the racks and from front to back once during baking. With a wide turner, immediately transfer the cookies to wire racks to cool completely.

6. Store in a tightly covered container, separating and cushioning the layers with sheets of waxed paper.

Yield: About 25 cookies

Shortbread Cutouts

Like a true shortbread, these cookies are tender-crumbly—more tender and less brittle than most rolled cookies. I usually restrain myself with these and don't decorate them at all or, at least, rather minimally. If you like, you can plop a nut on each one before baking. Rich macadamias or almonds would be good choices.

>   1 cup all-purpose flour
> $^3/_4$ cup cake flour (not self-rising flour)
> $^1/_4$ teaspoon baking powder
>   1 cup (2 sticks) salted butter or margarine,
>   at room temperature
> $^1/_3$ cup confectioners' sugar
>   1 teaspoon vanilla extract

1. Adjust two racks to divide the oven into thirds. Have ready two ungreased baking sheets. Also have ready an assortment of cookie cutters.

2. In a medium-size bowl, with a whisk, combine the all-purpose flour, cake flour, and baking powder until thoroughly combined.

3. In a large bowl, with an electric mixer at medium-high speed, beat together the butter, sugar, and vanilla until light and fluffy, 2 to 3 minutes. With the mixer at medium-low speed, gradually add the flour mixture, beating just until blended. Gather the dough into a ball and divide it into quarters. Wrap each quarter in plastic wrap and refrigerate until very cold and firm, 3 to 4 hours. (At this point the dough can be tightly wrapped in aluminum foil and refrigerated for up to one week or frozen for up to three months. If frozen, thaw in the refrigerator before proceeding.)

4. Preheat the oven to 350°.

5. On a lightly floured surface, roll one quarter of the dough to a $^1/_8$-inch thickness. (Leave the remaining dough in the refrigerator until you are ready to work with it.) Cut the dough into as many shapes as possible. Arrange the shapes on the ungreased baking sheets, spacing them about 1 inch apart. Gather the scraps of dough together and reroll once or twice.

6. Bake for 10 to 15 minutes until beginning to brown around the edges. Reverse the baking sheets on the racks and from front to back once during baking. With a wide turner, immediately transfer the cookies to wire racks to cool completely.

7. Repeat with the remaining dough.

8. Store in a tightly covered container.

Yield: 24 to 36 cookies

Linzer Hearts

These are classic Austrian cookies, usually made into heart shapes, but you can make them into wreaths or whatever you wish. Sometimes the bottom cookies are coated with melted chocolate, but raspberry jam, along with nuts, are the ingredients common to all Linzer cookies.

>   2 cups walnut pieces, toasted
>   2 $^1/_2$ cups all-purpose flour, divided
> $^1/_2$ cup cornstarch
>   1 cup (2 sticks) unsalted butter, at room
>   temperature
>   1 cup confectioners' sugar
>   2 large egg yolks
>   About 1 cup raspberry jam
>   Confectioners' sugar, for dusting cookies

1. In a food processor fitted with a steel blade, process the walnuts with 1 cup of the flour just until the nuts are finely ground.

2. In a medium-size bowl, with a whisk, combine the ground-walnut mixture, the remaining $1^1/_2$ cups flour, and the cornstarch until thoroughly mixed.

3. In a large bowl, with an electric mixer at medium-high speed, beat together the butter and confectioners' sugar until light and fluffy, 2 to 3 minutes. Beat in the egg yolks, one at a time, beating well after each addition. With the mixer at medium-low speed, gradually add the walnut

mixture, beating just until blended. Gather the dough into a ball and divide it into quarters. Wrap each quarter in plastic wrap and refrigerate for at least 8 hours or overnight. (At this point the dough can be tightly wrapped in aluminum foil and refrigerated for up to one week or frozen for up to three months. If frozen, thaw in the refrigerator before proceeding.)

4. Adjust two racks to divide the oven into thirds. Preheat the oven to 325°. Lightly grease two baking sheets. Have ready two heart-shaped cookie cutters, one 2½ inches in diameter and the other 1½ inches in diameter.

5. On a lightly floured surface, roll out one quarter of the dough to a ¼-inch thickness. (Leave the remaining dough in the refrigerator until you are ready to roll it.) Using the larger cutter, cut out as many hearts as possible. With a wide turner, transfer half of the heart-shaped cookies to one of the prepared baking sheets. Using the smaller cutter, cut out a heart shape from the center of the remaining heart-shaped cookies, creating frames to use as cookie tops. Transfer to the other baking sheet. (The small hearts that are created when the frames are cut will not be used. These can be baked separately until lightly browned, or the hearts can be gathered together, wrapped in plastic wrap and refrigerated. Later the dough can be rolled once, and cut into other shapes before baking.)

6. Bake the bottoms for about 15 minutes and the tops for about 12 minutes until barely golden. Reverse the baking sheets on the racks and from front to back once during baking. With a wide turner, transfer the cookies to wire racks to cool completely.

7. Repeat with the remaining dough.

8. Using a fine-mesh sieve, dust the heart frames evenly with the confectioners' sugar. With a small icing spatula, spread the solid hearts with jam. Place the dusted frames on top of the jam-covered hearts.

9. Store in a shallow, tightly covered container, separating the layers with crumpled sheets of waxed paper.

Yield: About 48 cookies

Tip

Rolling soft or sticky doughs between sheets of waxed paper makes the dough easier to handle. If the dough sticks to the waxed paper, chill for a few minutes and the waxed paper will peel off easily.

Old-Fashioned Gingerbread People

Gingerbread cookie dough cut into people shapes first became popular in Great Britain, where the cookies were called gingerbread husbands. It would be reasonable to assume that the recipe came to the United States with the English settlers and underwent a name change to gingerbread men. This is a good dough for cutting into shapes (people, animals, trees, wreaths, or whatever you like), but the real fun is decorating them. Gingerbread people are traditionally decorated with white or colored Royal Icing (page 29), which is piped on with a pastry tube.

> $^1/_2$ **cup sugar**
> $^3/_4$ **cup unsulphured molasses**
> **1 teaspoon ground cinnamon**
> **1 tablespoon ground ginger**
> $^1/_2$ **teaspoon ground cloves**
> $^1/_4$ **teaspoon ground nutmeg**
> $^1/_2$ **teaspoon salt**
> $^2/_3$ **cup (1 stick plus 3 tablespoons) salted butter or margarine**
> $^1/_2$ **teaspoon baking soda**
> **3 $^1/_4$ cups all-purpose flour**
> **1 large egg, lightly beaten**

1. In a large saucepan, combine the sugar, molasses, cinnamon, ginger, cloves, nutmeg, and salt. Bring to a boil over high heat. Remove from the heat and stir in the butter and baking soda until the butter melts. With a mixing spoon, stir in the flour and egg until well blended. Place the pan in the refrigerator until the batter is firm, about 3 hours. (At this point, the dough can be gathered into a ball and tightly wrapped in aluminum foil and refrigerated for up to one week or frozen for up to three months. If frozen, thaw in the refrigerator before proceeding.)

2. Adjust two racks to divide the oven into thirds. Preheat the oven to 350°. Lightly grease two baking sheets. Have ready a selection of cookie cutters in desired shapes and sizes.

3. Divide the cold dough in half. (Refrigerate the remaining half until you are ready to roll it.) Roll the cold dough between two sheets of waxed paper to a $^1/_4$-inch thickness. (For chewier cookies, roll $^3/_8$ inch thick.) Cut the dough into desired shapes. With a wide turner, arrange the cutouts on the prepared baking sheets. Gather the scraps of dough together and reroll once or twice. Repeat with the remaining dough.

4. Bake for about 12 minutes until slightly puffed and the edges are lightly browned. Reverse the baking sheets on the racks and from front to back once during baking. With a wide turner, immediately transfer the cookies to wire racks to cool completely.

5. Decorate the cookies as desired.

6. Store in a tightly covered container, separating the layers with crumpled sheets of waxed paper.

Yield: About 48 cookies in various sizes

How to Organize a Cookie Exchange

A cookie exchange is one of the easiest ways to have a diverse selection of cookies on hand for the holidays. To be successful there should be at least six participants. The premise is for each person to bake about a dozen extra cookies for each of the others. When the cookies are exchanged, each participant will have more than six different varieties of yummy, home-baked cookies.

Tip

To make "hair" and "whiskers" for Santa Claus or gingerbread people, or "fur" for animals, push little pieces of dough through a garlic press.

Spiced Swedish Animal Cookies

Granulated sugar instead of flour is used to keep this cookie dough from sticking while it's being rolled out. The sugar also gives the baked cookies a little extra crispness and a little sparkle. In Scandinavia, these cookies are baked in plain shapes year-round. Only at Christmas do they take on fanciful shapes, usually farm animals.

    3 cups all-purpose flour
    1 teaspoon salt
    1 teaspoon ground ginger
    1 teaspoon ground cinnamon
    1 teaspoon shredded and minced orange zest
    $^1/_2$ teaspoon baking soda
    1 cup (2 sticks) salted butter or margarine,
        at room temperature
    $^1/_2$ cup granulated sugar, plus additional for
        rolling cookies
    $^1/_4$ cup packed dark brown sugar
    $^1/_2$ cup unsulphured molasses
    1 large egg, lightly beaten

1. In a medium-size bowl, with a whisk, combine the flour, salt, ginger, cinnamon, orange zest, and baking soda until thoroughly mixed.

2. In a large bowl, with an electric mixer at medium-high speed, beat together the butter, $^1/_2$ cup granulated sugar, and brown sugar until creamy, 2 to 3 minutes. Beat in the molasses and egg until well blended. Gradually add the flour mixture to the butter mixture, beating just until blended. Gather the dough into a ball and divide it into quarters. Wrap each quarter in plastic wrap and refrigerate until very cold, at least 3 hours or overnight. (At this point the dough can be tightly wrapped in aluminum foil and refrigerated for up to one week or frozen for up to three months. Thaw in the refrigerator before proceeding.)

3. Adjust two racks to divide the oven into thirds. Preheat the oven to 375°. Have ready two ungreased baking sheets. Also have ready 3- to 4-inch-wide, animal-shaped cookie cutters.

4. Generously sprinkle a work surface with the additional granulated sugar. Work with one-quarter of the cold dough at a time. (Leave the remaining dough in the refrigerator until you are ready to roll it.) Sprinkle the top of the dough with granulated sugar. Roll the dough to a $^1/_8$-inch thickness. Cut the dough into as many shapes as possible. Arrange the shapes on an ungreased baking sheet, spacing them about 1 inch apart. Gather the scraps of dough together and reroll once or twice. The cookies can be decorated now or after baking. Repeat with the remaining dough.

5. Bake for 10 to 12 minutes until firm. Reverse the baking sheets on the racks and from front to back once during baking. With a wide turner, immediately transfer the cookies to wire racks to cool completely.

6. Store in a tightly covered container, separating and cushioning the layers with crumpled sheets of waxed paper.

Yield: About 65 cookies

Pennsylvania Dutch Butter Tiles

These pretty tile-shaped cookies are traditionally presented to Christmas carolers as they make their rounds from door to door. They are simply square sugar cookies that have been glazed and then decorated with little Christmas scenes.

- 2 ³/₄ cups all-purpose flour
- ¹/₂ teaspoon baking powder
- ¹/₂ teaspoon salt
- ³/₄ cup (1 ¹/₂ sticks) salted butter or margarine, at room temperature
- ¹/₂ cup sugar
- 1 large egg
- 1 large egg yolk
- 2 teaspoons vanilla extract

Glaze

- 3 cups confectioners' sugar
- About ¹/₄ cup milk

1. Adjust one rack to divide the oven in half. Preheat the oven to 350°. Lightly grease one large baking sheet.

2. In a medium-size bowl, with a whisk, combine the flour, baking powder, and salt until thoroughly mixed.

3. In a large bowl, with an electric mixer at high speed, beat the butter until creamy, about 1 minute. Add the sugar, egg, egg yolk, and vanilla and beat until light and fluffy, 2 to 3 minutes.

4. With the mixer at medium-low speed, gradually add the flour mixture, beating just until blended. Gather the dough into a ball. Wrap in plastic wrap and refrigerate for about 20 minutes. (At this point, the dough can be tightly wrapped in aluminum foil and refrigerated for up to one week or frozen for up to three months. If frozen, thaw in the refrigerator before proceeding.)

5. With a lightly floured rolling pin, roll the dough directly on the prepared baking sheet to make a 12-inch square, trimming the edges with a pizza wheel or a knife and ruler to make them straight. Cut the dough into sixteen 3-inch squares. *Do not separate the squares.*

6. Bake for 15 minutes until the dough at the outer edges is firm and lightly browned. Reverse the baking sheets on the racks and from front to back once during baking. Set the baking sheet on a wire rack. Recut the squares, if necessary, in order to separate them easily. Cool on the baking sheet for 5 minutes. With a wide turner, remove the outer-edge cookies from the baking sheet to a wire rack to cool completely. If the center cookies seem slightly underbaked, return them to the oven for an additional 4 minutes, or until firm and lightly browned around the edges. (The cookies may be made ahead up to this point. Seal in plastic bags and freeze for up to a month.)

7. Make the glaze: In a small bowl, stir together the confectioners' sugar and milk until smooth, adding more milk, if necessary, so that the glaze is thin enough to drizzle, but still firm enough to hold its shape. With an icing spatula or butter spreader, spread the glaze onto the cookies, covering evenly and completely. Set aside to dry for at least 2 hours or overnight.

8. Decorate the glazed cookies as desired with borders and simple Christmas motifs or scenes.

9. Store in a single layer in a tightly covered container.

Yield: 16 cookies

Variation

Quilt Cookies: Use the following diagrams to decorate the cookies to resemble quilt squares.

Flower for Quilt Cookies

Tree for Quilt Cookies

Holly for Quilt Cookies

Tulips for Quilt Cookies

Christmas Cookie Ornaments

Cookies as ornaments were an essential part of the nineteenth-century Christmas tree, and there's no reason why they can't be an essential part of your Christmas tree this year. They are particularly enchanting to kids, who love to eat them right off the tree. This is a particularly nice dough to use for cookie ornaments. It contains a large proportion of butter to flour, which means that the cookies will stay reasonably fresh on the tree.

> 1 cup (2 sticks) salted butter or margarine, at room temperature
> 1 cup sugar
> 3 large eggs, lightly beaten
> $^1/_3$ cup brandy or cognac (orange juice can be substituted)
> 1 teaspoon ground mace
> 4 cups all-purpose flour

1. In a large bowl, with an electric mixer at medium-high speed, beat the butter and sugar until light and fluffy, 2 to 3 minutes. Add the eggs, brandy, and mace and continue beating just until blended. The mixture will look curdled. With the mixer at medium-low speed, gradually add the flour, beating just until blended. Gather the dough into a ball and divide it in half. Wrap each half in plastic wrap and refrigerate until very cold, about 2 hours. (At this point, the dough can be tightly wrapped in aluminum foil and refrigerated for up to one week or frozen for up to three months. If frozen, thaw in the refrigerator before proceeding.)

2. Adjust two racks to divide the oven into thirds. Preheat the oven to 350°. Have ready two ungreased baking sheets. Also have ready a selection of large cookie cutters (about 4 × 3 inches).

3. On a lightly floured surface, roll half of the cold dough to a $^1/_8$-inch thickness. (Leave the remaining dough in the refrigerator until you are ready to roll it.) Cut the dough into as many shapes as possible. Arrange the shapes on the ungreased baking sheets, spacing them about 1 inch apart. Gather the scraps of dough together and reroll once. The cookies can be decorated now or after baking. With a thin skewer, make a hole near the top of each cookie to insert a narrow ribbon or string after baking. Repeat with the remaining dough.

4. Bake for 10 to 12 minutes until golden. Reverse the baking sheets on the racks and from front to back once during baking. With a wide turner, immediately transfer the cookies to wire racks to cool completely.

5. Slip a narrow ribbon or string through the hole in the decorated cookies and hang on the tree.

Yield: About 48 cookies

German Christmas Honey Cakes

These are traditionally made into thick star shapes and studded with almonds and candied cherries. They need to be aged for at least two or three weeks, so plan ahead.

> 3 $^1/_2$ cups all-purpose flour
> 1 tablespoon baking powder
> $^1/_8$ teaspoon salt
> 1 tablespoon unsweetened cocoa powder
> 2 teaspoons ground cinnamon
> $^1/_2$ teaspoon ground ginger
> $^1/_4$ teaspoon ground cloves
> 1 cup plus 2 tablespoons sugar
> $^2/_3$ cup honey
> $^1/_2$ cup (1 stick) salted butter or margarine
> 1 large egg, lightly beaten
> About 50 whole blanched almonds, for decorating cookies
> About 20 candied cherry halves, for decorating cookies

1. In a medium-size bowl, with a whisk, combine the flour, baking powder, salt, cocoa, cinnamon, ginger, and cloves until thoroughly mixed.

2. In a large, heavy saucepan, stir together the sugar, honey, and butter. Place over medium heat and stir constantly until melted and smooth. *Do not allow the mixture to boil.* Remove the pan from the heat. With a mixing spoon, and while the honey mixture is still hot, gradually stir in the flour mixture until well blended. Allow the mixture to cool for about 1 minute. Stir in the egg until well blended.

3. Turn the dough onto an unfloured surface and knead for 1 minute. If the dough is too sticky to handle, sprinkle about 1 teaspoon of flour over the dough while kneading. The dough will be very soft but will firm up as it stands. Form the dough into a disk and wrap it tightly in plastic wrap. Let stand overnight at room temperature. *Do not refrigerate.*

4. Adjust two racks to divide the oven into thirds. Preheat the oven to 350°. Lightly grease and flour two baking sheets. Have ready a 3½-inch, star-shaped cookie cutter.

5. Cut the dough in half. On an unfloured or *very lightly* floured surface, roll each half of the dough to a ⅓-inch thickness. Cut the dough into as many star shapes as possible. Gather the scraps of dough together and reroll once. Arrange the star shapes on the prepared baking sheets, spacing them about 1 inch apart. Stud the points of the stars with almonds and place candied cherry halves in the centers.

6. Bake for 15 to 17 minutes until lightly browned. Reverse the baking sheets on the racks and from front to back once during baking. With a wide turner, immediately transfer the cookies to wire racks to cool completely.

7. Store the cookies in a tightly covered container, separating the layers with sheets of waxed paper, for as long as two or three months. A slice of apple or raw potato placed in the container for a few days before serving will soften the cookies slightly so that they will be easier to eat. (Change the apple or potato slice every couple of days.)

Yield: 17 to 20 cookies

Tip

Reroll scraps of dough on a surface dusted with equal parts of flour and confectioners' sugar. This helps to keep the rerolled dough from getting tough and floury.

St. Nicholas Cookies

These heavily spiced, shiny-top cookies—crisp on the outside and slightly soft inside—are as Dutch as wooden shoes. In Holland they are called speculaas. The word is from the Latin speculum, or mirror. According to legend, speculaas originated as hard little cakes, pressed into and baked in hand-carved wooden molds in the shapes of people and animals. The cookies were then scattered in the fields as an offering to the spirits responsible for the success or failure of the crops.

These days, speculaas are usually cut into rectangles, and sometimes almond paste is sandwiched between two cookies. Speculaas are traditionally served on December 5, St. Nicholas's Eve. These cookies are best if left to mellow for a few days before serving.

    3 cups all-purpose flour
    1 tablespoon baking powder
    1 tablespoon ground cinnamon
    1 teaspoon ground nutmeg
    $^1/_2$ teaspoon ground cloves
    $^1/_2$ teaspoon anise seeds, crushed
    $^1/_2$ teaspoon ground white pepper
    $^1/_2$ teaspoon salt
    1 cup (2 sticks) salted butter or margarine,
       at room temperature
    1 $^1/_2$ cups packed dark brown sugar
    3 tablespoons milk
    1 large egg white, lightly beaten,
       for brushing on cookies
    $^1/_2$ cup blanched almond slices or slivers,
       for decorating cookies

1. Adjust two racks to divide the oven into thirds. Preheat the oven to 375°. Lightly grease two baking sheets.

2. Into a medium-size bowl, sift together the flour, baking powder, cinnamon, nutmeg, cloves, anise seeds, white pepper, and salt.

3. In a large bowl, with an electric mixer at medium-high speed, beat the butter until creamy,

about 1 minute. Add the brown sugar and continue beating until the mixture is light and creamy, 2 to 3 minutes. Beat in the milk until blended. With the mixer at medium-low speed, gradually add the flour mixture, beating just until blended. Gather the dough into a ball. (At this point, the dough can be tightly wrapped in aluminum foil and refrigerated for up to one week or frozen for up to three months. If frozen, thaw in the refrigerator and bring to room temperature before proceeding.)

4. On a generously floured surface, knead the dough until smooth. Roll the dough into a rectangle measuring about 15×12 inches that is $^1/_4$ inch thick. With a pizza wheel or the tip of a sharp knife and a ruler, cut the dough into rectangles measuring about $2^1/_2 \times 1^1/_2$ inches. Arrange the rectangles on the prepared baking sheets, spacing them about $^1/_2$ inch apart. With a pastry brush, brush the tops of the cookies with beaten egg white, then scatter a few pieces of almond over each cookie.

5. Bake for 12 to 15 minutes until firm and lightly browned. Reverse the baking sheets on the racks and from front to back once during baking. With a wide turner, immediately transfer the cookies to wire racks to cool completely.

6. Store in a tightly covered container.

Yield: About 48 cookies

Tip

After flour has been added to cookie batter, be careful not to overmix, which causes the gluten in the flour to develop and can produce tough cookies.

Sablés

The name of this French cookie is pronounced "saab-lay" and has nothing to do with furry little animals. Although the name makes these cookies sound very upscale, the translation is simply sand cookies, which refers to their tender, crumbly texture.

- $^3/_4$ **cup blanched, toasted almonds (page 16)**
- $^3/_4$ **cup ($1^1/_2$ sticks) salted butter or margarine, at room temperature**
- $^3/_4$ **cup confectioners' sugar**
- **1 large egg**
- **1 large egg yolk**
- **1 teaspoon vanilla extract**
- $^1/_4$ **teaspoon almond extract**
- $^1/_4$ **teaspoon salt**
- **2 $^3/_4$ cups all-purpose flour**

1. Adjust two racks to divide the oven into thirds. Preheat the oven to 350°. Have ready two ungreased baking sheets. Also have ready a $2^1/_2$-inch round, scalloped cookie cutter.

2. Place the almonds in a food processor fitted with a steel blade and process until finely ground, turning the processor off once and giving the nuts a good stir from the bottom to keep them from becoming pasty.

3. In large bowl, with an electric mixer at medium-high speed, beat the butter until creamy, about 1 minute. Add the confectioners' sugar, ground almonds, egg, egg yolk, vanilla, almond extract, and salt and beat until light and fluffy, 2 to 3 minutes. With the mixer at medium-low speed, gradually add the flour, beating just until blended. Gather the dough into a ball. (At this point, the dough can be tightly wrapped in aluminum foil and refrigerated for up to one week or frozen for up to three months. If frozen, thaw in the refrigerator. Bring to room temperature before proceeding.)

4. Divide the dough in half. Roll half of the dough between two sheets of waxed paper into a rectangle that is about $^1/_4$ inch thick. Slide an ungreased baking sheet under the dough and refrigerate until firm, about 20 minutes. Repeat with second half of the dough.

5. Remove one sheet of the dough from the refrigerator. Peel off the top sheet of waxed paper; replace loosely. Turn the dough over and discard the second sheet of waxed paper. Cut the dough into as many rounds as possible and place $^1/_2$ inch apart on the same ungreased baking sheet. Reroll the scraps between sheets of waxed paper and continue cutting out cookies. (If the dough becomes too warm to handle easily, refrigerate it for a few minutes.) Repeat with the second half of the dough.

6. Bake 11 to 12 minutes until lightly browned. Reverse the baking sheets on the racks and from front to back once during baking. With a wide turner, immediately transfer the cookies to wire racks to cool completely.

7. These cookies are not usually decorated, but are sometimes stamped with a design before baking.

8. Store in a tightly covered container, separating the layers with sheets of waxed paper.

Yield: About 48 cookies

Tip

Always use cool baking sheets. If the sheets are even slightly warm, the butter or other fat in the dough will start to melt before baking begins and the cookies will be flat and probably overbrowned on the bottoms.

Caramel Sour Cream Cookies

The original recipe for this delicate little cookie is a very old one that took some doing to get it to work with today's ingredients and methods. It is similar to a plain sugar cookie, but with a much richer flavor. Cut these cookies into fancy shapes, if you like, but I prefer to make them in scalloped rounds about 2 inches in diameter and with minimal, if any, decorations.

    2 1/2 cups all-purpose flour
    3/4 teaspoon baking powder
    1/4 teaspoon baking soda
    1/2 teaspoon ground nutmeg (optional)
    1/2 cup (1 stick) salted butter or margarine,
        at room temperature
    2/3 cup dark brown sugar
    1 large egg, lightly beaten
    1/2 cup sour cream

1. Adjust two racks to divide the oven into thirds. Lightly grease two baking sheets. Have ready an assortment of small, medium-size, and large cookie cutters.

2. In a medium-size bowl, with a whisk, combine the flour, baking powder, baking soda, and nutmeg until thoroughly mixed.

3. In a large bowl, with an electric mixer at medium-high speed, beat together the butter and brown sugar until very creamy, 2 to 3 minutes. Add the egg and the sour cream and beat until well blended. With the mixer at medium-low speed, gradually add the flour mixture, beating just until blended. Cover the bowl and chill until firm, about 1 hour. Divide the dough into quarters. Wrap each quarter separately in plastic wrap and refrigerate until chilled, about 1 hour. (At this point, the dough can be tightly wrapped in aluminum foil and refrigerated for up to one week or frozen for up to three months. If frozen, thaw in the refrigerator before proceeding.)

4. Preheat the oven to 350°.

5. Between two sheets of floured waxed paper, roll one quarter of the dough to a 1/8-inch thickness. (Leave the remaining dough in the refrigerator until you are ready to roll it.) Cut the dough into as many shapes as possible. Arrange the shapes on a prepared baking sheet, spacing them about 1 inch apart. Gather the scraps of dough together and reroll once or twice.

6. Bake for 8 to 10 minutes until the edges are lightly browned and firm to the touch. Reverse the baking sheets on the racks and from front to back once during baking. With a wide turner, immediately transfer the cookies to wire racks to cool completely.

7. Repeat with the remaining dough.

8. Store in a tightly covered container, separating and cushioning the layers with sheets of waxed paper.

Yield: About 80 cookies

Cocoa-Cinnamon Cutouts

This is an easy dough to work. It bakes into a very crisp little cookie that can be sandwiched together with a filling (pages 32–34), or decorated, or just enjoyed plain.

    2 cups all-purpose flour
    1/2 cup sugar
    2 tablespoons unsweetened cocoa powder
    1 tablespoon ground cinnamon
    1/2 cup (1 stick) salted butter or margarine,
        cut into large pieces
    1 large egg yolk, lightly beaten

1. In a large bowl, with a whisk, combine the flour, sugar, cocoa powder, and cinnamon until thoroughly mixed. With a pastry blender or two knives, cut in the butter until the mixture resembles small peas. With a mixing spoon, stir in the egg yolk just until well blended. Gather the dough into a ball and divide it in half. Wrap each half in plastic wrap and refrigerate until

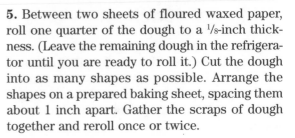

cold, about 1 hour. (At this point the dough can be tightly wrapped in aluminum foil and refrigerated for up to one week or frozen for up to three months. Thaw in the refrigerator before proceeding.)

2. Adjust two racks to divide the oven into thirds. Preheat the oven to 350°. Lightly grease two baking sheets; set aside. Have ready an assortment of 3-inch cookie cutters.

3. On a lightly floured surface, roll out half of the cold dough to a ⅛-inch thickness. (Leave the remaining dough in the refrigerator until you are ready to roll it.) Cut the dough into as many shapes as possible. Arrange the shapes on a prepared baking sheet, spacing them about ½ inch apart. Gather the scraps of dough together and reroll once or twice. The cookies can be decorated now or after baking. Repeat with the remaining dough.

4. Bake for about 12 minutes until firm. Reverse the baking sheets on the racks and from front to back once during baking. With a wide turner, immediately transfer the cookies to wire racks to cool completely.

5. Store in a tightly covered container.

Yield: About 40 cookies

AP's

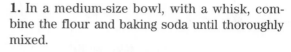

In this case, AP stands for Ann Page, a Colonial lady, who, according to popular legend, baked wonderful cookies. At some point she started selling them, marking her initials on top of the cookies before baking.

> 2 ½ **cups all-purpose flour**
> ½ **teaspoon baking soda**
> 1 **cup sugar**
> ½ **cup (1 stick) salted butter (not margarine), at room temperature**
> 2 **large eggs, well beaten**
> ½ **teaspoon vanilla extract**
> ¼ **cup sour cream**

1. In a medium-size bowl, with a whisk, combine the flour and baking soda until thoroughly mixed.

2. In a large bowl, with an electric mixer at medium-high speed, beat together the sugar and the butter until light and fluffy, 2 to 3 minutes. Beat in the eggs and vanilla until well blended. Beat in the sour cream until well blended. With the mixer at medium-low speed, gradually add the flour mixture, beating just until blended. Cover the bowl and chill until the dough is firm, about 2 hours. Divide the dough in half. Wrap each half in plastic wrap and refrigerate for at least 8 hours or overnight. (At this point the dough can be tightly wrapped in aluminum foil and refrigerated for up to one week or frozen for up to three months. If frozen, thaw in the refrigerator before proceeding.)

3. Adjust two racks to divide the oven in half. Preheat the oven to 350°. Have ready two ungreased baking sheets. Also have ready a 2½-inch round cookie cutter.

4. On heavily floured waxed paper, roll out half of the dough to a ¼-inch thickness. (Leave the remaining dough in the refrigerator until you are ready to work with it.) With the cookie cutter, cut into as many rounds as possible. Transfer the rounds to the ungreased baking sheets. With the tip of a wooden skewer, mark the tops deeply with Ann's initials—or yours. Gather the scraps of dough together and reroll once.

5. Bake for 8 to 10 minutes until firm to the touch and the edges are brown. Reverse the baking sheets on the racks and from front to back once during baking. With a wide turner, immediately transfer the cookies to wire racks to cool completely. Repeat with the remaining dough.

6. Store in a tightly covered container.

Yield: About 48 cookies

Tip

If using plastic cookie cutters, the cutting edge should be dipped in warm oil occasionally for cleaner, more defined edges.

Fans

Fan-shaped cookies were very popular in the Victorian era, when they were the nibble of choice to serve at afternoon teas and receptions.

2 cups all-purpose flour

1 teaspoon baking powder

³/₄ cup (1 ¹/₂ sticks) salted butter or margarine, at room temperature

¹/₂ teaspoon lemon or vanilla extract

¹/₂ cup packed light brown sugar

1 large egg yolk

Chocolate Dip

2 ounces (2 squares) semisweet chocolate

1 tablespoon heavy (whipping) cream

¹/₄ cup very finely chopped hazelnuts

1. In a medium-size bowl, with a whisk, combine the flour and baking powder until thoroughly mixed.

2. In a large bowl, with an electric mixer at medium-high speed, beat the butter with the lemon extract until creamy, about 1 minute. Add the brown sugar and the egg yolk. Beat until light and creamy, 2 to 3 minutes. With the mixer at medium-low speed, gradually add the flour mixture, beating just until blended. Gather the dough into a ball and divide it in half. Wrap each half in plastic wrap and refrigerate until very cold, about 2 hours. (At this point, the dough can be tightly wrapped in aluminum foil and refrigerated for up to one week or frozen for up to three months. If frozen, thaw in the refrigerator before proceeding.)

3. Adjust two racks to divide the oven into thirds. Preheat the oven to 325°. Lightly grease two baking sheets. Have ready a 3¹/₂-inch scalloped cookie cutter.

4. On a lightly floured surface, roll half of the cold dough to a ¹/₄-inch thickness. (Leave the remaining dough in the refrigerator until you are ready to roll it.) Cut the dough into as many rounds as possible. With the tip of a knife, cut each round into quarters. Arrange the quarters on a prepared baking sheet, spacing them about 1 inch apart. Use a butter spreader to lightly mark each quarter-round to resemble the folds in a fan. Gather the dough scraps together and reroll once. Repeat with the remaining dough.

5. Bake for 10 to 12 minutes until firm and lightly browned. Reverse the baking sheets on the racks and from front to back once during baking. With a wide turner, immediately transfer the cookies to wire racks to cool completely.

6. Make the chocolate dip: Place the chocolate and cream in a very small saucepan set over very low heat. Stir constantly until the mixture is smooth. Set aside to cool slightly. Place the hazelnuts in a small, deep bowl. When the cookies have cooled completely, dip the pointed ends into the chocolate and then into the hazelnuts. Set aside on a sheet of waxed paper until the chocolate has hardened, about 1 hour.

7. Store in a tightly covered container, separating the layers with sheets of waxed paper.

Yield: About 48 cookies

Buttery Butterscotch Cutouts

If you enjoy the flavor of butter as much as I do, I think you're going to like these crisp cutouts. Like all cutout cookies, these can be decorated any way you choose, before or after baking, plain or simple. I tend to like mine au naturel.

- 1 cup butterscotch-flavored chips
- 3 cups all-purpose flour
- 1/2 cup granulated sugar
- 1/2 cup packed light brown sugar
- 1 cup (2 sticks) salted butter, at room temperature
- 1 large egg
- 2 tablespoons milk
- 2 teaspoons vanilla extract
- Confectioners' sugar, for sprinkling on cookies
- Plain or colored granulated or crystal sugar, for sprinkling on cookies

1. Adjust two racks to divide the oven into thirds. Have ready two ungreased baking sheets. Also have ready an assortment of 2 1/2-inch cookie cutters.

2. In a small saucepan set over very low heat, melt the butterscotch-flavored chips, stirring constantly until smooth. Remove from the heat and set aside to cool slightly.

3. Scrape the melted chips into a large bowl. Add the flour, granulated sugar, brown sugar, butter, egg, milk, and vanilla. With an electric mixer at low speed, beat until well mixed, about 2 minutes, scraping the side of the bowl often with a rubber spatula. Gather the dough into a ball and divide it in half. Wrap each half of the dough in plastic wrap and refrigerate until firm, about 1 hour. (At this point the dough can be tightly wrapped in aluminum foil and refrigerated for up to one week or frozen for up to three months. If frozen, thaw in the refrigerator before proceeding.)

4. Preheat the oven to 375°.

5. On a well-floured surface, roll one half of the dough to a 1/8-inch thickness. (Leave the remaining dough in the refrigerator until you are ready to roll it.) Cut the dough into as many shapes as possible. Arrange the shapes on the ungreased baking sheets, spacing them about 1 inch apart. Gather the scraps of dough together and reroll once.

6. Bake for 5 to 8 minutes until the edges are lightly browned. Reverse the baking sheets on the racks and from front to back once during baking. With a wide turner, immediately transfer the cookies to wire racks to cool completely. Cool completely before sprinkling with sugars, or decorate as desired. Repeat with the remaining dough.

7. Store in a tightly covered container.

Yield: About 48 cookies

Tip

Cookies made with 100 percent corn oil margarine will be softer than those made with butter or regular margarine. Cookies made with vegetable shortening hold their shape better than those made with butter or margarine.

Brandy Gems

This is a very delicate little cookie, with a crisp, melt-in-the-mouth texture. The brandy flavoring is there, but very subtle.

- 2 cups all-purpose flour
- 3 hard-cooked large egg yolks
- 1 cup (2 sticks) salted butter or margarine, at room temperature
- 1/4 cup sugar
- 1 teaspoon shredded and minced lemon zest
- 1/4 cup brandy or cognac (orange juice can be substituted)
- 1 large egg, lightly beaten, for brushing cookies
- 3 tablespoons sugar and 1 teaspoon ground cinnamon, mixed together, for sprinkling on cookies
- About 1/2 cup finely chopped blanched almonds, for sprinkling on cookies

1. Adjust one rack to divide the oven in half. Preheat the oven to 350°. Have ready an ungreased baking sheet.

2. Sift the flour onto a large sheet of waxed paper. Press the hard-cooked egg yolks through a sieve onto another sheet of waxed paper.

3. In a large bowl, with an electric mixer at medium-high speed, beat the butter, sugar, and lemon zest together until light and fluffy, 2 to 3 minutes. With the mixer at medium speed, alternately beat in the flour and the brandy just until blended. Sprinkle the sieved egg yolks over the batter. With a mixing spoon, stir the yolks into the batter just until they disappear. Cover the bowl and refrigerate until the dough is cold, about 30 minutes. (At this point, the dough can be tightly wrapped in aluminum foil and refrigerated for up to one week or frozen for up to three months. If frozen, thaw in the refrigerator before proceeding.)

4. On a lightly floured surface, roll the dough into a 12 × 18-inch rectangle that is about 1/8 inch thick. With a pizza wheel or the tip of a sharp knife and

a ruler, cut the dough into 18 lengthwise strips that are 1 inch wide. Cut each strip into 3 pieces, each about 4 inches long. Arrange the pieces of dough on the baking sheet, spacing them about 1 inch apart. With a pastry brush, brush the top of each cookie with the beaten egg. Sprinkle each cookie with the sugar-and-cinnamon mixture. Scatter a few pieces of almond over each cookie.

5. Bake for 15 to 20 minutes until the cookies are firm when lightly touched. Reverse the baking sheet from front to back once during baking. With a wide turner, immediately transfer the cookies to wire racks to cool completely.

6. Store in a tightly covered container.

Yield: About 48 cookies

Hungarian Ne Plus Ultra Cookies

This recipe has been in my files for years. *Ne plus ultra* is Latin and means, approximately, "It doesn't get much better than this." Before making these delicious, crisp cookies, you might want to brush up on meringue making, which is explained on page 69.

1 cup all-purpose flour

¹/₂ cup (1 stick) plus 1 tablespoon cold butter, cut into small pieces

2 tablespoons granulated sugar

¹/₄ teaspoon salt

1 teaspoon vanilla extract

2 large egg yolks

About ¹/₃ cup peach or apricot preserves

Meringue

1 large egg white

¹/₈ teaspoon cream of tartar

¹/₄ cup confectioners' sugar

1. Adjust two racks to divide the oven into thirds. Have ready two ungreased baking sheets. Also have ready a 2-inch and a 1-inch round cookie or biscuit cutter.

2. In a very large bowl, with a pastry blender or two knives, blend the flour, butter, sugar, salt, vanilla, and egg yolks until the mixture begins to form a dough. Push the dough with the heel of your hand, right in the bowl, until the butter is well distributed. Gather the dough into a ball. Dust lightly with flour and wrap in plastic wrap. Place the dough in the refrigerator until it is very cold, at least 2 hours. (At this point, the dough can be tightly wrapped in aluminum foil and refrigerated for up to one week or frozen for up to three months. If frozen, thaw in the refrigerator before proceeding.)

3. Roll the cold dough between two sheets of waxed paper to a ¹/₄-inch thickness. With the larger cutter, cut the dough into 32 rounds, rerolling the scraps once. With the smaller cutter, cut the centers out of *half* of the rounds. (The small rounds that are left over will not be used for this recipe. They can be refrigerated and baked later.) Gather the scraps of dough together and reroll once. Place the rounds and rings on the ungreased baking sheets and refrigerate for 1 hour.

4. Preheat the oven to 350°.

5. Bake the cookies for 12 to 15 minutes until firm and lightly browned. Reverse the baking sheets on the racks and from front to back once during baking.

6. While the cookies are baking, make the meringue: In a small bowl, with an electric mixer at medium speed, beat the egg white with the cream of tartar until frothy. Gradually beat in the confectioners' sugar. Continue beating at high speed until the meringue is very thick and shiny and holds stiff peaks when the beaters are lifted.

7. Remove the cookies from the oven. Immediately close the oven door and turn off the heat. Working quickly, with a small spatula or a butter spreader, spread the rounds and the rings evenly with a thin coating of meringue. Return the cookies to the turned-off oven for about 20 minutes until the meringue is dry. With a wide turner, remove the cookies to wire racks to cool completely. Spread a thin layer of preserves on the plain undersides of the rounds, then set the rings on top, meringue side up.

8. Store at low humidity in a shallow, loosely covered container, separating and cushioning the layers with sheets of waxed paper.

Yield: 16 cookies

Tip

You can make your own custom cookie shapes by using a cardboard pattern and the tip of a sharp knife or a craft knife instead of cookie cutters.

Sweet Rolled Tea Cookies

This is another one of my favorite cookies, sweet and delicate, and positively scrumptious with hot tea. The filling can be tinted a pale color with a very few drops of liquid food coloring, if you like.

Dough

2 cups all-purpose flour

1 cup (2 sticks) salted butter, at room temperature

$^1/_3$ cup heavy (whipping) cream

About $^1/_2$ cup granulated sugar, for coating cookies

Filling

$^3/_4$ cup confectioners' sugar

$^1/_4$ cup ($^1/_2$ stick) salted butter, at room temperature

1 teaspoon vanilla extract

1 to 3 teaspoons heavy (whipping) cream

1. To make the dough, in a medium-size bowl, with an electric mixer at low speed, combine the flour, butter, and cream until well blended and the mixture forms a dough, 2 to 3 minutes. Gather the dough into a ball and divide it into thirds. Wrap each third in plastic wrap and refrigerate until firm, about 1 hour. (At this point the dough can be tightly wrapped in aluminum foil and refrigerated for up to one week or frozen for up to three months. If frozen, thaw in the refrigerator before proceeding.)

2. Adjust two racks to divide the oven in half. Preheat the oven to 375°. Have ready two ungreased baking sheets. Also have ready a 1$^1/_2$-inch round biscuit or cookie cutter. Sprinkle the granulated sugar on a sheet of waxed paper.

3. On a well-floured surface, roll one-third of the dough to a $^1/_8$-inch thickness. Cut into rounds with the cookie cutter. Dip both sides of each round in the granulated sugar. Place the sugared rounds on the ungreased baking sheets, spacing them about 1 inch apart. Prick the top of each cookie three times with the tines of a dinner fork.

4. Bake for 6 to 9 minutes until slightly puffed, but not brown. Reverse the baking sheets on the racks and from front to back once during baking. With a wide turner, immediately transfer the cookies to wire racks to cool completely. Repeat with the remaining dough.

5. While the cookies are cooling, make the filling: In a small bowl, with an electric mixer at medium speed, beat together the confectioners' sugar, butter, and vanilla until well blended. Gradually add the cream, beating until the mixture is fluffy and has reached a good spreading consistency.

6. With a small spatula or a butter spreader, spread about $^1/_2$ teaspoon of the filling on each of the bottoms of half the cookies. Top with the remaining cookies, flat sides against the filling.

7. Store in a tightly covered container.

Yield: About 54 cookies

Tip

When transferring cutout cookies to baking sheets, first lift off the scraps from around the cutout shapes.

Viennese Hazelnut Cookies

These are lovely, rich cookies as only European bakers can create them. Use salted butter or margarine instead of the unsalted variety, if you wish, but this is one cookie that I prefer to keep as pristine as it was intended to be. I even use unsalted butter to grease the baking sheet.

2 cups (4 sticks) unsalted butter, at room temperature

$^1/_4$ cup confectioners' sugar

$^1/_4$ cup granulated sugar

2 large eggs, separated

$^1/_2$ teaspoon vanilla extract

1 tablespoon shredded and minced lemon zest (1 small lemon)

2 $^1/_4$ cups sifted all-purpose flour

$^2/_3$ cup finely chopped, toasted hazelnuts (page 16)

1. In a large bowl, with an electric mixer at medium-high speed, beat together the butter with the confectioners' sugar and the granulated sugar until the mixture is pale and the granulated sugar is completely dissolved. (There should be no gritty feeling when a little of the mixture is rubbed between your fingers, so this may take a while, as much as 5 minutes.) Beat in the egg yolks, one at a time, until well blended. (Reserve the egg whites to brush on the unbaked cookies.) Beat in the vanilla and lemon zest. With a mixing spoon, stir in the flour, then mix the dough with your hands until it cleans the side of the bowl and can be gathered into a ball. Divide the dough into quarters. Wrap each quarter in plastic wrap. Refrigerate until very cold, about 2 hours. (At this point, the dough can be tightly wrapped in aluminum foil and refrigerated for up to one week or frozen for up to three months. If frozen, thaw in the refrigerator before proceeding.)

2. Adjust two racks to divide the oven into thirds. Preheat the oven to 400°. Lightly grease two baking sheets; set aside in a cool place. Have ready a 1$^1/_2$-inch round or scalloped cookie cutter.

3. Between two sheets of floured waxed paper, roll one-quarter of the dough to a $^1/_8$-inch thickness. (Leave the remaining dough in the refrigerator until you are ready to roll it.) Remove the top piece of waxed paper and cut the dough into as many rounds as possible. Arrange the rounds on the prepared baking sheets, spacing them about 1 inch apart. Gather the scraps of dough together and reroll once or twice. Repeat with the remaining dough. Lightly beat the reserved egg whites and, with a pastry brush, brush over the tops of the rounds. Sprinkle with the hazelnuts.

4. Bake for 8 to 10 minutes until the cookies are very lightly browned around the edges and have loosened from the baking sheet. Reverse the baking sheets on the racks and from front to back once during baking. With a wide turner, immediately transfer the cookies to wire racks to cool completely.

5. Store in a shallow, tightly covered container, separating the layers with sheets of waxed paper.

Yield: About 80 cookies

Honey Cookie-Bars

Make these cookies at least two weeks before you intend to serve them to give the flavors an opportunity to develop. Stored in an airtight container, they will keep for *months*.

1 1/3 cups honey

1/4 cup cognac or brandy (orange juice can be substituted)

1 cup superfine sugar

2 cups (about 8 ounces) shelled natural almonds, coarsely chopped

1/4 cup finely chopped candied orange peel

1/4 cup finely chopped candied lemon peel

1 tablespoon ground cinnamon

2 teaspoons shredded and minced lemon zest

1 teaspoon ground cloves

4 to 5 cups all-purpose flour

Glaze

1 cup sifted confectioners' sugar

1 to 2 tablespoons fresh lemon juice

1. Lightly butter and flour two baking sheets; set aside in a cool place.

2. In a large, heavy saucepan, heat the honey to boiling over medium heat. Remove from the heat and stir in the brandy. With a mixing spoon, stir in the superfine sugar until it is completely dissolved. Return the pan to low heat. Stir in the almonds, candied orange and lemon peels, cinnamon, lemon zest, and cloves until completely blended. Remove from the heat.

3. With a mixing spoon, begin stirring in the flour, starting with additions of 1/4 cup (different types of honey will require different amounts of flour). Continue stirring until the mixture cleans the side of the pan and begins to form a soft, but not sticky, dough.

4. Turn the dough onto a lightly floured surface. Knead in enough of the remaining flour, 1 tablespoon at a time, to form a dough that can be easily rolled. Divide the dough in half. Roll each half into a 16 × 6-inch rectangle that is about 1/4 inch thick. With a pizza wheel or the tip of a sharp knife and a ruler, cut the rectangle of dough in half lengthwise, forming two 16 × 3-inch rectangles. Cut each rectangle crosswise into sixteen 3 × 1-inch rectangles. Arrange the rectangles on the prepared baking sheets. Cover lightly with a kitchen towel and let stand at room temperature overnight. *Do not refrigerate.*

5. Adjust two racks to divide the oven into thirds. Preheat the oven to 350°.

6. Bake for 15 minutes until golden brown. Reverse the baking sheets on the racks and from front to back once during baking.

7. While the cookies are baking, make the glaze: In a small bowl, combine the confectioners' sugar and 1 tablespoon of the lemon juice. Add the remaining lemon juice, 1 teaspoon at a time, until the mixture reaches a thick spreading consistency. With a wide turner, immediately remove the cookies to wire racks. Immediately spread the tops of the warm cookies with glaze.

8. When the cookies have cooled completely, arrange them in a shallow, airtight container, separating the layers with sheets of waxed paper. Store 2 to 4 weeks at room temperature before serving.

Yield: 64 cookies

Tip

When measuring sticky liquids (honey, corn syrup, etc.), first wipe the inside of the measuring cup with oil. The liquid will flow freely and the cup will be easier to wash, too.

Chocolate-Hazelnut Cookies

Forget about these cookies for a few days after they are baked. They need a little time for the flavor to assert itself. The secret to working with this rich dough is to keep it as cold as possible at all times.

- 1 cup (about 4 ounces) shelled hazelnuts, skins removed (page 16)
- 1 1/4 cups all-purpose flour
- 1 cup cake flour (not self-rising flour)
- 1 1/2 tablespoons unsweetened cocoa powder
- 1 cup (2 sticks) salted butter or margarine, at room temperature
- 1/4 cup sugar
- 2 large egg yolks
- 1/4 teaspoon vanilla extract
- 4 ounces semisweet chocolate, ground in a food processor

1. Place the nuts in a food processor fitted with a steel blade and process until finely ground, turning the processor off once and giving the nuts a good stir from the bottom to keep them from becoming pasty.

2. In a medium-size bowl, with a whisk, combine the all-purpose flour, cake flour, and cocoa until thoroughly mixed.

3. In a large bowl, with an electric mixer at medium-high speed, beat together the butter and sugar until light and fluffy, 2 to 3 minutes. Beat in the egg yolks and vanilla until well blended. With a mixing spoon, stir in the ground chocolate and ground hazelnuts just until well blended. Add the flour mixture in three additions, stirring well after each addition. Knead the dough in the bowl until it is smooth and fairly stiff. Gather the dough into a ball and divide it in half. Wrap each half in plastic wrap and refrigerate until cold, about 1 hour. (At this point, the dough can be tightly wrapped in aluminum foil and refrigerated for up to one week or frozen for up to three months. If frozen, thaw in the refrigerator before proceeding.)

4. Adjust one rack to divide the oven in half. Preheat the oven to 375°. Lightly grease two baking sheets. Have ready a 1 1/2-inch round cookie cutter.

5. Place half of the cold dough on a work surface. (Leave the remaining dough in the refrigerator until you are ready to roll it.) With a rolling pin, pound the dough until it is malleable. Working quickly so that the dough stays cold, roll half of the dough between two sheets of floured waxed paper to a 1/8-inch thickness. Remove the top sheet of waxed paper. Cut the dough into as many rounds as possible. Arrange the rounds on the prepared baking sheet, spacing them about 1/2 inch apart. (The scraps can be gathered together and rerolled once. However, the dough must be chilled again before rerolling.) Repeat with the remaining dough.

6. Bake one sheet at a time for about 10 minutes until the cookies are pale and just set. Reverse the baking sheet from front to back once during baking. With a wide turner, immediately transfer the cookies to wire racks to cool completely. While the first batch of cookies is baking, prepare the second batch, making sure to keep the dough cold at all times.

7. Store the cookies in a tightly covered container, separating and cushioning the layers with sheets of waxed paper.

Yield: About 96 cookies

Tip

To keep waxed paper in place while rolling dough, dampen the counter before putting down the waxed paper.

Joe's Froggers

These cookies are an old New England favorite. According to legend, the funny name comes from the purported originator, an old man known as Uncle Joe who lived near a frog pond and who gave away his molasses cookies to anyone who brought him rum. The big, flat cookies are supposed to resemble the frogs in Joe's pond, and that is where they got their name.

    7 cups all-purpose flour
    1 tablespoon ground ginger
    1 teaspoon ground cloves
    1 teaspoon ground nutmeg
    1/2 teaspoon ground allspice
    1 teaspoon salt
    3/4 cup water
    1/4 cup dark rum
    2 cups unsulphured molasses
    2 teaspoons baking soda
    1 cup (2 sticks) salted butter or margarine,
        at room temperature
    2 cups sugar

1. In a large bowl, with a whisk, combine the flour, ginger, cloves, nutmeg, and allspice until thoroughly mixed.

2. In a 1-cup measure, dissolve the salt in the water and then stir in the rum. In a small bowl, mix the molasses with the baking soda. Stir the water mixture into the molasses mixture until blended.

3. In a large bowl, with an electric mixer at medium-high speed, beat together the butter and sugar until light and fluffy, 2 to 3 minutes. Add the molasses mixture alternately with the flour mixture, beating well after each addition just until blended. Cover the bowl and refrigerate the dough for at least 12 hours. (At this point, the dough can be gathered into a ball, tightly wrapped in aluminum foil, and refrigerated for up to one week or frozen for up to three months. If frozen, thaw in the refrigerator before proceeding.)

4. Adjust two racks to divide the oven into thirds. Preheat the oven to 375°. Lightly grease two baking sheets. Have ready a 4-inch round cookie cutter or other shapes of about the same size.

5. Divide the cold dough into quarters. On a lightly floured surface, roll one-quarter of the dough to a 1/3-inch thickness. (Keep the remaining dough refrigerated until you are ready to roll it.) Cut the dough into as many rounds or other shapes as possible. Arrange the rounds on the prepared baking sheets, spacing them about 2 inches apart. Gather the scraps of dough together and reroll once or twice. Repeat with the remaining dough.

6. Bake for about 12 minutes until crinkled and firm when lightly touched. Reverse the baking sheets on the racks and from front to back once during baking. With a wide turner, transfer the cookies to wire racks to cool completely.

7. Store in a tightly covered container, separating the layers with sheets of waxed paper.

Yield: About 40 cookies

Fruitcake Cookies

Huge, delicious, and *fun* are the words the tester used to describe these crisp, fruity molasses cookies. She says that if you eat just one for lunch with a glass of milk you won't be hungry until dinner. You'll be working with a large amount of batter, so bring out your very largest bowl.

> 5 ¹/₂ **cups all-purpose flour, divided**
>
> 1 ¹/₂ **teaspoons ground cloves**
>
> 1 ¹/₂ **teaspoons ground cinnamon**
>
> ³/₄ **teaspoon salt**
>
> 1 ¹/₂ **cups sugar**
>
> ¹/₂ **cup (1 stick) salted butter or margarine, cut into small pieces and softened slightly**
>
> ¹/₂ **cup honey**
>
> ¹/₂ **cup unsulphured molasses**
>
> ¹/₂ **cup plus 1 tablespoon cold water, divided**
>
> 1 ¹/₂ **cups finely chopped mixed candied fruits**
>
> 1 ¹/₂ **cups finely chopped pecans**
>
> 1 ¹/₂ **teaspoons baking soda**
>
> 1 **large egg and 1 large egg yolk, lightly beaten together**
>
> **Crystal sugar, for sprinkling on cookies**

1. Adjust two racks to divide the oven into thirds. Preheat the oven to 350°. Lightly grease two baking sheets. Have ready a 4-inch round cookie cutter.

2. In a very large bowl, with a whisk, combine 2 cups of the flour with the cloves, cinnamon, and salt until thoroughly mixed.

3. In a large, heavy saucepan or Dutch oven, with a mixing spoon, stir together the sugar, butter, honey, molasses, and 1 tablespoon of the water. Cook over low heat, stirring constantly, just until the butter is melted. Increase the heat to medium. When the mixture comes to a boil, boil for *exactly* 5 minutes without stirring.

4. Remove the pan from the heat and, with the spoon, beat in the flour-and-spice mixture all at once until well blended. Stir in the candied fruits and pecans until evenly distributed throughout the batter. Turn this mixture into a very large bowl and set aside until lukewarm.

5. In a small bowl, combine the remaining ¹/₂ cup water with the baking soda. With the spoon, beat the water mixture, egg, and egg yolk into the flour mixture until well blended. Beat in the remaining 2¹/₂ cups of flour, ¹/₂ cup at a time. Divide the dough into quarters.

6. On a lightly floured surface, roll one-quarter of the dough to a ¹/₄-inch thickness. Cut the dough into as many rounds as possible. Arrange the rounds on the prepared baking sheets. Sprinkle with sugar. Gather the scraps of dough together and reroll once. Repeat with the remaining dough.

7. Bake for 20 minutes until lightly browned and firm to the touch. Reverse the baking sheets on the racks and from front to back once during baking. With a wide turner, immediately transfer the cookies to wire racks to cool completely.

8. Store in a tightly covered container, separating the layers with sheets of waxed paper. A slice of apple or raw potato placed in the container and changed every other day or so will keep the cookies deliciously soft.

Yield: About 30 cookies

Tip

When rolling out cookie dough, always start at the center and roll outward in all directions.

Stage Planks

Even if you didn't know this was an old recipe, the ingredients would give you a clue. Stage planks were probably invented during a time when butter and eggs were relatively plentiful, but spices were not, and a single recipe calling for several spices was a sign of affluence.

- **3 cups all-purpose flour**
- **$1/2$ teaspoon ground ginger**
- **$1/2$ teaspoon ground cinnamon**
- **$1/2$ teaspoon ground cloves**
- **2 tablespoons salted butter or margarine,** at room temperature
- **$1/2$ cup packed light brown sugar**
- **$1/2$ cup unsulphured molasses**
- **$1/2$ teaspoon lemon extract**
- **$1/3$ cup buttermilk**
- **$1/2$ teaspoon baking soda**

1. In a medium-size bowl, with a whisk, combine the flour, ginger, cinnamon, and cloves until thoroughly mixed.

2. In a large bowl, with an electric mixer at medium-high speed, beat the butter with the brown sugar, molasses, and lemon extract until very creamy, 2 to 3 minutes. With the mixer at medium-low speed, add the flour mixture alternately with the buttermilk, adding the baking soda to the last addition of the buttermilk, and beating just until blended. Gather the dough into a ball and divide it in half. Wrap each half in plastic wrap and refrigerate until very cold, about 2 hours. (At this point, the dough can be tightly wrapped in aluminum foil and refrigerated for up to one week or frozen for up to three months. If frozen, thaw in the refrigerator before proceeding.)

3. Adjust two racks to divide the oven into thirds. Preheat the oven to 350°. Lightly grease two baking sheets.

4. On a lightly floured surface, roll half of the cold dough into a rectangle that is about $1/4$ inch thick. (Leave the remaining dough in the refrigerator until you are ready to roll it.) Trim the edges with a pizza wheel or a knife and a ruler to make them straight, then cut the dough into strips measuring about $2 \times 1^{1}/_{2}$ inches. Arrange the strips on a prepared baking sheet, spacing them about $1/2$ inch apart. Repeat with the remaining dough.

5. Bake for 10 to 12 minutes until firm and lightly browned. Reverse the baking sheets on the racks and from front to back once during baking. With a wide turner, immediately transfer the cookies to wire racks to cool completely.

6. Store in a tightly covered container, separating and cushioning the layers with sheets of waxed paper.

Yield: About 42 cookies

Tip

Did you know that ice cream cones are merely big flat cookies that have been rolled into the traditional cone shape?

Rye Rings

You can't always tell a book by its cover or a cookie by its ingredients. I was very ho-hum about this recipe when it crossed my desk, but after the tester sent me samples, it has become my cookie favorite of the moment, and I can't say enough good things about them. I especially enjoy these oatsy-flavored rings with a glass of milk.

- **1 $1/4$ cups rye flour**
- **1 $1/4$ cups all-purpose flour**
- **1 cup (2 sticks) salted butter or margarine,** at room temperature
- **$1/3$ cup packed light brown sugar**

1. Adjust one rack to divide the oven in half. Preheat the oven to 350°. Lightly grease two baking

sheets. Have ready a 2½-inch round cookie cutter with a scalloped or plain edge.

2. In a medium-size bowl, with a whisk, combine the rye flour and the all-purpose flour until thoroughly mixed.

3. In a large bowl, with an electric mixer at medium-high speed, beat the butter and brown sugar until creamy, 3 to 5 minutes. Add the flour mixture, about ½ cup at a time, beating after each addition just until blended. Gather the dough into a ball and divide it in half. Wrap each half in plastic wrap and refrigerate until slightly chilled, about 30 minutes. (At this point, the dough can be tightly wrapped in aluminum foil and refrigerated for up to one week or frozen for up to three months. If frozen, thaw in the refrigerator before proceeding.)

4. On a lightly floured surface, roll half of the dough to a ¼-inch thickness. Cut the dough into as many rounds as possible. Arrange the rounds on a prepared baking sheet, spacing them about 1 inch apart. Gather the scraps of dough together and reroll once or twice. Repeat with the remaining dough.

5. Bake for about 15 minutes until the cookies are lightly browned. Reverse the baking sheet from front to back once during baking. With a wide turner, immediately transfer the cookies to wire racks to cool completely.

6. Store in a tightly covered container.

Yield: About 40 cookies

Shrewsbury Cakes

Given the name, it would be safe to speculate that this crisp spice cookie probably originated in England. The dough is easy to work and requires no chilling before the cookies are cut, always a big plus if you are in a hurry. If you want larger cookies, use a 2½-inch cookie cutter, which will yield about 50 cookies.

2 cups all-purpose flour
½ cup sugar
½ teaspoon baking powder
½ teaspoon ground cinnamon
¼ teaspoon ground nutmeg
½ cup (1 stick) salted butter or margarine, at room temperature
1 large egg, lightly beaten
1 ½ teaspoons vanilla extract

1. Adjust two racks to divide the oven into thirds. Preheat the oven to 350°. Have ready two ungreased baking sheets. Also have ready a 1½-inch round biscuit or cookie cutter.

2. In a large bowl, with a whisk, combine the flour, sugar, baking powder, cinnamon, and nutmeg until thoroughly mixed. With a mixing spoon, stir in the butter until the mixture looks like coarse meal. Stir in the egg and vanilla. With your hands, mix the dough in the bowl until it is soft and pliable. Gather the dough into a ball and divide it in half. (At this point, the dough can be tightly wrapped in aluminum foil and refrigerated for up to one week or frozen for up to three months. If frozen, thaw in the refrigerator and bring to room temperature before proceeding.)

3. On a lightly floured surface, roll half of the dough to a thickness of ⅛ inch. Cut the dough into rounds with the cookie cutter. (Leave the remaining dough in the refrigerator until you are ready to roll it.) Arrange the rounds on the ungreased baking sheets, spacing them about ½ inch apart. Gather the scraps of dough together and reroll once or twice. Repeat with the remaining dough.

4. Bake for about 15 minutes until golden. Reverse the baking sheets on the racks and from front to back once during baking. With a wide turner, immediately transfer the cookies to wire racks to cool completely.

5. Store in a tightly covered container, separating and cushioning the layers with sheets of waxed paper.

Yield: About 108 cookies

English Oat Cakes

Don't let the rather stodgy name of these crumbly cookies put you off. They are *very* British, not too rich-tasting, and a fine accompaniment to an afternoon cup of tea or coffee. (And not bad for breakfast, either, as I once discovered.)

- 1 ¹/₂ cups regular (not quick-cooking or instant) rolled oats
- 1 ¹/₂ cups all-purpose flour
- 3 tablespoons granulated sugar
- 3 tablespoons packed dark brown sugar
- ¹/₂ teaspoon baking soda
- ¹/₂ cup (1 stick) plus 2 tablespoons cold salted butter or margarine, cut into ¹/₂-inch pieces
- 4 to 6 tablespoons ice water

1. In a large bowl, with a whisk, combine the oats, flour, granulated sugar, brown sugar, and baking soda until thoroughly mixed. Drop in the pieces of butter. With your fingertips, rub the dry ingredients and the butter together until the mixture resembles coarse crumbs. Add 4 tablespoons of the ice water all at once and toss the mixture together with your fingers until the ingredients come together and leave the side of the bowl. If the dough is too crumbly to hold together, gradually add up to 2 tablespoons of additional ice water. Gather the dough into a ball and divide it in half. Wrap each half in plastic wrap and refrigerate until cold, about 1 hour. (At this point, the dough can be tightly wrapped in aluminum foil and refrigerated for up to one week or frozen for up to three months. If frozen, thaw in the refrigerator before proceeding.)

2. Adjust two racks to divide the oven into thirds. Preheat the oven to 350°. Lightly grease two baking sheets. Have ready a 2-inch round cookie or biscuit cutter.

3. On a lightly floured surface, roll half of the cold dough to a thickness of about ¹/₈ inch. Cut the dough into as many rounds as possible. Arrange the rounds on the prepared baking sheets, spacing them about 1 inch apart. Gather the scraps of dough together and reroll once or twice. Repeat with the remaining dough.

4. Bake for 15 to 18 minutes until golden brown and firm when lightly touched. Reverse the baking sheets on the racks and from front to back once during baking. With a wide turner, immediately transfer the cookies to wire racks to cool completely.

5. Store in a tightly covered container.

Yield: About 40 cookies

Very Dainty Gingersnaps

The recipe for these bite-size gingersnaps, which first appeared in *The Thanksgiving Cookbook* (Macmillan), makes about 250 cookies. I know that sounds like a heck of a lot of cookies, but don't panic. They are very tiny and very, very easy to make, since the dough is rolled out directly on the baking sheet and the cookies are cut lickety-split with a pizza wheel right after they are baked. By the way, if you wonder about the black pepper in the list of ingredients, that's the spice that gives gingersnaps their characteristic bite. You can reduce the amount or omit it, if you want to.

- 2 cups all-purpose flour
- 2 teaspoons ground ginger
- 1 teaspoon baking soda
- 1 teaspoon salt
- ¹/₂ teaspoon ground allspice
- ¹/₄ to ¹/₂ teaspoon finely ground black pepper, or to taste
- ¹/₂ cup (1 stick) salted butter or margarine, at room temperature
- ¹/₂ cup packed light brown sugar
- ¹/₂ cup unsulphured molasses
- ¹/₄ cup very finely chopped crystallized ginger

1. In a medium-size bowl, with a whisk, combine the flour, ground ginger, baking soda, salt, allspice, and black pepper until thoroughly mixed.

2. In a large bowl, with an electric mixer at medium-high speed, beat together the butter and brown sugar until light and creamy, 2 to 3 minutes. With the mixer at medium speed, beat in the molasses until blended. With the mixer at medium-low speed, gradually add the flour mixture, beating just until blended. With a mixing spoon, stir in the crystallized ginger until well distributed throughout the batter. Gather the dough into a ball and divide it in half. Wrap each half in plastic wrap and refrigerate for 8 hours or overnight. (At this point the dough can be tightly wrapped in aluminum foil and refrigerated for up to one week or frozen for up to three months. Thaw in the refrigerator before proceeding.)

3. Adjust one rack to the upper third position in the oven. Preheat the oven to 350°. Lightly grease two large baking sheets.

4. Directly on one of the baking sheets, roll out half of the chilled dough until it is within about 1 inch of the edges of the baking sheet. With the tines of a dinner fork, prick the dough all over and no more than $1/2$ inch apart. (This is important, since it allows the heat to penetrate the dough and makes the cookies crisp.)

5. Bake for 10 to 12 minutes until firm when lightly touched. Reverse the baking sheet from front to back once during baking.

6. While the first batch of cookies is baking, roll out the second half of the dough on the other baking sheet. Bake the second batch as soon as the first is removed from the oven.

7. Remove the first batch of cookies from the oven and, with a pizza wheel or the tip of a sharp knife, immediately cut the baked dough into small diamond shapes right on the baking sheet. The easiest way to do this is to cut the dough lengthwise into long strips about 1 inch wide; then, starting at one corner, cut into diagonal strips about 1 inch wide (see illustration). With a wide turner, immediately transfer the cookies to wire racks to cool completely. They will become very crisp as they cool.

8. Store in a tightly covered container.

Yield: About 250 cookies

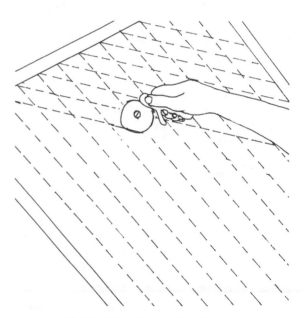

Cutting Very Dainty Gingersnaps

Filled Cookies

Rolled cookie dough can be shaped, twisted, and filled with wonderful things. Shapes can vary enormously, from plain foldovers to cookies that look like ravioli.

The technique of filling cookies is simple, and once you get the hang of it you can vary the fillings as much as you like, as long as they are thick and stable so they won't leak through the dough as they bake.

Prune-Filled Pinwheels

Pinwheel cookies look complicated, but they are merely squares of dough with the corners folded over the filling, and very simple to do. The prune filling in these cookies is delicious, although thick apricot, strawberry, or raspberry preserves could be used instead.

2 3/4 cups all-purpose flour
1/2 teaspoon baking soda
1 cup (2 sticks) salted butter or margarine, at room temperature
3/4 cup sugar
1 large egg
1 large egg yolk
1/2 teaspoon shredded and minced orange zest
1/2 cup plus 1 1/2 tablespoons prune filling (about half of a 12-ounce can)
1/4 teaspoon shredded and minced lemon zest
2 tablespoons chopped walnuts and colored nonpareils, for decoration

1. In a medium-size bowl, with a whisk, combine the flour with the baking soda until thoroughly mixed.

2. In a large bowl, with an electric mixer at medium-high speed, beat together the butter and the sugar until well blended, 2 to 3 minutes. Beat in the egg, egg yolk, and orange zest until blended.

3. Gradually add the flour mixture, beating on low speed or stirring in by hand, just until the flour is incorporated. Gather the dough into a ball and divide it in half. Wrap each half in plastic wrap and refrigerate until very cold, about 2 hours. (At this point, the dough can be tightly wrapped in aluminum foil and refrigerated for up to one week or frozen for up to three months; if frozen, thaw in the refrigerator before proceeding.)

4. Roll half of the dough between two sheets of waxed paper into a 1/4-inch-thick rectangle. Slide an ungreased baking sheet under the dough and refrigerate until firm, about 20 minutes. Repeat with the second half of the dough.

5. While the dough is chilling, in a small bowl with a mixing spoon, combine the prune filling and lemon zest; set aside.

6. Adjust two racks to divide oven into thirds. Preheat the oven to 375°. Lightly grease two baking sheets.

7. Slide one portion of the chilled dough onto a work surface. Peel off the top sheet of waxed paper; replace loosely. Turn the dough over; peel off and discard the second sheet of waxed paper. Using a fluted pastry wheel or a sharp knife and a ruler, cut the dough into 2 1/2-inch squares. With scissors, make a 1-inch cut in each square from each corner toward the center. After the corners are cut, place each square on a baking sheet, spacing them about 1 inch apart.

8. Spoon about 3/4 teaspoon of the prune filling in the center of each square. Lift up two diagonal corners of the square and fold them into the center. Repeat this procedure with the remaining two corners, pinching and pressing lightly to hold in place. Repeat with the remaining squares.

9. Reroll any dough scraps between sheets of waxed paper. Refrigerate until firm.

10. Bake for 7 to 10 minutes, or until lightly colored on top and golden brown around the edges, reversing the baking sheets on the racks and from front to back once during baking. Let

stand 2 minutes on the baking sheets set on wire racks. With a wide turner, transfer the cookies to wire racks to cool completely.

11. Repeat steps 7 and 8. Repeat steps 6, 7, and 8 with the remaining half of dough.

12. Store in a tightly covered container, separating the layers with sheets of waxed paper.

Yield: About 30 cookies

Windmills

These are very beautiful cookies, and will be especially so if you use a fluted pastry wheel to cut them.

> 2 $^3/_4$ cups all-purpose flour
> $^1/_4$ teaspoon baking soda
> $^1/_4$ teaspoon salt
> 1 cup (2 sticks) butter-flavored shortening
> $^2/_3$ cup sugar
> 1 large egg, lightly beaten
> About $^3/_4$ cup apricot, strawberry, or seedless raspberry preserves
> Confectioners' sugar, for dusting cookies

1. Adjust two racks to divide the oven into thirds. Have ready two ungreased baking sheets. Lightly grease two other baking sheets.

1. In a medium-size bowl, with a whisk, combine the flour, baking soda, and salt until thoroughly mixed.

2. In a large bowl, with an electric mixer at medium-high speed, beat together the shortening and sugar until light and creamy, 2 to 3 minutes. Beat in the egg until well blended. With the mixer at medium-low speed, gradually add the flour mixture, beating just until blended. Gather the dough into a ball and divide it in half.

3. On a very lightly floured surface, pat each half of the dough into a thick rectangle. Dust one rectangle with flour and place it between two sheets of waxed paper. Roll out to a 12 × 8-inch rectangle

that is about $^1/_8$ inch thick. Slide an ungreased baking sheet beneath the waxed-paper–encased rectangle and refrigerate for 20 minutes. Repeat with the remaining half of the dough.

4. Preheat the oven to 375°.

5. Place one of the chilled rectangles on a work surface. (Leave the other half of the dough in the refrigerator until you are ready to work with it.) Peel off the top sheet of waxed paper. With a fluted pastry wheel or the tip of a sharp knife and a ruler, cut the rectangle into 2$^1/_2$-inch squares. With a wide turner, transfer the squares to the prepared baking sheets, spacing them about 2 inches apart. With the pastry wheel or knife, cut four 1-inch slits in each square, starting at the corners and going in toward the center. Drop 1 measuring teaspoonful of the jam in the center of each square. Lift one corner of one square and bring the edge to the center, twisting it slightly. Do the same with the remaining three corners. Repeat this procedure with the remaining squares.

6. Bake for 7 to 10 minutes until the edges are golden brown. Reverse the baking sheets on the racks and from front to back once during baking. Cool for 2 minutes on the baking sheet. With a wide turner, transfer the cookies to wire racks to cool completely.

7. Repeat with the remaining half of the dough.

8. Store in a tightly covered container, separating the layers with sheets of waxed paper. Before serving, sprinkle very lightly with confectioners' sugar if desired.

Yield: About 36 cookies

 **Tip**

For fewer scraps and less rerolling, start cutting out cookie shapes from around the edge of the dough and work in toward the center.

Fruit-and-Nut-Filled Ravioli Cookies

When I got the bright idea to include ravioli cookies, I turned the development project over to Annie Bailey, who does this sort of thing so well. She did not disappoint me. These cookies are great!

Dough

2 cups all-purpose flour

1 1/2 teaspoons baking powder

2/3 cup (1 stick plus 3 tablespoons) salted butter or margarine, at room temperature

2/3 cup sugar

1 large egg

1/2 teaspoon vanilla extract

2 tablespoons milk

1 large egg, lightly beaten, for brushing on dough

Filling

1/3 cup chopped raisins

3 tablespoons strained fresh orange juice

2 tablespoons sugar

1 teaspoon all-purpose flour

1/8 teaspoon ground cinnamon

3 tablespoons finely chopped walnuts

1. Adjust two racks to divide the oven into thirds. Have ready two ungreased baking sheets.

2. In a medium-size bowl, with a whisk, combine the flour and baking powder.

3. In a large bowl, with an electric mixer at medium-high speed, beat together the butter and sugar until light and fluffy, 2 to 3 minutes. Beat in the egg and vanilla until light and fluffy, 2 to 3 minutes. With the mixer at medium-low speed, gradually add the flour mixture alternately with the milk, beating just until blended. Gather the dough into a ball and divide it in half. Wrap each half in plastic wrap and refrigerate until cold,

about 1 hour. (At this point, the dough can be gathered into a ball and tightly wrapped in aluminum foil and refrigerated for up to one week or frozen for up to three months. If frozen, thaw in the refrigerator before proceeding.)

4. While the dough is chilling, make the filling. In a small saucepan, combine the raisins, orange juice, sugar, flour, and cinnamon. Cook over medium-low heat, stirring constantly for about 2 minutes until the mixture comes to a boil. Remove from the heat and stir in the walnuts. Set aside to cool.

5. Preheat the oven to 350°.

6. Divide the dough in half. On a lightly floured surface, roll half of the dough into a rectangle measuring 11 × 9 inches. Trim the edges straight with a pastry wheel or the tip of a sharp knife and a ruler. Drop 30 measuring 1/2 teaspoonfuls of the filling mixture on the dough, spacing the drops 3/4 inch apart, making 5 rows across and 6 rows down. Brush the dough around the mounds of filling with the beaten egg.

7. Roll out the remaining half of the dough into a 12 × 10-inch rectangle. Trim the edges straight as before. Roll this dough up carefully on the rolling pin to lift it. Unroll the dough over the dough that is covered with the mounds of filling. With your fingers, press down gently around each mound of filling to seal the two doughs. With a fluted pastry wheel or the tip of a sharp knife, cut between the rows to make ravioli-shaped cookies. With a wide turner, carefully transfer the cookies to the ungreased baking sheets, spacing them about 1 inch apart.

8. Bake for 12 to 15 minutes until the edges are golden. Reverse the baking sheets on the racks and from front to back once during baking. With a wide turner, immediately transfer the cookies to wire racks to cool completely.

9. Store in a tightly covered container. Dust with confectioners' sugar just before serving, if desired.

Yield: 30 cookies

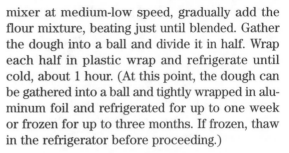

Chocolate Ravioli Cookies with Raspberry Filling

Each little ravioli is a couple of delicious mouthfuls. I like to serve these for dessert with fresh raspberries or sorbet.

   2 ounces (2 squares) semisweet chocolate, broken in half

   2 1/2 cups all-purpose flour

   1/4 teaspoon baking soda

   1 cup (2 sticks) salted butter or margarine, at room temperature

   1/2 cup sugar

   1 large egg, lightly beaten

   1 1/2 teaspoons vanilla extract

   About 1 1/4 cups seedless raspberry preserves

   Confectioners' sugar, for dusting cookies

1. Adjust two racks to divide the oven into thirds. Lightly grease two baking sheets.

2. In a small saucepan set over very low heat, melt the chocolate, stirring constantly until smooth. Remove from the heat and set aside to cool.

3. In a medium-size bowl, with a whisk, combine the flour and baking soda until thoroughly mixed.

4. In a large bowl, with an electric mixer at medium-high speed, beat together the butter and sugar until light and fluffy, 2 to 3 minutes. Beat in the egg and vanilla until well blended. With the mixer at medium-low speed, gradually add the flour mixture, beating just until blended. Gather the dough into a ball and divide it in half. Wrap each half in plastic wrap and refrigerate until cold, about 1 hour. (At this point, the dough can be gathered into a ball and tightly wrapped in aluminum foil and refrigerated for up to one week or frozen for up to three months. If frozen, thaw in the refrigerator before proceeding.)

5. Between two sheets of waxed paper, roll one-half of the dough into a 1/8-inch-thick rectangle. (Leave the remaining half of the dough in the refrigerator until you are ready to work with it. Remove the top sheet of waxed paper. With a pizza wheel or the tip of a sharp knife and a ruler, cut the dough into 1 1/2-inch squares. With a wide turner, transfer half the squares to the prepared baking sheets, spacing them about 2 inches apart. Drop 1/2 measuring teaspoonfuls of preserves in the center of the squares on the baking sheets. Top with a plain square. Seal around the edges with the tines of a dinner fork. Pierce the top of each square once with a wooden toothpick.

6. Bake for about 10 minutes until the edges are browned. Reverse the baking sheets on the racks and from front to back once during baking. With a wide turner, immediately transfer the cookies to wire racks to cool completely.

7. Repeat with the remaining half of the dough.

8. Store in a tightly covered container. Before serving, sprinkle lightly with confectioners' sugar, if desired.

Yield: About 72 cookies

Tip

   The quickest rolled cookies: Roll out the dough and cut into squares or strips with a fluted pastry wheel.

Jam-Filled Oatmeal Rounds

This is a neat little cookie to know about. It's rich and crunchy, and certainly a little different, but easy to make. The trick is to try to get as many rounds as possible out of the dough so it doesn't have to be rerolled. The scraps can be baked separately (for about half the time) after the filled cookies come out of the oven.

> 2 cups all-purpose flour
> 1 teaspoon baking powder
> 1 teaspoon salt
> $^1/_2$ teaspoon baking soda
> 2 $^1/_2$ cups quick-cooking (not regular or instant) rolled oats
> 1 cup (2 sticks) butter-flavored shortening
> 1 $^1/_2$ cups packed light brown sugar
> 2 large eggs, lightly beaten
> 2 teaspoons almond extract
> 1 cup finely chopped pecans
> One 12-ounce jar strawberry jam
> Crystal sugar, for spinkling on cookies

1. Adjust two racks to divide the oven into thirds. Lightly grease two baking sheets. Have ready a 2 $^1/_2$-inch round cookie cutter.

2. In a medium-size bowl, with a whisk, combine the flour, baking powder, salt, and baking soda.

3. In a large bowl, with an electric mixer at medium-high speed, beat together the shortening and brown sugar until creamy, 2 to 3 minutes. Beat in the eggs and almond extract until well blended. With the mixer at medium-low speed, gradually add the flour mixture, beating just until blended. With a mixing spoon, stir in the oats and nuts until well distributed throughout the batter. Gather the dough into a ball and divide it in half. Wrap each half in plastic wrap and refrigerate until cold, about 1 hour. (At this point, the dough can be tightly wrapped in aluminum foil and refrigerated for up to one week or frozen for up to three months. If frozen, thaw in the refrigerator before proceeding.)

4. Preheat the oven to 350°.

5. Divide the dough in half. On a lightly floured surface, roll half of the dough to a $^1/_4$-inch thickness. With the cookie cutter, cut out rounds as close together as possible. (You should have at least 24 rounds. If not, gather up the scraps and roll one more time.) In the center of 12 of the rounds, drop 1 measuring teaspoonful of the jam. Top with the remaining rounds. Seal around the edges with the tines of a dinner fork. Prick the center of each cookie once with the tines of the fork. Sprinkle with crystal sugar. With a wide turner, transfer the rounds to a prepared baking sheet, spacing them about 1 inch apart.

6. Bake for 12 to 15 minutes until lightly browned. Reverse the baking sheets on the racks and from front to back once during baking. Cool the cookies for 2 minutes on the baking sheets. With a wide turner, transfer the cookies to wire racks to cool completely.

7. Repeat this procedure with the remaining half of the dough.

8. Store in a tightly covered container, separating the layers with sheets of waxed paper.

Yield: 24 cookies

Pistachio Miracle Turnovers

The miracle here is that these turnover cookies are incredibly quick and easy to make.

> 1 cup all-purpose flour
> $^1/_2$ cup (1 stick) salted butter or margarine, cut into small pieces and then softened to room temperature
> 4 tablespoons sugar, divided
> $^1/_2$ cup whole pistachios
> $^1/_2$ cup golden raisins
> $^1/_4$ cup strained, fresh orange juice
> 2 teaspoons finely shredded and minced orange zest
> 1 large egg yolk, lightly beaten
> About 1 tablespoon very finely chopped pistachios, for sprinkling on cookies

1. Adjust two racks to divide the oven into thirds. Preheat the oven to 350°. Lightly grease two baking sheets; set aside. Have ready a 3-inch scalloped or plain cookie cutter.

2. In a large bowl, place the flour, butter, and 3 tablespoons of the sugar. With an electric mixer at medium speed, beat just until well blended. Gather the dough into a ball in the bowl and set aside.

3. Place the whole pistachios and raisins in a food processor fitted with a steel blade. Process until ground, turning off the processor once and giving the mixture a good stir from the bottom. Add the orange juice, orange zest, and the remaining tablespoon of sugar and process until well mixed.

4. On a lightly floured surface, roll the dough to a ¹/₈-inch thickness. Cut into as many rounds as possible. Spoon 2 teaspoons of the pistachio mixture onto one half of each round. Fold the other half of the rounds over the filling to make turnovers. (The dough may crack slightly.) With your fingertips, gently press down on the edges to seal. Place the turnovers on the prepared baking sheets, spacing them about 1 inch apart. (If there is any filling left, reroll the scraps and make as many more turnovers as possible.) With a pastry brush, brush each turnover with the egg yolk. Sprinkle with the finely chopped pistachios.

5. Bake for 15 minutes until lightly browned on the bottoms. Reverse the baking sheets on the racks and from front to back once during baking. With a wide turner, immediately transfer the turnovers to wire racks to cool completely.

6. Store in a tightly covered container, separating the layers with sheets of waxed paper.

Yield: About 18 turnovers

Sparklers

The cream cheese makes this dough very easy to work with and the cookies themselves are so simple to form that you might want to invite the kids to help make them.

1 ¹/₄ cups all-purpose flour

¹/₂ cup (1 stick) salted butter or margarine, at room temperature

One 3-ounce package cream cheese, at room temperature

1 ¹/₂ teaspoons finely shredded and minced orange zest

³/₄ cup multicolored milk chocolate candies (such as M&Ms), plus 16 additional candies for decoration

3 tablespoons raspberry preserves

Crystal sugar, for decoration

1. In a medium-size bowl, with a mixing spoon, stir together the flour, butter, cream cheese, and orange zest. Knead the mixture, right in the bowl, until smooth. Lightly cover the bowl and refrigerate until firm, about 1 hour.

2. While the dough is chilling, place ³/₄ cup of the candies in a large plastic bag and crush them with a rolling pin.

3. Adjust one rack to divide the oven in half. Preheat the oven to 350°. Lightly grease one large baking sheet.

4. On a lightly floured surface, roll the dough into a 12-inch square, trimming the edges with a knife and ruler to make them straight. Cut the dough into sixteen 3-inch squares, separating them slightly. Spread the center of each square with about ¹/₂ teaspoon of the jam, then sprinkle with about 1¹/₂ teaspoons of the crushed candy. Bring the corners of each square to the center. Press one whole candy in the center of each square to seal. Sprinkle with sugar. With a wide turner, arrange the squares on the prepared baking sheet.

6. Bake for 12 minutes until lightly browned. Reverse the baking sheet from front to back once during baking. With a wide turner, immediately transfer the squares to wire racks to cool completely.

7. Store in a tightly covered, shallow container, separating and cushioning the layers with sheets of waxed paper.

Yield: 16 cookies

Molded Cookies

Cookie molds, into which the dough is pressed before baking, produce a raised relief on the cookies. The art of molding cookies has been practiced for centuries.

Old cookie molds, which can have relatively simple or very intricate designs carved into them, were made out of wood. Now and then you may come across a couple of these old molds, but they are real collectors' items. Cookie molds these days are usually made out of ceramic.

To make molded cookies, you must use *a smooth, firm, rolled-cookie or refrigerator-cookie dough*. The dough must be well chilled before it is molded. Before using, the molds should be lightly coated with oil and then dusted with flour. Tap out the excess flour. Oiling the mold between cookies is usually not necessary, but re-flouring is.

Press a small amount of cold dough into the mold, making sure that it is well down into the pattern. Fill the mold with dough until it is even with the top of the mold. Turn the mold over and rap the edge several times on a block of wood or a wooden cutting board. After several raps, the cookie should fall out. Arrange the molded cookies on baking sheets and bake as the recipe you are using directs, although these cookies are usually thicker than most rolled or sliced cookies and may require a lower temperature and/or a longer baking time.

All of the makers of cookie molds that I know of *provide recipes that have been specially developed to work with the molds.* Look for cookie molds in well-stocked kitchenware stores. Cookie molds can also be ordered by mail and come with recipes to use with them. (See Appendix C, "Shopping and Mail-Order Sources.")

Chocolate-Filled Walnut Cookies

Of course, you don't *have* to sandwich these cookies with this soft, buttery, chocolatey filling, but I urge you to do it. They are, however, marvelous just plain, or drizzled with melted chocolate.

1 cup (about 4 ounces) shelled walnuts
1 1/2 cups all-purpose flour
1/4 teaspoon salt
3/4 cup (1 1/2 sticks) salted butter or margarine, at room temperature
1 large egg yolk
1 teaspoon vanilla extract
2/3 cup confectioners' sugar

Filling

1/2 cup (1 stick) cold butter, cut into several pieces
1/2 cup (3 ounces) semisweet chocolate chips
2 large eggs, well beaten
1/2 cup confectioners' sugar
1/2 teaspoon vanilla extract

1. Place the nuts in a food processor fitted with a steel blade and process until finely ground, turning the processor off once and giving the nuts a good stir from the bottom to keep them from becoming pasty.

2. In a medium-size bowl, with a whisk, combine the flour, ground walnuts, and salt until thoroughly mixed; set aside.

3. In a large bowl, with an electric mixer at medium-high speed, beat the butter until creamy, about 1 minute. Beat in the egg yolk, vanilla, and confectioners' sugar until well blended. With the mixer at medium-low speed, add the flour mixture, about 1/4 cup at a time, beating after each addition. Gather the dough into a ball. Divide the dough into quarters. Wrap each quarter in plastic wrap and refrigerate until very cold, at least 1 hour. (At this point, the dough can be tightly wrapped in aluminum foil and refrigerated for up to one week or frozen for up to three months. If frozen, thaw in the refrigerator before proceeding.)

4. Adjust one oven rack to divide the oven in half. Preheat the oven to 400°. Have ready two un-greased baking sheets. Also have ready a 1½-inch round cookie or biscuit cutter.

5. On a lightly floured surface, roll one-quarter of the dough to a ¼-inch thickness. (Leave the remaining dough in the refrigerator until you are ready to roll it.) Cut the dough into as many rounds as possible. Arrange the rounds on a baking sheet, spacing them about 1 inch apart. Gather the scraps of dough together and reroll once. Repeat with the remaining dough.

6. Bake one sheet at a time for 5 to 7 minutes until pale brown. Reverse the baking pan from front to back once during baking. With a wide turner, immediately transfer the cookies to wire racks to cool completely.

7. Make the filling: In a small, heavy saucepan, place the butter and chocolate. Cook over very low heat, stirring constantly until smooth. Remove from the heat and set aside to cool slightly. Beat in the eggs, confectioners' sugar, and vanilla until well blended. Return the pan to low heat and cook, stirring constantly, until thickened, 3 to 4 minutes. Set aside to cool.

8. With a small icing spatula or butter spreader, spread the bottoms of half of the cooled cookies with the chocolate filling. Sandwich together with the remaining halves, top sides up. If there is any chocolate filling left over, it can be drizzled off the tip of a spoon onto the tops of the cookies.

9. Store in a shallow, tightly covered container, separating the layers with sheets of waxed paper.

Yield: About 60 filled cookies

Tip

Rolling and cutting out cookies can very often be done right on the baking sheet, especially if the shapes are fairly simple. Lift the scraps off the baking sheets from around the cutouts.

COMPLETE GINGERBREAD HOUSE

Complete Gingerbread House

Gingerbread House Dough

1 cup (2 sticks) butter-flavored or plain
shortening

1 cup sugar

1 ¹/₂ cups regular or unsulphured molasses

6 cups all-purpose flour

1 ¹/₄ teaspoons salt

1 teaspoon baking soda

1 tablespoon ground ginger

1 tablespoon ground cinnamon

1 teaspoon ground nutmeg

1 teaspoon ground cloves

2 eggs, lightly beaten

Making the Dough

1. In a medium-size saucepan, combine the shortening, sugar, and molasses. Cook over medium-low heat, stirring constantly, just until the shortening is melted. Remove the pan from the heat and set aside to cool for 5 minutes.

2. In a large bowl, with a whisk, combine the flour, salt, baking soda, ginger, cinnamon, nutmeg, and cloves until thoroughly mixed.

3. With an electric mixer at low speed, beat the eggs and the slightly cooled shortening mixture into the flour mixture just until blended. (The batter will look like a thick syrup, but will become firm as it cools.) Pour the batter into a 13 × 9-inch metal baking pan or glass baking dish. Cover with plastic wrap and refrigerate until very firm, at least 4 hours.

Cutting and Baking

1. Enlarge the pattern pieces on sheets of sturdy paper, using the dimensions given on the diagrams. Cut out the patterns with scissors or a craft knife.

2. Preheat the oven to 375°. Adjust one rack to divide the oven in half. Lightly flour three large baking sheets.

3. With the tip of a sharp knife, cut the dough in the baking pan crosswise into three equal sections.

COMPLETE GINGERBREAD HOUSE

4. Remove one of the sections of dough and place it in the center on one of the prepared baking sheets. Lightly sprinkle the dough with flour. With a lightly floured rolling pin, roll the dough, on the baking sheet, to a ¼-inch thickness. Repeat this procedure two more times with the remaining thirds of the dough. If you can possibly make room for them in the refrigerator, keep the pans of rolled dough chilled until you are ready to work with them.

5. Working with one pan of dough at a time, place the pattern pieces directly on the rolled dough, spacing them about 1 inch apart, and keeping similar sizes together on separate sheets, since baking times will differ between large and small cutouts. Hold the pattern pieces down lightly on the dough, if necessary, and cut around each piece with the tip of a sharp knife.

6. Cut out one door and three windows from one of the two pieces of dough that will be the front of the house. (Or you may want to simply cut out little square or rectangular windows.)

7. Remove the strips of dough from around the patterns. Any remaining pieces of dough can be used to cut out front steps, shutters, walkway, etc.

8. Bake the large pieces of gingerbread for 10 to 12 minutes until firm. Bake smaller pieces for 6 to 8 minutes until firm. Reverse the baking sheet from front to back once during baking.

9. Immediately after baking, very carefully loosen the gingerbread pieces with a wide turner so they won't stick as they start to cool. *While the gingerbread is still warm and still on the baking sheet*, replace the pattern pieces on the gingerbread pieces and trim with the knife to *exactly match* the pattern. (Eat the scraps immediately with plenty of hot coffee!) Cool on the baking sheets for 10 minutes. Carefully transfer the pieces to wire racks and set them aside to dry for 24 hours.

Decorating and Assembling

Here is what you will need to decorate and construct the gingerbread house:

- Small and large icing spatulas
- Three pieces of corrugated cardboard, each measuring about 14 × 12 inches
- Masking tape
- Heavy-duty aluminum foil

Gingerbread House

We have the Grimm Brothers and their tale of Hansel and Gretel to thank for inspiring German bakers of many years ago to re-create the infamous witch's cookie-and-candy cottage. Over the years, making edible—or pseudo edible—witch cottages has become a holiday project that almost everyone has tried at least once: the Gingerbread House.

Gingerbread houses can be as simple or as complex and fanciful as the imagination and the artistic talent of the baker permits. Some of these houses actually end up being eaten, but most just sit around to be admired—sometimes year after year—until they eventually disintegrate.

For this gingerbread house and the very complete directions to make it, we have Annie Bailey and her girls, Megan and Mary Kate, to thank. The Baileys ended up building the house in February, when, according to Annie, it was much more appreciated than it would have been during the busy Christmas season. Annie says they now have plans to make an Easter gingerbread house. (I can see it now: tiny yellow dandelions popping up through green royal-icing grass, Lilliputian eggs hidden beneath the bushes, and a marshmallow bunny peeking around the corner of the house, which has since lost its snowy eaves. How wonderful it must be for Megan and Mary Kate to have such a neat mom.)

COMPLETE GINGERBREAD HOUSE

Tips for Beginners

If your first gingerbread house is a dismal failure, the chances are you will never make another. And that would be too bad, because a gingerbread house, when all goes reasonably well, is lots of fun to make.

- Read through the instructions carefully before you begin, sort of making the house in your mind first.
- Make up a batch of test dough and icing and practice the various procedures to familiarize yourself with the techniques before you start building the real house.
- Don't be too ambitious. Use ready-made patterns, or even a gingerbread-house mold, which is sold in a kit. Later on you can draw your own plans.
- Do not attempt to build a gingerbread house during humid weather. The gingerbread will not dry out properly and may very well crack. Royal icing will not perform well, either.
- Allow plenty of time. This is not a one-day endeavor. It is more like a week-long project to which you can keep coming back as time permits. A good idea is to set up the house-in-progress on a card table so that it can be moved out of the way into a quiet corner when you are not working on it.
- Enlist the aid of a helper, especially when you are setting up walls and roofs. An extra pair of hands is extremely useful at this point.
- If the house is for display only, spray it with shellac, which will help to keep it in good condition. A gingerbread house treated this way can be packed carefully in a box and saved from year to year.

- Pastry (decorating) bag
- Writing tip with a ⅛-inch opening
- Star or other tips with small openings
- Royal Icing (recipe follows) to use for decorating, gluing, and attaching details
- An assortment of candies and other small decorations, such as bite-size shredded wheat for a thatched roof

Tape the pieces of cardboard together securely to use as a sturdy base for the house. Cover the cardboard with foil; set aside.

Royal Icing

Make the royal icing shortly before you plan to use it. This icing dries out quickly. Keep it covered with a damp towel, pushed down into the bowl close to the icing, at all times. You will have to make new batches of the icing as you proceed through the building of the house. Do not try to save and use leftovers.

> **3 large egg whites, at room temperature**
> **½ teaspoon cream of tartar**
> **One 16-ounce box confectioners' sugar**

1. In a medium-size bowl, with an electric mixer at low speed, beat together the egg whites and cream of tartar until frothy. Gradually add the confectioners' sugar until blended. Beat at medium-high speed until the mixture becomes very stiff.

2. It is much easier to pipe the details on each piece of the house while it is laying flat on a work surface. (Small details can be glued on with the royal icing after the house has been constructed.) Fit a pastry bag with the appropriate tip. Fill the bag about two-thirds full of icing. (See page 30 for information about how to use a pastry bag.) Start

COMPLETE GINGERBREAD HOUSE

by decorating the corners of the house, roof lines, eaves, chimney, and around the doors and windows. After decorating, allow the icing time to dry completely, preferably overnight, before continuing.

3. To construct the house, ice the bottom edges and sides of the wall pieces. Set up front, back, and side walls together on the base. Hold each piece in place for a few minutes to give the icing a chance to set. Use small food cans set in strategic positions for support while the icing dries. (Curtains, if you are using them, should be glued behind the windows at this point.)

4. Pipe icing along the peaks, top edges of walls and the three unscalloped sides of each roof piece. Position one side of the roof so that it meets the house peaks and side wall. Hold this half in place and attach the other side of the roof. Adjust so that each side and the roof ridge meets evenly. Hold the roof in place for several minutes to give the icing a chance to set. Allow the roof to dry for at least two hours before continuing.

5. Attach the scalloped eave pieces to the front and back of the roof, holding them in place until the icing sets. Allow the eaves to dry for at least two hours before continuing.

6. With icing, secure the front and back of the chimney to the roof, holding them in place for a few minutes until the icing sets. Carefully attach the side pieces of the chimney the same way. Attach the door, slightly ajar, on one side of the door jamb. Attach front steps and shutters, if you are using them.

7. Now is the time to add the little details, using dabs of the icing to attach them.

8. Use swirls of icing on the base around the house to create a snowy front yard.

9. Glue a fluff of absorbent cotton to a toothpick and insert in the chimney for smoke.

Decorating Ideas

Start assembling little candies and other "findings" well before they are needed. Stop in a candy store and have a look around. Great house-decorating ideas are sure to pop into your head.

Roof: (If the roof is to be elaborately decorated, do this before it is assembled.) For roof tiles, use such goodies as overlapping, wafer candies (such as Necco's), nonpareils, sliced natural almonds, pretzel nuggets or sticks, tiny wafer cookies, or bite-sized shredded wheat biscuits. You can also make a snow-covered roof with royal icing, pulling it up with a spatula to make little drifts of snow. While the icing is still wet, sprinkle it with plain crystal sugar for a sparkling effect.

Curtains and windows: Use sticks of striped chewing gum or pieces of fruit rolls. Tiny pretzels, dipped in icing, make wonderful lace curtains. A short, birthday-size candle in every window is a nice touch. The candles can even be lit for a cheery glow on Christmas Eve, and can be replaced as often as you like.

Bushes and evergreens: Glue together clusters of green, sugar-coated gumdrops. Mound the icing into low bushes and sprinkle them with green sugar or green sprinkles.

Walkways and paths: Use tiny candies, such as cinnamon red-hots or little jelly beans, to pave a brick sidewalk.

Fences: Tiny candy canes or pretzel sticks make great fences. Pretzel sticks can also be stacked into a wood pile beside the house.

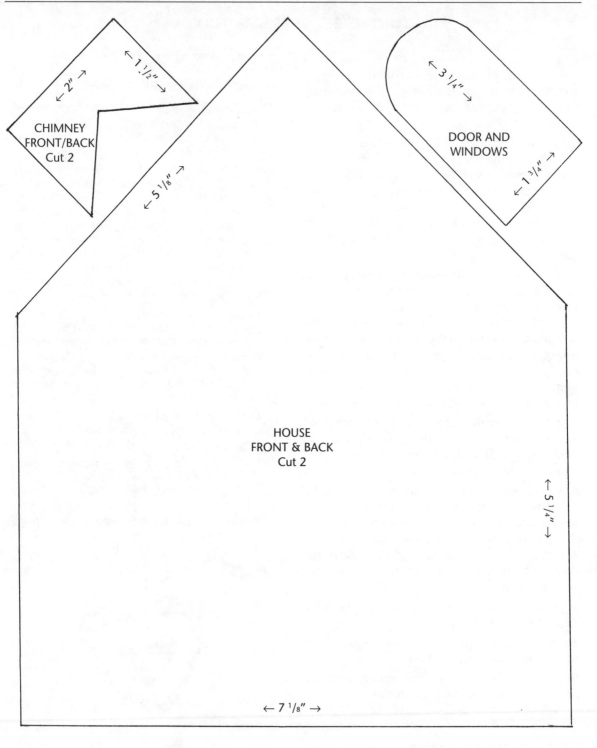

CHIMNEY
FRONT/BACK
Cut 2

← 2″ →

← 1.½″ →

← 5 ⅛″ →

DOOR AND
WINDOWS

← 3 ¼″ →

← 1 ¾″ →

HOUSE
FRONT & BACK
Cut 2

← 5 ¼″ →

← 7 ⅛″ →

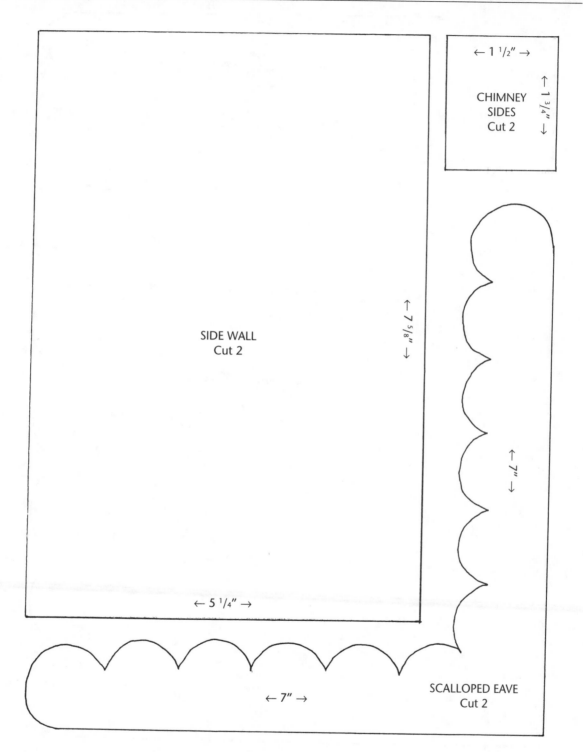

← 1 ¹/₂″ →

CHIMNEY
SIDES
Cut 2

← 1 ³/₄″ →

SIDE WALL
Cut 2

← 7 ⁵/₈″ →

← 7″ →

← 5 ¹/₄″ →

← 7″ →

SCALLOPED EAVE
Cut 2

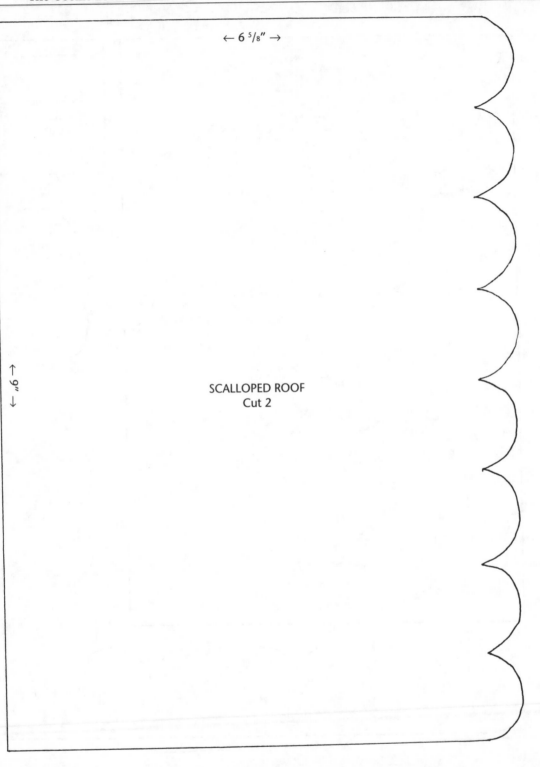

← 6 ⁵/₈″ →

↑ 9″ ↓

SCALLOPED ROOF
Cut 2

8
Icebox Cookies

After all these years, one would think that *icebox* cookies would be called *refrigerator* cookies. Occasionally they are, and sometimes they're called *sliced* cookies, but, for the most part, the old name sticks. Actually, I think the old-fashioned reference is rather endearing.

How miraculous it must have seemed to home bakers when they discovered that, thanks to the newly invented icebox, they could mix up a batch of cookie dough one day and then store it away to bake a day or two or three afterward.

THE ICEMAN COMETH

Not long ago, a young friend asked me exactly what an icebox was and how it worked. I would have liked to have told her that I am not *nearly* old enough to remember, but, in fact, I do vividly remember an icebox in action. My Aunt Dorothea hung on to hers until the late forties when the iceman's horse passed away.

The original iceboxes were made out of wood (usually golden oak, which makes them prized possessions these days, although I'm not exactly sure why, especially if you have ever gotten a whiff of the inside of one). The icebox had two insulated compartments lined in galvanized tin. In the top, perishables were stored. The bottom compartment held a gigantic piece of ice that could last for several days. Beneath the ice compartment was a drip tray that had to be tended carefully, another way of saying that it had to be emptied fairly often, especially in warm weather.

I suppose the old icebox did have a smidgen of charm, but not necessarily when the drip tray runneth over onto the kitchen floor.

SHAPING DOUGH FOR SLICING AND BAKING

The term *icebox cookie* means that the dough, or doughs, have been rolled into a cylinder, chilled until firm, then sliced and baked.

The obvious advantage to icebox cookies is that they are there when you want them. Refrigerated cookie doughs keep for up to a week, but I wouldn't recommend pushing it much beyond that, nor is there any reason to, since frozen cookie dough can be sliced almost as easily as cold dough. You can slice off as many cookies as you want, then return the remainder to the freezer.

Another plus for icebox cookies is that you don't need any special equipment to make them. Aside from the usual (bowls, baking sheets, and a mixer) you will *absolutely* need a long, sharp knife and plastic wrap, waxed paper, and aluminum foil.

Many icebox-cookie doughs can very easily be turned into rolled-cookie doughs and vice versa. After mixing the icebox-cookie dough and chilling it, the dough will, in most cases, be just as ready to roll out into a thin sheet that can be cut into shapes with cookie cutters.

Basic Vanilla Icebox Cookies

For families who love cookies, this is an excellent icebox-cookie dough to keep on hand in the refrigerator or freezer. The dough lends itself to a number of easy variations, which follow, and the cookies themselves are particularly fast to make, since the dough can be formed into cylinders right after it is mixed and needs to be chilled only once.

The baked cookies can be left plain, drizzled with or partially dipped into melted chocolate, or they can be sandwiched together with a filling (pages 32–34). If the cookies will be filled and sandwiched, cut the cylinders into 1/8-inch slices so that the sandwiched cookies won't be such a big mouthful. Also, if the baking time is calculated for 1/4-inch slices, it will have to be reduced by a couple of minutes.

3 cups all-purpose flour

1/2 teaspoon baking soda

1/4 teaspoon salt

1/2 cup (1 stick) salted butter or margarine, at room temperature

1/2 cup (1 stick) plain or butter-flavored shortening

1 cup sugar

1 large egg

2 tablespoons milk

1 teaspoon vanilla extract

1. In a medium-size bowl, with a whisk, combine the flour, baking soda, and salt until thoroughly mixed.

2. In a large bowl, with an electric mixer at medium-high speed, beat together the butter, shortening, and sugar until creamy, 2 to 3 minutes. Add the egg, milk, and vanilla and beat until very well blended. With the mixer at medium-low speed, gradually add the flour mixture, beating just until blended. Gather the dough into a ball and divide it in half.

3. On a very lightly floured surface, with your hands, roll and shape each dough half into an 8-inch cylinder. Wrap each cylinder in plastic wrap and refrigerate until very firm, about 4 hours. (At this point the dough can be tightly wrapped in aluminum foil and refrigerated for up to one week or frozen for up to three months.)

4. When ready to bake, adjust two racks to divide the oven into thirds. Preheat the oven to 375°. Have ready two ungreased baking sheets.

5. With a long, sharp knife, cut each cylinder into 1/4-inch slices. Arrange the slices on the ungreased baking sheets, spacing them about 2 inches apart.

6. Bake for 8 to 10 minutes until the edges are firm and the bottoms are lightly browned. Reverse the baking sheets on the racks and from front to back once during baking. With a wide turner, immediately transfer the cookies to wire racks to cool completely.

7. Store in a tightly covered container.

Yield: About 60 cookies

Variations

Spicy Icebox Cookies: Add 1 teaspoon ground cinnamon and 1/2 teaspoon ground nutmeg to the flour mixture.

Cardamom Cookies: Add 1 tablespoon ground cardamom to the flour mixture.

Caraway Cookies: Just before baking, sprinkle each cookie with a few caraway seeds.

Tips for Baking Icebox Cookies

- Read through the recipe before you begin to be sure that you understand the procedure and have all the ingredients and equipment you will need on hand.

- Most icebox-cookie doughs are not particularly sticky, but if some sticking should occur, the dough can always be rolled into cylinders on very lightly floured waxed paper.

- To keep the dough cylinders from forming a flat side, take them out of the refrigerator and roll them on a hard surface a couple of times while they are chilling.

- Icebox-cookie dough made with vegetable shortening, or a high percentage of shortening, will take about twice as long to become firm than cookie doughs made with butter or margarine.

- Plastic wrap is fine for short-term storage in the refrigerator, but strange flavors can seep into plastic-wrapped foods, even within a couple of days, I've found, and sometimes plastic tears or comes undone. For long-term refrigerator or freezer storage, aluminum foil is a better choice. Waxed paper tends to get soggy and comes undone easily. It is not a good choice for wrapping dough.

- If freezing, wrap the cylinders in aluminum foil *after* they are chilled and firm, so that they don't lose their shape in the wrapping. There is no need to remove the plastic wrap. Just overwrap the cylinder with the foil.

- Frozen dough cylinders do not have to be brought to refrigerator temperature before slicing. Frozen dough slices almost as easily as refrigerated dough and, if baked while the slices are still frozen, the cookies will actually be much crisper.

- It is important to use a long, sharp (and I do mean *sharp*) knife to slice the cylinders. Short, dull knives push the dough out of shape and, at best, you'll end up with lopsided cookies. At worst, filled cookies tend to come apart and the fillings fall out. If, despite your best efforts, the cookie slices do become a bit distorted as they are cut, simply push and press them back into shape with your fingers after transferring the slices to the baking sheet.

- If you want to sandwich two cookies with a filling, cut the slices only half as thick as you would for single cookies (usually $1/8$ inch instead of $1/4$ inch) so that the cookies are not so thick after they are baked and filled.

- It is important to keep icebox-cookie dough cold at all times. Bake two sheets at a time, leaving the dough you are not working with in the refrigerator until you are ready to slice and bake it.

- If the baking sheets are to be used for more than one batch of cookies, make sure they are completely cool and clean before reusing. Sometimes the baking sheets need to be rinsed with hot water, and other times it is enough to wipe them thoroughly with paper towels. If the baking sheet has only been wiped, the second greasing should be very light, and often it is not necessary at all.

Chocolate Icebox Cookies: Reduce the flour to $2\frac{1}{2}$ cups and add $\frac{1}{2}$ cup unsweetened cocoa powder to the flour mixture. Bake for 8 to 10 minutes until the tops look dry.

Orange Icebox Cookies: Omit the milk and vanilla extract. Add 2 tablespoons strained fresh orange juice and 2 tablespoons shredded and minced orange zest at the same time the egg is beaten into the batter.

Lemon Icebox Cookies: Omit the milk and vanilla extract. Add 2 tablespoons strained fresh lemon juice and 1 tablespoon shredded and minced lemon zest at the same time the egg is beaten into the batter.

Peppermint Icebox Cookies: Omit the vanilla extract. Add $\frac{1}{4}$ teaspoon peppermint extract at the same time the milk and egg are beaten into the batter. Add $\frac{1}{4}$ cup finely crushed peppermint candy at the same time the flour is added to the batter.

Date or Fig Cookies: Add about 1 cup minced, pitted dates or dried figs to the flour mixture.

Candied Cherry Slices: Add about 1 cup minced candied cherries or other candied fruit to the flour mixture.

Chocolate-Chip Slices: Substitute 1 cup packed light brown sugar for the granulated sugar. Finely chop 4 squares (4 ounces) semisweet chocolate in a food processor fitted with a steel blade. Stir into the dough after the flour is added.

Very Mocha Icebox Slices

I like to dip the ends of these cookies into two different chocolate glazes. First, dip a about a third of each cookie into Dark Chocolate Glaze (page 32). Set aside on a sheet of waxed paper until the chocolate is firm, about 1 hour. Then, using cool Milk Chocolate Glaze (page 32), rotate the cookie slightly and dip it into the white glaze, so that the two glazes overlap slightly. Set aside on waxed paper until firm, about 1 hour.

- 2 1/2 cups all-purpose flour
- 1/2 cup unsweetened cocoa powder
- 1 teaspoon ground cinnamon
- 1/2 teaspoon baking soda
- 1/4 teaspoon salt
- 1/2 cup (1 stick) salted butter or margarine, at room temperature
- 1/2 cup (1 stick) plain or butter-flavored shortening
- 1 tablespoon freeze-dried coffee granules mixed with 1 teaspoon hot water
- 1 cup sugar
- 1 large egg, lightly beaten
- 2 tablespoons milk
- 1 teaspoon vanilla extract

1. In a medium-size bowl, with a whisk, combine the flour, cocoa powder, cinnamon, baking soda, and salt until thoroughly mixed.

2. In a large bowl, with an electric mixer at medium-high speed, beat together the butter, shortening, coffee, and sugar until light and fluffy, 2 to 3 minutes. Add the egg, milk, and vanilla and beat until well blended. With the mixer at medium-low speed, gradually add the flour mixture, beating just until blended. Gather the dough into a ball.

3. Divide the dough in half. On a very lightly floured surface, with your hands, roll and shape each half into an 8-inch cylinder. Wrap each cylinder in plastic wrap and refrigerate until very firm, about 4 hours. (At this point the dough can be tightly wrapped in aluminum foil and refrigerated for up to one week or frozen for up to three months.)

4. When ready to bake, adjust two racks to divide the oven into thirds. Preheat the oven to 375°. Have ready two ungreased baking sheets.

5. With a long, sharp knife, cut each cylinder into 1/8-inch slices. Arrange the slices on the ungreased baking sheets, spacing them about 2 inches apart. Bake for 7 to 9 minutes until the tops look dry. Reverse the baking sheets on the racks and from front to back once during baking. With a wide turner, immediately transfer the cookies to wire racks to cool completely.

6. Store in a tightly covered container. If the cookies are glazed, separate the layers with sheets of waxed paper.

Yield: About 60 cookies

Citus Slices

. . . .

These are thick for icebox cookies, but have a wonderful texture and flavor. The glaze is important, so don't skip it. A Chocolate Glaze (page 32) would also be tasty with these cookies.

- ^{1}/$_2$ cup (1 stick) plus 2 tablespoons salted butter or margarine, at room temperature
- ^{1}/$_4$ cup confectioners' sugar
- ^{1}/$_4$ cup strained fresh lemon juice
- 1 ^{1}/$_2$ cups cake flour (not self-rising flour)
- ^{1}/$_4$ cup (about 4 ounces) minced candied orange peel

Orange Glaze
. . . .

- 1 cup confectioners' sugar
- 2 to 3 tablespoons strained fresh orange juice, at room temperature or slightly warm

1. In a medium-size bowl, with an electric mixer at medium-high speed, beat together the butter and sugar until light and fluffy, 2 to 3 minutes. Beat in the lemon juice until well blended. With the mixer at medium-low speed, gradually add the flour, beating just until blended. With a mixing spoon, stir in the orange peel until well distributed throughout the dough. Lightly cover the bowl and refrigerate until the dough is firm enough to handle, 1 to 2 hours. (The dough will still be slightly sticky.)

2. On a lightly floured surface, divide the dough in half. With lightly floured hands, roll and shape each half into a 14-inch cylinder. Wrap each cylinder separately in plastic wrap and refrigerate until firm, about 4 hours. (At this point the dough can be tightly wrapped in aluminum foil and refrigerated for up to one week or frozen for up to three months.)

3. When ready to bake, adjust two racks to divide the oven into thirds. Preheat the oven to 325°. Have ready two ungreased baking sheets.

4. With a long, sharp knife, cut the cylinders into ^{3}/$_4$-inch slices. Arrange the slices on the ungreased baking sheets, spacing them about 1^1/$_2$ inches apart.

5. Bake for about 15 minutes until just beginning to brown. Reverse the baking sheets on the racks and from front to back once during baking. Cool on the pan for 3 or 4 minutes. With a wide turner, transfer the cookies to wire racks to cool completely.

6. While the cookies are cooling, make the glaze. In a small bowl, mix the confectioners' sugar with 2 tablespoons of the orange juice until well blended. Beat in just enough of the remaining juice to give the mixture the proper consistency for coating the cookies.

7. Dip each cookie halfway into the glaze. Return to the wire racks until the glaze has hardened, 1 to 2 hours.

8. Store in a tightly covered container, separating the layers with sheets of waxed paper.

Yield: About 36 cookies

Tip

When baking an unfamiliar cookie recipe, it's always a good idea to withhold about an eighth of the flour called for before mixing the remainder with other dry ingredients (baking powder, spices, etc.). That way, you can be sure the batter will not be too dry and crumbly before adding the last bit of reserved flour. (Like salt, it's easy to add more flour, but difficult to take it away.)

Swedish Coconut Slices

One look at the ingredients tells you how rich and luscious these cookies are going to be, and you will not be disappointed if you bake them. For a change, the cookies are also wonderful sandwiched together with jam (I prefer raspberry) and sprinkled with confectioners' sugar.

- 3 ¹/₂ cups all-purpose flour
- 1 tablespoon baking powder
- 1 teaspoon baking soda
- 1 cup flaked coconut
- 2 cups (4 sticks) salted butter, at room temperature
- 2 cups sugar
- 1 teaspoon vanilla extract

1. In a medium-size bowl, with a whisk, combine the flour, baking powder, and baking soda until thoroughly mixed. Whisk in the coconut until well blended.

2. In a large bowl, with an electric mixer at medium-high speed, beat together the butter, sugar, and vanilla until light and fluffy, 2 to 3 minutes. With the mixer at medium-low speed, gradually add the flour mixture, beating just until blended. Gather the dough into a ball.

3. On a lightly floured surface, divide the dough into thirds. With lightly floured hands, roll and shape each third into an 8-inch cylinder. Wrap each cylinder separately in plastic wrap and refrigerate until firm, about 4 hours. (At this point the dough can be tightly wrapped in aluminum foil and refrigerated for up to one week or frozen for up to three months.)

4. When ready to bake, adjust two racks to divide the oven into thirds. Preheat the oven to 350°. Lightly grease two baking sheets.

5. With a long, sharp knife, cut the cylinders into ¹/₄-inch slices. Arrange the slices on the baking sheets, spacing them abut 2 inches apart.

6. Bake for about 12 minutes until the edges are lightly browned. Reverse the baking sheets on the racks and from front to back once during baking. With a wide turner, transfer the cookies to wire racks to cool completely.

7. Store in a tightly covered container.

Yield: About 96 cookies

Pangani

These chocolate-dipped vanilla wafers, flavored with cinnamon, are a traditional Christmas treat in Italy.

- 2 cups all-purpose flour
- ¹/₂ teaspoon ground cinnamon
- ¹/₈ teaspoon salt
- 1 cup (2 sticks) salted butter or margarine, at room temperature
- 1 cup sugar
- 2 large egg yolks
- 1 teaspoon vanilla extract

Chocolate Glaze

- 1 ¹/₂ cups semisweet chocolate chips
- 1 tablespoon plain shortening

1. In a medium-size bowl, with a whisk, combine the flour, cinnamon, and salt until thoroughly mixed.

2. In a large bowl, with an electric mixer at medium-high speed, beat together the butter and sugar until light and fluffy, 2 to 3 minutes. Add the egg yolks and vanilla and beat until well blended. With the mixer at medium-low speed, gradually add the flour mixture, beating just until blended. Gather the dough into a ball.

3. Divide the dough into quarters. On a very lightly floured surface, with your hands, roll and shape each quarter into an 8-inch cylinder. Wrap each cylinder separately in plastic wrap and refrigerate until very firm, about 4 hours. (At this point, the dough can be tightly wrapped in aluminum foil and refrigerated for up to one week or frozen for up to three months.)

4. When ready to bake, adjust two racks to divide the oven into thirds. Preheat the oven to 350°. Lightly grease two baking sheets.

5. With a long, sharp knife, cut the cylinders into ¼-inch slices. Arrange the slices on the prepared baking sheets, spacing them about 2 inches apart. Bake for about 5 minutes until lightly browned. Reverse the baking sheets on the racks and from front to back once during baking. Let cool on the baking sheets for 1 minute. With a wide turner, transfer the cookies to wire racks to cool completely.

6. While the cookies are cooling, make the glaze: In a small saucepan set over very low heat, melt together the chocolate and shortening, stirring constantly until smooth. Remove from the heat and set aside to cool slightly.

7. Dip each cookie halfway into the glaze, scraping off the bottom on the side of the pan. Place on wire racks until the chocolate is firm, about 1 hour.

8. Store in a tightly covered container, separating the layers with sheets of waxed paper.

Yield: About 120 cookies

Moroccan Sesame Slices

The extravagant use of sesame seeds in these cookies gives them an unusual, and very pleasant, nutty flavor and texture. And while we're on the subject of sesame seeds, when using this quantity, it would be wise to buy them in bulk from a health food store rather than in those little jars in the spice section. These cookies keep well for several weeks, although there's not a chance they would last that long.

> **1 cup sesame seeds**
> **1 ⅔ cups all-purpose flour**
> **2 teaspoons baking powder**
> **6 tablespoons (½ stick plus 2 tablespoons) salted butter or margarine, at room temperature**
> **½ cup packed light brown sugar**
> **1 large egg, lightly beaten**
> **½ teaspoon vanilla extract**

1. In a large, dry skillet set over medium heat, toast the sesame seeds, stirring constantly, until they are very aromatic and lightly browned. Remove from the heat and continue to stir for a few seconds until the seeds have cooled slightly.

2. In a small bowl, with a whisk, combine the flour and baking powder until thoroughly mixed.

3. In a medium-size bowl, with an electric mixer at medium-high speed, beat together the butter and brown sugar until creamy, 2 to 3 minutes. Beat in the egg and vanilla until well blended. With the mixer at low speed, gradually add the flour mixture, beating just until blended. With a mixing spoon, stir in the sesame seeds until well distributed throughout the dough. Turn the dough out onto a lightly floured surface and knead it for a minute or so. If the dough seems dry, gradually knead in a little water. If it seems sticky, knead in a little more flour. With your hands, roll and shape the dough into a 9-inch cylinder. Wrap the cylinder in plastic wrap and refrigerate until very firm, about 4 hours. (At this point the dough can be tightly wrapped in aluminum foil and refrigerated for up to one week or frozen for up to three months.)

4. When ready to bake, adjust two racks to divide the oven into thirds. Preheat the oven to 350°. Lightly grease two baking sheets.

5. With a long, sharp knife, cut the cylinder into ¼-inch slices. Arrange the slices on the prepared baking sheets, spacing them about 1 inch apart.

6. Bake for about 12 to 15 minutes until light golden. Reverse the baking sheets on the racks and from front to back once during baking. With a wide turner, immediately transfer the cookies to wire racks to cool completely.

7. Store in a tightly covered container.

Yield: About 36 cookies

Meltaways

It's confectioners' sugar and cornstarch that give these cookies their light, melt-in-the-mouth texture and their name. Plain meltaways are certainly meltingly delicious, but rather unexciting, so they are usually flavored with something, if only almond extract. In this recipe, the meltaways are flavored with either lemon or orange zest.

- 1 cup sifted all-purpose flour (measure after sifting)
- 1/2 cup cornstarch
- 3/4 cup (1 1/2 sticks) salted butter or margarine, at room temperature
- 1 cup sifted confectioners' sugar
- 1 teaspoon vanilla extract
- 4 teaspoons shredded and minced lemon or orange zest
- 1/4 cup granulated sugar

1. In a medium-size bowl, with a whisk, combine the flour and cornstarch until thoroughly mixed.

2. In a large bowl, with an electric mixer at medium-high speed, beat together the butter and confectioners' sugar until light and fluffy, 2 to 3 minutes. Beat in the vanilla until well blended. With the mixer at medium-low speed, gradually add the flour mixture, then the lemon or orange zest, beating just until blended. Gather the dough into a ball and flatten it into a 1-inch-thick disk. Wrap in plastic wrap and refrigerate until firm, about 1 hour.

3. On a very lightly floured surface, with your hands, roll and shape the dough into a 10-inch cylinder. Wrap the cylinder in plastic wrap and place in the freezer for 2 hours until solid. (At this point the dough can be tightly wrapped in aluminum foil and frozen for up to three months.)

4. When ready to bake, adjust two racks to divide the oven into thirds. Preheat the oven to 375°. Lightly grease two baking sheets. Sprinkle the granulated sugar onto a sheet of waxed paper.

5. Roll the cylinder back and forth in the granulated sugar. With a long, sharp knife, cut the frozen cylinder into 1/4-inch slices. Arrange the slices on the baking sheets, spacing them about 2 inches apart.

6. Bake for about 10 minutes until the edges are golden. Reverse the baking sheets on the racks and from front to back once during baking. With a wide turner, immediately transfer the cookies to wire racks to cool completely.

7. Store in a tightly covered container.

Yield: About 40 cookies

Lemony Nut Crisps

These cookies are a superb accompaniment to a light dessert, such as a fruit compote or sherbet.

- 2 cups all-purpose flour
- 1/4 teaspoon baking soda
- 1/4 teaspoon salt
- 1 cup (2 sticks) plain shortening
- 1/2 cup packed light or dark brown sugar
- 1/2 cup granulated sugar
- 1 large egg
- 1 tablespoon shredded and minced lemon zest
- 2 tablespoons strained fresh lemon juice
- 1/2 cup very finely chopped pecans

1. In a medium-size bowl, with a whisk, combine the flour, baking soda, and salt until thoroughly mixed.

2. In a large bowl, with an electric mixer at medium-high speed, beat the shortening with the brown sugar and granulated sugar just until well blended, about 1 minute. Add the egg, lemon zest, and lemon juice and beat until light and fluffy, 2 to 3 minutes. With the mixer at medium-low speed, gradually add the flour mixture, beating just until blended. With a mixing spoon, stir in the nuts until well distributed throughout the dough. Gather the dough into a ball.

3. On a lightly floured surface, with your hands, roll and shape the dough into a 10-inch cylinder.

Wrap the cylinder in plastic wrap and refrigerate until very firm, about 4 hours. (At this point the dough can be tightly wrapped in aluminum foil and refrigerated for up to one week or frozen for up to three months.)

4. When ready to bake, adjust two racks to divide the oven into thirds. Preheat the oven to 400°. Have ready two ungreased baking sheets.

5. With a long, sharp knife, cut the cylinder into ¼-inch slices. Arrange the slices on the ungreased baking sheets, spacing them about 2 inches apart.

6. Bake for 10 to 12 minutes until golden brown. Reverse the baking sheets on the racks and from front to back once during baking. With a wide turner, immediately transfer the cookies to wire racks to cool completely.

7. Store in a tightly covered container.

Yield: About 40 cookies

Potato-Chip Icebox Cookies

At one point in our nation's culinary history, potato chips were a popular addition to many recipes, from casseroles to cookies. The chips added a little salty flavor and a certain amount of crunch. Undoubtedly, the bright idea of doing something with potato chips other than eating them straight out of the bag came from the potato-chip manufacturers, who wanted to encourage sales. I remember buying bags of potato chips and then using a relatively small amount in the actual recipe. You know what happened to the rest of the chips. Just what their makers hoped for!

3 ½ cups all-purpose flour, divided

½ teaspoon baking soda

½ teaspoon ground cinnamon

½ cup (1 stick) salted butter or margarine, at room temperature

½ cup (1 stick) shortening

1 cup granulated sugar

½ cup light or dark brown sugar

1 large egg, lightly beaten

1 large egg yolk

1 tablespoon strained fresh lemon juice

¾ cup very finely chopped pecans

¼ cup crushed potato chips

1. In a medium-size bowl, with a whisk, combine 3 cups of the flour, the baking soda, and cinnamon until thoroughly mixed.

2. In a large bowl, with an electric mixer at medium-high speed, beat together the butter, shortening, granulated sugar, and brown sugar until light and fluffy, 2 to 3 minutes. Beat in the egg, egg yolk, and lemon juice until well blended. With the mixer at medium-low speed, gradually add the flour mixture, beating just until blended. With a mixing spoon, stir in the nuts and potato chips until well distributed throughout the dough. If needed, add a little more flour to give the dough a soft, but not sticky, consistency. Gather the dough into a ball.

3. Divide the dough into quarters. On a lightly floured surface, with your hands, roll and shape each quarter into an 8-inch cylinder. Wrap each cylinder in plastic wrap and refrigerate until firm, about 4 hours. (At this point the dough can be tightly wrapped in aluminum foil and refrigerated for up to one week or frozen for up to three months.)

4. When ready to bake, adjust two racks to divide the oven into thirds. Preheat the oven to 400°. Lightly grease two baking sheets.

5. With a long, sharp knife, cut the cylinders into ¼-inch slices. Arrange the slices on the prepared baking sheets, spacing them about 2 inches apart.

6. Bake for about 8 minutes until the edges are lightly browned. Reverse the baking sheets on the racks and from front to back once during baking. With a wide turner, immediately transfer the cookies to wire racks to cool completely.

7. Store in a tightly covered container.

Yield: About 128 cookies

Cereal Cookies

This recipe is an oldie but goodie. Cereal found its way into cookies about the same time as potato chips and probably for the same reasons: To promote sales. Nevertheless, this is a good, reliable cookie recipe, and the bran flakes do add some health benefits, I suppose.

> 3 cups all-purpose flour
> 2 teaspoons baking powder
> 1/4 teaspoon salt
> 1 cup (2 sticks) plain shortening
> 2 cups packed light brown sugar
> 2 large eggs
> 2 cups bran flakes ready-to-eat cereal

1. In a medium-size bowl, with a whisk, combine the flour, baking powder, and salt until thoroughly mixed.

2. In a large bowl, with an electric mixer at medium-high speed, beat together the shortening and brown sugar until very well blended, 2 to 3 minutes. Beat in the eggs until well blended. With the mixer at medium-low speed, gradually add the flour mixture, beating just until blended. With a mixing spoon, stir in the cereal until well blended. Gather the dough into a ball.

3. Divide the dough in half. On a lightly floured surface, with your hands, roll and shape each half into an 8-inch cylinder. Wrap the cylinders separately in plastic wrap and refrigerate until firm, about 4 hours. (At this point, the dough can be wrapped in aluminum foil and refrigerated for one week or frozen for up to three months.)

4. When ready to bake, adjust two racks to divide the oven into thirds. Preheat the oven to 375°. Have ready two ungreased baking sheets.

5. With a long, sharp knife, cut the cylinders into 1/4-inch slices. Arrange the slices on the ungreased baking sheets, spacing them about 2 inches apart.

6. Bake for 12 to 15 minutes until lightly browned. Reverse the baking sheets on the racks and from front to back once during baking. With a wide turner, immediately transfer the cookies to wire racks to cool completely.

7. Store in a tightly covered container.

Yield: About 64 cookies

Poor Man's Nut Cookies

Toasted shredded wheat gives this brown-sugar cookie its pleasant crunch—something like nuts— and, therefore, the name.

> 3/4 cup (1 1/2 sticks) plus 1 tablespoon salted butter or margarine, at room temperature, divided
> 1 cup crumbled shredded wheat biscuits
> 1 1/2 cups all-purpose flour
> 1 teaspoon baking powder
> 1 cup packed dark brown sugar
> 1 large egg, lightly beaten
> 1/2 teaspoon vanilla extract
> 1/2 cup raisins

1. In a large skillet, heat 1 tablespoon of the butter until foamy. Add the shredded wheat and stir almost constantly over medium-high heat until lightly browned. Remove from the heat and set aside.

2. In a medium-size bowl, with a whisk, combine the flour and baking powder until thoroughly mixed.

3. In a large bowl, with an electric mixer at medium-high speed, beat together the remaining 3/4 cup butter with the brown sugar until very creamy, 2 to 3 minutes. Add the egg and vanilla and beat until well blended. With the mixer at low speed, gradually add the flour mixture, beating just until blended. With a mixing spoon, stir in the reserved shredded wheat and the raisins until well distributed throughout the dough. Divide the dough in half.

4. On a lightly floured surface, with your hands, roll and shape each half into a 10-inch cylinder. Wrap each cylinder separately in plastic wrap and

refrigerate for at least 5 hours. (At this point, the cylinders can be tightly wrapped in aluminum foil and refrigerated for up to one week or frozen for up to three months.)

5. When ready to bake, adjust two racks to divide the oven into thirds. Preheat the oven to 375°. Have ready two ungreased baking sheets.

6. With a long, sharp knife, cut each roll into 1/4-inch slices. Arrange the slices on the ungreased baking sheets, spacing them about 2 inches apart.

7. Bake for 6 to 8 minutes until firm and lightly browned. Reverse the baking sheets on the racks and from front to back once during baking. With a wide turner, immediately transfer the cookies to wire racks to cool completely.

8. Store in a tightly covered container.

Yield: About 80 cookies

Chinese Almond Cookies

It may surprise you to learn that Chinese almond cookies are actually icebox cookies. It is *essential* to use lard in this recipe. (In case you've never purchased lard, which is rendered pork fat, it is usually sold someplace near the meat counter, packaged in a box in solid, one-pound blocks.) Unfortunately, shortening simply will not do for this recipe, and butter is absolutely *not* Chinese!

- 1 cup (1/2 pound) lard, at room temperature
- 1 cup sugar
- 1 large egg
- 1 tablespoon almond extract
- 1 1/2 teaspoons baking powder
- 1/4 teaspoon salt
- 2 1/4 cups all-purpose flour
- 1 cup blanched whole almonds, for decorating cookies
- 1 large egg, lightly beaten, for brushing on cookies

1. In a large bowl, with an electric mixer at medium-high speed, beat the lard until fluffy,

about 3 minutes. Gradually beat in the sugar until light and fluffy, 2 to 3 minutes. Beat in one of the eggs, the almond extract, baking powder, and salt until well blended. With the mixer at medium-low speed, gradually add the flour, 1/2 cup at a time, beating after each addition, just until blended. The dough will be grainy in texture. Divide the dough into 6 equal portions.

2. On a lightly floured surface, roll each portion of dough into a 6-inch cylinder with your hands. Wrap the cylinders separately in plastic wrap and refrigerate until firm, about 1 hour. (At this point, the cylinders can be tightly wrapped in aluminum foil and refrigerated for up to one week or frozen for up to three months.)

3. When ready to bake, adjust two racks to divide the oven into thirds. Preheat the oven to 375°. Lightly grease two baking sheets.

4. With a long, sharp knife, cut each cylinder into 1/2-inch slices. Arrange the slices on the prepared baking sheets, spacing them about 2 inches apart. Press an almond into the center of each slice, then, with a pastry brush, lightly brush each cookie with the beaten egg.

5. Bake for about 10 minutes until barely colored and lightly browned on the bottoms. Reverse the baking sheets on the racks and from front to back once during baking. With a wide turner, immediately transfer the cookies to wire racks to cool completely.

6. Store in an airtight container.

Yield: About 72 cookies

Tip

Rock-hard light or dark brown sugar can be softened in the microwave oven. Place the sugar in a glass bowl and sprinkle lightly with water. Cover loosely with microwave-safe plastic wrap. Microwave on high power until softened, checking every 15 seconds.

Classic Coconut Slices

The tasters raved about this little cookie. It has real melt-in-the-mouth texture and rich flavor.

1 ³/₄ cups all-purpose flour

¹/₂ teaspoon baking soda

1 cup (2 sticks) salted butter or margarine, at room temperature

1 cup sugar

1 large egg, lightly beaten

¹/₂ teaspoon vanilla extract

2 ¹/₄ cups shredded or flaked coconut, divided

1. In a medium-size bowl, with a whisk, combine the flour and baking soda until thoroughly mixed.

2. In a large bowl, with an electric mixer at medium-high speed, beat together the butter and sugar until light and fluffy, 2 to 3 minutes. Add the egg and vanilla and beat until well blended. With a mixing spoon, stir in 1³/₄ cups of the coconut. With the mixer at medium-low speed, gradually add the flour mixture, beating just until blended. Gather the dough into a ball and flatten it into a 1-inch-thick disk. Wrap the disk in plastic wrap and refrigerate until firm, about 1 hour.

3. Divide the dough into six equal parts. On an unfloured surface, with your hands, roll and shape each piece into a 6-inch cylinder. Sprinkle the remaining coconut onto a sheet of waxed paper. Roll each cylinder in the coconut to coat lightly. Wrap the cylinders separately in plastic wrap and refrigerate for at least 4 hours or overnight. (At this point, the dough can be tightly wrapped in aluminum foil and refrigerated for up to one week or frozen for up to three months.)

4. When ready to bake, adjust two racks to divide the oven into thirds. Preheat the oven to 325°. Lightly grease two baking sheets.

5. With a long sharp knife, cut each cylinder into ¹/₄-inch slices. Arrange the slices on the prepared baking sheets, spacing them about 2 inches apart.

6. Bake for 15 to 18 minutes until the cookies and coconut coating are lightly browned. Reverse the baking sheets on the racks and from front to back once during baking. With a wide turner, immediately transfer the cookies to wire racks to cool completely.

7. Store in a tightly covered container.

Yield: About 144 cookies

> **Tip**
>
> Different kinds of cookies stored together will end up tasting alike after a day or two. Store each type separately.

Alma Anderson's Icebox Cookies

My dear friend Vivian Manuel contributed this recipe, which comes from her Swedish grandmother. Vivian says she makes hundreds of these little cookies every Christmas, and keeps refilling her big, silver Revere bowl with them during the holidays. Her cute niece, Emily, says that Christmas wouldn't be Christmas without a bowl of "Aunt Boo's" cookies.

3 ¹/₂ cups all-purpose flour

3 teaspoons baking powder

¹/₂ teaspoon salt

1 cup walnuts

3 large eggs, lightly beaten

2 cups packed light brown sugar

³/₄ cup (1 ¹/₂ sticks) salted butter or margarine, melted and cooled

1 teaspoon vanilla extract

1. In a large bowl, with a whisk, combine the flour, baking powder, and salt until thoroughly mixed.

2. In the container of a food processor fitted with a steel blade, process the walnuts with on-off pulses until they are very finely chopped, but not ground; set aside.

3. In a large bowl, with an electric mixer at medium-high speed, beat together the eggs, brown sugar, cooled melted butter, and vanilla until light and fluffy, 2 to 3 minutes. With a mixing spoon, stir in the nuts until well blended. With the mixer at medium-low speed, gradually add the flour mixture, beating just until blended. Divide the dough into quarters.

4. On a lightly floured surface, with your hands, roll and shape each quarter into a 12-inch cylinder. Wrap the cylinders separately in plastic wrap and refrigerate until firm, at least 2 hours. (At this point, the cylinders can be tightly wrapped in aluminum foil and refrigerated for up to one week or frozen for up to three months.)

5. When ready to bake, adjust one rack to divide the oven in half. Preheat the oven to 375°. Lightly grease two baking sheets.

6. With a long, sharp knife, cut each cylinder into ¹/₂-inch slices. Arrange the slices on one of the prepared baking sheets, spacing them about 2 inches apart.

7. Bake one sheet at a time for about 10 minutes until golden brown. Reverse the baking sheet from front to back once during baking. With a wide turner, immediately transfer the cookies to wire racks to cool completely.

8. Store in a tightly covered container.

Yield: About 96 cookies

Pine Tree Shillings

These diminutive cookies are quite fetching with the little pine tree designs on the tops. As you might suspect, this is a very old recipe. The cookies are crisp and about the size of a quarter, just a little larger than the old English shilling, for which they are named.

1 ¹/₂ **cups all-purpose flour**
¹/₂ **teaspoon ground cinnamon**
¹/₄ **teaspoon ground ginger**
¹/₄ **teaspoon baking soda**
¹/₄ **teaspoon salt**
¹/₂ **cup unsulphured molasses**
¹/₄ **cup packed dark brown sugar**
¹/₄ **cup plain shortening**

1. In a medium-size bowl, with a whisk, combine the flour, cinnamon, ginger, baking soda, and salt until thoroughly mixed.

2. In a small bowl, with an electric mixer at medium-high speed, beat the molasses, brown sugar, and shortening together until creamy, 2 to 3 minutes. With the mixer at medium-low speed, gradually add the flour mixture, beating just until blended. Divide the dough into six parts.

3. On a lightly floured surface, with your hands, roll and shape each piece of dough into a 10-inch cylinder. Wrap each cylinder separately in plastic wrap and refrigerate until firm, about 4 hours. (At this point, the cylinders can be tightly wrapped in aluminum foil and refrigerated for up to one week or frozen for up to three months.)

4. When ready to bake, adjust two racks to divide the oven into thirds. Preheat the oven to 350°. Lightly grease two baking sheets.

5. With a long, sharp knife, cut the cylinders into ¹/₄-inch slices. Arrange the slices on the prepared baking sheets, spacing them about 2 inches apart. With your fingers or the bottom of a glass, gently press the slices until they are about ¹/₈-inch thick. With a wooden toothpick, draw a simple design of a pine tree on each cookie. (You can alternatively use a round cookie stamp to imprint the cookies with a design.)

6. Bake for 5 to 8 minutes until the edges are just starting to brown. Reverse the baking sheets on the racks and from front to back once during baking. With a wide turner, immediately transfer the cookies to wire racks to cool completely.

7. Store in a tightly covered container.

Yield: About 240 cookies

Almond-Butter Thins

"What a nice surprise that such a plain-looking, little cookie can taste so good," said the tasters. Because of all the butter they contain, these cookies keep like a dream for a long time, at least three weeks in a tightly covered container.

> 1/3 cup blanched whole almonds
> 1 cup (2 sticks) salted butter or margarine, at room temperature
> 1/2 cup sugar
> 2 cups all-purpose flour

1. In the container of a food processor fitted with a steel blade, process the almonds until finely ground, stopping the processor once and giving the nuts a good stir from the bottom to keep them from becoming pasty. You should have about 1/2 cup ground almonds.

2. In a large bowl, place the ground almonds, butter, sugar, and flour. Mix with your fingertips until the mixture forms a solid ball. Divide the dough in half.

3. On an unfloured surface, with your hands, roll and shape each half of the dough into a 12-inch cylinder. Wrap the cylinders separately in plastic wrap and refrigerate until very firm, about 2 hours. (At this point, the cylinders can be tightly wrapped in aluminum foil and refrigerated for up to one week or frozen for up to three months.)

4. When ready to bake, adjust two racks to divide the oven into thirds. Preheat the oven to 350°. Have ready two ungreased baking sheets.

5. With a long, sharp knife, cut each cylinder into 1/8-inch slices. Arrange the slices on the ungreased baking sheets, spacing them about 1 inch apart.

6. Bake for 10 to 12 minutes until very lightly browned. Reverse the baking sheets on the racks and from front to back once during baking. With a wide turner, immediately transfer the cookies to wire racks to cool completely.

7. Store in a tightly covered container.

Yield: About 120 cookies

Variation

Almond-Butter Buttons with Raspberry or Chocolate Filling: These cookies are somewhat fragile and should be handled carefully while you are filling them. Gently spread the bottom of one cookie with seedless raspberry preserves or melted and cooled semisweet chocolate chips, and sandwich with another cookie, flat sides together. (You may lose a few during this process, but they taste just as good broken.) If you are filling the cookies with chocolate, set these aside until the chocolate hardens, about 1 hour. Sprinkle both sides of the filled cookies with confectioners' sugar. Store in a tightly covered, shallow container, separating the layers with sheets of waxed paper. Sprinkle with confectioners' sugar again before serving.

Yield: About 60 filled cookies

Speckles

This is a cookie that appeals to just about everyone, probably because it contains so many popular ingredients: chocolate, nuts, oats, and even peanut butter.

> 1 1/2 cups all-purpose flour
> 1 cup sugar
> 1/2 teaspoon baking soda
> 1/2 teaspoon salt
> 1/4 teaspoon ground nutmeg
> 1/4 teaspoon ground cinnamon
> 1/2 cup (1 stick) plain shortening
> 1 large egg, lightly beaten
> 1/2 cup smooth peanut butter
> 1/2 cup water
> 1/2 cup regular or quick-cooking (not instant) rolled oats
> 1/2 cup very finely chopped walnuts
> 1 cup (6 ounces) semisweet chocolate chips, very finely chopped

1. In a medium-size bowl, with a whisk, combine the flour, sugar, baking soda, salt, nutmeg, and cinnamon until thoroughly mixed.

2. In a large bowl, with an electric mixer at medium-high speed, beat together the shortening, egg, peanut butter, and water until very light and fluffy, 2 to 3 minutes. With a mixing spoon, stir in the flour mixture, oats, walnuts, and chocolate until well blended. Gather the dough into a ball.

3. On a lightly floured surface, with your hands, roll and shape the dough into a 12-inch cylinder. Wrap the cylinder in plastic wrap and refrigerate until firm, 6 hours or overnight. (At this point the dough can be tightly wrapped in aluminum foil and refrigerated for up to one week or frozen for up to three months.)

4. When ready to bake, adjust two racks to divide the oven into thirds. Preheat the oven to 375°. Have ready two ungreased baking sheets.

5. With a long, sharp knife, cut the cylinder into ¼-inch slices. Arrange the slices on the ungreased baking sheets, spacing them about 2 inches apart.

6. Bake for 12 minutes until lightly brown and firm when lightly touched. Reverse the baking sheets on the racks and from front to back once during baking. With a wide turner, immediately transfer the cookies to wire racks to cool completely.

7. Store in a tightly covered container.

Yield: About 48 cookies

Oatmeal Icebox Cookies

If you thought that there was only one way to make oatmeal cookies, this recipe will come as a pleasant surprise: fresh-baked oatmeal cookies practically on demand!

- 1 ¾ cups all-purpose flour
- ½ teaspoon baking soda
- 1 cup (2 sticks) salted butter or margarine
- 1 cup packed light or dark brown sugar
- 1 large egg, lightly beaten
- 1 teaspoon vanilla extract
- 1 cup regular or quick-cooking (not instant) rolled oats

1. In a medium-size bowl, with a whisk, combine the flour and baking soda until thoroughly mixed.

2. In a large bowl, with an electric mixer at medium-high speed, beat together the butter and brown sugar until light and fluffy, 2 to 3 minutes. Add the egg and vanilla and beat until well blended. With the mixer at medium-low speed, gradually add the flour mixture, beating just until blended. With a mixing spoon, stir in the oats until well blended. Gather the dough into a ball.

3. Divide the dough in half. On a very lightly floured surface, with your hands, roll and shape each half into an 8-inch cylinder. Wrap the cylinders separately in plastic wrap and refrigerate until very firm, about 4 hours. (At this point the dough can be tightly wrapped in aluminum foil and refrigerated for up to one week or frozen for up to three months.)

4. When ready to bake, adjust two racks to divide the oven into thirds. Preheat the oven to 375°. Have ready two ungreased baking sheets.

5. With a long, sharp knife, cut each cylinder into ¼-inch slices. Arrange the slices on the ungreased baking sheets, spacing them about 2 inches apart. Bake for 7 to 9 minutes until the edges are lightly browned. Reverse the baking sheets on the racks and from front to back once during baking. Cool on the baking sheets for about 1 minute. With a wide turner, transfer the cookies to wire racks to cool completely.

6. Store in a tightly covered container.

Yield: About 60 cookies

Variations

Oatmeal-Nut Cookies: Stir ¼ cup very finely chopped pecans or other nuts into the dough at the same time the oats are added.

Oatmeal-Raisin Cookies: Stir ¼ cup very finely chopped raisins into the dough at the same time the oats are added.

Spicy Oatmeal Cookies: Add 1 teaspoon ground cinnamon and ¼ teaspoon ground cloves to the flour mixture.

Tip

To chop dried fruits more easily, lightly butter both sides of the knife first.

Butterscotch Dandies

Using a loaf pan to mold the cookies, instead of rolling them into a cylinder, is an even easier and faster way to shape icebox cookies. I often dip these cookies about halfway into melted chocolate (pages 11–12). If you want to take it one step further, sprinkle the chocolate with finely chopped pecans or other nuts, or colored sprinkles.

4 1/2 cups all-purpose flour

2 teaspoons baking powder

1 teaspoon baking soda

1 1/2 cups (3 sticks) salted butter or margarine, at room temperature

1 cup granulated sugar

1 cup packed light or dark brown sugar

3 large eggs, lightly beaten

1 teaspoon vanilla extract

1. Line two 8- or 9-inch loaf pans with aluminum foil, shiny side up; set aside.

2. In a medium-size bowl, with a whisk, combine the flour, baking powder, and baking soda until thoroughly mixed.

3. In a large bowl, with an electric mixer at medium-high speed, beat together the butter, granulated sugar, and brown sugar until light and fluffy, 2 to 3 minutes. Add the eggs and vanilla and beat until well blended. With the mixer at medium-low speed, gradually add the flour mixture, beating just until blended.

4. Divide the dough in half. Press each half into the bottoms of the loaf pans. Place the pans in the freezer until the dough is solid, at least 3 hours. (At this point, the dough can be removed from the pans, wrapped tightly in aluminum foil, and frozen for up to three months.)

5. When ready to bake, adjust two racks to divide the oven into thirds. Preheat the oven to 350°. Lightly grease two baking sheets.

6. Remove the dough from the pans and peel off the foil and discard. With a long, sharp knife, cut each portion of dough into 1/4-inch slices. Arrange the slices on the prepared baking sheets, spacing them abut 2 inches apart.

7. Bake for 8 to 12 minutes until golden brown. Reverse the baking sheets on the racks and from front to back once during baking. With a wide turner, immediately transfer the cookies to wire racks to cool completely.

8. Store in a tightly covered container.

Yield: About 65 cookies

Christmas Loaf Pan Cookies

This recipe requires more than the usual preparation work that most icebox cookies require, but once all the chopping and mixing is done, and the doughs are in the loaf pan, then it's all downhill to some really fabulous cookies.

Dark Dough

3 cups all-purpose flour, divided

1 teaspoon baking soda

1/2 teaspoon ground cinnamon

1/2 teaspoon ground cloves

1/4 teaspoon salt

1 cup (2 sticks) plain shortening

1 1/2 cups packed dark brown sugar

2 large eggs, lightly beaten

1 cup walnut pieces, very finely chopped

1 cup (6 ounces) semisweet chocolate chips, finely chopped

Light Dough

- 2 cups all-purpose flour, divided
- ¹/₄ teaspoon baking soda
- ¹/₄ teaspoon salt
- ¹/₂ cup (1 stick) plain shortening
- ³/₄ cup granulated sugar
- 1 large egg, lightly beaten
- 1 teaspoon vanilla extract (optional)
- ¹/₂ teaspoon almond extract
- 2 tablespoons water
- ³/₄ cup raisins, finely chopped
- 6 red candied cherries, finely chopped
- 6 green candied cherries, finely chopped

1. Line an 8- or 9-inch loaf pan with aluminum foil, shiny side up; set aside.

2. To make the dark dough: In a medium-size bowl, with a whisk, combine 2¹/₂ cups of the flour, the baking soda, cinnamon, cloves, and salt until thoroughly mixed.

3. In a large bowl, with an electric mixer at medium-high speed, beat together the shortening, brown sugar, and eggs until very creamy, 2 to 3 minutes. With the mixer at medium-low speed, gradually add the flour mixture, beating just until blended. Add enough of the remaining ¹/₂ cup flour to make a soft, but not sticky, dough. With a mixing spoon, stir in the nuts and chocolate until well distributed throughout the dough.

4. To make the light dough: In a medium-size bowl, with a whisk, combine 1³/₄ cups of the flour with the baking soda and salt until thoroughly mixed.

5. In a large bowl, with an electric mixer at medium-high speed, beat together the shortening and the sugar until very creamy. Add the egg, vanilla, almond extract, and water and continue beating until very light and fluffy, 2 to 3 minutes. With the mixer at medium-low speed, gradually add the flour mixture, beating just until blended. Add enough of the remaining ¹/₄ cup flour to make

a soft, but not sticky, dough. With a mixing spoon, stir in the raisins and cherries.

6. Pack *half* of the dark dough evenly into the loaf pan. Pack *all* of the light dough on top of the dark dough. Finally, pack the remaining half of the dark dough over the light dough. Cover the pan tightly with aluminum foil and refrigerate for at least 24 hours, or for up to one week. (At this point, the loaf can be turned out of the pan, tightly wrapped in aluminum foil, and frozen for up to three months.)

7. When ready to bake, adjust two racks to divide the oven into thirds. Preheat the oven to 400°. Have ready two ungreased baking sheets.

8. Turn the dough out of the loaf pan onto a work surface. Peel off the foil and discard. With a long sharp knife, cut the loaf lengthwise into thirds. Cut each long piece of dough crosswise into ¹/₄-inch slices. Arrange the slices on the ungreased baking sheets, spacing them about 2 inches apart.

9. Bake for 8 to 10 minutes until firm. Reverse the baking sheets on the racks and from front to back once during baking. With a wide turner, transfer the cookies to wire racks to cool completely.

10. Store in a tightly covered container.

Yield: About 100 cookies

Spirals, Swirls, and Other Pretty Cookie Patterns

The most remarkable thing about the icebox-cookie–making technique is that two or more contrasting colors of dough can be rolled together, or otherwise arranged in interesting configurations. Then, after chilling and slicing, out come cookies that are swirled, checkered, or in other eye-catching patterns that look very tricky to make, but aren't.

Sometimes, instead of a contrasting dough, fillings are rolled into the dough to make simple swirl patterns.

Basic Swirl Cookies

This is the classic single-swirl cookie made with two sheets of dough: plain and chocolate-flavored. As well as swirls, this dough can be used to make checkerboard cookies or mosaic cookies.

> 1 ¹/₂ cups all-purpose flour
>
> ¹/₄ teaspoon baking powder
>
> ³/₄ cup (1 ¹/₂ sticks) salted butter or margarine, at room temperature
>
> ³/₄ cup sugar
>
> 1 teaspoon vanilla extract
>
> 1 square (1 ounce) unsweetened or semi-sweet chocolate, melted and cooled (page 12)

Single swirl

1. In a medium-size bowl, with a whisk, combine the flour and baking powder until thoroughly mixed.

2. In a large bowl, with an electric mixer at medium-high speed, beat together the butter, sugar, and vanilla until light and fluffy, 2 to 3 minutes. With the mixer at medium-low speed, gradually add the flour mixture, beating just until blended. Divide the dough in half. Place half in the medium-size bowl. With the mixer at medium-low speed, beat the melted chocolate into the dough in the large bowl until evenly colored.

3. Roll the chocolate dough between two sheets of waxed paper into a 16 × 6-inch strip. Repeat with the plain dough. Remove the top sheets of waxed paper and evenly trim both strips with a pizza wheel or the tip of a sharp knife and a ruler. Invert the chocolate strip onto the plain strip. Peel off the waxed paper. With a rolling pin, roll very gently to press the doughs together. Starting with a long side, and using the bottom sheet of waxed paper to help you, roll up the dough into a cylinder. Wrap the cylinder in plastic wrap and refrigerate, seam side down, for at least 3 hours or overnight. (At this point the dough can be tightly wrapped in aluminum foil and refrigerated for up to one week or frozen for up to three months.)

4. When ready to bake, adjust two racks to divide the oven into thirds. Preheat the oven to 350°. Have ready two ungreased baking sheets.

5. With a long, sharp knife, cut the cylinder into ¹/₄-inch slices. Arrange the slices on the ungreased baking sheets, spacing them about 1 inch apart.

6. Bake for 8 to 10 minutes until firm when lightly touched. Reverse the baking sheets on the racks and from front to back once during baking. With a wide turner, immediately transfer the cookies to wire racks to cool completely.

7. Store in a tightly covered container.

Yield: About 64 cookies

Checkerboard Cookies

It is always interesting to note people's expressions when they contemplate a checkerboard cookie. You can almost read their minds: "How on earth was this done?" Actually, very simply. These cookies are made with the same ingredients as Basic Swirl Cookies.

1. In a medium-size bowl, with a whisk, combine the flour and baking powder until thoroughly mixed.

2. In a large bowl, with an electric mixer at medium-high speed, beat together the butter,

sugar, and vanilla until light and fluffy, 2 to 3 minutes. With the mixer at medium-low speed, gradually add the flour mixture, beating just until blended. Divide the dough in half. Place half in the medium-size bowl. With the mixer at medium-low speed, beat the melted chocolate into the dough in the large bowl until evenly colored.

3. Place the chocolate dough on a piece of plastic wrap. Using your hands and a long icing spatula, shape the dough into a 2-inch-square log. Repeat this procedure with the plain dough. Wrap both doughs fairly tightly in the plastic wrap (you don't want to disturb the shape in the wrapping) and refrigerate the logs until very firm, at least 4 hours or overnight. (As the dough begins to chill and become firm, you may want to remove the logs from the refrigerator once or twice and finesse the shape with your hands and the spatula, if you think the corners need a little sharpening up.)

4. Remove both doughs from the refrigerator. Working with one square log of dough at a time, using a long, sharp knife, cut the log lengthwise into thirds. Carefully separate the layers and lay them flat on the work surface. Cut each layer lengthwise into three strips. (You will have nine strips.) Repeat this procedure with the second log of dough. (Don't guess about any of this. Use a ruler and be reasonably precise. It is important that all the strips are the same size.)

5. On a sheet of plastic wrap, start arranging a checkerboard log. For the bottom layer, arrange three strips of dough, side by side, alternating plain and chocolate strips. Gently press the strips together. Make a second layer, starting with a different dough than the first layer. Make a third layer that is the same as the first layer. Wrap the checkerboard log in the sheet of plastic wrap. Make a second checkerboard log using the same procedure as the first log. Refrigerate both checkerboard logs for at least 4 hours or overnight until very firm. (At this point the dough can be tightly wrapped in aluminum foil and refrigerated for up to one week or frozen for up to three months.)

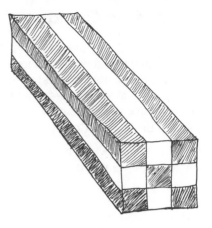

Checkerboard

6. When ready to bake, adjust two racks to divide the oven into thirds. Preheat the oven to 350°. Have ready two ungreased baking sheets.

7. With a long, sharp knife, cut the checkerboard logs into ¼-inch slices. Arrange the slices on the ungreased baking sheets, spacing them about 1 inch apart.

8. Bake for 8 to 10 minutes until firm when lightly touched. Reverse the baking sheets on the racks and from front to back once during baking. With a wide turner, immediately transfer the cookies to wire racks to cool completely.

9. Store in a tightly covered container.

Yield: About 64 cookies

Tip

To make perfectly square icebox cookies, line an empty aluminum-foil, waxed-paper, or plastic-wrap box with either foil or plastic wrap and pack the dough in tightly. Chill until firm before removing and slicing.

Mosaic Cookies

These cookies are slightly more time-consuming to make than plain refrigerator cookies. You will need very small, decorative cookie cutters, no more than about 1/2 inch in diameter at the widest point. These cookies are made with the same ingredients as Basic Swirl Cookies.

1. In a medium-size bowl, with a whisk, combine the flour and baking powder until thoroughly mixed.

2. In a large bowl, with an electric mixer at medium-high speed, beat together the butter, sugar, and vanilla until light and fluffy, 2 to 3 minutes. With the mixer at medium-low speed, gradually add the flour mixture, beating just until blended. Divide the dough in half. Place half in the medium-size bowl. With the mixer at medium-low speed, beat the melted chocolate into the dough in the large bowl until evenly colored.

3. Roll the chocolate dough between two sheets of waxed paper into a 16 × 6-inch strip. Repeat with the plain dough. Remove the top sheets of waxed paper and evenly trim both strips with a pizza wheel or the tip of a sharp knife and a ruler. Invert the chocolate strip onto the plain strip. Peel off the waxed paper. With a rolling pin, roll very gently to press the doughs together. Starting with a long side, and using the bottom sheet of waxed paper to help you, roll up the dough into a cylinder. Wrap the cylinder in plastic wrap and refrigerate for at least 3 hours or overnight until very firm. (At this point the dough can be tightly wrapped in aluminum foil and refrigerated for up to one week or frozen for up to three months.)

4. When ready to bake, adjust two racks to divide the oven into thirds. Preheat the oven to 350°. Have ready two ungreased baking sheets.

5. With a long, sharp knife, cut the cylinders into 1/4-inch slices. Use a tiny cutter to remove the center from a slice of plain dough and slice of chocolate dough. Place a chocolate center in a plain-dough center and vice versa, until all the slices have mosaic centers. Arrange the slices on

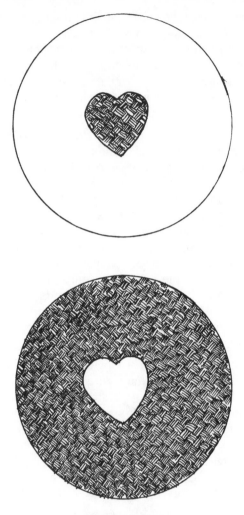

Mosaic cookies

the ungreased baking sheets, spacing them about 1 inch apart.

6. Bake for 8 to 10 minutes until firm when lightly touched. Reverse the baking sheets on the racks and from front to back once during baking. With a wide turner, immediately transfer the cookies to wire racks to cool completely.

7. Store in a tightly covered container.

Yield: About 64 cookies

Peanut Butter and Chocolate Swirls

For every type of cookie, there is at least one version that includes peanut butter as the main flavor. This recipe goes plain peanut butter one better and swirls in a layer of chocolate dough.

Peanut Butter Dough

- 1 cup all-purpose flour
- ¹/₂ teaspoon baking soda
- ¹/₄ cup (¹/₂ stick) salted butter or margarine, at room temperature
- ¹/₂ cup smooth peanut putter
- ³/₄ cup sugar
- 1 large egg
- ¹/₂ teaspoon vanilla extract

Chocolate Dough

- 1 ¹/₂ cups all-purpose flour
- 2 tablespoons unsweetened cocoa powder
- ¹/₂ teaspoon baking soda
- ¹/₄ teaspoon salt
- 6 tablespoons (³/₄ stick) salted butter or margarine, at room temperature
- ³/₄ cup sugar
- 1 large egg
- 1 teaspoon vanilla extract

1. To make the peanut butter dough, in a medium-size bowl, with a whisk, combine the flour and baking soda until thoroughly mixed.

2. In a large bowl, with an electric mixer at medium-high speed, beat together the butter, peanut butter, sugar, egg, and vanilla until light and fluffy, 2 to 3 minutes. With the mixer at medium-low speed, gradually beat in the flour mixture just until blended. Gather the dough into a ball and flatten it into a 1-inch-thick disk. Wrap in plastic wrap and refrigerate until firm, about 1 hour.

3. To make the chocolate dough: In the medium-size bowl, with a whisk, combine the flour, cocoa, baking soda, and salt until thoroughly mixed.

4. In the large bowl (no need to wash), with an electric mixer at medium-high speed, beat together the butter, sugar, egg, and vanilla until light and fluffy, 2 to 3 minutes. With the mixer at medium-low speed, gradually beat in the flour mixture just until blended. Gather the dough into a ball and flatten it into a 1-inch-thick disk. Wrap in plastic wrap and refrigerate until firm, about 1 hour.

5. Divide both disks of dough in half. On lightly floured sheets of waxed paper, with a floured rolling pin, roll each portion of dough into a rectangle measuring 12 × 6 inches. Trim the edges straight with a pizza wheel or the tip of a sharp knife and a ruler. Using the waxed paper to help you, invert each portion of peanut butter dough onto each portion of the chocolate dough. With a rolling pin, roll very gently to press the doughs together. Remove the top sheets of waxed paper. Starting with a 12-inch side, and using the bottom sheet of waxed paper to help you, roll each rectangle into a cylinder (see diagram, page 160). Wrap the cylinders separately in plastic wrap and refrigerate, seam sides down, until firm, about 1 hour. (At this point, the dough can be tightly wrapped in aluminum foil and refrigerated for up to one week or frozen for up to three months.)

6. When ready to bake, adjust two racks to divide the oven into thirds. Preheat the oven to 350°. Lightly grease two baking sheets.

7. With a long, sharp knife, cut each cylinder into ¹/₄-inch slices. Arrange the slices on the prepared baking sheets, spacing them about 1 inch apart. Bake for 8 to 10 minutes until lightly browned. Reverse the baking sheets on the racks and from front to back once during baking. With a wide turner, immediately transfer the cookies to wire racks to cool completely.

8. Store in a tightly covered container.

Yield: About 66 to 70 cookies

Black-and-White Double-Swirl Nut Cookies

This is a very showy cookie that looks far more difficult to make than it is. The dough is easy to work with and can just as easily be formed into any of the patterns shown in this chapter.

- 2 ounces (2 squares) unsweetened chocolate
- 2 1/2 cups all-purpose flour
- 1 teaspoon baking powder
- 3/4 cup (1 1/2 sticks) salted butter or margarine, at room temperature
- 1 1/4 cups sugar
- 1 teaspoon vanilla extract
- 2 large eggs
- 2/3 cup finely chopped walnuts, pecans, pistachio nuts, or hazelnuts, divided (see page 16 for instructions on how to remove the skins from pistachios and hazelnuts)
- 2 tablespoons milk

1. In a small saucepan set over very low heat, melt the chocolate, stirring constantly until smooth. Set aside to cool to room temperature.

2. In a medium-size bowl, with a whisk, combine the flour and the baking powder until thoroughly mixed.

3. In a large bowl, with an electric mixer at medium-high speed, beat together the butter, sugar, and vanilla until light and fluffy, 2 to 3 minutes. Add the eggs, one at a time, beating after each addition until blended. With the mixer at medium-low speed, gradually add the flour mixture, beating just until blended.

4. Remove half of the dough from the bowl and place it in the medium-size bowl. With a mixing spoon, stir in 1/3 cup of the nuts until well distributed throughout the dough. Gather the dough into a ball and flatten it into a 1-inch-thick disk. Wrap the disk in plastic wrap. To the other half of the dough, with the mixer at low speed, beat in the cooled chocolate and milk until well blended. With a mixing spoon, stir in the remaining 1/3 cup nuts until well distributed throughout the dough.

Gather the dough into a ball and flatten it into a 1-inch-thick disk. Wrap the disk in plastic wrap. Refrigerate both doughs until well chilled, 1 to 2 hours. (At this point, the dough can be tightly wrapped in aluminum foil and refrigerated for up to one week or frozen for up to three months.)

5. Between two sheets of waxed paper, roll the plain dough into a 12×8-inch rectangle. (If the dough cracks when it is rolled, let it stand for a few minutes until it warms up slightly.) Roll the chocolate dough between sheets of waxed paper into a rectangle measuring $11^{1/2} \times 8$ inches. Remove the top sheets of waxed paper. Trim the edges of the rectangles straight with a pizza wheel or the tip of a sharp knife and a ruler. Using the bottom sheet of waxed paper to help you, invert the chocolate dough onto the plain dough. (The rectangles should be the same length, but the chocolate dough should be about 1/4 inch from each long edge of the plain dough.) With a long, sharp knife, cut the dough in half crosswise to make two 6-inch pieces. (Cutting the dough in half makes it easier to handle.)

6. With the plain side up, using the bottom sheet of waxed paper to help you, roll one of the pieces of the layered dough from a long side just to the center. Turn the dough over and roll it from the opposite side to meet the other side at the center. Wrap the roll securely in plastic wrap, trying not to disturb the shape. Repeat with the second half of dough. Place both rolls in the refrigerator until they are very firm, about 2 hours. (At this point, the dough can be tightly wrapped in aluminum foil and refrigerated for up to one week or frozen for up to three months.)

7. When ready to bake, adjust two racks to divide the oven into thirds. Preheat the oven to 400°. Lightly grease two baking sheets.

8. With a long, sharp knife, cut each roll into 1/4-inch slices. Arrange the slices on the prepared baking sheets, spacing them about 1 inch apart.

9. Bake for about 8 minutes until firm to the touch and lightly browned. Reverse the baking sheets on the racks and from front to back once

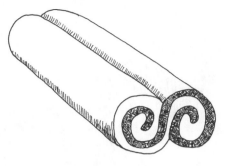

Double swirl

during baking. Leave the cookies on the baking sheet for 1 minute. With a wide turner, transfer the cookies to wire racks to cool completely.

10. Store in a tightly covered container.

Yield: About 48 cookies

Spicy Walnut Twirls

This is an unusual cookie, because the dough contains no sugar. All of the sweetness comes from the sugar-and-spice filling. I like to serve these cookies along with sorbet or fruit for dessert. A little drizzle of melted chocolate (page 12) on top of each one doesn't hurt a bit.

Dough

One 3-ounce package cream cheese, at room temperature
$^1/_2$ cup (1 stick) plus 2 tablespoons salted butter or margarine, at room temperature
1 teaspoon vanilla extract
1 cup all-purpose flour

Filling

$^3/_4$ cup chopped walnuts
$^1/_4$ cup sugar
2 teaspoons pumpkin pie spice
1 tablespoon salted butter or margarine, melted

1. To make the dough: In a large bowl, with an electric mixer at medium-high speed, beat the cream cheese, butter, and vanilla until light and fluffy, 2 to 3 minutes. With the mixer at medium-low speed, gradually add the flour, beating just until blended. Gather the dough into a ball and flatten it into a $^1/_2$-inch-thick disk. Wrap the disk in plastic wrap and refrigerate until firm, about 30 minutes.

2. While the dough is chilling, prepare the filling ingredients. Grind the walnuts in a blender or a food processor fitted with a steel blade, stopping the processor once to give the nuts a good stir from the bottom to keep them from becoming pasty; set aside. In a small bowl, with a fork, combine the sugar and pumpkin pie spice until blended.

3. On a lightly floured sheet of waxed paper, roll the dough into a rectangle measuring about 17 × 10 inches. Trim the edges straight with a pizza wheel or the tip of a sharp knife and a ruler. Brush the surface of the dough with the melted butter. Sprinkle the dough evenly with the sugar mixture. Sprinkle the ground walnuts over the sugar, pressing them very gently into the dough. Starting from a 17-inch side, and using the sheet of waxed paper to help you, roll the dough into a cylinder. Wrap the cylinder in plastic wrap and refrigerate, seam side down, until firm, about 1 hour. (At this point, the dough can be tightly wrapped in aluminum foil and refrigerated for up to one week or frozen for up to three months.)

4. When ready to bake, adjust two racks to divide the oven into thirds. Preheat the oven to 350°. Have ready two ungreased baking sheets.

5. With a long, sharp knife, cut the cylinder into $^1/_4$-inch slices. Arrange the slices on the ungreased baking sheets, spacing them about 2 inches apart.

6. Bake for about 10 minutes until golden. Reverse the baking sheets on the racks and from front to back once during baking. With a wide turner, immediately transfer the cookies to wire racks to cool completely.

7. Store in a tightly covered container.

Yield: About 42 cookies

Chocolate-Cherry Slice-and-Bake Cookies

This method of encasing one dough with another produces what professional bakers call a "bull's eye." But these cookies could just as easily be made into any other configuration that pleases you. This is a very pretty cookie, whether you choose to drizzle chocolate icing over it or not.

2 $^1/_4$ cups all-purpose flour

2 teaspoons baking powder

$^1/_2$ teaspoon salt

$^1/_3$ cup unsweetened cocoa powder

$^1/_4$ teaspoon baking soda

$^3/_4$ cup (1 $^1/_2$ sticks) salted butter or margarine, at room temperature

1 cup sugar

1 large egg

1 $^1/_2$ teaspoons vanilla extract

$^1/_4$ cup finely chopped maraschino cherries

Liquid red food coloring

4 teaspoons water

Cocoa Icing

2 tablespoons salted butter or margarine

2 tablespoons unsweetened cocoa powder

2 to 3 tablespoons water

1 cup sifted confectioners' sugar

1. In a medium-size bowl, with a whisk, combine the flour, baking powder, and salt until thoroughly mixed.

2. In a small bowl, with the whisk, combine the cocoa and baking soda until thoroughly mixed.

3. In a large bowl, with an electric mixer at medium-high speed, beat together the butter, sugar, egg, and vanilla until light and fluffy, 2 to 3 minutes. With the mixer at medium-low speed, gradually add the flour mixture, beating just until blended.

4. Remove 1$^1/_2$ cups of the dough from the bowl and place it in the medium-size bowl. In a small bowl, mix the cherries with about 6 drops of the

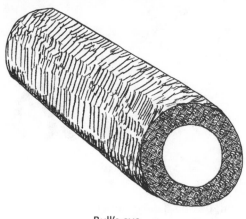

Bull's eye

red food coloring. With a mixing spoon, stir the cherry mixture into the dough until well blended and evenly colored.

5. To the dough remaining in the large bowl, with the mixer at medium speed, beat in the cocoa mixture and water until well blended and evenly colored.

6. Divide the chocolate dough in half. Roll each half of the dough between two sheets of waxed paper into two 12 × 4$^1/_2$-inch strips. Trim both strips straight with a pizza wheel or the tip of a sharp knife and a ruler; set aside.

7. Divide the cherry dough in half. On a work surface, with lightly floured hands, roll and shape each half of the cherry dough into a 12-inch cylinder.

8. Remove the top sheet of waxed paper from one of the strips of dough. Place one cylinder of the cherry dough lengthwise on the center of the strip. Using the bottom sheet of waxed paper to help you, wrap the chocolate dough around the cylinder to form one large roll. Pinch the ends of the chocolate dough where they meet to seal. Repeat with the remaining chocolate and cherry doughs. Wrap each roll in plastic wrap and refrigerate, seam sides down, for at least 6 hours, or for up to three days. (At this point, the dough can be tightly wrapped in aluminum foil and frozen for up to three months.)

9. When ready to bake, adjust two racks to divide the oven into thirds. Preheat the oven to 350°. Have ready two ungreased baking sheets.

10. With a long, sharp knife, cut the rolls into ¼-inch slices. Arrange the slices on the ungreased baking sheets, spacing them about 1 inch apart.

11. Bake for 7 minutes until set and nearly firm when lightly touched. Reverse the baking sheets on the racks and from front to back once during baking. Cool the cookies on the baking sheets for 1 minute. With a wide turner, transfer the cookies to wire racks to cool completely.

12. While the cookies are cooling, make the chocolate icing. In a small saucepan set over low heat, melt the butter. With a mixing spoon, stir in the cocoa and 2 tablespoons of the water. Cook for 5 minutes, stirring constantly, until thickened. Do not let the mixture boil. Remove from the heat and gradually stir in the confectioners' sugar. Beat with a whisk until smooth Add additional water, ½ teaspoon at a time, until the mixture is the right consistency to drizzle off the tip of a teaspoon.

13. When the cookies have cooled completely, drizzle with the icing. Set aside until the chocolate hardens, about 1 hour.

14. Store in a tightly covered container, separating the layers with sheets of waxed paper.

Yield: About 96 cookies

Aristocrats

Recipes for crisp, buttery Aristocrats, with their coating of sugar crystals, appear in some of the earliest cookbooks. These are very elegant "bull's eye" cookies.

¾ cup (1 ½ sticks) plus 2 tablespoons salted butter or margarine, at room temperature
⅔ cup sugar
1 large egg, lightly beaten
2 ½ cups all-purpose flour
⅓ cup very finely chopped walnuts
¼ cup (1 ½ ounces) very finely chopped semisweet chocolate
½ cup crystal sugar, for coating cylinders
1 large egg, lightly beaten, for brushing dough

1. In a large bowl, with an electric mixer at medium-high speed, beat together the butter and sugar until light and fluffy, 2 to 3 minutes. Beat in one egg until well blended. With the mixer at medium-low speed, gradually add the flour until the mixture cleans the side of the bowl and forms a dough. Divide the dough in half. Wrap one half in plastic wrap and refrigerate until firm, about 30 minutes.

2. Divide the remaining dough in half. On a very lightly floured surface, knead the walnuts into one half. Knead the chocolate into the other half. With very lightly floured hands, roll and shape each half into a 10-inch cylinder. Set the cylinders aside. Sprinkle the crystal sugar on a sheet of waxed paper.

3. On a very lightly floured surface, or between two sheets of waxed paper, roll the chilled dough into a rectangle measuring 11 × 9 inches. Trim the edges straight with a pizza wheel or the tip of a sharp knife and a ruler. Cut the rectangle in half lengthwise. Brush the surface of both halves with some of the second egg. Place one reserved cylinder lengthwise in the center of one of the halves of the rectangle. Repeat with the remaining cylinder and the remaining half rectangle. Wrap the dough around each cylinder to enclose it completely and form rolls. Pinch the edges and the ends of the dough together firmly to seal (see Bull's eye diagram, page 166). Brush the rolls with the remaining beaten egg. Roll the cylinders in the crystal sugar until they are well coated. Wrap each cylinder separately in plastic wrap and

refrigerate, seam sides down, until very firm, at least 4 hours. (At this point, the cylinders can be tightly wrapped in aluminum foil and refrigerated for up to a week or frozen for up to three months.)

4. When ready to bake, adjust two racks to divide the oven into thirds. Preheat the oven to 400°. Cover two baking sheets with aluminum foil. Lightly grease the foil.

5. With a long, sharp knife, cut the cylinders into ¼-inch slices. Arrange the slices on the prepared baking sheets, spacing them about 1 inch apart.

6. Bake for 10 to 12 minutes until golden. Reverse the baking sheets on the racks and from front to back once during baking. With a wide turner, immediately transfer the cookies to wire racks to cool completely.

7. Store in a tightly covered container.

Yield: About 80 cookies

Buttery Pastel Cloverleaf Slices

The point of cloverleaf cookies is to show off three or four different colors of dough. Sometimes the doughs can have different flavors, but usually they are made out of the same dough that has been tinted with food coloring.

> 1 ²/₃ cups all-purpose flour
> ¹/₂ cup flaked coconut
> 1 teaspoon shredded and minced lemon zest
> ¹/₂ teaspoon baking soda
> ¹/₂ cup (1 stick) salted butter, at room temperature
> ¹/₂ cup packed light brown sugar
> 1 large egg, lightly beaten
> 1 teaspoon vanilla extract
> Red, yellow, and green liquid or paste food coloring
> Colored sugar crystals (optional)

1. In a medium-size bowl, with a whisk, combine the flour, coconut, lemon zest, and baking soda until thoroughly mixed.

2. In a large bowl, with an electric mixer at medium-high speed, beat the butter and brown

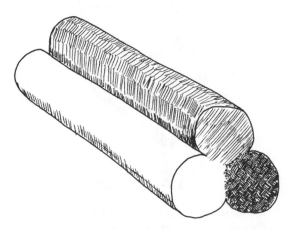

Three-leaf clover

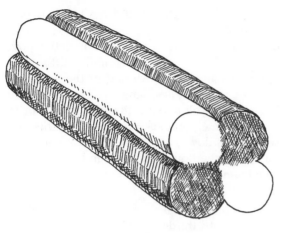

Four-leaf clover

sugar until very creamy, 2 to 3 minutes. Add the egg and vanilla and beat until well blended. With the mixer at medium-low speed, gradually add the flour mixture, beating just until blended. Gather the dough into a ball and divide it into three parts. Return one part of the dough to the large bowl. Place each of the other two parts of the dough in separate, medium-size bowls. Using a few drops of liquid food coloring, or a small amount of each color paste on the tips of toothpicks, tint one part of the dough pink, one part pale yellow, and one part pale green.

3. On a work surface, with your hands, roll each portion of the dough into a 16-inch cylinder. On a piece of plastic wrap, arrange the cylinders of dough together to form a three-leaf clover (see diagram on page 168), gently pressing them together. Wrap in plastic wrap and refrigerate for at least 3 hours or overnight until very firm. (At this point the dough can be tightly wrapped in aluminum foil and refrigerated for up to one week or frozen for up to three months.)

4. When ready to bake, adjust two racks to divide the oven into thirds. Preheat the oven to 375°. Have ready two ungreased baking sheets.

5. With a long, sharp knife, cut the cylinder into ¼-inch slices. Arrange the slices on the ungreased baking sheets, spacing them about 2 inches apart. Sprinkle with colored sugar crystals, if desired.

6. Bake for 6 to 8 minutes until firm to the touch. Reverse the baking sheets on the racks and from front to back once during baking. With a wide turner, immediately transfer the cookies to wire racks to cool completely.

7. Store in a tightly covered container.

Yield: About 64 cookies

Variation

Four-Leaf Clover: Divide the dough into four parts. Tint the fourth part another color. Arrange the cylinders into a four-leaf clover configuration (see diagram on this page). Add a minute or two to the baking time. The yield will be less, about 48 cookies.

 Tip

If using butter to grease baking sheets, use only unsalted butter and chances of the cookies sticking will be greatly lessened.

Peanut Butter and Chocolate Whirligigs

If you like the time-tested combination of chocolate and peanuts, you'll enjoy this crisp little cookie.

- $^3/_4$ cup salted or unsalted roasted peanuts
- 2 cups all-purpose flour
- $^1/_2$ cup (1 stick) salted butter or margarine, at room temperature
- $^1/_2$ cup (1 stick) plain shortening
- One 3-ounce package cream cheese, at room temperature
- 1 cup sugar
- 1 teaspoon vanilla extract

Filling

- 3 ounces (3 squares) semisweet chocolate or $^1/_2$ cup semisweet chocolate chips
- 2 tablespoons salted butter

1. In a food processor fitted with a steel blade, grind the peanuts, stopping the processor once and giving the nuts a good stir from the bottom to keep them from becoming pasty.

2. In a medium-size bowl, with a whisk, combine the ground peanuts and the flour until thoroughly mixed.

3. In a large bowl, with an electric mixer at medium-high speed, beat together the butter, shortening, cream cheese, sugar, and vanilla until fluffy, 2 to 3 minutes. With the mixer at low speed, gradually add the flour mixture, beating just until blended. Gather the dough into a ball and flatten it into a 1-inch-thick disk. Wrap the disk in plastic wrap and refrigerate until firm, about 2 hours.

4. Make the filling about 15 minutes before rolling out the dough. In a small saucepan set over very low heat, melt together the chocolate and the butter, stirring constantly until smooth. Remove from the heat and set aside.

5. Divide the dough in half. On a lightly floured sheet of waxed paper, roll each half into a 12×12-inch square. Trim the edges straight with a pizza wheel or the top of a sharp knife and a ruler. Spread each square with half of the chocolate mixture, stopping just barely short of the edges. Immediately roll into a cylinder. Wrap the cylinders separately in plastic wrap and refrigerate, seam sides down, until firm, about 2 hours. (At this point the dough can be tightly wrapped in aluminum foil and refrigerated for up to a week or frozen for up to three months.)

6. When ready to bake, adjust two racks to divide the oven into thirds. Preheat the oven to 375°. Lightly grease two baking sheets.

7. With a long, sharp knife, cut each cylinder into $^1/_8$-inch slices. Arrange the slices on the baking sheets, spacing them about 1 inch apart.

8. Bake for 8 to 10 minutes until golden brown. Reverse the baking sheets on the racks and from front to back once during baking. With a wide turner, immediately transfer the cookies to wire racks to cool completely.

9. Store in a tightly covered container.

Yield: About 192 cookies

Tip

When slicing a cylinder for icebox cookies, roll the cylinder after every third or fourth slice to keep the bottom from getting flat.

Apricot-Pistachio Twirls

This is a lovely cookie, with just a perfect balance between the tartness of the apricots in the filling and the delicate sweetness of the dough. Keep this cookie in the freezer, either baked or unbaked, for special occasions.

Filling

1 cup chopped dried apricots
$^3/_4$ cup water
$^1/_3$ cup sugar
1 teaspoon shredded and minced lemon zest
$^1/_2$ cup chopped pistachios

Dough

1 $^3/_4$ cups all-purpose flour
$^1/_2$ teaspoon baking soda
$^1/_2$ cup (1 stick) salted butter or margarine, at room temperature
$^1/_2$ cup granulated sugar
$^1/_2$ cup packed light or dark brown sugar
1 large egg, lightly beaten
$^1/_2$ teaspoon vanilla extract

1. To make the filling: In a medium-size saucepan, combine the apricots, water, sugar, and lemon zest. Over medium-high heat, bring the mixture to a boil, stirring frequently. Reduce the heat and simmer, stirring occasionally, until the apricots are tender and the mixture has thickened, about 15 minutes. Remove from the heat and cool slightly; stir in the pistachios.

2. To make the dough: In a medium-size bowl, with a whisk, combine the flour and baking soda until thoroughly mixed.

3. In a large bowl, beat together the butter, granulated sugar, and brown sugar until light and fluffy, 2 to 3 minutes. Add the egg and vanilla and beat until well blended. With the mixer at medium-low speed, gradually add the flour mixture, beating just until blended. Gather the dough into a ball and divide it in half.

4. Between sheets of waxed paper, roll each half of the dough into a rectangle measuring 10×8 inches. Remove the top sheets of waxed paper. Trim the edges straight with a pizza wheel or the tip of a sharp knife and a ruler. Spread each rectangle with half of the apricot mixture, stopping just short of the edges. Starting with a 10-inch edge, and using the bottom sheet of waxed paper to help you, roll each rectangle into a cylinder. Wrap the cylinders separately in plastic wrap and refrigerate, seam sides down, until very cold, about 2 hours. (At this point, the dough can be tightly wrapped in aluminum foil and refrigerated for up to one week or frozen for up to three months.)

5. When ready to bake, adjust two racks to divide the oven into thirds. Preheat the oven to 400°. Lightly grease two baking sheets.

6. With a long, sharp knife, cut each cylinder into $^1/_4$-inch slices. Arrange the slices on the prepared baking sheets, spacing them about 2 inches apart.

7. Bake for 8 to 10 minutes until lightly browned. Reverse the baking sheets on the racks and from front to back once during baking. With a wide turner, immediately transfer the cookies to wire racks to cool completely.

8. Store in a tightly covered container.

Yield: About 54 cookies

Tip

To speed up dough-chilling time, place the dough in the freezer and chill for 20 minutes for every hour needed in the refrigerator.

Sticky Bun Swirls

Everyone who has known me for longer than a week also knows that my last meal on earth would probably include sticky buns, which I learned to love—and still hanker for more than occasionally—when I was growing up in Reading, Pennsylvania. I've always wanted to make a cookie version of sweet, swirly buns, so I gave the job of developing such a recipe to Annie Bailey, who did her usual super job.

Dough

- 1 ¹/₂ cups all-purpose flour
- ¹/₂ teaspoon baking powder
- ¹/₄ teaspoon salt
- ¹/₂ cup (1 stick) salted butter or margarine, at room temperature
- One 3-ounce package cream cheese, at room temperature
- ¹/₃ cup granulated sugar

Filling

- 2 tablespoons light or dark brown sugar
- 1 teaspoon ground cinnamon
- 2 tablespoons melted butter or margarine, for brushing on dough
- 3 tablespoons dried currants
- 2 tablespoons finely chopped pecans

Glaze

- ¹/₃ cup sifted confectioners' sugar
- 1 ¹/₂ to 2 teaspoons milk

1. To make the dough: In a medium-size bowl, with a whisk, combine the flour, baking powder, and salt until thoroughly mixed.

2. In a large bowl, with an electric mixer at medium-high speed, beat together the butter, cream cheese, and granulated sugar until light and fluffy, 2 to 3 minutes. With the mixer at medium-low speed, gradually add the flour mixture, beating just until blended. Gather the dough into a ball and flatten it into a 1-inch-thick disk. Wrap the disk in plastic wrap and refrigerate until firm, about 1 hour.

3. While the dough is chilling, in a small bowl, combine the brown sugar and cinnamon.

4. On a lightly floured surface, roll the chilled dough into a rectangle measuring 12 × 10 inches. Trim the edges straight with a pizza wheel or the tip of a sharp knife and a ruler. Brush the dough with the melted butter, leaving a 1-inch border along one 12-inch edge. Sprinkle the brown-sugar mixture evenly over the butter. Sprinkle evenly with the currants and nuts.

5. Starting at the 12-inch side of the rectangle opposite the plain edge, roll the dough into a cylinder as tightly as possible without stretching the dough too much, up to the plain edge. Brush a little water on the plain edge and press it against the cylinder to seal. Wrap the cylinder in plastic wrap and refrigerate, seam side down, until firm enough to slice, about 1 hour. (At this point, the dough can be tightly wrapped in aluminum foil and frozen for up to three months.)

6. When ready to bake, adjust one rack to divide the oven in half. Preheat the oven to 350°. Lightly grease one large baking sheet.

7. With a long, sharp knife, cut the roll into ¹/₂-inch slices. Arrange the slices on the prepared baking sheet, spacing them about 1 inch apart.

8. Bake for 12 to 15 minutes until the edges are golden. Reverse the baking sheet from front to back once during baking.

9. While the cookies are baking, make the glaze. In a small bowl, stir together the confectioners' sugar and enough milk to make a glaze that is just thin enough to drizzle off the tip of a teaspoon.

10. When the cookies are removed from the oven, cool on the baking sheet for 2 minutes. With a wide turner, transfer the cookies to wire racks. While the cookies are still warm, but not hot, drizzle the glaze over each one, dividing evenly. Set aside on sheets of waxed paper until the cookies have cooled and the glaze is dry, about 1 hour.

11. Store in a tightly covered container, separating the layers with sheets of waxed paper.

Yield: About 24 cookies

Cranberry-Orange Rollups

Definitely the most delicious way I know to use leftover cranberry sauce, but also good enough to warrant opening a can of cranberry sauce.

Filling

- ³/₄ cup whole-berry cranberry sauce
- 1 tablespoon cornstarch
- ¹/₄ cup English orange marmalade
- 2 tablespoons orange liqueur or orange juice

Dough

- 1 ³/₄ cups all-purpose flour
- 1 teaspoon baking powder
- 1 teaspoon grated orange zest
- ¹/₄ teaspoon ground nutmeg
- ¹/₂ cup (1 stick) salted butter or margarine, at room temperature
- ³/₄ cup packed dark brown sugar
- 1 large egg
- ¹/₂ teaspoon vanilla extract

1. To make the filling: In a small saucepan combine the cranberry sauce, cornstarch, marmalade, and liqueur. Bring to a boil over medium-high heat, stirring constantly. Remove from the heat to cool. Cover and refrigerate until chilled, 2 to 3 hours.

2. To make the dough: In a medium-size bowl, with a whisk, combine the flour, baking powder, orange zest, and nutmeg until thoroughly mixed.

3. In a large bowl, with an electric mixer at medium-high speed, beat together the butter, brown sugar, egg, and vanilla until very creamy, 2 to 3 minutes. With the mixer at medium-low

speed, gradually add the flour mixture, beating just until blended. Cover the bowl and refrigerate until the dough is firm enough to handle, about 1 hour.

4. On a lightly floured surface, roll the dough into a 16 × 8-inch rectangle. Trim the edges even with a pizza wheel or the tip of a sharp knife and a ruler. With an icing spatula, spread the cold cranberry filling over the dough to within ¹/₄ inch of the edges. Starting at a 16-inch side, roll the dough into a cylinder. Cut in half to make two 8-inch cylinders. Wrap each cylinder separately in plastic wrap and refrigerate, seam side down, until very firm, 2 to 3 hours. (At this point, the cylinders can be tightly wrapped in aluminum foil and refrigerated for up to one week or frozen for up to three months.)

5. When ready to bake, adjust two racks to divide the oven into thirds. Preheat the oven to 375°. Cover two baking sheets with foil. Lightly grease the foil.

6. With a long, sharp knife, cut the cylinders into ¹/₂-inch slices. Arrange the slices on the baking sheets, spacing them about 2 inches apart.

7. Bake for about 12 minutes until the cookies are a light golden brown. Reverse the baking sheets on the racks and from front to back once during baking. With a wide turner, immediately transfer the cookies to wire racks to cool completely.

8. Store in a tightly covered container, separating the layers with sheets of waxed paper.

Yield: About 36 cookies

Tip

Shape dough into a flat disk rather than a ball to reduce the time it needs to chill through.

Indio Pinwheels

These cookies are named for the town of Indio in the Coachella Valley of California near Palm Springs, which is the center of the date-growing industry in that region. Date paste is a very traditional filling for swirl cookies.

Filling

One 8-ounce package (about 1 $\frac{1}{3}$ cups)
   whole pitted dates, coarsely chopped
$\frac{1}{3}$ cup sugar
$\frac{1}{2}$ cup water
2 tablespoons strained fresh lemon juice
$\frac{1}{2}$ teaspoon vanilla extract

Dough

3 cups all-purpose flour
$\frac{1}{2}$ teaspoon baking soda
1 cup (2 sticks) salted butter or margarine,
   at room temperature
$\frac{1}{2}$ cup granulated sugar
$\frac{1}{2}$ cup packed light brown sugar
1 large egg
3 tablespoons milk
1 teaspoon vanilla extract

1. To make the filling: In a medium-size saucepan, combine the dates, sugar, and water. Bring the mixture to a boil over medium-high heat, stirring frequently. Reduce the heat to medium and cook, stirring, until the mixture thickens, about 2 minutes. Remove from the heat and stir in the lemon juice and $\frac{1}{2}$ teaspoon of vanilla extract. Set aside to cool.

2. In a medium-size bowl, with a whisk, combine the flour and baking soda until thoroughly mixed.

3. In a large bowl, with an electric mixer at medium-high speed, beat together the butter, granulated sugar, and brown sugar until very creamy, 2 to 3 minutes. Add the egg, milk, and 1 teaspoon of the vanilla and beat until very well blended. With the mixer at medium-low speed, gradually add the flour mixture, beating just until blended. Gather the dough into a ball and flatten it into a 1-inch-thick disk. Wrap the disk in plastic wrap and refrigerate until firm, about 1 hour.

4. Divide the dough in half. Between two sheets of waxed paper, roll out each half of the dough into a rectangle measuring 12 × 10 inches. Remove the top sheets of waxed paper. Trim the edges straight with a pizza wheel or the tip of a sharp knife and a ruler. Spread both rectangles with the cooled filling, stopping just short of the edges and dividing evenly. Starting with a 12-inch side, and using the sheet of waxed paper to help you, roll each rectangle into a cylinder. Wrap the cylinders separately in plastic wrap and refrigerate, seam sides down, for at least 4 hours or overnight until very firm. (At this point, the dough can be tightly wrapped in aluminum foil and refrigerated for up to one week or frozen for up to three months.)

5. When ready to bake, adjust two racks to divide the oven into thirds. Preheat the oven to 375°. Lightly grease two baking sheets.

6. With a long, sharp knife, cut each cylinder into $\frac{1}{4}$-inch slices. Arrange the slices on the prepared baking sheets, spacing them about 2 inches apart.

7. Bake for 10 to 12 minutes until lightly browned. Reverse the baking sheets on the racks and from front to back once during baking. With a wide turner, immediately transfer the cookies to wire racks to cool completely.

8. Store in a tightly covered container, separating the layers with sheets of waxed paper.

Yield: About 80 cookies

Hungarian Poppy Seed Swirls

The sweetened poppy-seed paste used to fill these swirls is available in cans in European grocery stores, as well as at many specialty food stores. In eastern European countries, poppy-seed paste is used mainly as a strudel filling, but sometimes as a cookie filling, as well, especially at Christmas.

1 $^1/_3$ cups all-purpose flour

$^1/_2$ teaspoon baking soda

$^1/_4$ teaspoon ground cloves

$^1/_8$ teaspoon ground cinnamon

$^1/_2$ cup (1 stick) salted butter or margarine, at room temperature

$^1/_4$ cup sugar

1 large egg

$^1/_2$ teaspoon shredded and minced lemon zest

Half of a 12 $^1/_2$-ounce can ($^1/_2$ cup plus 1 tablespoon) poppy-seed paste (see note)

1. In a medium-size bowl, with a whisk, combine the flour, baking soda, cloves, and cinnamon until thoroughly mixed.

2. In a large bowl, with an electric mixer at medium-high speed, beat together the butter and sugar until light and fluffy, 2 to 3 minutes. Beat in the egg and lemon zest just until well blended. With the mixer at medium-low speed, gradually add the flour mixture, beating just until blended. Gather the dough into a ball and flatten it into a 1-inch-thick disk. Wrap the disk in plastic wrap and chill until firm, about 30 minutes, or for up to three days. (At this point, the dough can be tightly wrapped in aluminum foil and frozen for up to three months.)

3. Roll the dough between two sheets of waxed paper into a rectangle measuring 12×10 inches. Trim the edges straight with a pizza wheel or the tip of a sharp knife and a ruler. Slide an ungreased baking sheet under the dough and refrigerate until firm, about 30 minutes.

4. Slide the chilled dough onto a work surface. Peel off the top sheet of waxed paper; replace loosely. Turn the dough over; peel off and discard the second sheet of waxed paper. With a rubber spatula or the back of a mixing spoon, spread the poppy-seed paste to within $^1/_2$ inch of the edges of the dough. Starting from a 12-inch edge, and using the bottom piece of waxed paper to help you, roll the dough into a cylinder. Wrap the cylinder in plastic wrap and refrigerate, seam side down, for 30 minutes until firm. (At this point the dough can be tightly wrapped in aluminum foil and refrigerated for up to one week or frozen for up to three months.)

5. When ready to bake, adjust two racks to divide the oven into thirds. Preheat the oven to 350°. Lightly grease and flour two baking sheets.

6. With a long, sharp knife, cut the cylinder into $^1/_2$-inch slices. Place the slices on the prepared baking sheets, spacing them about 1 inch apart.

7. Bake for 11 to 13 minutes until lightly browned. Reverse the baking sheets on the racks and from front to back once during baking. Cool for about 5 minutes on the baking sheets set on wire racks. With a wide turner, transfer the cookies to wire racks to cool completely.

8. Store in a tightly covered container.

Yield: About 24 cookies

Tip

If you want to use the entire can of filling for the Swirls, then double the recipe and divide the dough in half. Proceed as directed, repeating the procedure with the second half of dough.

Raisin Wheels

Raisin pie (or funeral pie, as it is also called), is an old Pennsylvania Dutch recipe that I like a lot, and these cookies remind me of this pie.

> 2 cups all-purpose flour
> 1/2 teaspoon baking soda
> 1/2 teaspoon ground cinnamon
> 1/4 teaspoon salt
> 1/2 cup (1 stick) butter-flavored shortening
> 1 cup packed light brown sugar
> 1 tablespoon water
> 1 large egg, lightly beaten

Filling

> 1 cup finely chopped Muscat or other raisins
> 1/2 cup granulated sugar
> 1/2 cup water

1. In a medium-size bowl, with a whisk, combine the flour, baking soda, cinnamon, and salt until thoroughly mixed.

2. In a large bowl, with an electric mixer at medium-high speed, beat together the shortening, brown sugar, and 1 tablespoon water until very creamy, 2 to 3 minutes. Beat in the egg until well blended. With the mixer at medium-low speed, gradually add the flour mixture, beating just until blended. Gather the dough into a ball and flatten it into a 1-inch-thick disk. Wrap the disk in plastic wrap and refrigerate until firm, about 4 hours.

3. To make the filling: In a small saucepan, combine the raisins, sugar, and water. Cook over medium-high heat for about 10 minutes, stirring occasionally, until thickened. Remove from the heat and set aside to cool to room temperature.

4. Divide the dough in half. On a lightly floured surface, roll each half of the dough into a rectangle measuring 9 × 6 1/2 inches. Trim the edges straight with a pizza wheel or the tip of a sharp knife and a ruler. Spread the rectangles with the cooled filling, stopping just short of the edges and

dividing evenly. From a 6 1/2-inch side, roll each piece of dough into a cylinder. Wrap the cylinders separately in plastic wrap and refrigerate, seam sides down, until very firm, about 4 hours. (At this point, the dough can be tightly wrapped in aluminum foil and frozen for up to three months.)

5. When ready to bake, adjust two racks to divide the oven into thirds. Preheat the oven to 400°. Have ready two ungreased baking sheets.

6. With a long, sharp knife, cut the cylinders into 1/4-inch slices. Arrange the slices on the ungreased baking sheets, spacing them about 2 inches apart.

7. Bake for 8 to 10 minutes until lightly browned. Reverse the baking sheets on the racks and from front to back once during baking. With a wide turner, immediately transfer the cookies to wire racks to cool completely.

8. Store in a tightly covered container.

Yield: About 42 cookies

Jelly Swirls

You can use this recipe for filling to make plain jelly swirls in any flavor you wish. In that case, you omit the almonds and double the amount of jam or jelly and cornstarch so that the jelly layer is a little thicker.

> 2 3/4 cups all-purpose flour
> 1/2 teaspoon baking powder
> 1/2 cup (1 stick) salted butter or margarine, at room temperature
> 1 cup sugar
> 1 large egg
> 3 tablespoons milk
> 1 teaspoon vanilla extract

Filling

> 1/2 cup seedless raspberry or strawberry jam
> 1 1/2 teaspoons cornstarch
> 1/2 cup slivered or sliced almonds, toasted (page 16)

1. In a medium-size bowl, with a whisk, combine the flour and baking powder until thoroughly mixed.

2. In a large bowl, with an electric mixer at medium-high speed, beat the butter with the sugar until light and fluffy, 2 to 3 minutes. Add the egg, milk, and vanilla and beat until well blended. With the mixer at medium-low speed, gradually add the flour mixture, beating just until blended. Gather the dough into ball and flatten it into a 1-inch-thick disk. Wrap in plastic wrap and refrigerate until firm, about 1 hour.

3. While the dough is chilling, make the filling. In a small saucepan, combine the jam and the cornstarch. Cook over medium heat, stirring, until bubbly. Cook, stirring, for 1 minute longer. Remove from the heat and stir in the almonds. Cover and set aside to cool.

4. Divide the chilled dough in half. On sheets of waxed paper, with a floured rolling pin, roll each half into a rectangle measuring 18×12 inches. Trim the edges straight with a pizza wheel or a sharp knife and a ruler. Spread each rectangle with the cooled filling, stopping just short of the edges and dividing evenly. Starting with a 12-inch side, and using the sheet of waxed paper to help you, roll each rectangle into a cylinder. Wrap the cylinders separately in plastic wrap and refrigerate, seam sides down, for at least 4 hours or overnight until very firm. (At this point, the dough can be tightly wrapped in aluminum foil and refrigerated for up to one week or frozen for up to three months.)

5. When ready to bake, adjust two racks to divide the oven into thirds. Preheat the oven to 375°. Line two baking sheets with aluminum foil, shiny side up; lightly grease the foil.

6. With a long, sharp knife, cut each cylinder into ¼-inch slices. Arrange the slices on the prepared baking sheets, spacing them about 2 inches apart.

7. Bake for 9 to 11 minutes until the edges are firm when lightly touched and the bottoms are lightly browned. Reverse the baking sheets on the racks and from front to back once during baking. With a wide turner, immediately transfer the cookies to wire racks to cool completely.

8. Store in a tightly covered container, separating the layers with sheets of waxed paper.

Yield: About 60 cookies

9
Shaped Cookies

At least half of the cookies in the world fall into the category of shaped, which means that the dough is shaped before the cookies are baked. The shapes are usually simple: balls, crescents, and logs, for example, but they can be more elaborate, taking on the form of letters or even pretzels.

Most often the shaping is done with your own two hands, and other times by using a cookie press or a pastry bag fitted with a decorative tip. Sometimes the cookies are baked in muffin pans or cookie plaques, and they can also be pressed into ceramic or wooden molds, which gives them an "embossed" design, as well as a shape.

Shaped cookies are made with a stiff dough that is frequently chilled before the cookies are shaped. Chilling makes the dough easy to handle and also helps to keep the cookies from spreading too much as they bake.

Snow Drops

What makes these different from other kinds of flour-sugar-butter-nut cookies is the subtle flavors of coffee and cinnamon. These are what I think of as "tea party" cookies.

  2 cups all-purpose flour
  $^1/_3$ cup sugar
  1 cup (2 sticks) salted butter, at room temperature
  1 teaspoon instant-coffee powder (not granules)
  $^1/_2$ teaspoon ground cinnamon
  1 cup finely chopped pecans
  About $^1/_2$ cup confectioners' sugar, for coating cookies

1. Adjust two racks to divide the oven into thirds. Preheat the oven to 350°. Have ready two ungreased baking sheets. Sprinkle the confectioners' sugar onto a sheet of waxed paper.

2. In a large bowl, with an electric mixer at medium-low speed, combine the flour, sugar, butter, coffee powder, and cinnamon until light and fluffy, 2 to 3 minutes. With a mixing spoon, stir in the pecans until well distributed throughout the dough. Scoop the dough out of the bowl by heaping measuring teaspoonfuls and roll them between the palms of your hands into 1-inch balls. Arrange the balls on the ungreased baking sheets, spacing them about 2 inches apart.

3. Bake for 15 to 20 minutes until the edges are lightly browned. Reverse the baking sheets on the racks and from front to back once during baking. While the cookies are still warm, roll them in the confectioners' sugar. Cool the cookies completely on wire racks, then roll again in confectioners' sugar.

Yield: About 42 cookies

Giant Molasses Cookies

My Great-grandmother Hanners baked cookies very much like these for my father when he was a little boy, except that she used lard (which is rendered hog fat). However, shortening works very well. These cookies are definitely little-child size, that is to say big (about 4 inches in diameter), and are wonderfully soft and chewy, the perfect snack when served with a glass of milk. My tasters rated this cookie A-plus, which would not have surprised my father, who absolutely adored these molasses cookies above all others.

 3/4 cup sugar, divided
 2 1/4 cups all-purpose flour
 3/4 cup plain shortening, melted and cooled
 1/2 cup regular or unsulphured molasses
 2 teaspoons baking soda
 1 teaspoon ground ginger
 1/2 teaspoon ground cinnamon
 1/2 teaspoon ground cardamom
 1/4 teaspoon salt
 1 large egg, lightly beaten

1. Adjust two racks to divide the oven into thirds. Preheat the oven to 350°. Have ready two ungreased baking sheets. Sprinkle 1/4 cup of the sugar on a sheet of waxed paper.

2. In a large bowl, with an electric mixer at medium speed, beat together the remaining 1/2 cup sugar, the flour, shortening, molasses, baking soda, ginger, cinnamon, cardamom, salt, and egg until well blended, scraping the side of the bowl occasionally with a rubber spatula. (The dough will be very soft.)

3. Scoop 1/4 cupfuls of the dough out of the bowl and roll them into balls between the palms of your hands. Roll the balls in the sugar on the waxed paper. Arrange the balls on the baking sheets, spacing them about 3 inches apart.

4. Bake for about 15 minutes until puffed and the tops are crinkly. Reverse the baking sheets on the racks and from front to back once during baking. With a wide turner, immediately transfer the cookies to wire racks to cool completely.

5. Store in a tightly covered container, separating the layers with sheets of waxed paper.

Yield: About 10 big cookies

Hazelnut and Oatmeal-Apricot Cookies

Just when I was sure there couldn't possibly be a significantly different oatmeal cookie in the world, up pops this one, developed by the Hazelnut Marketing Board, and what a glorious use of hazelnuts this cookie is. My tasters and I especially liked the play of creamy white-chocolate chips against the tartness of the dried apricots.

 1 cup finely chopped dried apricots
 1 1/2 cups plus 1 tablespoon all-purpose flour, divided
 1 teaspoon baking soda
 1 cup (2 sticks) salted butter or margarine, at room temperature
 1 cup granulated sugar
 1 cup packed light brown sugar
 2 large eggs
 1 teaspoon vanilla extract
 2 1/2 cups regular or quick-cooking (not instant) rolled oats
 1 cup chopped hazelnuts
 1 cup vanilla-flavored white baking pieces

1. Adjust two racks to divide the oven into thirds. Preheat the oven to 350°. Lightly grease two baking sheets. In a small bowl, toss the apricots with 1 tablespoon of the flour; set aside.

2. In a medium-size bowl, with a whisk, combine the remaining 1 1/2 cups flour and the baking soda until thoroughly mixed.

Tips for Baking Shaped Cookies

- Read through the recipe completely to make sure that you have all the equipment and ingredients you will need.

- Baking sheets should be clean and cool. If the recipe calls for greasing the baking sheets, use a very light coating of grease or vegetable spray, otherwise the cookies can spread too much and even run into one another.

- If the recipe calls for the dough to be chilled, don't try to save time by skipping or skimping on this important step. In most cases the dough should be very cold when it is shaped. The exceptions are doughs that are put into a cookie press or piped with a pastry bag.

- Most shaped-cookie doughs are quite stiff and buttery and will roll easily between the palms of your hands without sticking. If some sticking occurs, dust your hands *very lightly* with flour.

- Don't overcrowd the baking sheets. If there are only a few cookies to be baked, spread them out evenly over the baking sheet so that no big empty spaces are exposed to the oven heat, or use a smaller baking sheet.

- Even though it may be a nuisance, reverse the baking sheets as instructed in the recipe. All ovens have "hot spots," and reversing the baking sheets helps the cookies to bake more evenly.

- Check the cookies for doneness at the first time given when there is a range of times. If only one time is given, set the timer for a couple of minutes before that time. Oven temperatures and other seemingly small factors can affect baking times significantly.

- Most shaped cookies should be removed from the baking sheet as soon as they come from the oven. If they stick a little, let them cool for a minute on the baking sheet and then try again.

- If the same baking sheet will be used for more than one batch of cookies, make sure that it is clean and completely cool before reusing. Often it is enough just to wipe the baking sheet with paper towels between batches. Sometimes it is necessary to rinse the sheet briefly in hot water and wipe it dry before regreasing. Occasionally there is enough grease left on the sheet so that regreasing isn't even necessary, but subsequent greasings should be extra light.

- All firm cookie doughs that can be shaped can be turned into dropped cookies by using a little less flour or adding a little liquid to the batter. Often the dough is soft enough to be dropped if the chilling step is omitted.

3. In a large bowl, with an electric mixer at medium speed, beat the butter, granulated sugar, brown sugar, eggs, and vanilla until light and fluffy, 2 to 3 minutes. With a mixing spoon, stir the flour mixture into the butter mixture until well blended. Stir in the oats, and then the hazelnuts, just until blended. Stir in the floured apricots, and then the white baking pieces until both are well distributed throughout the dough.

4. Scoop out heaping measuring tablespoonfuls of the dough and roll them into 1½-inch balls between the palms of your hands. Arrange the balls on the prepared baking sheets, spacing them about 2 inches apart. Flatten each ball slightly with your fingertips.

5. Bake for 11 to 13 minutes until just beginning to brown around the edges, but still slightly moist in the center. Reverse the baking sheets on the racks and from front to back once during baking. With a wide turner, immediately transfer the cookies to wire racks to cool completely.

6. Store in a tightly covered container.

Yield: About 36 cookies

Tip

For best baking results, bring whole eggs to room temperature before beating them into the batter.

Patti Hushon's Sugar-Raisin Cookies

After they are baked, these cookies turn into crinkly, chewy balls. The flavor develops and mellows nicely if they are stored for a day or two before eating.

- 3 1/2 cups all-purpose flour
- 2 teaspoons baking soda
- 1 1/4 cups granulated sugar, divided
- 1 cup (2 sticks) salted butter (not margarine), at room temperature
- 1 cup packed light or dark brown sugar
- 2 large eggs
- 1/4 cup milk
- 2 teaspoons vanilla extract
- 1 cup raisins

1. Adjust two racks to divide the oven into thirds. Preheat the oven to 375°. Lightly grease two baking sheets.

2. In a medium-size bowl, with a whisk, combine the flour and baking soda until thoroughly mixed. Sprinkle 1/4 cup of the granulated sugar onto a sheet of waxed paper.

3. In a large bowl, with an electric mixer at medium speed, beat together the butter, the remaining 1 cup of granulated sugar, and the brown sugar until light and fluffy, 2 to 3 minutes. Add the eggs, one at a time, beating well after each addition. Add the milk and the vanilla and beat until light and fluffy, about 2 minutes. With a mixing spoon, stir in together the flour mixture and the raisins just until blended and the raisins are well distributed throughout the dough.

4. Pinch off pieces of the dough and roll them into 1 1/4-inch balls between the palms of your hands. As they are formed, roll each ball in the granulated sugar on the sheet of waxed paper. Arrange the balls on the prepared baking sheets, spacing them about 1 inch apart.

5. Bake for 10 to 12 minutes until a light, golden color and the tops start to show cracks. Reverse the baking sheets on the racks and from front to back once during baking. With a wide turner, immediately transfer the cookies to wire racks to cool completely.

6. Store in a tightly covered container.

Yield: About 48 cookies

Glazed Sugar Thins

I call these nibbling cookies. They are the perfect companion for coffee or tea.

- 1/2 cup (1 stick) salted butter or margarine, at room temperature
- 1/2 cup sugar
- 1 large egg, separated, white lightly beaten
- 1/2 teaspoon vanilla extract
- 1/4 teaspoon salt
- 1 1/4 cups all-purpose flour, divided
- Cinnamon sugar (page 35), for sprinkling on cookies

1. In a small bowl, with an electric mixer at medium-high speed, beat together the butter and the sugar until light and fluffy, 2 to 3 minutes. Beat in the egg yolk, vanilla, and salt until fluffy, about 2 minutes. With a rubber spatula, gradually fold in 1 cup of the flour just until blended. Cover the bowl and refrigerate the dough until it is very cold, 1 to 2 hours.

2. Adjust two racks to divide the oven into thirds. Preheat the oven to 350°. Lightly grease two baking sheets. Sprinkle the remaining 1/4 cup flour on a sheet of waxed paper.

3. Scoop heaping teaspoonfuls of the cold dough out of the bowl and roll them between the palms of your hands into 1-inch balls. As they are made, arrange the balls on the prepared baking sheets, spacing them about 2 inches apart. Lightly press each ball into a thin round with the bottom of a drinking glass that has been dipped in the flour on the waxed paper. Brush the tops of the cookies with the egg white, then sprinkle very lightly with cinnamon sugar.

4. Bake for 8 to 10 minutes until golden. Reverse the baking sheets on the racks and from front to back once during baking. With a wide turner, immediately transfer the cookies to wire racks to cool completely.

5. Store in a tightly covered container.

Yield: About 48 cookies

Spotted Cows

In its original incarnation (circa 1940), these were sliced icebox cookies, and they still are in a sense, since the dough must be very cold and firm when it is baked. However, I found that the little chunks of chocolate in them made slicing the refrigerated cylinders a daunting task. So, I gave that up and rolled the cold dough into balls, and I liked the results very much. These cookies don't flatten out as they bake, but retain their shape, each one a big, delicious mouthful.

One 6-ounce piece semisweet chocolate
  or 1 cup chocolate chips
1 3/4 cups all-purpose flour
1/2 teaspoon baking powder
1/8 teaspoon salt
1/4 cup (1/2 stick) salted butter or margarine,
  at room temperature
1/4 cup (1/2 stick) plain shortening
1/4 cup granulated sugar
1/4 cup light brown sugar
1 large egg
1/2 teaspoon vanilla extract

1. On a cutting surface, with a long sharp knife, cut the chocolate into jagged 1/4- to 1/2-inch pieces. You should have about 1 cup. Place in the refrigerator until ready to use.

2. In a medium-size bowl, with a whisk, combine the flour, baking powder, and salt until thoroughly mixed.

3. In a large bowl, with an electric mixer at medium-high speed, beat together the butter and shortening with the granulated sugar, brown sugar, egg, and vanilla until very creamy, 2 to 3 minutes. With the mixer at medium-low speed, gradually add the flour mixture, beating just until blended. With a mixing spoon stir in the chilled chocolate pieces until well distributed throughout the dough. Cover the bowl and refrigerate until the dough is very cold and firm, about 2 hours. (At this point, the dough can be gathered into a ball, tightly wrapped in aluminum foil and refrigerated for up to one week or frozen for up to three months. If frozen, thaw in the refrigerator before proceeding.)

4. When ready to bake, adjust two racks to divide the oven into thirds. Preheat the oven to 350°. Lightly grease two baking sheets.

5. Scoop level measuring tablespoonfuls of the dough out of the bowl and roll them between the palms of your hands to make 1 1/4- to 1 1/2-inch balls.

6. Arrange the balls on the prepared baking sheets, spacing them about 1 inch apart. Bake for about 12 minutes until the bottoms are lightly browned and the cookies are rather soft when lightly pressed with a finger. (Be careful not to overbake or these cookies will get hard.) Reverse the baking sheets on the racks and from front to back once during baking. With a wide turner, immediately transfer the cookies to wire racks to cool completely.

7. Store in a tightly covered container.

Yield: About 36 cookies

Chocolate Crackles

These cookies are called crackles because that's what happens to them when they are baked. The cookies crack into a pattern of dark fissures in their snowy tops.

> 1/4 cup (1/2 stick) salted butter or margarine, at room temperature
> 4 ounces (4 squares) unsweetened chocolate
> 2 cups all-purpose flour, divided
> 2 cups granulated sugar
> 4 large eggs, lightly beaten
> 2 teaspoons baking powder
> 1/2 cup finely chopped pecans or walnuts (optional)
> About 1/3 cup confectioners' sugar

1. Adjust two racks to divide the oven into thirds. Lightly grease two baking sheets; set aside.

2. In a small saucepan set over very low heat, melt together the butter and chocolate, stirring constantly until smooth. Remove from the heat and set aside to cool slightly.

3. In a large bowl, with an electric mixer at medium speed, beat together the melted-chocolate mixture, 1 cup of the flour, the granulated sugar, eggs, and baking powder until well blended. With a mixing spoon, stir in the remaining 1 cup flour. Stir in the nuts until well distributed throughout the dough. Cover the bowl and refrigerate until the dough is firm, about 2 hours.

4. Preheat the oven to 300°.

5. Sprinkle the confectioners' sugar on a sheet of waxed paper. Scoop the dough by heaping measuring teaspoonfuls out of the bowl and roll them between the palms of your hands into 1-inch balls. Roll the balls in the confectioners' sugar. As they are rolled, arrange the balls on the prepared baking sheets, spacing them about 2 inches apart.

6. Bake for 12 to 15 minutes or until firm when lightly pressed. Reverse the baking sheets on the racks and from front to back once during baking. With a wide turner, immediately transfer the cookies to wire racks to cool completely.

7. Store in a tightly covered container, separating the layers with sheets of waxed paper.

Yield: About 48 cookies

Cracked Sugar Cookies

This is yet another of the seemingly endless versions of the all-time-favorite sugar cookie.

> 1 1/2 cups granulated sugar, divided
> 2 cups all-purpose flour
> 2 teaspoons baking soda
> 2 teaspoons cream of tartar
> 1 cup (2 sticks) butter-flavored shortening
> 1/2 cup packed light brown sugar
> 1 large egg, lightly beaten
> 1 teaspoon vanilla extract

1. Adjust two racks to divide the oven into thirds. Preheat the oven to 350°. Have ready two ungreased baking sheets. Sprinkle 1/2 cup of the granulated sugar onto a sheet of waxed paper.

2. In a medium-size bowl, with a whisk, combine the flour, baking soda, and cream of tartar until thoroughly mixed.

3. In a large bowl, with an electric mixer at medium-high speed, beat together the shortening, the remaining 1 cup granulated sugar, and the brown sugar until very creamy, 2 to 3 minutes. Beat in the egg and vanilla until well blended. With the mixer at medium-low speed, gradually add the flour mixture, beating just until blended. Scoop heaping measuring teaspoonfuls of dough out of the bowl and roll them between the palms of your hands into 1-inch balls. Roll the balls in the granulated sugar. Arrange on the ungreased baking sheets, spacing them about 2 inches apart. Flatten each ball slightly.

4. Bake for 8 to 10 minutes until golden. Reverse the baking sheets on the racks and from front to back once during baking. With a wide turner, immediately transfer the cookies to wire racks to cool completely.

5. Store in a tightly covered container.

Yield: About 60 cookies

3. In a large bowl, with an electric mixer at medium-high speed, beat together the butter and brown sugar until creamy, about 1 minute. Add the molasses and egg and beat until light and fluffy, 2 to 3 minutes. With the mixer at medium-low speed, gradually add the flour mixture, beating just until blended. With a mixing spoon, stir in the raisins, nuts, and cornflakes until well distributed throughout the batter. Cover the bowl and refrigerate until the dough is firm, 30 minutes to 1 hour.

4. Preheat the oven to 375°. Scoop rounded measuring tablespoonfuls of the dough out of the bowl and roll them into 1½-inch balls between the palms of your hands. Roll in the granulated sugar. As they are rolled, arrange the balls on the prepared baking sheets, spacing them about 2 inches apart.

5. Bake for 12 to 14 minutes until the edges are firm and the centers are still slightly soft when pressed with a finger. Reverse the baking sheets on the racks and from front to back once during baking. With a wide turner, immediately transfer the cookies to wire racks to cool completely.

6. Store in a tightly covered container.

Yield: About 24 cookies

Tip

To keep light and dark brown sugars soft, store in the freezer. As soon as the sugar thaws, it will be soft and ready to use.

Shaped Jumbles

A whole cookie cookbook could probably be devoted to jumbles alone, there are so many versions of this old American cookie. Jumbles, which originated in New England, can contain just a few ingredients, or many, which I imagine is how they got their name: A jumble of ingredients—whatever the baker happened to have in the larder—stirred into a plain, old-fashioned molasses or brown-sugar batter. You can stir in just about anything you like in place of the raisins, nuts, and cornflakes, as long as the total amount is not much more than 1½ cups.

> 2 ¼ cups all-purpose flour
> 2 teaspoons baking soda
> 1 teaspoon ground ginger
> 1 teaspoon ground cloves
> ³/₄ cup (1 ½ sticks) salted butter or margarine, at room temperature
> 1 cup packed light or dark brown sugar
> ¹/₄ cup regular or unsulphured molasses
> 1 large egg
> ¹/₂ cup raisins
> ¹/₂ cup finely chopped nuts
> ¹/₂ cup cornflakes cereal, crushed

1. Adjust two racks to divide the oven into thirds. Lightly grease two baking sheets; set aside.

2. In a medium-size bowl, with a whisk, combine the flour, baking soda, ginger, and cloves until thoroughly mixed.

Jumble Cookies II

This cookie must have been created by a baker who had a large selection of goodies on hand.

2 cups all-purpose flour

1 teaspoon baking soda

$^1/_2$ teaspoon baking powder

2 cups crisp-rice cereal

1 $^3/_4$ cups regular or quick-cooking (not instant) rolled oats

1 cup shredded or flaked coconut

1 cup (2 sticks) salted butter or margarine, at room temperature

1 cup granulated sugar

1 cup packed light or dark brown sugar

2 eggs, lightly beaten

1 teaspoon vanilla extract

1. Adjust two racks to divide the oven into thirds. Preheat the oven to 350°. Lightly grease two baking sheets.

2. In a large bowl, with a whisk, combine the flour, baking soda, and baking powder until thoroughly combined. With a mixing spoon, stir in the cereal, oats, and coconut.

3. In another large bowl, with an electric mixer at medium-high speed, beat together the butter, granulated sugar, and brown sugar until very creamy, 2 to 3 minutes. Beat in the eggs and vanilla until well blended. With a mixing spoon, gradually add the flour mixture, beating just until blended. Scoop heaping measuring teaspoonfuls of the dough out of the bowl and roll them between the palms of your hands into 1-inch balls. Arrange the balls on the baking sheets, spacing them about 2 inches apart. With a wide turner, slightly flatten each cookie to about 1½ inches in diameter.

4. Bake for about 10 minutes until lightly browned. Reverse the baking sheets on the racks and from front to back once during baking. With a wide turner, immediately transfer the cookies to wire racks to cool completely.

5. Store in a tightly covered container.

Yield: About 84 cookies

Snickerdoodles

Almost everyone knows that a snickerdoodle is a cookie with a nonsensical name. But few people know what's in a snickerdoodle, including me, until recently. For a cookie so famous, it really isn't very exciting.

2 $^3/_4$ cups all-purpose flour

1 teaspoon cream of tartar

$^1/_2$ teaspoon baking soda

1 $^1/_2$ cups sugar

$^1/_2$ cup (1 stick) salted butter or margarine, at room temperature

2 large eggs, lightly beaten

1 teaspoon vanilla extract

$^1/_4$ cup Cinnamon Sugar (page 35) for coating cookies

1. Adjust two racks to divide the oven into thirds. Preheat the oven to 400°. Have ready two ungreased baking sheets.

2. In a small bowl, with a whisk, combine the flour, cream of tartar, and baking soda until thoroughly mixed.

3. In a large bowl, with an electric mixer at medium-high speed, beat together the sugar and butter until light and fluffy, 2 to 3 minutes. Beat in the eggs and vanilla until well blended. With the mixer at medium-low speed, gradually add the flour mixture, beating just until blended. Sprinkle the cinnamon sugar on a piece of waxed paper.

4. Scoop heaping measuring teaspoonfuls of the dough out of the bowl and roll them between the palms of your hands into 1-inch balls. Roll the balls in the cinnamon sugar. As they are rolled, arrange the balls on the ungreased baking sheets, spacing them about 2 inches apart.

5. Bake for 8 to 10 minutes until fairly firm when lightly touched. Reverse the baking sheets on the racks and from front to back once during baking. With a wide turner, immediately transfer the cookies to wire racks to cool completely.

6. Store in a tightly covered container.

Yield: About 48 cookies

Greek Honey and Walnut Cookies

The Greeks pile these crumbly cookies in a pyramid and serve them drizzled with even more honey and sprinkled with a few chopped nuts.

- 1 cup (2 sticks) salted butter or margarine, at room temperature
- $^2/_3$ cup sugar
- 2 teaspoons vanilla extract
- 2 $^1/_2$ cups all-purpose flour
- 1 $^1/_2$ cups finely chopped walnuts, plus additional for sprinkling over cookies
- $^1/_2$ cup light cream
- $^1/_2$ cup honey, plus additional for brushing on or drizzling over cookies

1. In a large bowl, with an electric mixer at medium speed, beat together the butter, sugar, and vanilla until light and fluffy, 2 to 3 minutes. Add the flour all at once. With a pastry blender or two knives used in a crisscross fashion, combine the mixture until well blended and crumbly. With a mixing spoon, stir in 1½ cups of the walnuts until well distributed throughout the dough. Drizzle the cream over the flour mixture and mix with your fingertips until well blended. Turn the dough out onto a lightly floured surface and knead briefly. Gather the dough into a ball and wrap in plastic wrap. Refrigerate the dough until cold, about 1 hour.

2. Adjust two racks to divide the oven into thirds. Preheat the oven to 350°. Line two baking sheets with aluminum foil, shiny side up. Lightly grease the foil or coat with nonstick cooking spray.

3. Pinch off pieces of the cold dough and roll them into 1½-inch balls between the palms of your hands. As they are formed, arrange the balls on the prepared baking sheets, spacing them about 2 inches apart. Flatten each one slightly with the back of the tines of a dinner fork. Brush the tops with honey.

4. Bake for about 15 minutes until pale golden. Reverse the baking sheets on the racks and from front to back once during baking. With a wide turner, immediately transfer the cookies to wire racks to cool completely.

5. Store in a tightly covered container. Brush or drizzle with the additional honey and sprinkle with the additional walnuts, if desired, just before serving.

Yield: About 32 cookies

Tip

Flatten balls of dough with the bottom of a glass dipped in sugar for a flat cookie, a dinner fork for a ridged or crisscrossed top, or a cookie stamp for fancy designs.

Syrian Sesame Cookies

Bite into one of these cookies and you'll know it didn't come from Kansas. Actually, the memory of this cookie has haunted me ever since I tasted one very similar to it that my friends Gale Steves and Arlene Wanderman brought back from Syria, so I am thrilled to have found a recipe for them—and to share it with you. By the way, when using sesame seeds in this quantity, buy them at a Middle Eastern grocery store or a health food store. The little jars in the spice section at the supermarket are very costly.

>2 ¹/₂ cups sesame seeds
>
>1 ³/₄ cups all-purpose flour
>
>About ¹/₂ cup confectioners' sugar, for coating cookies
>
>1 tablespoon baking powder
>
>1 ¹/₄ cups superfine sugar
>
>2 teaspoons shredded and minced lemon zest
>
>5 large eggs
>
>Regular olive oil (not extra-virgin)

1. Adjust two racks to divide the oven into thirds. Preheat the oven to 350°. Heavily grease two baking sheets; set aside.

2. In a large, dry skillet set over medium heat, toast the sesame seeds, stirring constantly, until they are very aromatic and browned. Remove from the heat and continue stirring until the seeds have cooled slightly. Pour the seeds into a large bowl. Return the skillet to medium heat. Sprinkle the flour into the skillet and stir constantly until it is lightly browned. Remove from the heat and set aside to cool. Sprinkle the confectioners' sugar onto a sheet of waxed paper.

3. With a whisk, combine the browned flour with the baking powder until thoroughly mixed. Whisk in the toasted sesame seeds until well blended. Add the sugar and lemon zest, whisking the mixture until it is completely combined. Make a shallow crater in the center of the flour mixture and into it break the eggs. With a dinner fork, beat the eggs, trying to disturb the surrounding flour mixture as little as possible, then gradually start pulling the flour mixture from the side into the eggs, working the mixture as you do so until it forms a soft dough. If the dough seems especially sticky, add 1 to 3 tablespoon of flour. Grease the palms of your hands with oil. Scoop out level measuring tablespoonfuls of dough and roll them into balls between the palms of your hands. As they are formed, roll the balls in the confectioners' sugar and arrange them on the prepared baking sheets, spacing them about 2 inches apart. Flatten each ball with the palm of your hand to make 2-inch rounds.

4. Bake for 12 to 15 minutes until lightly browned and firm when pressed with a finger. Reverse the baking sheets on the racks and from front to back once during baking. With a wide turner, immediately transfer the cookies to wire racks to cool completely.

5. Store in a tightly covered container.

Yield: About 50 cookies

Lithuanian Mushroom Cookies

Don't let the length of this recipe put you off. Although there are a number of steps, each one is fairly easy and quick to do. These mildly spicy, crunchy cookies look so much like real mushrooms it's amazing. It does take some manual dexterity to shape the "caps" and "stems" and put them together. I like to tuck them here and there on a plate of more traditional cookies during the Christmas holidays, where they never fail to elicit small gasps of surprise.

>1 cup honey
>
>4 to 5 cups all-purpose flour
>
>1 ¹/₂ teaspoons baking powder
>
>1 teaspoon ground cinnamon
>
>¹/₂ teaspoon ground cloves
>
>¹/₂ teaspoon ground ginger
>
>¹/₂ teaspoon ground nutmeg
>
>¹/₂ teaspoon ground cardamom

$^{1}/_{4}$ cup ($^{1}/_{2}$ stick) salted butter or margarine, at room temperature

$^{1}/_{2}$ cup sugar

2 large eggs

$^{1}/_{4}$ cup sour cream

1 teaspoon shredded and minced lemon zest

1 teaspoon shredded and minced orange zest

Icing

5 teaspoons cold water

2 cups confectioners' sugar

4 teaspoons strained fresh lemon juice

2 teaspoons unsweetened cocoa powder

1. In a small saucepan, heat the honey over medium heat until small bubbles appear around the edge of the pan. Set aside to cool to lukewarm.

2. In a large bowl, with a whisk, combine the flour, baking powder, cinnamon, cloves, ginger, nutmeg, and cardamom until thoroughly mixed.

3. In a large bowl, with an electric mixer at medium-high speed, beat together the butter and sugar until light and fluffy, 2 to 3 minutes. Beat in the eggs, one at a time until thoroughly blended. Gradually add the lukewarm honey and sour cream, beating until well blended. With the mixer at low speed, add the flour mixture, $^{1}/_{4}$ cup at a time, beating after each addition, just until blended. With a mixing spoon, stir in the lemon and orange zests until well distributed throughout the dough. Gather the dough into a ball and divide it in half. Wrap each half in plastic wrap and refrigerate for 1 to 2 hours, or until very cold. (At this point, the dough can be tightly wrapped in aluminum foil and refrigerated for up to one week or frozen for up to three months; if frozen, thaw in the refrigerator before proceeding.)

4. Adjust one rack to divide the oven in half. Preheat the oven to 350°. Lightly grease two baking sheets.

5. Remove half of the dough from the refrigerator. Pinch off pieces of the cold dough and shape them into balls of varying sizes from 1 to 1$^{1}/_{2}$ inches in diameter. With your fingers, make an indentation in one side of each ball, then shape to resemble a mushroom cap. Place the "caps," rounded sides up, on a prepared baking sheet, spacing them about 2 inches apart.

6. Bake for about 10 minutes until lightly browned. Reverse the baking sheets on the racks and from front to back once during baking. With a wide turner, immediately transfer the "caps" to wire racks to cool completely.

7. Remove the second half of dough from the refrigerator. Pinch off pieces of dough of the same size as before and roll them between the palms of your hands and shape each one to resemble mushroom stems in various thicknesses, from 1 to 1$^{1}/_{2}$ inches in length. Place the "stems" on a prepared baking sheet, spacing them about 2 inches apart.

8. Bake for 10 minutes until lightly browned. Reverse the baking sheets on the racks and from front to back once during baking. With a wide turner, immediately transfer the "stems" to wire racks to cool completely.

9. While the cookie shapes are cooling, make the icing. In a medium-size bowl, with a mixing spoon, beat the water, 1 teaspoon at a time, into the confectioners' sugar until smooth. Beat in the lemon juice. Divide the icing in half, placing one half in a small bowl. Stir the cocoa into one half until completely blended.

10. When the cookie shapes are completely cool, use icing to fasten a stem into the underside of each cap. Set aside until completely dry. (While the icing dries, press a damp cloth directly onto the top of the remaining icing in each bowl to keep it from drying out.)

11. With a small spatula, lightly coat the stems and undersides of the caps with white icing; set aside to dry. With a small spatula, lightly ice the tops of the caps with the cocoa-tinted icing; set aside to dry.

12. To store, arrange carefully in a large, shallow tin or cardboard box, separating the layers with sheets of waxed paper.

Yield: About 30 cookies

Greek Orange Cookies

The Greeks do love their sweets, especially honey, which can almost always be found somewhere in their cookie recipes. These cookies are delicious served with fresh fruit, especially strawberries.

    3 1/2 cups all-purpose flour
    1 1/2 teaspoons baking powder
    1/2 teaspoon salt
    1 cup (2 sticks) salted butter or margarine,
      at room temperature
    3/4 cup confectioners' sugar
    1/2 cup olive oil or vegetable oil
    1 large egg, lightly beaten
    1/2 cup strained fresh orange juice
    2 teaspoons vanilla extract

Syrup

    1 cup granulated sugar
    3/4 cup water
    1/2 cup honey

Coating

    2 cups walnuts
    4 teaspoons ground cinnamon

1. Adjust two racks to divide the oven into thirds. Preheat the oven to 350°. Have ready two ungreased baking sheets.

2. In a large bowl, with a whisk, combine the flour, baking powder, and salt until thoroughly mixed.

3. In a large bowl, with an electric mixer at medium speed, beat the butter with the confectioners' sugar, scraping the side of the bowl often, until light and fluffy, 2 to 3 minutes. Beat in the oil, egg, orange juice, and vanilla until well blended. With the mixer at low speed, add the flour mixture, 1/2 cup at a time, beating after each addition, just until blended and the dough is soft and smooth.

4. Pinch off pieces of the dough and form them into ovals measuring about 2 inches long and

1/2 inch thick between the palms of your hands. Arrange the ovals on a baking sheet as they are formed, spacing them about 1 inch apart.

5. Bake for about 20 minutes until pale golden. Reverse the baking sheets on the racks and from front to back once during baking. With a wide turner, immediately transfer the cookies to wire racks to cool completely.

6. To make the syrup: In a medium-size saucepan, combine the sugar, water, and honey and bring to a boil over medium heat, stirring constantly until the sugar is dissolved. Boil the mixture, undisturbed, for *exactly* 20 minutes, adjusting the heat as necessary. Remove from the heat and set aside to cool to lukewarm.

7. To prepare the coating: Place the walnuts in a food processor fitted with a steel blade. Using on-off pulses, process the walnuts until very finely chopped, almost ground, stopping the processor once to give the nuts a good stir from the bottom to keep them from becoming pasty. In a wide, shallow bowl, mix the walnuts and cinnamon until completely blended.

8. With a slotted spoon, dip the cooled cookies into the lukewarm syrup, then immediately roll them in the nut mixture. Set aside on sheets of waxed paper for several hours to dry completely before serving or storing.

9. Store in a tightly covered container, separating the layers of cookies with sheets of waxed paper.

Yield: About 54 cookies

Central American Peanut Cookies

This cookie has all the same fine qualities as a good sugar, peanut, or oatmeal cookie rolled into one.

    1 1/2 cups all-purpose flour
    1 1/4 teaspoons baking powder
    1/4 teaspoon salt
    3/4 cup (1 1/2 sticks) salted butter or
      margarine, softened

3/4 cup packed light brown sugar

1 large egg, lightly beaten

One 3 1/2-ounce can sweetened flaked coconut

1 cup regular or quick-cooking (not instant) rolled oats

2/3 cup chopped, unsalted, roasted peanuts

1/4 cup granulated sugar

1. Adjust two racks to divide the oven into thirds. Preheat the oven to 350°. Lightly grease two baking sheets.

2. In a medium-size bowl, with a whisk, combine the flour, baking powder, and salt until thoroughly mixed.

3. In a large bowl, with an electric mixer at medium speed, beat together the butter and brown sugar until light and fluffy, 2 to 3 minutes. Beat in the egg until well blended.

4. With the mixer at low speed, gradually add the flour mixture, beating just until blended. With a mixing spoon, stir in the coconut, oats, and peanuts. Let stand for 5 minutes. Sprinkle the granulated sugar on a piece of waxed paper.

5. Pinch off pieces of the dough and roll them into 1 1/2-inch balls between the palms of your hands. Place the balls on the prepared baking sheets, spacing them about 2 1/2 inches apart. Press each ball with the bottom of a glass that has been dipped in the sugar on the waxed paper.

6. Bake for 13 to 15 minutes until golden brown around edges. Reverse the baking sheets on the racks and from front to back once during baking. Remove from the oven and let stand for 2 minutes on the baking sheets set on wire racks. With a wide turner, transfer the cookies to wire racks to cool completely.

7. Store in a tightly covered container.

Yield: About 36 cookies

Mexican Cornmeal Cookies

The cornmeal in these cookies is the first clue about where they come from, since cornmeal is an essential ingredient in many sweet and savory baked goods from Mexico and Central America.

3/4 cup (1 1/2 sticks) salted butter or margarine, at room temperature

2/3 cup sugar

2 large egg yolks

1 1/2 teaspoons vanilla extract

1 teaspoon shredded and minced lemon zest

1/2 cup yellow cornmeal

1 3/4 to 2 cups all-purpose flour

10 dried apricot halves, cut into thin strips

1. Adjust two racks to divide the oven into thirds. Preheat the oven to 350°. Lightly grease two baking sheets.

2. In a large bowl, with an electric mixer at medium speed, beat together the butter and the sugar until light and fluffy, 2 to 3 minutes. Beat in the egg yolks, vanilla, and lemon zest until blended. Add the cornmeal and beat at medium speed just until blended. Let the mixture stand for 2 minutes to allow the cornmeal to absorb some of the moisture in the batter.

3. With a mixing spoon, stir in 1 3/4 cups flour until well blended. Let the dough stand 5 minutes. Gather the dough into a ball. If it is too soft to hold its shape, stir in a few more tablespoons of flour, being careful not to add too much, since the cornmeal will continue to absorb moisture.

4. Pinch off pieces of the dough and shape them into 1-inch balls between the palms of your hands. Place the balls on the prepared baking sheets, spacing them about 1 1/2 inches apart. With your fingers, gently press the balls into 1 1/2-inch circles. Place a strip of apricot on each cookie.

5. Bake for 14 to 15 minutes until golden brown around the edges. Reverse the baking sheets on the racks and from front to back once during baking. Remove from the oven and let stand for 3 minutes on the baking sheets set on wire racks. With a wide turner, transfer the cookies to wire racks to cool completely.

6. Store in a tightly covered container.

Yield: About 48 cookies

Pfeffernusse

The German name translates to "pepper nuts," and every northern European country has its own version, but they are all quite similar. This recipe is the most typical.

About 2 cups confectioners' sugar for dusting cookies

2 1/4 cups all-purpose flour

1/2 teaspoon anise seeds, crushed

1/2 teaspoon ground black pepper

1/2 teaspoon ground cinnamon

1/4 teaspoon baking soda

1/4 teaspoon ground allspice

1/4 teaspoon ground nutmeg

1/8 teaspoon ground cloves

1/2 cup (1 stick) salted butter or margarine, at room temperature

3/4 cup packed light brown sugar

1/4 cup regular or unsulphured molasses

1 large egg, lightly beaten

1/2 teaspoon vanilla extract

1. Adjust two racks to divide the oven into thirds. Preheat the oven to 350°. Lightly grease two baking sheets. Place the confectioners' sugar in a brown paper bag.

2. In a medium-size bowl, with a whisk, combine the flour, anise seeds, black pepper, cinnamon, baking soda, allspice, nutmeg, and cloves until thoroughly mixed.

3. In a large bowl, with an electric mixer at medium-high speed, beat together the butter, brown sugar, and molasses until light and fluffy, 2 to 3 minutes. Beat in the egg and vanilla until well blended. With the mixer at medium-low speed, gradually add the flour mixture, beating just until blended. Scoop heaping measuring tablespoonfuls of dough out of the bowl and roll them between the palms of your hands into 1½-inch balls. Arrange the balls on the baking sheets, spacing them about 2 inches apart.

4. Bake for about 13 to 15 minutes until the balls are firm to the touch. Reverse the baking sheets on the racks and from front to back once during baking. Cool slightly on the baking sheets set on wire racks. Transfer a few warm cookies at a time to the paper bag containing the confectioners' sugar. Shake until the cookies are well coated. Place the coated cookies on wire racks to cool completely.

5. Store in a tightly covered container.

Yield: About 30 cookies

Ginger Nuts

It takes a few days for the flavor of these cookies to "mature," so plan to make them several days before you need them. Despite the name these cookies contain no nuts. The word refers to their texture, which is hard.

2 1/2 cups all-purpose flour

1 tablespoon ground ginger

1/2 cup (1 stick) salted butter or margarine, at room temperature

1/2 cup packed light brown sugar

3 tablespoons regular or unsulphured molasses

1 large egg

1/2 teaspoon baking soda

1 tablespoon water

1. Adjust two racks to divide the oven into thirds. Preheat the oven to 375°. Lightly grease two baking sheets.

2. In a medium-size bowl, with a whisk, combine the flour and ginger until thoroughly mixed.

3. In a large bowl, with an electric mixer at medium speed, beat the butter until creamy, about 1 minute. Beat in the sugar until light and fluffy, about 2 minutes. Beat in the molasses and egg until blended.

4. Dissolve the baking soda in the water and stir into the batter. With the mixer at low speed, gradually add the flour mixture, beating until the dough is smooth and stiff.

5. Scoop heaping measuring tablespoonfuls of the dough out of the bowl and roll them into $1^{1}/_{2}$-inch balls between the palms of your hands. Place the balls on the baking sheets, spacing them about 2 inches apart.

6. Bake for 15 minutes until the bottoms are a light, golden color. Reverse the baking sheets on the racks and from front to back once during baking. With a wide turner, immediately transfer the cookies to wire racks to cool completely.

7. Store in a tightly covered container. These cookies keep better than most, at least a month.

Yield: About 24 cookies

3. With lightly floured hands, pinch off pieces of the dough and roll them into 1-inch balls between the palms of your hands. Arrange the balls on the prepared baking sheets, spacing them about 1 inch apart.

4. Bake for 15 to 20 minutes until lightly browned. Reverse the sheets on the racks and from front to back once during baking. With a wide turner, immediately transfer the cookies from the baking sheets to wire racks to cool completely.

5. Store in a tightly covered container.

Yield: About 60 cookies

Dutch Spice Wafers

This is a very pleasing little cookie with a wonderful spicy flavor, which mellows and intensifies if the cookie is allowed to linger in the storage container for a couple of days before it is eaten.

> 2 cups sifted all-purpose flour
> $^{1}/_{2}$ teaspoon baking powder
> $^{1}/_{4}$ teaspoon anise seed, crushed (see Tip)
> $^{1}/_{4}$ teaspoon ground cardamom
> $^{1}/_{4}$ teaspoon ground cinnamon
> $^{1}/_{4}$ teaspoon ground nutmeg
> $^{1}/_{4}$ teaspoon salt
> 1 $^{1}/_{4}$ cups packed dark brown sugar
> 2 large eggs, lightly beaten
> 2 teaspoons finely chopped candied orange peel

1. Adjust two racks to divide the oven into thirds. Preheat the oven to 350°. Lightly grease two baking sheets.

2. Into a large bowl, sift together the flour, baking powder, anise seed, cardamom, cinnamon, nutmeg, and salt. With an electric mixer at medium speed, beat in the sugar, eggs, and orange peel until the mixture forms a soft dough. Add a little more flour, if necessary.

Tip

A mortar and pestle is the best way to crush anise seed. Lacking one of these, use something heavy, even a hammer, and crush the seeds in a plastic bag.

Mexican Wedding Cakes I

This is a cookie with many names, depending on what country you are in. In Russia there is a similar cookie known as Russian Tea Cakes (opposite page); in Greece they are called Powder Cookies; (page 196); and sometimes they are just called Crescents; but Mexican Wedding Cakes is the name that is most familiar. This is a very simple version of these cookies. Another more authentic version follows. (Also see JoAnn Macdonald's Monster Crescent Cookies on page 197.)

> 1 cup almond or pecan pieces
> 2 cups all-purpose flour, divided
> 1 cup confectioners' sugar, divided
> 1 cup (2 sticks) salted butter or margarine,
>   at room temperature
> 2 teaspoons vanilla extract

1. Adjust two racks to divide the oven into thirds. Preheat the oven to 325°. Have ready two ungreased baking sheets.

2. In a food processor fitted with a steel blade, process the nuts with ¼ cup of the flour, using on-off pulses until finely ground, stopping the processor once to give the nuts a good stir from the bottom to keep them from beccoming pasty.

3. In a medium-size bowl, with a whisk, combine the remaining 1¾ cups of flour and ground nuts until thoroughly mixed.

4. In a large bowl, with an electric mixer at medium-high speed, beat together ½ cup of the confectioners' sugar, butter, and vanilla until light and fluffy, 2 to 3 minutes. With the mixer at medium-low speed, gradually add the flour mixture, beating until the mixture forms a dough.

5. Sprinkle the remaining ½ cup confectioners' sugar on a sheet of waxed paper. Scoop the dough by heaping measuring teaspoonfuls out of the bowl and shape them into 1-inch balls between the palms of your hands. Arrange the balls on the ungreased baking sheets, spacing them about 1 inch apart.

6. Bake for about 18 minutes until set, but not brown. Reverse the baking sheets on the racks and from front to back once during baking. With a wide turner, immediately transfer the cookies to wire racks. Before they have had a chance to cool too much, roll each ball in the confectioners' sugar. Return to the wire racks to cool completely.

7. Store in a tightly covered container.

Yield: About 60 cookies

Mexican Wedding Cakes II

Masa harina, which is called for in this recipe, is a flour made from treated corn that is usually used to make tortillas. It can be found in Mexican grocery stores and many supermarkets.

> 1 cup all-purpose flour
> 2 tablespoons masa harina
> ½ cup (1 stick) salted butter or margarine,
>   at room temperature
> ⅓ cup confectioners' sugar, plus 2 cups for
>   coating cookies
> ½ teaspoon vanilla extract
> ¾ cup pecans, toasted (page 16), cooled and
>   minced or very finely chopped

1. Adjust two racks to divide the oven into thirds. Preheat the oven to 300°. Have ready two ungreased baking sheets. Place 2 cups of the confectioners' sugar in a brown paper bag.

2. In a small bowl, with a whisk, combine the flour and masa harina until thoroughly mixed.

3. In a large bowl, with an electric mixer at medium-high speed, beat together the butter, ⅓ cup confectioners' sugar, and vanilla extract until light and fluffy, 2 to 3 minutes. With the mixer at medium-low speed, gradually add the flour mixture, beating just until blended. With a mixing spoon, stir in the pecans until well distributed throughout the dough.

4. Scoop heaping measuring teaspoonfuls of the dough out of the bowl and roll them into 1-inch

balls between the palms of your hands. Arrange the balls on the ungreased baking sheets, spacing them about 1 inch apart.

5. Bake for about 25 minutes until the cookies just begin to turn golden. Reverse the baking sheets on the racks and from front to back once during baking. Cool slightly on the baking sheets set on wire racks. Transfer a few warm cookies at a time to the paper bag containing the confectioners' sugar. Shake until the cookies are well coated. Place the coated cookies on wire racks to cool completely.

6. Store in a tightly covered container.

Yield: About 24 cookies

Russian Tea Cakes

These little cookies are sort of like a ball-shaped shortbread, slightly crumbly with a real melt-in-the-mouth texture. Although a Russian probably wouldn't consider it, if you're a chocolate lover feel free to add $1/2$ cup of semisweet chocolate chips or chopped chocolate to the dough at the same time the nuts are added.

1 $1/2$ cups plus $1/3$ cup confectioners' sugar, divided

1 cup (2 sticks) salted butter or margarine, at room temperature

1 teaspoon vanilla extract

2 $1/4$ cups all-purpose flour

1 cup finely chopped walnuts, toasted (page 16)

1. Adjust two racks to divide the oven into thirds. Preheat the oven to 375°. Have ready two ungreased baking sheets. Place 1½ cups of the confectioners' sugar in a large bowl.

2. In a large bowl, with an electric mixer at medium speed, beat the butter until creamy, about 1 minute. Add the remaining $1/3$ cup of confectioners' sugar and the vanilla and beat until fluffy, 2 to 3 minutes. With the mixer at low speed,

gradually add the flour, beating just until blended. With a mixing spoon, stir in the nuts until well distributed throughout the dough. (At this point, the dough can be wrapped tightly in aluminum foil and refrigerated for one week or frozen for up to three months. If frozen, thaw in the refrigerator. Bring to room temperature before proceeding.)

3. Pinch off pieces of the dough and shape them into 1-inch balls between the palms of your hands. Place the balls on the baking sheets, spacing them about 2 inches apart.

4. Bake for 8 to 10 minutes until set, but not brown. Reverse the baking sheets on the racks and from front to back once during baking.

5. Working quickly, with a wide turner, remove a few of the hot cookies from a baking sheet and immediately drop them into the bowl of sugar; roll to coat them with the sugar. Transfer the coated cookies to wire racks to cool completely. Repeat with the remaining cookies. When the cookies have cooled, roll them again in the confectioners' sugar.

6. Store in a tightly covered container, separated by sheets of waxed paper.

Yield: About 48 cookies

Greek Powder Cookies (Kourambiethes)

In Greece, powder cookies (powder referring to a thick coating of "powdered" sugar) come in many sizes and shapes—round, triangular, crescents—depending on who is making them. They are popular throughout the year, and are certain to appear at all celebrations and on all holidays. At Christmas, a clove is stuck into the center to symbolize the spices the Wise Men brought to Bethlehem.

Considering the Greeks' collective sweet tooth, it's surprising that these cookies aren't more sweet than they are. They are, however, rolled in confectioners' sugar, and lots of it, just before they are served. I like to serve them on a big platter, garnished with fresh strawberries for dessert.

2 1/2 cups all-purpose flour
1/2 teaspoon baking powder
1 cup (2 sticks) unsalted butter (not margarine), at room temperature
1/4 cup confectioners' sugar, plus additional for sprinkling on cookies
1 large egg yolk
1/4 cup brandy
1/2 teaspoon vanilla extract
1/3 cup sliced or slivered almonds, toasted (page 16) and very finely chopped, but not pulverized
2 tablespoons granulated sugar
1/4 cup rose water (see Tip)

1. Adjust one rack to the lowest oven position. Preheat the oven to 250°. Have ready two ungreased baking sheets.

2. In a medium-size bowl, with a whisk, combine the flour and baking powder until thoroughly combined.

3. In a large bowl, with an electric mixer at medium speed, beat the butter until creamy, about 1 minute. Add the confectioners' sugar and egg yolk and continue beating until light and fluffy, 2 to 3 minutes. Beat in the brandy and vanilla. The mixture will look curdled. With the mixer at low speed, gradually add the flour mixture, beating just until blended. The dough will be soft and will leave the side of the bowl. With a mixing spoon, stir in the almonds and granulated sugar until well blended.

4. Using a heaping measuring tablespoonful of the dough for each cookie, roll into a ball between the palms of your hands and then flatten it to make a 1/2-inch-thick disk that measures about 1 1/2 inches in diameter. Arrange the cookies on the ungreased baking sheet, spacing them about 2 inches apart. With your thumb, make a fairly deep indentation in the center of each cookie. (These cookies must be baked one batch at a time. After one baking sheet is filled, cover the dough remaining in the bowl with plastic wrap. You can start forming the second batch of cookies a few minutes before the first batch is due to come out of the oven.)

5. Bake for about 30 minutes until the cookies have formed a crust and are just beginning to color, reversing the baking sheet from front to back once during baking. They will still feel slightly soft when lightly pressed. If you have any doubts, break a cookie in half. If it still looks unbaked in the center, bake for 5 minutes longer. With a wide turner, immediately transfer the cookies to wire racks to cool completely. While the cookies are still warm, place one drop of rose water on top of each.

6. Store the cookies in a tightly covered container, where they will keep nicely for several weeks. Before serving, roll the cookies in confectioners' sugar and stack them on a serving plate, sprinkling more confectioners' sugar between the layers.

Yield: About 24 cookies

Tip

Rose water is distilled from fresh rose petals, and can be found in specialty food stores that have a good stock of flavorings and extracts. If you can't find it, don't worry. The cookies are delicious without it.

JoAnn Macdonald's Monster Crescent Cookies

This is another cookie that my tasters rated A-plus.

- 1 cup pecan or walnut pieces
- 2 cups all-purpose flour, divided
- 1 cup (2 sticks) salted butter or margarine, at room temperature
- 1 teaspoon vanilla extract
- 1 cup confectioners' sugar, divided

1. Adjust two racks to divide the oven into thirds. Have ready two ungreased baking sheets.

2. In a food processor fitted with a steel blade, process the nuts with $\frac{1}{4}$ cup of the flour, using on-off pulses until finely ground.

3. In a medium-size bowl, with a whisk, combine the ground nuts and the remaining $1\frac{3}{4}$ cups of flour until thoroughly mixed.

4. In a large bowl, with an electric mixer at medium speed, beat the butter with the vanilla until creamy, about 1 minute. Add $\frac{1}{2}$ cup of the confectioners' sugar and beat until light and fluffy, about 2 minutes. With the mixer at low speed, gradually add the flour mixture, beating just until blended.

5. With a measuring tablespoon, scoop 2 tablespoon-size pieces of dough out of the bowl and shape them into crescents with your fingers. Arrange the crescents on the baking sheets, spacing them about $\frac{1}{2}$ inch apart. Place the baking sheets, uncovered, in the refrigerator until the crescents are firm, about 1 hour.

6. Preheat the oven to 350°.

7. Bake for about 20 minutes until barely colored and firm when lightly touched. Reverse the baking sheets on the racks and from front to back once during baking. With a wide turner, immediately transfer the cookies to wire racks. While the cookies are still warm, sift over them the remaining $\frac{1}{2}$ cup confectioners' sugar, which will melt and form a thin glaze. Allow the cookies to cool completely.

8. Store in a tightly covered container.

Yield: 18 to 24 cookies

Chocolate Crescents

- 1 $\frac{3}{4}$ cups all-purpose flour
- $\frac{1}{4}$ cup unsweetened cocoa powder
- 1 cup (2 sticks) salted butter or margarine
- 1 cup confectioners' sugar
- 1 teaspoon vanilla extract
- $\frac{1}{2}$ cup finely chopped almonds, walnuts, or pecans
- Confectioners' sugar for dusting cookies

1. Adjust two racks to divide the oven into thirds. Preheat the oven to 350°. Have ready two ungreased baking sheets.

2. In a medium-size bowl, with a whisk, combine the flour and the cocoa until thoroughly mixed.

3. In a large bowl, with an electric mixer at medium-high speed, beat together the butter, confectioners' sugar, and vanilla until light and fluffy, 2 to 3 minutes. With the mixer at medium-low speed, gradually add the flour mixture, beating just until blended. With a mixing spoon, stir in the nuts until evenly distributed throughout the dough. Scoop heaping teaspoonfuls of the dough out of the bowl and shape them into crescents with your fingers. Arrange the crescents on the ungreased baking sheets, spacing them about 2 inches apart.

4. Bake for 12 to 15 minutes until firm when lightly touched. Reverse the baking sheets on the racks and from front to back once during baking. With a wide turner, immediately transfer the cookies to wire racks to cool completely. Sprinkle lightly with confectioners' sugar while still warm.

5. Store in a tightly covered container.

Yield: About 48 cookies

Variation

Vanilla Crescents: Increase the flour by 2 tablespoons and omit the unsweetened cocoa powder.

Fuss Cookies

I can't imagine where this cookie got its funny name. All I know is that it's tender and melts in your mouth, and who could ask for more.

> 1 cup (2 sticks) salted butter or margarine, at room temperature
> $^1/_2$ cup sugar
> 2 teaspoons vanilla extract
> 3 $^1/_2$ cups cake flour (not self-rising flour)
> About 48 pecan halves
> Confectioners' sugar, for sprinkling on cookies

1. Adjust two racks to divide the oven into thirds. Preheat the oven to 325°. Lightly grease two baking sheets.

2. In a large bowl, with an electric mixer at medium-high speed, beat together the butter, sugar, and vanilla until light and fluffy, 2 to 3 minutes. With the mixer at medium-low speed, gradually add as much flour as possible. When the dough becomes too stiff for the electric mixer, work the remaining flour in by hand. The dough will be very stiff. Pinch off pieces of the dough and roll them into 1 inch balls. Arrange the balls on the prepared baking sheets, spacing them about 1$^1/_2$ inches apart. Press a pecan half into the center of each ball.

3. Bake for 12 to 15 minutes until pale brown. Reverse the baking sheets on the racks and from front to back once during baking. With a wide turner, immediately transfer the cookies to wire racks to cool completely.

4. Store in a tightly covered container. Sprinkle lavishly with confectioners' sugar before serving.

Yield: About 48 cookies

Christmas Candy Canes

Rolling two colors and flavors of dough into tiny ropes, then twisting them together and shaping them into candy-cane cookies, is a nifty family baking project for the holidays.

> $^1/_2$ cup granulated sugar
> $^1/_2$ cup crushed peppermint candy canes or hard peppermint candies
> $^1/_2$ cup (1 stick) salted butter or margarine, at room temperature
> $^1/_2$ cup plain or butter-flavored shortening
> 1 cup confectioners' sugar
> 1 large egg
> 1 teaspoon vanilla extract
> $^1/_2$ teaspoon peppermint extract
> 2 $^1/_2$ cups all-purpose flour
> $^1/_2$ teaspoon liquid red food coloring

1. Adjust two racks to divide the oven into thirds. Preheat the oven to 375°. Have ready two ungreased baking sheets. In a small bowl, mix the sugar with the crushed candy; set aside.

2. In a large bowl, with an electric mixer at medium-high speed, beat together the butter, shortening, confectioners' sugar, egg, vanilla, and peppermint extract until light and fluffy, 2 to 3 minutes. With the mixer at medium-low speed, gradually add the flour, beating just until blended. Remove half of the dough from the bowl and set aside on a sheet of waxed paper. To the dough remaining in the bowl, add the red food coloring and beat until evenly colored. (At this point both of the doughs can be tightly wrapped separately in aluminum foil and refrigerated for up to a week or frozen for up to three months. If frozen, thaw in the refrigerator and bring to room temperature before proceeding.)

3. For each candy cane, scoop 1 teaspoonful of the plain dough and the same amount of pink dough. Roll each scoop between the palms of your hands to make a 4-inch rope. Twist the ropes together and shape into a candy cane. As they are made, arrange the canes on an ungreased baking sheet, spacing them about 1 inch apart.

4. Bake for about 9 minutes until firm to the touch and barely golden. Reverse the baking sheets on the racks and from front to back once during baking. The moment the cookies come from the oven, sprinkle each one with the sugar-and-peppermint mixture. With a wide turner, immediately transfer the cookies to wire racks to cool completely.

5. Store in a tightly covered container, separating the layers with sheets of waxed paper.

Yield: About 48 cookies

Orange and Peanut Butter–Flavored Whole Wheat Cookies

These wholesome cookies are perfect for the kids' lunch boxes and also great as an after-school snack, served with milk and small bunches of seedless grapes or tangerines.

> $^1/_3$ cup plus 3 tablespoons granulated sugar, divided
>
> 1 $^1/_4$ cups whole wheat flour
>
> $^1/_2$ teaspoon baking powder
>
> $^1/_2$ teaspoon baking soda
>
> $^1/_2$ cup (1 stick) salted butter or margarine, at room temperature
>
> $^1/_2$ cup chunky peanut butter
>
> $^2/_3$ cup packed light brown sugar
>
> 1 large egg
>
> 2 teaspoons shredded and minced orange zest
>
> 1 teaspoon vanilla extract

1. Adjust two racks to divide the oven into thirds. Have ready two ungreased baking sheets. Place 3 tablespoons of the granulated sugar in a mound on a sheet of waxed paper; set aside.

2. In a medium-size bowl, with a whisk, combine the whole wheat flour, baking powder, and baking soda until thoroughly mixed.

3. In a large bowl, with an electric mixer at medium-high speed, beat together the butter and peanut butter until well blended, about 1 minute. Add the brown sugar and the remaining $^1/_3$ cup granulated sugar. Beat until well blended, about 1 minute. Add the egg, orange zest, and vanilla and beat again until light and fluffy, 2 to 3 minutes. With the mixer at medium-low speed, gradually add the flour mixture, beating just until blended. Cover the bowl and refrigerate until the dough is chilled, about 1 hour.

4. Preheat the oven to 350°.

5. Scoop heaping measuring teaspoonfuls of dough out of the bowl and roll them into 1-inch balls between the palms of your hands. As they are shaped, arrange the balls on the ungreased baking sheets, spacing them about 2 inches apart. Dip the tines of a dinner fork into the granulated sugar and gently press down on each ball twice, making a crisscross pattern.

6. Bake for about 12 minutes until lightly browned. Reverse the baking sheets on the racks and from front to back once during baking. With a wide turner, immediately transfer the cookies to wire racks to cool completely.

7. Store in a tightly covered container.

Yield: About 36 cookies

Bridal Shower Jewels

These buttery-rich, pale pink cookies are studded with bits of cherries, which makes them a pretty choice for a bridal shower table.

2 ¹/₄ cups all-purpose flour
¹/₂ teaspoon ground nutmeg
¹/₂ cup sugar
²/₃ cup (1 stick plus 3 tablespoons) salted butter, at room temperature
1 large egg, lightly beaten
¹/₂ teaspoon brandy extract
¹/₂ cup chopped maraschino cherries, well drained and patted dry
Confectioners' sugar, for dusting cookies

1. Adjust two racks to divide the oven into thirds. Preheat the oven to 350°. Have ready two ungreased baking sheets.

2. In a large bowl, with a whisk, combine the flour and nutmeg until thoroughly mixed. Add the sugar, butter, egg, brandy extract, and cherries. With the mixer at medium-low speed, beat until well blended, 2 to 3 minutes. Scoop the dough out of the bowl by heaping measuring teaspoonfuls and roll them between the palms of your hands into 1-inch balls. Arrange the balls on the ungreased baking sheets, spacing them about 2 inches apart.

3. Bake for 10 to 15 minutes until the edges are lightly browned. Reverse the baking sheets on the racks and from front to back once during baking. With a wide turner, immediately transfer the cookies to wire racks to cool completely.

4. Store in a tightly covered container. Dust with confectioners' sugar just before serving.

Yield: About 42 cookies

Monterey Cheese Cookies

These are definitely the cookies to make when you are tired of the same-old, same-old. This is basically one of those thousands of butter-sugar-flour cookie recipes with one important difference. Shredded cheese is added to the batter.

1 cup all-purpose flour
1 teaspoon baking powder
¹/₃ cup (¹/₂ stick plus 1 ¹/₂ tablespoons) salted butter or margarine, at room temperature
¹/₂ cup sugar
1 cup (4 ounces) shredded Monterey Jack cheese
1 large egg, lightly beaten, for brushing on cookies

1. Adjust two racks to divide the oven into thirds. Preheat the oven to 375°. Lightly grease two baking sheets.

2. In a small bowl, with a whisk, combine the flour and baking powder until thoroughly mixed.

3. In a medium-size bowl, with an electric mixer at medium-high speed, beat together the butter and sugar until light and fluffy, 2 to 3 minutes. With the mixer at medium-low speed, gradually add the flour mixture, beating just until blended. With a mixing spoon, stir in the cheese until well distributed throughout the dough.

4. Scoop out heaping measuring teaspoonfuls of the dough out of the bowl and roll them between the palms of your hands into little sticks measuring about 3 inches in length. Arrange the sticks on the baking sheets, spacing them about 2 inches apart. Press each one gently to flatten slightly. Brush with the beaten egg.

5. Bake for 8 to 10 minutes until lightly browned around the edges. Reverse the baking sheets on the racks and from front to back once during baking. With a wide turner, immediately transfer the cookies to wire racks to cool completely.

6. Store in a tightly covered container.

Yield: About 24 cookies

k very
erica's
ds have

rictly Ameri-
ow that they
and, depend-
re, have different
giveaway: a round
that can hold an
ngs. Too often we use
s when, in fact, almost
e little depression works
just as well. (See Chocolate Thumbprints on page 202 for more filling ideas.)

Classic Thumbprint Cookies

This is the thumbprint cookie that your great-grandmother used to make, and it is still one of the world's most perfect cookies.

- 2 cups all-purpose flour
- $1/2$ teaspoon baking powder
- 1 large egg, separated
- 1 $1/4$ cups finely chopped pecans, divided
- 1 cup (2 sticks) salted butter or margarine, at room temperature
- 1 $1/2$ teaspoons vanilla extract
- $1/2$ cup sugar
- 1 tablespoon milk
- Red or green maraschino or candied cherry halves

1. Adjust two racks to divide the oven into thirds. Preheat the oven to 350°. Have ready two ungreased baking sheets.

2. In a medium-size bowl, with a whisk, combine the flour and baking powder until thoroughly mixed. In a shallow bowl, with a fork, beat the egg white until foamy; set aside. Sprinkle $3/4$ cup of the pecans on a sheet of waxed paper.

3. In a large bowl, with an electric mixer at medium speed, beat the butter with the vanilla until creamy, about 1 minute. Gradually add the sugar and continue beating until light and fluffy, 2 to 3 minutes. Beat in the egg yolk and the milk until blended. With the mixer at low speed, gradually add the flour mixture, beating just until blended. With a mixing spoon, stir in the remaining $1/2$ cup of pecans until well distributed throughout the dough.

4. Pinch off pieces of the dough and roll them into 1-inch balls between the palms of your hands. As they are formed, dip the balls in the egg white, then roll in the pecans. As they are dipped and rolled, arrange the balls on the ungreased baking sheets, spacing them about 1 inch apart. With your thumb, make an indentation in each dough ball. Fill the indentations with cherry halves.

5. Bake for 15 to 18 minutes just until firm. Reverse the baking sheets on the racks and from front to back once during baking. With a wide turner, immediately transfer the cookies to wire racks to cool completely.

6. Store in a tightly covered, shallow container, separating the layers with sheets of waxed paper.

Yield: About 54 cookies

Variation

Sesame Thumbprint Cookies: Omit the egg-white coating. Roll the balls in sesame seeds, which have been sprinkled on a sheet of waxed paper. Fill the indentations with jelly or preserves, dropped from the tip of a spoon.

Chocolate Thumbprints

Like all thumbprints, these can be filled with any number of things besides the traditional preserves. Several easy variations follow at the end of the recipe.

> 3 ounces (3 squares) unsweetened chocolate
>
> 1 cup (2 sticks) salted butter or margarine, at room temperature
>
> 1 cup packed light brown sugar
>
> 2 large eggs, separated
>
> 2 teaspoons vanilla extract
>
> 1 $^3/_4$ cups all-purpose flour
>
> 1 cup finely chopped walnuts
>
> $^1/_3$ cup raspberry or strawberry jelly

1. In a small, heavy saucepan, melt the chocolate over very low heat, stirring constantly until smooth. Remove from the heat and set aside.

2. In a large bowl, with an electric mixer at medium-high speed, beat together the butter and sugar until light and fluffy, 2 to 3 minutes. Beat in the egg yolks, vanilla, and melted chocolate until blended. With the mixer at low speed, beat in the flour. Gather the dough into a ball. Wrap in plastic wrap and refrigerate for 30 minutes. (At this point, the dough can be tightly wrapped in aluminum foil and refrigerated for up to one week or frozen for up to three months. If frozen, thaw in the refrigerator before proceeding.)

3. Adjust two racks to divide the oven into thirds. Preheat the oven to 350°. Lightly grease two baking sheets.

4. In a shallow dish, with a fork, beat the egg whites until foamy. Pinch off pieces of the chilled dough and shape them into 1½-inch balls between the palms of your hands. Dip each ball into the egg white, then roll in the walnuts. Arrange the balls on the prepared baking sheets, spacing them about 1 inch apart. With your thumb, make an indentation in each dough ball. With the tip of a teaspoon, fill the indentation with jelly.

5. Bake for 12 to 14 minutes just until firm. Reverse the sheets on the racks and from front to back once during baking. With a wide turner, immediately transfer the cookies to wire racks to cool completely.

6. Store in a tightly covered, shallow container, separating the layers with sheets of waxed paper.

Yield: About 48 cookies

Variation

Candy Man Thumbprints: Roll the balls of dough in chocolate sprinkles, if desired, before placing them on the baking sheet. Fill with candy-coated chocolates, crushed peppermint, gum drops, jelly beans, whole chocolate kisses, or whole candied cherries.

Lemon Well Thumbprints

For an easy change, these thumbprints can be filled with jam or preserves instead of almonds. I like to use two or three kinds of preserves—apricot, raspberry, and blueberry, for instance—for color variation.

> 2 $^1/_2$ cups all-purpose flour
>
> 1 teaspoon baking powder
>
> 1 cup (2 sticks) salted butter or margarine, at room temperature
>
> 1 cup sugar
>
> 2 large egg yolks
>
> 2 teaspoons vanilla extract
>
> 2 teaspoons almond extract
>
> 1 teaspoon lemon extract
>
> About 35 whole blanched almonds

1. In a small bowl, with a whisk, combine the flour and baking powder until thoroughly mixed.

2. In a large bowl, with an electric mixer at medium speed, beat together the butter and sugar until light and fluffy, 2 to 3 minutes. Add egg yolks, one at a time, beating until blended after each addition. Beat in the vanilla, almond, and lemon extracts until blended. With the mixer at low speed, gradually beat in the flour mixture.

Gather the dough into a ball. Wrap in plastic wrap and refrigerate for 30 minutes. (At this point, the dough can be tightly wrapped in aluminum foil and refrigerated for up to one week or frozen for up to three months. If frozen, thaw in the refrigerator before proceeding.)

3. Adjust two racks to divide the oven into thirds. Preheat the oven to 225°. Have ready two ungreased baking sheets.

4. Roll the cold dough by tablespoonfuls between the palms of your hands into balls. Arrange the balls on the baking sheets, spacing them about 1½ inches apart. With your thumb, make an indentation in each dough ball. Place an almond in each indentation.

5. Bake for about 30 minutes until the bottoms of the cookies are dry and the tops are very pale colored. Reverse the baking sheets on the racks and from front to back once during baking. With a wide turner, immediately transfer the cookies to wire racks to cool completely.

6. Store in a tightly covered, shallow container, separating the layers with sheets of waxed paper.

Yield: About 36 cookies

Santa's Helpers

This is a thumbprint cookie, of sorts, but only if a giant makes the thumbprint.

Topping

½ cup packed light brown sugar

¼ cup sour cream

½ teaspoon ground cinnamon

1 cup coarsely chopped walnuts

Cookies

2 cups all-purpose flour

½ teaspoon baking soda

½ cup (1 stick) salted butter or margarine, at room temperature

1 cup packed light brown sugar

1 large egg

1 teaspoon vanilla extract

Icing

½ cup sifted confectioners' sugar

1 tablespoon water

1. Adjust two racks to divide the oven into thirds. Preheat the oven to 350°. Have ready two ungreased baking sheets.

2. To prepare the topping: In a small bowl, with a mixing spoon, stir together the sugar, sour cream, and cinnamon until smooth. Stir in the walnuts until blended; set aside.

3. To make the cookies: In a medium-size bowl, with a whisk, combine the flour and baking soda until thoroughly mixed.

4. In a large bowl, with an electric mixer at medium-high speed, beat together the butter and sugar until well blended. Add the egg and vanilla and beat until light and fluffy, 2 to 3 minutes. With the mixer at medium-low speed, gradually add the flour mixture, beating just until blended.

5. Gather the dough into a ball and flatten it into a 1-inch-thick disk. With a sharp knife, cut the disk into 12 equal parts. Roll each part into a ball between the palms of your hands. Arrange the balls on the baking sheets, spacing them about 3 inches apart. With your fingertips, make a wide, round depression in the center of each cookie that reaches almost to the edges, leaving a rim. Fill each depression with the topping, dividing evenly and mounding fairly high above the rims.

6. Bake for 15 to 20 minutes until the filling is set. Reverse the baking sheets on the racks and from front to back once during baking. With a wide turner, transfer the cookies to wire racks to cool completely. If you want to ice the cookies, in a small bowl, mix the confectioners' sugar and water until smooth. Drizzle the icing from the tip of a teaspoon over the rims of the cookies.

7. Store in a tightly covered, shallow container.

Yield: 12 cookies

Tip

If you want to make smaller cookies, form the dough into 24 balls and arrange 2 inches apart on the baking sheets. Fill and bake as directed above, although the baking time will be reduced.

Tiny Chocolate-Filled Almond-Button Thumbprints

Everyone loves these nutty-flavored, one-bite cookies. They literally melt in your mouth.

  1 cup blanched whole almonds, toasted (page 16)

  $^3/_4$ cup confectioners' sugar, divided

  2 cups all-purpose flour

  1 cup (2 sticks) salted butter or margarine, at room temperature

  1 teaspoon vanilla extract

  3 ounces (3 squares) semisweet chocolate

1. Place the almonds and $^1/_4$ cup of the confectioners' sugar in a food processor fitted with a steel blade. Process the almonds with on-off pulses, stopping the processor once and giving the almonds a good stir from the bottom to keep them from becoming pasty.

2. In a large bowl, with a whisk, combine the ground almonds, flour, and the remaining $^1/_2$ cup confectioners' sugar until thoroughly mixed. With a mixing spoon, stir in the butter and vanilla until a soft dough forms that is not at all crumbly. Cover the bowl and refrigerate until the dough is cold, about 1 hour.

3. Adjust two racks to divide the oven into thirds. Preheat the oven to 350°. Have ready two ungreased baking sheets.

4. Pinch off pieces of the cold dough and shape them into $^3/_4$-inch balls between the palms of your hands. Arrange the balls on the ungreased

baking sheets, spacing them about $^1/_2$ inch apart. With your finger, make a $^1/_2$-inch indentation in the top of each ball.

5. Bake for about 15 minutes until the cookies are only slightly colored. Reverse the baking sheets on the racks and from front to back once during baking. With a wide turner, immediately transfer the cookies to wire racks to cool completely.

6. While the cookies are cooling, in a small, heavy saucepan, melt the chocolate over very low heat, stirring constantly until smooth. With the tip of a teaspoon, spoon a small amount of chocolate into each indentation. Set aside until the chocolate is firm, about 2 hours.

7. Store in a tightly covered container, separating the layers with sheets of waxed paper.

Yield: About 96 cookies

Portugal Cakes

If you have visited Portugal, you will have undoubtedly succumbed to the temptation of these light and buttery cookies, which are invariably on display in every bakery window. They look more like tiny cakes than cookies, because they are baked in muffin pans.

  4 large eggs, separated, at room temperature

  1 cup (2 sticks) butter or margarine, at room temperature

  1 cup sugar

  $^1/_4$ cup dry port or sherry

  1 cup all-purpose flour

  $^1/_8$ teaspoon freshly grated nutmeg

  1 cup dried currants

1. Adjust two racks to divide the oven into thirds. Preheat the oven to 350°. Lightly grease forty-eight $1^1/_2$-inch minimuffin-pan cups.

2. In a medium-size bowl, with an electric mixer at low speed, beat the egg whites until frothy; beat at high speed just until stiff peaks form when the beaters are lifted.

3. In a large bowl, with the electric mixer at medium-high speed (there is no need to wash the beaters), beat together the butter and the sugar until light and fluffy, 2 to 3 minutes.

4. In a small bowl, beat the egg yolks with the port until blended; add to the butter mixture and beat at medium-high speed until very light and fluffy, 3 to 4 minutes. With a rubber spatula, fold the egg whites into the batter until no streaks of white remain. Sift together the flour and the nutmeg over the batter, folding as you sift, just until blended. Fold in the currants. Spoon the batter into the prepared cups, filling each one two-thirds full.

5. Bake for about 20 minutes until the tops are golden brown. Reverse the pans on the racks and from front to back once during baking. Cool in the pans set on wire racks for 5 minutes. Remove the cookies from the pans and arrange on wire racks to cool completely.

6. Store in an airtight container.

Yield: 48 cookies

American Pecan Tassies
· ·

Tartlike tassies are as American as pecan pie and probably originated in the South.

Dough

1 ¹/₂ cups all-purpose flour
³/₄ cup granulated sugar
³/₄ cup (1 ¹/₂ sticks) salted butter or margarine, cut into small pieces
1 large egg, lightly beaten

Filling

1 large egg
¹/₂ cup packed dark brown sugar
2 tablespoons light corn syrup
2 teaspoons vanilla extract
¹/₂ cup chopped pecans, toasted (page 16)
36 pecan halves

1. Adjust two racks to divide the oven into thirds. Preheat the oven to 350°. Insert paper liners in three 12-cup, 1¹/₂-inch mini-muffin pans.

2. To make the dough: In a medium-size bowl, with a whisk, combine the flour and sugar until thoroughly mixed. With a pastry blender or two knives, cut in the butter until the mixture resembles coarse crumbs. With a mixing spoon, stir in the egg, then use your hands to mix these ingredients into a dough. Gather the dough into a ball and wrap in waxed paper. Refrigerate the dough while preparing the filling. (At this point, the dough can be tightly wrapped in aluminum foil and refrigerated for up to one week or frozen for up to three months. If frozen, thaw in the refrigerator before proceeding.)

3. To make the filling: In a large bowl, with a fork, beat together the egg, brown sugar, corn syrup, and vanilla. Stir in the chopped pecans.

4. On a work surface, shape the dough into a rectangle. Cut the rectangle in half, then cut the halves in half. Continue in this manner until you have 36 equal-size pieces of dough. Press each piece into the bottoms and up the sides of the paper-lined muffin cups. Spoon 1 heaping teaspoonful of filling into each cup. Top each tassie with a pecan half.

5. Bake for 24 to 26 minutes until golden. Reverse the pans on the racks and from front to back once during baking. Cool in the muffin pans set on wire racks for 10 minutes. Carefully remove the tassies from the muffin pans to wire racks to cool completely.

6. Although tassies are best when served fresh—even warm—they can be stored at room temperature or in the refrigerator in a tightly covered, shallow pan for one or two days. For longer storage, wrap tightly and freeze. Thaw at room temperature for an hour or two before serving.

Yield: 36 tassies

Greek Letter Cookies

Traditional shapes for these cookies include rings, half circles, figure eights, S-curves, and even Greek letters. A food processor is necessary to make these cookies. Don't try to use a blender. It won't work.

- $^3/_4$ cup sugar
- 1 tablespoon shredded and minced orange zest
- 2 teaspoons shredded and minced lemon zest
- $^1/_3$ cup chopped walnuts, toasted (page 16)
- $^1/_2$ cup (1 stick) salted butter or margarine, at room temperature
- 1 large egg
- 1 large egg yolk
- 1 tablespoon water
- 2 cups all-purpose flour
- $^3/_4$ teaspoon baking powder
- $^1/_2$ teaspoon baking soda
- $^1/_4$ teaspoon salt

1. In a food processor fitted with a steel blade, combine the sugar and orange and lemon zests. Process until well blended, stopping once or twice to scrape down the side of the work bowl with a rubber spatula. Add the walnuts and process until finely chopped. Add the butter, egg, egg yolk, and water. Process until well blended. Add the flour, baking powder, baking soda, and salt. Process with on-off pulses just until blended.

2. Divide the dough in half and wrap each half in plastic wrap. Refrigerate until firm, about 2 hours. (At this point the dough can be tightly wrapped in aluminum foil and refrigerated for up to one week or frozen for up to three months. If frozen, thaw in refrigerator before proceeding.)

3. Adjust two racks to divide the oven into thirds. Preheat the oven to 350°. Lightly grease two baking sheets.

4. Working with half of the chilled dough at a time, pinch off heaping measuring tablespoonfuls of dough. Roll each piece on a lightly floured surface to form an 8-inch rope. (The dough will soften as it warms. If it becomes difficult to

handle, rechill it for a few minutes.) As they are formed, place the ropes on the prepared baking sheets and twist into desired shapes. Repeat with the remaining chilled dough.

5. Bake for 10 to 12 minutes until golden brown. Reverse the baking sheets on the racks and from front to back once during baking. Cool on the baking sheets set on wire racks for 3 minutes. With a wide turner, transfer the cookies to wire racks to cool completely.

6. Store in a tightly covered container.

Yield: About 44 cookies

Roman "S" Cookies

As well as the traditional "S," these Italian cookies are often shaped into the initials of the person to whom they are being given.

- 2 $^1/_2$ cups sifted all-purpose flour
- $^1/_4$ teaspoon salt
- $^3/_4$ cup (1 $^1/_2$ sticks) salted butter or margarine, at room temperature
- $^1/_2$ cup sugar
- 2 large eggs, divided
- 1 teaspoon shredded and minced lemon zest
- $^1/_4$ cup ground blanched almonds
- 1 tablespoon water
- $^1/_4$ cup finely chopped blanched almonds

1. In a medium-size bowl, with a whisk, combine the flour and salt until thoroughly mixed.

2. In a large bowl, with an electric mixer at medium-high speed, beat together the butter and sugar until light and fluffy, 2 to 3 minutes. Beat in one of the eggs until very well blended. With a mixing spoon, stir in the lemon zest. Add the flour mixture, $^1/_2$ cup at a time, beating just until blended after each addition. With the mixing spoon, stir in the ground almonds until well blended.

3. Shape the dough into a ball with lightly floured hands. Divide the dough into 8 equal parts. Wrap each piece in plastic wrap and refrigerate until very cold, 1 to 2 hours.

4. Adjust two racks to divide the oven into thirds. Preheat the oven to 325°. Lightly grease and flour two baking sheets. Whisk the remaining egg and the water in a small bowl; set aside. Sprinkle the almonds on a piece of waxed paper.

5. On a lightly floured surface, roll one piece of the chilled dough into a cylinder 4 inches long and 1 inch in diameter. (Keep the remaining dough refrigerated.) Cut each cylinder into eight ¹/₂-inch slices. Roll each slice of dough into a 4-inch rope. Brush each rope with the egg mixture and sprinkle with chopped almonds. Arrange the ropes on the prepared baking sheets, spacing them about 1 inch apart, at the same time shaping each one into an "S" or other initial.

6. Bake for 8 to 10 minutes until lightly browned on the bottoms with pale tops. Reverse the baking sheets on the racks and from front to back once during baking, With a wide turner, immediately transfer the cookies from the baking sheets to wire racks to cool completely.

7. Store in a tightly covered container.

Yield: About 64 cookies

Madeleines
· ·

These small, sponge-cake cookies, light, rich, and pure in flavor, have been popular in France for centuries. Like Marcel Proust, most visitors to Paris hope for at least one "remembrance of time past" when they nibble on madeleines dipped in tea. Although madeleines can be baked in small muffin-pan cups, you will probably be more pleased with the results if you bake them in real madeleine plaques, which are heavy baking sheets with shell-shaped depressions measuring about 3 inches long and ¹/₂ inch deep. Madeleine plaques are available in many well-stocked housewares departments, kitchenware stores, or by mail (page 353–354), and are not very expensive.

> **4 large eggs, separated, whites at room temperature**
> **¹/₈ teaspoon salt**
> **¹/₂ cup sugar**
> **1 tablespoon strained fresh orange juice**

> **1 teaspoon shredded and minced orange zest**
> **³/₄ cup all-purpose flour**
> **¹/₂ cup (1 stick) unsalted butter or margarine, melted and cooled**
> **Confectioners' sugar, for dusting madeleines**

1. Adjust one rack to the lowest oven position. Preheat the oven to 400°. Brush 24 madeleine molds with melted butter and turn them upside down on paper towels to drain. Have ready one large, ungreased baking sheet.

2. In a large bowl, with an electric mixer at low speed, beat the egg whites with the salt just until frothy; beat at high speed just until stiff peaks form when the beaters are lifted.

3. In a small bowl, with the mixer at medium-high speed (there is no need to wash the beaters), beat together the egg yolks and the sugar until pale yellow and thick, and a ribbon forms when the beaters are lifted, 2 to 3 minutes. Beat in the orange juice and zest just until blended. Fold about one-quarter of the egg whites into the yolk mixture until no streaks of white remain. Then pour the yolk mixture over the remaining whites and gradually sift in the flour, folding as you sift. Slowly pour the melted butter into the egg mixture, folding as you pour, and leaving behind the milky residue beneath the clear butter.

4. With a measuring tablespoon, fill each madeleine mold three-quarters full of batter. Place the filled molds on the baking sheet. Bake for 10 to 15 minutes until golden. Reverse the baking sheet from front to back once during baking. With the tip of a kitchen knife, immediately unmold the madeleines and transfer them to wire racks, shell side up, to cool completely.

5. Arrange the madeleines on a plate in a single layer and cover tightly. Just before serving, sprinkle sparingly with confectioners' sugar.

6. Madeleines do not keep very well, so those that are not going to be served the same day they are baked should be frozen in zipper-top plastic bags. Thaw in the bag at room temperature for an hour or so before serving.

Yield: 24 madeleines

German Sweet Pretzels

When anything is pretzel-shaped you can be reasonably certain it has its roots in Germany. These pretzel cookies, as well as the Chocolate Pretzels that follow, are no exception. Don't attempt to make these on a hot day or in an overheated kitchen, since the dough must be kept cool at all times while you are working with it.

Pretzel shape

> 1 ³/₄ cups all-purpose flour
>
> 1 cup confectioners' sugar
>
> ³/₄ cup (1 ¹/₂ sticks) cold salted butter or margarine, cut into very small pieces
>
> 2 tablespoons shredded and minced lemon zest
>
> 5 large egg yolks
>
> 1 teaspoon vanilla extract
>
> Egg wash (1 egg beaten with 1 tablespoon water), for brushing on pretzels
>
> Colored sugar crystals, for decoration

1. Into a large bowl, sift together the flour and the confectioners' sugar. Add the butter and lemon zest. Using the tips of your fingers, mix the ingredients together until crumbly.

2. In a small bowl, with a fork, beat the egg yolks with the vanilla just until well blended; add to the flour mixture. Blend the mixture with a dinner fork just until the dough comes together. Turn the dough out onto a lightly floured surface and knead it for about 30 seconds. Wrap the dough in plastic wrap and refrigerate until chilled, about 30 minutes.

3. Divide the dough in half and form it into 2 cylinders, each measuring 14 × 1¹/₂ inches. Tightly wrap each cylinder in plastic wrap and refrigerate for at least 8 hours or overnight. (At this point, the dough can be tightly wrapped in aluminum foil and refrigerated for up to one week or frozen for up to three months. If frozen, thaw in the refrigerator before proceeding.)

4. Lightly grease and flour two baking sheets. Remove one cylinder of dough from the refrigerator and cut it into ¹/₂-inch slices. Roll each slice into a small cylinder. On a lightly floured surface,

roll each small cylinder into a 7-inch rope. Twist each rope into a pretzel shape (see illustration) directly on a prepared baking sheet, spacing them about 1 inch apart. With a pastry brush, brush the cookies with egg wash; sprinkle generously with colored sugar crystals. Place the baking sheets with the cookies on them in the refrigerator until the dough is firm, at least 20 minutes.

5. Adjust two racks to divide the oven into thirds. Preheat the oven to 350°.

6. Bake the chilled cookies for 8 to 9 minutes until golden brown around the edges. Reverse the baking sheets on the racks and from front to back once during baking. With a wide turner, immediately transfer the cookies from the baking sheets to wire racks to cool completely.

7. Repeat steps 4, 5, and 6 with the second cylinder of dough.

8. Store the cookies in a tightly covered container, separating the layers with sheets of waxed paper.

Yield: About 56 cookies

Chocolate Pretzels

> 2 ²/₃ cups all-purpose flour
>
> ¹/₃ cup unsweetened cocoa powder
>
> ³/₄ cup granulated sugar
>
> 1 cup (2 sticks) cold salted butter or margarine, cut into very small pieces

2 large egg whites, lightly beaten

2 teaspoons vanilla extract

4 1/2 ounces (4 1/2 squares) unsweetened chocolate, coarsely chopped

1/3 cup strong coffee

1 cup sifted confectioners' sugar

1. Remove 2 tablespoons of the butter and set aside.

2. In a large bowl, with a whisk, combine the flour and the cocoa until thoroughly mixed; stir in the sugar; stir in all but the 2 tablespoons of reserved butter pieces; add the egg whites and vanilla. With a mixing spoon or your hands, toss the mixture until the egg whites are well incorporated into the dough. Form the dough into a ball. On a smooth surface, knead the dough lightly for a few seconds to distribute the butter evenly. Reform the dough into a ball; wrap in plastic wrap or waxed paper and chill until very cold, at least 1 hour. (At this point, the dough can be tightly wrapped in aluminum foil and refrigerated for up to one week or frozen for up to three months. If frozen, thaw in the refrigerator before proceeding.)

3. Adjust two racks to divide the oven into thirds. Preheat the oven to 375°. Lightly grease two baking sheets.

4. Divide the dough into thirds. Working with one piece of dough at a time, and leaving the other two-thirds refrigerated, roll into a cylinder about 5 inches long and 1½ inches in diameter; slice the cylinder crosswise into ½-inch pieces. Roll each piece to the thickness of a pencil and twist it into a pretzel shape (see illustration, page 208) directly on a prepared baking sheet, spacing them about 1 inch apart. Repeat with the remaining dough.

5. Bake for 15 to 20 minutes until the pretzels are dry and hard. With a wide turner, immediately transfer the pretzels to wire racks to cool completely.

6. In a small, heavy saucepan over very low heat, melt the chocolate with the coffee, stirring constantly until smooth. Remove from the heat. Stir in the reserved 2 tablespoons of butter and the confectioners' sugar until smooth. With a small spatula or a butter spreader, spread the icing on top of the pretzels. Allow the chocolate to harden before storing, about 2 hours.

7. Store in a tightly covered container, separating the layers with sheets of waxed paper.

Yield: About 30 cookies

Czechoslovakian Almond Strips

The flavor and texture of this cookie is somewhere between a meringue and a biscotti, with a tantalizing hint of orange and lemon flavors.

2 large eggs

2/3 cup sugar

1 cup all-purpose flour

3/4 cup sliced blanched almonds

1/2 cup semisweet chocolate chips

1/3 cup chopped candied orange peel

1 teaspoon ground cinnamon

2 tablespoons shredded and minced lemon zest

1. Adjust one rack to divide the oven in half. Preheat the oven to 350°. Lightly grease and flour one baking sheet.

2. In a small bowl, with an electric mixer at medium-high speed, beat together the eggs and sugar until the mixture is thick and pale-colored, 3 to 4 minutes. With a mixing spoon, stir in the flour, almonds, chocolate chips, candied orange peel, cinnamon, and lemon zest until the mixture is well blended.

3. With a large spoon, form three 2-inch-wide and 12-inch-long strips of dough on the prepared baking sheet.

4. Bake for about 20 minutes until the strips are pale gold. While they are still hot, cut each strip on the diagonal into ½-inch pieces right on the baking sheet. With a wide turner, immediately transfer the cookies to wire racks to cool completely.

5. Store in a tightly covered container.

Yield: About 36 cookies

Danish Jelly Ribbons

If packed carefully, these beautiful cookies, which are pictured on the cover, can travel quite a distance to enhance a friend or relative's cookie platter. In that case, I would suggest using chopped almonds instead of sliced almonds, placing them on only the jelly filling so that they stay in place. In Denmark, these tender cookies would be filled with lingonberry preserves, which are made from the tart Scandinavian berry. Lingonberry preserves are available in specialty food stores.

> 1 cup (2 sticks) salted butter or margarine, at room temperature
> 1/2 cup sugar
> 1 large egg
> 2 teaspoons almond extract
> 2 1/2 cups all-purpose flour
> 1/2 cup currant, raspberry, or strawberry jelly
> 1/2 cup sliced almonds

1. Adjust two racks to divide the oven into thirds. Have ready two ungreased baking sheets.

2. In a large bowl, with an electric mixer at medium-high speed, beat together the butter, sugar, egg, and almond extract until fluffy and pale colored, about 3 minutes. With the mixer at medium-low speed, gradually add the flour, beating just until blended. Gather the dough into a ball and divide it into eighths. Wrap each eighth in plastic wrap and refrigerate until firm, about 1 hour. (At this point, the dough can be tightly wrapped in aluminum foil and refrigerated for up to one week or frozen for up to three months. If frozen, thaw in the refrigerator before proceeding.)

3. Preheat the oven to 375°.

4. On a lightly floured surface, roll each piece of dough into a rope that is 10 inches long. (The ropes should not taper at the ends.) As they are formed, lay each rope on the ungreased baking sheets, spacing them an equal distance apart. With your fingers or the side of your hand, press a groove lengthwise down the center of each rope.

5. Bake for 10 minutes. Remove the ribbons from the oven. With the tip of a teaspoon, fill each groove with jelly; sprinkle with almonds. Return the ribbons to the oven for 5 to 10 minutes until the edges are golden. With a long, sharp knife, diagonally cut each ribbon into 2-inch pieces. With a wide turner, transfer the cut ribbons to wire racks to cool completely.

6. Store in a tightly covered container, separating the layers with sheets of waxed paper.

Yield: About 48 cookies

Rugelach

These cookies, usually filled with fruit and nuts, are customarily served on Jewish holidays. However, rugelach has achieved such worldwide popularity that it is not at all unusual to find them tucked among the traditional Christmas cookies in many American homes. Each filling makes enough for two dozen cookies. Double the filling ingredients if you want to make all of one kind.

Dough

> 1 cup (2 sticks) salted butter or margarine, at room temperature
> One 8-ounce package cream cheese, at room temperature
> 1/4 teaspoon salt
> 2 1/2 cups all-purpose flour

Chocolate-Walnut Filling

> 1/4 cup sugar
> 1 teaspoon ground cinnamon
> 1/4 cup miniature semisweet chocolate chips
> 1/4 cup finely chopped walnuts

Glaze

> 1 large egg yolk
> 1 teaspoon water
> 2 tablespoons sugar

Fruit-and-Nut Filling

- ¹/₄ cup sugar
- 1 teaspoon ground cinnamon
- ¹/₄ cup apricot, strawberry, or raspberry jam
- 3 tablespoons chopped raisins or dried currants
- ¹/₄ cup finely chopped walnuts

1. To make the dough: In a large bowl, with an electric mixer at medium speed, beat together the butter and the cream cheese until fluffy, about 2 minutes. Beat in the salt. With the mixer at low speed, gradually add the flour, beating just until the dough comes together. (If the dough begins to run up on the beaters, stir in the last bit of flour by hand.)

2. Divide the dough into four equal parts. Form each piece into a ball, flatten slightly, and wrap individually in plastic wrap. Refrigerate until very cold, 1 to 1¹/₂ hours. (At this point, the dough can be tightly wrapped in aluminum foil and refrigerated for up to one week or frozen for up to three months. If frozen, thaw in the refrigerator before proceeding.)

3. Adjust two racks to divide the oven into thirds. Preheat the oven to 350°. Have ready two or four ungreased baking sheets.

4. To make the Chocolate-Walnut Rugelach: On a lightly floured surface, roll one piece of the chilled dough into a 9-inch round. (Don't worry about a slightly uneven edge.) In a small bowl, combine the sugar and cinnamon. Sprinkle one-half of the sugar-cinnamon mixture over the dough to the edge. Sprinkle with half of the chocolate chips and half of the nuts, pressing them in lightly with a rolling pin. Repeat with a second piece of the dough.

5. With a long, sharp knife, cut each round of dough into 12 wedges. Roll up each wedge from the outside toward the point. Place the rugelach point sides down on two of the ungreased baking sheets, spacing them about 1 inch apart.

6. To make the glaze: Mix the egg yolk with the water. Brush the top of each rugelach with some of the glaze; sprinkle with a little of the sugar.

7. Bake for 32 to 35 minutes until golden. Reverse the baking sheets on the racks and from front to back once during baking. (While the first batch of rugelach bakes, it is a good time to repeat the cookie-making procedure.) With a wide turner, immediately transfer the rugelach to wire racks to cool completely.

8. To make the Fruit-and-Nut Rugelach: Roll out a third piece of the dough. In a small bowl, combine the sugar and cinnamon. Spread 2 tablespoons of the jam over the dough to the edge. Sprinkle one-half of the sugar-cinnamon mixture over the jam. Sprinkle with half of the raisins or currants and half of the nuts, pressing them in lightly as before. Repeat with the remaining piece of dough. Cut, roll, glaze, and bake as directed in steps 5, 6, and 7.

9. Store in a tightly covered container for two or three days. For longer storage, freeze in zipper-top plastic bags. Thaw at room temperature for an hour or so before serving.

Yield: About 48 rugelach

Scottish Shortbread Wedges with Chocolate-Nut Coating

Sometimes you may want to leave shortbread plain, but because this particular shortbread isn't all that sweet, most cookie lovers find the chocolate coating a nice addition.

- 1 cup (2 sticks) salted butter, at room temperature
- 2/3 cup confectioners' sugar
- 2 teaspoons vanilla extract
- 2 cups all-purpose flour

Coating

- 4 ounces (4 squares) semisweet chocolate
- 1/2 cup finely chopped California pistachio nuts, toasted (page 16)

1. Adjust two racks to divide the oven into thirds. Preheat the oven to 350°. Have ready two ungreased baking sheets. Sprinkle two additional baking sheets with flour.

Shortbread

In the baking vernacular, *short* is the word used to describe cookies and other baked goods that are rich, crumbly, and tender because they contain a disproportionately large amount of solid fat (for shortbread this is *always* butter) to flour and sugar. This happens because the fat acts to shorten the gluten strands in flour, which in turn tenderizes the cookie.

Shortbread is made in many shapes, but one of the most traditional forms is the wedge.

We can thank the Scots for shortbread. In Scotland (and in all of the United Kingdom), they call shortbread and most other cookies "biscuits" and prefer them a little less sweet than we do.

2. In a large bowl, with an electric mixer at medium-high speed, beat the butter until creamy, about 1 minute. Add the confectioners' sugar and vanilla and beat until light and fluffy, about 2 minutes. With the mixer at low speed, gradually add the flour, beating just until blended.

3. Divide the dough in half and shape into disks. (At this point, the dough can be tightly wrapped in aluminum foil and refrigerated for up to one week or frozen for up to three months. If frozen, thaw in the refrigerator and bring to room temperature before proceeding.)

4. Place one disk of dough on each of the two unfloured baking sheets. With your fingers, press each disk into an 8-inch round, which will be about 1/4 inch thick. Prick each round all over with the tines of a dinner fork. Then, use the tips of the back of the tines to press a decorative pattern around the edge of both rounds, dipping the tines in flour as often as necessary to prevent sticking. With a pizza cutter, pastry wheel, or a sharp knife, cut each round into 16 pie-shaped wedges. (Do not separate the wedges.) Place the cookie sheets in the freezer just until the dough is firm enough to handle, about 10 minutes.

5. Remove the cookie sheets from the freezer and separate the dough into wedges. With a wide turner, transfer the wedges to the floured baking sheets, spacing them about 1 inch apart.

6. Bake for 15 to 16 minutes until just brown around edges. Reverse the baking sheets on the racks and from front to back once during baking. Cool on the baking sheets set on wire racks for 10 minutes. With a wide turner, transfer the cookies to wire racks to cool completely.

7. To make the coating: In a small, heavy saucepan, melt the chocolate over very low heat, stirring constantly until smooth. Pour the melted chocolate into a shallow bowl and set aside to cool slightly. Place the nuts in a small bowl. Dip one long side of each cookie into the chocolate, covering about half of the cookie; sprinkle the chocolate with nuts. As they are dipped and sprinkled with nuts, place the cookies on a

baking sheet lined with waxed paper; refrigerate until the chocolate is set, about 15 minutes.

8. Store in single layers in a tightly covered, shallow container.

Yield: About 32 cookies

Variations

Easy Chocolate Shortbread: Reduce the flour to 1¾ cups and blend thoroughly with ½ cup unsweetened cocoa powder before adding to the batter. Bake for about 1 minute less than the plain version. Dip into the chocolate and coat with nuts, if desired.

Round Shortbread Cookies: Proceed with either recipe given above up to the point of shaping the dough in step 2. For step 3, on a piece of waxed paper, form the dough into the shape of a solid pound of butter (brick shape). (At this point, the dough can be tightly wrapped in aluminum foil and refrigerated for up to one week or frozen for up to three months. If frozen, thaw in the refrigerator. Bring to room temperature before proceeding.) Cut the dough into 8 crosswise slices, then cut each slice into 8 equal pieces. Roll each piece of dough between the palms of your hands to form a ball. Place the balls on two ungreased baking sheets, spacing them about 1 inch apart. With the back of the tines of a fork, press down on each ball to flatten it slightly. Bake for 15 to 20 minutes until the cookies are firm on the bottoms. Reverse the baking sheets on the racks and from front to back once during baking. With a wide turner, immediately transfer the cookies to wire racks to cool completely.

Coat the cookies with chocolate and nuts, or just chocolate, if desired. Store the cookies in an airtight container. The yield for these round cookies is about 64.

Pressed Shortbread

To make this shortbread, you will need a round ceramic dish that has elaborate indentations in the bottom, which produce a relief design when the baked shortbread is removed. The design also incorporates the traditional wedge shapes, so that the shortbread can easily be broken into neat pieces when it is served. Shortbread dishes can usually be found in stores specializing in baking equipment.

> 1 cup (2 sticks) salted butter, at room temperature
> ⅔ cup confectioners' sugar
> 2 teaspoons vanilla extract
> 2 cups all-purpose flour

1. Adjust one rack to divide the oven in half. Preheat the oven to 325°. Follow the manufacturer's instructions for preparing the shortbread dish, usually by brushing it with vegetable oil to season it and give it a patina.

2. To prepare the dough, follow the instructions in step 2 of Scottish Shortbread Wedges with Chocolate-Nut Coating or Easy Chocolate Shortbread (page 212).

3. With your fingers, spread the dough over the entire bottom of the dish, making sure that it is firmly pressed into every part.

4. Bake for about 45 minutes until lightly browned. Cool completely in the shortbread dish set on a wire rack. Carefully loosen around the edge with the tip of a small knife. Place a serving plate on top of the dish. Invert the two, then remove the dish.

5. Store in a tightly covered container.

Yield: Usually 8 wedges

Variation

Studded Pressed Shortbread: Stir into the flour ¼ cup finely chopped walnuts or pecans, or ¼ cup finely chopped raisins, or ¼ cup minisize semisweet chocolate chips.

Hawaiian Shortbread Cookies

This is the most luxurious shortbread cookie I have ever tasted, and one of my all-time favorites. It is tender and crumbly, full of the incomparable flavor of buttery macadamia nuts.

- 1 cup all-purpose flour
- ³/₄ cup confectioners' sugar
- ¹/₄ cup cornstarch
- ³/₄ cup (1 ¹/₂ sticks) salted butter, at room temperature
- 1 teaspoon vanilla extract
- 1 cup (about 4 ounces) finely chopped macadamia nuts
- 2 tablespoons minced macadamia nuts, for sprinkling on cookies

1. Adjust two racks to divide the oven into thirds. Preheat the oven to 300°. Have ready two ungreased baking sheets.

2. In a medium-size bowl, with a whisk, combine the flour, confectioners' sugar, and cornstarch until thoroughly mixed.

3. In a large bowl, with an electric mixer at medium-high speed, beat together the butter and vanilla until creamy, about 1 minute. With the mixer at medium-low speed, gradually add the flour mixture, beating just until blended. Scoop level measuring tablespoonfuls of dough out of the bowl and roll them into 1¹/₂-inch balls between the palms of your hands. Arrange the balls on the ungreased baking sheets, spacing them about 2 inches apart. Gently flatten the balls with the bottom of a glass. Sprinkle each cookie with about 1 teaspoon of the minced nuts.

4. Bake for 25 to 30 minutes until lightly browned around the edges. Reverse the baking sheets on the racks and from front to back once during baking. Cool the cookies on the baking sheets set on wire racks for 5 minutes. With a wide turner, transfer the cookies to wire racks to cool completely.

5. Store in a tightly covered container.

Yield: About 24 cookies

Tip

Coatings, such as chopped nuts, will adhere better to the cookies if the raw dough is first brushed with beaten egg white.

Easy Walnut Shortbread Cookies

All shortbread cookies are easy, this one especially so. Walnuts are traditional, but you can use any nuts that you like or that you happen to have on hand.

- 2 cups all-purpose flour
- ¹/₄ teaspoon baking powder
- 1 cup (2 sticks) salted butter, at room temperature
- ¹/₂ cup sifted confectioners' sugar
- ¹/₂ cup finely chopped walnuts
- About 30 walnut halves, for decorating cookies

1. In a medium-size bowl, with a whisk, mix the flour with the baking powder until thoroughly combined.

2. In a large bowl, with an electric mixer at medium-high speed, beat together the butter and the sugar until light and fluffy, 2 to 3 minutes. With the mixer on low speed, gradually add the flour mixture, beating just until blended. With a mixing spoon, stir in the chopped walnuts until they are well distributed throughout the dough. Cover the bowl and chill the dough until it is very cold, 1 to 2 hours.

3. Adjust two racks to divide the oven into thirds. Preheat the oven to 300°. Have ready two ungreased baking sheets.

4. Divide the chilled dough in half. Roll out each half on a lightly floured surface to a thickness of about ¹/₄ inch. Cut into simple shapes with 2- to 2¹/₂-inch cookie cutters. Arrange the cookies on

the baking sheets, spacing them about ¹/₂ inch apart. Press a walnut half onto each cookie. Gather the scraps of dough, roll out, and cut into shapes one more time.

5. Bake for 20 to 25 minutes until the edges are very lightly browned. Reverse the baking sheets on the racks and from front to back once during baking. With a wide turner, immediately transfer the cookies to wire racks to cool completely.

6. Store in a tightly covered container.

Yield: About 30 cookies

Oregon Hazelnut Whole Wheat Shortbread Squares

Using whole wheat flour in these shortbreads gives them a somewhat coarser texture than usual, but they are still very tender, with a rich, nutty flavor. If it's easier, you can cut the shortbreads into 2-inch rounds. They can also have a design pressed into them using a cookie stamp after they are cut and on the baking sheet.

> 1 cup whole shelled hazelnuts, toasted (page 16)
> ¹/₂ cup (1 stick) salted butter (not margarine), at room temperature
> ¹/₂ cup sugar
> 1 cup whole wheat flour

1. Adjust one rack to divide the oven in half. Preheat the oven to 350°. Have ready an ungreased baking sheet and a pizza or pastry wheel.

2. In a food processor fitted with a steel blade, process the hazelnuts until ground, stopping the processor once to give the nuts a good stir from the bottom.

3. In a large bowl, with an electric mixer at medium-high speed, beat together the butter and the sugar until light and fluffy, 2 to 3 minutes. With a mixing spoon, stir in the ground hazelnuts. Gradually add the flour, stirring after each addition, just until blended.

4. On a lightly floured surface, roll the dough into a ¹/₄-inch-thick square. With a pizza cutter or a pastry wheel, cut the dough into 2-inch squares. Arrange the squares on the ungreased baking sheet, spacing them about ¹/₂ inch apart.

5. Bake for 10 to 12 minutes until golden. Reverse the baking sheet from front to back once during baking. Cool for 5 minutes on the baking sheet set on a wire rack. With a wide turner, transfer the cookies to wire racks to cool completely.

6. Store in a tightly covered container.

Yield: About 24 cookies

Patti Hushon's Walnut Rounds

My daughter Kimberly discovered these cookies and the Sugar-Raisin Cookies on page 182 when she visited the Hushons' pretty farm near Delta, Pennsylvania, while she was on an open-house tour. Patti, whom I have corresponded with, but never met, must be the most gracious hostess in the county, since she offered her visitors a variety of cookies, as well as a tour of her house, and then was kind enough to give me the recipes for two of the cookies she served that day for this book. Kimberly pronounced this shortbread-style cookie one of the best she's ever eaten.

- 4 cups all-purpose flour
- 2 cups regular (not quick-cooking or instant) rolled oats
- 1 cup (about 4 ounces) finely chopped walnuts
- 2 cups (4 sticks) salted butter (not margarine), at room temperature
- 3 tablespoons vanilla extract
- 1 ³/₄ cups confectioners' sugar, divided

1. Adjust two racks to divide the oven into thirds. Preheat the oven to 325°. Have ready two ungreased baking sheets.

2. In a large bowl, with a whisk, combine the flour, oats, and walnuts until well mixed.

3. In another large bowl, with an electric mixer at medium-high speed, beat together the butter and vanilla until creamy, about 1 minute. Gradually add 1¹/₂ cups of the confectioners' sugar, beating until blended after each addition. Continue beating until the mixture is light and fluffy, about 3 minutes. With a mixing spoon, stir in the flour mixture just until well blended. Pinch off pieces of the dough and roll them into 1¹/₄- to 1¹/₂-inch balls between the palms of your hands. Arrange the balls on the ungreased baking sheets, spacing them about 1 inch apart.

4. Bake for 15 to 20 minutes until pale golden. Reverse the baking sheets on the racks and from front to back once during baking. With a wide turner, transfer the cookies to wire racks. While still warm, sift 2 tablespoons of the remaining confectioners' sugar over the cookies. After the cookies have cooled, sift the remaining 2 tablespoons confectioners' sugar over them.

5. Store in a tightly covered container.

Yield: About 64 cookies

Piped Lemon Strips

These are very adult cookies, tender and melting with very subtle flavor, that would be especially appropriate for fancy occasions, such as showers, teas, and wedding receptions.

- ¹/₂ cup (1 stick) salted butter (not margarine), at room temperature
- ¹/₂ cup sugar
- 3 large egg whites
- 1 cup all-purpose flour
- 2 tablespoons strained fresh lemon juice
- 2 teaspoons shredded and minced lemon zest
- Confectioners' sugar, for dusting cookies (optional)

1. Adjust two racks to divide the oven into thirds. Preheat the oven to 375°. Lightly grease and flour two baking sheets.

2. In a large bowl, with an electric mixer at medium-high speed, beat together the butter and sugar until light and fluffy, 2 to 3 minutes. Gradually beat in the egg whites. Continue to beat until very light and fluffy, about 2 minutes. With a mixing spoon, fold in the flour, lemon juice, and lemon zest.

3. Spoon the batter into a pastry bag fitted with a number 3 or a number 12 plain decorating tip. Pipe the batter in strips about 2¹/₂ inches long, spacing them about 1¹/₂ inches apart. (For more about how to use pastry bag, see page 30.)

4. Bake for 5 to 7 minutes until lightly browned around the edges. Reverse the baking sheets on the racks and from front to back once during baking. With a wide turner, immediately remove

the strips from the baking sheet to wire racks to cool completely.

5. Store in a tightly covered container. Dust very lightly with confectioners' sugar just before serving, if desired.

Yield: About 60 cookies

Lebkuchen Spritz Cookies

On the tattered card in my recipe file, these are known simply as "Snowflakes," probably because I always decorate them with white glaze, white nonpareils, and edible white glitter. Obviously, you can decorate them any way you like, or just leave them plain. By the way, *lebkuchen* is the German word for gingerbread.

>2 cups all-purpose flour
>1 teaspoon ground cinnamon
>$^1/_2$ teaspoon ground allspice
>$^1/_2$ teaspoon ground nutmeg
>$^1/_4$ teaspoon ground cloves
>$^1/_4$ teaspoon salt
>1 cup (2 sticks) salted butter or margarine, at room temperature
>$^2/_3$ cup granulated sugar
>1 large egg
>1 tablespoon strained fresh lemon juice

Glaze

>1 cup confectioners' sugar
>1 tablespoon milk
>$^1/_2$ teaspoon vanilla extract
>White nonpareils and white glitter

1. Adjust two racks to divide the oven into thirds. Preheat the oven to 375°. Lightly grease two baking sheets.

2. In a medium-size bowl, with a whisk, combine the flour, cinnamon, allspice, nutmeg, cloves, and salt until thoroughly mixed.

3. In a large bowl, with an electric mixer at medium-high speed, beat together the butter and granulated sugar until light and fluffy, 2 to 3 minutes. Beat in the egg and lemon juice until

blended. With the mixer at low speed, gradually add the flour mixture, beating just until blended.

4. Fit a cookie press with a shaping disc. Fill the barrel of the press with dough. Press into desired shapes on the prepared baking sheets, spacing them about 1 inch apart, and changing the disc as often as often as you want to change shapes.

5. Bake for 10 to 12 minutes until the edges are lightly browned. Reverse the baking sheets on the racks and from front to back once during baking. With a wide turner, immediately transfer the cookies to wire racks to cool completely.

6. To make the glaze: In a small bowl, stir together the confectioners' sugar, milk, and vanilla until smooth, adding more milk if necessary. (The glaze should be thin enough to drizzle, but still firm enough to hold its shape slightly.)

7. Drizzle the cooled cookies with glaze and immediately sprinkle with nonpareils and glitter, or decorate as desired.

Yield: About 60 cookies

Variation

Plain Spritz Cookies: Omit the cinnamon, allspice, nutmeg, cloves, and lemon juice; add 2 teaspoons of vanilla extract.

Spritz Cookies

Spritz (pronounced "schpritz") means that the dough is pushed through something to produce fancy shapes. There are two ways to do this: either with a cookie press (see box, page 220) or with a pastry tube fitted with a decorating tip (see "Piped Cookies," page 28). Pastry tubes and decorating tips used to be the way spritz cookies were formed, but these days a cookie press, fitted with any one of a number of shaping discs, does the job quickly and neatly.

Spritz cookies are easy and fun to make, a good parent-child project once you both get the hang of it and into the rhythm of pushing the dough through the press onto the baking sheet. If your first efforts are less than successful, simply scoop the dough back into the press and try again.

Piped cookies, for which a pastry bag and decorating tube are used, are simply a more aristocratic version of spritz cookies. The dough for piped cookies is more delicate, but the results can be very much the same as spritz cookies. (See "How to Use a Pastry Bag," page 30.)

Very-Almond Spritz Cookies

It is paste made with ground almonds that gives these spritz cookies their intense almond flavor.

- 1 ¹/₂ cups whole blanched almonds, toasted (page 16)
- 1 ¹/₂ cups confectioners' sugar
- 1 large egg, separated
- 1 teaspoon almond extract
- 2 cups all-purpose flour
- ¹/₂ cup sugar
- 1 cup (2 sticks) salted butter or margarine, cut into pieces
- 1 teaspoon vanilla extract
- Colored crystal sugar, for decoration (optional)

1. Adjust two racks to divide the oven into thirds. Preheat the oven to 350°. Lightly grease two baking sheets; set aside. Have ready a cookie press and shaping discs.

2. In a food processor fitted with a steel blade, grind the almonds, stopping the processor once and giving the nuts a good stir from the bottom to keep them from becoming pasty. Add the confectioners' sugar, the egg white, and almond extract and continue to process until a stiff paste forms. Add the flour and sugar and process until the mixture resembles coarse cornmeal. Add the butter, the egg yolk, and vanilla extract. Process with on-off pulses just until the ingredients are blended.

3. Fit a cookie press with a shaping disc. Fill the barrel of the press with dough. Press into desired shapes on the prepared baking sheets, spacing them about 1 inch apart, and changing the disc as often as often as you want to change shapes. Sprinkle with sugar crystals, if desired.

4. Bake for 8 to 10 minutes until barely golden. Reverse the baking sheets on the racks and from front to back once during baking. With a wide turner, immediately transfer the cookies to wire racks to cool completely.

5. Store in a tightly covered container.

Yield: About 60 cookies

Raspberry-Lemon Strips

These are very elegant cookies, and look especially pretty when arranged on a platter with similar fancy cookies, such as the Piped Lemon Strips on page 216. You'll need a cookie press (see box, page 220) to make these cookies.

- 1 cup raspberry or strawberry preserves
- 1 tablespoon berry-flavored liqueur, such as framboise or Chambord

¹/₂ **cup (1 stick) plus 6 tablespoons (³/₄ stick) salted butter or margarine, at room temperature**

³/₄ **cup sugar**

1 large egg, lightly beaten

2 teaspoons shredded and minced lemon zest

2 ¹/₄ cups sifted all-purpose flour, divided

1. Adjust two racks to divide the oven into thirds. Preheat the oven to 350°. Line four baking sheets with aluminum foil. Fit a cookie press with a disc that has a 1- to 1½-inch opening that is flat on one side and notched on the other. (If the only disc you have is notched at both sides, cover one with masking tape to make it smooth.)

2. In a small saucepan set over low heat, heat the preserves, stirring constantly until melted. Press the preserves through a sieve into a small bowl; discard the residue in the sieve. Stir the liqueur into the melted preserves; set aside.

3. In a small bowl, with an electric mixer at medium-high speed, beat together the butter and sugar until light and fluffy, 2 to 3 minutes. Beat in the egg and lemon zest until well combined. Add 2 cups of the flour to the butter mixture, ¹/₄ cup at a time, beating just until well blended after each addition. (The dough should be soft, but not sticky; if necessary, beat in a little more flour.) Shape the dough into a ball and set it on a sheet of waxed paper. Cover with an inverted bowl and leave at room temperature for 10 minutes.

4. Fill the cookie press with dough. Pipe four strips of dough, each 12 inches long, onto two of the prepared baking sheets.

5. Bake for 9 to 12 minutes until the edges begin to turn golden. Reverse the baking sheets on the racks and from front to back once during baking. Cool the strips on the baking sheets set on wire racks. Repeat the pressing and baking process with the remaining dough. When the second batch of strips has been removed from the oven, leave the oven on and set at 350°.

6. When the strips are completely cool, carefully remove them to a work surface. Invert every other strip so that the smooth side is up. Using a pastry brush, spread about 1 tablespoon of the preserves mixture on the smooth surface of each of the strips. Carefully sandwich two cookie strips, smooth sides together. With a wide turner, transfer four of the sandwiched strips to one of the baking sheets.

7. Return these four sandwiched strips to the oven until softened, about 3 minutes. Remove from the oven and, working quickly, transfer the sandwiched strips to a cutting surface. While still warm, using a sharp, thin-bladed knife, cut the strips on the diagonal into seven 1½-inch slices. Repeat with the remaining strips, heating only four strips at a time, since they must be warm when they are cut. With a wide turner, remove the cookies to wire racks to cool completely.

8. Store in airtight container, separated by sheets of waxed paper.

Yield: About 54 cookies

Cookie Press

A cookie press (sometimes called a cookie gun) is a barrel-shaped device with a plunger. Metal discs or plates with various designs cut out of them are fitted into the bottom of the barrel. Dough is placed in the barrel and then pressed through the discs with the plunger to form various shapes.

Cookie presses are easy to find in any store that carries a fairly complete line of baking equipment. The presses all have little differences in the way they work, and there are even electric and battery-operated models that do all the pushing for you.

Batons à l'Orange

Despite the fact that these are spritz cookies, batons originated in France, where they are, of course, piped onto the baking sheet with a pastry bag. Batons can be plain or flavored. In this case, orange flavorings have been added to the batter. A variation for plain batons follows.

3 ¹/₄ cups all-purpose flour
1 ¹/₂ teaspoons baking powder
1 cup sugar
¹/₂ cup (1 stick) salted butter or margarine, at room temperature
1 large egg, lightly beaten
Shredded and minced zest from one orange (about 1 tablespoon)
2 tablespoons orange liqueur
¹/₃ cup strained, fresh orange juice
Plain crystal sugar, for sprinkling on cookies

1. Adjust two racks to divide the oven into thirds. Lightly grease two baking sheets; set aside. Have ready a cookie press fitted with a rosette shaping disc.

2. In a medium-size bowl, with a whisk, combine the flour and baking powder until thoroughly mixed.

3. In a large bowl, with an electric mixer at medium-high speed, beat the sugar with the butter until light and fluffy, 2 to 3 minutes. Beat in the egg, zest, and liqueur until well blended. With the mixer at medium-low speed, add the flour mixture and orange juice alternately, beating after each addition until well blended. Cover the bowl and refrigerate it until the dough is cold, about 4 hours.

4. Preheat the oven to 350°.

5. Fill the barrel of the cookie press with the cold dough. Press out onto the prepared baking sheets into 3 × 1-inch strips, spacing them about 1 inch apart. Sprinkle with crystal sugar.

6. Bake for 10 to 12 minutes or until pale golden. Reverse the baking sheets on the racks and from front to back once during baking. With a wide turner, immediately transfer the cookies to wire racks to cool completely.

Yield: About 48 cookies

Variation

Vanilla Batons: Reduce the flour to 3 cups. Omit the orange zest and orange liqueur. Add 1 teaspoon vanilla extract at the same time the egg is beaten into the sugar-and-butter mixture. Substitute ¹/₃ cup milk for the orange juice. The tips of Vanilla Batons are often dipped into melted chocolate and sprinkled with minced walnuts or pistachios after baking.

Tip

When a recipe calls for liqueur or spirits, the flavor can be tamed by diluting with one-third water.

Peanut Butter and Jelly Spritz Cookies

It's amazing how this combination shows up in every kind of cookie.

 1 cup sifted confectioners' sugar
 $^1/_2$ cup (1 stick) salted butter or margarine, at room temperature
 $^1/_2$ cup creamy peanut butter
 1 large egg
 $^1/_2$ teaspoon vanilla extract
 2 $^1/_4$ cups all-purpose flour
 2 tablespoons Concord grape jelly

1. Adjust two racks to divide the oven into thirds. Preheat the oven to 375°. Have ready two ungreased baking sheets.

2. In a large bowl, with an electric mixer at medium-high speed, beat together the confectioners' sugar, butter, peanut butter, egg, and vanilla until light and fluffy, 2 to 3 minutes. With the mixer at low speed, gradually add the flour, beating just until blended.

3. Fit a cookie press with a shaping disc that makes a round cookie. Fill the barrel of the press with dough. Press onto the prepared baking sheets, spacing them about 1 inch apart.

4. Bake for 8 minutes until lightly browned. Reverse the baking sheets on the racks and from front to back once during baking. With a wide turner, immediately transfer the cookies to wire racks to cool completely. Just before serving, drop a dab of jelly from the tip of a teaspoon onto the center of each cookie.

5. Store in a tightly covered container.

Yield: About 60 cookies

Rainbow Spritz Cookies

This cookie is an example of how two or three doughs can be fitted together in a cookie press to produce a double- or triple-colored cookie. In this case, the same dough is used in different colors, but you can certainly use two or three spritz cookie doughs to achieve different flavors and/or colors.

 1 cup (2 sticks) salted butter or margarine, at room temperature
 $^1/_2$ cup sugar
 1 large egg
 1 teaspoon vanilla extract
 2 $^1/_4$ cups all-purpose flour
 Red liquid or paste food coloring
 Green liquid or paste food coloring

1. Adjust two racks to divide the oven into thirds. Preheat the oven to 350°. Have ready two ungreased baking sheets. Also have ready a cookie press and shaping discs.

2. In a large bowl, with an electric mixer at medium-high speed, beat together the butter and sugar until light and fluffy, 2 to 3 minutes. Beat in the egg and vanilla until well blended. With the mixer at medium-low speed, gradually add the flour, beating just until blended. Gather the dough into a ball and divide it into thirds. Place one-third back in the mixing bowl. (This part will remain untinted.) Place each of the other thirds in two medium-size bowls. Use either liquid or paste food coloring to tint one of the portions pink and one of the portions light green by kneading the colorings into the dough until evenly tinted. Shape each third of the dough into a cylinder that, when all three are grouped together, will fit into the barrel of the cookie press. Fill the cookie press with the plain and colored cylinders. Press the dough into desired shapes onto the ungreased baking sheets.

3. Bake for 8 to 10 minutes until firm, but not brown. Reverse the baking sheets on the racks and from front to back once during baking. With a wide turner, transfer the cookies to wire racks to cool completely.

4. Store in a tightly covered container.

Yield: About 48 cookies

Classic Italian Almond Biscotti

This is a true biscotti, very hard with a delicate, not-too-sweet flavor, the perfect biscotti for dipping into sweet wine, coffee, tea, or even cocoa.

1 ¹/₂ cups whole natural almonds, toasted (page 16) and divided
1 ¹/₂ cups all-purpose flour
¹/₂ teaspoon baking powder
¹/₂ teaspoon baking soda
¹/₄ teaspoon salt
³/₄ cup sugar
2 large eggs, at room temperature
1 tablespoon strained fresh lemon juice
1 teaspoon almond extract

1. In a food processor fitted with a steel blade, with on-off pulses, finely grind half of the almonds, stopping the processor once and giving the nuts a good stir from the bottom to keep them from becoming pasty. Coarsely chop the remaining almonds.

2. In a medium-size bowl, with a whisk, combine the flour, baking powder, baking soda, and salt until thoroughly mixed. With a mixing spoon, stir in the ground and chopped nuts until well blended.

3. In a large bowl, with an electric mixer at medium-high speed, beat together the sugar, eggs, lemon juice, and almond extract until well blended. With a mixing spoon, stir in the flour mixture just until blended. The dough will be sticky. Cover the bowl and chill the dough until firm, about 1 hour.

4. Adjust one rack to divide the oven in half. Preheat the oven to 350°. Lightly grease a large baking sheet.

5. Divide the chilled dough in half. On the prepared baking sheet, shape each piece of dough into a 10-inch log about 4 inches apart. With wet hands, pat and shape each log into a 10 × 2-inch loaf.

6. Bake for about 25 minutes until a toothpick inserted in the center comes out clean. Reverse

Biscotti

The word *biscotti* comes from the Italian *"bis,"* meaning "twice" or "again," and *"cuit"* or *"cotto,"* which means "cooked." What sets biscotti apart from other types of cookies is that they are baked twice: first, in a loaf form, then again after the loaves have been cut into diagonal slices. This process gives the biscotti its distinctive shape and a very crisp, almost hard texture. Traditionally, biscotti are served as a dipping cookie with sweet wine or coffee.

Americans have taken to biscotti like nothing since pizza, and the trendy little cookies are enjoying wild popularity these days. Biscotti lovers often ask me if it's possible to make a decent version of these chic cookies at home. The answer is unequivocally yes, and what's more, they are surprisingly easy to do.

True biscotti, the kind you find in Italy, are hard and dry, not especially sweet, and are usually made without the benefit of butter. But most biscotti made here contain butter and have more sugar added to appeal to American tastes.

In a tightly covered container, biscotti keep well, for several weeks, at least. Or they can be frozen in plastic bags and pulled out, piece by piece, as you want them.

the baking sheet from front to back once during baking. Cool on the baking sheet set on a wire rack for 15 minutes.

7. Remove the loaves from the baking sheet to a cutting surface. With a long, sharp knife, cut each loaf on the diagonal into ¹/₂-inch slices (see illustration below). Place the slices cut side down on the same baking sheet. (It's okay if they overlap a little.) Bake for about 15 minutes until crisp and golden, turning the slices once. Reverse the baking sheet from front to back once during baking. With a wide turner, immediately transfer the biscotti to wire racks to cool completely.

8. Store in a tightly covered container.

Yield: About 36 biscotti

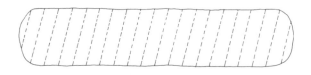

Biscotti loaf

Anise Biscotti

· ·

If you like licorice, you'll *adore* these.

- ³/₄ **cup sugar**
- 2 **tablespoons anise seeds**
- 2 ³/₄ **cups all-purpose flour**
- 1 ¹/₂ **teaspoons baking powder**
- ¹/₄ **teaspoon salt**
- 1 ¹/₂ **cups whole blanched almonds, toasted (page 16) and finely chopped**
- ¹/₂ **cup (1 stick) salted butter or margarine, at room temperature**
- 3 **large eggs, at room temperature**
- ¹/₄ **cup anise-flavored liqueur, such as Sambuca**

1. Place the sugar and anise seed in the container of an electric blender. Process until the seeds are chopped, but not pulverized.

2. In a medium-size bowl, with a whisk, combine the flour, baking powder, salt, and nuts until thoroughly mixed.

3. In a large bowl, with an electric mixer at medium-high speed, beat together the sugar mixture and the butter until light and fluffy, 2 to 3 minutes. Add the eggs and liqueur. Continue to beat until well blended. Add the flour mixture and beat just until blended. The dough will be sticky. Cover the bowl and chill until firm, about 1 hour.

4. Adjust one rack to divide the oven in half. Preheat the oven to 350°. Lightly grease a large baking sheet.

5. Divide the chilled dough in half. On the prepared baking sheet, shape each half into a 10-inch log, spacing about 4 inches apart. With wet hands, pat and shape each log into a $10 \times 2^{1}/_{2}$-inch loaf.

6. Bake for 30 minutes until a toothpick inserted in the center comes out clean. Reverse the baking sheet from front to back once during baking. (The loaves will have a few cracks in them.) Cool on the baking sheet set on a wire rack for 15 minutes.

7. Remove the loaves from the baking sheet to a cutting surface. With a long, sharp knife, cut each loaf on the diagonal into ¹/₂-inch slices (see illustration, opposite). Place the slices cut side down on the same baking sheet. (It's okay if they overlap a little.) Bake for 20 minutes until crisp, turning the slices once. Reverse the baking sheet from front to back once during baking. With a wide turner, transfer the biscotti to wire racks to cool completely.

8. Store in a tightly covered container.

Yield: About 54 biscotti

Variation

Anise-Spice Biscotti: Substitute 1 cup of walnuts for the almonds; add 1 teaspoon ground cinnamon, 1 teaspoon ground ginger, ¹/₂ teaspoon ground allspice, and ¹/₂ teaspoon ground cloves to the flour mixture.

 Tip

A small sieve makes it easy to dust cookies or bars with an even coating of cocoa powder or confectioners' sugar. Place in the sieve, then gently tap the side while moving the sieve over the area to be dusted.

Oatmeal-Raisin Biscotti

This is a very Americanized biscotti. If you like oatmeal cookies, this is your biscotti. After baking, plan to give this biscotti a day or so for the flavor to develop.

- 1 1/2 cups regular or quick-cooking (not instant) rolled oats
- 1 cup chopped walnuts
- 2 cups all-purpose flour
- 2 teaspoons ground cinnamon
- 1 teaspoon baking powder
- 1/2 teaspoon salt
- 1 cup packed light brown sugar
- 1/2 cup (1 stick) salted butter or margarine, at room temperature
- 2 large eggs, at room temperature
- 1 cup golden or dark raisins, coarsely chopped

1. Adjust one rack to divide the oven in half. Preheat the oven to 350°. Lightly grease a large baking sheet.

2. Spread the oats and walnuts in a large jelly-roll pan in a single layer. Bake for 10 minutes, stirring once, until golden and fragrant. Set aside to cool.

3. In a medium-size bowl, with a whisk, combine the flour, cinnamon, baking powder, and salt until thoroughly mixed.

4. In a large bowl, with an electric mixer at medium-high speed, beat together the brown sugar, butter, and eggs until light and fluffy, about 2 minutes. Add the flour mixture, the toasted oats and walnuts, and raisins. Continue beating just until well blended.

5. Divide the dough in half. On the prepared baking sheet, shape each half into a 10-inch log about 4 inches apart. With wet hands, pat and shape each log into a 10 × 2 1/2-inch loaf.

6. Bake for 25 minutes until the loaves are shiny and have many little cracks in them. Reverse the baking sheet from front to back once during baking. Cool on the baking sheet set on a wire rack for 15 minutes.

7. Remove the loaves from the baking sheet to a cutting surface. With a long, sharp knife, cut each loaf on the diagonal into 1/2-inch slices (see illustration, page 223). Handle the slices carefully, since the oats make them a little crumbly. Place the slices cut side down on the same baking sheet. (It's okay if they overlap a little.) Bake for 20 minutes until crisp, turning the slices once. Reverse the baking sheet from front to back once during baking. Cool on the baking sheet set on a wire rack for 10 minutes. With a wide turner, transfer the biscotti to wire racks to cool completely.

8. Store in a tightly covered container.

Yield: About 36 biscotti

Breakfast Biscotti

These have a delicate flavor and a more breadlike texture than most biscotti, which makes them ideal for a light breakfast. At least I think so. I keep them in a zipper-top bag in the freezer and take them out as I need them. They take only a few minutes to thaw, about the same time it takes to brew a pot of coffee and pour a glass of juice.

- 3 1/2 cups all-purpose flour
- 1 tablespoon baking powder
- 1/2 teaspoon salt
- 2 cups whole blanched almonds, toasted (page 16) and finely chopped
- 1/2 cup (1 stick) salted butter or margarine, at room temperature
- 1 1/4 cups sugar
- 5 large eggs, at room temperature
- 2 teaspoons almond extract

1. In a medium-size bowl, with a whisk, combine the flour, baking powder, salt, and almonds until thoroughly mixed.

2. In a large bowl, with an electric mixer at medium-high speed, beat together the butter and the sugar until light and fluffy, 2 to 3 minutes. Add the eggs and almond extract and continue

beating until well blended. With the mixer at low speed, add the flour mixture, beating just until blended. The dough will be sticky. Cover the bowl and chill until the dough is firm, about 1 hour.

3. Adjust two racks to divide the oven into thirds. Preheat the oven to 350°. Lightly grease two large baking sheets.

4. Divide the chilled dough into quarters. On each prepared baking sheet, shape two quarters of the dough into two 9-inch logs about 4 inches apart. With wet hands, pat and shape each log into a $9 \times 2^{1}/_{2}$-inch loaf.

5. Bake for 30 to 35 minutes until a toothpick inserted in the center comes out clean. Reverse the baking sheets on the racks and from front to back once during baking. Cool on the baking sheets set on wire racks for 15 minutes.

6. Remove the loaves from the baking sheets to a cutting surface. With a long, sharp knife, cut each loaf on the diagonal into $3/_4$-inch slices (see illustration, page 223). Place the slices cut side down on the same baking sheets. (It's okay if they overlap a little.) Bake for 18 to 20 minutes until golden and almost crisp, turning the slices once. Reverse the baking sheets on the racks and from front to back once during baking. With a wide turner, immediately transfer the biscotti to wire racks to cool completely.

7. Store in a tightly covered container.

Yield: About 42 biscotti

Lemon and Poppy Seed Biscotti

A friend of mine thought that the time-honored combination of lemon and poppy seeds was the result of my culinary genius. I didn't have the heart to tell her that I didn't invent it.

> 2 cups all-purpose flour
> 1 $^{1}/_{2}$ teaspoons baking powder
> $^{1}/_{4}$ teaspoon salt

> 2 tablespoons poppy seeds
> $^{3}/_{4}$ cup sugar
> $^{1}/_{4}$ cup ($^{1}/_{2}$ stick) salted butter or margarine, at room temperature
> 2 large eggs, at room temperature
> 2 teaspoons shredded and minced lemon zest
> 1 tablespoon lemon juice

1. In a medium-size bowl, with a whisk, combine the flour, baking powder, salt, and poppy seeds until thoroughly mixed.

2. In a large bowl, with an electric mixer at medium-high speed, beat together the sugar, butter, eggs, lemon zest, and lemon juice until light and foamy, about 3 minutes. With the mixer at medium speed, gradually add the flour mixture, beating just until blended. The batter will be sticky. Cover the bowl and chill the dough until firm, about 1 hour.

3. Adjust one rack to divide the oven in half. Preheat the oven to 350°. Lightly grease a large baking sheet.

4. Divide the chilled dough in half. On the prepared baking sheet, shape each half into a 10-inch log about 4 inches apart. With wet hands, pat and shape each log into a 10×3-inch loaf.

5. Bake for 25 minutes until a toothpick inserted in the center comes out clean. Reverse the baking sheet from front to back once during baking. The loaves will have small cracks in them. Cool on the baking sheet set on a wire rack.

6. Remove the loaves from the baking sheet to a cutting surface. With a long, sharp knife, cut each loaf into diagonal $^{1}/_{2}$-inch slices (see illustration, page 223). Place the slices cut side down on the same baking sheet. (It's okay if they overlap a little.) Bake for 15 minutes until crisp and golden, turning the slices once. Reverse the baking sheet from front to back once during baking. With a wide turner, immediately transfer the biscotti to wire racks to cool completely.

7. Store in an airtight container.

Yield: About 36 biscotti

Orange-Pecan Biscotti

These are my favorite biscotti, especially when they're glazed. I try to keep a bag of these in the freezer for all the many times I need a not-too-sweet little pick-me-up.

- 3 1/2 cups all-purpose flour
- 1 1/2 teaspoons baking powder
- 1/2 teaspoon salt
- 1/2 teaspoon ground cinnamon
- 1 cup granulated sugar
- 1/2 cup (1 stick) salted butter or margarine, at room temperature
- 1 tablespoon shredded and minced orange zest
- 2 large eggs, at room temperature
- 1 cup coarsely chopped pecans

Orange Glaze

- 1 cup confectioners' sugar
- 4 teaspoons orange juice

1. Adjust one rack to divide the oven in half. Preheat the oven to 350°. Lightly grease a large baking sheet.

2. In a medium-size bowl, with a whisk, combine the flour, baking powder, salt, and cinnamon until thoroughly mixed.

3. In a large bowl, with an electric mixer at medium-high speed, beat together the granulated sugar, butter, orange zest, and eggs until light and fluffy, about 2 minutes. With the mixer at medium speed, gradually add the flour mixture and beat just until blended. With a mixing spoon, stir in the pecans until well distributed throughout the dough. The dough will be crumbly. Gather the dough into a ball and divide it in half.

4. On a lightly floured surface, roll each piece of dough into a 10-inch log. Place the logs on the prepared baking sheet about 4 inches apart. With your hands, flatten each log to make a 10 × 3-inch loaf.

5. Bake for 25 minutes until a toothpick inserted in the center comes out clean. Reverse the baking sheet from front to back once during baking. Cool on the baking sheet set on a wire rack for 15 minutes.

6. Remove the loaves from the baking sheet to a cutting surface. With a long, sharp knife, cut each loaf on the diagonal into 1/2-inch slices (see illustration, page 223). Place the slices cut side down on the same baking sheet. (It's okay if they overlap a little.) Bake for 15 minutes until crisp and golden, turning the slices once. Reverse the baking sheet from front to back once during baking. With a wide turner, immediately transfer the biscotti to wire racks to cool completely.

7. To make the glaze: In a small bowl, combine the confectioners' sugar and orange juice. With a small spatula or a butter spreader, spread one side of each biscotti with a thin layer of glaze. Place glazed side up on a sheet of waxed paper until the glaze dries, about 1 hour.

8. Store in an airtight container, separating the layers with sheets of waxed paper.

Yield: About 48 biscotti

Variation

Cranberry-Orange Biscotti: Stir 1 cup of dried cranberries, coarsely chopped, into the batter at the same time the pecans are added.

Coconut Biscotti

Originally these were called toasted-coconut biscotti, but since the coconut is not actually toasted, I thought the name was misleading. However, the first flavor that hits you when you eat one of these biscotti is toasted coconut, which is wonderful.

1 ³/₄ cups all-purpose flour

1 teaspoon baking powder

¹/₄ teaspoon salt

1 ¹/₂ cups whole blanched almonds, toasted (page 16) and finely chopped

¹/₄ cup (¹/₂ stick) salted butter or margarine, at room temperature

¹/₂ cup sugar

2 large eggs, at room temperature

2 teaspoons coconut extract

1 teaspoon vanilla extract

One 3¹/₂-ounce can sweetened flaked coconut

Chocolate Dip

1 ¹/₂ cups (9 ounces) semisweet chocolate chips

1. In a medium-size bowl, with a whisk, combine the flour, baking powder, salt, and nuts until thoroughly mixed.

2. In a large bowl, with an electric mixer at medium-high speed, beat together the butter and the sugar until light and fluffy, 2 to 3 minutes. Add the eggs and the coconut and vanilla extracts. Continue to beat until well blended. Add the flour mixture and flaked coconut and beat just until blended. The dough will be sticky. Cover the bowl and chill the dough until firm, about 1 hour.

3. Adjust one rack to divide the oven in half. Preheat the oven to 350°. Lightly grease a large baking sheet.

4. Divide the chilled dough in half. On the prepared baking sheet, shape each half into a 10 × 2¹/₂-inch log about 4 inches apart. With wet hands, pat and shape each log into a 10 × 2-inch loaf.

5. Bake for 25 minutes until a toothpick inserted in the center comes out clean. Reverse the baking sheet from front to back once during baking. Cool on the baking sheet set on a wire rack for 15 minutes.

6. Remove the loaves from the baking sheet to a cutting surface. With a long, sharp knife, cut each loaf on the diagonal into ¹/₂-inch slices (see illustration, page 223). Place the slices cut side down on the same baking sheet. (It's okay if they overlap a little.) Bake for 15 minutes until crisp and golden, turning the slices once. Reverse the baking sheet from front to back once during baking. With a wide turner, immediately transfer the biscotti to wire racks to cool completely.

7. To make the dip: In a small, heavy saucepan, melt the chocolate over very low heat, stirring constantly until smooth. Set aside to cool slightly. Pour the chocolate into a narrow glass. Dip one end of each biscotti into the melted chocolate. Place the dipped biscotti on waxed paper until the chocolate hardens, about 2 hours.

8. Store in an airtight container, separating the layers with sheets of waxed paper.

Yield: About 30 biscotti

Ginger-Pear Biscotti

These are a very sophisticated and elegant biscotti, and one of my very favorites. They are sliced thinner than usual, which gives them a crisp and more cookielike texture.

   1 ³/₄ cups all-purpose flour
   1 teaspoon baking powder
   1 ¹/₄ teaspoons ground ginger
   ¹/₄ teaspoon salt
   ¹/₄ cup chopped walnuts, toasted (page 16)
   ¹/₄ cup (¹/₂ stick) salted butter or margarine, at room temperature
   ¹/₂ cup sugar
   1 large egg, at room temperature
   1 teaspoon vanilla extract
   One 2-ounce jar crystallized ginger, chopped
   ¹/₄ cup chopped dried pear

1. Adjust one rack to divide the oven in half. Preheat the oven to 350°. Lightly grease a large baking sheet.

2. In a medium-size bowl, with a whisk, combine the flour, baking powder, ground ginger, salt, and nuts until thoroughly mixed.

3. In a large bowl, with an electric mixer at medium-high speed, beat together the butter, sugar, egg, and vanilla until light and fluffy, about 2 minutes. With the mixer at medium speed, add the flour mixture, crystallized ginger, and pear, beating just until blended. The dough will be stiff. Gather the dough into a ball and divide it in half.

4. On a lightly floured surface, roll each piece of dough into an 8-inch log. Place the logs on the prepared baking sheet about 4 inches apart. With your hands, flatten each log to make an 8 × 2¹/₂-inch loaf.

5. Bake for 25 minutes until a toothpick inserted in the center comes out clean. Reverse the baking sheet from front to back once during baking. Cool on the baking sheet set on a wire rack for 15 minutes.

6. Remove the loaves from the baking sheet to a cutting surface. With a long, sharp knife, cut each loaf on the diagonal into ¹/₄-inch slices (see illustration, page 223). Place the slices cut side down on the same baking sheet. (It's okay if they overlap a little.) Bake for 10 minutes or until crisp (do not turn the slices). Reverse the baking sheet from front to back once during baking. With a wide turner, immediately transfer the biscotti to wire racks to cool completely.

7. Store in an airtight container.

Yield: About 44 biscotti

Chocolate-Hazelnut Biscotti

These biscotti are not quite as decadent as their name implies, since they contain no butter. They are especially good served along with fruit for dessert. Whether or not to coat the biscotti with chocolate is up to you. I usually do.

   2 ounces (2 squares) unsweetened chocolate
   1 ¹/₂ cups all-purpose flour
   1 teaspoon baking powder
   ¹/₂ teaspoon salt
   3 large eggs, at room temperature
   1 cup sugar
   1 teaspoon vanilla extract
   ¹/₂ cup chopped hazelnuts, toasted (page 16)

Chocolate Glaze

   1 cup (6 ounces) semisweet chocolate morsels

1. In a small, heavy saucepan, melt the 2 ounces of chocolate over very low heat, stirring constantly until smooth; set aside to cool to room temperature.

2. In a medium-size bowl, with a whisk, combine the flour, baking powder, and salt until thoroughly mixed.

3. In a large bowl, with an electric mixer at medium-high speed, beat the eggs until thick and lemon-colored, about 2 minutes. Gradually beat in the sugar and vanilla until very pale colored and the mixture forms a ribbon when the beaters are lifted, 2 to 3 minutes, stopping frequently to scrape down the side of the bowl. With the mixer at medium speed, beat in the melted chocolate until well blended. With a mixing spoon, stir in the flour mixture just until blended.

Stir in the nuts until well distributed throughout the dough. The dough will be sticky. Cover the bowl and chill until the dough is firm, about 1 hour.

4. Adjust one rack to divide the oven in half. Preheat the oven to 350°. Lightly grease a large baking sheet.

5. Divide the chilled dough in half. On the prepared baking sheet, shape each half into a 10-inch log about 4 inches apart. With wet hands, pat and shape each log into a 10 × 2-inch loaf.

6. Bake for 20 minutes until a toothpick inserted in the center comes out clean. Reverse the baking sheet from front to back once during baking. Cool on the baking sheet set on a wire rack for 15 minutes.

7. Remove the loaves from the baking sheet to a cutting surface. With a long, sharp knife, cut each loaf on the diagonal into 1/2-inch slices (see illustration, page 223). Place the slices cut side down on the same baking sheet. (It's okay if they overlap a little.) Bake for 10 minutes until crisp, turning the slices once. Reverse the baking sheet from front to back once during baking. With a wide turner, immediately transfer the biscotti to wire racks to cool completely.

8. To make the glaze: In a small, heavy saucepan, melt the chocolate morsels over very low heat, stirring constantly until smooth; set aside to cool slightly. With a small spatula or a butter spreader, spread one side of each biscotti with chocolate. Place chocolate side up on a sheet of waxed paper until the chocolate hardens, about 2 hours.

9. Store in a tightly covered container, separating the layers with sheets of waxed paper.

Yield: About 24 biscotti

Butter and Almond Strips

I think of these as a fake biscotti. They are easier to make, since the batter is first baked in a pan, like a cake, and then cut into strips for the second baking. These biscotti are just wonderful for dunking into coffee or tea during a midmorning or afternoon break.

2 cups all-purpose flour
1 teaspoon baking powder
1/4 cup (1/2 stick) salted butter or margarine, at room temperature
1 cup sugar
4 large eggs
1 cup slivered almonds, toasted (page 16)

1. Adjust one rack to divide the oven in half. Preheat the oven to 350° (325° if using glass loaf dishes). Lightly grease two 9 × 5-inch loaf pans or glass loaf dishes. Have ready two ungreased baking sheets.

2. In a medium-size bowl, with a whisk, combine the flour and baking powder until thoroughly mixed.

3. In a large bowl, with an electric mixer at medium speed, beat together the butter and sugar until light and fluffy, 2 to 3 minutes. Add the eggs, one at a time, beating well after each addition. With the mixer at medium-low speed, gradually add the flour mixture, beating just until blended. With a mixing spoon, stir in the almonds until well distributed throughout the batter. Turn the batter into the prepared loaf pans, dividing evenly and smoothing the tops with the back of a spoon.

4. Place the pans, side by side, on the oven rack. Bake for 30 to 35 minutes until the loaves are firm to the touch. Reverse the position of the pans and from front to back once during baking. Set the baking pans on wire racks to cool for 5 minutes. Remove the loaves from the pans and set on wire racks to cool completely.

5. Reduce the oven temperature to 250°.

6. With a long, sharp knife, cut each loaf in half lengthwise and vertically down the center; cut each half crosswise into strips about 3/4 inch wide. Arrange the strips cut sides down on the ungreased baking sheets.

7. Bake for 25 to 30 minutes until the strips are very dry. Reverse the baking sheets from front to back once during baking. With a wide turner, transfer the strips to wire racks to cool completely.

8. Store in a tightly covered container.

Yield: About 48 strips

Macaroons

Most macaroon cookies are dropped rather than shaped. Before starting to make Almond Cookies from Mykonos or Italian Almond and Pignoli-Studded Cookies that follow, you may want to read more about macaroons and how to make them, which is explained on pages 74–76 in the Drop Cookie chapter.

Almond Cookies from Mykonos (*Amygdalota*)

I first tasted a soft, chewy macaroon cookie very much like this one on a starry night, high on a hill on Mykonos in the Aegean Sea. As it turned out, the cookie was a local treat, made by a baker on the far side of the island, a place where tourists rarely go. I did a lot of "research" on the cookies during my days on Mykonos, and even brought home a hefty supply. But, despite all my best efforts, I never could quite manage to duplicate the ones I ate on the island. Maybe the missing ingredient is the starry night and the view of the harbor below. These are close, though.

- 4 $1/2$ cups blanched whole, sliced, or slivered almonds, divided
- 1 $1/2$ cups superfine sugar, divided
- 3 large egg whites, at room temperature
- $1/2$ teaspoon cream of tartar
- 1 teaspoon vanilla extract

1. Adjust one rack to divide the oven in half. Preheat the oven to 325°. Cover two baking sheets with aluminum foil, shiny side up. Lightly grease the foil with nonstick cooking spray.

2. Place $2^{1}/4$ cups of the almonds and $1/4$ cup of the sugar in a food processor fitted with a steel blade. Process with on-off pulses until the nuts are very finely ground, stopping the processor once and giving the nuts a good stir from the bottom to keep them from becoming pasty. Place the ground nuts in a small bowl. Repeat the grinding process with the remaining almonds and another $1/4$ cup of the sugar.

3. In a large bowl, with an electric mixer at medium-low speed, beat the eggs whites with the cream of tartar until frothy. Beat at medium-high speed until the whites form soft, curving peaks when the beaters are lifted. Add the remaining sugar, 1 tablespoon at a time, beating for about 1 minute after each addition. Add the vanilla and continue to beat until the mixture is very thick and shiny. With a mixing spoon, stir the almond mixture into the beaten egg whites. The batter will be very thick and very sticky.

4. Scoop heaping measuring tablespoonfuls of the batter out of the bowl and roll them into 1-inch balls between the palms of your hands. Arrange the balls as they are made on one of the prepared baking sheets, spacing them about 2 inches apart, and flattening each one slightly so that it measures about $1^{1}/2$ inches in diameter. (Rinsing and drying your hands between every few balls will help to make this process a little less messy.) As soon as one baking sheet is filled, place it in the oven and bake for 13 to 14 minutes until the cookies are barely colored. Bake one sheet at a time. Reverse the baking sheet from front to back once during baking. Cool on the baking sheet set on a wire rack. Remove the cooled cookies from the baking sheet with a wide turner.

5. Store in a tightly covered container for 3 or 4 days. The cookies can also be frozen in zipper-top plastic bags.

Yield: About 48 cookies

Tip

To evenly coat baked, ball-shaped cookies with sugar or cocoa powder, gently shake the two together in a brown paper bag.

Italian Almond and Pignoli-Studded Cookies

These are wonderfully soft and chewy meringue cookies.

½ cup flour

1 ½ cups blanched whole or slivered almonds

1 ½ cups superfine or granulated sugar, divided

2 large egg whites, at room temperature

1 teaspoon vanilla extract

³/₄ cup pine nuts (pignoli), finely chopped

1. Adjust one rack to divide the oven in half. Preheat the oven to 425°. Cover two baking sheets with aluminum foil, shiny side up. Grease the foil very lightly or coat it with nonstick cooking spray.

2. In a food processor fitted with a steel blade, finely grind the almonds with ½ cup of the sugar, stopping the processor once to give the almonds a good stir from the bottom.

3. In a large bowl, with an electric mixer at medium-low speed, beat the egg whites until frothy. Continue beating at high speed just until stiff peaks form when the beaters are lifted. With the mixer at medium speed, gradually beat in the almond mixture, and then the remaining 1 cup of sugar, 1 tablespoon at a time, beating for about 1 minute after each addition. Continue beating until the mixture is very thick and sticky, about 2 minutes. Beat in the vanilla until well blended.

4. Sprinkle the pine nuts on a sheet of waxed paper. Roll measuring tablespoonfuls of the almond mixture into 1-inch balls between the palms of your hands, then roll the balls in the pine nuts, pressing them into the dough. As they are formed, place the balls on one of the prepared baking sheets, spacing them about 3 inches apart. (Rinsing and drying your hands between every few balls will help to make the rolling process a little less messy.)

5. Bake the cookies one sheet at a time. Reverse the baking sheet from front to back once during baking. As soon as the first sheet is filled, place it in the oven and bake for 8 to 10 minutes until golden brown. Cool the cookies completely on the baking sheets set on wire racks. With a wide turner, remove the cookies from the baking sheets.

6. Store in a tightly covered container or plastic bag. The cookies will stay soft and chewy for 2 or 3 days, or they can be frozen in zipper-top plastic bags for longer storage.

Yield: 30 to 36 cookies

Ladyfingers

Ladyfingers are almost always used as part of something else. Rarely are they considered as just cookies to eat and enjoy by themselves, but they certainly are. You can, if you want to, split the ladyfingers and spread them with jam, then sandwich them back together.

> 4 large eggs, separated and at room temperature
> $^1/_8$ teaspoon cream of tartar
> $^3/_4$ cup superfine sugar, divided
> 1 teaspoon vanilla extract
> $^3/_4$ cup all-purpose flour
> Confectioners' sugar, for dusting ladyfingers

1. Adjust one rack to divide the oven in half. Preheat the oven to 350°. Lightly grease and flour two baking sheets; set aside. Fit a large pastry bag with a plain, large writing tube with a $^1/_2$-inch opening.

2. In a medium-size bowl, with an electric mixer at medium-low speed, beat together the egg whites and cream of tartar until frothy. With the mixer at high speed, add $^1/_4$ cup of the sugar, 1 tablespoon at a time, beating for about 1 minute after each addition. Continue beating until the whites are glossy and stand in stiff peaks when the beaters are lifted, 5 to 10 minutes.

3. In a large bowl, with the electric mixer at medium-high speed (no need to wash the beaters), beat together the egg yolks, the remaining $^1/_2$ cup sugar, and vanilla until thick and pale-colored, 2 to 3 minutes. With a mixing spoon, stir in the flour until well blended. Fold the beaten egg whites into the yolk mixture in three additions, just until blended.

4. Fill the prepared pastry bag with half of the batter. Pipe into 3-inch lengths on a prepared baking sheet, spacing them about 1 inch apart. For instructions about how to use a pastry bag, see page 000. Smooth the edges with a moistened fingertip into the traditional ladyfinger shape. Sprinkle each ladyfinger lightly with confectioners' sugar.

5. Bake one sheet at a time for 12 to 15 minutes until lightly browned. With a wide turner, immediately transfer the ladyfingers to wire racks to cool completely.

6. Repeat with the remaining batter.

7. Store in a tightly covered container.

Yield: About 48 cookies

SHAPED AND FILLED COOKIES

To take shaped cookies one step further, you can mold them around a confectionery filling, which is usually chocolate, or at least chocolate-based. The ruglelach fillings on page 211 also make good filling for shaped cookies. Almost any dough that can be shaped can be filled, although the dough may have to be chilled before filling to make it firmer. A few recipes follow that will undoubtedly inspire you to experiment with your own filled-cookie creations.

Glazed Bonbons

A row or two of these fancy, pink bonbons tucked into a gift box of cookies will make it a very luxe presentation.

> 1 $^3/_4$ cups all-purpose flour
> $^1/_2$ cup confectioners' sugar
> $^1/_2$ cup (1 stick) salted butter or margarine, at room temperature
> 2 tablespoons half-and-half or milk
> $^1/_2$ teaspoon almond extract
> 1 cup (6 ounces) semisweet chocolate morsels

Almond Glaze

> 2 $^1/_4$ cups confectioners' sugar
> 3 tablespoons water
> $^1/_4$ cup light corn syrup, divided
> 1 $^1/_2$ teaspoons vegetable oil
> $^3/_4$ teaspoon almond extract
> 3 to 4 drops red food coloring

1. Adjust two racks to divide the oven into thirds. Preheat the oven to 350°. Have ready two ungreased baking sheets.

2. In a medium-size bowl, knead together the flour, sugar, butter, half-and-half, and almond extract until well mixed.

3. Reserve 3 tablespoons of the chocolate morsels to use for decorating the tops of the finished bonbons. With your hands, shape about 2 rounded measuring teaspoonfuls of the dough around about 6 of the remaining chocolate morsels and roll into a ball between the palms of your hands. As they are made, arrange the balls on the ungreased baking sheets, spacing them about 1 inch apart. Press down on each ball gently to flatten it slightly on the bottom. With your fingers, shape the top of each ball into a slightly rounded peak.

4. Bake for about 15 minutes until the balls are firm, but not brown. Reverse the baking sheets on the racks and from front to back once during baking. With a wide turner, transfer the cookies to wire racks to cool completely.

5. To make the glaze: In a small bowl, with a mixing spoon, stir together the confectioners' sugar, water, 2 tablespoons of the corn syrup, oil, almond extract, and food coloring until smooth. Dip the cookies in the glaze, turning to coat them completely. Set on wire racks (over sheets of waxed paper to catch the drips) until dry, about 30 minutes.

6. In a small saucepan set over very low heat, melt together the 3 tablespoons of reserved chocolate morsels and the remaining 2 tablespoons corn syrup, stirring constantly until smooth. Drizzle off the tip of a spoon over the tops of the cookies in squiggles resembling those on top of chocolate candies. Set aside until the chocolate has hardened, about 15 minutes.

7. Store in a shallow, tightly covered container, separating the layers with sheets of waxed paper.

Yield: About 24 cookies

My Sister Ruth Howard's No-Bake Rum Balls

Rum Balls are easy to make (there's no baking), taste great, and keep well for several weeks, tasting better and better every day as they age and mellow. At one time this was a very avant-garde recipe and, as is always the way with good recipes, through the years there have been many variations of it. If you don't want to bother with the food processor to grind the vanilla wafers, you can simply put them into a plastic bag and pound them with a rolling pin until they are evenly crushed.

> About 8 ounces purchased vanilla wafers
> 1 1/2 cups confectioners' sugar divided
> 2 tablespoons unsweetened cocoa powder
> 1 cup finely chopped pecans
> 1/2 cup light corn syrup
> 1/4 cup rum

1. In the container of a food processor fitted with a steel blade, process the vanilla wafers until very finely ground.

2. In a large bowl, with a mixing spoon, combine the ground wafers, 1 cup of the confectioners' sugar, cocoa powder, and pecans until well blended. Stir in the corn syrup and rum until thoroughly blended.

3. Coat the palms of your hands with confectioners' sugar. Scoop out heaping measuring teaspoonfuls of the dough from the pan and roll them into 1-inch balls between the palms of your hands. Place the balls on waxed paper and set them aside to dry for about 1 hour.

4. Sprinkle the remaining 1/2 cup of confectioners' sugar onto a sheet of waxed paper. Roll each ball in the sugar.

5. Store in a tightly covered container, separating the layers with sheets of waxed paper.

Yield: About 30 balls

Chocolate-Filled Holiday Balls

These are one of my family's favorite Christmas cookies. I must also modestly tell you that they are especially well received when I give them away.

- 1 cup walnut pieces, divided
- 2/3 cup confectioners' sugar, divided
- 1 3/4 cups all-purpose flour
- 1 cup (2 sticks) salted butter or margarine, at room temperature
- 1 teaspoon vanilla extract

Chocolate Filling

- 1/2 cup (3 ounces) semisweet chocolate morsels
- 2 tablespoons salted butter or margarine
- 2 tablespoons heavy (whipping) cream
- 1/2 teaspoon vanilla extract
- 1 cup confectioners' sugar

1. Adjust two racks to divide the oven into thirds. Preheat the oven to 350°. Have ready two ungreased baking sheets.

2. In a food processor fitted with a steel blade, process the walnuts with 2 tablespoons of the confectioners' sugar until finely ground.

3. In a medium-size bowl, with a whisk, combine the flour and 3/4 cup of the ground-walnut mixture until thoroughly mixed.

4. In a large bowl, with an electric mixer at medium-high speed, beat together the butter, the remaining confectioners' sugar, and vanilla until creamy, 2 to 3 minutes. With the mixer at medium-low speed, gradually add the flour mixture, beating just until blended. Scoop heaping measuring teaspoonfuls of the dough out of the bowl and roll them into 1-inch balls between the palms of your hands. Arrange the balls on the baking sheets, spacing them about 2 inches apart.

5. Bake for about 11 minutes until golden around the edges. Reverse the baking sheets on the racks and from front to back once during baking. With a wide turner, immediately transfer the cookies to wire racks to cool completely.

6. While the cookies are cooling, make the filling. In a medium-size saucepan set over low heat, melt together the chocolate, butter, and cream, stirring constantly until smooth. Remove from the heat and set aside to cool slightly. Stir in the vanilla until blended. Gradually add the confectioners' sugar, beating until smooth.

7. Sprinkle the remaining walnut mixture on a sheet of waxed paper. When the cookies have cooled, spread the bottom side of each one with a generous teaspoon of the filling. Top with the remaining cookies, flat sides down on the filling. Roll the chocolate edges of the cookies into the walnut mixture.

8. Store in a tightly covered container, separating the layers with sheets of waxed paper.

Yield: About 18 sandwich cookies

Tip

Keep a constant check on the oven temperature (with an oven thermometer). In even the best ovens, heat build-up can occur, which causes subsequent batches of cookies after the first to bake more quickly.

Kiss Cookies

I'm sure you know what kind of kisses we're referring to.

1 ³/₄ cups all-purpose flour

1 cup very finely chopped walnuts or pecans

1 cup (2 sticks) salted butter or margarine, at room temperature

1 cup granulated sugar

1 teaspoon vanilla extract

¹/₃ cup confectioners' sugar

1 tablespoon unsweetened cocoa powder

About 36 foil-covered, milk-chocolate kisses

1. Adjust two racks to divide the oven into thirds. Have ready two ungreased baking sheets.

2. In a small bowl, with a whisk, combine the flour and walnuts until thoroughly mixed.

3. In a large bowl, with an electric mixer at medium-high speed, beat together the butter, granulated sugar, and vanilla until light and fluffy, 2 to 3 minutes. With the mixer at low speed, gradually add the flour mixture, beating just until blended. Cover the bowl and refrigerate until the dough is firm, 1 to 2 hours.

4. Preheat the oven to 375°.

5. Combine the confectioners' sugar and cocoa in a brown paper bag; set aside. Using about 1 measuring tablespoonful of dough for each cookie, shape the dough around a chocolate piece, covering it completely. Roll between the palms of your hands to make a ball. Arrange the balls on the ungreased baking sheets, spacing them about 2 inches apart.

6. Bake for 10 to 12 minutes until firm when lightly touched, but not brown. Reverse the baking sheets on the racks and from front to back once during baking. Cool on the baking sheets set on wire racks for a few minutes. Transfer a few warm cookies at a time to the paper bag containing the confectioners' sugar and cocoa. Shake until the cookies are well coated. Place the coated cookies on the wire racks to cool completely.

7. Store in a tightly covered container.

Yield: About 36 cookies

Variation

Lemon Kisses: Substitute 1¹/₂ teaspoons lemon extract for vanilla extract. A teaspoon or two of shredded and minced lemon zest can also be whisked into the flour mixture. Omit the cocoa from the confectioners' sugar coating, increasing the confectioners' sugar to about ¹/₂ cup.

10
Bar Cookies

I have never understood why bar cookies are called cookies at all, since they are obviously more like pieces of flat cake. However, there are some things in life better left unquestioned, and the business about whether bar cookies are or aren't may be one of them.

I like to imagine the original bar-cookie maker, who was intent on making some sort of traditional drop or shaped cookie, and got interrupted after the batter was mixed. What an ingenious idea it was to merely spread the batter in a pan and bake it. Wow! What a labor saver!

From this you have probably gathered that most bar-cookie batters, at least if they are the kind that are merely spread in a pan and baked, can be turned into drop cookies, or even shaped cookies, with only minor alterations, and sometimes no alterations, to the batter. Changes are usually just a matter of adding a little extra flour so that the batter will be the right consistency for dropping or shaping into balls. Perhaps all that's needed is for the batter to be chilled so that it stiffens up a bit.

VARIETY IS THE SPICE OF BARS

It's also incredibly easy to add your own touches to almost any bar cookie:

- Poke holes with a cake tester or thin skewer in the top of the still-warm bar cookies. Drizzle with a very small amount of liqueur or thawed, frozen juice concentrate. Chocolate batters take well to many flavors: citrus-, berry-, or coffee-flavored liqueurs, for instance; amaretto adds zing to almost any bar containing almonds; brandy does wonders for a batter that is a takeoff on a nut pie.

- Sprinkle dark bar cookies with confectioners' sugar or unsweetened cocoa powder on light bar cookies (through a paper doily for a lacy pattern).

- Chips (butterscotch, chocolate, white chocolate, or mint-flavored, for instance) can be sprinkled on top of the bars as soon as they have finished baking. Then run the pan back into the oven just until the chips are melted. They can be left looking melted, or they can be spread over the top to make a thin icing.

- Chopped nuts and flaked or shredded coconut are other easy toppers. Sprinkle these over the bar cookies about 5 minutes before the end of baking time, so that they have a few minutes in the oven to brown lightly. If you like, you can go a step further and mix the nuts or coconut with brown sugar and bake until bubbly.

- Bar cookies can be cut into many shapes besides squares, bars, and diamonds. You can use cookie cutters in various shapes. With this method, you will end up with a few scraps, but they're not likely to go to waste if they are put out on a plate for the family. Or crumble them onto ice cream or puddings.

STORING BAR COOKIES

Bar cookies have different storage requirements than other cookies, since they are more like pieces of cake and should be treated as such. After the bars are cut (usually after cooling) they can be stored right in the baking pan, tightly covered with aluminum foil or plastic wrap. If you prefer, the bars can be removed from the baking pan and each bar wrapped tightly in plastic wrap. For longer storage, wrap the bars individually in aluminum foil and freeze for up to six months. Thaw, in the wrapping, at room temperature for an hour or so before serving.

Bars can also be removed from the pan and stored in a tightly covered shallow container, separating the layers with sheets of waxed paper, since bar cookies tend to stick together.

Brownies

If there were ever a cookie to challenge the popularity of the chocolate-chip cookie, it must be the chocolate brownie. The brownie, a uniquely American confection, has triumphed through generations of mothers baking for their families, and are part of nearly everybody's sweetest childhood memories.

There may be as many brownie recipes as there are chocolate-chip cookie recipes, and everyone has his or her own special favorite. Whether the brownies are cakey or chewy, and whether or not there are nuts in the batter, for example, is usually the determining factor about what constitutes a good brownie and is just a matter of personal preference.

The brownies that follow are likely to suit every taste, and most of them are so simple, you'll wonder why anyone would ever bother to use a mix.

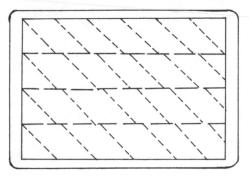

How to cut diamond-shaped bar cookies

The following tables provide general guidelines for how many bars can be cut from the most common sizes of baking pans.

13 x 9 x 2-INCH BAKING PAN

Number of Rows	Yield
6 × 6	36
8 × 5	40
8 × 6	48

8-INCH-SQUARE BAKING PAN*

Number of Rows	Yield
3 × 3	9
4 × 4	16
4 × 5	20
4 × 8	32
6 × 6	36

*A 9-inch-square baking pan will have the same yield, but the cookies will be slightly larger.

15 x 10 x 1-INCH JELLY-ROLL PAN

Number of Rows	Yield
7 × 5	35
10 × 4	40
12 × 4	48
8 × 6	48
10 × 5	50
9 × 6	54

Old-Fashioned Walnut Brownies

· ·

When you want an easy, reliable brownie recipe, this is it. The texture is somewhere between chewy and cakey, and it appeals to nearly everyone. Just remember not to beat the batter. Simply stir it with authority.

> **2 ounces (2 squares) unsweetened chocolate**
> **¹/₃ cup plain shortening**
> **2 large eggs**
> **1 cup sugar**
> **1 teaspoon vanilla extract**
> **¹/₄ teaspoon salt**
> **³/₄ cup all-purpose flour**
> **1 cup chopped walnuts**

1. Adjust one rack to divide the oven in half. Preheat the oven to 325°. Lightly grease an 8-inch-square metal baking pan.

2. In a small, heavy saucepan set over very low heat, melt the chocolate with the shortening, stirring constantly until smooth. Remove from the heat and set aside to cool to lukewarm.

3. In a large bowl, with a mixing spoon, beat the eggs lightly. Stir in the sugar, vanilla, and salt until well blended. Stir in the cooled chocolate mixture. Stir in the flour just until blended. Stir in the walnuts until well distributed throughout the batter. Turn the batter into the prepared pan, smoothing the top with the back of the spoon.

4. Bake for about 30 minutes just until the edges begin to pull away from the sides of the pan, but the center is still slightly soft when lightly pressed with a finger. Reverse the pan from front to back once during baking. Set the pan on a wire rack to cool completely before cutting into 4 × 4 rows.

5. Store in the baking pan, tightly covered with aluminum foil or plastic wrap.

Yield: 16 brownies

Tips for Baking Bar Cookies

- Read through the recipe completely to make sure that you have all of the equipment and ingredients you will need.

- Use the size pan that is called for in the recipe. If the pan is smaller, the bars may not bake correctly, or may be underbaked. If the pan is too large, the bars may be dry and overbaked.

- Metal baking pans and glass baking dishes can almost always be used interchangeably. However, because glass conducts heat differently than metal, the oven temperature must be reduced by 25° when using a glass baking dish.

- Use a light hand when greasing the baking pan or baking dish. A lavish coating of grease is not necessary in order for the bar cookies to come out of the pan easily.

- To press stiff doughs or crumb crusts into the pan, your fingers are the most efficient tool.

- Make sure to set the pan on a wire rack to cool. Without proper air circulation beneath the pan, the bottoms of the bar cookies will be soggy.

- When removing bar cookies from the pan, take out a corner piece first. Then use a wide turner or a narrow icing spatula to go beneath and loosen the surrounding bars.

- Bar cookies dry out more quickly than traditional cookies, so keep them tightly covered or wrapped after cooling.

Variations

Chocolate-Orange Brownies: Add ¹/₂ teaspoon shredded and minced orange zest and ¹/₂ teaspoon orange extract to the batter at the same time the vanilla is added.

Mint-Flavored Old-Fashioned Brownies: Add ¹/₄ teaspoon peppermint extract to the batter at the same time the vanilla is added; ¹/₂ cup crushed peppermint candies can also be stirred into the batter.

Mocha Brownies: Add 1 tablespoon instant-coffee granules (not powder) to the chocolate and shortening before melting.

Dark Chocolate Chewy Brownies

. . . .

For those who like their brownies very chocolatey and chewy, this is an excellent recipe. The peanut butter variation is wonderful, too, and both are quick to make.

- $^{1}/_{2}$ cup (1 stick) salted butter or margarine, cut into chunks
- 3 ounces (3 squares) unsweetened chocolate
- 1 $^{1}/_{3}$ cups sugar
- 2 large eggs, lightly beaten
- 1 teaspoon vanilla extract
- $^{1}/_{2}$ cup all-purpose flour
- $^{1}/_{2}$ cup of one or a mixture of toppings: chopped pecans, walnuts, or almonds; chopped semisweet or vanilla-flavored baking pieces

1. Adjust one rack to divide the oven in half. Preheat the oven to 350°. Lightly grease an 8-inch-square metal pan or a 9-inch round cake pan.

2. In a 2- to 3-quart saucepan set over very low heat, melt the butter with the unsweetened chocolate, stirring constantly until smooth. Remove from the heat. With a mixing spoon, stir in the sugar until blended. Stir in the eggs and vanilla until blended. Stir in the flour just until blended. Turn the batter into the prepared pan, spreading the top evenly with the back of the spoon. Sprinkle with one or a mix of any of the suggested toppings.

3. Bake for 25 to 30 minutes until the edges feel firm and the center springs back when gently pressed. Reverse the pan from front to back once during baking. Set the pan on a wire rack to cool completely before cutting into 4 × 4 rows or 16 wedges.

4. Store in the baking pan, tightly covered with aluminum foil or plastic wrap.

Yield: 16 bars or wedges

Variation

Peanut Butter Brownies: Reduce the melted butter to 5 tablespoons and omit the chocolate. Stir $^{3}/_{4}$ cup peanut butter into the melted butter. Reduce the sugar to 1 cup. Mix $^{1}/_{4}$ teaspoon baking powder with the flour. Instead of, or in addition to, the toppings, $^{1}/_{2}$ cup of chocolate chips can be stirred into the batter. Mix and bake as directed.

The World's Best Brownies

. . . .

I know, I know. This is a bold statement, and it's only my opinion, but the believing is in the tasting. Certainly these are *not* lunch-box brownies. They are very moist, rich with chocolate, butter, eggs, and very little else. Serve these brownies at room temperature, chilled, or even frozen. Sometimes I sprinkle them heavily with confectioners' sugar just before serving, and I also love them with strawberries or raspberries.

- 3 ounces (3 squares) unsweetened chocolate
- 3 ounces (3 squares) semisweet chocolate
- $^{1}/_{2}$ cup (1 stick) unsalted butter
- 1 $^{1}/_{4}$ cups sugar
- 2 large eggs, lightly beaten
- 1 teaspoon vanilla extract
- $^{1}/_{3}$ cup all-purpose flour
- 1 cup pecan pieces

1. Adjust one rack to divide the oven in half. Preheat the oven to 300°. Generously grease a 9-inch-square glass baking dish with unsalted butter.

2. In a medium-size, heavy saucepan set over very low heat, melt together the unsweetened chocolate, semisweet chocolate, and butter, stirring constantly until smooth. Remove from the heat. With a mixing spoon, stir in the sugar until well blended. Add the eggs, stirring until well blended. Add the vanilla and stir until blended. Add the flour, all at once, and beat with the spoon until the mixture is thick and shiny, about 1 minute.

Stir in the nuts until evenly distributed throughout the batter. Turn the batter into the prepared baking dish, smoothing the top with the back of the spoon.

3. Bake for about 45 minutes, or until the top looks dry and shiny and springs back when lightly pressed. Reverse the baking dish from front to back once during baking. Set the dish on a wire rack to cool completely before cutting into 4 × 4 or 6 × 4 rows.

4. Store in a tightly covered container, separating the layers with sheets of waxed paper.

Yield: 16 to 24 brownies

Chocolate-Mint Brownies

These are more cakelike than chewy, but still very moist. Be careful not to overbake them.

- 1 ¼ cups all-purpose flour
- ½ teaspoon baking soda
- ¾ cup sugar
- ½ cup (1 stick) salted butter or margarine, at room temperature
- 2 tablespoons water
- 1 ½ cups mint-flavored semisweet chocolate chips, divided
- 2 large eggs, lightly beaten
- 1 teaspoon vanilla extract
- 1 cup chopped walnuts
- Confectioners' sugar, for dusting brownies

1. Adjust one rack to divide the oven in half. Preheat the oven to 350° (or 325° if using a glass baking dish). Lightly grease a 9-inch-square metal baking pan or glass baking dish.

2. In a medium-size bowl, with a whisk, combine the flour and baking soda until thoroughly mixed.

3. In a small saucepan over medium heat, stir together the sugar, butter, and water. Bring to a boil and immediately remove from the heat. With a mixing spoon, stir in 1 cup of the chocolate chips until they are melted and the mixture is smooth.

4. Scrape the chocolate mixture into a large bowl. With the mixing spoon, stir in the eggs, one at a time, mixing well after each addition; stir in the vanilla. Stir in the flour mixture until well blended. Stir in the remaining 1 cup of chips and the walnuts until well distributed throughout the batter. Turn the batter into the prepared baking dish, smoothing the top with the back of the spoon.

5. Bake for 25 to 30 minutes until the center feels set, but still slightly soft, when lightly touched. Reverse the pan from front to back once during baking. Set the pan on a wire rack to cool completely before cutting into 4 × 4 rows.

6. Store in the baking pan, tightly covered with aluminum foil or plastic wrap. Just before serving, dust with confectioners' sugar.

Yield: 16 brownies

Rocky Road Brownies

Rocky road just happens to be one of my favorite ice-cream flavors. It's the nuts and marshmallows that I really like in the ice cream, and these bars have plenty of both in them.

1 3/4 cups all-purpose flour

1/4 cup unsweetened cocoa powder

1 teaspoon baking soda

1 cup (2 sticks) salted butter or margarine, at room temperature

1 cup packed light or dark brown sugar

2 large eggs

3 cups (18 ounces) semisweet chocolate chips, divided

1 cup blanched or natural whole almonds, coarsely chopped

1 cup miniature marshmallows

1. Adjust one rack to divide the oven in half. Preheat the oven to 350°. Line a 15 × 10-inch jelly-roll pan with foil, shiny side up, leaving about an inch of foil at each end to assist with the removal of the bars.

2. In a medium-size bowl, with a whisk, combine the flour, cocoa, and baking soda until thoroughly mixed.

3. In a large bowl, with an electric mixer at medium-high speed, beat together the butter and brown sugar until very creamy, 2 to 3 minutes. Beat in the eggs, one at a time, until well blended. With the mixer on medium-low speed, gradually add the flour mixture, beating after each addition just until blended. With a mixing spoon, stir in 2 cups of the chocolate chips and all of the almonds until well distributed throughout the batter. Spread the batter evenly in the prepared pan, smoothing the top with the back of the spoon.

4. Bake for about 15 minutes until set, but the center is still soft. Reverse the pan from front to back once during baking. Sprinkle evenly with the marshmallows and the remaining 1 cup of chocolate chips. Return to the oven for about 3 minutes

until the chocolate and marshmallows are soft. Cool in the pan on a wire rack for 5 minutes. Using the overlapping foil to assist, remove the baked batter to a cutting board; peel off the foil. With a long, sharp knife, cut into 10 × 5 rows. Transfer the bars to wire racks to cool completely.

5. Store in a tightly covered container, separating the layers with sheets of waxed paper.

Yield: 50 brownies

Tip

Most bar cookies cut more easily—and don't crumble—if they are completely cooled first.

Annie's Easy-as-Pie Brownies

What makes these so easy is that all the mixing is done in a saucepan. What makes them quick is that you don't even have to wait for the butter to soften. A great recipe when you want brownies *now*, not two hours from now.

4 ounces (4 squares) unsweetened chocolate

3/4 cup (1 1/2 sticks) salted butter or margarine

2 cups sugar

3 eggs, lightly beaten

1 teaspoon vanilla extract

1 cup all-purpose flour

1 cup coarsely chopped nuts (optional)

1. Adjust one rack to divide the oven in half. Preheat the oven to 350° (or 325° if using a glass baking dish). Lightly grease a 13 × 9-inch baking pan or glass baking dish.

2. In a 3-quart saucepan set over very low heat, melt together the chocolate and butter, stirring constantly until smooth. With a mixing spoon, immediately stir the sugar into the chocolate mix-

ture until well blended. Stir in the eggs and vanilla until completely blended. Stir in flour just until blended. Stir in nuts until well distributed throughout the batter. Turn into the prepared pan, smoothing the top with the back of the spoon.

3. Bake for 30 to 35 minutes until a wooden pick inserted in the center comes out almost clean. Reverse the pan from front to back once during baking. Set the pan on a wire rack to cool completely before cutting into 4 × 5 rows.

Yield: 20 brownies

Variations

Chippy Easy-as-Pie Brownies: Use 1 cup of semisweet chocolate chips in place of the optional nuts.

Extra-thick, Easy-as-Pie Brownies: Bake in a 9-inch-square pan for about 50 minutes.

Hocus Pocus Brownies

This is a very rich brownie that is topped with an easy vanilla frosting, chopped nuts, and melted chocolate. It is best to store these bars in the refrigerator, although it is not absolutely necessary.

Brownie Layer

  $^1/_2$ cup (1 stick) salted butter (not margarine), at room temperature
  2 ounces (2 squares) unsweetened chocolate
  1 cup sugar
  $^3/_4$ cup all-purpose flour
  2 large eggs, lightly beaten

Topping

  2 cups confectioners' sugar
  2 tablespoons salted butter, at room temperature
  2 tablespoons half-and-half or milk
  $^1/_2$ cup coarsely chopped peanuts, hazelnuts, or almonds

Drizzle

  $^1/_2$ cup semisweet chocolate chips

1. Adjust one rack to divide the oven in half. Preheat the oven to 350°. Lightly grease an 8-inch-square metal baking pan.

2. To make the brownie layer: In a 2-quart saucepan set over very low heat, melt together the butter and chocolate, stirring constantly until smooth. Remove from the heat. With a mixing spoon, stir in the sugar, flour, and eggs just until well blended. Turn into the prepared baking pan, smoothing the top with the back of the spoon.

3. Bake for 25 to 30 minutes until the brownies begin to pull away from the sides of the pan. (Be careful not to overbake.) Reverse the pan from front to back once during baking. Set the pan on a wire rack to cool completely.

4. To make the topping: In a small bowl, with an electric mixer at medium-high speed, beat together the confectioners' sugar, butter, and milk until smooth and creamy, 1 to 2 minutes. Spread this mixture over the cooled brownies. Sprinkle evenly with the nuts.

5. To make the drizzle: In a small saucepan set over very low heat, melt the chocolate, stirring constantly until smooth. Drizzle the chocolate off the tip of a teaspoon over the topping and nuts. Cover with aluminum foil or plastic wrap and refrigerate for 1 hour. Remove from the refrigerator and let stand at room temperature for 15 minutes before cutting into 4 × 4 rows.

6. Recover the pan and store in the refrigerator for up to 2 or 3 days.

Yield: 16 brownies

No-Bake Fudgy Brownies

I won't kid you. This isn't my recipe. It came to me years ago from the folks at Nestlé Food Company, who are constantly thinking up new and interesting ways to use their chocolate chips.

- 2 cups (12 ounces) semisweet chocolate chips
- One 14-ounce can regular or reduced-fat condensed (not evaporated) milk
- One 8 1/2-ounce package chocolate wafers, crushed
- 1 cup chopped walnuts, divided

1. Line an 8-inch-square metal baking pan with aluminum foil, allowing the foil to overhang slightly.

2. In the top of a double boiler set over hot (not boiling) water, melt the chocolate, stirring constantly until smooth. Remove the double boiler from the heat. With a mixing spoon, stir in the condensed milk, crushed wafers, and half of the nuts until well blended. Press this mixture into the prepared pan, patting it down evenly. Press the remaining 1/2 cup nuts evenly over the top.

3. Let stand at room temperature until firm, an hour or two. Cut into 4 × 4 rows.

4. Store in a tightly covered container, separating the layers with sheets of waxed paper.

Yield: 16 brownies

Party Brownies

Cut these super-rich bars into very small serving sizes to keep the calorie content from flying off the charts.

- 2 ounces (2 squares) unsweetened chocolate
- 1 1/2 cups all-purpose flour
- 1 teaspoon baking powder
- 1 cup (2 sticks) butter or margarine, softened
- 2 cups granulated sugar
- 4 large eggs
- 2 teaspoons vanilla extract
- 1 cup chopped walnuts

Topping

- 1/3 cup (1/2 stick plus 1 1/2 tablespoons) salted butter or margarine
- 3 cups sifted confectioners' sugar
- 3 tablespoons light cream or half-and-half
- 1 1/2 teaspoons vanilla extract

Drizzle Glaze

- 1 ounce (1 square) unsweetened chocolate
- 1 tablespoon butter
- 1 tablespoon confectioners' sugar

1. Adjust one rack to divide the oven in half. Preheat the oven to 350°. Lightly grease a 15 × 10 -inch jelly-roll pan.

2. In a small saucepan set over very low heat, melt the chocolate, stirring constantly until smooth. Remove from the heat and set aside.

3. In a medium-size bowl, with a whisk, combine the flour and baking powder until thoroughly mixed.

4. In a large bowl, with an electric mixer at medium-high speed, beat together the butter and sugar until light and fluffy, 2 to 3 minutes. Add the eggs, one at a time, beating after each addition. With a mixing spoon, stir in the melted chocolate and vanilla until well blended. With the mixer at medium-low speed, gradually add the flour mixture, beating just until blended. With the spoon, stir in the nuts until well distributed throughout the batter. Turn the batter into the prepared pan, smoothing the top with the back of the spoon.

5. Bake for 30 minutes until the edges are just starting to pull away from the sides of the pan. Reverse the pan from front to back once during baking. Set the pan on a wire rack to cool.

6. To make the topping: In a medium-size saucepan over medium heat, stir the butter until melted and browned, but not burned. Watch carefully. Remove from the heat and stir in the sugar, cream, and vanilla. Spread on the cooled cake.

7. To make the glaze: In a small saucepan set over very low heat, melt together the chocolate and

butter, stirring constantly. Remove from the heat and stir in the confectioners' sugar. Drizzle off the tip of a teaspoon over the topping. Cut into 10 × 4 rows.

8. Store in the baking pan, tightly covered with aluminum foil or plastic wrap.

Yield: 40 bars

Chocolate Mousse Brownies

Although these brownies are made in layers, they don't bake like that. They are very rich and fudgy, and the meringue topping is more like an icing.

Brownie Layer

$^1/_2$ cup (1 stick) salted butter or margarine

2 cups (12 ounces) semisweet chocolate chips

2 cups sugar

1 $^1/_4$ cups all-purpose flour

$^1/_2$ teaspoon baking powder

$^1/_2$ teaspoon salt

3 large eggs

2 teaspoons vanilla extract

$^1/_2$ cup chopped pecans

Mousse Layer

$^3/_4$ cup heavy (whipping) cream

1 cup (6 ounces) semisweet chocolate chips

3 large eggs

1 $^1/_2$ teaspoons vanilla extract

$^1/_2$ cup sugar

$^1/_4$ teaspoon salt

1 cup chopped pecans

1. Adjust one rack to divide the oven in half. Preheat the oven to 325°. Lightly grease a 13 × 9-inch glass baking dish.

2. To make the brownie layer: In a heavy, 4-quart saucepan set over very low heat, melt together the butter and chocolate chips, stirring constantly until smooth. Remove from the heat and set aside to cool to lukewarm.

3. In a large bowl, with a whisk, combine the sugar, flour, baking powder, and salt until thoroughly mixed.

4. In a small bowl, with a whisk, beat the eggs with the vanilla until frothy. With a mixing spoon, stir the beaten eggs into the cooled chocolate mixture just until blended. Gradually stir in the flour mixture. Stir in the pecans until well distributed throughout the batter. Turn the batter into the prepared baking dish, smoothing the top with the back of the spoon.

5. To make the mousse layer: In a small, heavy saucepan set over low heat, melt together the cream and the chocolate chips, stirring constantly until smooth. Remove from the heat and set aside to cool to lukewarm.

6. In a large bowl, with an electric mixer at medium-high speed, beat together the eggs, vanilla, sugar, and salt until thick and foamy, about 3 minutes. Gradually beat in the cooled chocolate mixture until well blended. Pour the mousse over the brownie mixture, smoothing the top with the back of the spoon. Sprinkle evenly with the chopped pecans.

7. Bake for 50 to 55 minutes until firm to the touch. Reverse the baking dish from front to back once during baking. Set the baking dish on a wire rack to cool completely before cutting into 6 × 6 rows.

8. Store in the baking dish, tightly covered with aluminum foil or plastic wrap.

Yield: 36 brownies

Chocolate-Raspberry Brownies

Chocolate and raspberries are a marriage made in heaven no matter how they're combined, and these slightly chewy brownies are no exception.

- $^2/_3$ **cup all-purpose flour**
- $^1/_4$ **teaspoon baking powder**
- $^1/_3$ **cup granulated sugar**
- **2 tablespoons salted butter or margarine**
- **2 tablespoons water**
- **2 cups (12 ounces) semisweet chocolate chips, divided**
- **1 large egg, lightly beaten**
- **1 teaspoon vanilla extract**
- $^1/_3$ **cup seedless raspberry preserves, stirred until softened**
- $^1/_2$ **cup finely chopped pecans**

1. Adjust one rack to divide the oven in half. Preheat the oven to 350°. Lightly grease an 8-inch-square metal baking pan.

2. In a medium-size bowl, with a whisk, combine the flour and baking powder until thoroughly mixed.

3. In a medium-size saucepan, combine the sugar, butter, and water. Cook over medium heat, stirring constantly, until the mixture boils. Remove from the heat and, with a mixing spoon, immediately stir in 1 cup of the chocolate chips until melted and smooth. Stir in the egg and vanilla until blended. Stir in the flour mixture and the remaining 1 cup of chocolate chips until well blended and the chips are well distributed throughout the batter. Turn into the prepared pan, smoothing the top with the back of a spoon. Place the pan in the freezer for 10 minutes. Spread the raspberry preserves over the chilled batter. Sprinkle the nuts evenly over the preserves.

4. Bake for 35 to 40 minutes until the brownies begin to pull away from the sides of the pan. Reverse the pan from front to back once during baking. Set the pan on a wire rack to cool completely before cutting into 4 × 4 rows.

5. Store in the baking pan, tightly covered with aluminum foil or plastic wrap.

Yield: 16 brownies

Chocolate-Raspberry Truffle Brownies Supreme

This divine recipe won fifth prize in the King Arthur Flour 1993 WinterBake contest. It was created by Sally Szymujko of Moultonboro, New Hampshire. After you taste these brownies, you will probably wonder, as I did, why they didn't win first prize. I cannot even begin to guess how many fabulous calories each one of these brownies must contain. This is a recipe for truly special occasions.

Brownie Base

- **1 $^1/_2$ cups unbleached, all-purpose flour**
- $^3/_4$ **teaspoon baking powder**
- $^1/_2$ **teaspoon salt**
- **2 cups (12 ounces) semisweet chocolate chips**
- $^1/_4$ **cup ($^1/_2$ stick) unsalted butter or margarine, at room temperature**
- **One 8-ounce package cream cheese, at room temperature**
- **1 $^3/_4$ cups sugar**
- **3 extra-large eggs**
- **2 teaspoons vanilla extract**
- **2 tablespoons raspberry liqueur**

Truffle Layer

- **1 cup (6 ounces) semisweet chocolate chips**
- $^2/_3$ **cup heavy (whipping) cream**
- **4 ounces cream cheese (half of an 8-ounce package), at room temperature**
- $^1/_2$ **cup raspberry jam**
- **3 extra-large eggs**

Topping

- **1 cup (6 ounces) semisweet chocolate chips**
- $^1/_4$ **cup heavy (whipping) cream**
- **2 tablespoons raspberry liqueur**

1. Adjust one rack to divide the oven in half. Preheat the oven to 350° (or 325° if using a glass baking dish). Lightly grease a 13 × 9-inch metal baking pan or glass baking dish.

2. To make the brownie base: In a medium-size bowl, with a whisk, combine the flour, baking powder, and salt until thoroughly mixed.

3. In a small saucepan set over very low heat, melt together the chocolate chips and butter, stirring constantly until smooth. Remove from the heat and set aside to cool slightly.

4. In a large bowl, with an electric mixer at medium-high speed, beat together the cream cheese and sugar until light and fluffy, 2 to 3 minutes. Add the eggs and vanilla and beat until well blended. With a mixing spoon, stir in the chocolate mixture and the raspberry liqueur until very well blended. With the mixer at medium-low speed, gradually add the flour mixture, beating just until blended. Turn the batter into the prepared pan, smoothing the top with the back of a spoon; set aside.

5. To make the truffle layer: In a small saucepan set over very low heat, melt together the chocolate chips and cream, stirring constantly until smooth. Remove from the heat and set aside to cool slightly.

6. In a medium-size bowl, with an electric mixer at medium-high speed, beat the cream cheese until fluffy, about 1 minute. With the mixer at medium speed, beat in the jam and the eggs until well blended. With a mixing spoon, stir in the chocolate mixture until well blended. Pour over the brownie base, tilting the baking pan in each direction to cover evenly.

7. Bake for 40 to 50 minutes until puffed and just set. (These brownies will not test for doneness by the usual methods.) Reverse the pan from front to back once during baking. Set the pan on a wire rack to cool completely.

8. To make the topping: In a small saucepan set over low heat, melt together the chocolate chips, cream, and liqueur, stirring constantly until smooth. Spread over the cooled brownies. Refrigerate until the topping is set, about 1 hour, before cutting into 6 × 6 rows.

9. Store in the baking pan, tightly covered with aluminum foil or plastic wrap.

Yield: 36 bars

Tip

To remove bars more easily from the baking pan, take out a corner piece first. This will enable you to slip a turner or icing spatula beneath the surrounding bars to loosen them.

Raspberry-Twirl Oat Brownies

The variations of brownies seem endless, but they are all so good that I want to include as many in this cookbook as possible.

1 ¹/₄ cups all-purpose flour

1 cup regular or quick-cooking (not instant) rolled oats

1 teaspoon baking powder

1 ¹/₂ cups (9 ounces) semisweet chocolate chips

²/₃ cup (1 stick plus 3 tablespoons) salted butter or margarine, at room temperature

1 cup sugar

2 large eggs

1 teaspoon vanilla extract

¹/₃ cup raspberry preserves

1. Adjust one rack to divide the oven in half. Preheat the oven to 350° (or 325° if using a glass baking dish). Lightly grease a 13 × 9-inch metal baking pan or glass baking dish.

2. In a medium-size bowl, with a whisk, combine the flour, oats, and baking powder until thoroughly mixed.

3. In a small saucepan set over very low heat, melt the chocolate, stirring constantly until smooth; set aside.

4. In a large bowl, with an electric mixer at medium-high speed, beat the butter, sugar, eggs, and vanilla until smooth. Stir in 1 cup of the melted chocolate until well blended. Turn the batter into the prepared pan, smoothing the top with the back of the spoon. Drop 16 measuring teaspoonfuls of the raspberry preserves evenly over the batter. With an icing spatula or a dinner knife, swirl the preserves into the batter.

5. Bake for 25 to 30 minutes until the edges pull away from the sides of the pan. Reverse the pan from front to back once during baking. Set on a wire rack to cool completely. Drizzle with the remaining ¹/₂ cup of melted chocolate. Cut into 6 × 6 rows.

6. Store in the baking pan, tightly covered with aluminum foil or plastic wrap.

Yield: 36 bars

Luscious Marbled Brownies

These bars are richness personified. However, they must be stored in the refrigerator, so don't count on them for any event during which they must remain at room temperature for very long.

Chocolate Crust

2 cups finely crushed purchased vanilla wafers (about 60)

¹/₃ cup unsweetened cocoa powder

¹/₂ cup confectioners' sugar

¹/₂ cup (1 stick) salted butter or margarine, melted

Filling

2 ounces (2 squares) unsweetened chocolate

Three 8-ounce packages cream cheese, at room temperature

One 14-ounce can regular or reduced-fat condensed (not evaporated) milk

3 large eggs, lightly beaten

2 teaspoons vanilla extract

1. Adjust one rack to divide the oven in half. Preheat the oven to 300°. Have ready an ungreased, 13 × 9-inch metal baking pan or glass baking dish.

2. To make the crust: In a medium-size bowl, with a whisk, combine the wafer crumbs, cocoa powder, and confectioners' sugar until thoroughly mixed. With a mixing spoon, stir in the melted butter until well blended. Press this mixture onto the bottom of the ungreased pan; set aside.

3. To make the filling: In a small saucepan set over very low heat, melt the chocolate, stirring constantly until smooth; set aside.

4. In a large bowl, with an electric mixer at medium-high speed, beat the cream cheese until

fluffy, 2 to 3 minutes. Gradually add the condensed milk, beating until smooth and creamy. Beat in the eggs and vanilla until well blended. Pour half of this mixture over the crust, smoothing the top with the back of the spoon. Stir the melted chocolate into the remaining cream cheese mixture until well blended. Spoon large dollops over the batter in the pan. With an icing spatula or a dinner knife, swirl the dollops gently through the batter for a marbled effect.

5. Bake for 45 to 50 minutes until set. Reverse the pan from front to back once during baking. Set the pan on a wire rack to cool completely before cutting into 6×6 rows.

6. Store in the baking pan in the refrigerator, tightly covered with aluminum foil or plastic wrap.

Yield: 36 bars

Real Blondies

Blondies have never achieved anything even approaching the popularity of their brunette sisters, but they are good, and a nice change—if you think you need a change—from chocolate brownies.

1 ³/₄ **cups all-purpose flour**
1 ¹/₄ **teaspoons baking powder**
¹/₂ **cup (1 stick) plus 2 tablespoons salted butter or margarine, at room temperature**
1 ¹/₂ **cups packed light brown sugar**
¹/₂ **cup granulated sugar**
1 ¹/₂ **teaspoons vanilla extract**
2 **large eggs**
1 **cup (6 ounces) semisweet chocolate chips**
1 **cup chopped pecans**

1. Adjust one rack to divide the oven in half. Preheat the oven to 350° (or 325° if using a glass baking dish). Lightly grease and flour a 13×9-inch metal baking pan or glass baking dish.

2. In a medium-size bowl, with a whisk, combine the flour and baking powder until thoroughly mixed.

3. In a large bowl, with an electric mixer at medium-high speed, beat together the butter, brown sugar, and granulated sugar until light and creamy, 2 to 3 minutes. Beat in the vanilla. Add the eggs, one at a time, beating until blended after each addition. With the mixer at medium-low speed, gradually add the flour mixture, beating just until blended. With a mixing spoon, stir in the chocolate chips and nuts until well distributed throughout the batter. Turn the batter into the prepared pan, smoothing the top with the back of the spoon.

4. Bake for 30 to 35 minutes until the edges just begin to pull away from the sides of the pan. Reverse the pan from front to back once during baking. Set the pan on a wire rack to cool completely before cutting into 6×6 rows.

5. Store in the baking pan, tightly covered with aluminum foil or plastic wrap.

Yield: 36 bars

Butterscotch-Pecan Blondies

These are the Dark Chocolate Chewy Brownies on page 240 that have had the chocolate removed and brown sugar substituted for the granulated sugar.

> $^1/_2$ cup (1 stick) salted butter or margarine, melted
>
> 1 $^1/_4$ cups packed light brown sugar
>
> 2 large eggs, lightly beaten
>
> 1 teaspoon vanilla extract
>
> 1 cup all-purpose flour
>
> $^1/_2$ cup pecan halves or pieces

1. Adjust one rack to divide the oven in half. Preheat the oven to 350°. Lightly grease an 8-inch-square metal baking pan or a 9-inch round cake pan.

2. In a medium-size bowl, with a mixing spoon, combine the melted butter and brown sugar until well blended. Stir in the eggs and vanilla until blended. Stir in the flour just until blended. Turn the batter into the prepared pan, smoothing the top with the back of the spoon. Arrange the pecan halves attractively over the top or sprinkle evenly with pecan pieces.

3. Bake for 25 to 30 minutes until the edges feel firm and the center springs back when gently pressed. Reverse the pan from front to back once during baking. Set the pan on a wire rack to cool completely before cutting into 4 × 4 rows or 16 wedges.

4. Store in the baking pan, tightly covered with aluminum foil or plastic wrap.

Yield: 16 brownies

White Chocolate "Brownies"

Isn't it interesting how brownies can suddenly turn white? Instead of sprinkling almonds over the top, you might prefer to glaze the brownies with a Chocolate Glaze (page 32) and leave it at that, or sprinkle the almonds over a chocolate frosting (page 32).

> 12 ounces vanilla-flavored white baking pieces
>
> 1 cup (2 sticks) salted butter or margarine
>
> 3 large eggs
>
> $^3/_4$ cup all-purpose flour
>
> 1 teaspoon vanilla extract
>
> $^1/_4$ teaspoon almond extract (optional)
>
> $^1/_2$ cup slivered or sliced almonds

1. Adjust one rack to divide the oven in half. Preheat the oven to 350° (or 325° if using a glass baking dish). Lightly grease and flour a 9-inch-square metal baking pan or glass baking dish.

2. In a large saucepan set over very low heat, melt together the white baking pieces and butter, stirring constantly. (Don't worry if the mixture separates.) Remove from the heat as soon as the baking pieces are melted.

3. In the same saucepan, with an electric mixer at medium speed, beat in the eggs until the mixture is smooth. Beat in the flour, vanilla, and almond extract until well blended. Turn the batter into the prepared pan, smoothing the top with the back of a spoon. Sprinkle the almonds evenly over the top of the batter.

4. Bake for 30 to 35 minutes until just set in the center and the top is golden brown. Reverse the pan from front to back once during baking. Set the pan on a wire rack to cool completely before cutting into 4 × 5 rows.

5. Store in the baking pan, tightly covered with aluminum foil or plastic wrap.

Yield: 20 bars

Fudge-Swirled Butterscotch Bars

2 cups (12 ounces) semisweet chocolate chips

1 cup (2 sticks) plus 2 tablespoons salted butter or margarine, divided

One 14-ounce can regular or reduced-fat condensed (not evaporated) milk

2 1/4 cups packed light or dark brown sugar

2 large eggs, lightly beaten

1 teaspoon vanilla extract

2 cups all-purpose flour

1 cup chopped pecans

1. Adjust one rack to divide the oven in half. Preheat the oven to 350°. Lightly grease a 15 × 10-inch jelly-roll pan.

2. In a medium-size saucepan, combine the chocolate chips, 2 tablespoons of the butter, and the condensed milk. Cook over low heat, stirring constantly, until the chocolate is melted and the mixture is smooth. Remove from the heat and set aside.

3. In a large saucepan, melt the remaining 1 cup butter; remove from the heat. With a mixing spoon, stir in the brown sugar, eggs, and vanilla until well blended. Stir in the flour just until blended. Stir in the pecans until well distributed throughout the batter. Evenly spread half of the batter in the prepared pan. With a measuring tablespoon, drop the chocolate mixture onto the batter. With an icing spatula, gently spread the chocolate to cover the batter. Drop the remaining batter by measuring teaspoonfuls over the chocolate. With the tip of the icing spatula, swirl the plain batter into the chocolate layer to create a marbled effect.

4. Bake for 25 to 35 minutes until light golden brown and the center is set when lightly touched. Reverse the pan from front to back once during baking. Set the pan on a wire rack to cool completely before cutting into 10 × 4 rows.

5. Store in the baking pan, tightly covered with aluminum foil or plastic wrap.

Yield: 40 bars

Tip

The number of eggs in brownies (and many other bar cookies) is the big determining factor in whether the bars will be cakey or chewy. The more eggs, the lighter the texture and the more cakelike the bars will be.

Layered Chocolate-Meringue Bars

There are three layers in this luscious bar: a bottom layer that is firm and cakelike, a middle layer of chocolate, and a chewy meringue topping. (If you're not familiar with how to make a meringue, you might want to turn to page 69, where this method of beating egg whites with sugar is explained.)

3 cups all-purpose flour

1 1/2 teaspoons baking powder

3/4 teaspoon baking soda

3/4 teaspoon salt

1 cup (2 sticks) salted butter or margarine, at room temperature

1 1/4 cups packed light brown sugar, divided

3/4 cup granulated sugar

3 large eggs, separated

1 1/2 tablespoons water

1 1/2 teaspoons vanilla extract

2 ounces (2 squares) unsweetened chocolate, grated

1. Adjust one rack to divide the oven in half. Preheat the oven to 350° (or 325° if using a glass baking dish). Lightly grease and flour a 13 × 9-inch metal baking pan or glass baking dish.

2. In a medium-size bowl, with a whisk, combine the flour, baking powder, baking soda, and salt until thoroughly mixed.

3. In a large bowl, with an electric mixer at medium speed, combine the butter with 3/4 cup of the brown sugar and the granulated sugar just until blended. Beat in the egg yolks, water, and vanilla. With the mixer at medium-high speed, beat the mixture until creamy, 3 to 4 minutes. With the mixer at medium-low speed, gradually add the flour mixture, beating just until blended. Press the dough into the prepared pan. Sprinkle evenly with the grated chocolate.

4. In a clean, medium-size bowl, with clean beaters, beat the egg whites at medium-low speed until frothy. With the mixer at medium-high

speed, add the remaining 1/2 cup brown sugar, 1 tablespoon at a time, beating for about 30 seconds after each addition. At high speed, beat until the mixture is smooth and glossy and stands in stiff peaks when the beaters are lifted. With a wide rubber spatula, spread the meringue evenly over the dough, pulling it up into a few little peaks, if you like.

5. Bake for 30 to 40 minutes until the meringue topping is light brown and firm when lightly touched. Reverse the pan from front to back once during baking. Set the pan on a wire rack to cool completely before cutting into 8 × 5 rows.

6. Store in the baking pan, tightly covered with aluminum foil or plastic wrap.

Yield: 40 bars

Elegant Raspberry-Meringue Bars

Keep this recipe for special occasions, when you want your reputation as a baker to be assured.

1/3 cup (1/2 stick plus 1 1/2 tablespoons) salted butter or margarine, at room temperature

1 cup all-purpose flour, divided

1/3 cup sugar

2 large eggs, separated

1/4 teaspoon cream of tartar

2/3 cup sifted confectioners' sugar

1 cup finely chopped almonds, toasted (page 16)

1/3 cup raspberry preserves

1. Adjust one rack to divide the oven in half. Preheat the oven to 350° (or 325° if using a glass baking dish). Have ready an ungreased 9-inch-square metal baking pan or glass baking dish.

2. In a medium-size bowl with an electric mixer at medium speed, beat the butter until creamy, about 1 minute. With the mixer at low speed, beat in 1/2 cup of the flour. Add the sugar and egg yolks. With the mixer at medium-high speed, beat until creamy, scraping the side of the bowl occasionally. With a mixing spoon, stir in the remaining

$^1/_2$ cup flour until well blended. Press this mixture onto the bottom of the ungreased pan. Bake for 15 minutes.

3. While the crust is baking, make the topping: In a clean, medium-size bowl with clean, dry beaters, beat the egg whites and cream of tartar at medium-low speed until frothy. Beat at medium-high speed until soft peaks form when the beaters are lifted. Gradually add the confectioners' sugar, beating at high speed until stiff peaks form when the beaters are lifted. With a rubber spatula or a mixing spoon, fold in the nuts.

4. Remove the crust from the oven. With an icing spatula, immediately spread the preserves over the hot crust. Drop the meringue over the preserves in large dollops, then gently spread it over the preserves, trying not to deflate the meringue any more than necessary.

5. Return to the oven and bake for about 20 minutes longer until the top is golden. Reverse the pan from front to back once during baking. Set the pan on a wire rack to cool completely before cutting into 4 × 4 rows.

6. Store in the baking pan, loosely covered in low humidity.

Yield: 16 bars

Irma Hyams's Walnut Bars

I have had this recipe in my cookie file for close to 30 years. Irma, who is one of the best bakers I know, first encountered a bar cookie similar to this one in a small town on the Dalmatian coast, of all places. She liked the little bar so much that she came home and developed her own recipe for a cookie just like the one she remembered. Clever Irma!

1 cup sifted cake flour
$^2/_3$ cup sifted confectioners' sugar
$^2/_3$ cup (1 stick plus 3 tablespoons) plus 1 tablespoon salted butter or margarine, at room temperature
1 egg, lightly beaten

Baked Topping

1 cup walnut pieces
$^1/_2$ cup granulated sugar
1 large egg beaten with 2 tablespoons milk
1 cup apricot or raspberry jam

1. Adjust one rack to divide the oven in half. Preheat the oven to 375°. Have ready an 8-inch-square metal baking pan.

2. In a medium-size bowl, with a whisk, combine the flour and confectioners' sugar until well blended. Add the butter and mix with your fingertips until the butter has been completely worked into the flour mixture. With a mixing spoon, stir in the egg until well blended. Spread this mixture over the bottom of the ungreased pan. Bake for 20 minutes. Remove from the oven and set aside.

3. To make the topping: Place the walnut pieces in a food processor fitted with a steel blade. Process until the nuts are finely ground, stopping the processor once and giving the nuts a good stir from the bottom to keep them from becoming pasty. In a small bowl, with a mixing spoon, mix the ground walnuts, sugar, and egg mixture.

4. With an icing spatula, spread the jam over the crust. Spread the walnut mixture over the jam. Return to the oven to bake for 20 to 25 minutes until golden. Reverse the pan from front to back once during the final baking period. Set the pan on a wire rack to cool completely before cutting into 4 × 8 rows.

5. Store in the baking pan, tightly covered with aluminum foil or plastic wrap.

Yield: 32 bars

Tip

Glass, enamel, stainless steel, or copper bowls are best for beating egg whites. Aluminum tends to darken them, and plastic bowls may harbor traces of grease.

Walnut-and-Oats Bars with Thick Chocolate Filling

These are mighty good bars, but it's the chocolate filling that really makes them stand-out special.

- 3 cups regular or quick-cooking (not instant) rolled oats
- 2 1/2 cups all-purpose flour
- 1 teaspoon baking soda
- 1 1/2 cups chopped walnuts, divided
- 1 cup (2 sticks) salted butter or margarine, at room temperature
- 2 cups packed light brown sugar
- 2 large eggs
- 1 teaspoon vanilla extract

Filling

- 1/2 cup (1 stick) salted butter or margarine
- 2/3 cup unsweetened cocoa powder
- 1/2 cup sugar
- One 14-ounce can regular or reduced-fat condensed (not evaporated) milk
- 1 1/2 teaspoons vanilla extract

1. Adjust one rack to divide the oven in half. Preheat the oven to 350°. Have ready a 15 × 10-inch jelly-roll pan.

2. In a medium-size bowl, with a whisk, combine the oats, flour, baking soda, and 1 cup of the walnuts until thoroughly mixed.

3. In a large bowl, with an electric mixer at medium-high speed, beat together the butter, brown sugar, eggs, and vanilla until light and fluffy, 2 to 3 minutes. With the mixer at medium-low speed, gradually add the oats mixture. When the batter becomes too stiff for the mixer, stir in the final amount with a mixing spoon. Remove 2 cups of the dough and set aside for the topping. Press the remaining dough evenly onto the bottom of the ungreased pan; set aside.

4. To make the filling: In a medium-size saucepan set over low heat, melt the butter. With a mixing spoon, stir in the cocoa and sugar until blended.

Stir in the condensed milk and cook, stirring constantly, until smooth and thick. Remove from the heat and stir in the vanilla.

5. Spread the filling evenly over the dough in the pan. Sprinkle the reserved oatmeal mixture evenly over the chocolate. Sprinkle evenly with the remaining 1/2 cup nuts.

6. Bake for 25 minutes until the top is golden. (The chocolate filling will be soft.) Reverse the pan from front to back once during baking. Set the pan on a wire rack to cool completely before cutting into 10 × 4 rows.

7. Store in the baking pan, tightly covered with aluminum foil or plastic wrap.

Yield: 40 bars

Maple-Walnut Shortbread Bars

The topping makes these bars a bit unusual, as well as especially scrumptious.

Shortbread

- 2 cups all-purpose flour
- 1/2 cup confectioners' sugar
- 1 teaspoon vanilla extract
- 1 cup (2 sticks) salted butter or margarine, cut into pieces
- 1/2 cup finely chopped walnuts

Topping

- 3/4 cup dark corn syrup
- 1/4 cup packed dark brown sugar
- 3 tablespoons all-purpose flour
- 1/4 teaspoon salt
- 2 large eggs, lightly beaten
- 2 teaspoons maple flavoring (optional)
- 1 cup finely chopped walnuts

1. Adjust one rack to divide the oven in half. Preheat the oven to 350° (or 325° if using a glass

baking dish). Have ready an ungreased, 13×9-inch metal baking pan or glass baking dish.

2. To make the shortbread: In a large bowl, with a whisk, combine the flour and sugar. Sprinkle with the vanilla. With a pastry blender (see page 22, "Cutting In") or two dinner knives used in a crisscross fashion, cut in the butter until the mixture resembles coarse crumbs. With a mixing spoon, stir in the walnuts until evenly distributed throughout the dough. Press this mixture onto the bottom of the ungreased pan. Bake for 15 minutes.

3. While the shortbread is baking, make the topping: In a medium-size bowl, with a mixing spoon, combine the corn syrup, brown sugar, flour, salt, eggs, and maple flavoring until well blended. Stir in the walnuts until well distributed throughout the topping. Remove the crust from the oven. Pour the topping evenly over the crust.

4. Return to the oven and bake for about 25 minutes longer until the topping is set and the edges are lightly browned. Reverse the pan from front to back once during the final baking period. Set the pan on a wire rack to cool completely before cutting into 8×6 rows.

5. Store in the baking pan, tightly covered with aluminum foil or plastic wrap, or remove from the pan and store in a tightly covered container.

Yield: About 48 bars

California Shortbread Bars

Almonds are called for in this recipe, but you can use whatever kind of nuts you happen to have on hand. By the way, the easy method given here for coating bar cookies with a thin chocolate icing can be used with almost any bar-cookie recipe.

1 cup (2 sticks) salted butter or margarine, at room temperature

1 cup light brown sugar

1 large egg yolk

1 teaspoon vanilla extract

$^1/_2$ teaspoon shredded and minced orange zest

$^1/_4$ teaspoon almond extract

2 cups all-purpose flour

1 cup chopped natural almonds, toasted (page 16) and divided

2 cups (12 ounces) semisweet chocolate chips

1. Adjust one rack to divide the oven in half. Preheat the oven to 350° (or 325° if using a glass baking dish). Generously grease a 13×9-inch metal baking pan or glass baking dish.

2. In a large bowl, with an electric mixer at medium-high speed, beat together the butter and brown sugar until very creamy, 2 to 3 minutes. Beat in the egg yolk, vanilla, orange zest, and almond extract until well blended. With a mixing spoon, stir in the flour just until blended. Stir in $^1/_2$ cup of the almonds until well distributed throughout the batter. Turn the batter into the prepared pan, smoothing the top with the back of a spoon.

3. Bake for about 25 minutes until firm and golden brown. Reverse the pan from front to back once during baking. Remove from the oven and sprinkle evenly with the chocolate chips. Return to the oven for 30 seconds. Remove from the oven and, with an icing spatula or the back of a large spoon, spread the melted chocolate over the surface. Sprinkle with the remaining $^1/_2$ cup of almonds. Set the pan on wire rack to cool completely before cutting into 6×6 rows.

4. Store in the baking pan, tightly covered with aluminum foil or plastic wrap.

Yield: 36 bars

Tip

Cold butter or margarine can be brought to room temperature quickly if it is shredded on a four-sided grater into the mixing bowl.

Maple Sugar Bars

My sister Suzanne Hanners, who lives in Florida, has had a love affair with maple sugar candy ever since I can remember. Nothing thrills her more than the sight of the UPS driver with a box from Vermont. These bars are for her.

    12 ounces maple sugar candy
    1 ¹/₂ cups finely chopped walnuts, divided
    1 ¹/₂ tablespoons salted butter or margarine,
        melted
    1 cup all-purpose flour
    1 teaspoon baking powder
    ¹/₄ cup (¹/₂ stick) salted butter or margarine,
        at room temperature
    1 large egg, lightly beaten

1. Adjust one rack to the upper third position in the oven. Preheat the oven to 350°. Lightly grease an 8-inch-square metal baking pan.

2. Place the maple sugar candy in a plastic bag and crush it using a heavy object, such as a rolling pin. You should have about 1¹/₂ cups. In a small bowl, mix ¹/₂ cup of the crushed maple sugar with ¹/₂ cup of the chopped walnuts and the melted butter; set aide.

3. In a medium-size bowl, with a whisk, combine the flour and baking powder until thoroughly mixed.

4. In a large bowl, with an electric mixer at medium-high speed, beat together the butter and the remaining 1 cup of maple sugar until creamy, 2 to 3 minutes. Beat in the egg until well blended. Turn the batter into the prepared baking pan, smoothing the top with the back of a spoon.

5. Bake for 25 to 30 minutes until a wooden pick inserted in the center comes out clean. Reverse the pan from front to back once during baking. Remove the cake from the oven. Set the oven temperature to broil. Spread the maple sugar-and-nut mixture evenly over the top of the cake. Return to the oven until the topping mixture is melted and golden, about 2 minutes. Set the pan on a wire rack to cool completely before cutting into 4 × 4 rows.

6. Store in the baking pan, tightly covered with aluminum foil or plastic wrap.

Yield: 16 bars

So-Simple Brown Sugar Chews

Yikes! The cupboard is nearly bare and there's no treat to stick in the lunch box tomorrow. Brown Sugar Chews to the rescue! Bake them tonight, cut them into bars in the morning. Wrap leftovers and stick them in the freezer for another day. Nothing could be more simple.

    ¹/₂ cup all-purpose flour
    ¹/₄ teaspoon salt
    ¹/₄ teaspoon baking soda
    1 large egg, lightly beaten
    1 cup packed light brown sugar
    ¹/₂ cup chopped walnuts
    ¹/₂ cup raisins

1. Adjust one rack to divide the oven in half. Preheat the oven to 350°. Lightly grease an 8-inch-square metal baking pan.

2. In a small bowl, with a whisk, combine the flour, salt, and baking soda until thoroughly mixed.

3. In a medium-size bowl, with a mixing spoon, stir together the egg and brown sugar until well blended. Add the flour mixture and beat until well blended. Stir in the walnuts and raisins until well distributed throughout the batter. Turn the batter into the prepared pan, smoothing the top with the back of the spoon.

4. Bake for 18 to 20 minutes until firm and the sides are just beginning to pull away from the sides of the pan. Reverse the pan from front to back once during baking. Set the pan on a wire rack to cool completely before cutting into 4 × 4 rows.

5. Store in the baking pan, tightly covered with aluminum foil or plastic wrap.

Yield: 16 bars

No-Roll Sugar Cookies

For those bakers who find rolling cookie dough a painful task, this recipe is a real stress reliever and time saver. I have suggested just a sprinkling of colored sugar on these cookies, but you can decorate them as elaborately as you like. They won't have the wonderful, whimsical shapes that cookie cutters provide, of course, but they can still look very pretty and festive.

- 1 ¹/₂ cups all-purpose flour
- 1 ¹/₂ teaspoons baking powder
- ³/₄ cup sugar
- ¹/₃ cup (¹/₂ stick plus 1 ¹/₂ tablespoons) salted butter or margarine, at room temperature
- ¹/₃ cup vegetable oil
- 1 large egg
- 1 tablespoon milk
- ¹/₂ teaspoon vanilla extract
- Tinted crystal sugar, for sprinkling on cookies

1. Adjust one rack to divide the oven in half. Preheat the oven to 375°. Have ready a 15 × 10-inch jelly-roll pan.

2. In a medium-size bowl, with a whisk, combine the flour and baking powder until thoroughly mixed.

3. In a large bowl, with an electric mixer at medium-high speed, beat together the sugar, butter, oil, egg, milk, and vanilla until light and fluffy, 2 to 3 minutes. With the mixer at medium-low speed, gradually add the flour mixture, beating just until blended. Spread the batter in the ungreased pan, smoothing the top with the back of a spoon. Sprinkle evenly with tinted sugar.

4. Bake for 10 to 12 minutes until golden. Reverse the pan from front to back once during baking. Cool in the pan for 5 minutes. Cut into 2¹/₂-inch squares, then cut the squares in half diagonally to make triangles. Remove the cookies from the pan.

5. Store in a tightly covered container.

Yield: 48 triangles

Chocolate-Chip and Oatmeal Bars

These chewy bars are great for snacking and they have tons of kid appeal, which makes them a good—as well as a reasonably nutritious—choice for the school lunch box.

- 1 ¹/₂ cups regular or quick-cooking (not instant) rolled oats
- ¹/₂ cup whole wheat flour
- 1 teaspoon baking powder
- ¹/₄ teaspoon salt
- ¹/₂ cup (1 stick) salted butter or margarine, at room temperature
- ¹/₂ cup packed light or dark brown sugar
- 2 large eggs, lightly beaten
- 1 ¹/₂ teaspoons vanilla extract
- 1 cup (6 ounces) semisweet chocolate chips
- ¹/₂ cup dark or golden raisins
- ¹/₂ cup coarsely chopped pecans

1. Adjust one rack to divide the oven in half. Preheat the oven to 350°. Lightly grease an 8-inch-square metal baking pan.

2. In a medium-size bowl, with a whisk, combine the oats, flour, baking powder, and salt until thoroughly mixed.

3. In a large bowl, with an electric mixer at medium-high speed, beat the butter and brown sugar until very creamy, 2 to 3 minutes. Add the eggs and the vanilla and beat until well blended. The mixture will look curdled. With a mixing spoon, stir in the oats mixture, chocolate chips, raisins, and pecans. Press this mixture evenly into the prepared pan.

4. Bake for 20 to 25 minutes until golden brown and the edges start pulling away from the sides of the pan. Reverse the baking pan from front to back once during baking. Set the pan on a wire rack to cool completely before cutting into 4 × 4 rows.

5. Store in the baking pan, tightly covered with aluminum foil or plastic wrap.

Yield: 16 bars

Oatmeal-Toffee Bars

Chopped, chocolate-covered toffee is what gives these bars crunch and buttery flavor.

- 1 cup all-purpose flour
- 1 cup regular or quick-cooking (not instant) rolled oats
- 2/3 cup packed light or dark brown sugar
- 2/3 cup (1 stick plus 3 tablespoons) salted butter or margarine, melted
- Five 1.4-ounce chocolate-covered toffee bars, chopped (about 1 1/2 cups)
- 2/3 cup chopped pecans
- 1/2 cup ready-to-serve butterscotch-caramel fudge topping

1. Adjust one rack to divide the oven in half. Preheat the oven to 350° (or 325° if using a glass baking dish). Lightly grease a 9-inch-square metal baking pan or glass baking dish.

2. In a medium-size bowl, with a mixing spoon, combine the flour, oats, and brown sugar until thoroughly mixed. Add the melted butter and stir until crumbly. Remove 3/4 cup of the oats mixture and set aside to use for the topping. Press the remaining oats mixture onto the bottom of the baking pan.

3. Bake for 15 minutes until the crust is firm. Sprinkle the chopped toffee and nuts evenly over the crust. Drizzle the topping off the tip of a teaspoon over the toffee and nuts to within 1/2 inch of the edges. Sprinkle evenly with the reserved oats mixture. Continue to bake for 22 to 25 minutes until golden brown. Reverse the pan from front to back once during the final baking period. Set the pan on wire rack to cool completely before cutting into 4 × 4 rows.

4. Store in the baking pan, tightly covered with aluminum foil or plastic wrap.

Yield: 16 bars

Granola Goodies

Because they're loaded with nutritious ingredients, these bars qualify as a good-for-you snack.

- 1/2 cup all-purpose flour
- 1/2 teaspoon baking soda
- 2 1/4 cups plain granola-type, ready-to-eat cereal
- 1/2 cup slivered or sliced almonds
- 1/2 cup raisins
- 1/4 cup packed dark brown sugar
- 1/2 cup (1 stick) salted butter or margarine, at room temperature
- 1/4 cup honey

1. Adjust one rack to divide the oven in half. Preheat the oven to 350° (or 325° if using a glass baking dish). Have ready a 9-inch-square metal baking pan or glass baking dish.

2. In a medium-size bowl, with a whisk, combine the flour and baking soda until thoroughly mixed.

3. In a large bowl, with an electric mixer at low speed, combine the cereal, flour mixture, almonds, raisins, brown sugar, butter, and honey until well blended, 1 to 2 minutes. Press this mixture evenly onto the bottom of the ungreased pan.

4. Bake for 20 to 25 minutes until the edges are brown. Reverse the pan from front to back once during baking. Set the pan on a wire rack to cool completely before cutting into 4 × 4 rows.

5. Store in the baking pan, tightly covered with aluminum foil or plastic wrap.

Yield: 16 bars

Peanut Butter and Oats Bars

Wholesome cookie bars may be the best reward for a good report card. These are just right for school lunches or an afternoon snack.

2 cups regular or quick-cooking (not instant) rolled oats

1 ½ cups all-purpose flour

1 teaspoon baking powder

¼ teaspoon salt

⅔ cup chunky or smooth peanut butter

2 tablespoons salted butter or margarine, at room temperature

1 cup sugar

⅓ cup dark corn syrup

2 large eggs

1 teaspoon vanilla extract

2 cups raisins

1. Adjust one rack to divide the oven in half. Preheat the oven to 400°. Sprinkle the oats in a single layer in a jelly-roll pan. Bake for 8 to 10 minutes, stirring occasionally, until lightly toasted; set aside. Reduce the oven heat to 350° (or 325° if using a glass baking dish). Lightly grease a 13 × 9-inch baking pan or glass baking dish.

2. In a medium-size bowl, with a whisk, combine the flour, baking powder, and salt until thoroughly mixed.

3. In a large bowl, with an electric mixer at medium-high speed, beat together the peanut butter and butter until smooth, about 1 minute. Beat in the sugar, corn syrup, eggs, and vanilla until light and fluffy, 2 to 3 minutes. With the mixer at medium-low speed, gradually add the flour mixture, beating just until blended. With a mixing spoon, stir in the raisins until well distributed throughout the batter. Spread the batter evenly in the prepared pan, smoothing the top with the back of the spoon.

4. Bake for about 25 minutes until a wooden pick inserted in the center comes out clean. Reverse the pan from front to back once during baking. Set the pan on a wire rack to cool completely before cutting into 6 × 6 rows.

5. Store in the baking pan, tightly covered with aluminum foil or plastic wrap.

Yield: 36 bars

Variation

Extra-Peanutty Peanut Butter and Oats Bars: Substitute 1 cup of the raisins with 1 cup coarsely chopped peanuts or 1 cup peanut butter chips.

Peanut Butter and Chocolate-Coconut Bars

These are very sweet and chewy, and also very easy to make, since it's just a matter of sprinkling and drizzling things over the crust.

¼ cup (½ stick) salted butter or margarine, melted

1 cup graham cracker crumbs

One 6-ounce bag (1 cup) semisweet chocolate chips

1 cup peanut butter chips

1 cup flaked coconut

One 14-ounce can regular or low-fat sweetened condensed milk

1 cup chopped roasted peanuts (salted or unsalted)

1. Adjust one rack to divide the oven in half. Preheat the oven to 350° (or 325° if using a glass baking dish). Have ready a 13 × 9-inch metal baking pan or glass baking dish.

2. In a small bowl, with a fork, combine the melted butter with the graham cracker crumbs until thoroughly mixed. Press this mixture evenly onto the bottom of the ungreased pan. Sprinkle evenly with a mixture of the chocolate chips, peanut butter chips, and coconut. Drizzle the condensed milk evenly over all, then sprinkle with the chopped peanuts.

3. Bake for 25 to 30 minutes until bubbly and the top is golden brown. Reverse the pan from front to back once during baking. Set the pan on a wire rack to cool completely before cutting into 6 × 6 rows.

4. Store in the baking pan, tightly covered with aluminum foil or plastic wrap.

Yield: 36 bars

Easy Peanut Buddy Bars

I think of this a learning recipe because it's a very good starter for children who want to learn how to bake. Even the frosting makes itself.

> 1 cup smooth peanut butter
>
> 6 tablespoons (³/₄ stick) salted butter or margarine, at room temperature
>
> 1 ¹/₄ cups sugar
>
> 3 large eggs
>
> 1 teaspoon vanilla extract
>
> 1 cup all-purpose flour
>
> 2 cups milk-chocolate chips, divided

1. Adjust one rack to divide the oven in half. Preheat the oven to 350° (or 325° if using a glass baking dish). Have ready a 13 × 9-inch metal baking pan or glass baking dish.

2. In a large bowl, with an electric mixer at medium-high speed, beat together the peanut butter and butter until smooth, about 1 minute. Add the sugar, eggs, and vanilla and beat until creamy, about 1 minute. With the mixer at medium-low speed, gradually add the flour, beating just until blended. With a mixing spoon, stir in 1 cup of the milk-chocolate chips. Turn the batter into the ungreased pan, smoothing the top with the back of the spoon.

3. Bake for 25 to 30 minutes until the edges start to brown. Reverse the pan from front to back once during baking. Remove from the oven and immediately sprinkle the remaining 1 cup of milk-chocolate chips evenly over the top. Set the pan on a wire rack for about 5 minutes until the chips become shiny and soft. With an icing spatula, spread the chips evenly over the surface to make a frosting. Cool completely before cutting into 6 × 6 rows.

4. Store in the baking pan, tightly covered with aluminum foil or plastic wrap.

Yield: 36 bars

Chewy Peanut Bars

Anything chewy and peanutty is usually received with great pleasure. These bars are not only very good, but they are easy to make and can be mixed, baked, cooled, and ready to eat in just about an hour. If you like, a Chocolate Glaze (page 32) can be drizzled over the cooled bars.

Crust

> ³/₄ cup all-purpose flour
>
> ¹/₄ teaspoon baking powder
>
> ¹/₄ cup (¹/₂ stick) salted butter or margarine, at room temperature
>
> ¹/₄ cup granulated sugar

Topping

> 1 large egg
>
> ¹/₃ cup light or dark corn syrup
>
> 2 tablespoons dark brown sugar
>
> ¹/₂ teaspoon vanilla extract
>
> 1 cup chopped peanuts

1. Adjust one rack to divide the oven in half. Preheat the oven to 375° (or 350° if using a glass baking dish). Lightly grease an 9-inch-square metal baking pan or glass baking dish.

2. To make the crust: In a small bowl, with a whisk, combine the flour and baking powder until thoroughly mixed.

3. In a medium-size bowl, with an electric mixer at medium-high speed, beat together the butter and sugar until light and fluffy, 2 to 3 minutes. With the mixer at medium-low speed, gradually add the flour mixture, beating just until blended. Press this mixture onto the bottom of the prepared pan; set aside.

4. To make the topping: In a medium-size bowl, with the electric mixer at medium speed, beat the egg until frothy. Beat in the corn syrup, brown sugar, and vanilla until well blended. With a mixing spoon, stir in the peanuts until evenly distributed throughout the batter; set aside.

5. Bake the crust for 4 minutes. Remove from the oven and pour the topping over the partially baked crust. Bake for about 18 minutes longer until puffy and set. Reverse the pan from front to back once during the final baking period. Set the pan on a wire rack to cool completely before cutting into 3×3 rows.

6. Store in the baking pan, tightly covered with aluminum foil or plastic wrap.

Yield: 9 bars

Very Easy Rocky Road Bars

This bar cookie is a good baking project for older kids, who can easily make them after school.

- 1 ¹/₂ cups finely crushed unsalted pretzels
- ³/₄ cup (1 ¹/₂ sticks) salted butter or margarine, melted
- One 14-ounce can regular or reduced-fat condensed (not evaporated) milk
- 2 cups miniature marshmallows
- 1 cup butterscotch-flavor chips
- 1 cup semisweet chocolate chips
- 1 cup flaked coconut
- ³/₄ cup chopped pecans

1. Adjust one rack to divide the oven in half. Preheat the oven to 350° (or 325° if using a glass baking dish). Have ready a 13×9-inch metal baking pan or glass baking dish.

2. In a small bowl, combine the crushed pretzels and melted butter. Press this mixture onto the bottom of the ungreased pan. Pour the condensed milk evenly over the crust, spreading evenly with the back of a spoon. Scatter over the condensed-milk layer in the order given, marshmallows, butterscotch chips, chocolate chips, coconut, and pecans. Press the toppings down firmly into the condensed milk.

3. Bake for 25 to 30 minutes until lightly browned. Reverse the pan from front to back once during baking. Set the pan on a wire rack to cool completely. Cut into 6×6 rows.

4. Store in the baking pan, tightly covered with aluminum foil or plastic wrap.

Yield: 36 bars

Tip

Use the correct pan size for bar cookies. Bar cookies baked in a pan that is too large can be dry. If the pan is too small, the center may be underbaked.

Chocolate-Caramel-Pecan Bars

My grandkids say these cookies are like chocolate turtles. In other words, they taste as good as the name implies.

Crust

    1/2 cup confectioners' sugar
    1/2 cup (1 stick) salted butter or margarine, at room temperature
    1 tablespoon heavy (whipping) cream
    1 cup all-purpose flour

Caramel Filling

    24 caramels, unwrapped
    1/3 cup heavy (whipping) cream
    2 cups pecan halves

Chocolate Topping

    1/2 cup milk-chocolate or semisweet chocolate chips
    1 teaspoon butter or margarine
    2 tablespoons heavy (whipping) cream

1. Adjust one rack to divide the oven in half. Preheat the oven to 325°. Grease a 9-inch-square baking pan.

2. To make the crust: In a medium-size bowl, with a mixing spoon, combine the sugar, butter, and cream until well blended. Add the flour and mix until crumbly. Press this mixture evenly onto the bottom of the prepared baking pan. Bake for 15 to 20 minutes until firm to the touch. Reverse the pan from front to back once during baking.

3. While the crust is baking, make the filling. In a medium-size saucepan set over low heat, combine the caramels and cream, stirring frequently until the caramels are melted and the mixture is smooth. Remove from the heat. Stir in the pecans until well coated. Remove the crust from the oven. Immediately spoon the filling over the crust, spreading evenly.

4. To make the topping: In a small saucepan set over very low heat, melt the chocolate, butter, and cream together, stirring constantly until smooth. Drizzle over the filling from the tip of a teaspoon. Refrigerate until the filling is firm, about 1 hour. Cut into 4 × 5 rows.

5. Store in the baking pan, tightly covered with aluminum foil or plastic wrap.

Yield: 20 bars

Hazelnut Pie Bars

If you like rich nut pies, this is a bar cookie you're bound to enjoy. The topping is made with hazelnuts, a nice change from the more familiar pecans.

    1 cup plus 1 tablespoon all-purpose flour, divided
    1/2 cup regular or quick-cooking (not instant) rolled oats
    3/4 cup packed light brown sugar, divided
    1/2 cup (1 stick) cold salted butter or margarine, cut into pieces
    4 large eggs
    3/4 cup honey
    1 teaspoon vanilla extract
    1 cup coarsely chopped skinned hazelnuts, toasted (page 16)

1. Adjust one rack to divide the oven in half. Preheat the oven to 350° (or 325° if using a glass baking dish). Lightly grease a 13 × 9-inch metal baking pan or glass baking dish.

2. In a large bowl, with a whisk, combine 1 cup of the flour, the oats, and 1/4 cup of the brown sugar until thoroughly mixed. With a pastry blender or two knives used in a crisscross fashion, cut in the butter until the mixture resembles coarse crumbs. Press this mixture onto the bottom of the prepared pan.

3. Bake for 15 minutes.

4. While the crust is baking, in a medium-size bowl, with an electric mixer at medium speed, beat the eggs until frothy. With a mixing spoon,

stir in the remaining ¹/₂ cup brown sugar and 1 tablespoon flour, the honey, and vanilla until well blended. Stir in the hazelnuts until they are well distributed throughout the batter. Pour this mixture over the partially baked crust.

5. Bake for about 25 minutes until firm. Reverse the pan from front to back once during final baking period. Set the pan on a wire rack to cool completely before cutting into 6 × 6 rows.

6. Store in the baking pan, tightly covered with aluminum foil or plastic wrap.

Yield: 36 bars

New Orleans Date and Nut Bars

If you can manage to keep everybody's mitts off them for that long, give these bars a day or two to allow the flavors to become better acquainted before serving.

> 1 cup finely chopped dates
> 2 tablespoons bourbon or orange juice
> ¹/₄ cup all-purpose flour
> ¹/₂ teaspoon baking powder
> 2 large eggs
> ¹/₂ cup sugar
> 1 cup coarsely chopped walnuts or pecans

1. Adjust one rack to divide the oven in half. Preheat the oven to 350°. Lightly grease and flour an 8-inch-square metal baking pan.

2. In a small bowl, mix the dates with the bourbon. Onto a sheet of waxed paper, sift the flour with the baking powder.

3. In a small bowl, with an electric mixer at medium speed, beat the eggs until frothy. Gradually beat in the sugar. Continue beating until thick and lemon colored, 2 to 3 minutes. With a mixing spoon, stir in the flour mixture, nuts, and bourbon-soaked dates just until blended. Turn the batter into the prepared pan, smoothing the top with the back of a spoon.

4. Bake for about 30 minutes until light brown and crusty. Reverse the pan from front to back once during baking. Cool in the pan set on a wire rack for 10 minutes before cutting into 4 × 4 rows.

5. Store in the baking pan, tightly covered with aluminum foil or plastic wrap.

Yield: 16 bars

Tip

Nuts can be skinned easily by using one of two methods: either blanching or dry heating. To blanch nuts, drop in boiling water for 1 to 2 minutes. Remove with a slotted spoon and slip the skin off with your fingers. Or place the nuts in a single layer on a baking sheet and heat in a 350° oven for about 10 minutes or until the skins shrivel. Place the nuts on one half of a dish towel; cover with the other half of the towel. Roll the towel back and forth over the nuts until the skins, or at least most of them, come off.

Linzer Lattice Bars

Anything "Linzer" harks back to the great Austrian Linzertorte, which, according to culinary legend, originated in the city of Linz. In my research for these cookies, I found that there seems to be no definitive recipe for either Linzertorte or Linzer cookies. The only thing they have in common is a buttery dough that sometimes includes nuts and spices, and sometimes doesn't, and a filling, usually made with raspberries, but sometimes not. Frequently Linzer cookies are dusted with confectioners' sugar before they are served, and other times they aren't. Recipes for other forms of Linzer cookies can be found in the index.

- 2/3 cup blanched almonds, toasted (page 16)
- 1 1/2 cups all-purpose flour
- 1 teaspoon baking powder
- 1/4 teaspoon ground cinnamon
- 1/8 teaspoon ground cloves
- 1/2 cup (1 stick) salted butter or margarine, at room temperature
- 1/2 cup packed light brown sugar
- 1/4 cup granulated sugar
- 1 large egg, lightly beaten
- 1/4 cup raspberry preserves

1. Adjust one rack to divide the oven in half. Preheat the oven to 375°. Have ready an 8-inch-square metal baking pan.

2. In a food processor fitted with a steel blade, grind the almonds, stopping the processor once and giving the nuts a good stir from the bottom to keep them from becoming pasty; set aside.

3. In a medium-size bowl, with a whisk, combine the flour, baking powder, cinnamon, and cloves.

4. In a large bowl, with an electric mixer at medium-high speed, beat together the butter, brown sugar, and granulated sugar until light and creamy, 2 to 3 minutes. With a mixing spoon, stir in the egg and ground almonds until well blended. Divide the dough into thirds.

5. Between two sheets of waxed paper, roll out one third of the dough to a thickness of 1/8 inch.

Place the dough, still between the sheets of waxed paper, in the refrigerator until chilled, about 15 minutes. Press the remaining two-thirds of the dough evenly into the ungreased pan. With an icing spatula, spread the preserves evenly over the dough.

6. Remove the chilled dough from the refrigerator. Peel off the top sheet of waxed paper and discard. With a pizza wheel or the tip of a sharp knife and a ruler, cut the dough into 1-inch strips. Arrange the strips in a lattice pattern over the jam-covered dough.

7. Bake for 30 minutes until golden brown. Reverse the pan from front to back once during baking. Set the pan on a wire rack to cool completely before cutting into 4×5 rows with a serrated knife.

8. Store in the baking pan, tightly covered with aluminum foil or plastic wrap.

Yield: 20 bars

Strawberry Wonders

If you prefer raspberry preserves (or any other) beneath the streusel, go ahead and make the substitution.

Crumb Topping

- 1 1/2 cups all-purpose flour
- 1/2 cup regular or quick-cooking (not instant) rolled oats
- 1/2 cup granulated sugar
- 3/4 cup (1 1/2 sticks) salted butter or margarine, at room temperature
- 1/2 teaspoon baking soda

Filling

- 2 tablespoons salted butter or margarine, at room temperature
- 1/4 cup all-purpose flour
- 1/4 cup packed light brown sugar
- 3/4 cup flaked coconut

³/₄ cup chopped walnuts

¹/₂ teaspoon ground cinnamon

One 10-ounce jar strawberry preserves

1. Adjust one rack to divide the oven in half. Preheat the oven to 350° (or 325° if using a glass baking dish). Lightly grease a 13 × 9-inch metal baking pan or glass baking dish.

2. To make the topping: In a large bowl, with an electric mixer at low speed, beat together the flour, oats, sugar, butter, and baking soda, scraping the side of the bowl often until the mixture is crumbly, 1 to 2 minutes. Press this mixture onto the bottom of the prepared pan. Bake for 18 to 22 minutes until the edges are lightly browned.

3. To make the filling: In the same large bowl, with the electric mixer at medium-low speed, beat together the butter, flour, brown sugar, coconut, walnuts, and cinnamon, scraping the side of the bowl often until well blended, 1 to 2 minutes. Spread the preserves over the hot crust to within ¹/₄-inch of the edges. Spread the topping evenly over the preserves, smoothing with the back of a spoon. Return to the oven and continue baking for 18 to 22 minutes until the edges are lightly browned. Reverse the pan from front to back once during the final baking period. Set the pan on a wire rack to cool completely before cutting into 6 × 6 rows.

4. Store in the baking pan, tightly covered with aluminum foil or plastic wrap.

Yield: 36 bars

Merry Cherry Bars

Cherry liqueur is what gives these chocolate bars a spirited lift. If you prefer not to use it, then simply increase the milk to ¹/₄ cup. The bars will still be wonderful.

¹/₂ cup drained and chopped red maraschino cherries

2 tablespoons cherry liqueur

One 8-ounce package cream cheese, at room temperature

¹/₂ cup granulated sugar

¹/₃ cup unsweetened cocoa powder

2 tablespoons milk

1 large egg

¹/₂ teaspoon vanilla extract

1 cup all-purpose flour

¹/₃ cup (1 stick plus 1 ¹/₂ tablespoons) salted butter or margarine, at room temperature

¹/₂ cup packed light brown sugar

¹/₂ cup very finely chopped almonds

1. Adjust one rack to divide the oven in half. Preheat the oven to 375° (or 325° if using a glass baking dish). Have ready a 9-inch-square metal baking pan or glass baking dish.

2. In a small bowl, combine the cherries with the liqueur; set aside.

3. In a medium-size bowl, with an electric mixer at medium-high speed, beat together the cream cheese and granulated sugar until light and fluffy, 2 to 3 minutes. Add the cocoa, milk, egg, and vanilla and beat until smooth. With a mixing spoon, stir in the cherry mixture until well distributed throughout the batter.

4. In a large bowl, place the flour, butter, and brown sugar. Using clean beaters, beat the mixture at low speed until fine crumbs form, 2 to 3 minutes. Beat in the almonds until blended. Measure out ³/₄ cup of the crumb mixture and set aside. Press the remaining crumbs onto the bottom of the ungreased pan. Bake for 10 minutes until lightly browned. Evenly spread the batter over the warm crust, smoothing the top with the back of a spoon. Sprinkle with the reserved ³/₄ cup crumbs.

5. Bake for 25 minutes until lightly browned. Reverse the pan from front to back once during the final baking period. Set the pan on a wire rack to cool completely before cutting into 4 × 4 rows.

6. Store in the baking pan in the refrigerator, tightly covered with aluminum foil or plastic wrap.

Yield: 16 bars

Fresh Lemon Bars

These thin, delicate bars can also be made with orange juice and orange zest. In that case, you might want to sprinkle the baked bars with equal amounts of cocoa powder and confectioners' sugar. Don't mix the two together; sprinkle them on separately.

- $1/2$ cup (1 stick) cold salted butter or margarine
- 1 cup plus 2 tablespoons all-purpose flour, divided
- $1/4$ cup confectioners' sugar
- 2 large eggs
- 1 cup granulated sugar
- 2 tablespoons strained fresh lemon juice
- 1 teaspoon shredded and minced lemon zest
- Confectioners' sugar, for sprinkling on bars

1. Adjust one rack to divide the oven in half. Preheat the oven to 350° (or 325° if using a glass baking dish). Have ready a 9-inch-square metal baking pan or glass baking dish.

2. In a medium-size bowl, with a pastry blender or two knives used in a crisscross fashion, cut the butter into 1 cup of the flour and the confectioners' sugar until large crumbs form. Press this mixture evenly onto the bottom of the ungreased pan. Bake for about 20 minutes until pale brown.

3. While the crust is baking, prepare the topping. In a medium-size bowl, with a mixing spoon, combine the eggs, granulated sugar, lemon juice, lemon zest, and the remaining 2 tablespoons of flour until well blended.

4. Remove the crust from the oven and immediately pour the topping mixture evenly over the crust. Return to the oven to bake for about 25 minutes until the topping is firm. Reverse the pan from front to back once during the final baking period. Set the pan on a wire rack to cool completely before cutting into 4 × 4 rows.

5. Store in the baking pan, tightly covered with aluminum foil or plastic wrap. Sprinkle lavishly with confectioners' sugar just before serving.

Yield: 16 bars

Back-to-School Apple Bars

There are a whole lot of good ingredients here, but they all combine swiftly in one big bowl.

- $1/2$ cup whole wheat flour
- $1/2$ cup all-purpose flour
- $1/2$ cup packed light or dark brown sugar
- 2 teaspoons ground cinnamon
- $1/2$ teaspoon ground nutmeg
- $1/2$ teaspoon baking soda
- $1/4$ teaspoon salt
- 4 cups cornflakes cereal
- 2 small unpeeled apples, cored and shredded (1 $1/2$ cups)
- $1/2$ cup dark or golden raisins
- 1 large egg, lightly beaten
- $1/3$ cup light corn syrup
- 2 tablespoons vegetable oil
- 1 tablespoon confectioners' sugar

1. Adjust one rack to divide the oven in half. Preheat the oven to 350° (or 325° if using a glass baking dish). Lightly grease a 9-inch-square metal baking pan or glass baking dish.

2. In a large bowl, with a whisk, combine the whole wheat flour, all-purpose flour, brown sugar, cinnamon, nutmeg, baking soda, and salt until thoroughly mixed. With a mixing spoon, stir in the cornflakes, apples, raisins, egg, corn syrup, and oil. Turn into the prepared baking pan, smoothing the top with the back of the spoon.

3. Bake for about 35 minutes until a wooden pick inserted in the center comes out clean. Reverse the pan from front to back once during baking. Set the pan on a wire rack to cool completely. Sprinkle lightly with confectioners' sugar. Cut into 5 × 4 rows.

4. Store in the baking pan, tightly covered with aluminum foil or plastic wrap.

Yield: 20 bars

Apple Pie Bars

In the reading, this recipe looks a lot like an apple pie. Actually, it ends up as a rather flat bar, and a very good one, at that.

Crust

Milk
1 large egg, separated (reserve the w hite for the filling)
2 ¹/₂ cups all-purpose flour
1 teaspoon salt
1 cup (2 sticks) cold salted butter or margarine, cut into small pieces

Apple Filling

1 cup crushed cornflakes cereal
8 to 10 medium-size McIntosh or Granny Smith apples, peeled, cored, and cut into ¹/₄-inch slices (about 8 cups)
1 cup plus 2 tablespoons granulated sugar, divided
1 teaspoon ground cinnamon, divided
¹/₂ teaspoon ground nutmeg
Reserved egg white (from crust)

Lemon Glaze

1 cup confectioners' sugar
1 tablespoon strained fresh lemon juice
¹/₂ teaspoon vanilla extract
About 1 tablespoon milk

1. Adjust one rack to divide the oven in half. Preheat the oven to 350°. Have ready a 15 × 10-inch jelly-roll pan.

2. To make the crust: In a 1-cup glass measure, mix enough milk with the egg yolk to make ²/₃ cup; set aside.

3. In a medium-size bowl, with a whisk, combine the flour and salt until thoroughly mixed. With a pastry blender or two knives used in crisscross fashion, cut in the butter until the mixture forms small crumbs. With a fork, stir in the yolk mixture until the dough forms a ball. Divide the

dough in half. On a lightly floured surface, roll half of the dough into a 15 × 10-inch rectangle. Trim the edges straight with a pizza wheel or the tip of a sharp knife and a ruler. Place the dough on the bottom of the ungreased pan. Set the other half of the dough aside.

4. To make the filling: Sprinkle the cornflakes evenly over the crust in the pan. Layer the apples over the corn flakes. In a small bowl, combine 1 cup of the sugar with ¹/₂ teaspoon of the cinnamon and the nutmeg. Sprinkle evenly over the apples.

5. Roll the remaining half of the dough and trim as before. Place the top crust over the filling. In a small bowl, with a fork, beat the egg white until foamy. Brush over the top crust. In a small cup, mix the remaining 2 tablespoons of sugar and the remaining ¹/₂ teaspoon cinnamon. Sprinkle evenly over the crust.

6. Bake for 45 to 60 minutes until lightly browned. Reverse the pan from front to back once during baking.

7. While the bars are baking, make the glaze. In a small bowl, stir together the confectioner's sugar, lemon juice, vanilla, and enough milk to give the glaze a good drizzling consistency. Remove the bars from the oven and immediately drizzle with the glaze, dribbling it off the tip of a teaspoon. Set the pan on a wire rack to cool completely before cutting into 10 × 4 rows.

8. Store in the baking pan, tightly covered with aluminum foil or plastic wrap.

Yield: 40 bars

Tip

Lemons and oranges will yield as much as twice the amount of juice if they are microwaved on high power until just warm to the touch, 20 to 40 seconds. Alternate method: Submerge in very hot water for 15 minutes.

Applesauce Bars

These are a classic American bar cookie—real comfort food.

  1 ¼ cups all-purpose flour
  1 teaspoon baking powder
  ½ teaspoon ground cinnamon
  ½ teaspoon salt
  ¼ teaspoon baking soda
  ¼ teaspoon ground nutmeg
  ½ cup (1 stick) plus 2 tablespoons salted
      butter or margarine
  1 cup packed light brown sugar
  ½ cup unsweetened applesauce
  1 large egg
  1 teaspoon vanilla extract
  ½ cup chopped walnuts
  ½ cup dark or golden raisins
  Orange Glaze (page 147)

1. Adjust one rack to divide the oven in half. Preheat the oven to 350° (or 325° if using a glass baking dish). Lightly grease a 13 × 9-inch metal baking pan or glass baking dish.

2. In a medium-size bowl, with a whisk, combine the flour, baking powder, cinnamon, salt, baking soda, and nutmeg until thoroughly mixed.

3. In a medium-size saucepan set over low heat, melt the butter. Remove from the heat. With a mixing spoon, stir in the brown sugar, applesauce, egg, and vanilla until well blended. Gradually add the flour mixture, stirring just until blended. Stir in the walnuts and the raisins until well distributed throughout the batter. Spread evenly in the prepared pan, smoothing the top with the back of the spoon.

4. Bake for about 25 minutes until a wooden pick inserted in the center comes out clean. Reverse the pan from front to back once during baking. Set the pan on a wire rack to cool completely. Spread with Orange Glaze. Cut into 6 × 6 rows.

5. Store in the baking pan, tightly covered with aluminum foil or plastic wrap.

Yield: 36 bars

Easy Cranberry-Crumb Bars

Bars like these are fun to make with the kids. Everything needed can be assembled in a jiffy and the mixing and putting together goes quickly, too. Only the baking seems to take forever, particularly for hungry kids, who are anxious to sample the fruits of their efforts.

  2 ¼ cups all-purpose flour, divided
  1 ½ cups regular or quick-cooking (not
      instant) rolled oats
  1 cup sugar
  1 cup (2 sticks) salted butter or margarine,
      at room temperature
  One 16-ounce can whole-berry cranberry
      sauce
  ¾ cup orange marmalade
  ½ cup slivered almonds

1. Adjust one rack to divide the oven in half. Preheat the oven to 350° (or 325° if using a glass baking dish). Lightly grease a 13 × 9-inch metal baking pan or glass baking dish.

2. In a large bowl, with an electric mixer at low speed, combine 2 cups of the flour with the oats, sugar, and butter until crumbly. Measure out 1½ cups of the oats mixture and set aside to use as a topping. Press the remaining mixture onto the bottom of the prepared pan. Bake for 15 minutes.

3. While the crust is baking, prepare the filling. In a small bowl, with a mixing spoon, mix together the cranberry sauce, marmalade, almonds, and the remaining ¼ cup of flour.

4. Remove the crust from the oven and spread with the filling mixture, smoothing the top with the back of the spoon. Sprinkle with the reserved oats mixture.

5. Continue to bake for 45 minutes until golden. Reverse the pan from front to back once during the final baking period. Set the pan on a wire rack and cool completely before cutting into 6 × 6 rows.

6. Store in the baking pan, tightly covered with aluminum foil or plastic wrap.

Yield: 36 bars

Cranberry-Fig Bars

Cranberries are a wonderful ingredient to use in sweet baked goods. Their tartness against the very rich crust and topping in these bars is a good flavor and texture contrast.

> 2 cups all-purpose flour
>
> 2 cups regular or quick-cooking (not instant) rolled oats
>
> 1 ½ cups packed light brown sugar
>
> ½ teaspoon baking soda
>
> ½ teaspoon ground cinnamon
>
> 1 cup (2 sticks) salted butter or margarine, melted
>
> One 12-ounce bag cranberries, rinsed, drained, and patted dry
>
> 1 cup finely cut dried figs (scissors work best for cutting figs)
>
> 6 tablespoons honey
>
> 1 teaspoon vanilla extract

Lemon Glaze

> 1 ½ cups sifted confectioners' sugar
>
> 2 tablespoons fresh strained lemon juice

1. Adjust one rack to divide the oven in half. Preheat the oven to 350° (or 325° if using a glass baking dish). Have ready a 13 × 9-inch metal baking pan or glass baking dish.

2. In a large bowl, with a whisk, combine the flour, oats, brown sugar, baking soda, and cinnamon until thoroughly mixed. With a mixing spoon, stir in the melted butter. Pat half of this mixture evenly on the bottom of the ungreased pan. Bake for 8 minutes.

3. In a large saucepan, combine the cranberries, figs, and honey. Bring to a boil over high heat. Lower the heat and cook, covered, stirring often until the cranberries pop. Remove from the heat and cool slightly. Stir in the vanilla.

4. Remove the partially baked crust from the oven. Spread the cranberry filling over the crust. Sprinkle the remaining flour mixture evenly over the filling. Return to the oven and bake for 20 minutes until golden. Reverse the pan from front to back during the final baking period. Set the pan on a wire rack to cool completely.

5. To make the glaze: In a small bowl, stir together the confectioners' sugar and lemon juice. Drizzle the glaze from the tip of a teaspoon over the top of the baked crumb layer. Cut into 8 × 5 rows.

6. Store in the baking pan, tightly covered with aluminum foil or plastic wrap.

Yield: 40 bars

Tip

So-called airtight or tightly covered containers include zipper-top plastic bags, cookie tins, screw-top jars or jars with gasket lids, rigid plastic containers, and even tightly sealed foil packets.

Chewy California Fig Bars

The more I use figs in my baking, the more I like what they do for the end results. Figs make cookies and bars especially chewy and rich-tasting, and also help to keep them moist and fresh-tasting.

Filling

One 8-ounce package dried figs
1 cup granulated sugar
$^1/_2$ cup hot water
$^1/_2$ cup chopped nuts

Crumb Crust and Topping

1 cup (2 sticks) salted butter or margarine, at room temperature
1 cup light brown sugar
$^1/_2$ teaspoon salt
$^1/_2$ teaspoon vanilla extract
1 $^3/_4$ cups all-purpose flour
1 $^3/_4$ cups regular or quick-cooking (not instant) rolled oats

1. Adjust one rack to divide the oven in half. Preheat the oven to 350° (or 325° if using a glass baking dish). Have ready a 13 × 9-inch metal baking pan or glass baking dish.

2. To make the filling: With scissors, cut the figs into small pieces. In a medium-size saucepan, combine the figs, sugar, water, and nuts. Heat to boiling. Reduce the heat and simmer, stirring frequently, until thickened, about 10 minutes. Set aside to cool.

3. To make the crust and topping: In a large bowl, with an electric mixer at medium-high speed, beat the butter, brown sugar, salt, and vanilla until very creamy, 2 to 3 minutes. With a mixing spoon, stir in the flour and oats until well blended and crumbly. Press two-thirds of this mixture evenly onto the bottom of the ungreased pan. Spread the filling over the top. Crumble the remaining crust mixture over the filling.

4. Bake for 25 to 30 minutes until lightly browned. Reverse the pan from front to back once during baking. Set the pan on a wire rack to cool completely before cutting into 6 × 6 rows.

5. Store in the baking pan, tightly covered with aluminum foil or plastic wrap.

Yield: 36 bars

Very Interesting Apricot Bars

What makes these bars interesting and sort of fun to make is that part of the dough is frozen and then shredded and sprinkled over the top of the bars to make a crusty topping.

3 cups all-purpose flour
2 teaspoons baking powder
$^1/_2$ cup (1 stick) salted butter or margarine, at room temperature
$^1/_4$ cup ($^1/_2$ stick) plain or butter-flavored shortening
1 cup sugar
1 large egg, lightly beaten
$^1/_4$ cup fresh strained lemon juice
1 teaspoon shredded and minced lemon zest
About 1 cup apricot preserves

1. Adjust one rack to divide the oven in half. Lightly grease a 13 × 9-inch metal baking pan or glass baking dish.

2. In a medium-size bowl, with a whisk, combine the flour and baking powder until thoroughly mixed.

3. In a large bowl, with an electric mixer at medium-high speed, beat together the butter, shortening, and sugar until light and creamy, 2 to 3 minutes. Beat in the egg and then the lemon juice and lemon zest until well blended. With the mixer at medium-low speed, gradually add the flour mixture, beating just until blended. Remove about one-quarter of the dough and wrap it loosely in plastic wrap. Place in the freezer until frozen solid, about 1 hour. Lightly cover the bowl containing the remaining dough and place in the refrigerator until firm, about 1 hour.

4. Preheat the oven to 350° (or 325° if using a glass baking dish).

5. Press the chilled dough onto the bottom of the prepared pan. With an icing spatula, spread the preserves over the dough to within ¼ inch of the edges. Using a four-sided grater, shred the frozen dough onto a sheet of waxed paper. Sprinkle evenly over the preserves.

6. Bake for 30 to 35 minutes until the shredded-dough topping is browned. Reverse the pan from front to back once during baking. Set the pan on a wire rack to cool completely before cutting into 6 × 6 rows.

7. Store in the baking pan, tightly covered with aluminum foil or plastic wrap.

Yield: 36 bars

Dreamy Coconut and Raisin Squares

It's the gooey filling that makes these three-layer bars so memorable.

- ½ cup (1 stick) salted butter or margarine, at room temperature
- ½ cup sifted confectioners' sugar
- 1 cup all-purpose flour
- One 7-ounce can or bag (2 ⅔ cups) shredded or flaked coconut, divided
- 2 large eggs
- 1 teaspoon vanilla extract
- 1 cup packed light or dark brown sugar
- 1 teaspoon baking powder mixed with 2 tablespoons all-purpose flour
- ⅔ cup dark or golden raisins
- ½ cup semisweet chocolate chips

1. Adjust one rack to divide the oven in half. Preheat the oven to 350° (or 325° if using a glass baking dish). Have ready an ungreased 9-inch-square metal baking pan or glass baking dish.

2. In a medium-size bowl, with an electric mixer at medium-high speed, beat together the butter and confectioners' sugar until light and fluffy, 2 to 3 minutes. With a mixing spoon, stir the flour and ⅔ cup of the coconut until well blended. Press this mixture onto the bottom of the ungreased pan. Bake for 20 minutes until golden.

3. While the crust is baking, in a medium-size bowl, with the electric mixer at medium speed, beat together the eggs and vanilla. Gradually beat in the brown sugar until well blended, about 1 minute. With the mixing spoon, stir in the mixture of baking powder and flour until well blended. Stir in the raisins and 1 cup of the remaining coconut until well distributed throughout the batter. Remove the crust from the oven. Pour the batter over the crust, smoothing the top with the back of the spoon.

4. Bake for 30 minutes longer until the filling is set. Reverse the pan from front to back once during the final baking period. Remove from the oven and immediately sprinkle evenly with the chocolate chips. Cover the pan with aluminum foil and let stand for 2 to 3 minutes until the chips become shiny and soft. With an icing spatula, spread the chocolate evenly over the surface to make a frosting. Sprinkle evenly with the remaining 1 cup of coconut. Cool completely in the pan set on a wire rack before cutting into 4 × 4 rows.

5. Store in the baking pan, tightly covered with aluminum foil or plastic wrap.

Yield: 16 bars

Chocolate Fruit Bars

Christmas is a good time to make these candylike bars, which look very merry, dotted with pieces of red and green candied cherries.

> 2 cups finely crushed purchased vanilla wafers (about 60)
>
> 1/2 cup unsweetened cocoa powder
>
> 3 tablespoons granulated sugar
>
> 2/3 cup (1 stick plus 3 tablespoons) cold salted butter or margarine
>
> 1 cup peanut butter chips
>
> 1 cup mixed red and green candied cherries, cut in half
>
> 1/2 cup chopped dates
>
> One 14-ounce can sweetened condensed (not evaporated) milk
>
> 3/4 cup coarsely chopped pecans

1. Adjust one rack to divide the oven in half. Preheat the oven to 350° (or 325° if using a glass baking dish). Have ready a 13 × 9-inch baking pan or glass baking dish.

2. In a large bowl, with a mixing spoon, stir together the wafers, cocoa, and sugar. With a pastry blender or two knives used in a crisscross fashion, cut in the butter until the mixture forms small crumbs. Press this mixture onto the bottom and 1/2 inch up the sides of the ungreased pan. Sprinkle the peanut butter chips, cherries, and dates evenly over the crust. Drizzle the condensed milk evenly over the fruit. Sprinkle with the pecans.

3. Bake for 25 to 30 minutes until the edges of the filling are lightly browned and the center is bubbly. Reverse the pan from front to back once during baking. Set the pan on a wire rack to cool completely. Cover tightly with aluminum foil or plastic wrap and let stand at room temperature for about 8 hours before cutting into 6 × 6 rows.

4. Store in the baking pan, tightly covered with aluminum foil or plastic wrap.

Yield: 36 bars

Zucchini Bars

I often wonder who got the idea of adding vegetables to baked goods, but it was a good one. Besides making them a trifle more nutritious, vegetables add moisture to the batter and help to retain it after baking. The frosting is strictly optional, but very good.

> 2 cups all-purpose flour
>
> 1 1/2 teaspoons baking powder
>
> 1 cup sugar
>
> 3/4 cup (1 1/2 sticks) salted butter or margarine, at room temperature
>
> 2 large eggs, lightly beaten
>
> 1 teaspoon vanilla extract
>
> 2 cups shredded zucchini
>
> 3/4 cup shredded coconut
>
> 1 cup golden raisins

Brown Sugar Frosting

> 3 tablespoons salted butter or margarine, at room temperature
>
> 1/2 cup firmly packed light brown sugar
>
> 1/4 cup milk
>
> 2 to 2 1/2 cups confectioners' sugar

1. Adjust one rack to divide the oven in half. Preheat the oven to 350°. Lightly grease a 15 × 10-inch jelly-roll pan.

2. In a medium-size bowl, with a whisk, combine the flour and baking powder until thoroughly mixed.

3. In a large bowl, with an electric mixer at medium-high speed, beat together the sugar and butter until light and fluffy, 2 to 3 minutes. Add the eggs and vanilla and beat until well blended. With the mixer at medium-low speed, gradually add the flour mixture, beating just until blended. With a mixing spoon, stir in the zucchini, coconut, and raisins until well distributed throughout the batter. Turn into the prepared pan, smoothing the top with the back of the spoon.

4. Bake for 20 to 30 minutes until light golden brown. Reverse the pan from front to back once during baking. Set the pan on a wire rack to cool completely.

5. To make the frosting: In a medium-size saucepan, combine the butter and brown sugar. Bring to a boil, stirring constantly, over medium-high heat. Reduce the heat to medium and cook, stirring, for 1 minute until slightly thickened. Remove the pan from the heat and cool for 10 minutes. Add the milk and beat until smooth. Beat in 1½ cups of the confectioners' sugar until smooth. Add enough of the remaining confectioners' sugar to give the mixture a good spreading consistency. With an icing spatula, spread the frosting over the cooled cake. When the frosting has set, about 1 hour, cut into 10 × 4 rows.

6. Store in the baking pan, tightly covered with aluminum foil or plastic wrap.

Yield: 40 bars

Evelyne Newman's Cheesecake Diamonds

Everybody loves these bars, but they do have to be kept refrigerated after they are cooled. This is not anything like a dessert cheesecake. The topping is very thin.

- 5 tablespoons (½ stick plus 1 tablespoon) salted butter or margarine, at room temperature
- ⅓ cup light or dark brown sugar
- 1 cup all-purpose flour
- ¼ cup chopped walnuts
- ½ cup granulated sugar
- One 8-ounce package cream cheese, at room temperature
- 1 large egg, lightly beaten
- 2 tablespoons milk
- 1 tablespoon strained fresh lemon juice
- ½ teaspoon vanilla extract

1. Adjust one rack to divide the oven in half. Preheat the oven to 350°. Have ready an 8-inch-square metal baking pan.

2. In a medium-size bowl, with an electric mixer at medium-high speed, beat together the butter and brown sugar until light and fluffy, 2 to 3 minutes. With a mixing spoon, stir in the flour and walnuts. Remove ½ cup of this mixture and set aside for topping. Press the remainder onto the bottom of the ungreased pan.

3. Bake for 12 to 15 minutes until the crust is firm.

4. While the crust is baking, make the filling. In a medium-size bowl, with an electric mixer at medium-high speed, beat the granulated sugar and cream cheese until smooth. Add the egg, milk, lemon juice, and vanilla. Beat until thoroughly blended. Spread over the partially baked crust. Sprinkle evenly with the reserved butter mixture. Reverse the pan from front to back and continue to bake for 25 minutes until the topping is a golden brown. Set the pan on a wire rack to cool completely before cutting into 2-inch diamonds (see diagram on page 238).

5. Cover the pan with aluminum foil or plastic wrap and refrigerate for up to 2 or 3 days.

Yield: 16 diamond-shaped bars

Old-Fashioned Cheesecake Bars

I don't consider cheesecake bars to be cookies in the strictest sense, but so many people do that I've decided I would be remiss not to include a classic version of the old favorite. Depending on the holiday or the occasion, these bars can be left plain, with only a chocolate drizzle, perhaps, or decorated to the nines with all kinds of sweeties.

> 1 $^1/_2$ cups shortbread crumbs (5 $^1/_2$ to 6 ounces shortbread cookies, your own or purchased)
>
> $^1/_2$ cup finely chopped walnuts
>
> $^1/_4$ cup ($^1/_2$ stick) salted butter or margarine, melted
>
> Three 8-ounce packages cream cheese, at room temperature
>
> $^3/_4$ cup sugar
>
> 1 tablespoon all-purpose flour
>
> 3 large eggs, lightly beaten
>
> $^3/_4$ cup heavy (whipping) cream
>
> 2 teaspoons vanilla extract
>
> Suggested toppings: Drizzled, melted dark or white chocolate, chopped candy bars, chopped chocolate-mint wafers, nonpareils, plain or chocolate-dipped whole nuts, jellied fruit slice wedges, gumdrops, jelly beans, sliced or chopped nuts, toasted coconut, chopped dried or candied fruit, grated chocolate, or chocolate curls

1. Adjust one rack to divide the oven in half. Preheat the oven to 325°. Line a 9-inch-square metal baking pan with foil, shiny side up, allowing the foil to overhang slightly. Lightly grease the foil.

2. In a small bowl, with a fork, combine the cookie crumbs, walnuts, and butter. Press this mixture onto the bottom of the prepared baking pan. Bake for 5 to 6 minutes until golden. Remove from the oven and set aside to cool slightly.

3. In a large bowl, with an electric mixer at medium speed, beat together the cream cheese, sugar, and flour until smooth. Beat in the eggs, cream, and vanilla until well blended. Pour over the partially baked crust. Return to the oven and bake for 25 to 30 minutes until the cheesecake appears to be set. Reverse the pan from front to back once during baking. Turn off the oven and leave the cheesecake in the oven with the door ajar for about 30 minutes until the top of the cheesecake feels firm when lightly pressed. Set the pan on a wire rack to cool for about 1 hour. Cover and refrigerate for about 4 hours until well chilled.

4. Remove the cheesecake from the pan by lifting up the foil. With a long, sharp knife, cut the cheesecake into 4 × 4 rows. Decorate by lightly pressing assorted toppings onto the surface.

5. Store in a tightly covered container in the refrigerator for up to 4 days, or freeze for up to 2 weeks. (If freezing the bars, decorate with the toppings after thawing the bars in the refrigerator.)

Yield: 16 bars

Variations

Marbled Chocolate-Cheesecake Bars: Substitute 1$^1/_2$ cups chocolate-wafer crumbs for the shortbread crumbs. For the batter, increase the sugar to 1 cup. After mixing, remove 3 cups of the batter to a medium-size bowl. To the remaining batter, beat in 2 tablespoons unsweetened cocoa powder. Alternately spoon the plain and chocolate batters over the partially baked crust. Run an icing spatula or a dinner knife through the batter to create a marbled effect. Bake as directed above.

Minty Marbled Chocolate-Cheesecake Bars: Add $^1/_2$ teaspoon peppermint extract to the chocolate batter.

Glazed Lebkuchen Diamonds

If stored in a tightly covered container, these bars will keep very nicely for about a month, during which time the flavor will only mellow and intensify, making them better with every passing day. These are absolutely fabulous when served with plain hot tea.

2 ³/₄ cups all-purpose flour

¹/₂ teaspoon baking soda

1 teaspoon ground cinnamon

1 teaspoon ground cloves

1 teaspoon ground nutmeg

¹/₂ teaspoon salt

³/₄ cup packed light or dark brown sugar

1 large egg

1 cup honey

1 tablespoon shredded and minced lemon zest

1 teaspoon strained fresh lemon juice

1 cup golden raisins

1 cup blanched slivered almonds, toasted (page 16)

¹/₂ cup chopped mixed candied fruit

¹/₂ cup chopped citron (the candied peel of a thick-skinned, lemonlike fruit)

Lemon Glaze

1 cup sifted confectioners' sugar

1 ¹/₂ to 2 tablespoons strained fresh lemon juice

About 24 candied cherries, cut in half, for decoration (optional)

1. Adjust one rack to divide the oven in half. Preheat the oven to 375°. Lightly grease a 15 × 10-inch jelly roll pan.

2. In a medium-size bowl, with a whisk, combine the flour, baking soda, cinnamon, cloves, nutmeg, and salt until thoroughly mixed.

3. In a large bowl, with an electric mixer at medium-high speed, beat together the brown sugar and egg until light and creamy, 2 to 3 minutes. Add the honey, lemon zest, and lemon juice and beat until well blended. With the mixer at medium-low speed, gradually add the flour mixture, beating just until blended. With a mixing spoon, stir in the raisins, almonds, candied fruit, and citron until evenly distributed throughout the batter. Turn the batter into the prepared pan, smoothing the top with the back of the spoon.

4. Bake for 20 minutes until lightly browned. Reverse the pan from front to back once during baking.

5. While the lebkuchen is baking, make the glaze. In a small bowl, with a whisk, combine the confectioners' sugar and enough lemon juice to make a thin glaze.

6. When the lebkuchen is removed from the oven, set the pan on a wire rack to cool slightly. While still warm, spread with the glaze. Cool completely before cutting into 7 × 5 rows. Decorate each bar with a candied cherry half, if desired.

7. Store in a single layer in a tightly covered container.

Yield: 35 bars

Coconut Macaroon Bars

Fresh bread crumbs used to play a more important part in baking back in olden times than they do now. In those days, whenever possible, bread crumbs were used in place of flour, a more precious commodity than leftover bread, which never went to waste.

>   1 ¼ cups graham-cracker crumbs
>   1 cup slivered almonds, toasted (page 16) and finely chopped
>   2 tablespoons sugar
>   ½ cup (1 stick) salted butter or margarine, melted
>   One 14-ounce can regular or reduced-fat condensed (not evaporated) milk
>   One 7-ounce package flaked coconut (2 ⅔ cups)
>   2 cups fresh white bread crumbs (4 to 5 slices whirled briefly in a blender or a food processor)
>   2 large eggs
>   2 teaspoons vanilla extract
>   1 ½ teaspoons almond extract

1. Adjust one rack to divide the oven in half. Preheat the oven to 350° (or 325° if using a glass baking dish). Have ready a 13 × 9-inch metal baking pan or glass baking dish.

2. In a small bowl, with a fork, combine the graham-cracker crumbs, almonds, sugar, and butter until well blended. Press this mixture firmly onto the bottom of the ungreased pan. Bake for 15 minutes.

3. In a medium-size bowl, with an electric mixer at low speed, beat together the condensed milk, coconut, bread crumbs, eggs, vanilla, and almond extract until well blended.

4. Remove the pan from the oven. Spread the coconut mixture evenly over the partially baked crust. Return to the oven to bake for about 30 minutes longer until lightly browned. Reverse the pan from front to back once during the final baking period. Set the pan on a wire rack to cool completely before cutting into 6 × 6 rows.

5. Store in the baking pan in the refrigerator, tightly covered with aluminum foil or plastic wrap.

Yield: 36 bars

Scandinavian Cardamom Bars

Cardamom is a pungent spice from India, therefore quite rare and expensive in the faraway Scandinavian countries, at least in earlier times. It was the addition of this precious spice that made these bars so special that they were rarely baked at any time of the year other than Christmas. You might want to treat yourself to these delicate bars more often.

>   2 cups sifted all-purpose flour
>   ¼ teaspoon ground cardamom
>   1 cup (2 sticks) salted butter or margarine
>   1 cup sugar
>   2 large egg yolks
>   1 teaspoon vanilla extract
>   ½ cup finely chopped walnuts
>   ½ cup lingonberry preserves (see Tip)

1. Adjust one rack to divide the oven in half. Preheat the oven to 325°. Lightly grease an 8-inch-square metal baking pan.

2. In a medium-size bowl, with a whisk, combine the flour and cardamom until thoroughly mixed.

3. In a large bowl, with an electric mixer at medium-high speed, beat together the butter and sugar until light and fluffy. Add the egg yolks and vanilla and beat until well blended. With a mixing spoon, stir in the chopped walnuts until well distributed throughout the batter. Spoon half of the batter into the prepared pan, smoothing the top with the back of the spoon. With an icing spatula, lightly spread the preserves over the batter. Add the remaining batter, spreading evenly.

4. Bake for about 30 minutes until lightly browned. Reverse the pan from front to back once during baking. Set the pan on a wire rack to cool for about 15 minutes before cutting into 4 × 4 rows, then cool completely.

5. Store in the baking pan, tightly covered with aluminum foil or plastic wrap.

Yield: 16 bars

Tip

Lingonberry preserves can be found in specialty food stores. Strawberry or raspberry preserves can be substituted.

English Toffee Bars

This is the cookie version of chocolate-covered toffee candy bars. If you're a toffee lover, these bars will often be baking in your oven.

- 1 ³/₄ cups all-purpose flour
- 1 teaspoon ground cinnamon
- 1 cup (2 sticks) salted butter or margarine, at room temperature
- 1 cup sugar
- 1 large egg, separated
- 1 cup finely chopped pecans
- 3 tablespoons milk
- 1 teaspoon instant-coffee granules or powder
- 2 ounces (2 squares) semisweet chocolate, broken in half

1. Adjust one rack to divide the oven in half. Preheat the oven to 275°. Lightly grease a 15 × 10-inch jelly-roll pan.

2. In a medium-size bowl, with a whisk, combine the flour and cinnamon until thoroughly mixed.

3. In a large bowl, with an electric mixer at medium-high speed, beat together the butter and sugar until light and fluffy, 2 to 3 minutes. Beat in the egg yolk until well blended. With the mixer at medium-low speed, gradually add the flour mixture, beating just until blended. Press this mixture evenly onto the bottom of the prepared pan. In a small bowl, lightly beat the egg white and brush it over the dough. Sprinkle with the pecans, pressing them lightly into the dough.

4. Bake for 1 hour until firm and the edges are just beginning to brown. Reverse the pan from front to back once during baking. Set the pan on a wire rack to cool for about 5 minutes before cutting into 7 × 5 rows.

5. While the bars are baking, in a small saucepan, heat the milk until tiny bubbles appear around the edge. Remove from the heat and stir in the instant coffee granules until dissolved. Add the chocolate. Return to low heat and cook, stirring, until the chocolate is melted and the mixture is smooth. Drizzle the chocolate mixture off the tip of a teaspoon onto the bars.

6. Store in the baking pan, tightly covered with aluminum foil or plastic wrap.

Yield: 35 bars

Halfway Bars

Halfway to what, I can't help but wonder. Halfway to making traditional chocolate-chip cookies and then the baker got tired and baked the dough in a pan? In any case, this is a delicious bar.

- 1 cup all-purpose flour
- $^1/_2$ teaspoon baking powder
- $^1/_4$ teaspoon salt
- $^1/_8$ teaspoon baking soda
- $^1/_2$ cup (1 stick) plain shortening
- $^3/_4$ cup packed dark brown sugar, divided
- $^1/_4$ cup granulated sugar
- 1 large egg, separated
- 1 teaspoon vanilla extract
- $^1/_2$ cup semisweet chocolate chips

1. Adjust one rack to divide the oven in half. Preheat the oven to 375° (or 350° if using a glass baking dish). Lightly grease a 13 × 9-inch metal baking pan or glass baking dish.

2. In a medium-size bowl, with a whisk, combine the flour, baking powder, salt, and baking soda until thoroughly mixed.

3. In a large bowl, with an electric mixer at medium-high speed, beat together the shortening, $^1/_4$ cup of the brown sugar, and the granulated sugar until creamy, 2 to 3 minutes. Add the egg yolk and the vanilla and beat until blended. With the mixer at medium-low speed, gradually add the flour mixture, beating just until blended to make a soft dough. Pat the dough evenly into the prepared pan. Sprinkle evenly with the chocolate chips.

4. In a small, clean bowl with clean beaters, beat the egg white at medium-low speed until frothy. Increase the speed to high and beat until stiff peaks form when the beaters are lifted. Gradually beat in the remaining $^1/_2$ cup brown sugar until well combined. Spoon the egg-white mixture over the chocolate chips. With an icing spatula, spread evenly over the surface.

5. Bake for about 25 minutes until dry looking and firm when lightly touched. Reverse the pan from front to back once during baking. Set the pan on a wire rack to cool completely. While still warm cut into 6 × 6 rows.

6. Store in the baking pan, tightly covered with aluminum foil or plastic wrap.

Yield: 36 bars

Hermit Bars

Hermits, so the story goes, originated in Cape Cod, Massachusetts, back in the days of clipper ships, when they were taken along on long sea voyages. These moist cookie bars, rich with spices from the West Indies, taste just as good and travel just as well today as they did then.

- One 14-ounce can regular or low-fat sweetened condensed (not evaporated) milk
- $^1/_3$ cup all-purpose flour
- 1 large egg
- 1 teaspoon vanilla extract
- 1 teaspoon ground cinnamon
- $^1/_2$ teaspoon ground ginger
- $^1/_2$ teaspoon ground cloves
- $^1/_2$ cup golden raisins
- 1 cup coarsely chopped walnuts

1. Adjust one rack to divide the oven in half. Preheat the oven to 350°. Have ready an ungreased 8-inch-square metal baking pan.

2. In a medium-size bowl, with a mixing spoon, combine the condensed milk, flour, egg, vanilla, cinnamon, ginger, cloves, raisins, and walnuts until thoroughly mixed. Spread the batter in the baking pan, smoothing the top with the back of the spoon.

3. Bake for 25 minutes until golden brown. Reverse the pan from front to back once during baking. Set the pan on a wire rack to cool completely. Cover and chill before cutting into 4 × 4 rows.

4. Store in the baking pan, tightly covered with aluminum foil or plastic wrap.

Yield: 16 bars

Chocolate S'more Bars

These bars satisfy sudden urges for something good to eat and easy to make. About the only way to cut these bars is with a wet knife, rewetting it when it begins to stick.

6 whole graham crackers
$^2/_3$ cup all-purpose flour
$^1/_8$ teaspoon baking soda
$^1/_3$ cup ($^1/_2$ stick plus 1$^1/_2$ tablespoons) salted butter or margarine
$^1/_4$ cup sugar
2 tablespoons light corn syrup
1 teaspoon vanilla extract
1 large egg, lightly beaten
1 cup canned or bottled chocolate syrup
2 cups miniature marshmallows

1. Adjust one rack to the upper third position in the oven. Preheat the oven to 325°. Line the bottom of a 9-inch-square glass baking dish with the graham crackers, cutting the crackers with a serrated knife to make them fit.

2. In a medium-size bowl, with a whisk, combine the flour and baking soda until thoroughly mixed.

3. In a large bowl, with an electric mixer at medium-high speed, beat together the butter, sugar, corn syrup, and vanilla until light and fluffy, 2 to 3 minutes. Beat in the egg until blended. With the mixer at medium-low speed, gradually add the flour mixture alternately with the chocolate syrup, beating just until blended. Turn the batter into the prepared baking dish, smoothing the top with the back of a spoon.

4. Bake for about 35 minutes until the edges begin to pull away from the sides of the pan. Reverse the pan from front to back once during baking. Remove the pan from the oven and raise the oven temperature to broil. Immediately scatter the marshmallows over the top, dividing evenly. Place the pan under the broiler until the marshmallows are toasted. Set the pan on a wire rack to cool for about 20 minutes. With a wet knife, cut into 4 × 4 rows. Serve while still warm.

Yield: 16 bars

No-Bake Orange Buttercream Squares

The refrigerator "bakes" these bars, which makes them the ideal choice for hot days.

Crust

1 $^1/_4$ cups crushed chocolate wafer cookies
$^1/_3$ cup ($^1/_2$ stick plus 1$^1/_2$ tablespoons) salted butter or margarine, at room temperature

Filling

1 $^1/_2$ cups confectioners' sugar
$^1/_3$ cup ($^1/_2$ stick plus 1$^1/_2$ tablespoons) salted butter or margarine, at room temperature
1 tablespoon milk
2 teaspoons finely shredded and minced orange zest
$^1/_2$ teaspoon vanilla extract

Glaze

1 tablespoon unsweetened cocoa powder
1 tablespoon salted butter or margarine, melted

1. To make the crust: In a medium-size bowl, stir together the cookie crumbs and the butter. Press onto the bottom of a 9-inch-square glass baking dish. Refrigerate until firm, about 1 hour.

2. To make the filling: In a medium-size bowl, with an electric mixer at medium-low speed, beat together the confectioners' sugar, butter, milk, orange zest, and vanilla. Beat at medium-high speed, scraping the side of the bowl often, until light and fluffy, 2 to 3 minutes. Spread this mixture over the firm crust.

3. To make the glaze: In a small bowl, stir together the cocoa and butter. Drizzle over the filling from the tip of a teaspoon. Refrigerate until firm, about 2 hours, before cutting into 8 × 4 rows.

4. Store in the baking dish in the refrigerator, tightly covered with aluminum foil or plastic wrap.

Yield: 32 bars

Cream-Filled Chocolate Bars

Here is the closest I can get to a dense, frosted, and filled chocolate cake in the handy form of a bar cookie.

- 1/4 cup (1/2 stick) salted butter or margarine, softened
- 1 ounce (1 square) unsweetened chocolate, broken in half
- 1 large egg
- 1/2 cup sugar
- 1/4 cup all-purpose flour
- 1/2 teaspoon vanilla extract
- 1/2 cup chopped almonds

Vanilla Cream Filling

- 1/2 cup confectioners' sugar
- 1 tablespoon salted butter or margarine, at room temperature
- 1 1/2 teaspoons milk
- 1/4 teaspoon vanilla extract

Chocolate Glaze

- 2 tablespoons sugar
- 1 tablespoon water
- 1/4 cup semisweet chocolate chips
- About 1/2 cup sliced or slivered almonds, toasted (page 16)

1. Adjust one rack to divide the oven in half. Preheat the oven to 375°. Line a 9-inch-square glass baking dish with foil, shiny side up. Lightly grease the foil.

2. In a small saucepan set over very low heat, melt together the butter and chocolate, stirring constantly until smooth. Set aside to cool slightly.

3. To make the bars: In a medium-size bowl, with an electric mixer at medium-high speed, beat the egg until frothy. Beat in the sugar and flour until well blended. With a mixing spoon, stir in the chocolate mixture and the vanilla until very well blended. Stir in the almonds until evenly distributed throughout the batter. Turn into the prepared

baking dish, smoothing the top with the back of the spoon.

4. Bake for 10 to 12 minutes until the edges begin to pull away from the sides of the pan. Reverse the baking dish from front to back once during baking. Set the baking dish on a wire rack to cool completely. Invert onto a cutting surface and peel away the foil.

5. To make the filling: In a small bowl, with an electric mixer at medium-high speed, beat together the confectioners' sugar, butter, milk, and vanilla. Beat until creamy with a good spreading consistency.

6. With a long, serrated knife, cut the cake in half to make two layers. Spread one cut side with filling. Set the other layer over the filling, cut side down.

7. To make the glaze: In a very small saucepan, bring the sugar and water to a boil. Remove from the heat and immediately stir in the chocolate chips until melted and smooth. Spread over the top of the cake while still warm. Sprinkle with the sliced almonds. Set aside until the chocolate is firm before cutting into 3 × 3 rows.

8. Store in a single layer in a tightly covered, shallow container.

Yield: 9 bars

Miss Anthony's Chocolate Pan Cookies

Clara Anthony was a nursing supervisor at Hunterdon Medical Center in Flemington, New Jersey, during the years I worked there in the public information department. Miss Anthony often brought these cookie bars to small staff celebrations, and she was kind enough to share the recipe with me. They are rather flat and crisp, and not awfully sweet.

- 2 ounces (2 squares) semisweet chocolate
- 1/2 cup (1 stick) salted butter or margarine
- 1 cup sugar

2 large eggs, lightly beaten
$^1/_2$ cup all-purpose flour
$^1/_4$ teaspoon salt
$^1/_2$ teaspoon vanilla extract
$^2/_3$ cup finely chopped nuts

1. Adjust two racks to divide the oven into thirds. Preheat the oven to 400°. Lightly grease two 8-inch-square metal baking pans.

2. In a small, heavy saucepan set over very low heat, melt together the chocolate and the butter, stirring constantly until smooth. Pour the melted chocolate mixture into a large bowl and set aside to cool to lukewarm.

3. With a mixing spoon, stir the sugar, eggs, flour, salt, and vanilla into the cooled chocolate mixture just until well blended. Spread the batter into the prepared pans, dividing evenly. Smooth the tops with the back of the spoon. Sprinkle evenly with the nuts.

4. Bake on separate racks for about 12 minutes until the edges begin to pull away from the sides of the pans, and the surface is firm to the touch. Reverse the pans on the racks and from front to back once during baking. Set the pans on wire racks to cool slightly before cutting each pan into 4 × 4 rows. (If they cool too much they will not cut neatly.)

5. Store in the baking pan, tightly covered with aluminum foil or plastic wrap.

Yield: 32 bars

Pan-Cookie Cinnamon Triangles

Pan cookies aren't quite the same as bars. They are thinner and crisper, but the method for making them is about the same. These are very nice cookies to serve during the holidays, especially if they are decorated with candied red and green cherries.

2 cups all-purpose flour
1 $^1/_2$ teaspoons ground cinnamon
1 cup (2 sticks) salted butter or margarine, at room temperature
$^3/_4$ cup packed light brown sugar
1 large egg, separated
$^1/_2$ cup chopped pecans
12 whole red candied cherries, cut in half
12 whole green candied cherries, cut in half

1. Adjust one rack to divide the oven in half. Preheat the oven to 275°. Have ready an ungreased, 15 × 10-inch jelly-roll pan.

2. In a medium-size bowl, with a whisk, combine the flour and cinnamon until thoroughly mixed.

3. In a large bowl, with an electric mixer at medium-high speed, beat together the butter, brown sugar, and egg yolk until very creamy, 2 to 3 minutes. With the mixer at medium-low speed, gradually add the flour mixture, beating just until blended. (If the dough becomes too stiff for the electric mixer, use your hands to mix in the remainder of the flour.) Spread and press the dough evenly in the ungreased pan. In a small bowl, with a fork, beat the egg white until frothy. Brush the top of the dough with the egg white. With the tip of a sharp knife and a ruler, score the dough into 2$^1/_2$-inch squares. Score the squares in half diagonally to make triangles. Sprinkle with the nuts and then place a cherry half in the center of each triangle.

4. Bake for about 1 hour until golden. Reverse the pan from front to back once during baking. Remove the pan from the oven and, with a sharp knife, cut into triangles, following the score marks. Cool completely in the pan set on a wire rack.

5. Store in the baking pan, tightly covered with aluminum foil or plastic wrap.

Yield: 48 cookies

Pizza Pan Cookies

No cookie cookbook today would be complete without this recipe, which is on its way to becoming an American classic for kids of all ages. Besides the toppings given here, the "pizza" can be sprinkled with all kinds of goodies: peanuts, raisins, jelly beans, and other little candies, whatever strikes your fancy and happens to be in the cupboard.

>1 cup (2 sticks) salted butter or margarine, at room temperature
>1/2 cup granulated sugar
>1/2 cup packed light or dark brown sugar
>1 large egg, lightly beaten
>2 teaspoons vanilla extract
>1 3/4 cups all-purpose flour
>1 1/2 cups (8 ounces) semisweet chocolate chips
>1/2 cup pecan pieces
>2 cups miniature marshmallows

1. Adjust one rack to divide the oven in half. Preheat the oven to 350°. Lightly grease and flour a 12-inch pizza pan.

2. In a large bowl, with an electric mixer at medium-high speed, beat the butter, granulated sugar, and brown sugar until light and creamy, 2 to 3 minutes. Beat in the egg and vanilla until well blended. With the mixer at medium-low speed, gradually add the flour, beating just until blended. Spread the dough evenly in the prepared pan.

3. Bake for about 20 minutes until just firm to the touch. Remove from the oven and immediately sprinkle evenly with the chocolate chips, pecan pieces, and marshmallows. Return to the oven and bake until the marshmallows are melting and lightly browned, about 15 minutes. Reverse the pan from front to back once during baking. Set the pan on a wire rack and cool for about 10 minutes. With a long, serrated knife, cut the pizza into 12 wedges. Serve warm or cool.

4. Store in the pizza pan, tightly covered with aluminum foil or plastic wrap.

Yield: 12 cookies

Marzipan Bars

Almond paste, the main ingredient in marzipan, is something that most people either really like or dislike, and I'm afraid I fall into the latter group. However, even I think these bars are good, so if you love marzipan, you'll be crazy about these bars.

Crust

>1/2 cup (1 stick) salted butter or margarine, at room temperature
>1/2 cup packed light brown sugar
>1 teaspoon vanilla extract
>1 1/2 cups all-purpose flour
>3/4 cup raspberry jam, stirred until soft

Filling

>1 1/3 cups almond paste (page 35)
>1/2 cup sugar
>1 teaspoon vanilla extract
>3 large eggs

Frosting

>1 ounce (1 square) semisweet chocolate, melted
>2 tablespoons salted butter or margarine, at room temperature
>1 1/2 cups confectioners' sugar
>2 tablespoons whole milk
>1 teaspoon vanilla extract

1. Adjust one rack to divide the oven in half. Preheat the oven to 350° (or 325° if using a glass baking dish). Have ready an ungreased 13 × 9-inch metal baking pan or glass baking dish.

2. To make the crust: In a medium-size bowl, with an electric mixer at medium speed, beat together the butter, brown sugar, and vanilla until light and fluffy, 2 to 3 minutes. With the mixer at medium-low speed, gradually add the flour, beating just until the mixture forms a soft dough. Press the dough onto the bottom of the ungreased pan. Spread the dough evenly with the jam.

3. To make the filling: In a medium-size bowl, with an electric mixer at medium speed, beat together the almond paste and sugar until smooth. Beat in the vanilla. Add the eggs, one at a time, beating well after each addition. Spread the filling over the jam.

4. Bake for 20 to 25 minutes until the filling is pale golden. Reverse the pan from front to back once during baking. Set the pan on a wire rack to cool completely.

5. To make the frosting: In a small, heavy saucepan set over very low heat, melt the chocolate, stirring constantly until smooth. Remove from the heat and set aside to cool slightly.

6. In a medium-size bowl, with an electric mixer at medium speed, beat together the butter, confectioners' sugar, milk, and vanilla until smooth. Beat in the cooled chocolate until well blended. Spread the frosting over the filling. Cover and chill for 1 hour before cutting into 6×6 rows.

7. Store in the baking pan, tightly covered with aluminum foil or plastic wrap.

Yield: 36 bars

11
Special Cookies

As I was writing this cookbook I came to a point when I had to find a home for those orphan recipes that had been tossed around from chapter to chapter. At one point they ended up as small congregations that wouldn't support a chapter on their own. But I just couldn't bear to leave them out, considering the emotional bond I had developed with them.

And so, in this chapter, you'll find a collection of seemingly unrelated recipes, including those for healthful cookies, "unscratch" cookies, children's recipes, and even dog cookies. But they all have at least one thing in common: They might just be among the best recipes in the book.

HEALTHFUL COOKIES

As I've mentioned elsewhere in this book, and maybe more than once, I don't consider cookies to be particularly unhealthful. Yes, they are sweet. Yes, the majority of them do contain fat. But simply by virtue of their size, diet-damage control is pretty much up to the eater, and in my opinion, a few cookies a week on the average is not likely to shorten your life span by a whole lot, and will certainly make it more pleasant.

Chances are that if you are on a severely restricted diet, you're not going to keep this book at your elbow. But for those times when you're on a weight-loss program, or want to send over something low-fat and delicious to a friend who has recently had bypass surgery, or you just want to have some cookies around that you can eat in a reasonably unrestrained manner, these recipes may be useful.

There are some steps you can take on your own to make cookie recipes more healthful. However, I would warn against monkeying around too much with baking recipes unless you really know your stuff. There is a lot of chemistry involved in baking, and random substitutions can't be made as if the batter were a pot of stew.

Harvest Oat Drops

These cookies are crisp when you bring them out of the oven, but soften upon standing. I am sure that each one must have at least a day's worth of dietary fiber, so I would advise against eating too many at one time.

- 1/2 pound pitted prunes, chopped
- 1/2 cup water
- 2/3 cup canola oil
- 1 large apple, cored and shredded (about 1 cup)
- 1/2 teaspoon salt
- 1 teaspoon vanilla extract
- 3 cups regular or quick-cooking (not instant) rolled oats
- 1/8 teaspoon ground cinnamon
- 1/2 cup finely chopped walnuts

1. Adjust two racks to divide the oven into thirds. Preheat the oven to 350°. Have ready two ungreased baking sheets.

2. In a medium-size saucepan, combine the prunes with the water. Cook over medium heat, stirring occasionally, until soft. Remove from the heat. With an electric mixer at medium speed, beat the prunes until smooth. Beat in the oil until well blended. With a mixing spoon, stir in the apple, salt, and vanilla until well blended. Stir in the oats, cinnamon, and walnuts until completely blended. Drop by measuring tablespoonfuls onto the ungreased baking sheets, spacing the drops about 1 inch apart.

3. Bake for 15 to 20 minutes until lightly browned. Reverse the baking sheets on the racks and from front to back once during baking. With a wide turner, immediately transfer the cookies to wire racks to cool completely.

4. Store in a tightly covered container.

Yield: About 36 cookies

Nutrition information per cookie: 91 calories; 2 grams protein; 9 grams carbohydrate; 6 grams fat; 0 milligrams cholesterol; 33 milligrams sodium.

Oatmeal-Apple-Raisin Cookies

You can feel good about giving these cookies to your kids. I considered adding a little toasted wheat germ (about a tablespoon to the dry ingredients), but then didn't. You can, if you want to. It certainly won't hurt.

- 1 1/2 cups regular or quick-cooking (not instant) rolled oats
- 3/4 cup all-purpose flour
- 1/2 cup whole wheat flour
- 3/4 teaspoon baking soda
- 1/2 teaspoon salt
- 1/2 teaspoon ground cinnamon
- 1/2 teaspoon ground cardamom
- 1/8 teaspoon ground nutmeg
- 1/8 teaspoon ground cloves
- 1/2 cup plus 2 tablespoons (1 1/4 sticks) salted butter or margarine, at room temperature
- 1 cup plus 2 tablespoons packed light brown sugar
- 1 large egg
- 1/2 cup shredded peeled apple
- 1 teaspoon vanilla extract
- 1 cup dark or golden raisins

1. Adjust two racks to divide the oven into thirds. Preheat the oven to 350°. Lightly grease two baking sheets.

2. In a large bowl, with a whisk, combine the oats, all-purpose flour, whole wheat flour, baking soda, salt, and spices until mixed.

3. In a medium-size bowl, with an electric mixer at medium-high speed, beat the butter and brown sugar until very creamy, 2 to 3 minutes. Beat in the egg, apple, and vanilla until very well blended. Gradually add the flour mixture, beating just until blended. With a mixing spoon, stir in the raisins until they are well distributed throughout the batter. Drop by rounded teaspoonfuls onto the prepared baking sheets, spacing the drops about 2 inches apart.

4. Bake for about 10 minutes, or until the edges are golden brown. Reverse the baking sheets on the racks and from front to back once during baking. With a wide turner, immediately transfer the cookies to wire racks to cool completely.

5. Store in a tightly covered container, separating the layers with sheets of waxed paper.

Yield: About 60 cookies

Nutrition information per cookie: 60 calories; 1 gram protein; 10 grams carbohydrate; 2 grams fat; 9 milligrams cholesterol; 53 milligrams sodium.

Zero-Fat Chewy Chocolate Cookies

If you know someone who is on a severely restricted, low-fat diet, these cookies would be deeply appreciated. They have a richness and depth of flavor that is almost always missing in fat-free baked goods. The chewiness of these cookies depends on not overbaking them, so watch carefully toward the end of baking time. This recipe is so remarkable that I feel compelled to give praise and thanks to Jane Uetz and the home economists in the test kitchens at Best Foods for having developed it.

> 1 ½ **cups all-purpose flour**
> ½ **cup sugar**
> ½ **cup unsweetened cocoa powder**
> ½ **teaspoon baking soda**
> ½ **teaspoon salt**
> ½ **cup light or dark corn syrup**
> 3 **large egg whites**
> **Confectioners' sugar, for dusting cookies**

1. Adjust one rack to the lowest oven position. Preheat the oven to 350°. Lightly coat two baking sheets with vegetable cooking spray.

2. In a large bowl, with a whisk, combine the flour, sugar, cocoa, baking soda, and salt until thoroughly mixed. With a mixing spoon, stir in the corn syrup and egg whites until thoroughly blended. The dough will be thick and slightly sticky. Drop the dough by rounded measuring teaspoonfuls onto one of the prepared baking sheets, spacing them about 1 inch apart. (Bake one batch at a time. The second sheet of cookies can be prepared while the first is baking.)

3. Bake for 7 to 9 minutes just until set. The cookies will be soft when lightly pressed. (Be careful not to overbake them.) Reverse the baking sheet from front to back once during baking. With a wide turner, immediately transfer the cookies to wire racks to cool completely. Dust very lightly with confectioners' sugar before serving.

4. Store in an airtight container for up to 3 days. For longer storage, freeze in zipper-top plastic bags for up to six months.

Yield: About 30 cookies

Nutrition information per cookie: 60 calories; 1 gram protein; 13 grams carbohydrate; 0 grams fat; 0 milligrams cholesterol; 61 milligrams sodium.

Tip

To coat cookies evenly with confectioners' sugar, place the sugar and the warm cookies together in a brown bag and gently shake the bag up and down.

Low-Cal Black-and-White Cookies

A traditional recipe for these favorite cookies appears elsewhere in this book. Consult the index.

> One 18$^1/_4$- or 18$^1/_2$-ounce box light yellow cake mix
> $^1/_2$ cup low-fat lemon yogurt
> 3 large egg whites

Icings

> 1 cup confectioners' sugar
> 2 tablespoons light corn syrup
> 1 tablespoon plus $^1/_2$ to 1 teaspoon milk
> $^1/_4$ cup semisweet chocolate chips, melted (page 12)

1. Adjust two racks to divide the oven into thirds. Preheat the oven to 350°. Coat two baking sheets with nonstick cooking spray.

2. In a large bowl, with a mixing spoon, combine the cake mix, yogurt, and egg whites. With an electric mixer at low speed, beat until well blended, 1 to 2 minutes. Increase the speed to medium and beat 2 minutes longer. Drop by $^1/_4$ cupfuls onto the prepared baking sheets, spacing the drops about 3 inches apart.

3. Bake for 15 to 20 minutes until light golden. Reverse the baking sheets on the racks and from front to back once during baking. Set the baking pans on wire racks until the cookies are completely cool.

4. While the cookies are cooling, make the icings. In a small bowl, stir together the confectioners' sugar, corn syrup, and 1 tablespoon of the milk. Pour half of this mixture into another small bowl and stir in the melted chocolate chips. If needed, add another $^1/_4$ to $^1/_2$ teaspoon of milk to either icing for a good spreading consistency.

5. With a small icing spatula or a butter spreader, coat half of the flat bottom side of each cookie with the white icing; coat the other half with chocolate icing. Set aside until the icing is firm, 15 to 30 minutes.

6. Store in a tightly covered container, separating the layers with sheets of waxed paper.

Yield: About 14 cookies

Nutrition information per cookie: 216 calories; 2 grams protein; 44 grams carbohydrate; 3 grams fat; 1 milligram cholesterol; 286 milligrams sodium.

Low-Fat Ginger Cookies

These are nice little cookies to have in the jar. They have lots of intense flavor and just enough fat to appease a craving for "something good."

> $^1/_4$ cup granulated sugar (optional)
> 3 cups uncooked oat-bran cereal
> $^3/_4$ cup all-purpose flour
> 1 teaspoon baking soda
> 2 teaspoons ground ginger
> 1 teaspoon ground cinnamon
> $^3/_4$ cup packed light or dark brown sugar
> $^1/_2$ cup light corn syrup
> $^1/_2$ cup (1 stick) salted margarine or butter, at room temperature
> 2 large egg whites

1. Adjust two racks to divide the oven into thirds. Preheat the oven to 350°. Have ready two ungreased baking sheets. If using the granulated sugar, sprinkle it onto a sheet of waxed paper.

2. In a medium-size bowl, with a whisk, combine the oat bran, flour, baking soda, ginger, and cinnamon until thoroughly mixed.

3. In a large bowl, with an electric mixer at medium-high speed, beat together the brown sugar, corn syrup, and margarine until very well blended. Add the egg whites and beat until well blended. With the mixer at medium-low speed, gradually add the flour mixture, beating just until blended. Scoop heaping measuring teaspoonfuls of the dough out of the bowl and roll into 1-inch balls between the palms of your hands. Roll the balls in the granulated sugar. As you roll them, arrange the balls on the ungreased baking sheets,

spacing them about 2 inches apart. With your fingers gently flatten each ball into a 2-inch round.

4. Bake for 11 to 13 minutes until light golden brown. Reverse the baking sheets on the racks from front to back once during baking. Cool for 1 minute on the baking sheets. With a wide turner, transfer the cookies to wire racks to cool completely.

5. Store in a tightly covered container.

Yield: About 42 cookies

Nutrition information per cookie: 82 calories; 3 grams fat; 13 grams carbohydrates; 0 milligrams cholesterol (if using margarine); 2 grams protein; 50 milligrams sodium.

Peanut Butter Shortbread

A true Scotsman would probably faint at this version of shortbread, flavored with peanut butter, of all things, and much lower in fat than a real shortbread. But don't expect it to have the same melt-in-the-mouth, crumbly texture as the real thing, which has an even higher ratio of butter to flour.

> $^1/_2$ **cup (1 stick) salted margarine or butter, at room temperature**
>
> $^1/_2$ **cup sugar**
>
> $^1/_4$ **cup smooth peanut butter**
>
> **2 cups all-purpose flour**
>
> **2 tablespoons superfine sugar, for sprinkling on shortbread**

1. Adjust two racks to divide the oven into thirds. Preheat the oven to 300°. Lightly grease two 8-inch-round cake pans.

2. In a large bowl, with an electric mixer at medium speed, beat together the margarine, sugar, and peanut butter until smooth, about 1 minute. With your fingertips, blend in the flour until the mixture resembles coarse meal. Gather the dough together and gently press into a ball.

3. Divide the dough in half. Press each half of the dough evenly into the bottom of the prepared

cake pans. With the tines of a dinner fork, press the outer edges to form a decorative pattern. With the tip of a knife, lightly score each pan of shortbread into 8 wedges. Sprinkle the top of each evenly with superfine sugar.

4. Stagger the pans on the oven racks and bake for about 45 minutes until very lightly browned. Reverse the pans on the racks once during baking. With the tip of a sharp knife, immediately cut each pan or shortbread into wedges on the score marks. Set the pans on wire racks to cool completely.

5. Store in a tightly covered container.

Yield: 16 cookies

Nutrition information per cookie: 155 calories; 8 grams fat; 19 grams carbohydrates; 0 milligrams cholesterol (if using margarine); 3 grams protein; 19 milligrams sodium.

Granny's Graham Crackers

These are not going to taste like the graham crackers you snacked on in grade school with a carton of milk. They have a rough-and-ready texture with lots of wheat flavor, and have a better-developed taste after they have been allowed to languish in the cookie jar for a couple of days.

    1 tablespoon cider vinegar
    1 cup heavy (whipping) cream
    1 cup sugar
    2 tablespoons salted butter or margarine, melted
    1 teaspoon baking soda
    3 to 4 cups whole wheat flour

1. Adjust two racks to divide the oven into thirds. Preheat the oven to 450°. Lightly grease two baking sheets.

2. In a large bowl, stir the vinegar into the cream. Set aside until the cream thickens and turns sour, about 5 minutes. With a mixing spoon, stir in the sugar, melted butter, and baking soda, stirring until the mixture is very well blended, about 2 minutes. Gradually stir in 3 cups of the flour, stirring just until blended. Add as much more flour as necessary until the dough comes together and leaves the side of the bowl.

3. On a lightly floured surface, roll the dough into a 20 × 12-inch rectangle. With a pizza wheel or the tip of a sharp knife and a ruler cut the dough into 2 × 3-inch rectangles. Prick the cookies all over with the tines of a fork. Arrange the cookies on the prepared baking sheets, spacing them about 1½ inches apart.

4. Bake for 10 to 12 minutes until nicely browned and firm when lightly touched. Reverse the baking sheets on the racks and from front to back once during baking. With a wide turner, immediately transfer the cookies to wire racks to cool completely.

5. Store in a tightly covered container.

Yield: About 40 cookies

Nutrition information per cookie: 75 calories; 1 gram protein; 11 grams carbohydrate; 3 grams fat; 10 milligrams cholesterol; 29 milligrams sodium.

Peach Crunchies

I consider these bars to be quite a healthful snack, even though they do contain margarine or butter. There's less than a teaspoon per bar, which does contribute quite a lot to the flavor.

    2 cups granola
    1 cup all-purpose flour
    1 cup whole wheat flour
    ½ cup packed dark brown sugar
    ½ cup honey
    ½ cup (1 stick) salted or unsalted butter or margarine, melted
    ⅔ cup peach or apricot preserves

1. Adjust one rack to divide the oven in half. Preheat the oven to 325°. Lightly grease an 11 × 7-inch glass baking dish.

2. In a large bowl, with a whisk, combine the granola, all-purpose flour, whole wheat flour, and brown sugar until thoroughly mixed. With a mixing spoon, stir in the honey and melted butter until well blended. The mixture will be crumbly. Press half of the granola mixture into the prepared baking dish. Spread the preserves evenly over the top. Sprinkle the remaining granola mixture evenly over the preserves.

3. Bake for 30 minutes until the granola topping is nicely browned. Reverse the baking dish from front to back once during baking. Set the pan on a wire rack to cool completely before cutting into 6 × 5 rows.

4. Store in the baking pan, tightly covered with aluminum foil or plastic wrap.

Yield: 30 bars

Nutrition information per bar: 142 calories; 2 grams protein; 24 grams carbohydrate; 5 grams fat; 9 milligrams cholesterol; 37 milligrams sodium.

Cut the Fat, Hang on to the Flavor

The tips that follow will help you increase the nutrition or reduce the fat and calories in many cookie recipes:

- Up to one-fourth of the all-purpose flour in any cookie recipe can be replaced with whole wheat flour.

- Up to 1 cup of wheat germ can be substituted for 1 cup of flour in any cookie recipe.

- Two egg whites can be substituted for one whole egg, or an egg substitute can be substituted for whole eggs, measure for measure.

- Sugar substitutes cannot be used in place of natural sweeteners. Recipes for artificially sweetened baked goods must be specially formulated.

- Chocolate chips, nuts, and other high-fat stir-ins can be replaced with chopped dried fruit or even soft, fat-free candies. (Consider the more exotic dried fruits, such as cherries, blueberries, or cranberries.)

- Substitute half the amount of miniature chocolate chips for the whole amount of regular-size chips. The little chips give the illusion of more chocolate because they can be better distributed throughout the batter.

- Prune, date, and fig purees can almost always be substituted for the fat in any baking recipe, measure for measure. To make dried-fruit puree, combine 1 cup (about 6 ounces, pitted, if necessary) chopped, dried fruit in a blender or food processor with ¹/₄ cup water. Process until reasonably smooth. The yield is just about 1 cup, which can be used, for instance, in place of 2 sticks of butter or margarine, or solid shortening, or oil. Miraculous, isn't it? The puree can also be substituted for half of the fat instead of all of it for richer flavor.

- Use unflavored or butter-flavored nonstick vegetable spray to grease baking sheets and baking pans.

- And the easiest way of all to cut the fat in half in any cookie recipe: Make the cookies or bars only half the size that the recipe calls for.

One-Bowl Vanilla-Chip Lemon Bars

These are not only reasonably low in fat, but they're also easy to make.

> 1 ¹/₄ cups all-purpose flour, divided
> 1 cup sugar, divided
> ¹/₃ cup (¹/₂ stick plus 1 ¹/₂ tablespoons) salted butter or margarine, at room temperature
> ³/₄ cup vanilla-flavored white baking pieces
> ¹/₂ cup egg substitute
> ¹/₄ cup strained fresh lemon juice
> 2 teaspoons finely shredded and minced lemon zest
> Confectioners' sugar

1. Adjust one rack to divide the oven in half. Preheat the oven to 350°. Have ready a 9-inch-square metal baking pan.

2. In a medium-size bowl, with a whisk, combine 1 cup of the flour and ¹/₄ cup of the sugar until thoroughly mixed. With a pastry blender or two knives used in a crisscross fashion, cut in the butter until the mixture resembles coarse crumbs. Press this mixture into the bottom of the ungreased pan. Bake for 15 minutes or until lightly browned. Remove from the oven and immediately sprinkle evenly with the white baking pieces; set aside.

3. In the same medium-size bowl, stir together the egg substitute, lemon juice, lemon zest, the remaining ¹/₄ cup flour, and the remaining ³/₄ cup sugar. Pour evenly over the baking pieces.

4. Bake for 15 minutes until set. Reverse the baking pan from front to back once during baking. Cool for about 5 minutes in the pan set on a wire rack, then sprinkle with confectioners' sugar. Cool completely before cutting into 6 × 6 rows.

5. Store in the baking pan, tightly covered with aluminum foil or plastic wrap.

Yield: 36 bars

Nutrition information per bar: 72 calories; 1 gram protein; 10 grams carbohydrate; 3 grams fat; 5 milligrams cholesterol; 25 milligrams sodium.

Low-Fat, Extremely Fudgy Brownies

No one believes me when I tell them the fat content of these fabulous brownies. I'm not usually a big fan of low-fat. But, quite honestly, I'd just as soon eat these brownies as any other. This is another recipe that is so good that I must give credit to the California Date Administration Committee, which developed the recipe.

³/₄ cup unsweetened cocoa powder

¹/₂ cup all-purpose flour

¹/₂ teaspoon baking soda

¹/₂ teaspoon salt

6 ounces (1 cup) pitted California dates

¹/₄ cup water

2 tablespoons canola oil

1 cup sugar

1 large egg

1 teaspoon vanilla extract

¹/₄ cup semisweet chocolate chips

2 tablespoons chopped walnuts

1. Adjust one rack to divide the oven in half. Preheat the oven to 350°. Lightly coat an 8- or 9-inch square metal baking pan with vegetable cooking spray.

2. In a medium-size bowl, with a whisk, combine the cocoa, flour, baking soda, and salt until thoroughly mixed.

3. In a food processor fitted with a steel blade, combine the dates and water; process until smooth (you should have about ³/₄ cup of purée).

4. In a large bowl, with an electric mixer at medium speed, beat together the date puree, oil, sugar, egg, and vanilla until thoroughly blended. With the mixer at medium-low speed, gradually add the flour mixture, beating until well blended. With a mixing spoon, stir in the chocolate chips. Spread the batter into the prepared pan, smoothing the top with the back of the spoon. Sprinkle evenly with the walnuts.

5. Bake for 25 to 35 minutes just until the center springs back when lightly touched. Reverse the pan from front to back once during baking. Cool in the pan on a wire rack before cutting into 4 × 4 rows.

Yield: 16 bars

Nutrition information per bar: 130 calories; 2 grams protein; 26 grams carbohydrates; 3 grams fat; 15 milligrams cholesterol; 133 milligrams sodium.

(Almost) Guilt-Free Brownies

Although not quite as chewy and gooey as Low-Fat, Extremely Fudgy Brownies, these brownies are a little quicker and a little easier to make. One of these brownies, served with a dollop of frozen vanilla yogurt and a couple of tablespoons of chocolate syrup, makes a terrific dessert. I know because I eat this combination often. (Surprisingly, chocolate syrup—at least Hershey's—contains only a minuscule amount of fat.)

3 ounces (3 squares) unsweetened chocolate

1 cup sugar

³/₄ cup all-purpose flour

³/₄ cup nonfat cottage cheese

3 large egg whites

1 teaspoon vanilla extract

¹/₄ teaspoon salt

Confectioners' sugar, for sprinkling on brownies

1. Adjust one rack to divide the oven in half. Preheat the oven to 350°. Lightly coat an 8-inch-square metal baking pan with nonstick vegetable cooking spray.

2. In a small saucepan set over very low heat, melt the chocolate, stirring constantly until smooth. Remove from the heat and set aside to cool slightly.

3. In the container of a food processor fitted with a steel blade, process together the sugar, flour, cottage cheese, egg whites, vanilla, and salt until

smooth. Add the cooled chocolate and process briefly to blend thoroughly. Turn the batter into the prepared pan, smoothing the top with the back of a spoon.

4. Bake for 20 to 25 minutes until the edges look dry and the center feels firm to the touch. Reverse the pan from front to back once during baking. Set the pan on a wire rack to cool completely before cutting into 4 × 4 rows.

5. Store in a tightly covered container, separating the layers with sheets of waxed paper. Sprinkle lightly with confectioners' sugar just before serving.

Yield: 16 bars

Nutrition information per bar: 108 calories; 3 grams protein; 19 grams carbohydrate; 3 grams fat; 1 milligram cholesterol; 87 milligrams sodium.

California Dried Fruit Bars

If you look at this recipe carefully, you will recognize it as a version of the chocolate-chip cookie, with lots of dried fruit instead of the chips and most of the nuts. (You can omit the nuts and reduce the fat a little more, if you want to.)

> 1 ³/₄ cups all-purpose flour
> ¹/₂ teaspoon baking powder
> ¹/₂ teaspoon salt
> ¹/₄ teaspoon ground cinnamon
> ¹/₈ teaspoon ground nutmeg
> ¹/₃ cup golden raisins
> ¹/₃ cup dried apricots, coarsely chopped
> ¹/₃ cup pitted prunes, coarsely chopped
> ¹/₂ cup (1 stick) salted margarine or butter, at room temperature
> 1 cup packed light brown sugar
> 1 large egg
> 1 teaspoon vanilla extract
> ¹/₂ cup coarsely chopped pecans

1. Adjust one rack to divide the oven in half. Preheat the oven to 350° (or 325° if using a glass baking dish). Lightly grease a 13 × 9-inch metal baking pan or glass baking dish.

2. In a medium-size bowl, with a whisk, combine the flour, baking powder, salt, cinnamon, and nutmeg until thoroughly mixed.

3. In a small bowl, combine the raisins, apricots, and prunes. Toss 1 tablespoon of the flour mixture with the fruit.

4. In a large bowl, with an electric mixer at medium-high speed, beat together the margarine, brown sugar, egg, and vanilla until light and fluffy, 2 to 3 minutes. With a mixing spoon, stir in the flour mixture until well combined. (The batter will be very dry and stiff.) Stir in the dried-fruit mixture and the nuts until well distributed throughout the dough. Turn the dough into the prepared pan, patting it down evenly with your fingers.

5. Bake for 18 to 20 minutes until the edges begin to brown slightly. Reverse the pan from front to back once during baking. Cool in the pan on a wire rack before cutting into 6 × 4 rows.

6. Store in the baking pan, tightly covered with plastic wrap or aluminum foil.

Yield: 24 bars

Nutrition information per bar: 141 calories; 2 grams protein; 21 grams carbohydrate; 6 grams fat; 20 milligrams cholesterol; 122 milligrams sodium.

High-Low-No Pistachio and Oat Bran Bars

High fiber, low sodium, no cholesterol. These are great backpack bars and provide quick energy for runners, hikers, and bikers.

  1 cup chopped California pistachios, divided
  1 cup oat bran
  1 cup whole wheat flour
  1 1/2 teaspoons baking soda
  1/2 cup regular or unsulphured molasses
  1 1/3 cups boiling water
  1/2 cup raisins or chopped pitted prunes
  1 tablespoon vegetable oil

1. Adjust one rack to divide the oven in half. Preheat the oven to 350° (or 325° if using a glass baking dish). Coat an 8-inch-square metal baking pan or 9-inch-square glass baking dish with nonstick cooking spray.

2. In a large bowl, with a mixing spoon, combine 3/4 cup of the pistachios with the oat bran, whole wheat flour, baking soda, molasses, boiling water, raisins, and oil until very well blended. Turn the batter into the prepared pan, smoothing the top with the back of the spoon.

3. Bake for 30 minutes until the center is set. Reverse the pan from front to back once during baking. Set the pan on a wire rack to cool completely before cutting into 4 × 4 rows.

4. Store in the baking pan, tightly covered with aluminum foil or plastic wrap.

Yield: 16 bars

Nutrition information per bar: 140 calories; 3 grams protein; 21 grams carbohydrate; 6 grams fat; 0 milligrams cholesterol; 142 milligrams sodium.

Tip

Confectioners' sugar sticks better to the cookies if they are sprinkled while still warm from the oven.

Pat Baird's Old-Fashioned Raisin Bars

When I told Pat that I was writing a 400-cookie cookbook, she immediately offered to contribute a recipe and this is it. "Only 399 to go," she wrote at the top of the recipe. Pat is a registered dietitian and is frequently called upon by members of the food industry for her opinions and advice in matters of nutrition, especially when taste-appeal and convenience matter. Pat uses applesauce in these bars to replace fat and add moisture.

  1 3/4 cups all-purpose flour
  2 teaspoons pumpkin pie spice
  1 teaspoon baking soda
  1/4 teaspoon salt
  1 1/4 cups applesauce
  2 tablespoons vegetable oil
  1 cup packed light brown sugar
  1 cup raisins
  1 teaspoon shredded and minced orange zest
  Confectioners' sugar, for sprinkling on bars

1. Adjust one rack to divide the oven in half. Preheat the oven to 350° (or 325° if using a glass baking dish). Lightly grease a 13 × 9-inch metal baking pan or glass baking dish.

2. In a large bowl, with a whisk, combine the flour, pumpkin pie spice, baking soda, and salt until thoroughly mixed.

3. In a medium-size bowl, with an electric mixer at low speed, beat together the applesauce, oil, brown sugar, raisins, and orange zest until well combined. Gradually add the flour mixture, beating just until blended. Turn the batter into the prepared pan, smoothing the top with the back of a spoon.

4. Bake for 25 to 30 minutes until a wooden pick inserted in the center comes out clean. Reverse the pan from front to back once during baking. Set the pan on a wire rack to cool completely before cutting into 7 × 4 rows.

5. Store in the baking pan, tightly covered with aluminum foil or plastic wrap. Just before serving, sprinkle with confectioners' sugar.

Yield: 28 bars

Nutrition information per bar: 94 calories; 1 gram protein; 21 grams carbohydrate; 1 gram fat; 0 milligrams cholesterol; 53 milligrams sodium.

No-Bake Raisin-Peanut Bars

Kids not only like these, but they can also help to make them.

> **2 tablespoons salted or unsalted margarine**
> **¹/₄ cup sugar**
> **¹/₄ cup honey**
> **2 cups cornflakes cereal**
> **1 cup raisins**
> **¹/₃ cup coarsely chopped, dry-roasted, unsalted peanuts**

1. Coat a 9-inch-square metal baking pan or glass baking dish with vegetable cooking spray.

2. In a medium-size saucepan, combine the margarine, sugar, and honey. Bring to a boil over medium-high heat, stirring constantly. Reduce the heat and simmer, stirring, for 3 minutes. Remove from the heat and stir in the cornflakes, raisins, and peanuts until well coated. Press this mixture evenly in the prepared baking pan. Set aside until cool and firm, 1 to 2 hours. Cut into 9 × 3 rows.

Yield: 27 bars

Nutrition information per bar: 56 calories; 1 gram protein; 10 grams carbohydrate; 2 grams fat; 0 milligrams cholesterol; 29 milligrams sodium.

SAVORY COOKIES AND CRACKERS

You know my theory by now, at least if you have worked your way from the front to the back of this book: If it looks like a cookie, and it tastes like a cookie, then it must be a cookie. Sugar, in my opinion, should not be the sole criterion for what constitutes a cookie.

Mary Murray's Crispy Cocktail Cookies

Mary trots out these savory cookies to accompany predinner drinks. I am honored to be able to use this recipe, because Mary has never before shared it, at least for publication.

> **³/₄ cup plus 2 tablespoons all-purpose flour, divided**
> **2 cups shredded sharp white cheddar cheese**
> **¹/₂ cup (1 stick) unsalted butter or margarine, at room temperature**
> **1 teaspoon Worcestershire sauce**
> **¹/₈ teaspoon liquid red-pepper seasoning**
> **2 cups crisp rice cereal**

1. Adjust two racks to divide the oven into thirds. Preheat the oven to 375°. Lightly grease two baking sheets. Sprinkle 2 tablespoons of the flour on a sheet of waxed paper.

2. In a large bowl, with an electric mixer at medium speed, beat together the cheese, butter, Worcestershire sauce, and red-pepper seasoning until thoroughly combined. With the mixer at low speed, gradually add the remaining ³/₄ cup flour, beating just until blended. With your fingertips, mix the cereal into the dough until well blended. Pinch off pieces of the dough and roll them into 1¹/₂-inch balls between the palms of your hands. Arrange the balls on the prepared baking sheets, spacing them about 2 inches apart. Flatten each ball with the back of a dinner fork, dipping the back of the tines into the flour on the waxed paper to keep the fork from sticking to the dough.

3. Bake for 10 to 12 minutes, or until golden brown. Reverse the baking sheets on the racks and from front to back once during baking. With a wide turner, immediately transfer the cookies to wire racks to cool completely.

4. Store in an airtight container.

Yield: About 30 cookies

Soda Crackers

I do believe the word *Saltines* has been trade-marked, but that is what these are, or at least what soda crackers used to be before they became a packaged product.

    3 1/2 cups all-purpose flour, divided
    One 1/4-ounce package fast-rising yeast
    1/2 teaspoon sugar
    1/2 teaspoon baking soda
    1/2 teaspoon salt
    2/3 cup water
    1/4 cup vegetable oil
    1 egg white beaten with 1 tablespoon water
    Coarse salt

1. In a large bowl, with a whisk, combine 2 cups of the flour, yeast, sugar, baking soda, and salt until thoroughly mixed.

2. In a small saucepan, combine the water and oil. Cook over medium heat until very warm (120° to 130°). With a mixing spoon, immediately stir into the flour mixture until well blended. Gradually add enough of the remaining flour to make a stiff dough.

3. Turn the dough out onto a lightly floured surface. Knead until smooth and elastic, adding more flour as needed. Cover and let stand 20 minutes.

4. On a lightly floured surface, roll the dough into a 12 × 10-inch rectangle. Brush off excess flour. Fold the dough crosswise into thirds to form a 10 × 4-inch rectangle. Repeat the procedure of rolling into a 12 × 10-inch rectangle and folding into thirds two more times for a total of three times. Cover the dough and let rest 10 minutes.

5. Adjust two racks to divide the oven into thirds. Preheat the oven to 350°. Lightly grease two baking sheets.

6. Divide the dough into thirds. On a lightly floured surface, roll one third of the dough to a 14 × 10-inch rectangle. With a pizza wheel or the tip of a knife and a ruler, cut the dough into 2-inch squares. Prick each cracker several times with the tines of a fork. Arrange the squares on the prepared baking sheets, spacing them about 1 inch apart. Repeat with the remaining dough. Brush the top of each cracker with the egg white mixture. Sprinkle with salt to taste.

7. Bake for 8 to 10 minutes until barely light brown. Reverse the baking sheets on the racks from front to back once during baking. With a wide turner, immediately transfer the crackers to wire racks to cool completely.

8. Store in a tightly covered container.

Yield: About 120 crackers

Variations

Other toppings: Instead of salt, sprinkle the crackers with grated Parmesan cheese, toasted wheat germ, toasted sesame seeds, or dried herbs or seeds.

Cheese Bites

These biscuitlike cookies are particularly nice to serve with before-dinner drinks. They are quite rich, so you don't have to worry about spreading them with anything. They are also a good accompaniment for soup or salad.

    5 ounces (half of a 10-ounce bar) extra-sharp
        cheddar cheese, cut into pieces
    1/2 cup (1 stick) salted or unsalted butter or
        margarine, at room temperature
    1 cup all-purpose flour
    1/8 teaspoon paprika
    1/2 teaspoon Worcestershire sauce
    1/2 teaspoon liquid red- or green-pepper
        seasoning

1. Place the cheese pieces in the container of a food processor or blender. Process until very finely chopped, almost to the point of being ground.

2. In a medium-size bowl, with a mixing spoon, combine the chopped cheese, butter, flour, paprika, Worcestershire sauce, and pepper seasoning

until very well blended. Gather the mixture into a ball and divide it into quarters.

3. On an unfloured surface, roll and shape each quarter into a 10-inch cylinder. Wrap the cylinders separately in plastic wrap and refrigerate until very cold, about 2 hours. (At this point, the dough can be tightly wrapped in aluminum foil and refrigerated for up to one week or frozen for up to three months. If frozen, thaw in the refrigerator before proceeding.)

4. When ready to bake, adjust two racks to divide the oven into thirds. Preheat the oven to 350°. Lightly grease two baking sheets.

5. With a long, sharp knife, cut the cylinders into 1/4-inch slices. Arrange the slices on the prepared baking sheets, spacing them about 1 inch apart.

6. Bake for 10 to 12 minutes until firm and golden. Reverse the baking sheets on the racks and from front to back once during baking. With a wide turner, immediately transfer the cookies to wire racks to cool completely.

7. Store in a tightly covered container for up to two weeks. Freeze for longer storage and thaw at room temperature.

Yield: About 264 crackers

Cornmeal Crispies

I keep these frozen in small batches in zipper-top plastic bags. Then, when I need a good, crisp, fresh-tasting cracker, I pull out a bag or two and in just a few minutes they are at room temperature and ready to serve.

> **1 cup all-purpose flour**
> **1/2 cup yellow cornmeal**
> **1/2 teaspoon salt**
> **1/8 teaspoon pepper**
> **5 tablespoons (1/2 stick plus 1 tablespoon) cold salted butter or margarine, cut into pieces**
> **1/2 cup shredded cheddar cheese**
> **1/4 cup milk**

1. Adjust two racks to divide the oven into thirds. Preheat the oven to 350°. Lightly grease two baking sheets. Have ready a 1½-inch round biscuit or cookie cutter.

2. In a medium-size bowl, with a whisk, combine the flour, cornmeal, salt, and pepper until thoroughly mixed. With a pastry blender or two knives used in a crisscross fashion, cut the butter into the flour mixture until the mixture resembles coarse crumbs. With a dinner fork, stir in the cheese and milk until the mixture is moist and holds together. Turn out onto a lightly floured surface and knead about 15 times. Divide the dough into quarters.

3. On a lightly floured surface, roll each quarter to a 1/4-inch thickness. Cut into as many rounds as possible with the biscuit cutter, placing each one as it is cut on a prepared baking sheet.

4. Bake for 12 to 15 minutes until crisp and lightly browned. Reverse the baking sheets on the racks and from front to back once during baking. With a wide turner immediately transfer the cookies to wire racks to cool completely.

5. Store in a tightly covered container for up to two weeks. Freeze for longer storage and thaw at room temperature.

Yield: About 48 crackers

Chile-Cheese Biscotti

I became so intrigued with the seemingly limitless possibilities of biscotti during the testing and writing of this book that I asked Annie Bailey, who developed all of the biscotti recipes, if she could do a savory version. In her notes at the top of the recipe, she says the results are somewhere between a biscotti and a breadstick, good enough to eat on their own, but also great with drinks. According to Annie, you can underbake the slices by a few minutes and they will be more like breadsticks, crisp on the outside and soft and breadlike on the inside.

    3 1/4 cups all-purpose flour
    1 tablespoon baking powder
    1 teaspoon salt
    1/2 teaspoon black pepper
    1/4 cup (1/2 stick) salted butter or margarine,
        at room temperature
    1 cup shredded Monterey Jack cheese
    1 cup grated Parmesan cheese
    One 7 1/2-ounce can diced green chilies, very
        well drained
    1 large egg, at room temperature
    2/3 cup whole milk

1. Adjust two racks to divide the oven into thirds. Lightly grease two large baking sheets; set aside.

2. In a medium-size bowl, with a whisk, combine the flour, baking powder, salt, and pepper until thoroughly mixed.

3. In a large bowl, with an electric mixer at medium-high speed, beat together the butter, jack cheese, and Parmesan cheese until very well blended, 2 to 3 minutes. Add the chilies, egg, and milk and beat at medium speed until well blended. Gradually add the flour mixture, beating just until blended. The dough will be slightly sticky. Lightly cover the bowl and chill the dough until cold and firm, about 1 hour.

4. Preheat the oven to 350°.

5. Divide the chilled dough into quarters. On each prepared baking sheet shape two pieces of the dough into two 9-inch logs about 4 inches apart. With your hands, pat and shape each log into a 9 × 3-inch loaf.

6. Bake for 30 to 35 minutes, or until a toothpick inserted in the center comes out clean. Reverse the baking sheets on the racks and from front to back once during baking. Transfer the loaves to wire racks to cool for 15 minutes.

7. On a cutting surface, with a long, sharp knife, cut each loaf into 1/2-inch diagonal slices (see illustration on page 223). Place the slices cut side down on the same baking sheets. (It's okay if they overlap a little.) Bake for about 20 minutes, or until golden and crisp, turning the slices once and reversing the baking sheets on the racks and from front to back once during baking. With a wide turner, immediately transfer the biscotti to wire racks to cool completely.

8. Store in a tightly covered container.

Yield: About 56 biscotti

Linda Greenhouse's Matzo

You don't have to be Jewish to love matzo—or to bake it. Some years ago, my good friends and neighbors Linda and Barry Greenhouse prepared a Seder dinner for Passover and invited my husband, Gerry, and me to join them and their families. Linda, who is a truly gifted cook, was not content to merely serve packaged matzo. She decided to make her own. She did and this is the recipe. Besides being an important religious symbol, matzo is wonderful to use as a plain cracker, spread with almost anything you like. If you want to, I suppose there is no reason you couldn't stir some dried or fresh herbs into the batter, or to sprinkle the matzo with a little salt when you turn it to bake the second side.

    About 2 cups unbleached all-purpose flour
    1/2 teaspoon salt (optional)
    1/2 to 3/4 cup water

1. Adjust one rack to the lower third of the oven. Preheat the oven to 500°. Have ready two ungreased baking sheets.

2. If using the salt, in a very large, wide bowl, with a whisk, combine the flour and the salt until thoroughly mixed. Otherwise, simply place the flour in the bowl. Gather the flour into a mound in the bowl and make a little crater in the center. Add ½ cup of the water and stir the mixture with a fork, gradually bringing in the flour from around the side of the bowl. Add more water, as needed, just enough to make a soft and very slightly sticky dough.

3. Turn the dough onto a lightly floured surface and knead it about 10 times, adding a little more flour, if necessary, so that it can be rolled easily. Don't overdo the kneading, since you don't want to get the gluten in the flour all agitated. Divide the dough into quarters.

4. On a lightly floured surface, roll each quarter of the dough to a 7-inch round that is no more than ⅛ inch thick and preferably a little thinner. (Some unevenness around the edge is to be expected, and marks it as true, homemade matzo.) With the tines of a dinner fork, prick the round all over, right down to the work surface. This helps the matzo bake evenly and prevents it from bubbling and buckling. Roll the dough onto the rolling pin. Unroll it onto the center of one of the ungreased baking sheets.

5. Bake one sheet at a time for about 10 minutes until the matzo shows some brownish patches and looks very dry. With a wide turner, flip the matzo to the other side and bake for 5 to 8 minutes until a light, golden brown. With a wide turner, transfer the matzo to a wire rack to cool completely.

6. While the first matzo is baking, make the second matzo and have it ready to go into the oven as soon as the first one comes out. Do not roll the matzo dough until you are ready to bake it.

7. To store, wrap the matzo loosely in aluminum foil. It can be recrisped, if necessary, in a 350° oven for about 3 minutes.

Yield: 4 matzos

Tip

Short on baking sheets? Turn over metal jelly-roll pans, large roasting pans, pizza pans, lasagna pans, etc. Cover with aluminum foil, shiny side up, and bake away!

Linda Greenhouse's Lavash

Linda decided to make her own lavash while we were all on a Middle Eastern restaurant kick a number of years ago. She succeeded admirably, of course. This Middle Eastern sesame cracker should be baked on the floor of a gas oven to simulate a brick oven. These turn out much better and it is certainly less time-consuming to make the lavash in a gas oven rather than in an electric oven.

> About 5 cups unbleached all-purpose flour
>
> 1 envelope dry yeast
>
> 2 teaspoons salt
>
> 1 teaspoon sugar
>
> $^1/_4$ cup ($^1/_2$ stick) salted butter, melted
>
> 1 $^1/_2$ cups warm (105° to 130°) water
>
> About 1 cup sesame seeds (see note)

1. Use a little softened butter or vegetable shortening to grease the inside of a large bowl; set aside.

2. In another large bowl, with a whisk, combine the flour, yeast, salt, and sugar until thoroughly mixed. In a 2-cup measure, stir the melted butter into the warm water. Gradually stir and beat 1$^1/_4$ cups of the water mixture into the flour mixture, adding as much of the remaining water mixture as necessary until the flour mixture holds together and leaves the side of the bowl. Knead the dough in the bowl until it is smooth and springy. Transfer the dough to the greased bowl, turning to coat the surface. Cover with plastic wrap and place a hot, damp towel over the plastic wrap. Set aside in a warm place until doubled in bulk, 1 to 2 hours.

3. Remove the racks from a gas oven. If using an electric oven, place one rack as close to the bottom of the oven as possible and place a heavy baking sheet on the rack. Preheat a gas oven to 350°; preheat an electric oven to 375°.

4. Divide the dough into 12 equal parts and cover with a damp towel. Sprinkle the sesame seeds over a work surface. Working with one piece of dough at a time, and keeping the remaining pieces covered, roll the dough out over the sesame seeds into a round that is as thin as you can possibly make it without tearing the dough. Roll the dough around the rolling pin. Unroll the dough onto the bottom of the gas oven or onto the baking sheet in an electric oven.

5. Bake one at a time until light golden with a few dark-brown patches. In a gas oven this will take 2 to 3 minutes; in the electric oven about 13 minutes. With a wide turner, transfer the lavash to a wire rack to cool completely.

6. While one lavash is baking, roll out another so that it is ready to go into the oven as soon as the previous one comes out.

7. Store wrapped loosely in aluminum foil.

Yield: 12 lavash

Tip

When using sesame seeds in this quantity, buy them loose from a health food store or at a Middle Eastern grocery, where they are a lot less expensive than those in the little jars.

French Twists

I think commercially prepared frozen puff pastry is one of the world's great inventions. A Frenchman would probably sniff at the idea of using such a product, but how many cooks are actually going to start from scratch to make the real thing in this day and age?

> $^1/_3$ cup freshly grated Parmesan or Romano cheese
>
> 1 $^1/_2$ teaspoons chili powder
>
> One sheet of frozen puff pastry from a 17 $^1/_4$-ounce package, thawed according to package directions
>
> 1 large egg, lightly beaten

1. Adjust two racks to divide the oven into thirds. Preheat the oven to 425°. Have ready two ungreased baking sheets.

2. In a small bowl, combine the cheese and chili powder; set aside.

3. Unfold the puff pastry on a sheet of waxed paper. Brush half of the beaten egg over the surface. Sprinkle half of the cheese mixture over the egg-brushed pastry, pressing it in lightly with your fingers. Cover the pastry with another sheet of waxed paper and invert. Peel off the top sheet of waxed paper and prepare the second side of the pastry with the egg and cheese mixture as before.

4. Fold the pastry in half lengthwise and remove the bottom sheet of waxed paper. With a pizza wheel or the tip of a sharp knife, cut the pastry crosswise into ³/₈-inch strips to make 20 strips.

5. Pick up one of the strips and unfold it. Twist the strip, while holding both ends. Lay the twist on an ungreased baking sheet, pressing both ends of the twist onto the baking sheet to anchor it. Repeat with the remaining strips, placing 10 twists on each baking sheet. Place the baking sheets in the freezer for 10 minutes.

6. Bake for 7 to 8 minutes until crisp and golden. Reverse the baking sheets on the racks and from front to back once during baking. With a wide turner, carefully transfer the twists to wire racks to cool completely.

7. Store in a tightly covered container for up to a week. The twists can be warmed or recrisped in a 400° oven for about 5 minutes.

Yield: 20 twists

COOKIES FOR KIDS

Cookies and kids go together like peanut butter and jelly. During my years as the food editor for *Parents Magazine*, we spent quite a lot of time and devoted many pages to the subject.

All cookies are for kids, who seem to enjoy making them almost as much as they love eating them. The pleasant memories of cookie-making sessions with Mom (or Dad, in this era) are ones that many of us treasure for a lifetime. I can't imagine a child who wouldn't love to come into the kitchen to help with cookie making. Even the youngest tot can make some contributions to the effort and really enjoy doing it.

Most of the cookies in this book are certainly simple enough for children to assist in the making. This chapter has been assembled as a quick guide to no-bake, supersimple, and other particularly kid-pleasing cookies.

I believe that we all should know how to cook and to nourish ourselves properly. Helping to make cookies at a tender age may be one of the best ways to learn.

HOW KIDS CAN HELP AND WHEN

Ages 3 to 5

Stir

Crush

Dump premeasured ingredients into bowls

Choose and use cookie cutters

Apply simple decorations

Ages 5 to 7

Learn how to read a recipe

Learn how to measure

Grease baking sheets

Break eggs

Blend and mix with a spoon

Use an electric mixer

Roll dough into balls

Drop or push batter off a spoon

Help arrange cookies on baking sheets

Fill the barrel of a cookie press; press spritz cookies onto a baking sheet

Do simple decorations with little or no assistance

Ages 7 to 10

Read the recipe and assemble the supplies
and ingredients

Measure accurately

Learn to roll dough

Cut out cookies and arrange on baking sheets

Learn to use a pastry bag

Do more advanced cookie decorations

Learn to use the oven and handle knives
safely

Ages 11 to 13

At this point, most children are usually
capable of baking simple to moderately
difficult cookies with only some grown-up
supervision and a little help, if needed.

Ages 14 and Up

Point kids in the direction of the cookbooks
and kitchen and tell them you'll be in for
samples later.

My Very Own Cookies

Remember what fun it was to roll pieces of soft
bread in your hands to make little doughy rounds?
With this dough, children can make cookies using
the same technique. Trees, wreaths, candy canes,
and snowmen, even animals, alphabet letters, and
other shapes quickly take shape on the baking
sheet. These cookies are ideal for Christmas and
other holidays, of course, but they can be baked
year-round in whatever shapes your child pleases
or that reflect the season.

1 ounce (1 square) unsweetened chocolate,
    broken in half

2 1/4 cups all-purpose flour

1 teaspoon baking powder

1 cup sugar

3/4 cup (1 1/2 sticks) salted butter or
    margarine, at room temperature

1 large egg

2 teaspoons vanilla extract

5 to 6 drops liquid food coloring

For decorations: colored sugars, crystal
    sugars, multicolored sprinkles, tiny candies,
    confectioners' sugar, etc.

1. Adjust two racks to divide the oven into thirds.
Preheat the oven to 375°. Lightly grease two baking sheets.

2. In a small saucepan set over very low heat,
melt the chocolate, stirring constantly until
smooth. Remove from the heat and set aside
to cool.

3. In a medium-size bowl, with a whisk, combine
the flour and baking powder until thoroughly
mixed.

4. In a large bowl, with an electric mixer at
medium-high speed, beat together the sugar, butter, egg, and vanilla until thick and pale-colored,
2 to 3 minutes. With the mixer at medium-low
speed, gradually add the flour mixture, beating
just until blended. Gather the dough into a ball
and divide it into three equal portions. Leave one
portion in the mixing bowl. Place the other two
portions of dough in two separate bowls. Add the
food coloring to the dough in the mixing bowl and
beat at medium speed until evenly tinted. To one
of the portions of plain dough, with a mixing
spoon, add the melted chocolate and stir until
evenly colored.

5. To shape the cookies, pull off pieces of the
dough and roll into balls about 1/4 to 1/2 inch in
diameter. Arrange the balls on the baking sheets
in the desired forms. The balls should touch
each other.

6. Bake for 7 or 8 minutes until the balls feel
fairly firm when lightly touched. Reverse the baking sheets on the racks and from front to back
once during baking. Cool for 1 minute on the baking sheet. With a wide turner, transfer the cookies to wire racks to cool completely.

7. Store in a tightly covered container.

**Yield: About 36 to 60 balls,
depending on the size**

How to Organize a Cookie-Decorating Party

At holiday time, cookie making can become a social event for the junior set, and having a cookie baking and decorating party one afternoon before the holidays would likely be the thrill of a lifetime for any child. If you are brave enough to do it, here are a few time-tested suggestions to make sure that everything goes smoothly.

- Decide in advance which cookie cutters will be used, and how the cookies will be decorated. You don't want too much going on at once. The cookie shapes should probably be fairly large and straightforward. Decorating should also be limited to one fairly basic technique.

- Because kids just naturally have short attention spans, and don't like to spend too long on grunt work, it's best to have the dough made and everything ready to go when the little bakers arrive. Don't plan to devote too much time to any one step or procedure.

- Depending on how many kids are participating, having a parent's helper on hand may also be a smart idea.

- Set up two areas: One for baking and another for decorating.

- Cookies can be decorated either before or after they are baked, and it's usually best to choose one or the other method for a decorating party.

- After the first few batches of cookies have been cut (or cut, rolled, and baked, if they are to be decorated after baking), go on to the decorating phase.

- Depending on which decorating method will be used, an assortment of appropriate supplies should be in a central location. Each child can be given paper plates and cups for the decorations he or she wants to use. Or set these up in advance at each child's decorating place.

- Have plenty of wet sponges or paper towels ready. You can count on a lot of little messes to clean up.

- Remember to take pictures.

- Provide the children with bags or tins to take home the cookies they have baked and decorated.

Variations

Trees: On the baking sheet, place 10 green or plain balls to form a solid triangle, with the balls touching. Use 1 chocolate ball for the tree trunk. Decorate as desired.

Wreaths: On the baking sheet, place 8 green, chocolate, and plain balls to form a circle, with the balls touching. Decorate as desired.

Candy Canes: On the baking sheet, place 7 chocolate or plain balls to form a candy cane, with the balls touching. Decorate as desired, or sprinkle with confectioners' sugar while the cookies are still warm to form a glaze.

Snowmen: Roll the dough into 1- or 2-inch balls. On the baking sheet, arrange 3 balls to form each snowman, with the balls touching. With the bottom of a glass that has been buttered and dipped in sugar, lightly flatten each ball into slightly different sizes to make the head and upper and lower torso. Decorate as desired.

Tip

Unless the recipe directs otherwise, always grease baking sheets lightly. Overgreasing causes the cookies to spread too much and the bottoms will be overbrowned.

Mittens and Gloves

The shapes of these cookies are made from your child's own hand. This is a good dough for kids to learn with, since it's easy to make and easy to roll. In the beginning, roll the dough out thicker than usual, about $1/4$ inch thick. All sorts of free-form shapes can be cut from this dough, or you can use cookie cutters.

> $1/2$ cup (1 stick) salted butter or margarine, at room temperature
> $3/4$ cup sugar
> 1 large egg
> 1 teaspoon vanilla extract
> 2 cups all-purpose flour
> Tubes of cake-decorating frosting in various colors

1. In a large bowl, with an electric mixer at medium-high speed, beat together the butter and sugar until light and fluffy, 2 to 3 minutes. Add the egg and vanilla and beat until smooth, about 1 minute. With the mixer at medium-low speed, gradually add the flour, beating just until blended and the mixture forms a dough. Gather the dough into a ball.

2. Divide the dough in half. Shape each half into a 1-inch-thick disk. Wrap in plastic wrap and refrigerate until cold and firm, about 1 hour. (At this point the dough can be tightly wrapped in aluminum foil and refrigerated for up to one week or frozen for up to three months. If frozen, thaw in the refrigerator before proceeding.)

3. Adjust two racks to divide the oven into thirds. Preheat the oven to 350°. Lightly grease two baking sheets.

4. Remove one disk of dough from the refrigerator. Place a sheet of waxed paper on a dampened work surface (to keep the waxed paper from sliding). Place the dough on the waxed paper. Cover it with another sheet of waxed paper. Roll the dough out between the sheets of waxed paper to a $1/4$-inch thickness. Remove the top sheet of waxed paper.

5. To make mittens and gloves, have your child place her or his hand on the dough with fingers closed. Working quickly (so the dough doesn't get soft), cut around the hand with a dull knife to make a mitten shape, or have your child spread her or his fingers and cut around each finger to make a glove. (If the dough begins to get soft, simply place it in the refrigerator for a few minutes.) With a wide turner, transfer the shapes to the prepared baking sheets, spacing them about $1\frac{1}{2}$ inches apart. Reroll the scraps and cut out.

6. Bake for 6 to 8 minutes, depending on the size, until golden. Reverse the baking sheets on the racks and from front to back once during baking. With a wide turner, immediately transfer the cookies to wire racks to cool completely.

7. Decorate the cooled cookies using purchased tubes of frosting. Since this frosting will not dry very hard, it's best to leave these cookies on a tray, lightly covered with waxed paper.

Yield: 8 to 14 cookies

Lollipops

What makes these particular cookies so kid-alluring is the shape they finally take. This technique for making lollipop cookies can be used with almost any cookie that is rolled into a ball before baking. For giving away, wrap the cookie top of each lollipop in plastic wrap or cellophane. Tie with ribbon around the stick just below the cookie. These cookies can also be decorated to look like flowers and stuck into a flower pot filled with florists' foam. If you like, the wooden sticks can be tinted with diluted food coloring.

> 2 cups all-purpose flour
> 1 $1/2$ teaspoons baking powder
> $1/4$ teaspoon salt
> $2/3$ cup (1 stick plus 3 tablespoons) butter-flavored shortening
> $3/4$ cup sugar

4 teaspoons milk

1 teaspoon vanilla extract

1 large egg, lightly beaten

24 to 30 flat wooden sticks

Decorations: chocolate, butterscotch, peanut butter, and vanilla chips; raisins, diced dried fruit, flaked coconut; tiny candies, such as red hots, colored sugars and sprinkles, dragees, etc.

1. In a medium-size bowl, with a whisk, combine the flour, baking powder, and salt until thoroughly mixed.

2. In a large bowl, with an electric mixer at medium-high speed, beat together the shortening, sugar, milk, and vanilla until creamy, 2 to 3 minutes. Beat in the egg until well blended. With the mixer at medium-low speed, gradually add the flour mixture, beating just until blended. Cover the bowl and refrigerate until the dough is very firm, several hours or overnight.

3. When ready to bake, adjust two racks to divide the oven into thirds. Preheat the oven to 375°. Have ready two ungreased baking sheets.

4. Scoop heaping measuring tablespoonfuls of dough out of the bowl and form them into 1½-inch balls between the palms of your hands. Push an ice cream stick into the center of each ball. Arrange the balls on the baking sheets, spacing them about 3 inches apart. With the bottom of a wide, smooth turner that has been lightly greased and floured, flatten each ball until it is about ½ inch thick and 3 inches in diameter. Decorate as desired, pressing the decorations lightly into the dough.

5. Bake for 8 to 10 minutes or until firm and barely colored. Reverse the baking sheets on the racks and from front to back once during baking. Cool for 2 minutes on the baking sheet. With a wide spatula, transfer the cookies to wire racks to cool completely.

6. Store in a shallow, tightly covered container.

Yield: About 24 cookies

Flying Saucers

The sheer size of these cookies is just one thing that makes them so appealing to kids.

1 ½ cups all-purpose flour

¼ cup unsweetened cocoa powder

1 teaspoon baking soda

1 cup (2 sticks) salted butter or margarine, at room temperature

1 cup packed light brown sugar

½ cup granulated sugar

2 large eggs

1 teaspoon vanilla extract

1 cup (6 ounces) semisweet chocolate chips

¾ cup raisins

¾ cup chopped walnuts or pecans

1. Adjust two racks to divide the oven in half. Preheat the oven to 350°. Lightly grease two baking sheets and then dust them with flour.

2. In a medium-size bowl, with a whisk, combine the flour, cocoa, and baking soda until thoroughly mixed.

3. In a large bowl, with an electric mixer at medium-high speed, beat together the butter, brown sugar, and granulated sugar until creamy, about 1 minute. Add the eggs and vanilla and beat until light and very creamy, 2 to 3 minutes. With the mixer at medium-low speed, gradually add the flour mixture, beating just until blended. With a mixing spoon, stir in the chocolate chips, raisins, and nuts until well distributed throughout the batter.

4. Scoop ½ cupfuls of the batter out of the bowl and drop onto the prepared baking sheets, spacing the drops about 5 inches apart. Using a small spatula dipped in water, smooth the mounds of dough into rounds measuring about 3½ inches.

5. Bake for 10 to 12 minutes until golden. Reverse the baking sheets on the racks and from front to back once during baking. With a wide turner, immediately transfer the cookies to wire racks to cool completely.

Yield: About 16 cookies

Monkey Business

Older children should be able to make these simple bars completely unassisted.

- 3 cups miniature marshmallows
- 1/2 cup honey
- 1/3 cup (1/2 stick plus 1 1/2 tablespoons) salted butter or margarine
- 1/4 cup peanut butter
- 2 teaspoons vanilla extract
- 4 cups ready-to-eat crisp rice cereal
- 2 cups quick-cooking (not instant) rolled oats
- 1/2 cup shredded or flaked coconut
- 1/4 cup coarsely chopped peanuts

1. In a medium-size saucepan over medium heat, combine the marshmallows, honey, butter, peanut butter, and vanilla. Cook, stirring constantly, until the marshmallows are melted and the mixture is smooth.

2. In a large bowl, with a mixing spoon, gently toss together the rice cereal, oats, coconut, and peanuts until well combined. Spread evenly in a 13 × 9-inch baking dish. Pour the hot melted marshmallow mixture over the cereal mixture and mix gently until well coated. With your fingers, pat the mixture down into the baking dish. Set aside until cool and firm, 1 to 2 hours, before cutting into 8 × 5 rows.

3. Store in the baking dish, tightly covered with aluminum foil or plastic wrap.

Yield: 40 bars

Tip
Brush melted jelly on baked cookies for a quick glaze and some gloss.

No-Bake Brownies

For little kids, adult assistance will be needed in melting the chocolate chips and lining the pan with foil. Other than that, this is a recipe that 5- to 7-year-olds can feel proud about having made all by themselves.

- 2 cups (12 ounces) semisweet chocolate chips
- One 14-ounce can regular or reduced-fat condensed (not evaporated) milk
- One 8 1/2-ounce package chocolate wafers, finely crushed
- 1 cup chopped walnuts, divided

1. Line an 8-inch-square metal baking pan with foil, shiny side up.

2. In a medium-size saucepan set over very low heat, melt the chocolate, stirring constantly until smooth. Remove from the heat and stir in the condensed milk, crushed wafers, and 1/2 cup of the nuts. Press this mixture into the prepared pan. Press the remaining 1/2 cup nuts evenly over the top. Let stand at room temperature until firm, about 2 hours. Cut into 4 × 4 rows.

3. Store in the pan, tightly covered with aluminum foil or plastic wrap.

Yield: 16 brownies

Caramel-Apple Cereal Bars

Apples are one dried fruit that isn't often included in baked goods, and I'm not sure why. They have a wonderful sweet-tart flavor and a nice chewy texture. Make sure you have more on hand than what is needed to make these squares, since the kids are likely to eat them before they ever make it into the bars.

- 6 cups bite-size rice cereal squares
- 2 cups chopped dried apples
- 1/2 cup peanuts
- One 14-ounce package caramels, unwrapped
- 1/4 cup milk

1. Lightly grease a 13×9-inch baking pan or glass baking dish.

2. In a large bowl, with your hands, combine the cereal, apples, and peanuts.

3. In a small saucepan, combine the caramels and milk. Cook over low heat, stirring constantly until the caramels are melted and smooth. Pour the caramel mixture over the cereal and toss with a mixing spoon until well coated. Press evenly into the prepared pan. Set aside until firm, about 1 hour, before cutting into 4×5 rows.

4. Store in the baking pan, tightly covered with aluminum foil or plastic wrap.

Yield: 20 bars

Crisp Chocolate Bars

These no-bake bars are a good spur-of-the-moment project, since you are very likely to have the ingredients on hand.

> 1 cup (6 ounces) semisweet chocolate chips
> $^1/_2$ cup (1 stick) salted butter or margarine
> One 10-ounce package marshmallows
> 6 cups ready-to-eat crisp rice cereal

1. Lightly grease a 13×9-inch metal baking pan or glass baking dish.

2. In a large saucepan set over very low heat, melt together the chocolate and butter, stirring constantly until smooth. Add the marshmallows and stir until melted. Remove the pan from the heat. Add the cereal and stir gently until evenly coated with the chocolate mixture. Press evenly into the prepared baking pan. Set aside until completely cool. Cut into 6×6 rows.

3. Store in the baking pan, tightly covered with plastic wrap or aluminum foil.

Yield: 36 bars

No-Bake Fruit and Honey Bars

In a pinch, one or two of these cookies served with a glass of milk makes a fast and complete breakfast.

> $^1/_4$ cup sugar
> $^1/_4$ cup ($^1/_2$ stick) salted butter or margarine
> $^1/_3$ cup honey
> 1 teaspoon ground cinnamon
> One 6-ounce package dried fruit bits
> 1 $^1/_2$ cups sweetened rice cereal with real cocoa
> 1 cup quick-cooking (not instant) rolled oats

1. Have ready an 8-inch ungreased metal baking pan.

2. In a medium-size saucepan, combine the sugar, butter, honey, and cinnamon. Bring to a boil over medium heat. Boil for 1 minute, stirring constantly. Remove from the heat and add the fruit bits, cereal, and oats. Stir gently until well coated. Press evenly into the ungreased pan. Refrigerate until set, about 1 hour. Cut into 4×4 rows.

3. Store in the baking pan, tightly covered with aluminum foil or plastic wrap.

Yield: 16 squares

Tip

In general, cookies baked on a greased baking sheet will spread more and be thinner than those baked on an ungreased sheet.

No-Bake Honey-Butterscotch Bars

Young children can do all the measuring, stirring, pressing, and spreading for these chewy bars.

    1 cup butterscotch-flavored chips
    1/2 cup honey
    1/2 cup smooth or chunky peanut butter
    2 cups ready-to-eat crisp rice cereal
    1 cup (6 ounces) semisweet chocolate chips

1. Preheat the oven broiler. Adjust one rack a few inches below the heat source. Lightly grease an 8-inch metal baking pan.

2. In a microwave-safe, 4-cup measure, combine the butterscotch chips, honey, and peanut butter. Microwave on high (100 percent power) until the mixture has softened enough to be stirred smooth, 1 to 2 minutes; set aside.

3. In a large bowl, with a mixing spoon, combine the cereal and butterscotch mixture until well blended. Press this mixture evenly into the prepared pan. Sprinkle evenly with the chocolate chips.

4. Place the pan beneath the broiler and broil for 2 minutes, or until the chips are soft enough to spread. Spread the melted chips evenly over the top of the cereal mixture. Set aside until completely cool before cutting into 4 × 4 rows.

5. Store in the baking pan, tightly covered with plastic wrap or aluminum foil.

Yield: 16 bars

Haystacks

This is a no-bake cookie that has been popular with several generations of children.

    One 6-ounce package butterscotch chips
    1/4 cup smooth or chunky peanut butter
    1 cup coarsely crushed potato chips or chow
        mein noodles
    1 cup miniature marshmallows

1. Line a baking sheet with waxed paper.

2. Place the butterscotch chips in a large, microwave-safe bowl. Cook on high (100 percent power) for 1 minute; stir. Microwave 10 to 20 seconds longer until the chips are melted; stir until smooth. Stir in the peanut butter until well blended. Stir in the potato chips and marshmallows until well distributed throughout the batter. Drop by level measuring tablespoonfuls onto the prepared baking sheet. Let stand until firm, about 2 hours.

3. Store in a tightly covered container, separating the layers with sheets of waxed paper.

Yield: About 22 cookies

No-Bake Chocolate-Lemon Chews

I know this looks like a very strange combination of ingredients for cookies, but the results are really quite delicious. The recipe calls for lemon candies, but you can certainly use any hard candy you like: peppermint, butterscotch, orange, or anything, although my family has always preferred the slight tang of lemon with the chocolate.

    1/2 cup (about 4 ounces) hard lemon candies
    1 cup (6 ounces) semisweet chocolate chips
    2 tablespoons salted butter or margarine
    1 cup quick-cooking rolled oats
    1/4 cup confectioners' sugar, for coating
        cookies

1. Place the lemon candies in a zipper-top plastic bag; seal the bag. With a rolling pin, pound the candies until they are more or less evenly pulverized. (You should have about 1/2 cup crushed candy.)

2. In a medium-size saucepan set over low heat, stir together the chocolate and butter until melted and smooth. Remove from the heat. Stir in the crushed candies until well blended. Stir in the oats until well blended.

3. Sprinkle the confectioners' sugar onto a sheet of waxed paper. Scoop heaping measuring teaspoonfuls of the chocolate mixture out of the pan and roll and press them into 1-inch balls between the palms of your hands. (It helps if you stop every third or fourth ball and wash and dry your hands.) Roll each ball in confectioners' sugar as it is formed. Set aside on waxed paper until cool and firm, about 2 hours.

4. Store in a tightly covered container, separating the layers with sheets of waxed paper. These cookies will keep very well for at least a week.

Yield: About 18 cookies

Louise Johnson's Miracle Peanut Butter Cookies

Louise is the mother of one of my dearest friends, Linda Johnson. These cookies really are miraculous. Once you decide that you want to make them it takes only about 30 minutes until you can pop one into your mouth. Louise usually makes these cookies when her granddaughter Kaitlyn comes to visit. Kaitlyn doesn't like peanut butter, but she *loves* to make these cookies.

> 1 cup smooth or chunky peanut butter
> 1 ¹/₃ cups sugar, divided
> 1 large egg
> 1 ¹/₂ teaspoons vanilla extract

1. Adjust two racks to divide the oven into thirds. Preheat the oven to 325°. Lightly grease two baking sheets.

2. In a large bowl, with an electric mixer at medium-high speed, beat together the peanut butter, 1 cup of the sugar, egg, and vanilla until the mixture forms a dough and cleans the side of the bowl. Sprinkle the remaining ¹/₃ cup of sugar onto a piece of waxed paper.

3. Scoop the batter out of the bowl by heaping teaspoonfuls and roll into 1-inch balls between the palms of your hands. Arrange on the prepared baking sheets, spacing them about 3 inches apart.

Dip the bottom of a glass into the sugar and use it to slightly flatten each cookie, dipping the bottom of the glass into the sugar between each cookie.

4. Bake for about 14 minutes or until the cookies look dry and are lightly browned on the bottom. Reverse the baking sheets on the racks and from front to back once during baking. With a wide turner, immediately transfer the cookies to wire racks to cool completely.

5. Store in a tightly covered container.

Yield: About 30 cookies

Magic Meringues

These cookie-meringues are great fun to make, and even more fun to watch through the microwave door as they bake. They are a wonderful project for those days when the children are bored and looking for something new and novel to do. This recipe is nothing like baked-in-the-oven meringues, so don't be tempted to try making them in a conventional oven.

> 1 egg white, at room temperature
> ¹/₂ teaspoon vanilla extract
> 2 to 2 ¹/₂ cups sifted confectioners' sugar

1. In a medium-size bowl, with a dinner fork, beat the egg white with the vanilla just until frothy. Gradually add the sugar, mixing with the fork at first and then with your hands, until enough sugar has been added so that the mixture is still pliable, but *very* stiff. Pinch off pieces of the mixture and roll them into 1-inch balls between the palms of your hands. Arrange about 6 balls on a flat, microwave-safe plate, spacing them 2 to 3 inches apart.

2. Microwave on high (100 percent power) for 1 to 1¹/₂ minutes until the balls have puffed to three or four times their original size. Leave in the microwave oven for 3 minutes, then transfer to wire racks to cool completely. Repeat with the remaining mixture.

Yield: 12 to 16 meringues

Peanut Butter and Chocolate Puffs

These will remind you a lot of the very popular chocolate-covered marshmallow cookies, and that's not bad.

    24 purchased chocolate wafer cookies,
       divided
    1/4 cup smooth peanut butter
    12 large marshmallows

1. Spread each of the bottoms of 12 cookies with 1 teaspoon of the peanut butter; set aside.

2. On a large, microwave-safe plate, arrange the remaining 12 cookies, bottom sides up. Top each cookie with a marshmallow. Microwave on high (100 percent power) for 10 to 12 seconds or until the marshmallows begin to puff. Remove from the microwave oven and immediately top with the remaining cookies, peanut butter side down.

3. Store the cookies on the plate, lightly covered with plastic wrap.

Yield: 12 sandwich cookies

Chocolate Bird Nests

Little kids will love to play Easter Bunny helpers with these goodies at Easter time—and any other time of the year, as well.

    2 1/2 cups chow mein noodles
    2 cups coarsely crushed cornflakes cereal
    3 cups (18 ounces) semisweet chocolate chips
    54 jelly beans in various colors

1. Line a large baking sheet with waxed paper.

2. In a large bowl, with your hands, toss together the noodles and cereal.

3. In a medium-size saucepan set over low heat, melt the chocolate, stirring constantly until smooth. Pour over the noodle mixture and toss gently with a mixing spoon until evenly coated.

4. For each nest, mound 2 tablespoonfuls of the cereal mixture on the prepared baking sheet. With your fingers, make an indentation in each mound, shaping the mixture into nests. Press three jelly beans in each indentation. Set aside until firm, about 2 hours.

Yield: About 18 cookies

Snowmen

There's a simple construction project here that just happens to be good to eat.

    8 whole graham crackers (5 × 2 1/2 inches)
    Vanilla buttercream frosting (page 32) or
       vanilla ready-to-spread frosting
    Decorations: multicolored sprinkles, black
       licorice whips, slivered almonds, mini-
       chocolate chips, red writing gel, tiny
       cinnamon candies
    One 9-ounce package white and pink
       marshmallow-and-coconut–topped cookies

1. Lay the graham crackers out on a work surface. Spread one side of each cracker with a layer of frosting. Sprinkle the moist frosting with multicolored sprinkles.

2. Place a dab of frosting on the bottom of each marshmallow cookie to act as "glue." Immediately place two cookies on each prepared graham cracker to resemble a snowman. (Place the first cookie close to one end of the graham cracker so that when the second cookie is put in place there is room at the top for a hat.)

3. Arrange a piece of the licorice strip crosswise on top of the head to resemble a hat brim. Arrange two short pieces of licorice vertically over the brim to resemble the crown of the hat. On the top cookie, use mini-chocolate chips for the eyes and a piece of slivered almond for the nose. Pipe a smiling mouth with the writing gel. Place three cinnamon candies on the bottom cookie for buttons.

Yield: 8 cookies

STOVE-TOP COOKIES

Not every cookie in the world is baked. Some very traditional and popular cookies are made on the stove top.

Keep in mind that back in the old days, firing up the oven was a big deal, and to heat the oven to make a batch of cookies would have been a preposterous idea. Baking was usually reserved for one day a week, so fried breads, pastries, and even cookielike confections were not unusual. Every country in the world has its own version of a fried cookie, and every one that I have ever tasted has been wonderful.

Spanish Fried Pastries

If you like the flavor of licorice, use the anise seeds. If not, don't use them.

 3/4 cup regular olive oil
 Peel from 1 small orange, cut into strips (be sure to cut or scrape away the bitter white pith just beneath the peel)
 1/3 cup dry sherry
 1/3 cup sweet sherry
 3 tablespoons fresh strained orange juice
 2 teaspoons sesame seeds
 1 teaspoon anise seeds
 3 1/2 cups all-purpose flour
 Vegetable oil, for frying
 Confectioners' sugar, for sprinkling on cookies

Syrup

 1 cup honey
 1/4 cup water

1. In a small saucepan set over medium heat, combine the olive oil and orange peel. Cook until the peel is dark brown, about 5 minutes. Remove the peel with tongs or a slotted spoon and discard. Set the oil aside to cool to lukewarm.

2. In a large bowl, combine the orange-flavored oil with both wines, the orange juice, sesame seeds, and anise seeds. With a mixing spoon, gradually stir in 3 cups of the flour until a sticky dough is formed.

3. Turn the dough out onto a lightly floured surface. Knead the dough until it is smooth and springy, adding as much flour as necessary to prevent sticking. Cover the dough with a clean dish towel and allow it to rest at room temperature for 30 minutes.

4. Pull off small pieces of the dough. Between the palms of your hands, form the dough into 3/4-inch balls. On a work surface, flatten each ball, then stretch it carefully into an oval measuring about 4 × 2 inches and 1/8 inch thick. As they are shaped, arrange the ovals in a single layer on large baking sheets.

5. Pour enough vegetable oil into an electric skillet or a large, heavy skillet to measure about 1/2 inch. Set the thermostat on the skillet at 360°. If using a regular skillet, heat the oil over medium heat until it registers 360° on a deep-fry thermometer. With a slotted spoon, slip the ovals, one at a time, into the hot oil, being careful not to crowd them. Fry, turning each oval once, until lightly browned on both sides, about 1 1/2 minutes total frying time. With the slotted spoon, transfer the fried cookies to paper towels to drain. Repeat with the remaining ovals.

6. To make the syrup: In a small saucepan, heat the honey and water together over medium heat just until the mixture boils. Reduce the heat to low and simmer, uncovered, for 5 minutes.

7. Working with two or three fried cookies at a time, with tongs, place the cookies in the honey mixture. Immediately lift out, allowing the excess to drip back into the pan. Place the dipped cookies on wire racks that have been set over foil or baking sheets to catch the drips. Repeat dipping with the remaining cookies. Let stand until dry to the touch, 1 to 2 hours.

8. Store in a tightly covered container, separating the layers with sheets of waxed paper. Lightly sprinkle with confectioners' sugar just before serving.

Yield: About 60 cookies

Italian Crostoli

Using a fluted pastry wheel to cut the dough for this Italian specialty is a nice touch that makes this little fried pastry look especially delicate and pretty.

    1 1/2 cups all-purpose flour
    1 1/2 teaspoons baking powder
    1/2 teaspoon salt
    1/3 cup milk
    1 tablespoon brandy
    1 teaspoon vanilla extract
    2 tablespoons sugar
    1 tablespoon butter, melted and cooled
    1 teaspoon shredded and minced lemon zest
    1 large egg yolk
    Vegetable oil, for frying
    Confectioners' sugar, for dusting cookies

1. In a medium-size bowl, with a whisk, combine the flour, baking powder, and salt until thoroughly mixed.

2. In a small bowl, with a table fork, beat the milk, brandy, vanilla, sugar, butter, lemon zest, and egg yolk until blended. With a mixing spoon, gradually stir the milk mixture into the flour mixture until thoroughly blended and a dough has formed.

3. Turn the dough out onto a lightly floured surface. Knead the dough gently about 20 times until smooth.

4. On a lightly floured surface, roll the dough into a 14 × 10-inch rectangle. With a fluted pastry wheel or a pizza cutter and a ruler, cut the dough into 2 × 1-inch strips, then cut a 1-inch slit in the center of each strip.

5. Pour enough vegetable oil into an electric skillet or a large, heavy skillet to measure about 2 inches. Set the thermostat on the skillet at 375°. If using a regular skillet, heat the oil over medium heat until it registers 375° on a deep-fry thermometer. Carefully drop about 6 of the crostoli into the hot oil and fry until golden, about 2 minutes.

With a slotted spoon, remove the crostoli from the oil to drain and cool on paper towels. Repeat with the remaining strips.

6. Store in a tightly covered, shallow container for several days. (The cookies should not be stacked more than three deep.) The crostoli can also be frozen in airtight plastic bags. If necessary, recrisp in a 300° oven for 3 to 5 minutes. Dust with confectioners' sugar before storing or just before serving.

Yield: About 60 crostoli

Variation

Fried Bow Ties: Cut the dough into 4 × 1½-inch strips, then cut a 1-inch slit in the center of each strip as before. Thread one end of the rectangle through the slit and pull gently to make a bow tie. Heat the oil to 350°. Continue as directed for Crostoli.

American Funnel Cakes

These funny fried cookies are a Pennsylvania Dutch specialty. Pouring the batter through a funnel into hot oil produces free-form, squiggly cookies that are as fun to make as they are to eat. Funnel-cake batter contains no sugar. Their sweetness depends entirely on the amount of confectioners' sugar that is sprinkled on the cookies after they are made.

    3 cups all-purpose flour
    1 teaspoon baking powder
    1/2 teaspoon salt
    2 cups milk
    2 large eggs
    Vegetable oil or plain vegetable shortening,
        for frying
    Confectioners' sugar, for dusting cookies

1. In a medium-size bowl, with a whisk, combine the flour, baking powder, and salt until thoroughly mixed. In a small bowl, with the whisk, beat the milk and eggs together. Whisk them into the flour mixture to form a smooth batter.

2. Pour the oil into an electric skillet or a heavy, medium-size skillet to a depth of about 1 inch. Set the thermostat on the skillet at 400°. If using a regular skillet, heat the oil over medium heat until it registers 400° on a deep-fry thermometer.

3. Fill a funnel with batter, holding a finger over the opening at the bottom of the funnel. (The size of the opening in the funnel will determine how fat the funnel cakes will be.) Hold the funnel above the hot oil and then remove your finger to let the batter flow, making swirls, coils, and other shapes 3 to 5 inches in diameter. Keep the funnel moving and use your finger to control the flow. Fry the cakes 1 to 2 minutes on each side until golden. With tongs or a wide, slotted turner, remove the cakes from the oil to drain on paper towels. Once you become adept at making funnel cakes, you can do three or four at a time. However, in the beginning, make them one or two at a time until you get the hang of it.

4. Cool the cookies completely on paper towels or wire racks. Store in a tightly covered, shallow container. (The cookies should not be stacked more than three deep.) Dust with confectioners' sugar just before serving. Funnel cakes can also be frozen in airtight plastic bags. If necessary, recrisp in a 300° oven for 3 to 5 minutes.

Yield: About 48 cookies

Rosettes

To make these fried cookies you will need a rosette iron. This little gadget, which usually comes packaged as a set, has a wooden or plastic handle with one or two wire rods onto which are attached metal forms, usually about 3 inches in diameter, in fancy designs. To make the rosettes, the forms are first dipped into hot oil to heat them. The hot forms are then dipped into a thin batter, which is picked up onto the hot form, and then immersed in the hot oil to finish cooking. This produces airy, wafflelike cookies. It takes a little practice to get the timing and the knack of doing this down pat. Rosette sets, which can be found in most kitchenware stores, come with very explicit directions about how they are to be used. When making rosettes for the first time, here are some helpful tips:

- If batter gets on top of the molds, fry as directed, then gently scrape it off with a knife.

- If the batter does not adhere to the molds, the oil may be either too hot or too cold.

- If the rosettes don't seem crisp enough, the batter may be too thick; thin with a little milk. Also check the temperature of the oil and the mold.

  2 large eggs
  2 teaspoons sugar
  1 cup milk
  1 cup sifted all-purpose flour
  1/4 teaspoon salt
  1 tablespoon vanilla or lemon extract
  Vegetable oil, regular olive oil, or plain vegetable shortening, for frying
  Confectioners' sugar or cinnamon sugar (page 35), for dusting cookies

1. Attach the mold or molds to the rosette iron; set aside.

2. In a medium-size bowl, with a whisk, mix the eggs with the sugar, then beat in the milk until well blended. Whisk in the flour, salt, and vanilla to make a smooth batter that is the consistency of heavy cream. Refrigerate the batter until it is chilled, about 1 hour. When ready to proceed, you may want to pour the batter into a loaf pan to make dipping easier.

3. Pour the oil into an electric skillet or a heavy, medium-size saucepan to a depth of about 2 inches. Set the thermostat on the skillet at 375°. If using a saucepan, heat the oil over medium heat until it registers 375° on a deep-fry thermometer. Immerse the mold in the hot oil until very hot, about 30 to 45 seconds. Lift the iron out and blot it on paper toweling. Immediately dip the mold into the batter only to the depth of the mold. (Try not to get batter on top of the mold.) Immerse the batter-covered mold in the hot oil, covering it completely. When the bubbling stops and the rosettes are a delicate brown, lift the iron out of the oil, allowing the excess oil to drip back into the pan. Over paper towels, gently tap the top of the mold with a wooden spoon to release the rosette. Repeat this procedure with the remaining batter, but remember always to reheat the iron before making additional cookies.

4. Cool the cookies completely, with the more open sides down, on paper towels. Store in a tightly covered, shallow container. (The cookies should not be stacked more than three deep.) Dust with confectioners' sugar or cinnamon sugar before storing or just before serving.

5. Store in a tightly covered container for several days. The cookies can also be frozen in airtight plastic bags. If necessary, recrisp in a 300° oven for 3 to 5 minutes.

Yield: About 50 rosettes

Mexican Fritters

These are made the same way as Rosettes. Only the batter and the yield are different.

3 egg yolks
$1/2$ cup milk
$1/2$ cup all-purpose flour
$1/4$ teaspoon baking powder
$1/2$ cup superfine sugar
1 teaspoon ground cinnamon
$1/8$ teaspoon ground cloves

1. In a medium-size bowl, beat the egg yolks lightly with a whisk. Whisk in the milk, flour, and baking powder. Refrigerate the batter until it is chilled, about 1 hour.

2. Fry the fritters as directed for Rosettes. In a small bowl, mix the sugar, cinnamon, and cloves. Dip both sides of each fried cookie in this mixture.

Yield: About 24 fritters

Pizzelles

In Italy, pizzelles are usually broken into the wedges that are stamped into the iron. They are not generally eaten by themselves, but are served with something else, such as spumoni, granita (Italian ice), or as part of a fruit plate.

3 $1/2$ cups all-purpose flour
1 $1/2$ cups sugar
4 teaspoons baking powder
1 cup (2 sticks) salted butter or margarine, melted and cooled
2 tablespoons anise extract
6 large eggs, lightly beaten

1. In a medium-size bowl, with a whisk, combine the flour, sugar, and baking powder until thoroughly mixed. With an electric mixer at low speed, beat in the butter, anise extract, and eggs until thoroughly blended, scraping the side of the bowl several times with a rubber spatula.

2. Preheat a 7-inch pizzelle iron over medium heat until a drop of water bounces around on the surface. (If using an electric model, preheat as the manufacturer directs.)

3. Pour 2 tablespoons of the batter slightly off center to the rear of the iron. Close the iron, squeezing the handles together to distribute the batter evenly over the surface. Any excess batter that oozes out the side of the iron should be scraped off with a knife. Close and bake for about 30 seconds on each side, or as the manufacturer directs. (Do not lift the cover during baking.) Lift the cover and use a fork to loosen the pizzelle. Transfer to a wire rack to cool completely. When the pizzelles have cooled, break each one into 4 wedge-shaped pieces, or leave them whole, if you like.

4. Store in a tightly covered container.

Yield: About 96 wedges

Pizzelle and Krumkake Irons

These hinged devices, with designs imprinted into the metal baking surfaces, are made in both electric and nonelectric models. If you plan to make either one of these cookies very often, it will probably pay to invest in an electric model, which makes things go infinitely easier. Both irons can be purchased in kitchenware stores or ordered by mail from Sur La Table and other mail order companies, as well (see Appendix C, "Shopping and Mail-Order Sources").

Follow the manufacturer's directions for seasoning the iron before using it for the first time.

There is a certain knack for making pizzelles and krumkakes, and you might lose a couple or three in the learning process. Once you get a feel for it, though, they can be turned out very quickly.

Norwegian Krumkakes

Krumkakes are Scandinavia's answer to Italy's pizzelle, and are imprinted with a design made by using a krumkake iron (see box on page 315). The cookies can be left flat and sprinkled with confectioners' sugar, which is not traditional, or they can be rolled while still hot on a tapered cone and later filled with whipped cream and fruit, which is the way they are served in Norway. A cone is sometimes included with the iron, or it can be purchased separately.

Follow the directions that come with the krumkake iron for seasoning it, or coat both surfaces very lightly with nonstick cooking spray before making the first cookie. After that it does not need seasoning.

1/2 cup all-purpose flour
1/8 teaspoon ground or freshly grated nutmeg
1/2 cup sugar
3 large eggs
1 teaspoon vanilla extract
1/2 cup clarified butter

1. In a small bowl, with a whisk, combine the flour and nutmeg until thoroughly mixed.

2. In a large bowl, with an electric mixer at medium speed, beat together the sugar, eggs, and vanilla until very well blended, 1 to 2 minutes. Add the flour mixture and beat just until smooth.

3. Preheat a seasoned krumkake iron over medium heat until a drop of water bounces around on the surface. (If using an electric model, preheat as the manufacturer directs.) Ladle between 2 and 3 teaspoons of the batter slightly off center to the rear of the iron. (The exact amount will depend on the size of the iron. Consult the manufacturer's directions.) Close the iron, squeezing the handles together to distribute the batter evenly over the surface. Any excess batter that oozes out the side of the iron should be scraped off with a knife. Over medium heat, bake for 30 seconds. Turn the iron over and bake for 30 seconds on the other side. Open the iron and remove

the wafer with the tip of a small knife or an icing spatula to a wire rack to cool completely. The warm wafer can also be rolled into a cylinder about 1 inch in diameter, either by hand or using a rolling cone. Transfer the roll to a wire rack, seam side down, to cool. Repeat this procedure with the remaining batter. Just before serving, the rolled wafers can be filled with lightly sweetened whipped cream that has been mixed with cut fruit or whole berries.

Yield: About 24 krumkakes

Welsh Skillet Cookies

I remember so well the first time I made these cookies. They didn't seem like they would be anything special. Was I ever surprised! One or two are never enough, so you might as well go ahead and double the recipe while you're at it.

2 cups sifted all-purpose flour
1 cup sugar
2 teaspoons baking powder
1/2 cup (1 stick) cold salted butter or margarine, cut into pieces
3/4 cup golden raisins
3/4 cup chopped walnuts
2 large eggs, lightly beaten
1 teaspoon vanilla extract

1. In a large bowl, with a whisk, combine the sifted flour, sugar, and baking powder until thoroughly mixed. With a pastry blender or two knives used in a crisscross fashion, cut in the butter until the mixture resembles coarse crumbs. With a mixing spoon, stir in the raisins and walnuts. Stir in the eggs and vanilla until well blended. (The mixture will be dry.)

2. Turn the dough out onto a lightly floured surface and pat down into a 1/4-inch thickness. With a floured, 2-inch biscuit cutter, cut into as many rounds as possible. Gather the scraps of dough together. Pat out and cut into rounds one more time.

3. Preheat an ungreased griddle or large skillet over medium heat until the skillet is medium-hot. Place as many cutouts on the griddle as possible without crowding them. Bake for 4 to 5 minutes on the first side. With a wide turner, flip the cookies and bake for 3 to 4 minutes on the second side. The cookies should be well browned on both sides. With the turner, transfer the cookies to wire racks to cool completely. Repeat with the remaining unbaked cookies.

4. Store in a tightly covered container. Sprinkle with confectioners' sugar before serving, if desired.

Yield: About 40 cookies

UNSCRATCH COOKIES

Convenience foods started appearing on grocery store shelves shortly after World War II. In great part, it *was* the effort to keep the troops well fed that led to a convenience phenomenon that just keeps growing and shows no signs of stopping.

I'm certain it didn't take long for inventive bakers to start coming up with shortcuts made from shortcuts, so to speak. Recipes for cookies made with cake mixes, for example, started appearing in women's magazines and home pages in the newspapers very soon after the cake mixes themselves.

Cookies are so simple to make, I often wonder why we ever have the need to make them any simpler. Nevertheless, cookies made with various forms of convenience foods do abound.

Cake-mix cookies and pudding cookies, in particular, have become a part of the history of American cookies. The recipes that follow are a sampling of some of the best and most popular.

The Old Cake Mix Cookie

I think this is the first cake mix cookie from the days when there were probably only two or three kinds of mix: white, yellow, and chocolate. Devil's food cake and angel food cake mixes came later. These days, as you well know, there are many, many more, but I suspect this formula would work with all of them, as long as the volume of dry mix is about the same.

> 1/2 cup (1 stick) salted butter or margarine, at room temperature
> 1 large egg
> One package any plain cake mix, weighing between 18 and 19 ounces

1. Adjust two racks to divide the oven into thirds. Preheat the oven to 350°. Have ready two ungreased baking sheets.

2. In a large bowl, with an electric mixer at medium-high speed, beat the butter and egg until creamy, about 1 minute. With the mixer at medium-low speed, gradually add the cake mix, beating until well blended. (If the batter is too thick to drop easily, gradually beat in a tablespoon or two of milk or water.) Drop by rounded measuring tablespoonfuls onto the ungreased baking sheets, spacing the drops about 2 inches apart.

3. Bake for 9 to 12 minutes until firm when lightly touched. Reverse the baking sheets on the racks and from front to back once during baking. With a wide turner, transfer the cookies to wire racks to cool completely.

4. Store in a tightly covered container.

Yield: About 30 cookies

Pudding Cookies

The more commonly known name for buttermilk baking mix (or biscuit mix) is Bisquick™. Since so many people ask, I just thought I'd tell you right up front and end the confusion. These are nice cookies, crisp and crunchy all the way through. And, heaven knows, they're easy.

> 1 cup buttermilk baking mix
> One 4-serving box any flavor instant pudding
> 1 large egg, lightly beaten
> 1/4 cup vegetable oil
> Granulated sugar

1. Adjust two racks to divide the oven into thirds. Preheat the oven to 350°. Lightly grease two baking sheets.

2. In a large bowl, with an electric mixer at medium-high speed, beat together the baking mix, dry pudding mix, egg, and vegetable oil until a crumbly dough forms. Gather the dough into a ball.

3. Sprinkle the granulated sugar onto a sheet of waxed paper. Scoop heaping teaspoonfuls of the dough out of the bowl and roll them into 1-inch balls between the palms of your hands. Arrange the balls on the prepared baking sheets, spacing them about 2 inches apart. Lightly grease the bottom of a flat-bottom glass with butter or margarine. Dip the glass bottom into the sugar, then press the glass onto a dough ball and flatten to a 1/4-inch-thick cookie that is about 2 inches in diameter. Repeat with remaining dough balls.

4. Bake for about 10 minutes until the edges are golden brown. Reverse the baking sheets on the racks and from front to back once during baking. With a wide turner, immediately transfer the cookies to wire racks to cool completely.

5. Store in an airtight container.

Yield: About 20 cookies

Pound Cake and Pumpkin Bars

Someone brought these to a Thanksgiving dinner I attended a few years ago. I thought they were pretty good and asked for the recipe. I was surprised that the crust, which is very crumbly and delicious, was made from a mix.

> One 16-ounce package pound cake mix
> 3 large eggs, divided
> 2 tablespoons salted butter or margarine, melted
> 4 teaspoons pumpkin pie spice, divided
> One 8-ounce package cream cheese, at room temperature
> One 14-ounce can sweetened regular or low-fat condensed (not evaporated) milk
> 3/4 cup solid-pack pumpkin
> 1 cup finely chopped hazelnuts

1. Adjust one rack to divide the oven in half. Preheat the oven to 350°. Have ready a 15 × 10-inch jelly-roll pan.

2. In a large bowl, with an electric mixer at low speed, combine the cake mix, 1 of the eggs, the butter, and 2 teaspoons of the pumpkin pie spice until crumbly. Press this mixture evenly into the bottom of the jelly-roll pan.

3. In the same bowl, beat the cream cheese until fluffy, 2 to 3 minutes. Gradually beat in the condensed milk, pumpkin, and the remaining 2 teaspoons of pumpkin pie spice until blended. Pour over the crust, tilting the pan until the batter covers the crust evenly. Sprinkle with the nuts.

4. Bake for 30 to 35 minutes until set. Reverse the pan from front to back once during baking. Cool in the pan on a wire rack. Refrigerate until cold before cutting into 5 × 5 rows.

5. Remove the bars from the pan and arrange them in a shallow container, separating the layers with sheets of waxed paper. Cover and store in the refrigerator.

Yield: 25 bars

Hazelnut-Coconut Squares

It takes one bowl and about 5 minutes and these delectable bars are ready to go into the oven.

> **2 large eggs, lightly beaten**
> **2 ¹/₂ cups packed light brown sugar**
> **1 cup buttermilk baking mix**
> **¹/₂ cup flaked coconut**
> **¹/₂ cup chopped hazelnuts, toasted (page 16)**

1. Adjust one rack to divide the oven in half. Preheat the oven to 350°. Lightly grease a 9-inch-square glass baking dish.

2. In a large bowl, place the eggs and the brown sugar. With an electric mixer at medium speed, beat until well blended. Add the baking mix and beat until smooth. With a mixing spoon, stir in the coconut and nuts. Turn the batter into the prepared baking pan, smoothing the top with the back of the spoon.

3. Bake for 30 to 35 minutes until golden brown. Reverse the pan from front to back on the rack once during baking. Set the pan on a wire rack to cool only slightly before cutting into 6 × 6 rows.

4. Store in the baking dish, tightly covered with aluminum foil or plastic wrap.

Yield: 36 squares

FROZEN PUFF PASTRY

Frozen puff pastry is my all-time favorite convenience food, and I use it constantly to make cookies and other confections. These are my favorites.

Tip

Can't find an oval cookie cutter? Neither could I, so I bought a 4-inch round cutter and bent it into an oval shape.

Shoe Soles

You would be most likely find these unusual cookies in a Bavarian pastry shop.

> **Granulated sugar, for sprinkling on rolling surface**
> **One 17 ¹/₄-ounce package frozen puff pastry, thawed as package directs**
> **Confectioners' sugar, for sprinkling on cookies**

1. Adjust two racks to divide the oven into thirds. Preheat the oven to 400°. Lightly coat two baking sheets with nonstick vegetable spray. Have ready a 4- to 4¹/₂-inch oval cookie cutter (see Tip).

2. Sprinkle a generous coating of granulated sugar on a rolling surface. Unfold one sheet of the pastry and roll to a ¹/₈-inch thickness. Cut the pastry into as many ovals as possible. Lightly roll out each oval to the size of a small shoe sole, about 5¹/₂ to 6 × 3 inches. With the back of a long knife, lightly press a waffle pattern into each oval to resemble shoe soles. Arrange the ovals, pattern side down, on a prepared baking sheet. Repeat with the remaining sheet of pastry. Just before placing the baking sheets in the oven, dust each cookie heavily with confectioners' sugar.

3. Bake for 8 to 10 minutes, or until the cookies are glazed and lightly browned, watching carefully, since the glaze burns easily. Reverse the baking sheets on the racks and from front to back once during baking. With a wide turner, transfer the cookies to wire racks to cool completely.

4. Store in a loosely covered container, separating the layers with sheets of waxed paper.

Yield: About 16 cookies

Palmiers

This is one French confection that I could not live without for too long, and I suspect you will end up feeling the same way after you make them once. Sometimes, if I am really feeling particularly evil, I will sandwich a few of these together with raspberry jam and sprinkle them with confectioners' sugar. Yum!

> One 17 1/4-ounce package frozen puff pastry, thawed as package directs
>
> Granulated sugar, for sprinkling on rolling surface and pastry

1. Adjust two racks to divide the oven into thirds. Preheat the oven to 400°. Lightly coat two baking sheets with nonstick vegetable spray.

2. Unfold one sheet of the pastry and cut it in half lengthwise to make two $9^{1}/_{2} \times 4^{1}/_{2}$-inch strips.

3. Sprinkle the work surface heavily with granulated sugar. Roll one of the strips into a 12×5-inch strip. Sprinkle fairly heavily with granulated sugar. Turn in each long side almost to the center, then fold in half lengthwise. Roll this piece very lightly with the rolling pin. With a long, sharp knife, cut into $1/_{4}$-inch slices. Arrange the slices on the prepared baking sheets, cut side up, spacing them about 1 inch apart.

4. Bake for 7 to 10 minutes until golden brown. With a wide turner, flip the pastries over and bake 1 to 2 minutes longer until the second side is lightly browned. Reverse the baking sheet from front to back when the palmiers are turned. With a wide turner, transfer the palmiers to wire racks to cool completely. Repeat this procedure with the remaining sheet of puff pastry while the first batch of palmiers is baking.

Yield: 192 tiny palmiers

French Bow Ties

This is another tricky little maneuver with puff pastry.

> One 17 1/4-ounce package frozen puff pastry, thawed as package directs
>
> 1 egg yolk mixed with 1 tablespoon water
>
> Confectioners' sugar, for sprinkling on cookies

1. Adjust two racks to divide the oven into thirds. Preheat the oven to 400°. Lightly grease two baking sheets with nonstick vegetable spray.

2. On a lightly floured surface, gently roll one sheet of the pastry to a 12×10-inch rectangle. With a pizza wheel or the tip of a sharp knife and a ruler, cut the pastry into four 3×10-inch strips.

3. With a narrow pastry brush, brush a strip of the egg yolk mixture down the center of three of the strips. Stack the strips on top of each other. Top with the remaining unbrushed strip, keeping all of the edges even. (The egg yolk will act as a "glue" to keep the strips together.) To fuse the layers, lay a heavy rolling pin lengthwise on the center of the stack and press down firmly. *It is important that the edges on either side remain separate.* With a long, sharp knife, cut the stack into $1/_{2}$-inch slices.

4. To shape, pick up one strip and hold it at the center. Gently spread out the edges at one end to form a fan with the edges facing upward. Repeat at the other end. As they are shaped, arrange the bow ties on the baking sheet, spacing them about 1 inch apart. Place the baking sheets in the refrigerator for 20 minutes.

5. Bake for 6 to 7 minutes until lightly browned. With a wide turner, flip the bow ties over and bake 3 to 4 minutes longer until lightly browned. With a wide turner, immediately transfer the bow ties to wire racks to cool completely.

6. Store in a loosely covered container. Sprinkle with confectioners' sugar just before serving.

Yield: About 40 bow ties

Puffy Nut Twists

Back in the old days—or at least in the days before frozen puff pastry was invented—these twists would have been a two-day project.

Walnut Filling

3/4 **cup walnut pieces**

1 **large egg, lightly beaten**

1/4 **cup packed light brown sugar**

1/8 **teaspoon salt**

One sheet of frozen puff pastry from a 17 1/2-ounce package, thawed as package directs

Glaze

1 **cup sifted confectioners' sugar**

1/8 **teaspoon lemon extract or** 1/4 **teaspoon vanilla extract**

1 **to 2 tablespoons milk**

1. Adjust one rack to divide the oven in half. Preheat the oven to 400°. Have ready one ungreased baking sheet.

2. To make the filling: Place the nuts in a food processor fitted with a steel blade. Process until finely ground, turning off the processor once and giving the nuts a good stir from the bottom to keep them from becoming pasty. In a small saucepan, combine the egg, ground nuts, brown sugar, and salt. Set over medium heat and stir constantly until the mixture thickens. Remove from the heat and set aside.

3. Roll the pastry into a 14-inch square. Cut the square in half with a pizza wheel or the tip of a sharp knife and a ruler. Spread the filling evenly over one of the pastry halves. Place the remaining half of the pastry over the filling. With the wheel and the ruler, cut the filled pastry lengthwise into seven 1-inch strips. Then cut each strip crosswise into 4 pieces. Pick up each piece and twist it twice, placing each piece on the ungreased baking sheet as it is twisted, spacing them about 1 inch apart.

4. Bake for 12 to 15 minutes until crisp and golden. With a wide turner, immediately transfer the twists to wire racks to cool completely.

5. To make the glaze: In a small bowl, with a mixing spoon, combine the confectioners' sugar, lemon extract, and enough milk so that the glaze is the proper consistency to drizzle off the tip of a spoon. Drizzle the glaze onto the twists. Set aside until the glaze is firm, about 30 minutes.

6. Store for a day or two in a single layer in a loosely covered container.

Yield: 28 twists

Puffy Pecan Crisps

These are sort of a French version of American Southern Pecan Tassies.

1/2 **cup packed light or dark brown sugar**

2 **tablespoons salted butter or margarine, melted**

1/3 **cup finely chopped pecans**

One sheet of frozen puff pastry from a 17 1/4-ounce package, thawed as package directs

Confectioners' sugar, for dusting crisps

1. Adjust one rack to divide the oven in half. Preheat the oven to 400°. Have ready two or three pans of 3-inch muffin cups. In a small bowl, combine the sugar, melted butter, and pecans.

2. Unfold the pastry on a lightly floured surface. Roll into a 15 × 12-inch rectangle. With a pizza wheel or the tip of a sharp knife and a ruler, cut the pastry lengthwise into five 3-inch strips. Cut the strips crosswise into four 3-inch pieces to make 20 squares. Press the squares into the bottoms of 20 muffin-pan cups. Place 1 heaping teaspoon of the pecan mixture in each cup.

3. Bake for 12 minutes until golden. Set the pans on wire racks to cool completely. Carefully remove the crisps from the muffin pans.

4. Store in a tightly covered, shallow container. Sprinkle with confectioners' sugar just before serving.

Yield: 20 crisps

CANINE COOKIES

Dog fancier that I am, I had to include a little something for Fido. Actually, these recipes are not a whim. Even before it was socially responsible to do so, I have always been concerned with what my family ate. I feel the same way about my dogs. This is not to say that they don't get some store-bought pet goodies. I must warn you, though, that during the course of perfecting the recipes for these cookies, I have almost ruined my own dogs' tastes for any kind of commercial bones or cookies. They come racing to the kitchen whenever they smell either of these baking. They love warm cookies!

Whole Wheat Butter Bites

I tested these little biscuit-cookies on every dog I know (and I have quite a few dog friends besides my own Taco and Ginger) and they all loved them. Even the Holbrooke cats next door thought they were good enough to leave only the scraps of a plastic bag after I slid a few samples through their mail slot late one night.

2 1/2 cups whole wheat flour

2 tablespoons wheat germ

1/2 teaspoon salt

6 tablespoons (3/4 stick) salted butter or margarine, at room temperature

1 large egg

3/4 cup skim milk

1. Adjust two racks to divide the oven into thirds. Lightly grease two baking sheets. Have ready a 1 1/2-inch round cookie or biscuit cutter.

2. In a medium-size bowl, with a whisk, combine the flour, wheat germ, and salt until thoroughly mixed.

3. In a large bowl, with an electric mixer at medium-high speed, beat together the butter and egg until fairly well blended. (There will be some flecks of butter in the mixture.) With the mixer at medium-low speed, gradually add the flour mixture and the milk alternately to the butter mixture, starting and ending with the flour, and beating just until blended after each addition. Gather the dough into a ball. If it seems crumbly, add a few drops of water; if it seems sticky, add a little more flour. Wrap the dough in plastic wrap and refrigerate until cold, about 1 hour.

4. Preheat the oven to 350°.

5. Divide the dough in half. On a lightly floured surface, roll half of the dough to a 1/8-inch thickness. With the cookie cutter, cut into rounds. Arrange the rounds on a prepared baking sheet, spacing them about 1 inch apart. Gather the dough scraps together, reroll, and cut as many more rounds as possible. Repeat with the remaining half of the dough.

6. Bake for about 20 minutes until puffy, but still slightly soft when pressed with a finger, and the bottoms are just starting to color. Reverse the baking sheets on the racks and from front to back once during baking. Slide the cookies off the baking sheets onto wire racks to cool completely.

7. Store in a tightly covered container for several weeks. For longer storage, freeze in tightly sealed, zipper-top plastic bags.

Yield: About 94 cookies

Hoovers

· ·

I used to call these crunchy, aromatic bones Woofers, but I changed the name in memory of my very dear friend Hoover, a noble, intelligent, and sweet-tempered Golden Retriever. He could devour these nearly as fast as I could take them out of the oven. These bones smell so good when you open the container that you will be tempted to spread one with cream cheese and have it yourself.

> 1 cup whole wheat flour
>
> 1 cup cornmeal
>
> $^1/_4$ cup wheat germ
>
> 2 tablespoons dried parsley flakes or $^1/_4$ cup minced fresh parsley
>
> $^1/_2$ teaspoon salt
>
> 2 large cloves garlic, peeled and put through a garlic press
>
> $^1/_4$ cup olive or vegetable oil
>
> $^2/_3$ cup water

1. Adjust two racks to divide the oven into thirds. Preheat the oven to 425°. Lightly grease two baking sheets. Have ready small, medium, and/or large cookie cutters (see Tip).

2. In a large bowl, with an electric mixer at medium speed, combine the flour, cornmeal, wheat germ, parsley, salt, garlic, and oil until the mixture resembles small crumbs. Add the water and beat until the dough leaves the side of the bowl and can be gathered into a ball. Divide the dough in half.

3. On a very lightly floured surface (this dough is very easy to work); roll half of the dough to a $^1/_4$-inch thickness. With the cutters, cut the dough into shapes. With a wide turner, transfer the cutouts to the prepared baking sheets, spacing them about 1 inch apart. Gather the dough scraps together and reroll. Cut as many more shapes as possible. Repeat with the remaining half of the dough.

4. Bake for 16 to 20 minutes depending on the size of the bones, until fairly firm when lightly touched. Reverse the baking sheets on the racks and from front to back once during baking. With a wide turner, immediately transfer the cookies to wire racks to cool completely.

5. Store in an airtight container. These cookies keep well for several weeks. For longer storage, freeze in zipper-top plastic bags.

Yield: About 20 small cookies, 16 medium-size cookies, or 14 large cookies

Tip

When I make these, I use a set of three bone-shaped cookie cutters. The small cutter measures $1^3/_4 \times ^3/_4$ inch; the medium-size cutter $2^1/_2 \times 1^1/_4$ inches, and the large cutter $3^1/_2 \times 1^1/_4$ inches.

12
Favorite Cookies from Friends

Three years ago, I realized just how fortunate I am to have such good friends. During my husband's, Gerry Repp, long illness, and after his death, I was surrounded and supported by some very caring people, a great many of whom are, in one way or another, part of the food community to which we all belong, or "foodies" as we often refer to each other. Not that I was surprised. In a conversation I had a few weeks ago with another food writer, we marveled at how generous food professionals can be with one another. We concluded that, because food is a subject so close to everyone's heart, those who make a career of it are just naturally inclined to be kind-spirited and open-handed.

When the thought occurred to me to ask some of my "foodie" friends to participate in this book by each sharing one of their favorite cookie recipes for a special chapter, they were, without exception, eager to comply.

I think some of these names will be familiar to you, especially if you look at the covers of cookbooks and the mastheads of some of the leading magazines.

Not surprisingly, either, many of these recipes are hand-me-downs from moms and childhood favorites. So, what else is new?

Enjoy!

Elizabeth Alston's Dutch Peppernuts

Elizabeth is the warm and engaging food editor of *Woman's Day* magazine. I've known her since her days as the food editor of *Redbook* magazine many years ago. Elizabeth says that these diminutive cookies can be stored for up to 3 weeks and the flavor keeps getting better and better and better.

1 1/2 cups plus 2 1/2 tablespoons all-purpose flour
1 tablespoon baking powder
1/4 teaspoon ground cinnamon
1/4 teaspoon ground cloves
1/4 teaspoon ground mace
1/4 teaspoon ground nutmeg
1 cup packed light or dark brown sugar
1/2 cup (1 stick) salted butter or margarine, at room temperature
1 large egg
1/2 teaspoon anise extract

1. In a medium-size bowl, with a whisk, combine 1½ cups of the flour, the baking powder, cinnamon, cloves, mace, and nutmeg until thoroughly mixed.

2. In a large bowl, with an electric mixer at medium-high speed, beat together the brown sugar, butter, egg, and anise extract until thick and pale-colored, 2 to 3 minutes. With the mixer at medium-low speed, gradually add the flour mixture, beating until well blended. Gather the dough into a ball and divide it into quarters. Wrap each quarter separately in plastic wrap and refrigerate until firm, about 2 hours. (At this point, the dough can be tightly wrapped in aluminum foil and refrigerated for up to 1 week or frozen for up to 3 months. If frozen, thaw in the refrigerator before proceeding.)

3. Adjust two racks to divide the oven into thirds. Preheat the oven to 350°. Have ready at least two ungreased baking sheets.

4. Lay a 12-inch strip of waxed paper on a slightly dampened work surface (to keep the waxed paper from sliding around). Lightly dust the waxed paper with flour. With a lightly floured rolling pin, roll one quarter of the dough on the waxed paper into an 8-inch square. (Leave the remaining dough in the refrigerator until you are ready to work with it.) Slide an ungreased baking sheet beneath the waxed paper and freeze for 10 minutes until the dough is very firm. (Meanwhile, start rolling the remaining quarters of dough the same way.)

5. Slide the waxed paper from the cookie sheet onto a cutting surface. With a pizza wheel or the tip of a sharp knife and a ruler, cut the dough into 1/2-inch squares. (These do not have to be absolutely exact.) Scatter the little squares of dough about 1/4 inch apart on an ungreased baking sheet.

6. Bake two sheets at a time for 9 to 10 minutes until firm to the touch and very lightly browned. Reverse the baking sheets on the racks and from front to back once during baking. With a wide turner, transfer the cookies to wire racks or a countertop to cool completely.

7. Repeat the cutting and baking with the remaining dough.

8. Store in a tightly covered container.

Yield: About 500 tiny cookies

Annie Bailey's Butterscotch-Oatmeal Shortbread

. . . .

"I can't possibly decide which is my *one* favorite cookie recipe," Annie said to me. "I have so many." Annie, who is a whiz in the kitchen, developed many of the recipes in this book, including the biscotti recipes and the gingerbread house. I met her on a food editors' trip in 1983 when she was working for *Redbook*. A couple of years later she came to work as the test kitchen director at *Parents Magazine*. Annie's wit and good humor, to say nothing of her incredible cooking skills, made it a pleasure for me to come to work. These days Annie stays fairly close to home with her husband, Michael, and their two daughters, Megan and Mary Kate. Annie must undoubtedly be the cookie-bakingest and most favorite mom on the block.

- 1 ¹/₂ cups all-purpose flour
- ³/₄ cup packed light brown sugar
- 1 cup regular or quick-cooking (not instant) rolled oats
- 1 cup (2 sticks) salted butter or margarine, at room temperature
- 2 tablespoons granulated sugar

1. In a large bowl, with an electric mixer at low speed, beat together the flour, brown sugar, oats, and butter just until the mixture starts to come together. Increase the speed to medium and beat until the mixture becomes very crumbly and then comes together into a stiff dough. Gather the dough into a ball.

2. Divide the dough in half. Sprinkle the granulated sugar onto a sheet of waxed paper. With your hands, shape each half of the dough into an 8-inch cylinder. Roll the cylinders in the granulated sugar. Wrap each cylinder separately in plastic wrap and freeze for about 1 hour, or until very cold and firm.

3. Adjust two racks to divide the oven into thirds. Preheat the oven to 350°. Have ready two ungreased baking sheets.

4. With a long, sharp knife, cut the cylinders into ³/₈-inch slices. Arrange the slices on the ungreased baking sheets, spacing them about 1 inch apart.

5. Bake for 14 to 16 minutes until golden. Reverse the baking sheets on the racks and from front to back once during baking. With a wide turner, immediately transfer the cookies to wire racks to cool completely.

6. Store in a tightly covered container.

Yield: About 48 cookies

 Tip
For a slightly different flavor, Annie suggests adding about ³/₄ teaspoon shredded and minced orange zest.

Jeanne Bauer's Ginger Genies

"If you like ginger, you're going to love these cookies," says Jeanne. Jeanne, who is a consultant to the food and beverage industry, a former public relations executive, and, when I first knew her, the food editor for the McFadden group of women's magazines. Jeanne says she usually makes these cookies either soft or crisp. The soft ones she likes to use as a coffee dipper. The crisp cookies she crumbles—or uses the crumbs from the cookie tin—to scatter over fresh pineapple slices or chunks, lemon sherbet or sorbet, or ice cream. Other times she stirs the crumbs into plain or vanilla yogurt.

    2 1/2 cups all-purpose flour
    1 tablespoon ground ginger
    1 tablespoon baking soda
    3/4 cup (1 1/2 sticks) salted butter or
        margarine, at room temperature
    1 cup light or dark brown sugar
    1/2 cup unsulphured molasses
    1 large egg
    3 tablespoons minced fresh ginger root
    3/4 cup finely chopped crystallized ginger

1. In a medium-size bowl, with a whisk, combine the flour, ground ginger, and baking soda until thoroughly mixed.

2. In a large bowl, with an electric mixer at medium-high speed, beat together the butter and brown sugar until very well blended, 2 to 3 minutes. Add the molasses and egg and beat until smooth. With the mixer at medium-low speed, gradually add the flour mixture, beating just until blended. With a mixing spoon, stir in the fresh ginger and crystallized ginger until well distributed throughout the batter. Cover the bowl and refrigerate for several hours or overnight.

3. Adjust two racks to divide the oven into thirds. Preheat the oven to 350°. Lightly grease two baking sheets.

4. Scoop heaping teaspoonfuls of the batter out of the bowl and roll them into 1-inch balls between the palms of your hands. Arrange the balls on the prepared baking sheets, spacing them about 2 inches apart.

5. Bake for 10 to 12 minutes depending on whether you like your cookies soft (10 minutes), crisp (12 minutes), or something in between (11 minutes). Reverse the baking sheets on the racks and from front to back once during baking. With a wide turner, immediately transfer the cookies to wire racks to cool completely.

6. Store in a tightly covered container.

Yield: About 48 cookies

Marla Bazar's Beloved Mondelbrud

Marla is the food editor at *Parents Magazine*, so if you have little kids and read *Parents*, now you know who is responsible for all the good advice about dealing with picky eaters, lunch-box food, and magical birthday cake constructions. This filled cylinder cookie is baked and then sliced and will remind you of rugelah, although it is quicker and easier.

    3 cups all-purpose flour
    2 teaspoons baking powder
    1/2 cup (1 stick) unsalted butter
    1 cup granulated sugar
    3 large eggs

Filling

    3 tablespoons strawberry or apricot preserves
    3/4 cup finely chopped walnuts
    3/4 cup raisins
    Ground cinnamon

1. In a medium-size bowl, with a whisk, combine the flour and baking powder until thoroughly mixed.

2. In a large bowl, with an electric mixer at medium-high speed, beat the butter with the

sugar until light and fluffy, 2 to 3 minutes. Beat in the eggs, one at a time, until blended. With the mixer at medium-low speed, gradually add the flour mixture, beating just until blended. Divide the dough into thirds. Wrap each third in plastic wrap and refrigerate until firm, about 1 hour.

3. Adjust one rack to divide the oven in half. Preheat the oven to 350°. Lightly grease one large baking sheet.

4. On a lightly floured surface, roll out each third of the dough into a 10-inch oval shape. Spread each oval with 1 tablespoon of the preserves, leaving a ¹/₂-inch border. Sprinkle each oval with ¹/₄ cup of the walnuts and ¹/₄ cup of the raisins over the preserves. Sprinkle generously with cinnamon. From a long side, roll up each oval of dough, pinching the ends to seal. Arrange all three rolls, seam sides down, on the prepared baking sheet.

5. Bake for 50 to 60 minutes until lightly browned on top. Reverse the baking sheet from front to back once during baking. Remove the baking sheet from the oven. With a wide turner, immediately remove the rolls to a cutting surface. With a long, serrated knife, cut each roll into about 20 diagonal slices.

6. Store in a tightly covered container, separating the layers with sheets of waxed paper.

Yield: About 60 cookies

Betty Bianconi's Toffee-Cookie Bars

"It was my mom, years ago, who invented this mouthwatering cookie recipe when she started baking as a hobby after she retired," writes Betty. "After sampling the thin, crisp, chocolate-coated cookie, it immediately went on my list of favorites and has stayed there." Betty, who is the former food editor of *Woman's World*, also happens to be the talented and versatile baker who tested—and often had to rework—many of the recipes in this

book, not an easy job, and in record time. She also did the food styling for the glorious photo of the cookies on the cover.

> 1 cup (2 sticks) salted butter or margarine, at room temperature
> 1 cup packed light or dark brown sugar
> 1 cup all-purpose flour
> 1 large egg yolk
> One 6-ounce bag (1 cup) semisweet chocolate chips
> ¹/₂ cup chopped nuts

1. Adjust one rack to divide the oven in half. Preheat the oven to 350°. Lightly grease a 15 × 9-inch jelly-roll pan; set aside.

2. In a large bowl, with an electric mixer at medium-high speed, beat together the butter and brown sugar until very well blended, 2 to 3 minutes. With a mixing spoon, stir in the flour and egg yolk until the mixture forms a dough. Turn the dough into the prepared jelly-roll pan. With the palm of your hand or the back of the spoon, press the dough evenly into the pan.

3. Bake for about 20 minutes until lightly browned. Reverse the baking sheet from front to back once during baking. Remove the pan from the oven to a wire rack and immediately sprinkle the chocolate chips evenly over the baked dough. Let stand about 5 minutes until the chips have melted. With a spatula, spread and smooth the chocolate into an even layer. Sprinkle evenly with the nuts. Allow to cool slightly. While still warm, cut into 6 × 7 rows; cool completely.

4. Store in a tightly covered container, separating the layers with sheets of waxed paper.

Yield: 42 bars

Babs Chernetz's Nutty Squares

Babs is the food editor of *McCall's*, and also the undisputed expert among us about what's hot to eat and where to eat it. She has a bulging file of write-ups on restaurants she has tried, or intends to try, in both the United States and Europe. So, if I'm going anywhere, the first thing to do is call Babs and ask her where to eat. Babs has a scrupulous palate, and when we travel together it's fun to follow her from restaurant to restaurant, and listen and learn while she critiques the food. Babs says these cookies are among her "faves" and easy, too. There are precious few cookie recipes that I want to run into the kitchen and make, but this is one of them.

- 1 cup all-purpose flour
- ¹/₂ cup (1 stick) cold, unsalted butter, divided
- ¹/₂ cup granulated sugar
- ¹/₂ cup packed light or dark brown sugar
- 2 tablespoons honey
- ¹/₄ cup heavy (whipping) cream
- 2 cups unsalted mixed nuts (with or without peanuts), coarsely chopped

1. Adjust one rack to divide the oven in half. Preheat the oven to 350°. Grease a 9-inch-square, metal baking pan and line it with aluminum foil, shiny side up, allowing the ends to extend over the rim of the pan; grease the foil.

2. In a food processor fitted with a steel blade, mix the flour, ¹/₄ cup of the butter, and the granulated sugar until crumbly. Press this mixture over the foil in the bottom of the pan. Bake for 10 minutes. Remove from the oven and set aside.

3. In a medium-size saucepan, heat the remaining ¹/₄ cup butter, brown sugar, and honey until melted and bubbly. Boil for 1 minute; remove from the heat. Stir in the cream and then the nuts. Pour into the pan over the crust.

4. Bake for about 20 minutes until bubbly. Cool the cookies in the pan set on a wire rack. Using the foil to help you, lift the cookies out of the pan. Peel off the foil. Cut the cookies into 8 × 8 rows.

5. Store in a tightly covered container.

Yield: About 64 cookies

Pat Cobe's Ginger Crisps

"I became attached to these cookies during my first job, working in the test kitchen at *Good Housekeeping* magazine," says Pat. "One of our staff was from Scandinavia and she baked these cookies during the holidays . . . and any other time we all felt that we needed a cookie break, which was often." In 1980, Pat went out on her own as a freelance writer, editor, and author. In 1992 Fawcett/Columbine published her *International Kosher Cookbook*. Now and then Pat and I have the opportunity to collaborate on various magazine projects, and it is always such a pleasure to work with her. I hope she feels the same about me.

- 2 cups all-purpose flour
- 1 ¹/₂ cups sugar, divided
- 1 ¹/₂ teaspoons ground ginger
- 1 ¹/₂ teaspoons ground cinnamon
- 1 teaspoon baking soda
- ¹/₂ teaspoon salt
- ¹/₂ teaspoon ground nutmeg
- ³/₄ cup (1 ¹/₂ sticks) unsalted butter, at room temperature
- ¹/₂ cup dark molasses
- 1 large egg

1. In a large bowl, with a whisk, combine the flour, 1 cup of the sugar, ginger, cinnamon, baking soda, salt, and nutmeg until thoroughly mixed. Add the butter, molasses, and egg all at once. With an electric mixer at low speed, beat the mixture just until blended. With the mixer at medium-high speed, beat for 2 minutes, occasionally scraping the side of the bowl with a rubber spatula. Gather the dough into a ball. Wrap in plastic wrap and refrigerate until well chilled, about 1 hour.

2. Adjust two racks to divide the oven into thirds. Preheat the oven to 375°. Lightly grease two baking sheets. Sprinkle the remaining ¹/₂ cup sugar onto a sheet of waxed paper.

3. Working on a lightly floured surface, pull off small pieces of the dough and roll them into 1-inch balls between the palms of your hands. Arrange the balls on the prepared baking sheets, spacing them about 2 inches apart. With the bottom of a glass dipped in the sugar, flatten each ball into a ¹/₈-inch-thick round.

4. Bake for 8 to 10 minutes until lightly browned around the edges. Cool the cookies on the baking sheets for 2 minutes. With a wide turner, transfer the cookies to wire racks to cool completely.

5. Store in a tightly covered container.

Yield: About 72 cookies

Tip

Butter can be brought to room temperature in a microwave oven. Place one stick of cold butter or margarine on a glass plate. Microwave at 30 percent power (medium-low) for 1 to 2 minutes, rotating the dish and testing the butter every 30 seconds. (Be careful! The butter can very suddenly melt if it's not carefully watched.)

Stephanie Curtis's Macarons au Chocolat (Chocolate Macaroons)

When I am visiting in Paris with my dear and long-time friend Stephanie, we would while away many an afternoon drinking little cups of strong coffee accompanied by these divine macaroons. When Stephanie lived in New York, she was an editor at

Food & Wine magazine, mostly covering the restaurant beat. She moved to Paris about ten years ago, where she thrives as a correspondent for many food publications. Stephanie, who is my personal expert regarding matters of French food and restaurants, tells me that the true mark of a perfect French macaroon is a smooth, shiny, crisp exterior with a soft, moist center. These macaroons can be served singly, if you like, but they are divine when sandwiched together with Raspberry Filling. Before starting on this recipe, you may want to read about how to use a pastry tube on page 30, and do not make them during humid weather.

> 1 ¹/₂ **cups slivered almonds**
> 1 ³/₄ **cups sifted confectioners' sugar**
> 1 ¹/₂ **tablespoons sifted unsweetened cocoa powder**
> 6 **large egg whites, at room temperature**
> 2 **tablespoons superfine sugar**
> ¹/₂ **teaspoon vanilla extract**

Filling

> ¹/₂ **pint fresh raspberries**
> ¹/₄ **cup heavy (whipping) cream**
> 8 **ounces (8 squares) semisweet chocolate**
> 2 **tablespoons unsalted butter (not margarine), at room temperature**
> 1 **tablespoon raspberry liqueur**

1. Adjust two racks to divide the oven into thirds. Line two baking sheets with aluminum foil, shiny side up. Place another baking sheet beneath each lined sheet. Fit a pastry bag with a plain, number 6 decorating tip.

2. In a food processor fitted with a steel blade, process the nuts until finely ground, stopping the processor once to give the nuts a good stir from the bottom to keep them from becoming pasty. You should have *exactly* 1¹/₃ cups of ground almonds.

3. In a medium-size bowl, with a whisk, combine the ground almonds, confectioners' sugar, and cocoa until thoroughly mixed.

4. In a large bowl, with an electric mixer at medium-low speed, beat the egg whites until frothy. Continue to beat at high speed until soft peaks form when the beaters are lifted. Add the superfine sugar, 1 tablespoon at a time, beating for about 1 minute between each addition. Continue to beat until stiff peaks form when the beaters are lifted. Add the vanilla and beat for about 1 minute. Sprinkle the confectioners' sugar mixture over the egg whites and fold in with a rubber spatula.

5. Fill the prepared pastry bag with the batter. Pipe out even-size rounds, about 1 inch in diameter, onto the prepared baking sheets, staggering the mounds and keeping them about 1 inch apart. Set the sheet of macaroons aside at room temperature until a light crust forms on them, about 15 minutes.

6. Preheat the oven to 350°.

7. Bake for 15 minutes, leaving the oven door slightly ajar (this allows the steam to escape), until firm when lightly touched and the bottom edges are pale brown.

8. Cool on the baking sheets set on wire racks. Lift the macaroons off the baking sheets with your fingers.

9. To make the filling: In a small, heavy saucepan, combine the raspberries and cream. Cook over medium heat, stirring and mashing the berries into the cream, for 5 minutes, or until thickened; set aside.

10. In a medium-size, heavy saucepan set over very low heat, melt the chocolate, stirring constantly until smooth. Off the heat, stir the butter and the liqueur into the melted chocolate. Add the raspberry mixture to the chocolate mixture and stir until well combined. Transfer the filling to a bowl. Cover and chill until set.

11. To form filled cookies, using a small spatula or a butter spreader, smooth a thin layer of the filling on the bottom of one macaroon. Top with another macaroon, bottom sides together, to form a sandwich. Repeat with the remaining macaroons and filling.

12. Arrange the filled macaroons in one or two layers in a shallow container. Cover and store in the refrigerator. (If the macaroons are not filled, they can be stored at room temperature in a tightly covered container, separating the layers with sheets of waxed paper.)

Yield: About 42 filled macaroons

Tip

Plastic bowls are slightly porous, so they can retain minute amounts of fat. Don't use them for beating egg whites, since even the smallest amount of fat can deflate them.

Nathalie Dupree's Pecan Cookies

Nathalie is one of the busiest women I know, and also one of the nicest. She has a popular cooking series on public television and when she's not taping, she's writing magazine articles, consulting, or crisscrossing the country for book tours and personal appearances. In 1976, Nathalie founded Rich's Cooking School in Atlanta, and I think she may have given Paul Prudhomme his first spot in the limelight. Nathalie and I became friends while we were judges one year at the National Broiler Council's chicken cooking contest. She says these shortbread cookies are terrific eaten plain, but they're also great with sweet, juicy Georgia peaches. About 30 minutes before serving, she sandwiches whipped cream and peaches between two of these cookies and chills them. Just before serving, she decorates them with a little more whipped cream or sprinkles them with confectioners' sugar.

1 ½ **cups all-purpose flour**
⅓ **teaspoon salt**
1 ¼ **cups finely chopped and toasted pecans (page 16)**

¹/₂ cup (1 stick) plus 2 tablespoons unsalted butter, at room temperature

¹/₂ cup sugar

1. Adjust two racks to divide the oven into thirds. Have ready two ungreased baking sheets. Also have ready a 3-inch round cookie cutter with a plain or scalloped edge.

2. In a small bowl, with a whisk, combine the flour and salt until thoroughly mixed. With a mixing spoon, stir in the pecans until well distributed throughout the flour mixture.

3. In a medium-size bowl, with an electric mixer at medium-high speed, beat together the butter and sugar until light and fluffy, 2 to 3 minutes. With the mixing spoon, stir in the flour mixture just until blended and a dough forms. Divide the dough into quarters.

4. Place each quarter of the dough between two sheets of waxed paper. Roll each quarter to a ¹/₈-inch thickness. Place the encased pieces of dough in the refrigerator and chill until firm, about 30 minutes.

5. Preheat the oven to 375°.

6. Remove the dough from the refrigerator; remove the top sheet of waxed paper. Cut into 3-inch rounds. Arrange the rounds on the ungreased baking sheets.

7. Bake for about 10 minutes just until the edges begin to brown. Reverse the baking sheets on the racks and from front to back once during baking. The cookies will be soft even though fully baked and will harden as they cool. When the cookies are nearly hard, with a wide turner, transfer them to wire racks to cool completely.

8. Store in a tightly covered container.

Yield: About 14 cookies

Carol Gelles's Cottage Cheese Rugelach

I don't know why Carol's rugelach tastes better than any other. It's much easier to make than others, mainly because Carol has adapted it for the food processor. She says these are a hit whenever she serves them, and they freeze beautifully, which means she can always have some on hand. Carol and I used to work together when she was one of New York's premier food stylists. Now we are fellow authors with the same publishing house. Carol's newest book, *1,000 Vegetarian Recipes*, was published by Macmillan last spring.

One 8-ounce container full-fat cottage cheese

1 cup (2 sticks) salted butter (not margarine), at room temperature

2 cups all-purpose flour

2 tablespoons butter, melted

1 cup dark brown sugar

³/₄ teaspoon ground cinnamon

³/₄ cup chopped walnuts

¹/₂ cup raisins

1 large egg, beaten with 1 tablespoon water, for brushing on rugelach

1. Adjust two racks to divide the oven into thirds. Preheat the oven to 350°. Lightly grease two baking sheets.

2. In a food processor fitted with a steel blade, process the cottage cheese until smooth. Add the butter and process until completely combined. Add the flour and pulse-process until a dough forms.

3. Divide the dough into three equal parts. If the dough is too soft to roll out, refrigerate until it reaches rolling consistency.

4. On a well-floured surface, roll each part of the dough into a 10-inch circle. Brush each circle with melted butter.

5. In a small bowl, combine the brown sugar and the cinnamon. Sprinkle each circle with the cinnamon mixture, dividing evenly. Sprinkle with walnuts and raisins, dividing evenly. With a pastry wheel or the tip of a sharp knife, cut each circle into 16 pie-shaped wedges. Beginning at the wide end, roll up each wedge. Arrange the roll-ups on the baking sheets, seam sides down. For a shiny finish, brush each roll-up with the egg mixture.

6. Bake for 30 to 35 minutes until browned. Reverse the baking sheets on the racks and from front to back once during baking. With a wide turner, remove the rugelach to wire racks to cool completely.

7. Store in a tightly covered container, separating the layers with sheets of waxed paper.

Yield: 48 rugelach

Margaret Happel's Mexican Cookie Bars

Margaret has had a long and distinguished career in the food industry. Before I knew her, she was the food editor of the *Ladies' Home Journal*, as well as the editor for the original *Good Food* magazine published by *TV Guide*. Later, Margaret went on to become consumer affairs director for Nabisco and was most recently the food editor at *Redbook*. She has written seven cookbooks and is a trustee and chairman for the Educational Policy Committee for the Culinary Institute of America.

> One 6-ounce package butterscotch-flavored chips
> $^1/_2$ cup (1 stick) salted butter or margarine
> $^1/_2$ cup packed dark brown sugar
> 1 $^1/_2$ cups all-purpose flour
> 1 teaspoon baking powder
> $^1/_2$ teaspoon salt
> 1 cup chopped, toasted almonds (page 16)
> $^1/_2$ cup finely chopped mixed candied fruits
> $^1/_2$ cup currants or chopped raisins
> 2 large eggs, lightly beaten
> 1 tablespoon minced and shredded orange zest
> $^1/_8$ teaspoon chili powder (optional)

1. Adjust one rack to divide the oven in half. Preheat the oven to 350° (or 325° if using a glass baking dish). Lightly grease a 13 × 9-inch metal baking pan or glass baking dish; set aside.

2. In a medium-size saucepan set over low heat, combine the butterscotch chips, butter, and brown sugar. With a mixing spoon, stir constantly until melted and smooth. Remove from the heat and set aside.

3. In a medium-size bowl, with a whisk, combine the flour, baking powder, and salt until thoroughly mixed. With the mixing spoon, stir the flour mixture into the butterscotch mixture until just blended. Turn the batter into the prepared pan, spreading it with the back of the spoon to make an even layer.

4. Bake for 20 minutes. While the bars are baking, in a medium-size bowl, combine the almonds, candied fruits, currants, eggs, orange zest, and chili powder; set aside.

5. Remove the pan of partially baked dough from the oven and spread the almond mixture evenly over the hot dough. Return to the oven, reversing the pan from front to back at the same time, and bake for 20 minutes longer. Set the pan on a wire rack to cool completely before cutting into 9 × 6 rows.

6. Store in the baking pan, tightly covered with aluminum foil or plastic wrap.

Yield: 54 bars

Jan Hazard's Sarah Bernhardts

"I have just the cookie for you," Jan told me, and this is the recipe she sent—an indulgent macaroon cookie that is a triple treat of mouthwatering ingredients. Jan is the food editor of the *Ladies' Home Journal*, as well as the mother of two, although I can't imagine her putting *these* cookies in a school lunch box, especially if they've been gold-leafed! This recipe has appeared in the *Journal* under the heading of "Cookie Dazzlers." That's for sure.

Dough

> One 7-ounce tube or one 8-ounce can
>   almond paste
> $^1/_2$ cup granulated sugar
> 2 large egg whites
> $^1/_4$ teaspoon almond extract
> Pinch of salt

Filling

> $^3/_4$ cup heavy (whipping) cream
> 16 ounces (16 squares) semisweet chocolate,
>   chopped and divided
> 2 tablespoons unsalted butter
>   (no substitutions)
> 1 teaspoon dark rum
> Edible gold leaf (see Tip)

1. Adjust two racks to divide the oven into thirds. Preheat the oven to 350°. Line three baking sheets with aluminum foil, shiny side up. Fit a large pastry bag with a $^1/_4$-inch plain tip.

2. In a large bowl, with a mixing spoon, combine the almond paste, sugar, egg whites, almond extract, and salt. With an electric mixer at medium speed, beat the mixture until smooth. Increase the speed to high and beat for 2 minutes. Spoon the batter into the pastry bag and pipe $^3/_4$-inch rounds on the prepared baking sheets.

3. Bake for 10 to 12 minutes until light golden. Reverse the baking sheets on the racks and from front to back once during baking. (Bake the third sheet in the center of the oven, reversing the baking sheet from front to back once during baking.) Set the baking sheets on wire racks until the cookies are completely cool. Carefully peel the cookies from the foil and set aside.

4. While the cookies are cooling, make the filling. In a medium-size saucepan heat the cream over medium heat just to boiling. Remove the pan from the heat. Add 8 ounces of the chocolate and the butter and rum. Stir until smooth. Let stand, stirring occasionally, until thick enough to pipe, about 40 minutes.

5. Fit a pastry bag with a $^1/_2$-inch plain tip. Spoon in the filling and pipe a small mound on the flat side of each cookie. Place the cookies on the baking sheets, chocolate side up, and refrigerate until firm, about 1 hour.

6. In a small saucepan set over very low heat, melt the remaining 8 ounces of chocolate, stirring until smooth. Remove from the heat. Set aside and keep warm.

7. Dip each cookie, filling side down, in the chocolate to coat. Place the cookie, chocolate side up, on a jelly-roll pan or a tray. Refrigerate until firm. Decorate each cookie with a small piece of gold leaf, if desired.

8. Store in a tightly covered container, separating the layers with sheets of waxed paper. The cookies can also be frozen for up to 3 months.

Yield: About 96 cookies

Tip

    Edible gold leaf (along with instructions for using it) is available in stores that specialize in fancy baking products. It can also be ordered by mail. (See Appendix C, "Shopping and Mail-Order Sources.")

Howard Helmer's Rutgers University Cookies

For many years, Howard has been the incredibly popular spokesperson and goodwill ambassador for the American Egg Board. Howard and I go back a long time, almost 30 years. One of his claims to fame is that he is in the *Guinness Book of World Records* as the world's fastest omelet maker: 427 omelets in 30 minutes, a record he set in 1990 that has yet to be broken. When Howard's son, Michael, was a student at Rutgers a few years ago, these cookies were great favorites on campus, and probably still are.

To make the cookies you need one box of Duncan Hines chocolate-chip cookie mix and "a whole lot of candy bars," anything you love, from Milky Ways, to Snickers, to Fifth Avenues, to Heath Bars. Follow the directions on the box for mixing the cookies. Then, stir in the candy bars that have been cut or broken into small pieces. "Done right," Howard says, "you can actually double the yield of the cookies." Bake according to the package directions, although the time may have to be adjusted to allow for the addition of the candy. "The candy bars get all gooey and run together, and the cookies are fantastic," sighs Howard.

 **Tip**

A slice of apple or a piece of soft bread do a remarkably good job of keeping soft cookies soft, and softening cookies that have gotten too hard. Place the apple or bread slice with the cookies in an airtight container. Replace the apple or bread every couple of days. By this method, it takes about 24 hours to soften hard cookies.

Irma Hyams's Apricot Nut Squares with Chocolate Chips

Irma Hyams is one of the first food professionals I met when I came into the business as the food editor for *Lady's Circle* magazine in the late sixties. At the time, Irma was the vice president of a public relations agency, but was known around town as "the chocolate lady," because she handled the account for the Chocolate Manufacturers' Association. Irma is my main source for chocolate information and lore. These bars, she says, keep well and freeze well and, not to my surprise, contain some chocolate.

> Fine, dry bread crumbs, for coating baking pan
> Boiling water
> $^1/_2$ cup dried apricots, cut in half
> $^3/_4$ cup plus 2 tablespoons all-purpose flour
> $^1/_2$ teaspoon (scant) baking powder
> $^1/_2$ teaspoon (scant) baking soda
> 6 tablespoons ($^1/_2$ stick plus 2 tablespoons) salted butter
> $^1/_2$ cup sugar
> 1 large egg
> $^1/_2$ teaspoon almond extract
> $^1/_2$ cup (3 ounces) semisweet chocolate chips
> $^1/_2$ cup chopped pecans or walnuts
> Confectioners' sugar, for dusting bars

1. Adjust one rack to divide the oven in half. Lightly grease an 8-inch-square metal baking pan and dust with bread crumbs, shaking out the excess.

2. In a small bowl, pour enough boiling water over the apricots just to cover them; let stand 30 minutes.

3. Adjust one rack to divide the oven in half. Preheat the oven to 350°.

4. In a medium-size bowl, with a whisk, combine the flour, baking powder, and baking soda until thoroughly mixed.

5. In a large bowl, with an electric mixer at medium-high speed, beat together the butter and sugar until light and fluffy, 2 to 3 minutes. Beat in the egg and almond extract until well blended. With a mixing spoon, stir in the apricots with the liquid. With the spoon, gradually beat in the flour mixture until well blended with the liquid ingredients. Pour the batter into the prepared pan, spreading it evenly over the bottom and into the corners. Scatter the chocolate chips and chopped nuts over the surface. (They will disappear during baking.)

6. Bake for 40 to 45 minutes until the dough shrinks from the sides of the pan. Reverse the pan from front to back once during baking. Set the pan on a wire rack to cool completely. Sprinkle with confectioners' sugar. Cut into 4 × 5 rows.

7. Store in the baking pan, tightly covered with aluminum foil or plastic wrap.

Yield: 20 bars

Linda Johnson's Southwestern Brownies

Besides being the "mother" of Hoover, the Golden Retriever for whom the dog bones on page 323 are named, Linda is one of my closest friends. She doesn't consider herself a "foodie," but I do. Linda is a prop stylist who works mainly with food, gathering all the beautiful tableware and accessories that go into the gorgeous food photographs you see in magazines and cookbooks. Her husband, Marty Jacobs, is a well-known food photographer, who just happens to have taken the picture that appears on the cover of this book. These brownies are like no others you have ever tasted. Linda suggests serving a spoonful of vanilla ice cream with each serving to help put out the fire!

4 ounces (4 squares) unsweetened chocolate
6 tablespoons (³/₄ stick) unsalted butter, at room temperature
1 ¹/₄ cups packed light brown sugar

1 teaspoon instant espresso powder
1 teaspoon ground cinnamon
¹/₂ to ³/₄ teaspoon ground red pepper
¹/₈ teaspoon salt
1 teaspoon vanilla extract
3 large eggs
³/₄ cup sifted all-purpose flour

1. Adjust one rack to divide the oven in half. Preheat the oven to 375°. Line an 8-inch-square metal baking pan with foil.

2. In a small saucepan set over very low heat, melt the chocolate, stirring constantly until smooth; set aside.

3. In a large bowl, with an electric mixer at medium-high speed, beat the butter until creamy, about 1 minute. Add the brown sugar, espresso powder, cinnamon, red pepper, salt, and vanilla and beat until blended. Add the eggs, one at a time, beating until blended after each addition. With the mixer at medium-low speed, gradually add the flour and then the melted chocolate, beating just until well blended. Turn the batter into the prepared pan, smoothing the top with the back of a spoon.

4. Bake for about 25 minutes until a toothpick inserted in the center comes out clean. Reverse the pan from front to back once during baking. Cool in the pan set on a wire rack for about 20 minutes. Turn out of the pan and peel away the foil. With a sharp knife, cut into 2-inch squares.

5. Store in a tightly covered container.

Yield: 16 brownies

Tip
All cookies on the same baking sheet should be about the same size so that they bake in the same amount of time. For the same reason, don't bake two sheets of different-size cookies at the same time.

Phyllis Kohn's Peanut Butter Chocolate Chippers

As fellow cookbook authors and food writers, Phyllis and I spend a lot of time on the telephone bouncing ideas off one another. Her most recent cookbook, *365 Delicious Low-Fat Recipes*, was published last year by HarperCollins. But when it came to a favorite cookie, Phyllis took a higher-fat route and sent this recipe for the cookies she says she used to make by the gross and send to her two sons when they were away at college. (She does add that reduced-fat peanut spread can be substituted for the peanut butter.) As a time-saving technique, Phyllis suggests measuring out all the dough before shaping it into balls.

    1 cup smooth peanut butter
    2/3 cup granulated sugar
    1 large egg
    1/3 cup miniature chocolate chips

1. Adjust two racks to divide the oven into thirds. Preheat the oven to 350°. Lightly grease two large baking sheets.

2. In a large bowl, with a mixing spoon, mix together the peanut butter, sugar, and egg until thoroughly combined. Stir in the chocolate chips until evenly distributed throughout the batter. Scoop out level measuring tablespoonfuls of the dough and shape between the palms of your hands into balls measuring about 1 inch in diameter. Arrange the balls on the prepared baking sheets, spacing them about 1½ inches apart. With a dinner fork, flatten each cookie in a crisscross pattern.

3. Bake for 12 to 14 minutes until lightly browned. Reverse the baking sheets on the racks and from front to back once during baking. With a wide turner, immediately transfer the cookies to wire racks to cool completely.

4. Store in a tightly covered container.

Yield: About 32 cookies

Nicola Kotsoni's Mother's Quick Honey Puffs

When you see the beautiful and stylish Nicola breezing in and out of her New York restaurants (Periyali, Il Cantinori, and, until recently, Aureole), it's hard to believe that she is also a terrific cook. These Greek fritters, called *tighanites*, are a quick version of *loukoumathes*, which her mother always made to serve on Nicola's name day. (In Greece, children are named after the saint on whose day they are born.) The only tricky part about making these fritters is shaping the dough so that the puffs come out in neat little rounds, which takes some practice. But they taste great no matter how they look.

    1 ½ cups all-purpose flour
    3 tablespoons sugar
    2 teaspoons baking powder
    2 large eggs
    1/2 cup milk
    Regular (not virgin or extra-virgin) olive oil or
        vegetable oil, for frying
    Honey, for drizzling over fritters
    Ground cinnamon, for sprinkling on fritters
    Sesame seeds, for sprinkling on fritters

1. Line a shallow pan with several thicknesses of paper towels. Preheat the oven to 200°.

2. In a large bowl, with a whisk, combine the flour, sugar, and baking powder until thoroughly mixed. In a small bowl, with a fork, lightly beat the eggs with the milk. With a mixing spoon, stir the egg mixture into the flour mixture to make a very soft dough.

3. Pour enough oil into a deep, wide pan to measure about 4 inches. Set the pan over high heat until the oil registers 365° on a deep-fry thermometer.

4. To make the puffs, place a big spoonful of the dough in the palm of your left hand (assuming you are right-handed) and make a fist. Tighten your fist so that a little "bubble" of dough, about

the size of a walnut, comes up next to your thumb. With a regular teaspoon held in your right hand, cut the bubble off with the edge of the spoon and carefully lower it into the hot oil. Fry about six puffs at a time until golden. (You can usually get two or three puffs out of each fistful of dough. When the spoon begins to get sticky—about every third puff—dip it into hot water, but be careful not to let any drops of water fall into the hot oil or it will splatter.) Remove the fritters with a slotted spoon to the paper-lined pan and place in the oven to keep warm while the remaining fritters are fried.

5. Arrange the warm fritters in a stack on a serving plate and drizzle them with honey. Sprinkle with cinnamon and/or sesame seeds.

Yield: About 36 fritters

Tip

Tighanites are best when they are served immediately after they are fried and still warm. However, they can be made ahead, cooled, and then frozen in a plastic bag or tightly wrapped in aluminum foil. Unwrap and place the frozen fritters on a baking sheet. Reheat at 300° for 10 to 12 minutes until very warm. Drizzle with honey and sprinkle with cinnamon and/or sesame seeds and serve immediately. If there are any leftover honey-coated fritters, they can be rewarmed in a skillet with a little more honey and a few drops of water. Cook over very low heat, stirring frequently, until warm.

Christine Smith Koury's Extraordinary Brownies

"I'm the brownie expert extraordinaire," writes Chris in introducing her recipe, and after you try these rich, fudgy delights you'll believe it. Chris followed me as the food editor at *Parents Magazine*, and now she is the food editor at *Redbook*. In matters of food, there are few things about which Chris and I disagree, except lentils. Certainly we are of one mind when it comes to chocolate.

> 1 cup all-purpose flour
> $^1/_2$ cup unsweetened cocoa powder
> $^1/_4$ teaspoon salt
> $^2/_3$ cup (1 stick plus 3 tablespoons) salted butter or margarine, melted
> 1 $^1/_3$ cups sugar
> 2 large eggs
> 1 $^1/_2$ teaspoons vanilla extract
> $^1/_2$ cup chopped, toasted walnuts, divided (optional)

1. Adjust one rack to divide the oven in half. Preheat the oven to 350°. Lightly grease an 8-inch-square baking pan.

2. In a small bowl, with a whisk, combine the flour, cocoa, and salt until thoroughly mixed.

3. In a medium-size bowl, with a mixing spoon, stir together the butter, sugar, eggs, and vanilla until well blended. Stir in the flour mixture just until blended. Stir in half of the walnuts until well distributed throughout the batter. Turn the batter into the prepared pan, spreading it evenly and smoothing the top with the back of the spoon. Sprinkle evenly with the remaining walnuts.

4. Bake for about 30 minutes until the top appears dry and the center is set. Reverse the pan from front to back once during baking. Set the pan on a wire rack to cool completely before cutting into 4 × 4 rows.

5. Store in the baking pan, tightly covered with aluminum foil or plastic wrap.

Yield: 16 brownies

Marianne Langan's
Lemon-Coconut Smoothies

Marianne and I met about ten years ago shortly after she became the food editor of *McCall's* magazine. Before that, I only knew her by reputation as a top-notch food stylist, one of those talented people who make food look so glorious for photography. Marianne not only styles food exquisitely, but the "real food" she cooks always tastes as wonderful as it looks. These days, Marianne is running her own public relations agency in Florida. She prefers the lemon-lime variation of these bar cookies, but admits that most people like just plain lemon. She also says that the coconut can be omitted.

Crust

1/4 cup plus 2 tablespoons (3/4 stick) unsalted butter or margarine, at room temperature

1/4 cup packed light brown sugar

1/8 teaspoon salt

1 cup all-purpose flour

4 teaspoons shredded and minced lemon zest (from 1 large lemon), divided

Topping

2 large eggs

2/3 cup granulated sugar

2 tablespoons all-purpose flour

1/4 teaspoon baking powder

1/4 cup fresh strained lemon juice

1 cup shredded or flaked coconut

Confectioners' sugar, for dusting on bars

1. Adjust one rack to divide the oven in half. Preheat the oven to 350° (or 325° if using a glass baking dish). Lightly grease and flour a 13 × 9-inch metal baking pan or glass baking dish.

2. To make the crust: In a medium-size bowl, with an electric mixer at medium-high speed, beat together the butter, brown sugar, and salt until very well blended, 2 to 3 minutes. With the mixer at medium-low speed, gradually add the flour and 1/2 teaspoon of the lemon zest, beating just until blended. Spread this mixture evenly in the bottom of the prepared pan.

3. Bake for 12 minutes until lightly browned.

4. To make the topping: While the crust is baking, in a small bowl, with the electric mixer at medium-high speed (no need to wash the beaters), beat the eggs until frothy. Gradually beat in the granulated sugar, flour, and baking powder. With a mixing spoon, stir in the remaining 3 1/2 teaspoons of lemon zest and the lemon juice.

5. Sprinkle the coconut evenly over the baked crust. Pour the lemon topping evenly over the coconut. Bake for 20 minutes longer until the top is dry to the touch. Cool completely in the pan set on a wire rack. Generously dust with confectioners' sugar before cutting into 7 × 3 rows.

6. These cookies can be stored in the baking pan, tightly covered with aluminum foil or plastic wrap, in the refrigerator or at room temperature. Storing the bars in the refrigerator makes them firmer and lightens the lemon flavor. At room temperature, the topping is softer and more flavorful. A good compromise is to store the bars in the refrigerator and hold them at room temperature for about 30 minutes before serving.

Yield: 21 bars

Variations

Lemon-Lime: Reduce the lemon zest to 2 teaspoons and add 2 teaspoons shredded and minced lime zest to the topping. Reduce the lemon juice to 2 tablespoons and add 2 tablespoons lime juice.

Lime: Substitute lime zest and lime juice for the lemon.

Marion Lyons's Dutch Butter Cookies

Marion is one of the most versatile and capable writers and editors I know. For years she worked for *Woman's Day*, putting together many of their special-interest magazines. Not only did she deal with food topics, she was equally at home doing gardening and crafts issues. Marion says, "My mother's recipe for these cookies called for 1 pound butter, 4 cups flour, and a cup of everything else, but I can't fit that amount into any known pan size. These are scrumptious cookies if they're not overbaked. Sometimes they come out crisp, sometimes chewy, but no matter which way, they're always delicious."

1 ¹/₂ cups (3 sticks) salted butter, at room temperature

3 cups all-purpose flour

³/₄ cup packed light brown sugar

³/₄ cup granulated sugar

³/₄ cup coarsely ground almonds, divided

1 teaspoon ground cinnamon

Milk, for brushing on dough

1. Adjust two racks to divide the oven into thirds. Preheat the oven to 375°. Have ready three 8-inch-square metal baking pans.

2. In a large bowl, place the butter, flour, brown sugar, granulated sugar, ¹/₂ cup of the almonds, and the cinnamon. Working with your hands, toss and rub the mixture between your fingertips until it forms a dough. Divide the dough evenly among the baking pans, patting it down evenly. (The depth of the dough in the pan should be about ¹/₂ inch.) Brush the tops of the dough in the pans with the milk. Scatter the reserved almonds over top, dividing evenly.

3. Bake for 12 or 13 minutes until brown, watching carefully toward the end of the baking time so that the cookies don't overbake. Reverse the pans on the racks and from front to back once during baking. Remove from the oven and cut each pan into 6 × 4 rows while still hot. Cool in the pans set on wire racks.

4. Store in a tightly covered container.

Yield: 72 cookies

Marianne Bellon Marinelli's Almond Spice Tiles

"Several years ago, I tasted a wonderful spice cookie in a restaurant and decided to develop a similar recipe of my own," writes Marianne. And who better to do it than Marianne, one of the most naturally gifted and talented young food professionals I know. "Since then," she continues, "these cookies have become my trademark, and many of my friends look forward to eating them, especially at Christmas." Marianne suggests keeping a couple of bricks of dough in the freezer at all times. When you want these fresh-baked cookies, simply slice as many as you want and return the brick to the freezer. These cookies also freeze well in airtight plastic bags after they are baked.

- 1 cup (2 sticks) unsalted butter, at room temperature
- 1 cup granulated sugar
- ³/₄ cup packed dark brown sugar
- 1 tablespoon ground cinnamon
- 1 teaspoon ground cloves
- 1 teaspoon baking soda
- ³/₄ teaspoon ground nutmeg
- ¹/₂ teaspoon salt
- 2 large eggs
- 1 teaspoon vanilla extract
- 3 ¹/₂ cups all-purpose flour
- 2 cups sliced blanched or natural almonds

1. In a large bowl, with an electric mixer at medium-high speed, beat the butter, granulated sugar, and brown sugar until light and fluffy, 2 to 3 minutes. Add the cinnamon, cloves, baking soda, nutmeg, and salt. Beat at medium speed until combined. Add the eggs and vanilla and beat until well blended.

2. With the mixer at medium-low speed, gradually add 2 cups of the flour, beating until the flour is almost incorporated into the dough. With a mixing spoon, stir in the remaining 1¹/₂ cups of flour and the almonds. *The dough will be very stiff.*

You can use your hands if necessary. Some of the almonds will undoubtedly break while stirring them into the dough, but that doesn't matter. Gather the dough into a ball.

3. Divide the dough in half. With your hands and the aid of an icing spatula or a wide turner, shape each half into a 10 × 3 × 1-inch brick. Wrap the bricks separately in plastic wrap and refrigerate until very cold and firm, at least 2 hours. (At this point the dough can be tightly wrapped in aluminum foil and frozen for up to three months.)

4. When ready to bake, adjust two racks to divide the oven into thirds. Preheat the oven to 375°. Have ready two ungreased baking sheets.

5. With a long, sharp knife, cut the bricks into slightly less than ¹/₄-inch slices. Arrange the slices on the ungreased baking sheets, spacing them about 1 inch apart.

6. Bake for 10 to 13 minutes until brown around the edges. Reverse the baking sheets on the racks and from front to back once during baking. With a wide turner, immediately transfer the cookies to wire racks to cool completely.

7. Store in a tightly covered container.

Yield: About 80 cookies

Susan McQuillan's Mother's Empire Biscuits

Susan and I worked together on a magazine project a few years ago and have remained good friends since. Susan became a registered dietitian and is now food editor for *American Health* magazine. "My mother, Irene McQuillan, makes these cookies every year for Christmas," Susan says, "and sometimes for other special occasions, like weddings and birthdays. She uses margarine and shortening; I use butter and shortening when I make them. I also sneak in a half cup or so of wheat germ (and omit about ¼ cup of the flour), or I use 1 cup of whole wheat flour in place of the same amount of white flour. I have to admit that I really like these cookies better with all white flour, but now that I'm a nutritionist my conscience won't let me bake that way anymore."

- 4 cups all-purpose flour
- 2 teaspoons cream of tartar
- 1 teaspoon baking soda
- ¹/₂ cup (1 stick) salted butter or margarine, at room temperature
- ¹/₂ cup (1 stick) plain or butter-flavored shortening
- ¹/₂ cup sugar
- 2 large eggs
- 2 tablespoons milk

Filling and Frosting

- ¹/₂ cup confectioners' sugar
- 2 to 3 teaspoons milk
- ¹/₄ cup strawberry or seedless raspberry jam

1. Adjust two racks to divide the oven into thirds. Preheat the oven to 350°. Lightly grease two baking sheets. Have ready a 2-inch round cookie cutter.

2. In a medium-size bowl, with a whisk, combine the flour, cream of tartar, and baking soda.

3. In a large bowl, with an electric mixer at medium-high speed, beat together the butter, shortening, and sugar until very well blended, 2 to 3 minutes. Add the eggs and the milk and continue to beat just until blended. With the mixer at medium-low speed, gradually add the flour mixture, beating just until blended.

4. On a lightly floured surface, roll the dough to a ¹/₈-inch thickness. Cut into rounds. Arrange the cookies on the prepared baking sheets, spacing them about 1 inch apart. Gather the scraps of dough together and reroll once.

5. Bake for 10 to 12 minutes until barely golden. Reverse the baking sheets on the racks and from front to back once during baking. With a wide turner, immediately transfer the cookies to wire racks to cool completely.

6. While the cookies are cooling, make the frosting. In a small bowl, mix together the confectioners' sugar and milk. When the cookies have cooled, sandwich them in pairs with the jam, bottom sides together. Spread the tops thinly with frosting. Set aside until the icing is dry, about 1 hour.

7. Store in a tightly covered container, separating the layers with sheets of waxed paper.

Yield: About 25 sandwich cookies

Regina Ragone's Sicilian Fig Cookies

Regina is the food editor for *Weight Watchers* magazine. I gave Regina her first magazine job in 1988 and I take enormous pride in her career. This recipe came to Regina via her sister, Angela Ragone, who got it from her mother-in-law, Frances D'Onofrio.

2 ¹/₄ cups all-purpose flour
¹/₂ cup sugar
Pinch of salt
¹/₂ cup plus 6 tablespoons (1 ³/₄ sticks) cold, unsalted butter, cut into small pieces
1 large egg
1 large egg yolk
1 teaspoon vanilla extract
Shredded and minced zest of 1 lemon

Filling

1 cup chopped dried figs
1 cup blanched almonds, finely chopped
1 cup raisins
Shredded and minced zest of 1 tangerine or 1 small juice orange
1 tablespoon honey
1 tablespoon sugar
3 tablespoons strained fresh tangerine or orange juice
¹/₂ cup semisweet chocolate chips

Glaze

1 large egg beaten with 1 tablespoon water

1. Adjust one rack to divide the oven in half. Lightly grease one large baking sheet.

2. To make the dough: In a large bowl, with a whisk, combine the flour, sugar, and salt until thoroughly mixed. Add the butter. With a pastry blender or two knives used in a crisscross fashion, cut in the butter until the mixture resembles coarse crumbs. With a mixing spoon, stir in the egg, egg yolk, vanilla, and lemon zest. Turn out onto a lightly floured surface and knead just until

the dough comes together. Shape into a disk. Wrap in plastic wrap and refrigerate for 1 hour.

3. While the dough is chilling, make the filling. In a medium-size saucepan, combine the figs, almonds, raisins, tangerine zest, honey, sugar, and tangerine juice. Cook over medium-low heat, stirring occasionally, until the mixture forms a paste, about 10 minutes. Remove from the heat and stir in the chocolate chips. Set aside to cool slightly.

4. Preheat the oven to 350°.

5. On a lightly floured surface, with a floured rolling pin, roll out the chilled dough to a thickness of ¹/₈ inch. With a pizza wheel or the tip of a sharp knife and a ruler, cut the dough into 3-inch-wide strips.

6. Roll pieces of the fig mixture between the palms of your hands into logs measuring ¹/₂ inch in diameter that are the same length as the strips of dough. Place the logs in the centers of the dough strips; roll the dough around the filling so that it meets at the center. With your fingers press down the seam and sort of pinch it together just enough so that it holds. With a long, sharp knife, cut each roll into 1³/₄-inch pieces. Arrange the pieces seam sides down on the prepared baking sheet, spacing them about 1¹/₂ inches apart. Brush the tops with the egg glaze.

7. Bake for about 20 minutes until nicely browned. Reverse the baking sheet from front to back once during baking. With a wide turner, immediately transfer the cookies to wire racks to cool completely.

8. Store in a tightly covered container, separating the layers with sheets of waxed paper.

Yield: About 30 cookies

Tip

Make an easy filling for cookies this way: Grind nuts or dried fruits in a food processor, then bind with honey.

David Ricketts's Double Chocolate-Chunk Cookies

"Here is one of my favorite cookie recipes, which I included in the *Family Circle Cookbook*," writes David, fellow cookbook author and food writer. "It is one of the recipes I demonstrated when I was touring for the book. The cookies were always a hit, no matter what time of the day. Sometimes I would bring a plateful to radio interviews, usually a mistake, since the sound of cookies crunching as the hosts inhaled them often drowned me out."

> 6 squares (1 ounce each) semisweet chocolate, divided
>
> 1 1/4 cups all-purpose flour
>
> 1/2 teaspoon baking soda
>
> 1/4 teaspoon salt
>
> 1/2 cup (1 stick) unsalted butter, at room temperature
>
> 1/2 cup granulated sugar
>
> 1/2 cup packed light brown sugar
>
> 1 large egg
>
> 1 teaspoon vanilla extract
>
> 1 cup coarsely chopped pecans

1. Adjust one rack to divide the oven in half. Preheat the oven to 375°. Have ready one or two ungreased baking sheets.

2. In a small saucepan over very low heat, stir 1 square of the chocolate until melted and smooth. Chop the remaining 5 squares of chocolate into 1/2-inch chunks.

3. In a medium-size bowl, with a whisk, combine the flour, baking soda, and salt until thoroughly mixed.

4. In a large bowl, with an electric mixer at medium-high speed, beat the butter until creamy, about 1 minute. Gradually beat in the granulated sugar and brown sugar until very well blended, 2 to 3 minutes. Beat in the egg and vanilla. Beat in the melted chocolate until well blended. With a mixing spoon, stir in the chopped chocolate and

pecans. Drop the dough by rounded tablespoonfuls onto the prepared baking sheets, spacing them about 2 inches apart.

5. Bake for 10 to 12 minutes until slightly browned around the edges. Reverse the baking sheet from front to back once during baking. With a wide turner, immediately transfer the cookies to wire racks to cool completely.

6. Store in a tightly covered container.

Yield: About 24 cookies

Excerpted from *The Family Circle Cookbook: New Tastes for New Times*, by the editors of *Family Circle* and David Ricketts. Copyright©1992 by The Family Circle, Inc., Published by Simon & Schuster, Inc.

Olga Rigsby's Merenguitos de Mani (Peanut Meringues)

Olga is our Cuban bombshell, a fun and funny lady who was for many years the food editor at *Seventeen* magazine. These days she edits and translates cookbooks, and works as a food consultant for the Hispanic and Latino market. Olga has also served as a judge for the prestigious James Beard Book Awards for many years. "Growing up in Cuba, we all loved any form of meringues. Parties—even children's parties—would not have seemed festive without some little 'meringuito' piled high on a platter."

> 2 large egg whites, at room temperature
> 1/8 teaspoon cream of tartar
> 1/2 cup superfine sugar
> 1/2 cup chopped peanuts

1. Adjust one rack to divide the oven in half. Preheat the oven to 200°. Cover one large baking sheet with aluminum foil, shiny side up.

2. In a medium-size bowl, with an electric mixer at medium-low speed, beat together the egg whites and cream of tartar until frothy. Increase the speed to medium-high and add the sugar, 1 tablespoon at a time, beating for a minute or two after each addition. Continue to beat until the eggs whites stand in stiff, glossy peaks when the beaters are lifted. With a rubber spatula or a large spoon, fold in the peanuts until well distributed throughout the meringue.

3. Fit a pastry bag with a fairly large, plain tube and pipe out little round meringues, about 1 inch apart, on the prepared baking sheets. (Or you can use two teaspoons to shape the meringues.)

4. Bake for 1 hour. With a wide turner, immediately remove the meringues from the baking sheet and transfer to wire racks to cool completely.

Yield: About 36 meringues

Arthur Schwartz's Fifties-Style Crisp Peanut Butter Cookies

When Arthur and I first met many years ago, we were both looking pretty silly wearing 10-gallon hats and standing around with one foot on the bottom rail of a corral fence while we learned about the Colorado cattle industry. At the time, I was the food editor of *Parents Magazine* and Arthur was the food editor and restaurant critic for the *New York Daily News*. These days he hosts a popular food talk show on WOR Radio in New York City. While Arthur was growing up in Brooklyn most of the cookies he ate came from the corner bakery. On the infrequent occasions when his mom baked cookies, it was almost always this peanut butter cookie, which is still one of his favorites. Arthur says they are wonderful when eaten warm, but are even better when they are allowed to cool and get crisp.

> 2 1/2 cups all-purpose flour
> 1 teaspoon baking powder
> 1 teaspoon baking soda
> 1 teaspoon salt
> 1 cup (2 sticks) salted butter or margarine, at room temperature
> 1 cup creamy or chunky peanut butter
> 1 cup granulated sugar
> 1 cup packed light or dark brown sugar
> 2 large eggs, lightly beaten
> 1 teaspoon vanilla extract

1. Adjust two racks to divide the oven into thirds. Preheat the oven to 375°. Have ready two ungreased baking sheets.

2. In a medium-size bowl, with a whisk, combine the flour, baking powder, baking soda, and salt until thoroughly mixed.

3. In a large bowl, with an electric mixer at medium-high speed, beat together the butter and peanut butter until well blended and smooth, about 1 minute. Beat in the granulated sugar and

brown sugar until very well blended, 2 to 3 minutes. Beat in the eggs and vanilla until well combined. With the mixer at medium-low speed, gradually add the flour mixture, beating just until blended.

4. Scoop teaspoonfuls of dough out of the bowl and roll them into 1-inch balls between the palms of your hands. As they are shaped, arrange the balls on the ungreased baking sheets, spacing them about 2 inches apart. With the tines of a fork, flatten each ball making a crisscross pattern on the dough.

5. Bake for about 12 minutes until lightly browned. Reverse the baking sheets on the racks and from front to back once during baking. With a wide turner, immediately transfer the cookies to wire racks to cool completely.

6. Store in a tightly covered container.

Yield: About 65 cookies

Gale Steves's Chipper Nuts

Even though Gale is now vice president and editor-in-chief of *HOME Magazine*, I still consider her to be very much a food person, which is what she was when we first met and before she changed editorial gears. We have worked together on several food magazines, and I've always admired her knowledge of food and cooking skills. "My mother was very creative in making up names for the recipes she prepared," she writes. "These were special favorites of my brother's and mine. When I found the recipe recently in an old file I inherited after Mother died, it was a poignant moment . . . and a family reunion of sorts."

2 ^{1}/$_2$ cups all-purpose flour

1 teaspoon baking soda

1 teaspoon salt

^{3}/$_4$ cup (1 ^{1}/$_2$ sticks) unsalted butter, at room temperature

^{3}/$_4$ cup packed light or dark brown sugar

^{2}/$_3$ cup confectioners' sugar

1 large egg

^{1}/$_2$ teaspoon vanilla extract

One 12-ounce package (2 cups) semisweet chocolate chips

1 ^{1}/$_3$ cups coarsely chopped pecans

1. Adjust two racks to divide the oven into thirds. Have ready two ungreased baking sheets.

2. In a medium-size bowl, with a whisk, combine the flour, baking soda, and salt until thoroughly mixed.

3. In a large bowl, with an electric mixer at medium-high speed, beat together the butter, brown sugar, and confectioners' sugar until light and fluffy, 2 to 3 minutes. Beat in the egg and vanilla until well blended, about 1 minute. With the mixer at medium-low speed, gradually add the flour mixture, beating just until blended. Divide the dough in half. On two 16-inch sheets of waxed paper, spoon each half of the dough in a 12-inch strip down the center. With your hands, shape each strip into a 12-inch cylinder. Roll the waxed paper around the cylinder and twist the ends. Refrigerate the cylinders until firm and very cold, 1 to 2 hours, or for up to three days. (At this point the cylinders can be tightly wrapped in aluminum foil and frozen for up to three months. If frozen, soften slightly in the refrigerator before cutting into slices.)

4. Preheat the oven to 325°.

5. With a long, sharp knife, cut the cylinders into ^{1}/$_2$-inch slices. Arrange the slices on the ungreased baking sheets. Bake for 12 to 14 minutes until golden brown. Reverse the baking sheets on the racks and from front to back once during baking. Remove the baking sheets from the oven and set them on wire racks for 5 minutes. With a wide turner, transfer the cookies to wire racks to cool completely.

6. Store in a tightly covered container.

Yield: About 48 cookies

Arlene Wanderman's Cenci

I've known Arlene since she was the food editor of the *Ladies' Home Journal*. Now she heads her own food communications company, which represents, among others, the International Olive Oil Council. I consider Arlene to be the undisputed expert in matters of European, Mediterranean, and Middle Eastern cookery. So I wasn't surprised when she sent me this cookie recipe, and said it was one of her favorites. The method for making these cookies is very much Old World. If the thought of dumping and mixing flour and other ingredients on the counter is a little intimidating, there is probably no reason you can't do the mixing in a very large bowl and then turn the dough out onto the counter to be kneaded.

> 1 pound (4 cups) all-purpose flour
> 1/3 cup sugar
> Pinch of salt
> Shredded and minced zest from 1 lemon (about 1 tablespoon)
> 4 large eggs
> 2 tablespoons unsalted butter, melted and cooled
> 1 tablespoon grappa (brandy distilled from the skins, seeds, and stalks of grapes) or other brandy
> 1 cup regular olive oil, for frying
> Confectioners' sugar, for dusting cookies

1. Place the flour on a clean work surface. With your hands, mix the sugar, salt, and lemon zest into the flour until thoroughly mixed. Push the flour mixture into a mound and make a crater in the center. Break the eggs into the crater, then pour the cooled, melted butter over the eggs. With a fork, lightly mix the eggs and butter together without disturbing the shape of the mound. Gradually mix the flour into the egg mixture, bringing flour from the rim into the center, while at the same time working the mixture to the outside. When most of the flour has been absorbed by the butter and eggs, add the brandy. Knead for 10 minutes. Gather the dough into a ball and place in a bowl. Cover with a clean kitchen towel and set aside to rest for 1 hour.

2. Divide the dough in half. Turn out one half onto a work surface and roll to a 1/8-inch thickness. Cut into any shapes desired with 2-inch cookie cutters. (Diamond, round, and rectangular shapes are the most traditional.) Set the shapes aside on sheets of waxed paper until you have finished all of the cutting. Repeat with the remaining half of the dough.

3. In a large skillet, heat the olive oil. When it is hot, add the dough shapes to the skillet, a few at a time, and fry until golden brown, turning and adjusting the heat as necessary. Drain on paper towels. Dust with confectioners' sugar before serving.

Yield: About 25 cookies

Susan Westmoreland's Stem Ginger Cookies

Susan is the food director at *Good Housekeeping* magazine, as well as the mother of a young son, so you know she has had plenty of cookie-making experience. Susan was working for *Glamour* magazine when we first met, and before that she worked as a chef. She was so young then that I can't believe she's been in the business for more than 15 years. Susan admits to loving the flavor of ginger, so it's not surprising that one of her favorite cookie recipes would include plenty of it.

> 2 3/4 cups all-purpose flour
> 2 teaspoons cream of tartar
> 1 1/2 teaspoons ground ginger
> 1 teaspoon baking soda
> 1/2 teaspoon salt
> 1 cup (2 sticks) unsalted butter
> 3/4 cup light or dark brown sugar
> 2 large eggs
> 1 teaspoon vanilla extract
> 1/2 cup finely chopped crystallized (stem) ginger

1. Adjust two racks to divide the oven into thirds. Preheat the oven to 375°. Have ready two ungreased baking sheets.

2. In a medium-size bowl, with a whisk, combine the flour, cream of tartar, ground ginger, baking soda, and salt until thoroughly mixed.

3. In a large bowl, with an electric mixer at medium-high speed, beat together the butter and brown sugar until very well combined, 2 to 3 minutes. Add the eggs, one at a time, beating well after each addition. Beat in the vanilla. With the mixer at medium-low speed, gradually add the flour mixture, beating just until blended. With a mixing spoon, stir in the crystallized ginger until well distributed throughout the batter.

4. Scoop teaspoonfuls of batter out of the bowl and roll them into 1-inch balls between the palms of your hands. As they are shaped, arrange the balls on the ungreased baking sheets, spacing them at least 3 inches apart (they spread a lot).

5. Bake for 8 to 10 minutes until pale golden. Reverse the baking sheets on the racks and from front to back once during baking. With a wide turner, immediately transfer the cookies to wire racks to cool completely.

Yield: About 48 cookies

Mildred Ying's Oatmeal Crackles

. . . .

"You certainly are brave to commit to over 400 cookie recipes," writes this very special friend, and the former long-time food editor of *Good Housekeeping.* "Many years ago I decided to do 101 cookie recipes for a December issue of *GH.* Each cookie had to be completely different and we photographed them all. My staff almost murdered me by the time we completed the story!" Mildred says she made five batches of these jumbo cookies at Christmas, and her two grown sons devoured them down to the last crumbs.

2 cups all-purpose flour

1 ¹/₂ teaspoons baking soda

1 teaspoon salt

1 ¹/₂ cups packed light brown sugar

1 cup vegetable oil

1 tablespoon vanilla extract

2 large eggs

3 cups quick-cooking (not instant) rolled oats

¹/₄ cup granulated sugar

1. Adjust two racks to divide the oven into thirds. Preheat the oven to 375°. Lightly grease two baking sheets.

2. In a medium-size bowl, with a whisk, combine the flour, baking soda, and salt until thoroughly mixed.

3. In a large bowl, with an electric mixer at medium-high speed, beat the brown sugar, oil, vanilla, and eggs until smooth, about 2 minutes. With the mixer at medium-low speed, gradually add the flour mixture, beating just until blended. With a mixing spoon, stir in the oats until very well blended. (The mixture will be very thick.)

4. Place the granulated sugar in a wide, shallow bowl. Scoop slightly rounded tablespoonfuls of dough out of the bowl and roll them into 1¹/₄-inch balls between the palms of your hands. Roll the balls in the sugar and then arrange them on the prepared baking sheets, spacing them about 2 inches apart.

5. Bake for about 15 minutes until golden. Reverse the baking sheets on the racks and from front to back once during baking. With a wide turner, immediately transfer the cookies to wire racks to cool completely.

6. Store in a tightly covered container.

Yield: About 30 cookies

Appendix A   Equivalents

After you've been cooking and baking long enough, the most-often used equivalents become second nature. You don't have to think twice to know that there are 4 tablespoons in ¼ cup, or that chocolate chips come in 6- and 12-ounce bags, and that 6 ounces of chips measures one cup.

MEASUREMENT EQUIVALENTS

Dash=Less than ⅛ teaspoon

Pinch (dry ingredient)=⅛ teaspoon

1½ teaspoons=½ tablespoon

3 teaspoons=1 tablespoon

4 tablespoons=¼ cup

5 tablespoons plus 1 teaspoon=⅓ cup

8 tablespoons=½ cup

16 tablespoons=1 cup

2 cups=1 pint

2 pints=1 quart

4 quarts=1 gallon

SELECTED FOOD EQUIVALENTS

Butter, Margarine, and Shortening (Stick)

½ stick=4 tablespoons=¼ cup

1 stick=8 tablespoons=½ cup

2 sticks=1 cup=8 ounces

4 sticks=2 cups=1 pound

Butter and Margarine (Whipped)

1 cup=4 ounces

Chocolate

Chocolate chips (6 ounces)=1 cup

Unsweetened or semisweet chocolate (1 ounce, 1 square)=about 4 tablespoons shredded, grated or finely chopped

Dried Fruit

Dates, pitted (8 ounces)=1⅓ cups chopped

Prunes (1 pound)=2½ cups

Raisins, seeded (1 pound)=3¼ cups

Raisins, seedless (1 pound)= 2¾ cups

Flour

All-purpose flour (1 pound)=3½ to 4 cups

Whole wheat flour(1 pound)=3¾ to 4 cups

Nuts

Almonds, in-shell (1 pound)=1 cup shelled; ¾ cup sliced or slivered

Almonds, shelled (1 pound)=3 cups whole

Hazelnuts, shelled (1 pound)=3 cups whole

Hazelnuts, shelled (1 pound)=3½ cups, coarsely chopped

Peanuts, in-shell (1 pound)=1¼ cups whole; 1 cup chopped

Pecans, in-shell (1 pound)=1⅓ cups halves

Pecans, shelled (1 pound)=4 cups halves

Pistachios, in-shell (8 ounces)=1 cup nutmeats

Walnuts, in-shell (1 pound)=1⅔ cups halves

Walnuts, shelled (1 pound)=1½ cups chopped

Sugar

Brown sugar (1 pound)=about 2¼ cups packed

Confectioners' sugar (1 pound)=3½ to 4 cups

Granulated sugar (1 pound)=about 2 cups

Citrus Fruit

Lemon (medium-size)=2 to 3 tablespoons juice and 2 to 3 teaspoons shredded zest

Orange (medium-size)=about ⅓ cup juice and 2 to 3 tablespoons shredded zest

Appendix B Substitutions

It is always best, of course, to try to have the exact ingredient called for in a recipe, especially a baking recipe, but no one is infallible.

For	Substitute
Baking powder (1 teaspoon)	$\frac{1}{2}$ teaspoon cream of tartar plus $\frac{1}{4}$ teaspoon baking soda
Buttermilk (1 cup)	1 cup plain yogurt or 1 tablespoon lemon juice stirred into a cup whole milk; let stand 5 minutes

Chocolate

Unsweetened chocolate (1 ounce)	3 tablespoons cocoa plus 2 teaspoons shortening
Semisweet chocolate (1 ounce)	1 ounce unsweetened chocolate plus 1 tablespoon granulated sugar *or* 3 tablespoons chocolate chips
Cream, heavy or whipping (1 cup)	$\frac{1}{3}$ cup melted butter plus $\frac{3}{4}$ cup whole milk
Egg, whole	2 egg yolks plus 1 tablespoon water
Honey	Light corn syrup (although corn syrup is not as sweet as honey)
Molasses (1 cup)	Honey or dark corn syrup
Sour cream (1 cup)	3 tablespoons melted butter stirred into buttermilk or plain yogurt to make 1 cup
Whole milk (1 cup)	equal parts evaporated (not condensed) milk and water, or 2 teaspoons butter plus 1 cup skim milk or water

Appendix C   Shopping and Mail-Order Sources

There is nothing so unique called for in this book that you should have much trouble finding it. In fact, most of the stuff is probably right there in your cabinets. Just in case you really get stuck for something, however, here is a list of stores and mail-order companies that specialize in various kinds of baking and cooking equipment and ingredients.

All of these companies will send catalogs, which are fascinating to browse through. Even if you don't need a thing, I dare you not to order *something*. Sometimes there is a charge for the catalog, which may be deductible from the first order, but from then on you will probably be on the mailing list forever.

EQUIPMENT

Bridge Kitchenware
214 East 52nd Street
New York, NY 10022
1-800-274-3435 (outside New York area)
1-212-688-4220

Offers a complete line of professional, European culinary equipment. Charge for catalog, which is deductible from the first order.

E. Dehillerin
18-20, rue Coquilliére
75001 Paris, France
(33-1) 42.36.53.13

On your next trip to Paris, be sure to stop by Dehillerin in the historic Les Halles area, formerly the city's central food market. Dehillerin specializes in cooking utensils and baking equipment as only the French can. Catalog available.

Sweet Celebrations (formerly Maid of Scandinavia)
7009 Washington Avenue South
Edina, MN 55439
1-800-328-6722

Offers a complete line of baking equipment and supplies, from very ordinary and functional to very specialized and

unique pieces of European bakeware and accessories. The emphasis here is on cake decorating and candy-making supplies. Charge for catalog.

Sur La Table
84 Pine Street
Pike Place Farmers' Market
Seattle, WA 09101
1-800-243-0852

Offers a complete line of baking equipment, supplies, and appliances. Handmade copper cookware is a specialty. Catalog available.

Wilton Industries
2240 West 57th Street
Woodridge, IL 60517
1-800-794-5866 (outside Illinois)
1-708-963-7100

Caters to the home baker with a complete line of decorating supplies, cookie-making equipment; an excellent source for food coloring, dragées, sprinkles, and ready-made royal icing decorations, with emphasis on holiday products. Wilton products are also available in many kitchenware stores. A variety of catalogs available.

EQUIPMENT AND INGREDIENTS

New York Cake and Baking Distributors
(formerly The Chocolate Gallery)
56 West 22nd Street
New York, NY 10010
1-800-675-CAKE (outside New York area)
1-212-675-CAKE

Specializes in decorating supplies; also one of the best sources for food coloring, dragées, sprinkles, and ready-made royal icing decorations. Catalog available.

King Arthur Flour Baker's Catalog
P.O. Box 876
Norwich, VT 05055-0876
1-800-827-6836

Offers equipment and ingredients especially for home bakers, including their own brand of flours, from all-purpose to a blend that is specially formulated for bread machines. Catalog is free.

Williams-Sonoma
P.O. Box 7456
San Francisco, CA 94120-7456
1-800-541-2233
With stores everywhere in the United States, and more
opening all the time, Williams-Sonoma carries everything
the gourmet might pine for, from interesting gadgets
and special foods to high-end stoves. Catalog available.

Appendix D   Author's Choice

Although there is a very complete index in this book, for easy reference here are some of my own cookie favorites for special occasions.

Cookies for Chocolate Lovers

Cookies for Kids to (Help) Make

Cookie Jar Classics

International Cookies

Christmas Cookies

Index